DISCOVERING
POETRY

DISCOVERING POETRY

HANS P. GUTH
GABRIELE L. RICO

San Jose State University

A BLAIR PRESS BOOK

PRENTICE HALL, ENGLEWOOD CLIFFS, NJ 07632

Library of Congress Cataloging-in-Publication Data

Guth, Hans Paul
        Discovering poetry / Hans P. Guth and Gabriele L. Rico.
            p.   cm.
        "A Blair Press book."
        Includes index.
        ISBN 0-13-221987-5
            1. English language—Rhetoric.   2. Poetry—Collections.
        3. College readers.   I. Rico, Gabriele L.   II. Title.
        PE1417.G867   1993
        808.1—dc20   92-26686
                                                                                                CIP

Cover designer: Thomas Nery
Prepress buyer: Herb Klein
Manufacturing buyers: Robert Anderson and Patrice Fraccio
Photo researchers: Joelle Burrows and Lori Morris-Nantz
Cover art: William Blake, *The Ancient of Days* (detail from the frontispiece of *Europe: A Prophecy*). Hand colored print. Fitzwilliam Museum, Cambridge. Diego Rivera, The Flower Vendor (detail), 1949. Museo Espaniol de Arte Contemporaneo, Madrid.

Acknowledgments appear on pages 522–530, which constitute
a continuation of the copyright page.

Blair Press
The Statler Building
20 Park Plaza, Suite 1113
Boston, MA 02116-4399

    © 1993 by Prentice Hall, Inc.
        A Simon & Schuster Company
        Englewood Cliffs, NJ 07632

Printed in the United States of America
10 9

ISBN 0-13-221987-5

Prentice-Hall International (UK) Limited, *London*
Prentice-Hall of Australia Pty. Limited, *Sydney*
Prentice-Hall Canada Inc., *Toronto*
Prentice-Hall Hispanoamericana, S.A., *Mexico*
Prentice-Hall of India Private Limited, *New Delhi*
Prentice-Hall of Japan, Inc., *Tokyo*
Simon & Schuster Asia Pte. Ltd., *Singapore*
Editora Prentice-Hall do Brasil, Ltda., *Rio de Janerio*

PREFACE
To the Instructor

Everything is new under the sun.
CZESLAW MILOSZ

Silence is the real crime against humanity.
NADYEZHDA MANDELSHTAM

The purpose of *Discovering Poetry* is to help today's students discover the life of the imagination and the power of literature. In this book we set out

♦ to help students (many of them non-readers) become active and responsive readers;

♦ to do justice to the emotional and imaginative as well as the intellectual dimensions of literature;

♦ to contribute to the task of redefining the canon, making works by women and by authors from culturally diverse backgrounds an integral part of the study of literature;

♦ to help students bring their own imagination and creativity into play;

♦ to talk to today's students in a lively, supportive, and accessible style designed to demystify traditional terms and categories;

♦ to provide more motivation, guidance, and student models for writing about literature than any comparable text.

REDEFINING THE CANON

Discovering Poetry provides balanced coverage of the rich diversity of our literary culture. We have aimed at a fruitful interaction of classics and moderns (and we have included many modern classics). We have aimed at a balance of women and men. We frequently juxtapose traditional or mainstream authors with writers from culturally diverse backgrounds.

Rediscovering the Heritage   Classics are works that speak to readers across distances in time or place. Our reward as teachers comes when classics are rediscovered by a new generation of students. *Discovering Poetry* tries to make students sense the enduring freshness and power of classic poems by Donne,

Hopkins, and Millay. The book features fresh readings of authors like Emily Dickinson and Robert Frost.

Tomorrow's Classics We take special pride in recognizing contemporary writers who write with integrity and passion. The book highlights poems by poets like Sharon Olds, Denise Levertov, William Stafford, and Gwendolyn Brooks.

Multicultural Literacy A central aim of teaching literature is the broadening of imaginative sympathy. This book is rich in selections by authors who broaden our horizons—Third World writers like Wole Soyinka and Federico García Lorca as well as writers who dramatize the meeting of cultures, like Lorna Dee Cervantes and Louise Erdrich.

Juxtapositions Paired readings help students see the presence of the past or the continuity of perennial themes in works rooted in diverse cultural traditions. Often a classic is seen in a fresh light as it is juxtaposed with a modern poem on the same theme. Often juxtapositions help students see the continuity between canonized traditional readings and newer voices—as when a poem by John Donne is juxtaposed with one by N. Scott Momaday.

Authors Covered in Depth Featured authors are covered in depth with a rich array of biographical and critical materials. Major featured poets are Emily Dickinson (with focus on the poet's voice), Robert Frost (with focus on poet and persona), and Gwendolyn Brooks (with focus on commitment and universality).

THE ACTIVE READER

The questions and activities following literary selections promote the ideal of the active, involved, empathetic reader. Several strands intermesh in the after-selection apparatus: "The Receptive Reader"—promoting close, attentive reading; "The Personal Response"—validating the personal connection that makes the literature meaningful for readers; and "The Creative Dimension"— fostering the creative participation that brings the readers' own imaginations into play and helps them enter imaginatively into a writer's world.

The Receptive Reader This strand promotes close reading (and rereading) of a poem, encouraging openness to the difficult and new. Questions and discussions focus on how details and formal elements serve the larger whole. (The questions encourage exploration not only of the what but also of the why and so what.)

The Personal Response Questions and activities under this heading validate the reader's personal response, doing justice to the imaginative and emotional as well as the intellectual appeal of literature. Students are encouraged to find the personal connection, to relate what they read to their own experience.

The Creative Dimension   Creative activities following many selections bring the reader's imagination into play. Students are invited, for instance, to re-create a haunting image or dominant impression or to write a response to a classic poem.

A DYNAMIC CRITICAL PERSPECTIVE

This book owes a special debt to the dynamic variety of contemporary literary criticism and literary theory. We are indebted to provocative recent readings of authors like Emily Dickinson and to eloquent discussions of their craft by poets such as Dylan Thomas and Audre Lorde.

Updating the Critical Tradition   For decades, literature texts in the tradition of the New Criticism taught the elements of literature as if they were ends in themselves (contrary to the spirit of the best New Critics). The best current criticism has moved beyond a formalistic preoccupation with the technical workings of literature—without abandoning the tradition of close, faithful attention to the text that is the major legacy of the twentieth-century critical tradition. Throughout this book, we aim at the right balance of close reading, personal engagement, and creative participation.

Correlating Form and Meaning   In teaching students to respond to the formal elements of literature, we focus on how point of view, image, metaphor, or form serves its larger human meaning. Point of view, for example, is more than a technical concern; when we study point of view, we become aware of the window a poem opens on the world.

The Range of Interpretation   As Pablo Neruda has said, it takes two poets to make a poem: The poet who wrote it and the poet-reader who brings the letters on the page to life in the theater of the mind. This book explores the range of both critics' reactions and students' responses to key works. Major critical trends are shown in exceptionally accessible critical excerpts representing the range of interpretation for selected authors.

A TEXT FOR TEACHERS AND LEARNERS

Our aim is to help teachers find *a way into* literature for their students—regardless of the students' previous experience or the preconceptions they bring to the reading. We have made it our special concern to help teachers overcome negative attitudes that students may bring with them from previous encounters with poetry.

A Lively, Accessible Style   To make key terms and categories come to life for today's students means initiating students who tend to be unschooled in mastering demanding concepts or new terms. We try not to give students technically correct "dictionary definitions" purporting to take care of key terms once and for all. Instead, we try to make students see the need for or the vital significance of a key term. We focus on essentials first, having students discover complications and finer points later. We provide the reinforcement needed if students are to make key concepts their own.

A Learning Sequence   The organization of the book often leads students from the more accessible to the more challenging. Literal chronological sequence is one thing; the dynamics of learning and discovery are another.

Cross-References   "Cross-references" for discussion or writing invite students to explore connections between selections related in theme or form—helping them discover recurrent patterns and illuminating contrasts, helping them see a familiar selection from a fresh perspective.

WRITING ABOUT LITERATURE

We have tried to provide more guidance, encouragement, and recognition for student writing than any comparable text. Guidelines for writing about literature and sample student papers do not appear in a one-size-fits-all writing chapter or as an afterthought in an appendix. Instead, they come with *each* chapter.

Writing Workshops   The writing workshops following each chapter focus on the process that makes substantial, purposeful, live student writing take shape. Students repeatedly see sample assignments move from prewriting (journal writing, note-taking, clustering, brainstorming) to drafting and from there to instructor response and peer critique and then to revision and final editing.

The Imaginative Dimension   As part of both after-selection apparatus and the writing workshops, imaginative writing opportunities enable students to give voice to their own experience and bring their own creativity into play.

Model Student Papers   A wealth of motivated, well-developed student writing provides models for class discussion of writing strategies and for peer review. Emphasis is on the potential, the promise, of student writing. Peer editors are encouraged to help student writers build on their strengths as well as to correct their weaknesses.

Research and Documentation   *Discovering Poetry* initiates students into library research and sets up an ample choice of research paper projects on literary topics. The text provides guidelines and a model of a documented paper. Pointed instructions elucidate for the student the mysteries of the current MLA documentation style, clarifying the rationale while giving a wealth of sample entries.

ACKNOWLEDGMENTS

Working on this book has been a privilege and a joy. We owe special thanks to Kathleen Evans, who did first-rate work while helping us with many editing and writing tasks. Nancy Perry of Blair Press had the vision to make this book possible, and she and Denise Wydra accomplished the impossible in coordinating the work of perceptive, dedicated reviewers and shepherding a complex enterprise. We owe a special debt to the admirable patience and competence of Julie Sullivan, who saw the book through production.

We are indebted to students whose intelligence, curiosity, and imagination have kept alive our faith in the power of literature and in the human enterprise. Of the many students from whose writing we have learned and who have allowed us to use or adapt their papers, we want to thank especially Debbie Nishimura, Andrea Sandke, Olivia Nunez, Francia Stephens, Mike DeAngelis, Dea Nelson, Kam Chieu, Greg Grewell, Johanna Wright, Merritt Ireland, Linda Spencer, Elizabeth Kerns, Conard Mangrum, Joyce Halenar, Marilyn Johnson, Michael Guth, John Newman, Judith Gardner, Pamela Cox, Rita Farkas, Barbara Hill, Melody Brune, Paul Francois, Ruth Randall, Katheryn Crayton-Shay, Dorothy Overstreet, Bill Irwin, Ruth Veerkamp, Martha Kell, Kevin McCabe, Thomas Perez-Jewell, Janelle Ciraulo, Irina Raicu, Joyce Sandoval, Catherine Hooper, Gail Bowman, Todd Marvin, and Catherine Russell.

Among the colleagues who pored over the manuscript and shared with us their enthusiasms and apprehensions, we want to thank especially William E. Cain, Wellesley College; Patricia E. Connors, Memphis State University; John L. Davis, The University of Texas at San Antonio; Kitty Chen Dean, Nassau Community College; Carla Johnson, St. Mary's College; Bob Mayberry, University of Nevada at Las Vegas; Susan J. Miller, Santa Fe Community College; Melita Schaum, University of Michigan, Dearborn; and William E. Sheidley, University of Connecticut.

Working with colleagues from around the country has renewed our faith in our common task. As members of our profession, in spite of the political and theoretical allegiances that divide us, we share the love of learning, the love of language, and the love of literature. May this book give pleasure to those who teach and learn from it.

HANS P. GUTH
GABRIELE L. RICO

BRIEF CONTENTS

CONTENTS

3   IMAGE   *The Open Eye*   69

4   METAPHOR   *Making Connections*   90

WRITING ABOUT LITERATURE
Writing Workshops at a Glance

DISCOVERING POETRY

1 PREVIEW
What Is Poetry?

The poet, lacking the impediment of speech with which the rest of us are afflicted, gazes, records, diagnoses, and prophecies.

RICHARD SELZER

I dwell in Possibility—
A fairer House than Prose—
More numerous of Windows—
Superior—for Doors—

EMILY DICKINSON

Sei que canto. E a canção é tudo.
Tem sangue eterno e asa ritmada.
E um dia sei que estarei mudo:
—mais nada.

I know that I sing. And song is all for me.
Its heart beats forever as it flies on rhythmic wing.
And I also know that one day my voice will fall silent—
Never to be heard again.

CECÍLIA MEIRELES

FOCUS ON POETRY

What is poetry? Cautious readers might start by saying that poems are surrounded by more white space on the page than prose. (Poems are usually made up of lines that stop short of the margin.) Obviously, such a definition does not do justice to the pleasure poetry gives its readers, to its power to move, or to its power to take readers beyond what they already think and feel. The gift of language is what makes us human, and poets make the fullest use of it. They often seem to write with a heightened sense of awareness, with a special intensity—"in a fine frenzy," in Shakespeare's words.

Poets are in love with words. One way to define poetry is to call it language at its best: Poets use its full potential, using more of it and using it to better advantage than we usually do. Poets mobilize to the fullest the image-making capacity of language. ("This morning," Javier Gálvez says, "the sun broke/my window/and came in laughing.") Poetry has the ability to delight the ear and the power to stir our emotions. It has the potential, if we let it, of making us more responsive and thoughtful human beings.

Read a short poem first of all as a communication from one fellow human being to another. Listen to the human voice speaking in the poem. That voice may be speaking about anything within the realm of human experience, real or imagined. Here is a modern American poet speaking to us about the pain of separation.

W. S. MERWIN   (born 1927)

Separation   1963

Your absence has gone through me
Like thread through a needle.
Everything I do is stitched with its color.

What helps make this a poem rather than ordinary prose?

✧ First of all, out of the confusing flow of experience, the poet has brought something into *focus*. For a moment, we stop hurrying to whatever we were doing next. We stop to pay attention. We linger for a while—to contemplate, to take something in.

✧ Secondly, what we take in is not just talk. We are helped to *imagine* what separation is like. The poem gives us something to visualize, to take in with the mind's eye. It is as if our days, like a piece of embroidery, were stitched through with a continuing thread—of missing the other person. A sewing needle does not jab the fabric once and then think about something else. It does its work by making one stitch after the other, stitching in the thread that will hold the fabric together or that will shape a pattern in a piece of embroidered material.

✧ Thirdly, the poem does not just give us information to feed into a data bank. We are not expected to record the message with no more emotion than a fax machine. Writing poetry is an act of faith: The poet assumes that we are capable of caring one way or the other. We are capable of entering imaginatively into the poet's *feelings*, of sharing his sense of loss.

✧ Finally, the poem is printed as lines of verse. These measure out or mark off units of thought, laying out the message in a satisfying *pattern* (that we can take in at a glance). When we finish reading, we have the satisfying sense of having taken in a complete whole.

Poetry comes to us as one of our oldest heirlooms as human beings. Civilization began when the first artists painted bison on the walls of caves and the first poets chanted songs about the exploits of the tribe or the creation of all living things. In many early cultures, a dominant form, or genre, was the **epic,** a long poem that spoke to its listeners in an elevated style and embodied their values, aspirations, and traumas. Often, the traditional epic focused on a high point in the history of a people, the way Homer in the *Iliad* sang the Greek expedition to besiege and destroy the fabled city of Troy:

> As the many tribes of winged birds—
> The geese, the cranes, and the long-throated swans—
> Make their flight this way and that
> And then settle in fluttering swarms
> While a vast field echoes with their cries,
> So these many tribes poured out from their ships
> Onto the plain of Troy.

When we talk about poetry today, we usually think of a more personal kind of writing. We think of a fairly short poem that communicates personal observations, feelings, and thoughts. We call such a short poem the **lyric,** named after the lyre, or small harp, that the poets of ancient Greece played as they recited their verses.

USING THE IMAGINATION

Memory does not retain all, but only what strikes the spirit.
ÉMILE BERNARD

To find the raw material for poems, you don't need to backpack to Katmandu. No doubt some have done so and returned knowing less than Emily Dickinson knew from watching hummingbirds and garter snakes in the meadow across the road past her home.
X. J. KENNEDY

A real poet can make everything into poetry, including his or her own life.
DIANE WAKOSKI

Poets ask us to use our imagination. Although they make us think, they first of all ask us to imagine. They make us see, they make us feel, and they make us think. A dictionary definition of the word *presentiment* would tell us that it is a sudden fleeting feeling of anxiety—a sudden, passing sense of fore-boding, a premonition that something hurtful is going to happen. Unlike a dictionary definition, the following poem does not *state* this idea; it brings it to life.

EMILY DICKINSON (1830–1886)

Presentiment   1863

Presentiment—is that long shadow—on the lawn—
Indicative that Suns go down—
The notice to the startled Grass
That Darkness—is about to pass—

This poem makes us *see*. The poem starts with a striking **image:** On a sunny day, we all of a sudden notice the dark shadow on the lawn that announces (or is an indication of) the coming of evening. The poem makes us *feel:* Like the grass, we may be startled, afraid of darkness. We may share in a shuddery feeling. The poem makes us *think:* We are reminded that "suns go down." We may reflect that, like them, sunny parts of our lives must sooner or later alternate with darkness.

The following poem is one of the best loved (and most often discussed) in the English language. What experience does it ask you to share? What does the poem invite you to see, feel, and think?

ROBERT FROST (1874–1963)

Stopping by Woods on a Snowy Evening   1923

Whose woods these are I think I know.
His house is in the village though;
He will not see me stopping here
To watch his woods fill up with snow.

My little horse must think it queer   5
To stop without a farmhouse near
Between the woods and frozen lake
The darkest evening of the year.

He gives his harness bells a shake
To ask if there is some mistake.   10
The only other sound's the sweep
Of easy wind and downy flake.

The woods are lovely, dark and deep.
But I have promises to keep,
And miles to go before I sleep,   15
And miles to go before I sleep.

In this poem, we find ourselves on a deserted rural road in the wintertime, away from the nearest village or farmhouse, with the driver of the horse-drawn vehicle stopping to look at the woods filling up with snow. It is cold enough for the lake to have frozen over, and the evening is getting very dark, so the normal thing would be to hurry on home. (The horse certainly seems to think so, wondering "if there is some mistake.")

But something strange happens in this poem: It is very quiet, the wind is an "easy wind," and the snowflakes are "downy," like a down-filled pillow beckoning us toward rest. The snow-covered woods look "lovely." It would be tempting not to go on—to go to sleep in the soft snow. It would be restful to push out of mind whatever cares, responsibilities, or pressures are waiting in the village. In the end, tempting as the thought may be of dropping out, of going to "sleep," the speaker in the poem is kept going by the thought of "promises to keep." There are still "miles to go," as the speaker says twice, "miles to go."

Perhaps the secret of this poem's appeal is its apparent simplicity. It sets up a situation that many different readers can in their own way find mirrored in their experience: It is likely to make them share the longing for rest, but at the same time it is likely to make them sense the need to go on. Some readers of this poem will remember the word *promises* especially: What "promises" does the speaker have to keep? Different readers might think of responsibilities to family, obligations to friends, debts to be repaid. Some readers will be haunted by the beckoning dark woods. One student said: "The horse does not know we are going to die, but the poet does."

THE RECEPTIVE READER

What kind of "promises" do you think the speaker had in mind? ✧ Critics have argued whether or not the dark woods in this poem are a symbol of death. What would be your answer to this question, and how would you support it? ✧ What is the effect of the poet's repeating the last line?

The images in a poem bring an experience to life for us by appealing to our senses—by making us see, hear, smell, taste, and touch. Vivid, graphic images re-create for us the **concrete** texture of experience, that is, the visible, tangible quality of the world we take in through our senses. At the same time, the images in a poem often carry meanings beyond their literal surface impact. They become a language of speaking and moving images, suggesting meanings that would remain pale or incomplete when spelled out in more literal terms. The most basic device poets use to convey meanings beyond those of ordinary literal speech is the **metaphor.** It "carries us beyond" ordinary literal meanings to something else. One of Shakespeare's best-known sonnets begins,

Let me not to the marriage of true minds
Admit impediments.

The poet is saying that no obstacles should be allowed to interfere with (to "impede") the marriage of minds sincerely meaning to be faithful to one another. Metaphorically, marriage here evokes a true meeting of minds, a perfect union of the kind we envision an ideal marriage to be. The marriage metaphor here carries a richer meaning than the literal word *union:* Traditionally, marriage has been a solemn occasion, surrounded by pomp and circumstance, sanctified by religion, and carrying with it the promise of lifelong devotion.

As you read and study poems, you will again and again encounter other features of the poet's language that make it richer and more imaginative than language for everyday use:

◇ If we read the woods in Frost's poem not as a place for a temporary rest but as a beckoning toward the final long rest of death, we are reading them as a **symbol.** The marriage in the Shakespeare sonnet need not literally take place; the poet very likely brought it into the poem as a metaphor. However, the woods in the Frost poem are literally there; we may choose to give them a larger symbolic significance.

◇ Poets use words rich in **connotation** and shades of meaning. They use words that carry the right overtones or emotional associations. In the Dickinson poem, *startled* says more than *surprised,* since we can be mildly surprised, whereas we find it hard to be mildly startled.

◇ Modern poets especially are likely to be sensitive to **irony;** they are likely to explore the puzzles posed by **paradox.** Irony goes counter to expectation, leaving us in varying degrees bemused and amused. It is ironic that in the Frost poem the horse, and not its human owner, thinks it's time to go on home. Paradox confronts us with contradictions that may make sense on second thought. It is paradoxical that in Frost's poem the snow, hostile to life, comes down in "downy" flakes (soft like the feathers used in pillows) and that the woods (which may be a symbol of death) are "lovely." On second thought, we may realize that to a harried person death could begin to seem restful and beautiful.

◇ Poets may call up a whole range of memories by way of **allusion.** A modern feminist poet referring to Helen may trust the brief mention to call up a whole range of associations with the legendary Helen of Troy—celebrated for her beauty, reviled for leaving her Greek husband for a Trojan prince, blamed for the war that destroyed Troy.

EXPLORATIONS

A Fresh Look

The following poems invite you to take a fresh look at something familiar—the human body, the rain, the moon. What do you look at in each poem, and how is the poet's angle of vision different or new? What new or unexpected connections does the poem establish? What new meanings does the poet find in familiar sights or familiar facts? What does the poet make you see and feel that a less imaginative observer might have missed?

AUDRE LORDE (born 1934)

Coping 1968

It has rained for five days
running
the world is
a round puddle
of sunless water 5
where small islands
are only beginning
to cope
a young boy
in my garden 10
is bailing out water
from his flower patch
when I ask him why
he tells me
young seeds that have not seen sun 15
forget
and drown easily.

THE RECEPTIVE READER

1. What is *ordinary* about the situation described in this poem? What is *imaginative* about the way this poet looks at the rain? What gives the seeds a significance beyond their ordinary literal meaning?

2. What is the central word in this poem? How does the poet highlight it? What is its full meaning?

FEDERICO GARCÍA LORCA (1898–1936)

Half Moon 1928

TRANSLATED BY W. S. MERWIN

The moon goes over the water.
How tranquil the sky is!
She goes scything slowly
the old shimmer from the river;
meanwhile a young frog 5
takes her for a little mirror.

THE RECEPTIVE READER

What does this poem by a well-known Spanish poet ask you to visualize, to imagine? What makes the imaginative comparisons in the poem new or unexpected? What makes them fitting?

AL YOUNG   (born 1939)

Chemistry   1968

What connects me to this moon
is legendary, and what connects
the moon to me is as
momentary as the night is
long before it burns away like   5
that fire in the eyes of lovers
when, spent, they turn
from one another and fall against
the dark sides of their pillows
to let their blood color cool.   10

You too know well the nature of
our chemistry: 65% oxygen,
18% carbon, 10% hydrogen,
3% nitrogen, a touch of calcium,
phosphorus and other elements.   15
But largely (by 70%) we're water:
2 parts hydrogen to 1 part oxygen,
and mostly we're still all wet—
9 parts fear chained to 1 part joy.
Is this why we're given to drowning   20
ourselves in pools of tears,
long on sorrow and shallow on laughter;
drowning ourselves in sugar and salt
as it were, as we are, as the treasured
substance of a former fish's life   25
can never be technically measured?

This chemistry we swim and skim
is what connects all light with me
olympically,° for real life   *in a godlike way*
science will forever be proving   30
this radiant suspension to be love
in but one of its bubbling mutations.

THE RECEPTIVE READER

1. In this poem, what is the connection between the moon and the lovers?

2. What knowledge of biology, or "life science," does the poet expect of his readers? What new and imaginative use does he make of biological facts? What is the connection he establishes between our body chemistry and our feelings? How would you sum up what he means by "real life science"?

THE PERSONAL RESPONSE

Audre Lorde and Al Young are among the best-known African American poets. Does knowing this biographical fact make a difference to the way you respond to the poems?

RHYMED OR UNRHYMED POETRY?

Talking becomes poetry as walking becomes dancing.
JOSEPHINE MILES

Does a poem have to rhyme? For the uninitiated reader, rhyme and meter are often the external signals that a writer is writing poetry. They are noticeable formal features of much traditional poetry, but they became more and more optional during the twentieth century. **Rhyme** is an echo effect produced when a poet repeats the same sounds at the end of the final syllables (sometimes whole final words) of two or more lines:

> The grizzly bear whose potent HUG
> Was feared by all is now a RUG.
> Arthur Guiterman

Rhyme keeps alive the delight in repetition, in finding recurrent patterns, that children first experience when they recite "Hickory-dickory-DOCK / The mouse ran up the CLOCK." At the same time, rhyme helps a poet create patterns by marking off regular intervals, by measuring off lines of verse. At the end of a set of lines, rhyme gives us a sense of **closure,** of having arrived at a satisfying conclusion. This sense of a pleasing completeness is especially strong in a **closed couplet** (rhymed set of two lines), like the one Alexander Pope (1688–1744) wrote about Sir Isaac Newton, master physicist of the eighteenth century and pioneer of the modern theory of light:

> Nature and Nature's laws lay hid in NIGHT.
> God said, "Let Newton be!" and all was LIGHT.

Rhyme can help a poet give shape to a **stanza,** a set of related lines with a pattern that may be repeated in other such stanzas in the same poem. In the following opening stanza of a song from a Shakespeare play, we see an interlaced rhyme scheme: The first and third lines rhyme (SUN/DONE). So do the second and fourth, as well as the fifth and sixth (giving us a pattern of ababcc):

Fear no more the heat of the SUN,	a
Nor the furious winter's RAGES.	b
Thou thy worldly task hast DONE,	a
Home art gone, and taken thy WAGES.	b
Golden lads and girls all MUST,	c
As chimney-sweepers, come do DUST.	c

Serious students of poetry take stock of different kinds of rhyme and trace in detail the role they play in determining the texture and shape of poems. (See Chapter 7 for a closer, more technical look.) However, most poets of our century (and some earlier ones) have done *without* rhyme. They have moved from traditional form, with consistent use of rhyme and an underlying regular beat, or meter, toward **open form** (earlier also called **free verse**). They lay out their poems and give shape to them by other means.

In the following unrhymed modern poem, the layout of the lines on the page guides us in setting up the pauses that shape the rhythm of the poem as a whole.

WILLIAM CARLOS WILLIAMS (1883–1963)

This Is Just to Say 1934

I have eaten
the plums
that were in
the icebox

and which 5
you were probably
saving
for breakfast

Forgive me
they were delicious 10
so sweet
and so cold.

THE CREATIVE DIMENSION

Have you ever felt like leaving a message that might begin "This is just to say"? Look at the following student-written response to the Williams poem. How or how well did the student reader get into the spirit of the original poem? Then write a "This-is-just-to-say" message of your own.

This is just to say

I used
the last of
the gas
in your car

you will probably be in
a rush tomorrow
and won't have
time
to refill the
tank

I'm sorry
but I had
no money
and I so

detest the
smell of gas
on my
hands

JUXTAPOSITIONS ⟺─────────────────

To Rhyme or Not to Rhyme

The two poems that follow deal with a similar topic but are different in form. The first poem is by an eighteenth-century English poet who uses rhyme extensively. Lines and stanzas are neatly marked off and packaged. The second poem is by a twentieth-century poet who does without regular rhyme and whose lines move freely in an irregular pattern. How does the difference in form affect your response as a reader?

WILLIAM COWPER (1731–1800)

The Snail   before 1800

Give but his horns the slightest touch,
His self-collective power is such,
He shrinks into his house with much
    Displeasure.

Wherever he dwells, he dwells alone,   5
Except himself, has chattels° none,   *goods*
Well satisfied to be his own
    Whole treasure.

Thus hermit-like his life he leads,
Nor partner of his banquet needs,°   *nor does he need*   10
And if he meets one, only feeds
    The faster.

Who seeks him must be worse than blind
—He and his house are so combined—
If finding it, he fails to find   15
    Its master.

THE RECEPTIVE READER

1. What in the outward form of this poem mirrors the shrinking of the snail as it withdraws into the shell?

2. How does this poet go beyond the simplest use of rhyme—two consecutive lines that rhyme? Can you read this poem out loud so as to do justice to the echo effect of rhyme and to the spilling over of the sense (or the sentence) from the third into the fourth line of each stanza?

3. In how many ways does this poem compare the snail to a human being? With what effect? How are we reminded in the poem that the animal is *different* from a human being?

4. What is witty about this poem? Does it have a serious point?

MAY SWENSON   (born 1919)

Living Tenderly   1963

My body a rounded stone
with a pattern of smooth seams.
My head a short snake
retractive, projective.°   *able to pull in and jut out*
My legs come out of their sleeves   5
or shrink within,
and so does my chin.
My eyelids are quick clamps.
My back is my roof.
I am always at home.   10
I travel where my house walks.
It is a smooth stone.
It floats within the lake,
or rests in the dust.
My flesh lives tenderly   15
inside its bone.

THE RECEPTIVE READER

1. Modern poems doing without a regular rhyme scheme may nevertheless use *occasional* rhyme and echo effects similar to rhyme. How does this poet use rhyme and other repetition or echoing of sound?

2. What *other* kinds of repetition, and of lining up of opposites, help give shape to this poem?

3. What makes the last two lines a high point or fitting *conclusion* of the poem?

THE PERSONAL RESPONSE

Which of the two poems do you like better and why? (Are you inclined to favor the traditional or the modern?)

THE CREATIVE DIMENSION

Try your hand at writing a riddle poem similar to May Swenson's "Living Tenderly." Make sure to furnish your reader with vivid, revealing clues.

METER AND FREE VERSE

*Poetry withers and dries out when it leaves music, or at
least imagined music, too far behind.*

EZRA POUND

*The poem exists in the whole body of the person absorbing
it, and particularly in the mouth that holds the intimate
sounds touching each other, and in the leg that dances the
rhythm.*

DONALD HALL

Anyone who breathes is in the rhythm business.

WILLIAM STAFFORD

Does poetry have to have a strong regular rhythm, or meter? In traditional kinds of poetry, rhyme and meter go hand in hand in helping to shape
the poem. **Meter** regulates the free-flowing irregular rhythms of ordinary
speech. It sets up a regular underlying beat of the kind that in music we
could accentuate by a drumbeat (or by tapping our toes and clapping our
hands). Much modern poetry has moved toward freer, more irregular
rhythms—hard to chart, or scan, as a regular beat. Many modern poets, like
the poet Donald Hall, tend to think of meter not as a constraint but as "a
loose set of probabilities."

Meter has an enticing (and sometimes hypnotic) effect because it mirrors
basic rhythms of life: the lub DUB, lub-DUB, lub-DUB of the heart; the one-two,
one-two of walking or running; the in-and-out of deep breathing. The following lines from the poem by Robert Frost that you read earlier have an exceptionally regular beat. Each second syllable has a stronger stress than the
first—with the exception of the fourth word in the first and second lines and
the second word in the third line. However, since the basic underlying beat
goes on, we sense these words as a departure from, or a variation on, the basic
meter. These variations keep the basic four-beat line from becoming monotonous, like the tick-tack of a metronome:

Whose WOODS these <u>are</u> I THINK I KNOW
His HOUSE is <u>in</u> the VILLage, THOUGH.
He <u>will</u> not SEE me STOPPing HERE
To WATCH his WOODS fill UP with SNOW.

The fourth and last line shows the underlying four-beat rhythm most
clearly. (The return to the basic regular meter often signals a return to the
basic theme or point, or an answer after questions or doubts.) To chart the
basic meter, we can cut up the line into four pairs of syllables, each with an *unstressed* or weak syllable first and a *stressed* or emphasized syllable second:

To WATCH | his WOODS | fill UP | with SNOW.

Each of these four segments (one stressed syllable each) is called a **foot.** A foot with only two syllables and the stress last is still called by its original Greek name. It is an **iambic** foot, and the "DeTROIT—DeTROIT—DeTROIT" meter it sets up (rather than "BOSton—BOSton—BOSton") is called iambic meter. Over the centuries, iambic meter with four or five beats to the line has become the dominant or most common meter in poetry written in English. (See Chapter 7 for a closer and more technical look at meter.)

Strongly metrical poetry, rhymed or unrhymed, was the norm till well into the nineteenth century. However, in true poetry meter is never merely mechanical. It provides only the underlying beat, not the music. The following poem is by Alfred, Lord Tennyson, in his time perhaps the most widely read poet of the Victorian Age (roughly the mid-nineteenth century). Read the poem out loud or hear it read out loud. Which lines come closest to a regular four-beat iambic meter? What makes the second and third lines different?

ALFRED, LORD TENNYSON (1809–1892)
The Eagle   1851

He clasps the crag with crooked hands;
Close to the sun in lonely lands,
Ringed with the azure° world, he stands.   *deep sky-blue*

The wrinkled sea beneath him crawls;
He watches from his mountain walls,   5
And like a thunderbolt he falls.

The first line of the poem (like the fourth) has a very regular beat:

He CLASPS | the CRAG | with CROOK | ed HANDS

But in the second line (as in the third), the stress pattern is reversed at the beginning of the line. This reversal, or inversion, sets up the kind of counter-rhythm that keeps meter from becoming too mechanical. (See Chapter 7 for more on this common **trochaic** inversion.)

CLOSE to | the SUN | in LONE | ly LANDS

In each stanza, there is a slowing down at the end as we rest momentarily on a final word that is crucial to the meaning and at the same time accentuated by rhyme: ". . . he STANDS"; ". . . he FALLS."

THE RECEPTIVE READER

1. How should this poem sound when read aloud? Listen as several classmates read the poem. Which of them comes closest to the right balance—making the reader sense the underlying rhythm without making it mechanical or obtrusive?

2. The eagle, although almost extinct, is everywhere in traditional lore and public symbols. What images, ideas, or associations does the eagle bring to mind? Are any of them echoed in Tennyson's poem? Is there anything new or different about the way Tennyson asks us to imagine the eagle in this poem?

Even in Tennyson's time, poets were experimenting with less regular rhythms. Here is an example of **free verse** by the American poet Walt Whitman (the "poet of democracy"). Whitman's free verse has a strong rhythm, but it does not have an easily charted regular beat. The lines vary greatly in length. (Some lines are short, but others go on and on.) There is nothing tidy or measured about Whitman's verse. He saw himself as the prophet of a new national consciousness and a new spirituality, and his lines have the flow and sweep of a prophet's inspirations.

Try to read the poem first with exaggerated stress on strongly stressed or accentuated syllables. Although there is no strong regular beat or meter, an irregular rhythmic pattern emerges. We can imagine that we are hearing the poet chant these lines. In the words of one student reader, "The almost chanting, yet not mesmerizingly regular rhythm elevates the tone of the poem and gives it almost oracular power."

WALT WHITMAN (1819–1892)
A Noiseless Patient Spider   1881

A noiseless patient spider
I marked where on a little promontory° it stood isolated,   *outcropping*
Marked how to explore the vacant vast surrounding
It launched forth filament, filament, filament out of itself,
Ever unreeling them, ever tirelessly speeding them.   5
And you O my soul where you stand,
Surrounded, detached, in measureless oceans of space,
Ceaselessly musing, venturing, throwing, seeking the
    spheres to connect them,
Till the bridge you will need be formed, till the
    ductile° anchor hold,   *easily bent*
Till the gossamer thread you fling catch somewhere,
    O my soul.   10

This poem revolves around the parallel between "the noiseless patient spider" and the human soul. The spider stands "isolated" as if on a cliff jutting out into the sea, encircled by what is, for the spider, the "vacant vast surrounding." Similarly, the soul finds itself "detached, in measureless oceans of space"—in the vast spaces our thoughts can travel without finding a firm support or rest. The spider with tireless repetition spins and launches forth "filament, filament, filament," hoping they will catch at points beyond the empty space to allow it to anchor its net. (The word *launch* implies exploration, as when we launch a space probe into the reaches of outer space.) Similarly, the human soul, "ceaselessly musing, venturing, throwing, seeking," launches forth the thoughts that will allow it to find a firm point of rest or to connect with what gives meaning to our lives.

The slow, solemn rhythm of the lines suits the elevated subject: our search for spiritual fulfillment, our faith in our ability to find a spiritual anchor in what at first seems a vast meaningless universe. Here is how you might mark the stresses that account for the rhythm of the first three lines:

A NOISEless PATient SPIDer
I MARKed where on a LITTle PROMontory it STOOD ISolated,
MARKed how to exPLORE the VACant VAST surROUNDing

THE RECEPTIVE READER

1. How well do you respond to the *rhythm* of Whitman's verse? Can you chart the major stressed syllables in the rest of the poem? Do you and your classmates agree on the rhythmic patterns of the lines?

2. What ideas or associations do spiders usually bring to mind? What is *different* about the way Whitman looks at the spider in this poem?

3. What is the connection between the spider and the poet's *soul*? What is the "bridge" the soul will need? What is the "gossamer thread" the soul flings in this poem?

4. Why does the poet start with the *image* of the patient spider—rather than with the central idea of the poem? What does the poet lose or gain by not letting us know till halfway through the poem that it is addressed to his soul?

Much later free verse has a less strong, less chanting rhythm than Whitman's poems. The following lines are from a poem by Daniela Gioseffi, an American poet and playwright writing a century later. Her lines illustrate the irregular length of line and the underplayed, almost conversational rhythm of much current poetry. The poet is not speaking from a podium or preaching from a pulpit; she is talking with us easily and confidentially. (Try to identify stressed or accented syllables as you read.)

A silver watch you've worn for years
is suddenly gone
leaving a pale white stripe
blazing on your wrist.

JUXTAPOSITIONS ━━━━━━━━━━

Meter and Free Verse

The following two poems are by poets who choose to use traditional rhyme and meter in some of their poems and modern free verse in others. Most readers know Edna St. Vincent Millay for poems on traditional themes, mourning lost happiness and the passing of love. However, she also wrote intensely personal poems in a less traditional mold and passionate indictments of war and oppression. Her poem, the first of the two reprinted here, is a sonnet, a traditional fourteen-line poem, elaborately crafted, and often addressed to a lover. (You will be able to take a closer look at the sonnet form in Chapter 7.) Gwendolyn Brooks is best known for eloquent poems about the injustices suffered by black Americans, although many of her poems are loving portraits of people she cherished. In the first poem, look closely at the workings of traditional rhyme and meter. In the second poem, look at the workings of modern free verse.

EDNA ST. VINCENT MILLAY   (1892–1950)

Pity me not because the light of day   1917

Pity me not because the light of day
At close of day no longer walks the sky;
Pity me not for beauties passed away
From field and thicket as the years go by;
Pity me not the waning of the moon,   5
Nor that the ebbing tide goes out to sea,
Nor that man's desire is hushed so soon,
And you no longer look with love on me.
This have I known always: Love is no more
Than the wide blossom which the wind assails,   10
Than the great tide that treads the shifting shore,
Strewing fresh wreckage gathered in the gales:
Pity me that the heart is slow to learn
What the swift mind beholds at every turn.

THE RECEPTIVE READER

1. A key feature of the sonnet is its interlaced *rhyme scheme*. Which lines rhyme in this sonnet?

2. Another traditional feature is the five-beat iambic meter (called *iambic pentameter,* after the Greek word for five). Which lines have the most regular iambic beat, on the "DeTROIT-DeTROIT-DeTROIT" model? Which lines vary the beat by starting with a strongly accented first syllable?

3. The rhyme scheme and the traditional meter help make a sonnet a unified, finished whole. In this poem, how do the *repetition* of phrases and the use of parallel, similar sentence structure contribute to the same effect?

4. What *images* does the poet draw on to help you imagine the nature of love? What do these images have in common?

5. As in many other sonnets, the final *couplet* provides a turning point, an answer to a question raised earlier. Here, we go on from the "Pity me not . . ." pattern of the earlier lines to what *does* deserve our pity. What is the difference between the slow heart and the swift mind?

THE PERSONAL RESPONSE

Millay was out of fashion for a time but is being rediscovered by a new generation of readers. Can you relate to the mood or the predominant feeling of this sonnet? Why or why not?

GWENDOLYN BROOKS   (born 1917)

Truth   1949

And if sun comes
How shall we greet him?
Shall we not dread him,
Shall we not fear him
After so lengthy a   5
Session with shade?

Though we have wept for him,
Though we have prayed
All through the night-years—
What if we wake one shimmering morning to   10
Hear the fierce hammering
Of his firm knuckles
Hard on the door?

Shall we not shudder?—
Shall we not flee   15
Into the shelter, the dear thick shelter
Of the familiar
Propitious° haze?   *promising good fortune*

Sweet is it, sweet is it
To sleep in the coolness   20
Of snug unawareness.

The dark hangs heavily
Over the eyes.

THE RECEPTIVE READER

1. This poem does not use traditional rhyme and meter. It nevertheless has a stronger rhythm than much modern free verse. What guides you in reading the poem with the *right rhythm*? Point out examples of the poet's repeating phrases or sentence frames. Can you show how this repetition sets up patterns that help make the poem a unified whole? What is the effect of the frequent repetition or echoing on you as the reader?

2. Traditional guidelines for rhyme ruled out the repetition of identical words at the end of lines. Modern critics know it occurs in contemporary poetry; they sometimes call it *para-rhyme* (a rhyme that is not really a rhyme but something like it). Where does it occur in this poem? They also call pairs of words that do not rhyme but more distantly sound alike *half-rhymes* or *slant rhymes*. Where do you find these in the poem?

3. How are the images and feelings associated with the sun in this poem different from more familiar or predictable ones? How are the images and feelings associated with the dark, its opposite, different from what we might expect?

4. What "fierce" and feared or dreaded truths do you think the poet had in mind? What kind of "night-years" may the poet have been thinking about?

THE PERSONAL RESPONSE

Many readers read Brooks' poetry in the context of the civil rights struggle of the sixties and seventies. Does this poem's perspective on truth apply to other contexts, other situations? (Is the poem both timely and timeless at the same time?)

THE CREATIVE DIMENSION

Suppose you were asked to draw up five questions designed to test your respondents' loyalty to the truth. What would your questions be?

CLOSE READING AND THE PERSONAL RESPONSE

The poem must provoke its readers: force them to hear—to hear themselves.
                                                    OCTAVIO PAZ

The purpose of poetry is to remind us how difficult it is to remain just one person, for our house is open, there are no keys in the doors, and invisible guests come in and out at will.
                    CZESLAW MILOSZ, "THE POETIC VOICE IN US"

May God us keep / From single vision.
                    WILLIAM BLAKE

What is your role as the reader? A poem is not like an art object in a glass case in a museum, with a sign that says "Do not touch the artifacts." A successful poem does something for you as the reader: It may open a new perspective. It may shake you up; it may move you to laughter or to tears. The poem ceases to be just words on a page when it triggers this kind of interaction between the poet and you as the reader.

Some readers get much out of even a fairly short or simple poem. It is as if their antennas were especially well equipped to pick up the signals the poem sends. To make the most of your reading, consider guidelines like the following:

✦ *Give the poem a close reading.* Take in as much as you can; be open to whatever the poem has to offer. Many readers start with a fairly quick reading of the whole poem to get an overall impression. But then they go back to take in important details. They linger over a key line. They weigh the impact of a key image. They puzzle over apparent contradictions.

✦ *Get your bearings.* Who is speaking in the poem? What is the situation or occasion? What seems to be the agenda? For instance, are we looking at a scene from the world of nature? Are we witnessing a confrontation between parent and child? Is a lover talking to the beloved?

✧ *Respond to the poem as a whole.* Try to get a sense of its overall pattern. Look for key words or phrases that echo in the poem. Look at how the poem as a whole takes shape. For instance, does it move from now to then (and then perhaps back again to now)? Does it play off two different ways of looking at our world? Does it set up polarities—for instance, does it move from innocence to experience? Does it travel between city life and nature?

✧ *Get into the spirit of the poem.* We are disappointed when someone reading a poem aloud reads without expression, without feeling. We want the reader's face, gestures, and body language to act out the mood, the rhythm, or the overall shape of the poem. Even when reading silently, a receptive reader may betray by nods and frowns and gestures that the poem is being experienced, acted out, in the reader's mind.

✧ *Be ready for a personal response.* We do not read poetry in order to analyze poems that leave us cold. Writing poetry is an act of faith assuming that the poet's observations and experiences will find an echo in the experience of the reader. A poem that is reprinted and reread time and again has touched a chord in many different readers. To be moved by a poem about the loss of a father, we need not have lost a father ourselves, but the poem may remind us of the loss of somebody or something dear to us.

Give the following short poem a careful, patient, line-by-line reading. Then look at one student reader's close reading of the poem. What did you miss that the student reader noticed? What in turn did you notice that she apparently missed?

LINDA PASTAN   (born 1932)

Sometimes in Winter   1991

when I look into
the fragile faces
of those I love,

I long to be
one of those people who skate   5
over the surface

of their lives, scoring
the ice with patterns
of their own making,

people who have   10
no children.
who are attached

to earth only by
silver blades moving
at high speed,   15

who have learned to use
the medium of the cold
to dance in.

Compare the reading in the following sample student paper with your own reading of the poem.

SAMPLE STUDENT PAPER

Dancing in the Medium of the Cold

In the poem "Sometimes in Winter," we are asked to explore the relationship between life and ice-skating. Taken out of context, the metaphor of life as skating over ice might not appear to be entirely serious. But the images that are used in this poem make us think seriously about the comparison. The comparison is followed up in a chain of related words and images: winter, cold, a surface that can be scored but not penetrated, patterns sketched in the ice, silver blades speeding across the ice.

On the surface, the sight of the "silver blades moving / at high speed" across the ice is very appealing. The skaters score "the ice with patterns / of their own making." They seem in charge, in control, deciding for themselves whether they want to score in the ice a figure 8 or some other kind of graceful loop. What a relief it would be to be a free-floating skater and not to have to worry about the needs and demands of others who depend on us.

However, the person speaking to us in the poem cannot be like an ice-skater skimming over the surface of life. For her, love means attachment. Looking into the "fragile" faces of those she loves, she sees how vulnerable they are. The speaker implies that love for children holds her to the earth when she says that people who have no children are attached to the earth only by "silver blades moving / at high speed." Is this connection enough to hold a person to the earth for very long? What happens to the ice-skater when this tenuous connection is severed? Does she fly off the earth? Does she cease to exist? That is what the metaphor implies. People who are not attached to loved ones are not fully participating in life; they only glide over the surface. They dance on top of life, but they do not enter into it.

The speaker in the poem says that she longs to be one of the people who skate over the surface of life, but the metaphor she uses belies or contradicts that claim. She may be attracted to the speed and flash of the ice-skater, but the images we see make us realize that the flash is all on the surface. The skaters are adapting to the medium in which they live; they are surrounded by the cold, so they have learned to dance (live) in it. If they were allowed to choose all over again, might they not say that they long to be attached to the earth by something more than silver blades moving at high speed?

Bickering, emergency phone calls, and disrupted schedules make life in close contact with others very different from skating gracefully over the ice. But could we stand "the medium of the cold" if we severed our ties?

QUESTIONS

Does this reading explain why there is so much ice and cold in this poem? What do the "silver blades" make you see or feel? Were you surprised by the use of the word *fragile* at the beginning of the poem? (Does the student writer do enough to explain how it makes us feel?) How do you explain that the skaters are "dancing"?

To judge from this student paper, our personal response to this poem will depend at least in part on how we feel about living in a close web of personal relationships as against the free-floating loneliness of the skater. But the student writer's own personal answer is only implied. (One reader started a more personal response to this poem by saying, "Not just sometimes in winter but several times a day I muse how I might be better off on my own.")

The two responses that follow the next poem (by an Irish poet) are by one reader. The first response is again the kind of close reading that tries to do justice to the poem in front of us on the page. The second response, however, goes a step further. The reader asked: What does this poem mean to me personally? Is there any personal connection between this poem and something in my own life? Study the two different dimensions of this reader's response. How are they different? How are they related?

SEAMUS HEANEY   (born 1939)

Valediction   1966

Lady with the frilled blouse
And simple tartan skirt,
Since you have left the house
Its emptiness has hurt
All thought. In your presence   5
Time rode easy, anchored
On a smile; but absence
Rocked love's balance, unmoored
The days. They buck and bound
Across the calendar   10
Pitched from the quiet sound
Of your flower-tender
Voice. Need breaks on my strand;°   *beach, shore*
You've gone, I am at sea.
Until you resume command   15
Self is in mutiny.

Look at the way the following reading pulls out and interprets significant details in the poem:

CLOSE READING: The poem "Valediction" describes the emotional experience of a man whose female companion (probably his wife) has left him. The poet uses a central metaphor to explain the speaker's emotional state, a metaphor he develops in a variety of ways, to describe exactly how the man in the poem is affected by her absence.

The metaphor in the poem is that of a boat on a lake or an ocean. When the "lady with the frilled blouse / And simple tartan skirt" was present, the boat was "anchored" secure in its mooring. "Time rode easy," suggesting the placid setting and the speaker's previously peaceful state of mind. With her absence, however, the calmness is lost: "love's balance," which existed in her presence, is "rocked," and the days "unmoored." Time is no longer safe at anchor but cast off, wild. The days now "buck" and "bound" as the boat pitches in the water; there is nothing smooth about the man's existence anymore.

Meanwhile, the waves have started to break on the beach. The waves are the man's "need," the beach his "strand." With the lady gone, the speaker is truly "at sea." He can only visualize calm in his life once more if she will return to "command" the boat that is the speaker himself. Until that time the boat is doomed to be "in mutiny," that is, beyond his control, at the mercy of time and the waves.

THE RECEPTIVE READER

What details in the poem follow up the contrast between the calm before and the turmoil after the woman's departure? Were you surprised by the phrase "resume command"? What do you think it shows about the relationship between the two people? Did this reader miss any significant details in this poem?

Look at the way the following response by the same reader relates the poem to the reader's own experience. A paper anchored in close reading but going on to the personal connection would answer both basic questions: What does this poem mean—to perhaps a majority of perceptive readers? And what does the poem mean to me?

PERSONAL RESPONSE: It is easy to identify with a poem that carries such an obvious central metaphor. It uses the boat rocked by waves as the metaphor for an event disturbing the equilibrium of someone's life. While I have never experienced what it is like to have the most important person in my life walk out on me, curiously enough, I dreamed about this happening to me just a few nights ago. In my dream I was in college, and J. had just left me. (As is common with dreams, there was no obvious reason for this occurrence.)

I experienced total and utter despair. Although several close friends and family were with me, they were unable, even unwilling, to help me through the experience. I was truly "at sea." I started out into the streets, attempting to find my way "home" to J. A wind started to roar toward me, hindering my steps, and the flat road suddenly became a hill. My last impression before awaking involved a clear realization that I never would succeed in reaching the crest of the hill and passing over to the other side.

Thinking about this dream, I have become aware that I fear greatly this absence that Heaney describes in his poem. I find myself believing that I would act like the man he describes and like the person I appeared to be in my dream. Fortunately for me, I have the warning ahead of time—never to take your loved ones for granted.

THE RECEPTIVE READER

How do you explain this reader's dream? What is the connection between the dream and the poem? Did this poem bring any personal associations or memories to your mind? How did you personally react to the poem?

EXPLORATIONS

The Personal Response

Of the following poems, choose the one that speaks to you most directly or that means most to you personally. First, read the poem carefully, paying special attention to details that might seem difficult or unexpected on first reading. Present your own close reading of the poem in such a way that it could lead a fellow reader to a fuller understanding and appreciation of the poem. Then present your personal response to the poem, explaining your personal reaction or showing why the poem has a special meaning for you as a reader.

ALICE WALKER (born 1944)

New Face 1972

I have learned not to worry about love;
but to honor its coming
with all my heart.
To examine the dark mysteries
of the blood 5
with headless heed and
swirl,
to know the rush of feelings
swift and flowing
as water. 10
The source appears to be
some inexhaustible
spring
within our twin and triple
selves; 15
the new face I turn up
to you
no one else on earth
has ever
seen. 20

THE RECEPTIVE READER

1. What is the focus of this poem? What sets it in motion?
2. Although this poem addresses a large recurrent question in our lives, it translates the poet's feelings and ideas into strong graphic images. What are striking examples? What gives them special force?
3. This poem comes to a close with a beautiful fresh image. What is its meaning?

WALLACE STEVENS (1879–1955)
Disillusionment of Ten O'clock   1923

The houses are haunted
By white nightgowns.
None are green,
Or purple with green rings,
Or green with yellow rings,   5
Or yellow with blue rings.
None of them are strange,
With socks of lace
And beaded ceintures.°   *fancy sashes*
People are not going   10
To dream of baboons and periwinkles.°   *cone-shaped snails*
Only, here and there, an old sailor,
Drunk and asleep in his boots,
Catches tigers
In red weather.   15

THE RECEPTIVE READER

1. Why is this poet "disillusioned"? About what?
2. What is funny about the idea of these houses being "haunted"? Why does the color of people's nightgowns matter in this poem? The critic Irving Howe said that the nightgowns are the "uniform of ordinariness and sober nights." What did he mean?
3. Why do *dreams* matter in this poem? What do the people's dreams and their nightgowns have in common?
4. Does the poet share the conventional attitude toward *drunks*? Howe said that the sailor is the one person in this poem who "stands outside the perimeter of busy dullness." What did he mean?

THE CREATIVE DIMENSION

Most poets would be content if their readers were to give a poem a close, careful reading and allow it to activate a personal reaction. Their readers would thus already be moving beyond the stage of mere passive, uninvolved reading. However, a third way of "getting into" a poem is to allow it to trigger a creative response, to bring your own creativity into play. One way to get into the spirit of a poem is to write a similar poem of your own or a passage of your own triggered in some way by the poem. This way you get to know the poem "from the inside"—the way a person playing an instrument or acting a part in amateur performance ceases to be a passive spectator.

For instance, we know that a student has understood and appreciated the Wallace Stevens poem when we see the following student-written re-creation. How or how well does the student poem capture the mood and intention of the original? How close is it to the original in pattern or form?

Disenchantment at the Dance

The dance is crowded
With blue denim.
There are no dresses
Of shiny, red satin
Or shimmering silk.
No bright feathered hats
No rhinestone buttons.
People aren't dancing
The foxtrot or cha cha.
Only, once in a while,
A few underclassmen
In T-shirts and jeans
Clap their hands
Shuffle their feet.

When a poem moves you in a special way, it may trigger a creative effort of your own—a poem, a prose passage, a drawing, a photograph. Such a creative response or re-creation may sum up a personal impression, or it may pursue a train of thought set in motion by something in the original poem. It may focus on a haunting image or take off from a provocative phrase. It may talk back to the original poem. One basic function of poetry is to keep alive the poet in each of us. We are not likely to become good readers of poetry if we seldom use our own imagination.

EXPLORATIONS ⟨━━━━━━━━━━━━━━━━━━━━━━━━━━━

Reading and Writing Haiku

> As we know from the Japanese experience of the haiku, as well as the experience of many brief poems in the Western tradition, poetry can be present in fifteen words, or in ten words. Length or meter or rhyme have nothing to do with it.
> ROBERT BLY

> Boy with dollar cries
> Sign in poetry shop reads:
> "No haiku today"
> STUDENT HAIKU

Several traditional kinds of Japanese poetry work on the principle of "much in little." They give you snapshots (or **vignettes**) of three lines or five lines each—very short poems that focus your attention on something that is worth looking at but that busy, harried people might overlook. Reading and re-creating these short poems can help you move from passive to more active and appreciative reading.

The best known of these centuries-old short forms is the three-liner, or **haiku**. It fixes a sight or observation in a beautifully crafted form, the way amber encases and preserves an insect caught in the sap of a tree. (One early translator said that haiku about dragonflies are almost as numerous as the dragonflies themselves in the early autumn.)

A giant firefly
that way, this way, that way, this—
and it passes by.

In its strict traditional form, the haiku arranges exactly seventeen syllables in three lines of five, seven, and five syllables each. Count the syllables in the following example. (The *m* in the last line counts as a separate syllable.)

Kumonosu no	5	Ah! Unsuspecting	5
Atari ni asobu	7	the whir of the dragonfly	7
To-m-bo kana!	5	Near the spider's net	5

The most famous of haiku poets is Basho, and his most famous haiku, often translated, is the following.

BASHO   (1644–1694)

Furuike ya	5	An old quiet pond—	5
kawazu tobikomu	7	Frog splashes into water,	7
mizu no oto	5	Breaking the silence	5

Most modern re-creations keep the basic three-line format but do not observe the strict syllable count. The following translations preserve the short-long-short of the haiku without the strict five-seven-five pattern. Both originals were written by women, who "dominated the early years of the literary tradition in Japan not only in numbers, but in formal, aesthetic terms as well" (Rob Swigart).

UKIHASHI   (17th century)

TRANSLATED BY KENNETH REXROTH AND IKUKO ATSUMI

Whether I sit or lie
My empty mosquito net
Is too large.

KAWAI CHIGETSU-NI (1632–1736)

TRANSLATED BY KENNETH REXROTH AND IKUKO ATSUMI

Grasshoppers
Chirping in the sleeves
Of a scarecrow.

Study the following student-written examples of modernized haiku. Then try your hand at some of your own. Note that the focus in the poems themselves is on what we see—although we as readers may take the poem as a starting point for thoughts and feelings. Note the focus on thought-provoking specifics—the absence of blank-check words like *beautiful, sweet, innocent.* The first two examples are formal haiku observing the 5-7-5 pattern:

FORMAL:	A seed yearning for the dark warm earth to moisten must practice patience.	Husband's warm body, Comforting hum of furnace— I drift back to sleep.
INFORMAL:	An old woman looking at granddaughter reminisces	Bright yellow cranes, Old building standing Condemned to die.
	Tranquil is the garden of Eden before the inevitable intrusion Of the stealthy reptile	

A related Japanese form, fixing a moment in time, is the five-liner (or **tanka**). In the strict traditional form, it adds two seven-syllable lines, giving the poet a little more elbowroom. (Historically, the haiku is actually an abbreviated tanka, first written by poets who considered the five-liner too wordy.) The following translation does not observe the strict syllable count.

LADY HORIKAWA (12th century)

TRANSLATED BY KENNETH REXROTH AND IKUKO ATSUMI

How long will it last?
I do not know
his heart.
This morning my thoughts are tangled
as my black hair.

The following student-written tanka does rise to the challenge of the traditional 5-7-5-7-7 pattern:

On the bottom shelf	5
the cheese from three months ago	7
has grown pale-blue fur	5
and I think I heard it growl	7
I'm pretty sure it was cheese.	7

The following student-written five-liners vary the traditional pattern. Try writing some five-line poems of your own.

Batman
flits across my rooftop,
sits on my TV antenna
and pretends
he's a 200-pound pigeon.

Honey
Comb, the Queen Bee,
Reigns with trifling, stoic
Elegance, keeping her left eye
Droneward.

WRITING ABOUT LITERATURE

1. Keeping a Poetry Journal (Suggestions for Writing)

Cover done by MAC
Inside done by IBM
Each word is a joy
"WORD PROCESSING HAIKU," STUDENT JOURNAL

The Writing Workshop   Keeping a poetry journal helps you become a more responsive, more thoughtful reader. Your journal can also be the place where you do much of the **prewriting** for more structured formal papers. In writing a paper, you will be able to turn to your journal for tentative ideas, relevant evidence, and background information.

◇ Your journal gives you a chance to formulate your *overall impression* of a poem. You may start with first impressions, trying to organize them into some preliminary pattern. You may try to get down and organize some of the free-floating associations and reactions that the poem activates on first reading. Keeping a journal will get you into the habit of thinking about the significance, shape, and tone of a poem as a whole.

◇ Your journal enables you to keep a rough record of what you take in as you read. You may want to use part of your journal for a *running commentary*, highlighting striking passages, key images, or notes struck more than once in a poem. In your journal, you can focus on a question that bothers you or on puzzling details. Your journal then serves as the record of your close reading of a poem, as you get involved in the way it takes shape and as you try to do justice to nuances and shades of meaning.

◇ Your journal gives you a chance to formulate your *personal response*. Some poems move us strongly. They strike a powerful chord. We seem to be listening to a kindred spirit. Other poems are impressive or thought provoking, but we read them from a respectful distance. Still other poems we fight, because they seem to be looking at our world through the wrong end of the telescope. Or they may make us confront topics or issues we have been trying to avoid. In your journal, you can begin to explain and justify to yourself your own personal interaction with a poem.

The following sample entries from student journals illustrate possible topics and formats for your own journal. Note that the entries show evidence of careful firsthand reading—weaving into the text quoted words and phrases, half lines and whole lines, from the poems being discussed.

Focus on Words A large part of careful close reading is trying to decode fully the shades of meaning, the overtones, and the associations of the poet's words. In a short poem, each word counts. (It has been estimated that the weight per word is five to ten times in a poem what it would be in ordinary casual prose.) The author of the following journal entry "read out" of the poet's choice of words considerably more than their bare dictionary meaning:

> William Carlos Williams in "The Dance" makes us see the peasants making merry in a painting by Breughel, a sixteenth-century Flemish painter of peasant life. Right away we see that the people in the painting are big, beefy, corpulent, solid peasant types. The poet uses the word *round* several times ("the dancers go round, they go round and / around"). The poet compares their bellies to the "thick- / sided glasses whose wash they impound."
>
> Williams uses words like *squeal* and *blare* and *tweedle* to describe the music of the bagpipes. These words are not normally used to describe music; in fact, they have connotations of being really annoying sounds. *Squeal* brings to mind pictures of stuck pigs, angry children, or the air being let out of tires. *Blare* makes us hear the horns of frustrated drivers, the sound a donkey makes, unwelcome stereos at 3 a.m., or a charging elephant. *Tweedle* to me is an annoying, monotonous sound that alternates between two high-pitched notes, back and forth, back and forth. The choice of these words gives us an idea that the dancers are not a noble bunch. These are people whose children probably don't wear shoes; these dancers dance to loud music and drink and belch and don't give a second thought. Just from these word choices, I see big bellies that shirts don't quite cover. I see women with enormous hips. Food in enormous quantities is being eaten, perhaps without utensils or even plates. Faces are being wiped on sleeves, not napkins or towels. These people are hard workers, and they celebrate hard, with great happiness.

Focus on Metaphor Often a poem comes into focus for us as we begin to see the full meaning of a central metaphor or organizing symbol. The following journal entry traces in detail the possible ramifications of a haunting central image:

> Spiders usually bring associations of haunted, spooky places inhabited by ghosts, witches, and skeletons. Spiders are often thought of as cruel beings who suck the blood out of poor trapped helpless bugs. On the other hand,

spiders also bring visions of beautiful, sparkling, intricate webs. In his poem "A Noiseless Patient Spider," Walt Whitman takes us way beyond the ordinary associations. He sees the spider sympathetically as it noiselessly and patiently performs the simple life-supporting function of sending out its web in search of its needs. So Whitman can easily slip into the parallel search of each person (not just poets!). "Ceaselessly musing, venturing, throwing," we search for the ideas, beliefs, values, or mission that can be the anchor of our lives. The "gossamer threads" that the soul flings are the searching thoughts, the trial and error, the seeking that each person performs to find a happy or at least bearable environment in which the mind and heart can live. The bridge each soul seeks to build will take it to a meaning that imposes order on the universe, which without it remains an incomprehensible, dangerous place.

The Reader's Background   A poem is a transaction between the poet and the reader. A poem is not sufficient unto itself. It activates and shapes what the reader brings to the poem—in the way of memories, associations, overtones of words, shared values, or cultural heritage. The student author of the following entry was able to get into the spirit of a poem because it stimulated a range of relevant associations. She was able to make the right connections:

> In his poem "Pied Beauty," G. M. Hopkins writes about beauty that is not smooth and boring but instead dappled, freckled, "counter, original, spare, strange." The poem cites as an example different occupations or trades with their "gear and tackle and trim." I thought right away of a friend who was a rock climber—he had a fascinating variety of ropes, clips, wedges, "helpers," with the ropes and slings in bright, varied colors. I also thought of painters or roofers, with their trucks loaded down with various gear—ladders, paint cans with paint dripping down the sides, plastic coverings, drop cloths spattered with paint. Hopkins looked with wonder and delight at asymmetrical things that to him became a symbol of the color and variety of God's creation.

The student who wrote the following entry felt he had a special way into a poem because of his regional background:

> An image is the picture that is worth a thousand words. But do images communicate equally effectively with different readers? If the reader does not have the background that a poet assumes, does the significance of the poem suffer? I cannot help feeling that something is lost if people are not aware of what it takes to rise on a bitter cold winter morning as "imaged" in Robert Hayden's poem "Those Winter Sundays." In the "blueblack cold," the father, with cracked hands that ached from his weekday labor, made the "banked fires blaze"—but "no one ever thanked him" for this labor of love. As an Easterner transplanted to Southern California, I know it is difficult to explain bitter cold, or the glory of thunderstorms, or the bite of the air on a crisp autumn day. Here there is no weather. Spirits cannot be brought down by yearning for a weekend that is then rained out—two months in a row. Spirits

cannot be raised by the first sight of buds on the trees, the first call of spring birds. There are no major mood swings.

The Personal Response   How we as readers experience a poem depends on our private agendas, emotional needs, and moral values. A poem can have a powerful impact on us if it gives voice and direction to what we already strongly feel:

> In his poem "London," William Blake takes us to an eighteenth-century city where we hear the "infant's cry of fear," "the hapless soldier's sigh," and the "youthful harlot's curse" among soot-blackened churches and castles whose walls are figuratively covered with blood. Every day my own point of view toward today's cities comes closer to Blake's. Cities today are filled with poverty, violence, and hunger. I cannot walk to school without seeing the lines of people in the naturalization offices, the children waiting in line at the rescue mission, or the homeless and mentally challenged sleeping on the grass outside Grace Baptist Church. I honestly don't know why I get so upset about all the poverty in the city. I guess I feel so guilty because of all the advantages I have had. And when I see the children lining up to get at least one real meal, the guilt sets in.

The Creative Dimension   A poem may serve as a stimulus or catalyst for a creative effort of your own that spins off from the original. The student author of the following entry had read Thomas Hardy's end-of-the-century poem "The Darkling Thrush"—the century being the nineteenth century (p. 42). She wrote the following farewell poem for the twentieth century:

> An Epitaph for the Twentieth Century by 438-11-7322
>
> Nine digits we're linked to
> from birth
> A number that stays with us
> till our last day on earth
>
> Without a number
> You can have no card
> Without a card
> All business retards
>
> Whether you're a king, queen, or jack
> Hinges on where your card fits into the stack
>
> In the future they'll remark:
> Humankind gave the digit a high place
> and did much to erase
> Fingerprint and face.

How to Cite Poetry   In writing your journal entries, practice the conventions that you will have to observe in more formal papers.

✧ Put the title of the poem in quotation marks; *italicize* (<u>underscore</u> on an old-fashioned typewriter) the book or collection in which it appears.

> Judy Grahn's poem "Paris and Helen" appears in her collection *The Queen of Wands.*

✧ When you run in lines of poetry as part of your own text, use a **slash** (with a space on either side) to show line breaks in the original poem:

> Asked to let anger out of its cage, the speaker in the poem says that anger, once loose, "may / turn on me, maul / my face, draw blood."

✧ Normally set off three or more lines of verse as a **block quotation**—indent and center on page, *no* quotation marks. (You may choose to set off even a single line or two lines to make them stand out.)

> The rose plays a somewhat unusual role in the opening lines of Gwendolyn Brooks' poem "A Song in the Front Yard":
>
> I've stayed in the front yard all my life.
> I want to peek at the back
> Where it's rough and untended and hungry weeds grow.
> A girl gets sick of a rose.

✧ Use double quotation marks for ordinary quotations; use **single quotation marks** for a quote-within-a-quote:

> In her introduction to Janet Lewis' *Poems Old and New: 1918–1978,* Helen Trimpi says that Lewis' poetry has a drive "toward balance—to 'bind despair and joy / into a stable whole'—in life as well as in music and art."

2 PATTERN
The Whole Poem

The person who writes out of an inner need is trying to order his corner of the universe; very often the meaning of an experience or an emotion becomes clear only in this way.

MAXINE KUMIN

When I was young, to make something in language, a poem that was all of a piece, a poem that could stand for what I was at the time—that seemed to be the most miraculous thing in the world.

THEODORE ROETHKE

FOCUS ON PATTERN

Poetry, like its sister arts, springs from the human impulse to give shape to experience. A poem opens, moves forward, and comes to a close. It has an overall pattern; it has a design. When we read attentively, we sense how the poem takes shape. As we read and reread, we begin to see how details work in **context**—as part of a web of meanings. Parts that seemed puzzling at first may slowly fall into place. They become part of the whole—they help make up the poem's overall shape, or configuration. A configuration is a fitting together of parts in a distinctive pattern. When we see the New York City skyline with the twin towers of the World Trade Center and the tapered tip of the Empire State Building, we are not likely to say: "Chicago!" We recognize a distinct silhouette, unmistakable like a signature.

The following is a poem that many readers have found beautifully finished, complete in itself. When they finish reading it, the poem has satisfied the expectations it has created. It has accomplished its agenda, unlike a conversation that has lost its thread.

WENDELL BERRY   (born 1934)

The Peace of Wild Things   1968

When the despair of the world grows in me
and I wake in the night at the least sound
in fear of what my life and my children's life may be,
I go and lie down where the wood drake°   *male duck with brilliant plumage*
rests in his beauty on the water, and the great heron feeds.   5
I come into the peace of wild things
who do not tax their lives with forethought
of grief. I come into the presence of still water.
And I feel above me the day-blind stars
waiting with their light. For a time   10
I rest in the grace of the world, and am free.

What gives this poem its satisfying shape? The poet takes us on a journey of the mind—a journey from one state of mind to another. The poem focuses on a need—the need for an antidote to anxiety and despair. This is the need the speaker in the poem feels while lying awake in the dark of night, worrying about a threatening future. The poem as a whole then fills that need, leaving the speaker ("for a time") at peace and at rest, feeling "free."

Each detail in this poem is part of this larger pattern. The speaker in the poem wakes up at night from an uneasy, fearful sleep "at the least sound" that might suggest threat or danger. The unknown, nameless threats that the future holds for him and his children fill him with anxiety and despair. He then seeks and finds in nature images that inspire a healing sense of calm—the wood drake that "rests in his beauty on the water," the great heron feeding, the "still water." The "wild things" of nature (although perhaps themselves living in a threatening world) are not troubled by "forethought / of grief." The starlight, entirely above the turmoil of knotted human emotions, calms and lifts the spirit. The keynote—the central term that sums up much of the meaning or goal of the poem—is the word *peace*. It appears first in the title, and it appears again at a pivotal point in the poem when we "come into the peace of wild things."

The poet raises a question and gives an answer. That answer may not be the last word on the issue (it may work only "for a time"). It will not suit everyone. However, the poem gives us a strong sense that the poet finished what he had started. The poet has done his part. When a poem gives us this satisfying sense of completeness, we say that it has achieved **closure.** Something worthwhile has been accomplished or completed.

THE RECEPTIVE READER

1. What associations with or reactions to *nature* do you bring to this poem? (How do you usually think and feel about nature?) Does the poet's relation to nature (or, more precisely, that of the speaker in the poem) seem strange or understandable to you?

2. How are the stars "day-blind," and how are they nevertheless a consoling presence in this poem?

3. The word *grace* has several possible meanings, from "gracefulness" to "divine grace." What does the word mean in the context of the last line?

4. In this poem, how is *sound* related to sense? Does this poem sound neatly packaged—or does it sound free-flowing to you? Does it have a soothing effect on the reader? When read out loud, should it sound challenging, desperate, quiet, angry, defiant, passionate?

THE PERSONAL RESPONSE

What do you think are the fears that keep the speaker in the poem awake at night? Do you think people can find ways to escape from "forethought" or worry about the future?

As a potter takes formless clay and shapes it into a lovely lasting pitcher or jar, so the poet uses words to give a satisfying shape to the miscellaneous flow of experience. Something previously blurred comes into focus; something that might have gone unnoticed receives attention. Things that were disjointed fit together. They become part of a shape or configuration; they become part of a pattern.

THE POWER OF ATTENTION

A poem is a momentary stay against confusion.
ROBERT FROST

How do poems organize the miscellaneous flow of experience? How do they give shape to what is often shapeless, unsorted? First of all, poems focus our attention. Too often we are hurried, unable to pay undivided attention to any one thing. The poet asks us to slow down, to stop for a closer look. The poem, for a time, brings part of our human reality into **focus.** For instance, it may ask us to focus on a place, a person, or an event in order to fix a moment in time. The following poem is like a freeze frame capturing a picture that, though mute, has something to say to us. What does the poem make you see? What does it make you feel? What does it make you think?

WILLIAM CARLOS WILLIAMS (1883–1963)

Between Walls   1934

the back wings
of the

hospital where
nothing

will grow lie   5
cinders

in which shine
the broken

pieces of a green bottle

THE RECEPTIVE READER

1. Why do you think the poet bypassed the rest of the building and of the hospital grounds to focus your attention where he does?

2. Some of the key words in this poem are *hospital, nothing,* and *cinders.* Why are they key words? How does the poem make them stand out?

3. What is the lone touch of *color* in these lines? What does it make you feel or think?

4. This poem uses bare-minimum lines, with no chance for lush rhythms to develop. Why?

The following poem is by a poet who became well known in the eighties. What do you see in the frame the poet sets up in the poem? Is there a movement or a mental journey to give a pattern to the poem as a whole?

S H A R O N   O L D S   (born 1942)

The Possessive   1980

My daughter—as if I
owned her—that girl with the
hair wispy as a frayed bellpull

has been to the barber, that knife grinder,
and had the edge of her hair sharpened.   5

Each strand now cuts
both ways. The blade of new bangs
hangs over her red-brown eyes
like carbon steel.

       All the little   10
spliced ropes are sliced. The curtain of
dark paper-cuts veils the face that
started from next to nothing in my body—

My body. My daughter. I'll have to find
another word. In her bright helmet   15
she looks at me as if across a
great distance. Distant fires can be
glimpsed in the resin light of her eyes:

the watch fires of an enemy, a while before
the war starts.   20

This poem focuses on a crucial stage in the relationship between mother and daughter: The distance seems to be growing between mother and child. We come in at a turning point when the daughter is moving from a non-threatening wispy-hair or curly-hair stage to a new helmetlike hairdo, with bangs that remind the mother of sharpened blades, hinting at future hostility and aggressiveness. The poem leaves us with the uneasy sense of a coming confrontation. Parent and child are headed for a future where they will be like two armies, each waiting around its campfires on the evening before battle.

THE RECEPTIVE READER

1. How does hair become an issue in this poem? (What exactly did the barber do to the girl's hair?)
2. How many words in the poem remind you of *weapons* used to fend off or hurt an enemy?
3. Possessive pronouns show where or to whom something belongs: *my* daughter, *your* son, *her* briefcase. Where and how does a possessive pronoun become an issue in this poem?

THE PERSONAL RESPONSE

A sixties musical celebrating the spirit of protest of a new generation was called *Hair*. Why or how does hair become an issue in the confrontation between the generations? Do adults overreact to the hairstyles of the young?

THE CREATIVE DIMENSION

Often what lingers in the mind after we read a poem is something that appeals strongly to the visual imagination—a central image or a key metaphor (or a web of related metaphors). What did the student author of the following re-creation carry away from the poem? Do a similar brief re-creation of a central image or metaphor in this or in an earlier poem in this chapter.

> My daughter has pulled on a helmet
> as protection from sharp words.
> She hears nothing but feels
> > all.
> Her eyes look out from behind the blades
> of her new bangs.
> Behind their curtain
> she prepares for battle.

The following poem again focuses on a significant moment. A poet from the Southwest, who published a book of poems called *Hijo del Pueblo*—Son of the Pueblo, remembers an encounter that acquires a new meaning in retrospect. What is that meaning?

LEROY V. QUINTANA   (born 1944)

Legacy II   1976

Grandfather never went to school
spoke only a few words of English,
a quiet man; when he talked
talked about simple things
planting corn or about the weather   5
sometimes about herding sheep as a child.
One day pointed to the four directions
taught me their names

        El Norte
Poniente   Oriente   10
        El Sur

He spoke their names as if they were
one of only a handful of things
a man needed to know

Now I look back   15
only two generations removed
realize I am nothing but a poor fool
who went to college

trying to find my way back
to the center of the world   20
where Grandfather stood
that day

THE RECEPTIVE READER

1. *El Norte* and *El Sur* are Spanish for north and south; *Poniente* means west ("where the sun sets") and *Oriente* means east ("where the sun rises"). Poems that use the physical arrangement of words on a page to mirror meaning are often called *concrete poetry*. How does the arrangement of the Spanish names on the page help the poet make the main point of the poem?

2. How are we supposed to feel about or toward the grandfather who is at the center of this poem?

3. How does the treatment of the grandfather-grandson relationship compare with the treatment of the mother-daughter relationship in the poem by Sharon Olds?

THE PERSONAL RESPONSE

A central issue in our growing up is how we accept or reject the heritage of family tradition, regional ties, or ethnic roots. Write about your relation to one major part of your own "legacy."

JUXTAPOSITIONS ══════════════════════════════

To Look on Nature

The two following poems observe a similar pattern: Both focus on a scene from the natural world. This scene then inspires feelings and reflections. Both poems project human feelings and thoughts into nature's creatures, as if to break down the barrier that usually separates us from the creatures of the animal kingdom. Thomas Hardy, an English poet and novelist who had become well known by the 1880s and 1890s, wrote the first of the two following poems on the last day of the nineteenth century. During the preceding decades, there had been much questioning of traditional religious faith. What was the poet's end-of-century mood? (The thrush is a small bird known as an excellent singer.)

THOMAS HARDY   (1840–1928)

The Darkling Thrush   1900

I leant upon a coppice° gate	*grove of small trees*
When Frost was specter-gray,	
And Winter's dregs made desolate	
The weakening eye of day.	
The tangled bine-stems° scored the sky	*shoots of climbers* 5
Like strings of broken lyres,°	*small (poet's) harps*
And all mankind that haunted nigh°	*near*
Had sought their household fires.	
The land's sharp features seemed to be	
The Century's corpse outleant,	10
His crypt the cloudy canopy,°	*raised cloth covering*
The wind his death-lament.	
The ancient pulse of germ and birth	
Was shrunken hard and dry,	
And every spirit upon earth	15
Seemed fervorless° as I.	*without passion*
At once a voice arose among	
The bleak twigs overhead	
In a full-hearted evensong°	*sung evening prayer*
Of joy illimited;°	*unlimited* 20
An aged thrush, frail, gaunt, and small,	
In blast-beruffled plume,°	*feathers, plumage*
Had chosen thus to fling his soul	
Upon the growing gloom.	
So little cause for carolings	25
Of such ecstatic sounds	
Was written on terrestrial° things	*earthly*
Afar or nigh around,	

That I could think there trembled through
    His happy good-night air   30
Some blessed Hope, whereof he knew
    And I was unaware.

THE RECEPTIVE READER

1. Take a close look at the poet's *language:* What is "the weakening eye of day"? What is the "cloudy canopy"? What is the "ancient pulse of germ and birth"? How was the bird's plumage "blast-beruffled"?

2. Where did you expect this poem to lead you as the reader? What details help make the *setting* unpromising for what happens later in the poem?

3. Where does this poem leave you? What makes the thrush in this poem a good *symbol* for hope?

4. Which words in the poem have religious overtones or *connotations*? Do you think the poet is religious?

THE CREATIVE DIMENSION

Assume today is the last day of another century, a hundred years after Hardy wrote his poem. Write your own epitaph for the *twentieth* century.

Compare the following poem with the poem by Hardy. Compare and contrast the natural scenes the two poets bring into focus, the emotions they invite you to share, and the thoughts they inspire.

SYLVIA PLATH   (1932–1963)

Frog Autumn   1959

Summer grows old, cold-blooded mother.
The insects are scant, skinny.
In these palustral° homes we only   *swampy*
Croak and wither.

Mornings dissipate in somnolence.°   *sleepiness*   5
The sun brightens tardily
Among the pithless° reeds. Flies fail us.   *weak-stemmed*
The fen° sickens.   *bog, swamp*

Frost drops even the spider. Clearly
The genius of plenitude°   *bountifulness* 10
Houses himself elsewhere. Our folk thin
Lamentably.

THE RECEPTIVE READER

1. Who is speaking in this poem? To whom? How does the choice of speaker change our usual *perspective* on life in the bog? What details make us imagine real creatures of the fen or swamp?

2. Some of the sentences in this poem are very sparse yet charged with meaning. What are some striking examples? (Why is a sparse, bare-bones sentence style appropriate to this poem?)

3. The word *lamentably* points to something to be lamented, to be mourned and deplored. How does the poet make the word stand out? How does the rest of the poem lead up to it?

THE PERSONAL RESPONSE

Do you consider the poem complete? Do you want it to go on—for instance, to find out what happens to the bog dwellers? Why or why not?

CROSS-REFERENCES—For Discussion or Writing

Many poets have turned to nature as an oracle, listening intently for its message. In this chapter, three poets—Berry, Hardy, and Plath—look in the mirror of nature and each see a different face. Compare and contrast the poets' relationship to nature in these three poems.

THE SHAPE OF THE POEM

To know one thing, you must know its opposite just as much; else you don't know that one thing.
HENRY MOORE

Each poem has its own unique shape. There is no standard formula to guide the poet's creative imagination. Nevertheless, when we look at a finished poem, we often see shaping forces at work that we recognize. The ability to focus, to concentrate, takes us a first big step toward bringing order into the bewildering flow of experience. A second organizing strategy that poets employ is intentional, purposeful **repetition**. Repetition can be thoughtless or mechanical; it then grates on our ears. Repetition is purposeful when the poet uses it to highlight, to emphasize. It is illuminating when it lines up like and like, when it confronts like and unlike.

By merely looking at the following poem from a distance, you can see that the poet repeats exactly the way each set of lines, or stanza, is laid out on the page. What are the uses of repetition in the poem?

DOROTHY PARKER   (1893–1967)

Solace   1931

There was a rose that faded young;
I saw its shattered beauty hung
   Upon a broken stem.

I heard them say, "What need to care
With roses budding everywhere?"   5
    I did not answer them.

There was a bird, brought down to die;
They said, "A hundred fill the sky—
    What reason to be sad?"
There was a girl, whose lover fled;   10
I did not wait, the while they said:
    "There's many another lad."

This poem, like much poetry traditional in form, uses repetition at the
most basic level to create sound patterns pleasing to the ear. End rhymes, in an
interlaced rhyme scheme, mark off lines of similar length and help punctuate
the poet's words. Lines with a recurrent underlying iambic meter (there WAS a
ROSE that FADed YOUNG) alternate with a three-beat line (uPON a BROKen
STEM). These formal features serve to reinforce a pattern of repetition that
helps guide our thoughts and feelings in the poem as a whole. The same sentence frame—"*There was a* rose"; "*There was a* bird"; "*There was a* girl"—in-
troduces each of the three parts of the poem. These sentences are **parallel** in
grammatical form—a signal to the reader that the three scenarios they introduce might also be parallel in content or in meaning. And so they are—they
each tell different versions of the same basic story.

THE RECEPTIVE READER

1. What is the same basic story that is repeated in the three parts of the poem?
What is the reaction of the speaker in the poem?

2. Can you trace the close similarity in the way each parallel mini-event is patterned beyond the first half of the opening lines?

THE PERSONAL RESPONSE

Are you inclined to side with the "I" or the "they" of the poem?

Repetition sets up the routine of our lives. It helps us identify the constants that enable us to chart our course. Other basic patternings are similarly
rooted in common human experience. For instance, our minds are prepared to
see a sequence of events build up to a **climax**. We are geared to see a series of
preparatory steps lead up to a high point. Clouds slowly darken the sky until a
climactic thunderstorm releases crashing thunder and pouring rain. Tensions
in a marriage slowly build up until they explode in a divorce. Much of what we
plan and do is **cumulative**—we build on what has gone before till we reach a
destination.

Look at the way the following poem builds up to a climax. (Sleepers in
rural communities used to be awakened by the bugling, blaring cockadoodle-
doo of the rooster stretching its neck and throwing back its head to greet the
morning.)

ARCHIBALD MACLEISH   (1892–1982)

The Genius   1933

Waked by the pale pink
Intimation° to the eastward,   *first hint*
Cock, the prey of every beast,
Takes breath upon the hen-house rafter,
Leans above the fiery brink   5
And shrieks in brazen obscene burst
On burst of uncontrollable derisive° laughter: *contemptuous*
Cock has seen the sun! He first! He first!

THE RECEPTIVE READER

1. To build up to a *climax,* we often start slowly and in a low key. Then we gradually pile up strong and stronger details until we reach the high point. How does the poem follow this pattern? How does the poet give extra force to the high point?

2. Like earlier poems in this chapter, this poem is a striking example of *personification*—of treating objects or animals as if they were persons. The poet reads human attitudes and feelings into our cousins of the animal world. What human feelings and attitudes does he dramatize in this poem?

3. What do you think the poet meant by the *title?*

In the following poem, repetition and climactic order combine with a third organizing strategy: The poem hinges on a pivotal *but* that provides the turning point. We go from point to **counterpoint,** from statement to counterstatement.

WILLIAM MEREDITH   (born 1919)

A Major Work   1958

Poems are hard to read
Pictures are hard to see
Music is hard to hear
And people are hard to love

But whether from brute need   5
Or divine energy
At last mind eye and ear
And the great sloth heart will move.

In the first four lines, the basic sentence frame ("_____ are hard to _____") is repeated four times. We sense that all four grammatically **parallel** statements are part of the same pattern. They are parallel not only in structure but also in *meaning:* Our minds are slow to grapple with a serious poem. Our eyes only slowly take in the rich texture in the painting of an old master (or puzzle over the strange shapes in the work of a modern). The untrained ear resists Beethoven. And finally, people—no less complicated than a sonnet or a sonata—are also hard to read and love.

Here, however, we come to the reversal or counterpoint: As we again look at mind, eye, ear, and heart in the same parallel order, we see them overcome resistance or inertia. When we come to the inertia-ridden and slothful "great sloth heart," we realize that the order of the four test cases was not accidental but *cumulative*. It is the slowness of the human heart to be moved to love that most concerns the poet. The last line is climactic; the poem as a whole has led up to this weighty, emphatically stressed line: "And the GREAT | SLOTH | HEART | WILL | MOVE."

THE RECEPTIVE READER

1. What does the phrase "from brute need / Or divine energy" mean?
2. If the poet were asked to spell out how, why, where, or when the "great sloth heart will move," what do you think he would say?

In much of our living and thinking, we see the play of opposites. When we can line them up as clearly defined polar opposites, we call them **polarities.** Polarities help us organize our thoughts; they help us draw our mental maps. They are built into the basic texture of our lives: man and woman, night and day, land and sea, arrival and departure, storm and calm, then and now. We chart our course between opposite poles: work and play, success and failure, dependence and independence, freedom and commitment. The following passage from the King James Bible rehearses age-old polarities that are constants in human experience.

ECCLESIASTES (3:1-8)

To every thing there is a season

To every thing there is a season, and a time to every purpose under the heaven:
A time to be born, and a time to die; a time to plant, and a time to pluck up that which
    is planted;
A time to kill, and a time to heal; a time to break down, and a time to build up;
A time to weep, and a time to laugh; a time to mourn, and a time to dance;
A time to cast away stones, and a time to gather stones together; a time to embrace,
    and a time to refrain from embracing;   5
A time to get, and a time to lose; a time to keep, and a time to cast away;
A time to rend, and a time to sew; a time to keep silence, and a time to speak;
A time to love, and a time to hate; a time of war, and a time of peace.

THE RECEPTIVE READER

Which of these opposed pairs from biblical times still play a major role in our lives? For those that seem dated or obsolete, what would be a modern counterpart?

THE CREATIVE DIMENSION

How would *you* fill in the frame "A time to . . . a time to . . ."? Write your own updated catalog of modern polarities.

The following poem lines up polar opposites in an exactly parallel pattern. Which opposing details are exceptionally neatly balanced?

JON SWAN
The Opening   1959

Seed said to flower:
    You are too rich and wide.
    You spend too soon and loosely
    That grave and spacious beauty
    I keep secret, inside.   5
    You will die of your pride.

Flower said to seed:
    Each opens, gladly
    Or in defeat. Clenched, close,
    You hold a hidden rose   10
    That will break you to be
    Free of your dark modesty.

In this poem, we listen to a dialogue between two opposed points of view. The poet allots nearly equal time to the two sides. The parallel openings ("Seed said to flower" / "Flower said to seed") are a signal that the poet's exploration of the same issue is continuing.

THE RECEPTIVE READER

As the poet presents both sides of the dialogue, which details are for you most telling or significant? In this confrontation, is there something to be said on both sides? What side is the poet on, and how can you tell? What side are you on, and why?

JUXTAPOSITIONS ━━━━━━━━━━━━━━
Point and Counterpoint

Look for the uses of repetition and the play of point and counterpoint in the following poems. First, study the uses of repetition in the following lines from a longer poem by New England's first poet.

ANNE BRADSTREET   (about 1612–1672)
From *The Vanity of All Worldly Things*   1650

As he said "vanity!" so "vain!" say I,
"Oh! vanity, O vain all under sky."

Where is the man can say,° "Lo, I have found   *who can say*
On brittle earth a consolation sound"?
What is't in honor to be set on high?°   *raised to high station*   5
No, they like beasts and sons of men shall die,
And whilst they live, how oft doth turn their fate;
He's now a captive that was king of late.°   *only recently*
What is't in wealth great treasures to obtain?
No, that's but labor, anxious care, and pain.   10
He heaps up riches, and he heaps up sorrow,
It's his today, but who's his heir tomorrow?
What then? Content in pleasure canst thou find?
More vain than all, that's but to grasp the wind.
The sensual senses for a time they please,   15
Meanwhile the conscience rage, who shall appease?
What is't in beauty? No, that's but a snare,
They're foul° enough today that once were fair.   *ugly*
What is't in flowering youth or manly age?
The first is prone to vice, the last to rage.   20
Where is it then, in wisdom, learning, arts?
Sure, if on earth, it must be in those parts;
Yet these the wisest man of men did find
But vanity, vexation of mind.

THE RECEPTIVE READER

1. The poet's first line takes up the words of the preacher who repeated the biblical "Vanity of vanities; all is vanity." Can you show that the parts making up this excerpt are *parallel* both in wording and in meaning?

2. What examples of *point and counterpoint* can you find in these lines?

3. Religion in Bradstreet's time was often more demanding than in ours. How much of her outlook is strange and how much is familiar to you as a modern reader?

The second poem was written by a poet who was a collector and editor of black American poetry. What is the role of repetition and of point and counterpoint in this poem?

ARNA BONTEMPS   (1902–1973)

A Black Man Talks of Reaping   1940

I have sown beside all waters in my day.
I planted deep, within my heart the fear
That wind or fowl would take the grain away.
I planted safe against this stark, lean year.

I scattered seed enough to plant the land   5
In rows from Canada to Mexico,
But for my reaping only what the hand
Can hold at once is all that I can show.

Yet what I sowed and what the orchard yields
My brother's sons are gathering stalk and root,
Small wonder then my children glean in fields
They have not sown, and feed on bitter fruit.

10

THE RECEPTIVE READER

1. How is the central claim the speaker in this poem makes reinforced or reiterated by sentences *parallel* in form and meaning?

2. Where does the countermovement start in this poem, and how is it sustained or reinforced? (How is "gleaning" different from "reaping"?)

3. A rhyme word at the end of a line, a group of lines, or the whole poem can highlight a crucial idea and make us pause and ponder its significance. How does the poem as a whole lead up to the phrase "bitter fruit"?

4. The imaginative comparisons around which the poem is built are the harvest metaphor and the family metaphor. What gives them special force? (Do you remember any traditional lore or biblical quotations that involve sowing and reaping?)

THE CREATIVE DIMENSION

We call a heightened and compressed playing off of opposites an *antithesis*. (*Thesis* and *antithesis* are the original Greek words for statement and counterstatement.) Study the following examples of antithesis. For each, write one or more imitations (close or approximate) of your own.

1. To err is human; to forgive, divine. (Alexander Pope)
   SAMPLE IMITATION: To whine is childish; to ask, adult.

2. There are a thousand hacking at the branches of evil to one who is striking at the root. (Henry David Thoreau)
   SAMPLE IMITATION: There are a thousand correcting with red ink to one who writes an encouraging word.

3. It is a miserable state of mind to have few things to desire and many things to fear. (Sir Francis Bacon)

A SENSE OF PATTERN

The mysteries remain,
I keep the same
cycle of seed-time
and of sun and rain.
H. D. (HILDA DOOLITTLE), "THE MYSTERIES REMAIN"

A sense of pattern is in our bones. At times, the patterning that gives shape to a poem seems to be directly inspired by the patterns of nature or of ordinary human life. Sometimes the patterns that organize a poem seem to echo lived rhythms from afar. And sometimes the poet seems to play variations on, or intentionally go counter to, patterns built into common human experience. One of the constants in human experience is the daily cycle from night to dawn to noon to dusk and back to night. The title of the following poem means "dawn." In early medieval poetry, night was the friend and dawn the enemy of lovers. (In a medieval castle, a *bower* was the private room of a lady.) Ezra Pound, one of the great early moderns, often re-created the poetic styles of earlier periods in his poems.

EZRA POUND   (1885–1972)
Alba   1926

When the nightingale to his mate
Sings day-long and night late
My love and I keep state
In bower
In flower   5
Till the watchman on tower
Cry:
   "Up! Thou rascal, Rise,
   I see the white
    Light   10
   And the night
     Flies."

THE RECEPTIVE READER

 1. How does rhyme in this poem highlight the alternation between night and day? How does it emphasize the watchman's (and the poem's) message?

 2. Pound often turned to the literature of distant places and distant centuries for inspiration. In the setting of this poem, do you find yourself a total stranger?

 The following poem reminds us of the cycle of the seasons, but it uses thoughts about the falling leaves of October as a springboard for reflections on the similar cycle of youth and age. Autumn with the falling of leaves is a major way station of the passing year, just as the realization of approaching age is a major way station in human life. The sumac mentioned in the poem is a shrub whose leaves turn a brilliant dark red in the fall.

KAY BOYLE   (born 1903)
October 1954   1954

Now the time of year has come for the leaves to be burning.
October, and the months fill me with grief
For the girl who used to run with the black dogs through them,

Singing, before they burned. Light as a leaf
Her heart, and her mouth red as the sumac turning.   5

Oh, girl, come back to tell them with your bell-like singing
That you are this figure who stands alone, watching
                the dead leaves burn.
(The wind is high in the trees, and the clang of bluejay
                voices ringing   10
Turns the air to metal. This is not a month for anyone
                who grieves.)
For they would say that a witch had passed in fury if
                I should turn,
Gray-haired and brooding, and run now as once I ran   15
                through the leaves.

THE RECEPTIVE READER

1. How does the poet focus our attention on the burning leaves? What do they stand for as a central symbol in the poem? How does the poet use *repetition* to make the key words echo through the poem?

2. How many details help develop the *polarity* of youth and age?

3. Why is October "not a month for anyone who grieves"?

THE PERSONAL RESPONSE

To some people, the cycle of the changing seasons has come to mean very little. What does it mean in your own life?

The following poem is by e. e. cummings, a poet who often seems to march to a different drummer. But he then often turns out to be exceptionally attuned to basic rhythms that shape our lives. This poem focuses on two entirely anonymous and representative people: "anyone" (somebody who could be *anyone*) and "noone" (somebody who was *no one* in particular). Noone loved anyone while other someones married those who were everybody or everything to them. (Are you keeping up with the games cummings plays with pronouns?) How does the poem trace the life cycle of "anyone" and "noone"?

E. E. CUMMINGS (1894–1963)

anyone lived in a pretty how town   1940

anyone lived in a pretty how town
(with up so many floating bells down)
spring summer autumn winter
he sang his didn't he danced his did.

Women and men (both little and small)   5
cared for anyone not at all

they sowed their isn't they reaped their same
sun moon stars rain

children guessed (but only a few
and down they forgot as up they grew   10
autumn winter spring summer)
that noone loved him more by more

when by now and tree by leaf
she laughed his joy she cried his grief
bird by snow and stir by still   15
anyone's any was all to her

someones married their everyones
laughed their cryings and did their dance
(sleep wake hope and then) they
said their nevers they slept their dream   20

stars rain sun moon
(and only the snow can begin to explain
how children are apt to forget to remember
with up so floating many bells down)

one day anyone died i guess   25
(and noone stooped to kiss his face)
busy folk buried them side by side
little by little and was by was

all by all and deep by deep
and more by more they dream their sleep   30
noone and anyone earth by april
wish by spirit and if by yes.

Women and men (both dong and ding)
summer autumn winter spring
reaped their sowing and went their came   35
sun moon stars rain

cummings (the lower case is the original author's) is a favorite of readers
who delight in **word play.** He syncopates the English language the way a jazz
musician syncopates a melody. We hear echoes of the original melody, but they
are broken up and come back in snatches, played back against the grain. The
fourth line, for instance, might read in ordinary peoplespeak as follows: "He
sang (talked about?) what he didn't do and danced (acted out?) what he did."

The poet delights in the play of opposites, as when in the third stanza people who grow "up" forget "down." We might say in ordinary language that
women and men reaped what they had sown and that they first came into this
world but finally went from it again like everybody else. The poet (at the end
of the poem) says that they "reaped their sowing and went their came."

Embedded in the word play and repetitions like those of a nursery rhyme
are the way stations in the uneventful ordinary lives of the anonymous "anyone" and "noone." Apparently the latter loved the former, and they shared joy

and grief. "Anyone" eventually died, mourned by "noone" (who kissed his face), and they were finally buried side by side, while around them the cycles of sowing and reaping, symbolic of our life cycles, continue.

THE RECEPTIVE READER

1. The names of the four seasons echo through this poem like a *refrain* (or like a bell). Why? Why do they appear in changing, rotating order? What other set of four terms serves a similar function in the poem? How?

2. This poet delights in playing off *polarities* that make up the web of anyone's experience, such as joy and grief. What other such polarities can you find in the poem?

3. The *form* of the poem—with its simple four-line stanzas, its occasional simple or predictable rhymes, the poet's fondness for repetition—has some of the simple child-like quality of a nursery rhyme or childhood jingle. Do form and meaning go together in this poem? How?

THE PERSONAL RESPONSE

For you, is this a sad poem? a funny poem? What would you say to readers who want to dismiss it as a nonsense poem?

THE CREATIVE DIMENSION

In a Quaker reading, members of a group each take turns reading part of a text. With your classmates, do a Quaker reading of cummings' poem, perhaps changing readers at each stanza break.

JUXTAPOSITIONS ⟅━━━━━━━━━

The Daily Cycle

Both of the following poems follow the ever-recurring daily cycle from dawn through noon to dusk and night. One makes us trace it in wonder and awe, as if we were the first people on earth. The other plays variations on it that are part serious, part tongue in cheek. The first poem is by a poet of Kiowa ancestry who grew up in Oklahoma; his poems often draw on the legends and ways of the tribal life of the past.

N. SCOTT MOMADAY   (born 1934)

New World   1976

1.
First Man,
behold:
the earth
glitters   5
with leaves;
the sky
glistens
with rain.   2.
Pollen   At dawn   10
is borne   eagles
on winds   hie and
that low   hover
and lean   above   3.
upon   the plain   At noon   15
mountains.   where light   turtles
Cedars   gathers   enter
blacken   in pools.   slowly
the slopes—   Grasses   into
and pines.   shimmer   the warm   4.
                   and shine.   dark loam.   At dusk   20
                   Shadows   Bees hold   the gray
                   withdraw   the swarm.   foxes
                   and lie   Meadows   stiffen
                   away   recede   in cold;
                   like smoke.   through planes blackbirds   25
                                   of heat   are fixed
                                   and pure   in the
                                   distance.   branches.
                                                  Rivers
                                                  follow   30
                                                  the moon,
                                                  the long
                                                  white track
                                                  of the
                                                  full moon.   35

THE RECEPTIVE READER

1. For people living closer to nature than we do, each stage of the day (like each stage in the cycle of the seasons) had its own characteristic feel or atmosphere. What is the morning feeling in this poem? How do the details selected by the poet conjure up the feeling of high noon? What is striking about the visual images that bring up dusk?

2. How does the sense of an immemorial cycle that gives shape to this poem affect you as a reader? What feelings are you left with as you finish the poem?

THE CREATIVE DIMENSION

What are the three (four? five?) stages of the day in your own present-day world? Bring them to life for your reader in a poem or prose passage.

The second poem is by an English poet of the early seventeenth century who rewrote conventions and crossed established boundaries. He was one of the **metaphysical** poets of his time, passionate, but at the same forever analyzing and rationalizing their emotions. What use does the poet make of the familiar stages of the daily cycle? How does he impose his own perspective and priorities?

JOHN DONNE (1572–1631)

A Lecture upon the Shadow   1635

Stand still, and I will read to thee
A lecture, love, in Love's philosophy.
    These three hours that we have spent
    Walking here, two shadows went
Along with us, which we ourselves produced;   5
    But, now° the sun is just above our head,   *now that*
    We do those shadows° tread,   *on those shadows*
And to brave clearness all things are reduced.
    So, whilst° our infant loves did grow,   *while*
    Disguises did and shadows flow   10
    From us and our cares,° but now 'tis not so.   *our fears*

That love hath not attained the highest degree
Which is still diligent lest others° see.   *so others won't*

Except° our loves at this noon stay,   *unless*
We shall new shadows make the other way.   15
    As the first were made to blind
    Others, these which come behind
Will work upon ourselves, and blind our eyes.
    If our loves faint and westwardly decline,
    To me thou° falsely thine,   *you . . . your*   20
And I to thee mine, actions shall disguise.
    The morning shadows wear away,
    But these grow longer all the day;
But oh, love's day is short, if love decay.

Love is a growing or full constant light,   25
And his first minute after noon is night.

THE RECEPTIVE READER

1. The shadow cast by the sun becomes the central *metaphor* in this poem. What were the shadows in the morning? (What were the "cares" and "disguises" of the morning?) What happens to the shadows at high noon? What is the crucial difference between the morning shadows and the shadows after noon?

2. How does this poem ask you to revise your usual sense of the daily cycle? What familiar associations of dawn, noon, and night does the poem preserve? How does it depart from them?

THE PERSONAL RESPONSE

How do you react to the three student-written responses that follow? Which comes closest to your own response to the poem and why? Which do you disagree with and why?

1. John Donne did not write flowery, sickening-sweet love poetry but instead took his images from areas like philosophy, botany, or astronomy. The link between the shadow and love is not a worn-out comparison like spring or a rough road. What could be less permanent or more fleeting and transitory than a shadow? Just as a day ages and changes, so do the lovers age and change, and so does their love. Naturally the sun will not obey the lovers' wants and commands. It follows a cyclical pattern: Love grows, reaches a high point, and then declines and dies. This poem leaves me unsettled. I keep getting the idea that as soon as I fall in love I better steel myself so that I will not be disappointed when the shadows reappear.

2. I like the beginning of this poem much more than the end. As the sun moves through the sky, the shadows cast according to the position of the sun change, just as love in a relationship is different when it is young and when it is tried and true. At first, we hide behind shadows or façades instead of showing our true selves, but after a while we can put our disguises away just as at noon we can walk on our shadows. However, in the afternoon, love might grow weary and turn false, with the afternoon shadows pointing forward to the night and the end of love. The reason I would rather focus on the first half of the poem is that I think love should continue to grow and build on itself. If love grows weary, making "new shadows" the other way, I don't think it was love in the first place. I have never heard a parent say: "I have fallen out of love with my children; I think I will find a more suitable child elsewhere." Would that be true love?

3. This poem takes a very intellectual approach. It fuses "reason" and "love" to create an intellectual's love poetry. The very first sentence commands his lover to "stand still" so that the speaker can give a lecture on "love's philosophy." This is an unusual way to begin a poem, since the word *lecture* makes us expect to be preached to and given a lesson. Donne seems to say that the sun can be held in check, not physically in the actual universe around us, but spiritually by an effort of our minds that preserves love's full noon. But his philosophy is an "all-or-nothing" philosophy, since the "first minute after noon" is already night. As we see the lengthening shadows and observe deceit creeping into our love, we realize our vulnerability. The lecturer sounded very cool and intellectual at the beginning, but he ends by being naked and vulnerable. Having chosen the sun as a symbol of love, what can he do to avoid the evening and night?

CROSS-REFERENCES—For Discussion or Writing

John Donne's "A Lecture upon the Shadow" and Marge Piercy's "Simple Song" (p. 59), though separated by three centuries, focus on our yearning for full and complete communication with another human being and the obstacles that defeat or thwart us in our quest. Compare and contrast the two poems.

EXPLORATIONS ━━━━━

Concrete Poetry

In **concrete poetry,** the external shape of the poem mirrors its meaning. The external layout—otherwise usually a simple series of lines of equal or varying length—speaks to us and makes a statement. A poem about a bell is bell-shaped; a poem about the wings of angels is printed in the shape of wings. The following poem, by a native Alaskan whose native language is Tlingit, uses many repetitions of the Tlingit word for apple (*x'aax'*) to make up the shape of an apple. At the top of the apple, we see a little squiggle making up the stem—it's the Tlingit word for stem (*akat'ani*). The poem also uses the native word for worm (*tl'ukwx̱*). Where is the worm?

N O R A   D A U E N H A U E R   (born 1927)

Tlingit Concrete Poem   1984

```
                                  t ' a n
                             a               i
                            a    k
              x ' aax ' x ' aax ' x ' aax ' x ' aax ' x ' aax
            aax ' x ' aax ' x ' aax ' x ' aax ' x ' aax ' x ' aax ' x
          ' x ' aax ' x ' aax ' x ' aax ' x ' aax ' x ' aax ' x ' a
        x ' x ' aax ' x ' aax ' x ' aax ' x ' aax ' x ' aax ' x ' aax
       aax ' x ' aax ' x ' aax ' x ' aax ' x ' aax ' x ' aax ' x ' aax '
      ' aax ' x ' aax ' x ' aax ' x ' aax ' x ' aax ' x ' aax ' x ' aax ' x
     x ' aax ' x ' aax ' x ' aax ' x ' aax ' x ' aax ' x ' aax ' x ' aax ' x '
    ' x ' aax ' x ' aax ' x ' aax ' x ' aax ' x ' aax ' x ' aax ' x ' aax ' x '
    ' x ' aax ' x ' aax ' x ' aax ' x ' aax ' x ' aax ' x ' aax ' x ' aax ' x ' a
    ' x ' aax ' x ' aax ' x ' aax ' x ' aax ' x ' aax ' x ' aax ' x ' aax ' x ' a
   x ' x ' aax ' x ' aax ' x ' aax ' x ' aax ' x ' aax ' x ' aax ' x ' aax ' x ' a
   x ' x ' aax ' x ' aax ' x ' aax ' x ' aax ' x ' aax ' x ' aax ' x ' aax ' x ' a
   x ' x ' aax ' x ' aax ' x ' aax ' x ' aax ' x ' aax ' x ' aax ' x ' aax ' x ' a
   x ' x ' aax ' x ' aax ' x ' aax ' x ' aax ' x ' aax ' x ' aax ' x ' aax ' x ' a
    ' x ' aax ' x ' aax ' x ' aax ' x ' aax ' x ' aax ' x ' aax ' x ' aax ' x ' a
    ' x ' aax ' x ' aax ' x ' aax ' x ' aax ' x ' aax ' x ' aax ' x ' aax ' x '
    ' x ' aax ' x ' aax ' x ' aax ' x ' aax ' x ' aax ' x ' aax ' x ' aax ' x '
     x ' aax ' x ' aax ' x ' aax ' x ' aax ' x ' aax ' x ' aax ' x ' aax ' x '
      ' aax ' x ' aax ' x ' aax ' x ' aax ' x ' aax ' x ' aax ' x ' aax ' x
       ' aax ' x ' aax ' x ' aax ' x ' aax ' x ' aax ' x ' aax ' x ' aax '
        aax ' x ' aax ' x ' aax ' x ' aax ' x ' aax ' tl' uk w x̱ ' aax ' x ' aax '
        ax ' x ' aax ' x ' aax ' x ' aax ' x ' aax ' x ' aax ' x ' aax ' x ' aax
         x ' x ' aax ' x ' aax ' x ' aax ' x ' aax ' x ' aax ' x ' aax ' x ' aa
          ' x ' aax ' x ' aax ' x ' aax ' x ' aax ' x ' aax ' x ' aax ' x ' a
           ' aax ' x ' aax ' x ' aax ' x ' aax ' x ' aax ' x ' aax ' x
            ax ' x ' aax ' x ' aax ' x ' aax ' x ' aax ' x ' aax
             ' x ' aax ' x ' aax ' x ' aax ' x ' aax ' x ' a
              ' aax ' x ' aax ' x ' aax ' x ' aax ' x '
               ' x ' aax ' x ' aax ' x ' aa
                ' x ' aa
```

POEMS FOR FURTHER STUDY

In reading the following poems, pay special attention to features that give shape to the poem as a whole. For instance, where does the poem focus your attention? Is there a playing off of opposites? Is there a movement from then to now, or from question to answer? What makes the poem a complete, finished whole?

MARGE PIERCY   (born 1936)

Simple Song   1968

When we are going toward someone we say
You are just like me
your thoughts are my brothers
word matches word
how easy to be together.   5

When we are leaving someone we say:
how strange you are
we cannot communicate
we can never agree
how hard, hard and weary to be together.   10

We are not different nor alike
But each strange in his leather body
sealed in skin and reaching out clumsy hands
and loving is an act
that cannot outlive   15
the open hand
the open eye
the door in the chest standing open.

THE RECEPTIVE READER

1. What is simple about this "simple song"?
2. What does the poet mean by "your thoughts are my brothers"? (Or by "word matches word"?) What are we supposed to think or feel when we are told that we are in a "leather body" and "sealed in skin"? What is the role or significance of the open hand, the open eye, the open door?
3. How does this poem use *parallelism* to line up opposites and to bond things that are similar?
4. How would you chart the overall *development* or shape of this poem?

THE CREATIVE DIMENSION

Some poems leave an exceptionally clear or compelling pattern imprinted on our minds. Choose one such poem. Can you sum up the pattern as briefly as the student author did in the following response to the Piercy poem? (Can you do so without oversimplifying?)

When we agree
I like you
we are one.
When we disagree
I don't like you
we are separate.
You are my enemy.

GARY SOTO   (born 1952)

We are beginning to see the work of **bilingual** poets—American poets who speak English as a second language or who are part of the first generation in their family to speak mainly English while another language is still the language of the home. The following poem is by a Chicano poet who grew up in a Mexican-American neighborhood in Fresno, California. One listener at one of Soto's poetry readings said that he "was funny, and humble, and touching, and completely terrific."

Oranges   1985

The first time I talked
With a girl, I was twelve,
Cold, and weighted down
With two oranges in my jacket.
December. Frost cracking   5
Beneath my steps, my breath
Before me, then gone,
As I walked toward
Her house, the one whose
Porch light burned yellow   10
Night and day, in any weather.
A dog barked at me, until
She came out pulling
At her gloves, face bright
With rouge. I smiled,   15
Touched her shoulder, and led
Her down the street, across
A used car lot and a line
Of newly planted trees,
Until we were breathing   20
Before a drugstore. We
Entered, the tiny bell
Bringing a saleslady
Down a narrow aisle of goods.
I turned to the candies   25
Tiered like bleachers
And asked what she wanted—
Light in her eyes, a smile

Starting at the corners
Of her mouth. I fingered   30
A nickel in my pocket,
And when she lifted a chocolate
That cost a dime,
I didn't say anything.
I took the nickel from   35
My pocket, then an orange,
And set them quietly on
The counter. When I looked up,
The lady's eyes met mine,
And held them, knowing   40
Very well what it was all
About.

      Outside,
A few cars hissing past,
Fog hanging like old   45
Coats between the trees.
I took my girl's hand
In mine for two blocks,
Then released it to let
Her unwrap the chocolate   50
That was so bright against
The grey of December
That, from some distance,
Someone might have thought
I was making a fire in my hands.   55

THE RECEPTIVE READER

1. This poet has an uncanny gift for recalling the small revealing details that conjure up scenes from the past. What are striking examples in this poem?

2. How does this poem develop and take shape? What is the overall pattern? What are major stages or high points? What helps the reader experience a sense of completion?

3. Gary Soto is known for poems presenting candid and bittersweet childhood memories in understated and wryly humorous fashion. How does this poem show these qualities?

JAMES LAUGHLIN   (born 1914)
Junk Mail   1986

is a pleasure to at least
one person a dear old man

in our town who is drift-
ing into irreality he

walks each morning to the   5
post office to dig the

treasure from his box he
spreads it out on the lob-

by counter and goes through
it with care and delight.   10

THE RECEPTIVE READER

1. A *vignette* is a snapshot (using words or a picture) that captures a moment in time. It makes us focus briefly on something worth attention, or it makes us look at something from a fresh perspective. Does the above vignette fit this definition?

2. Is there any movement or development in this poem? From what to what?

R O B E R T   F R O S T   (1874–1963)

Fire and Ice   1923

Some say the world will end in fire,
Some say in ice.
From what I've tasted of desire
I hold with those who favor fire.
But if I had to perish twice   5
I think I know enough of hate
To say that for destruction ice
Is also great
And would suffice.

THE RECEPTIVE READER

1. How is Frost playing off opposites in this poem? How well do fire and ice fit the emotions for which they serve as symbols in this poem?

2. How does the rhyme scheme in this poem serve to highlight the polar opposites?

THE PERSONAL RESPONSE

Where have you encountered the destructiveness of desire as a theme in your reading or viewing?

A D R I E N N E   R I C H   (born 1929)

Novella   1967

Two people in a room, speaking harshly.
One gets up, goes out to walk.
(That is the man.)

The other goes out into the next room
and washes the dishes, cracking one.   5
(That is the woman.)
It gets dark outside.
The children quarrel in the attic.
She has no blood left in her heart.
The man comes back to a dark house.   10
The only light is in the attic.
He has forgotten his key.
He rings at his own door
and hears sobbing on the stairs.
The lights go on in the house.   15
The door closes behind him.
Outside, separate as minds,
the stars too come alight.

THE RECEPTIVE READER

1. From what perspective or vantage point are we watching the scene unfolding in this poem?

2. Many of the sentences in this poem are spare and factual. What are striking examples? Where and how do the powerful emotions involved in what we observe shine through?

3. A *novella* is a story that is shorter and more pointed than a full-length novel. Does the poet expect us to read this poem as the story of two specific individuals? Or are the people in this poem representative or even archetypal—standing for an age-old, often-repeated pattern?

4. The final two lines bring the poem to a close by serving as a summing up and last word. How?

WRITING ABOUT LITERATURE

2. *The Whole Paper (From Notes to Revision)*

The Writing Workshop   How does a successful paper about a poem take shape? A well-worked-out paper will not arrive on your desk ready-made. Think of your writing as a process that starts with your first reading of a poem and ends with a revised final draft. Be prepared to take a paper through overlapping stages: careful reading, note taking, thinking about the poem, planning your strategy, preparing a rough first draft, working on a more polished revision, final editing and proofreading.

Remember that false starts and blind alleys are part of a writer's day. Be prepared to change direction as necessary. Always go back to the poem itself as your main source of ideas and evidence.

Reading Notes   Suppose you are working on a paper about Marge Piercy's "Simple Song" (p. 59). Allow time for the preliminary note-taking stage. Many readers find it useful to jot down a running commentary as they work their way through a poem. Here they note key phrases and striking images, questions that arise in the reader's mind, or possible clues to the poet's intention or the larger meaning of the poem. Your **reading notes** for the poem might look like this:

> title: why "Simple Song"? Words in the poem are very simple (none need to be looked up in a dictionary)
>
> (line 5) it's "easy to be together" because they don't really see who's there
>
> second stanza is exactly parallel in layout to the first—but now we exit from the relationship
>
> (line 7) "how strange you are"—the other person was not really known to begin with
>
> (line 10) last lines in first and second stanzas are parallel: "how easy . . ."; "how hard . . ." But the same line in second stanza is longer, more drawn-out ("how hard, hard and weary . . .") to make the point of how hard and weary it is to stay together when love is gone
>
> (line 12) "leather body"—leather used as a protection since early times; it's tough, more impenetrable than human skin
>
> (line 17) the "open eye"—we really see others for what they are?
>
> (line 18) "door in the chest standing open"—willingness to let someone in

Reading Journal   A journal entry will often record your interpretation of a poem—the way you make sense of it—and your more personal reaction. It may also note your queries—your attempts to puzzle out difficult passages, your tentative answers to unsolved questions. In your paper, you will then be able to draw on some of the more unstructured and informal material in your journal. A journal entry for the Piercy poem might look as follows:

> I felt in reading this poem that most people operate exactly the way the first ten lines of this poem describe. In the early stages of courtship, all is euphoria. People focus on everything they can share and agree on. They say, "how easy to be together." Then they slowly let down their guard. They let their differences come to the surface; they become impatient with each other. They start calling each other weird and "strange." Getting along becomes "hard, hard and weary." Although this poem seems to talk mainly about romantic or sexual relationships, I believe the pattern applies to friendships as well.

Planning the Paper   Even while taking notes and recording tentative reactions, you will be thinking about how to lay out your material in a paper. You will be pushing toward an overall impression or keynote—a key idea or ideas that will make your details add up. You will be sketching out a master plan— the major stages through which you will take your reader. Give special thought to the following way stations in the itinerary to be traveled by your reader:

✦ *Introduction, or lead*   How are you going to attract and focus the attention of your reader? You may want to lead your readers into the poem from a biographical fact, such as a revealing detail about the poet's war experience or family history that could serve to illuminate the poem. You may want to start with a striking quote from the poet, illuminating his or her intention. You may want to dramatize the setting or the time, vividly re-creating the context of the poem.

✦ *Overview*   What is going to be your central focus? If possible, let a graphic, vivid introduction lead your readers directly to your main point. State it as your **thesis** and then devote your paper to developing and supporting it. A thesis sums up in a short, memorable statement what the paper as a whole is trying to prove. (Sometimes, however, you will prefer to raise a question to be pondered by the reader and to be answered by the paper as a whole. Or you may want to state a tentative claim or working hypothesis to be tested or modified by your paper.)

Give the kind of preview or overview here that will point your readers in the right direction. Help them find their bearings. Often a thesis statement already broadly hints at the major stages in the writer's master plan. It furnishes the reader with a capsule itinerary for the journey ahead.

✦ *Plan*   How are you going to follow up your thesis? For the body of a short paper, try to sketch out a three-step or four-point plan to serve as your grand design. Make sure that you arrive at a clear agenda: first this, next this, then that. Highlight the transitions from one major point or stage to the next, so your readers will not get lost in detail. Signal turning points, crucial objections, clinching arguments: "on the other hand"; "readers hostile to easy answers may object . . ."; "however, such objections will carry much less weight when we realize. . . ."

Often the way the poem itself takes shape will provide a tentative blueprint for all or part of your paper. The "Simple Song" poem swings from the extreme of euphoria, of being blissfully and uncritically in love, to the opposite extreme of sour disappointment and failure to communicate. We may well look to the third and last part of the poem for some middle ground, or for some lesson to be learned, or for some sort of answer. The paper, like the poem, could go from point to counterpoint and then toward some kind of resolution.

✦ *Follow-up*   Whatever your claims or generalizations, remember that each general statement you make is a promise to your readers: "This is what I claim, and here is the evidence to support it." Much of your text should show a rich texture of quotation, explication (close, careful explanation), and interpretation. Choose brief revealing quotations (but don't rip them out of context, omitting essential ifs and buts). Explain what your quotations say and how they say it; explore their overtones and implications. Relate them to the larger context of the poem: What role do they play in the poem as a whole?

❖ *Conclusion* End on a strong note. Pull together essentials of your argument. Put them in the perspective of today, or of your own experience, or of the readers' lives. Or relate the individual poem to the larger patterns of the poet's work. Aim for a wrap-up or a clincher sentence that your readers will remember.

❖ *Title* Writers are often content with a dull working title while drafting a paper ("Structure in Marge Piercy's 'Simple Song'"). Then, first things last, they hit on the title that is both informative and provocative. An effective title is serious enough to do justice to the topic but also interesting enough to beckon to the reader. A thought-provoking quote can attract the reader's attention. A play on a key word or an allusion to a figure from myth or legend can make a title stand out from the mass of unread material that harried readers pass by each day.

Read the following student paper to see how it lives up to the criteria sketched in these guidelines.

SAMPLE STUDENT PAPER

The Real Act of Love

In her introduction to *Circle on the Water,* a book of her selected poems, Marge Piercy writes that a poem should "function for us in the ordinary chaos of our lives." Her intention in writing her poems is to "give voice to something in the experience of life. . . . To find ourselves spoken for in art gives dignity to our pain, our anger, our lust, our losses."

Her poem "Simple Song" achieves these goals for me. The poem asks us to face the most terrifying and difficult of human activities: loving another person and opening ourselves to love in return. The title promises us a "simple song." The simplicity promised in the title is carried out in the three-part structure of the poem and conveyed in its simple language. By focusing on the essentials of a very complex issue, the poem helps us see first the lacking sense of reality and second the inevitable alienation that defeats us when we "reach out" to others. It then takes us to a third stage that explains the dilemma and may offer a way out.

The poem filters out all intermediate stages to focus on the two phases that are like turning points in our lives: "going toward" and "leaving." The first group of five lines makes us feel the sweetness and newness of someone we have just met. This is the state of falling in love when we feel totally in harmony with the other person. We say, "You are just like me / your thoughts are my brothers / word matches word / how easy to be together." We feel we have found the perfect soulmate, who thinks and speaks like us.

However, anyone with experience can already forecast the exact opposite stage. In the next set of five lines, we are leaving. The other person has become "strange": "we cannot communicate / we can never agree / how hard, hard and weary to be together." Here we have a feeling of loss, a feeling of confusion and defeat as for some reason we stop loving. The lines in this second stanza are arranged in parallel fashion to those in the first; they serve as a mirror image to those in the first. "You are just like me" turns into "how strange you are." "Word matches word" turns into "we cannot communicate." These contrasting lines give us a clue that maybe our "going toward" was not a clear-eyed move but at least in part self-deception. It did not make allowance for hard times or unexpected problems. Did we know the person whom we told "your thoughts are my brothers" in any real sense?

The last stanza moves beyond the dilemma that confronts us in the first two stanzas and points toward a possible solution to our confusion and pain. The first three lines of the stanza say, "We are not different nor alike / But each strange in his leather body / sealed in skin and reaching out clumsy hands." Our problem is not that we are different from each other. We are all "strange." We are each in a leather body, which sounds tough, isolated from human touch like an animal. To be "sealed in skin" sounds sterile, like being put in a vacuum plastic pouch. We are impenetrable, isolated human beings, groping for contact with "clumsy hands." But we are too thick-skinned to let in another in order to know the soft-skinned person inside the leather covering.

The last five lines may be pointing to a course between the polar opposites of uncritical acceptance and resentful rejection. The poem says, "loving is an act / that cannot outlive / the open hand / the open eye / the door in the chest standing open." The image of the open hand may imply an opening up of our fist to show what's there and let the other person see who we really are. But it may also imply the willingness to accept what the other person has to offer, without illusions that we create about the other person in our minds. The "open eye" implies willingness to see others as they really are, to see that rarely does "word match word" and that it not "easy to be together" on a continuous basis. We have to risk the open door if we do not want to be satisfied with the less fearful business of having someone fill a temporary need for companionship.

The type of love in the first stanza cannot last because it makes us imagine a perfect merging of people who are really unique and strange. When we exaggerate everything we have in common, we already program ourselves for the disappointment acted out in the second stanza. I read a book recently that talks about a "matching game"—trying to build a relationship on everything that makes two people alike. The real key is to teach our "clumsy hands" to be more accepting of what makes us different. This way we can be in love with a real person rather than with a creation of our own minds.

QUESTIONS

How effectively do title and introduction lead toward the main point of the paper? What overview or preview does the paper provide—how effectively does it prepare you for what is to come? How clear does the structure or shape of the poem become to the reader? What important details stand out, and how well does the writer explain them? What does the conclusion do that the rest of the paper has not already done? Where do you agree and where do you part company with the student writer?

A Checklist for Revision It is usually ill-advised to complete a first draft and act as if it were a finished paper. If at all possible, let your draft lie on your desk or sit in your computer. To revise and polish your paper, you will need some distance, some perspective. For a day or two, enjoy the relief of having pulled your material into preliminary shape. Then reread your first draft. Look at it through the reader's eye. Ask yourself questions like the following:

1. Is the introduction too colorless and dutiful? Does it say things like "In this paper, I will examine important similarities and differences between two poems"? When revising, dramatize and highlight one key difference or similarity to give your readers a foretaste of what your paper will cover.

2. Does your paper have a clear enough focus? Can you point to a sentence that spells out in so many words your main point or your overall perspective? Does it stand out as a **thesis statement** early in your paper or as a well-earned conclusion at the end?

3. Does your preview or overview give your readers enough of a sense of direction? For instance, does it alert your readers that your paper will be built around a contrast of then and now, or around a turning from dejection to a renewal of hope?

4. As your paper develops, is your master plan clear enough to your readers? Revision is your chance to smooth out apparent detours, backtrackings, or leads that lead nowhere. Can you sum up your strategy in a three-point or four-point (maybe a five-point) outline? If not, try to streamline your overall plan of organization.

5. Do you signal major way stations in your paper clearly enough? (Try not to make your readers slog through an unmarked, uncharted line-by-line reading.) Check for lame **transitions** like "also" or "another point we might mention." Spell out why the next point is the logical next step in your paper. For instance, does it introduce clinching evidence for a claim you made earlier? Does it raise an important objection? Does it defuse charges by others who disagree with you?

6. Do you make enough use of striking, revealing quotations? Do you use striking short quotations early enough in the paper to get the reader into the spirit of the poem (or poems)? For example, in writing about Gwendolyn Brooks' poem "Truth," do you early in the paper make your readers hear "the fierce hammering" of the knuckles of Truth on the door, awakening the people sheltered in the "propitious haze" of unawareness?

7. Do you tie your personal reactions closely enough to a detailed reading of the text? Or are you using isolated phrases and images as a launching pad to spin you out on mental journeys of your own? When you make much of a key word or a key line of the poem, make sure you pay attention to how it works in the context of the poem as a whole.

8. Have you found the happy medium between a hyperformal and a supercasual use of words? Make sure the language of a poem, alive with image and rhythm, does not clash with your own stodgy, overwritten impersonal style. ("A deep look at the whole poem gives overwhelming reference to the plight of alienation and illuminates the poet's transcendent purpose.") Skirt the opposite extreme of discussing a poem about humanity's spiritual quest in the language in which you would ask for pretzels in the pub. ("Wait a minute! I thought this was a poem about a spider!")

9. Does your conclusion bring your paper to a satisfying close? Does it leave your readers with a point, an image, or a question to remember? Revise a conclusion that will seem too interchangeable—saying things that could be said about many different poems. ("This poem asks readers to be more aware of their environment and to be more critical of themselves.") Make sure your conclusion sounds as if it were custom-made for your subject today, for a specific poem or poems.

3 IMAGE
The Open Eye

Great literature, if we read it well, opens us up to the world. It makes us more sensitive to it, as if we acquired eyes that could see through things and ears that could hear smaller sounds.

DONALD HALL

FOCUS ON IMAGE

Poets take you into a world of images. An **image** is a vividly imagined detail that speaks to your sense of sight, hearing, smell, taste, or touch. Poets expect you to read their poems with open eyes and willing ears. They write with a heightened awareness, making you take in more of the world around you than people do who see only the stretch of asphalt in front of their cars. Poets ask you to look, to marvel at what you see. It is as if the poet were clearing a fogged-over windshield to help you take a closer look at your world—to take in the texture and shape of clouds, the look on faces in the crowd, the dartings and peckings of birds.

The following poem centers on a memorable image. It asks you focus on and take in a striking sight. If you let it, the central image in this poem will etch itself on your memory. It will start a chain of associations activating disturbing thoughts and feelings. It may come back to haunt you at unexpected moments.

WILLIAM STAFFORD (born 1914)

At the Bomb Testing Site   1960

At noon in the desert a panting lizard
waited for history, its elbows tense,
watching the curve of a particular road
as if something might happen.

It was looking for something farther off   5
than people could see, an important scene
acted in stone for little selves
at the flute end of consequences.

There was just a continent without much on it
under a sky that never cared less.   10
Ready for a change, the elbows waited.
The hands gripped hard on the desert.

This poem begins and ends with the sight the poet calls up before our
eyes: the panting watchful lizard, its elbows tense, gripping the desert floor
hard with its hands, surrounded by the empty desert (like a "continent without
much on it"), under the empty uncaring cloudless sky. This is a striking image,
and the poet takes the time to let it sink in.

At the same time, as often with poetic images, there is more to the lizard
than meets the eye. Our first hint is that the panting lizard "waited for history." We *are* at a bomb testing site. Something disastrous might happen to the
desert life at any moment. The lizard, part of life that has existed on this earth
for untold millions of years, might presently perish in the blinding flash of a
nuclear holocaust.

From there the chain of associations and forebodings will take each of us
to our own personal version of the distant "important scene" at the "flute end
of consequences"—where our common history will be channeled as toward
the end of a flute toward its final destination. We each will have our own version of the journey to the time when both the lizard and we ourselves will be
history, destroyed by the self-important machinations of our busybody johnny-
come-lately species. However, whatever our fears or speculations, we are left to
ponder the image of the lizard, survivor from the dim prehistoric past, now endangered. The poem does not preach; the image of the lizard is mute and eloquent at the same time.

THE RECEPTIVE READER

1. Does it make any difference to the poem as a whole that the time is noon? that
the lizard is watching a curve in the road? Why is the "important scene" in the future
acted out for "little selves"?

2. For many people, lizards, like other reptiles, seem alien, remote from human
beings in the chain of evolution. For you, does the lizard make a good central image
for this poem? Why or not? (What for you would have been a better choice?)

VISUAL AND OTHER IMAGES

Images in verse are not mere decoration, but the very essence of an intuitive language.

T. E. HULME

It is better to present one image in a lifetime than to produce voluminous works.

EZRA POUND

I am an instrument in the shape of a woman trying to translate pulsations into images

ADRIENNE RICH, "PLANETARIUM"

Vivid and thought-provoking imagery satisfies what for many modern readers is the test of true poetry: A poem should not merely verbalize ideas but translate ideas and feelings into graphic images. It should not tell us about an experience but act it out for us. It should not take inventory of feelings but make us share in them. Look for the striking visual images in the following poem. What does the poem make you see? What does it make you feel? What does it make you think?

MARY OLIVER (born 1935)

The Black Snake   1979

When the black snake
flashed onto the morning road,
and the truck could not swerve—
death, that is how it happens.

Now he lies looped and useless   5
as an old bicycle tire.
I stop the car
and carry him into the bushes.

He is as cool and gleaming
as a braided whip, he is as beautiful and quiet   10
as a dead brother.
I leave him under the leaves

and drive on, thinking,
about *death:* its suddenness,
its terrible weight,   15
its certain coming. Yet under

reason burns a brighter fire, which the bones
have always preferred.
It is the story of endless good fortune.
It says to oblivion: not me!   20

It is the light at the center of every cell.
It is what sent the snake coiling and flowing forward
happily all spring through the green leaves before
he came to the road.

The speaker in this poem is thinking about what keeps us going in face of the knowledge that disaster may strike. Death may lurk at any turn in the road. (The one thing sure about death is its "certain coming.") However, the person speaking does her thinking in vivid images. The poem focuses on the black snake—which has to become real for us if the poem is to carry its true weight. We need to imagine the snake as it moves "happily . . . through the green leaves" until it meets sudden death in the road. Perhaps then we will be ready to say with the poet: "That is how it happens." The snake apparently is not some alien creature "out there." *We* are like the snake, moving through life merrily until of a sudden something terrible overtakes us. We feel the "terrible weight" of that knowledge.

Paradoxically, however, the poem will leave many readers not with the image of the dead snake but with the image of the live snake moving "happily all spring through the green leaves." The poem does not move from life to death but from the experience of death to an affirmation of life. To keep going, we have to believe that we are special and therefore deserving of survival. When oblivion threatens to erase the memory of our existence, we feel deep down: "not me!" Deep down we believe in "endless good fortune." This faith in our own invulnerability enables us to say no to "oblivion"—to the inevitable future when we will be forgotten.

THE RECEPTIVE READER

1. What graphic images make you see the way the snake moved when it was alive? What images help you see the way it looked after it had been hit?

2. How is what "reason" says in this poem different from what people know (or prefer to believe) in their "bones"? What striking image helps you visualize the intense vital energy of that knowledge?

3. What is "the light at the center of every cell"? What do you know about cells that can help you understand this phrase and its role in the poem?

THE PERSONAL RESPONSE

Does it strike you as strange that both Stafford and Oliver choose a reptilian for the central image in a poem raising questions about life and death?

By *image,* we usually mean a picture we see with the mind's eye. However, we also use the word more generally for any detail that speaks to our senses, whether of sight, hearing, smell, taste, or touch. Most poetic images are visual images—something we can see the way we look in a mirror and see an image of ourselves. However, others are sound images, like the rustling of leaves or the pounding of the surf. Still others are taste images—like the sourness of a lemon that makes the mouth pucker. Still others might be touch images, like the sensation we feel when we run our fingers over the rough bark of a tree.

The images we grasp with our senses make poetry **concrete**—they bring our eyes and ears and nerve ends into play. Concrete, sensory details take us into a world of sights, sounds, smells, tastes, and sensations. Concrete details are at the opposite end of the spectrum from **abstract** ideas. Abstract ideas like happiness, freedom, and honor "draw us away" from concrete experience toward large categories and general labels. The American poet Theodore Roethke had a special gift for using the image-making language of poetry to re-create the rich texture of sensory experience. In the following poem, Roethke uses visual images, but he also uses images that speak strongly to other senses. What does the poem make you see? And how does the poet go *beyond* visual images to include other kinds of sensory detail? What sensations and feelings does the boy experience?

THEODORE ROETHKE   (1908–1963)
My Papa's Waltz   1948

The whiskey on your breath
Could make a small boy dizzy;
But I hung on like death:
Such waltzing was not easy.

We romped until the pans   5
Slid from the kitchen shelf;
My mother's countenance
Could not unfrown itself.

The hand that held my wrist
Was battered on one knuckle;   10
At every step you missed
My right ear scraped a buckle.

You beat time on my head
With a palm caked hard by dirt,
Then waltzed me off to bed   15
Still clinging to your shirt.

THE RECEPTIVE READER

1. What does this poem make you see? What details in the poem bring senses *other* than sight into play?

2. What helps you put yourself in the boy's place? Where and how do *you* share in what the boy sensed and felt?

THE RANGE OF INTERPRETATION

Many readers find that this poem makes them relive the experience but does not really tell them what to make of it. Critics have read the poem different ways. *Romp* is usually an approving word; it makes us think of a happy, boisterous, energetic kind of running or dancing. Do you think the boy liked the romp in this poem? As he looks back, how does the speaker in the poem feel about his father? Is he critical of the father? Or is he expressing feelings of love for him?

EXPLORATIONS

The Range of Imagery

The following poem starts out to give general advice but almost immediately begins translating it into striking imagery. Which images are visual, and which represent other kinds?

ANN DARR   (born 1920)

Advice I Wish Someone Had Given Me   1971

Be strange if it is necessary, be
quiet, kindly as you can without
feeling the heel marks on your head.
Be expert in some way that pleasures
you, story-telling, baking, bed;   5
marvel at the marvelous
in leaves, stones, intercepted light;
put truth and people in their right-
full angle in the sun . . . find the shadow,
what it falls upon.   10
Trust everyone a little, no one much.
Care carefully.
Thicken your skin to hints and hurts, be
allergic to the soul scrapers.

THE RECEPTIVE READER

1. Explain the striking *visual* images in this poem. How would we put "truth and people in their right- / full angle in the sun"? What is the "shadow" that we are asked to find?

2. Which images are visual while at the same time bringing bodily *sensations* into play? What sensations are we made to experience by the "heel marks" (and what caused them)? Who are the "soul scrapers"? What sensations or feelings does the phrase bring into play?

3. What is contradictory or paradoxical about the *play on words* in "Care carefully"? Does this piece of advice make sense to you? Does any of the advice in this poem have a special meaning for you?

4. This poet makes minimal and somewhat unusual use of *rhyme*. How?

IMAGES AND FEELINGS

If. . . it makes my whole body so cold no fire can ever
warm me, I know that is poetry. If I feel physically as if the
top of my head were taken off, I know that is poetry.
                                        EMILY DICKINSON

Poetic images have the power to stir our emotions. At times, the poet may seem to adopt the stance of the neutral, unemotional reporter. The poet's eye then is the objective camera eye, recording dispassionately what it sees. However, many poems travel without warning from what the poet saw to what the poet felt and thought. The scene we find ourselves reenacting in the following poem has the hallucinatory intensity of a dream. What feeling or feelings does it invite you to share?

URSULA K. LE GUIN (born 1929)
The Old Falling Down   1988

In the old falling-down
house of my childhood
I go down-
stairs to sleep out-
side on the porch   5
under stars and dream
of trying to go up-
stairs but there are no
stairs so I climb
hand over hand clambering   10
scared and when I get there
to my high room, find
no bed, no chair, bare floor.

THE RECEPTIVE READER

1. What for you is the dominant *emotion* in this poem? (Does it make you share in mixed or contradictory emotions?) What haunting images create the emotional effect?

2. What is the difference between "climbing" and "clambering"?

3. Several split or *divided words* in this poem make us move on from the end of a line to the next without the break or rest we would normally expect. Do you see any connection between this extra effort required of the reader and the subject of the poem?

THE CREATIVE DIMENSION

Do you recognize the feeling or feelings pervading this poem? Have you ever had a similar dream? Write a passage (or poem) about a haunting and perhaps recurrent dream.

Poets vary greatly in how fully they signal their emotions. Often, like Theodore Roethke in "My Papa's Waltz," they let the experience speak for itself. Whether the boy in the poem felt a sickening fear or a mad dizzy joy is for our own emotional antennas to pick up. Contrast the Roethke poem with another father-son poem by Robert Hayden, who in other poems has written eloquently about the heritage of African-Americans. What feelings does the poet express in response to the scenes he dramatizes in this poem?

ROBERT HAYDEN (1913–1980)

Those Winter Sundays   1962

Sundays too my father got up early,
and put his clothes on in the blueblack cold,
then with cracked hands that ached
from labor in the weekday weather made
banked fires blaze. No one ever thanked him.   5

I'd wake and hear the cold splintering, breaking.
When the rooms were warm, he'd call,
and slowly I would rise and dress,
fearing the chronic angers of that house.

Speaking indifferently to him,   10
who had driven out the cold
and polished my good shoes as well.
What did I know, what did I know
of love's austere and lonely offices?

In this poem, the poet makes us suffer the bitter cold by appealing to our senses of sight and touch. We can visualize the "blueblack cold" and feel the "cracked hands that ached." When the blazing fire drives out the icy cold, our sense of hearing is brought into play: As the blazing wood shifts and splits, we seem to "hear the cold splintering, breaking." Speaking of his father, the poet early sounds a note of regret: "No one ever thanked him." Frightened by the constant angry quarrels in his parents' house, the boy acted indifferent, retreating into a shell. He never responded to the love the father showed by the "lonely offices" or services of every day.

THE RECEPTIVE READER

1. As the poet steers your emotions in this poem, what are your feelings toward the lonely father?

2. The word *austere* means being self-denying but at the same time being proud to be so, holding aloof. How does this key word fit into the poem?

3. Why does the poet repeat the question "What did I know?" in the next to the last line of the poem?

THE CREATIVE DIMENSION

Most of us can think of an occasion or person that we did not appreciate properly. We remember lost opportunities, occasions for regret. Write a passage or poem on the theme of "What did I know, what did I know."

JUXTAPOSITIONS

The Sense of Place

Both of the following poems take you to a place to which the poet has strong emotional ties. What images make the setting real for you? How do the poets communicate their feelings? Can you share in the feelings expressed in these poems?

WILLIAM STAFFORD   (born 1914)

One Home   1963

Mine was a Midwest home—you can keep your world.
Plain black hats rode the thoughts that made our code.
We sang hymns in the house; the roof was near God.

The light bulb that hung in the pantry made a wan light,
but we could read by it the names of preserves—   5
outside, the buffalo grass, and the wind in the night.

A wildcat sprang at Grandpa on the Fourth of July
when he was cutting plum bushes for fuel,
before Indians pulled the West over the edge of the sky.

To anyone who looked at us we said, "My friend";   10
liking the cut of a thought, we could say, "Hello."
(But plain black hats rode the thoughts that made our code.)

The sun was over our town; it was like a blade.
Kicking cottonwood leaves we ran toward storms.
Wherever we looked the land would hold us up.   15

THE RECEPTIVE READER

1. What striking images put us in the Midwest that was the poet's home? Where do the poet's feelings about the land show? Where do his feelings about the people show? How?

2. Like much earlier traditional poetry, this twentieth-century poem is divided into *stanzas,* or sets of lines that each follow a similar pattern, like the verses of a song. Can you show that each stanza (or almost each stanza) focuses on one dimension or aspect of the midwestern tradition or mentality that is the subject of this poem?

3. In some songlike poems, the same line (or group of lines) comes back in each stanza as a *refrain.* In this poem, a key line is repeated only once. Why is it important enough for the poet to repeat it?

4. This poem makes some limited, low-key use of rhyme. Where and how? The poem also uses lines of roughly similar length, with a steady underlying beat. Can you find some lines that have a clear five-beat rhythm? (Note that usually *more than one* unstressed syllable comes between beats.) Why is it not surprising that this poet would like a style that is low-key but has a steady underlying beat?

The second poem about a favorite place takes us to the now-empty and fenced-in lots under a raised freeway in California, with the small houses gone and the fruit trees and vegetable patches running wild. The Hispanic poet talking here about childhood scenes slides from English into Spanish (the language of her childhood) and back, moving easily between two languages like other bilingual Americans.

LORNA DEE CERVANTES   (born 1954)
Freeway 280   1981

Las casitas° near the gray cannery	*the little houses*
nestled amid wild abrazos° of climbing roses	*hugs*
and man-high red geraniums	
are gone now. The freeway conceals it	
all beneath a raised scar.	5
But under the fake windsounds of the open lanes,	
in the abandoned lots below, new grasses sprout,	
wild mustard remembers, old gardens	
come back stronger than they were,	
trees have been left standing in their yards.	10
Albaricoqueros, cerezos, nogales° . . .	*apricot, cherry, walnut*
Viejitas° come here with paper bags to gather greens.	*little old women*
Espinaca, verdolagas, yerbabuena° . . .	*spinach, purslane, mint*

I scramble over the wire fence
that would have kept me out.   15
Once, I wanted out, wanted the rigid lanes
to take me to a place without sun,
without the smell of tomatoes burning
on swing shift in the greasy summer air.

Maybe it's here	20
en los campos extranos de esta ciudad°	*in the strange fields of this city*
where I'll find it, that part of me	
mown under	
like a corpse	
or a loose seed.	25

THE RECEPTIVE READER

1. What is the "raised scar"? What are the "windsounds," and why are they "fake"? How does the poet feel about the freeway?

2. How did the poet feel about this setting when she grew up there? What role

did the cannery play in her childhood or adolescence?

    3. What are her feelings as she returns to this setting? What does she mean when she says that "wild mustard remembers"?

    4. Students of language use the term *code-switching* for shifting from one language, or linguistic code, to the other. At what points in the poem does the poet shift back to the Spanish of her childhood? What might have been lost if she had used the literal English translations here printed in the margin?

THE PERSONAL RESPONSE

Do you think the part of the poet (or of her past) that was "mown under" will prove a "corpse" or a "seed"? What images of continuing growth earlier in this poem might help you answer this question?

THE CREATIVE DIMENSION

Most people have intense personal associations—positive or negative—with a childhood setting that may haunt them in their dreams. Write a poem or prose passage about a childhood setting or favorite place recalled in vivid memories or revisited in a dream.

POETRY AND PARAPHRASE

*I think that the one thing that's been consistently true
about my poetry is this determination to get authenticity of
detail.*

MAXINE KUMIN

For many modern poets, insisting on concrete images, anchored in authentic firsthand observation, has been a safeguard against secondhand ideas. They are likely to speak in vivid images even when making a general point about life or about people. They are likely to remind us that the poem and a prose translation, or **paraphrase,** are not the same. Look at the relation between idea and image in the following example.

KENNETH REXROTH   (born 1905)

Trout   1956

The trout is taken when he
Bites an artificial fly.
Confronted with fraud, keep your
Mouth shut, and don't volunteer.

How is fraud like fishing for trout? What would be lost if this poet had given us only the last two lines? The trout is totally without guile, going about its legitimate business as nature prompts it. People producing the artificial fly used in trout fishing invest great ingenuity and resourcefulness in producing something to fool an unsuspecting victim that has done them no harm. By dramatizing the relationship between the perpetrator and the victim of fraud, the poet makes us "see it feelingly"; we know how it feels to be hooked.

In a paraphrase, we put someone else's ideas into our own words, thus making sure we understand the plain literal meaning. But we must try not to reduce something that was alive with human feelings and purposes to a residue of inert ideas. We can often paraphrase a poem to extract its prose meaning, but in the process much of what the poem does to involve our senses, our hearts, and our minds is likely to be lost. In reading the following poem, pay special attention to the images that make the speaker's thoughts and feelings real for us. What makes the poem different from the paraphrase that follows it?

EDNA ST. VINCENT MILLAY (1892–1950)
Childhood Is the Kingdom Where Nobody Dies 1937

Childhood is not from birth to a certain age and at a certain age
The child is grown, and puts away childish things.
Childhood is the kingdom where nobody dies.

Nobody that matters, that is. Distant relatives of course
Die, whom one never has seen or has seen for an hour, 5
And they gave one candy in a pink-and-green striped bag, or a jack-knife,
And went away, and cannot really be said to have lived at all.

And cats die. They lie on the floor and lash their tails,
And their reticent fur is suddenly all in motion
With fleas that one never knew were there, 10
Polished and brown, knowing all there is to know,
Trekking off into the living world.
You fetch a shoe-box, but it's much too small, because she won't curl up now:
So you find a bigger box, and bury her in the yard, and weep.

But you do not wake up a month from then, two months, 15
A year from then, two years, in the middle of the night
And weep, with your knuckles in your mouth, and say Oh, God! Oh, God!
Childhood is the kingdom where nobody dies that matters,—mothers and fathers
    don't die.

And if you have said, "For heaven's sake, must you always be kissing a person?"
Or, "I do wish to gracious you'd stop tapping on the window with your thimble!" 20
Tomorrow, or even the day after tomorrow if you're busy having fun,
Is plenty of time to say, "I'm sorry, mother."

To be grown up is to sit at the table with people who have died, who neither listen nor
    speak;
Who do not drink their tea, though they always said
Tea was such a comfort. 25

Run down into the cellar and bring up the last jar of raspberries;
    they are not tempted.
Flatter them, ask them what was it they said exactly
That time, to the bishop, or to the overseer, or to Mrs. Mason;
They are not taken in.
Shout at them, get red in the face, rise,   30
Drag them up out of their chairs by their stiff shoulders and shake them and yell
    at them;
They are not startled, they are not even embarrassed;
    they slide back into their chairs.

Your tea is cold now.
You drink it standing up,
And leave the house.   35

A short prose paraphrase of the flow of thought in this poem might read like this:

> Childhood is not a matter of chronology; we leave it behind when we become aware of the reality of death. During childhood, death is not real. Death is not real when distant relatives die whom we have known only from short visits. Childhood pets die and are buried, but they do not cause wild passionate grief that lasts for months and years. Our childhood continues as long as our parents are spared and there is plenty of time to apologize and make amends after a temporary estrangement. We know that we have passed from childhood to adulthood when we are forced to accept the fact that people who were close to us and part of our lives are gone forever. They and their familiar mannerisms may be so vivid in our memories that they may seem to be in the room with us, but we are forever cut off from communicating with them. We find ourselves alone in an empty house; we have no reason to linger there to be with someone close to us.

This paraphrase can serve as a chart to the poet's thoughts, but we must remember that it is different from the real poem, just as a map of a river is different from the river. In the paraphrase, the relatives, the pets, the parents, and grief for their loss all remain abstractions, as different from the living currency of thought and feeling as the figures in a checkbook are from the actual currency we spend.

THE RECEPTIVE READER

What striking images make the relatives and childhood perceptions of them real for the reader? What graphic, unexpected images dramatize the death of childhood pets? What images make the speaker's grief real when people die who "matter"? How does the poet dramatize the feeling of being cut off from human contact with the dead?

THE PERSONAL RESPONSE

Millay was widely admired in her day but fell from favor when critical trends encouraged distance and control in the expression of personal emotions. Feminist critics today praise her as women writers increasingly use poetry as a medium for coming to terms with intensely felt personal experience. How do you respond to the emotions expressed in this poem?

POEMS FOR FURTHER STUDY

In reading the following poems, pay special attention to imagery that brings a scene or a natural setting to life for the reader. How does it appeal to the senses? What does it do for the reader?

PETER MEINKE (born 1932)

Sunday at the Apple Market

1977

Apple-smell everywhere!
Haralson McIntosh Fireside Rome
old ciderpresses weathering in the shed
old ladders tilting at empty branches
boxes and bins of apples by the cartload   5
yellow and green and red
piled crazy in the storehouse barn
miraculous profusion, the crowd
around the testing table laughing rolling
the cool applechunks in their mouths   10
dogs barking at children in the appletrees
couples holding hands, so many people

out in the country carrying bushels
and baskets and bags and boxes of apples
to their cars, the smell of apples   15
making us for one Sunday afternoon free
and happy as people must have been meant to be.

THE RECEPTIVE READER

1. What are striking realistic details that only an observer who knows the scene well could have noticed? What senses *other* than sight does the poem bring into play? Which images in this poem stay with you after you finish reading?

2. Some poems early strike a *keynote* that sets the tone and recurs through the poem like the tolling of a bell. What is the keynote in this poem, and how does it echo through the poem?

THE PERSONAL RESPONSE

Why does the apple market become a symbol of happiness for the poet? Are you the kind of person who would have shared in the happy feeling? Why or why not?

JOHN KEATS   (1795–1821)

To Autumn   1819

Season of mists and mellow fruitfulness,
   Close bosom-friend of the maturing sun;
Conspiring with him how to load and bless
   With fruit the vines that round the thatch-eaves° run;   *of thatched roofs*
To bend with apples the mossed cottage-trees,   5
   And fill all fruit with ripeness to the core;
      To swell the gourd, and plump the hazel shells
With a sweet kernel; to set budding more,
   And still more, later flowers for the bees,
   Until they think warm days will never cease,   10
      For summer has o'er-brimmed their clammy cells.

Who hath not seen thee oft amid thy store?
   Sometimes whoever seeks abroad may find
Thee sitting careless on a granary floor,
   Thy hair soft-lifted by the winnowing wind;   15
Or on a half-reaped furrow half asleep,
   Drowsed with the fume of poppies, while thy hook
      Spares the next swath and all its twinèd flowers:
And sometimes like a gleaner thou dost keep
   Steady thy laden head across a brook;   20
   Or by a cider-press with patient look
      Thou watchest the last oozings hours by hours.

Where are the songs of Spring? Aye, where are they?
   Think not of them, thou hast thy music too—
While barrèd° clouds bloom the soft-dying day,   *streaked*   25
   And touch the stubble-plains with rosy hue;
Then in a wailful choir the small gnats mourn
   Among the river sallows,° borne aloft   *low willow trees*
      Or sinking as the light wind lives or dies;
And full-grown lambs loud bleat from hilly bourn;°   *field*   30
   Hedge crickets sing; and now with treble soft
The redbreast whistles from a garden-croft;°   *small plot*
      And gathering swallows twitter in the skies.

THE RECEPTIVE READER

1. Readers have long turned to Keats' poetry for its rich sensuous imagery. How much of Keats' *harvest imagery* does the modern reader still recognize? (Can you visualize the reaper cutting a swath through the wheat interspersed with flowers? Can you visualize the wind winnowing the grain—by blowing the lighter chaff away as the grain is thrown into the air?)

2. What words and images in this poem help create the prevailing *mood*—the rich harvest mood of things coming to fruition, offering a feast to the senses? (Which images are visual images? Which are sound images? Which involve sensations—touch,

taste?) What does Keats' way of looking at the nuts, the bees, or the cider press contribute to the characteristic feeling that pervades the poem?

3. Why are the swallows gathering? Is it a mere coincidence that Keats mentions them last in the poem?

THE PERSONAL RESPONSE

Keats, like other Romantic poets of the early nineteenth century, saw the healing influence of nature as an antidote to the ills of city civilization. Can you get into the spirit of his nature poetry? Is your own relationship with nature similar or different?

T. S. ELIOT (1888–1965)
Preludes
1917

1
The winter evening settles down
With smell of steaks in passageways.
Six o'clock.
The burnt-out ends of smoky days.
And now a gusty shower wraps   5
The grimy scraps
Of withered leaves about your feet
And newspapers from vacant lots;
The showers beat
On broken blinds and chimney-pots,   10
At the corner of the street
A lonely cab-horse steams and stamps.
And then the lighting of the lamps.

2
The morning comes to consciousness
Of faint stale smells of beer   15
From the sawdust-trampled street
With all its muddy feet that press
To early coffee-stands.
With the other masquerades
That time resumes,   20
One thinks of all the hands
That are raising dingy shades
In a thousand furnished rooms.

3
You tossed a blanket from the bed,
You lay upon your back, and waited;   25
You dozed, and watched the night revealing
The thousand sordid images
Of which your soul was constituted;
They flickered against the ceiling.
And when all the world came back   30

And the light crept up between the shutters
And you heard the sparrows in the gutters,
You had such a vision of the street
As the street hardly understands;
Sitting along the bed's edge, where   35
You curled the papers from your hair,
Or clasped the yellow soles of feet
In the palms of both soiled hands.

4
His soul stretched tight across the skies
That fade behind a city block,   40
Or trampled by insistent feet
At four and five and six o'clock;
And short square fingers stuffing pipes,
And evening newspapers, and eyes
Assured of certain certainties,   45
The conscience of a blackened street
Impatient to assume the world.

I am moved by fancies that are curled
Around these images, and cling:
The notion of some infinitely gentle   50
Infinitely suffering thing.

Wipe your hand across your mouth, and laugh;
The worlds revolve like ancient women
Gathering fuel in vacant lots.

THE RECEPTIVE READER

1. T. S. Eliot was one of the leaders in the early modern rebellion against the conventionally beautiful or superficially pretty in poetry. How many of the images make this poem head in the opposite direction? Which are most striking or memorable for you, and why?

2. How does the "you" addressed in the poem relate to the "sordid" images shown in this poem? How does the "I" that is speaking? How do you?

THE CREATIVE DIMENSION

Much modern poetry explores negative or mixed emotions about the urban landscape or cityscape in which most of us live. Write a passage or poem packed with images that project your own feelings about the city or about the American small town. How do you react to the following example?

After the first rain, the city's smells only reek louder and damper: damp wool, wet newspapers, the oily dirty street. The smell of yesterday's meatloaf wafts from the neighboring apartment when I open the window to smell the wet cement. Today will be like yesterday. I open a thousand locks on the front door and lock a thousand behind me.

DANA GIOIA   (born 1950)

California Hills in August   1982

I can imagine someone who found
these fields unbearable, who climbed
the hillside in the heat, cursing the dust,
cracking the brittle weeds underfoot,
wishing a few more trees for shade.   5

An Easterner especially, who would scorn
the meagreness of summer, the dry
twisted shapes of black elm,
scrub oak, and chaparral—a landscape
August has already drained of green.   10

One who would hurry over the clinging
thistle, foxtail, golden poppy,
knowing everything was just a weed,
unable to conceive that these trees
And sparse brown bushes were alive.   15

And hate the bright stillness of the noon,
without wind, without motion,
the only other living thing
a hawk, hungry for prey, suspended
in the blinding, sunlit blue.   20

And yet how gentle it seems to someone
raised in a landscape short of rain—
the skyline of a hill broken by no more
trees than one can count, the grass,
the empty sky, the wish for water.   25

THE RECEPTIVE READER

1. What is the task the poet set herself in this poem? Why does she make us look at the landscape familiar to her through the eyes of the *outsider*?

2. What images or details make the landscape real for you? Were you surprised when the poem reached its turning point at the beginning of the last stanza?

3. What phrase or phrases would you nominate as the key to the characteristic quality of the landscape in this poem?

4. Do your sympathies lie with the Easterner or the Westerner in this poem?

THE CREATIVE DIMENSION

Have you ever felt defensive about a place dear to your heart? Write about it, first from the point of view of the outsider and then from your own point of view. For a possible model, look at the following re-creation of the Gioia poem.

To the outsider, the August hills are dry, barren,
brittle, devoid of life.
But in those dusty landscapes I see the

promise of emerald hills sparkling with dew
orange and yellow poppies
lupine and mustard.
I imagine warm and humid days alive
with the hum of insects.
I know beauty is just a rain away.

WRITING ABOUT LITERATURE

3. Looking at Imagery (Using Detail)

The Writing Workshop   You need to read a poem with an open eye and a willing ear. One of your first questions will be: "What does the poet want me to see and hear? What does the poet want me to visualize, to imagine?" You have to be receptive to the signals that are designed to call up vivid images on your mental screen. If you are a reader with a technical bent, you will have to shift from a number-crunching or data-collecting mode to a mode of recording images and decoding their meanings.

In preparing a paper on the imagery of a poem, ask yourself questions like the following:

✧ How does the poet make the *setting* real for you? Where is the poem taking you? What revealing details bring the place, the people, or the situation to life for you?

✧ What *key images* are particularly striking or revealing? What sights seem to stand out? Why are they important in the poem as a whole? Quote phrases, half-lines, or lines to make your reader see key images and how they come back or find an echo at other points in the poem.

✧ Does the poem appeal to more than your sense of sight? Does it bring *other senses* into play—your hearing, your sense of smell, or your sense of touch? One way to organize your paper might be to sort out the different kinds of imagery.

✧ What *emotions* do the images in the poem stir in the reader? What attitudes do they bring into play? Do they in any way trigger contradictory feelings or mixed emotions? One way to organize your paper might be to look first at images that steer the reader's reactions one way and to look later at images that point in a different direction.

✧ Is the poem unified by a prevailing *mood*? Or does it move through stages as images shift or as the associations and implications of key images change? One way to organize your paper might be to mark off major stages in the way the poem shapes the reader's thoughts and feelings.

✧ In reading the poem, do you remain caught up in the surface texture of vivid graphic imagery? Or does the poem raise issues that go beyond a particular scene? Does the poem imply more *general meanings*? (Does the poem make you think?)

Study the following student paper focused on a poem's imagery. How does the writer set her paper in motion? Is there a preview or hint of her general strategy? Does the paper follow up what you took to be the writer's overall plan? What use does she make of short, apt quotations? How does she wind up her paper?

SAMPLE STUDENT PAPER

At Peter Meinke's Apple Market

"Apple-smell everywhere!" So starts Peter Meinke's poem, "Sunday at the Apple Market." Apples of all kinds (Haralson, McIntosh, Fireside, Rome), apple smells, and the paraphernalia of the apple harvest are everywhere in this poem—in "miraculous profusion." The poet could simply have said, "The apple market was busy Sunday afternoon with lots of people buying tons of apples of different colors and kinds." Instead, Peter Meinke assaults our senses with a feast of concrete imagery. We can choose to let this poem simply "be," as Archibald MacLeish says—to let it simply exist and speak for itself. Or we can choose to look behind the images to find a larger meaning. Either way, we cannot help relishing the rich sensuous quality of its "being."

Poems often display vivid visual and auditory imagery, and this poem does so in exceptional profusion. We see yellow, green, and red apples "piled crazy in the storehouse barn (7), apples in "bushels / and baskets and bags and boxes" (13–14), "apples by the cartload" (5). We hear "the crowd / around the testing table laughing" (8–9) and the "dogs barking at children in the appletrees (11)."

However, this poem appeals to all the senses; indeed, apple smell is everywhere, from the beginning to the "smell of apples" at the end (l5). We experience taste along with smell as the people around the testing table roll "the cool applechunks in their mouths" (10) or as we recall the juice made by the "old ciderpresses weathering in the shed" (3). We can imagine ourselves holding hands as the couples do in the poem; we carry the weight of bushels, baskets, bags, and boxes.

Why is the crowd laughing; why are the people happy? We see them at the apple market at the time of harvest, of ripeness and fruition. All the previous stages, from winter and pruning of the trees through blossom time, have led up to this stage of fullness and culmination. We can imagine the harvest cycle as parallel to our own journey through life, since all the stages of our own growth are represented: We see the children in the apple trees; we see the couples holding hands; we see the children's parents carrying apples back to their cars. We can enjoy a sense of cycle that leads up to this moment when we enjoy the fruits of our journey through life.

However, the poem does not stop there. Contrasting with the dominating concrete images of the ample harvest are hints of a further stage in the cycle. The "old ciderpresses weathering in the shed" (3) suggest fermentation and aging. The "old ladders tilting at empty branches" (4) foreshadow the end of fertility, with the coming of barrenness and decay—the inevitable continuation of the process we experience at the high point of the cycle in this poem. We see "so many people / out in the country" (13) on this Sunday to capture and carry back with them this happy moment of fulfillment that cannot last. For "one Sunday afternoon" these people are "free / and happy as people must have been meant to be" (16–17).

Reading the poem, I was struck by the image of the dogs barking at the children in the apple trees. It brought to mind a time when my grandparents' orchard was for me a "free and happy" world of its own. I remember a Sunday when I was hiding from my cousins in my grandmother's apple tree, stifling giggles on a high branch, my Sunday dress torn on the rough bark. I wrote a brief poem recalling the experience; it ends as follows:

In Sunday black and white like spotted puppies
they sniff and search under apple carts
and behind the stacked up empty wooden crates.
Behind heavy leaves red apples hide.
I hide, too.

QUESTIONS

1. How does the student writer set the scene or the tone? How well does she get into the spirit of the poem?

2. Does she provide the evidence needed to support her conclusions?

3. How do you react to the way she winds up her paper?

4. Is your response to the poem different from that of the student writer? Do you disagree with any of her conclusions?

4 METAPHOR
Making Connections

FOCUS ON METAPHOR

Poets use striking imaginative comparisons to go beyond the resources of literal speech. They take us into a world of vivid visual images, but often there is more to the image than meets the eye. When a poet says, "The bird of love is on the wing," the line is meant to call up a vivid visual image before the mind's eye. But the poem is not literally talking about a bird. Instead, it *compares* the feeling of falling in love to the exhilaration a bird might experience in flight.

The bird here is an example of **metaphor,** language used imaginatively to carry ideas and feelings that otherwise might be hard to put into words. A metaphor is a brief, compressed comparison that talks about one thing as if it were another. The comparison is implied and not spelled out. It comes into the poem unannounced, without the words *like* or *as* to signal that something is not literally a bird but only in some way like a bird. (A close cousin of metaphor, which signals the comparison by words such as *like* or *as if,* is called a **simile.**)

The following poem shows the way metaphors come into a poem.

EMILY DICKINSON   (1830–1886)
Apparently with no surprise   1884

Apparently with no surprise
to any happy Flower
The Frost beheads it at its play—
In accidental power—
The blonde Assassin passes on—   5
The Sun proceeds unmoved
To measure off another Day
For an approving God.

As we read this poem, our first hint that the poet is speaking metaphorically is the word *happy* applied to the flower. Flowers are not literally happy or
unhappy. They have no feelings, just as they do not "play" (any more than
they go about serious business). These metaphors are each built on an implied
as if: It is *as if* the flower had been happily and innocently at play when it was
attacked by the frost. It is *as if* the killer frost were an executioner who "beheads" the condemned victim. It is *as if* the frost were an "assassin," thus
adding the idea of treachery to the brutality of the victim's execution.

The metaphors in this poem make us think of both the frost and the
flower as if they were human beings, acting out a grim minidrama that stirs our
sympathies and raises troubling questions in our minds. (This kind of
metaphor, which treats things or plants as if they were persons, is called **personification.**) Metaphor here serves functions that make it a vital part of the
poet's language:

❖ First, metaphor has the power to call up striking visual *images*. We see
with the mind's eye the flower at play, the murderous frost beheading it, the
"blonde" assassin (not a stereotypical beetle-browed villain) passing on non-
chalantly. We see (or imagine) the sun proceeding on its course as if nothing
special had occurred. Metaphor is one of the poet's chief means of living up
to the ideal that "a poem does not talk about ideas; it *enacts* them" (John
Ciardi).

❖ Second, metaphor has the power to stir our *feelings:* We are likely to
shudder at the swift destruction of the helpless, harmless flower. We should
feel at least a twinge of terror at seeing it destroyed. The ability of metaphor to
engage our emotions makes for a key difference between poetic language on
the one hand and scientific or other kinds of emotionally neutral language on
the other. The English Romantic poet Samuel Taylor Coleridge voiced a re-
quirement echoed by many moderns when he said that poetry should "be sensuous, and by its imagery elicit truth at a flash, and be able to move our
feelings and awaken our affections."

✧ Third, metaphor has the power to make us *think*. Since we are thinking beings, it is hard for us to watch the spectacle of the killer frost without asking ourselves uneasy questions. Is it true that only we, sentimental humans, care? Do only we feel forebodings of sudden death as the frost does its killer job? The poem gives us pause. It raises questions to which it does not provide easy answers.

What is the difference between image and metaphor? The poet's *images* can make us feel more fully alive, more alert to our surroundings. The poet's image making invites us to respond to the rich sensuous or sensory surface of the world. In Peter Meinke's "Sunday at the Apple Market," we visualize apples, we smell apples, we roll apple chunks around in our mouths. There are apples literally everywhere in the poem. Whatever associations they bring into play, they are first of all literal apples.

By contrast, in Emily Dickinson's poem there are no literal beheadings or assassins; the sun does not literally measure off a day the way a tailor measures off cloth. These are *metaphors*. The images they make us see have their meaning beyond what meets the eye. We have to decode the metaphors in order to understand what they stand for in the world of real flowers, real frost, and the real sun.

THE RECEPTIVE READER

Dickinson's poems often have puzzling, provocative phrases tucked away in them that become more meaningful on second thought and on second reading. Why "accidental power"? Why "blonde assassin"? Is the scene being watched by an "approving God"?

READING FOR METAPHOR

Without metaphor, language would lose its lifeblood and stiffen into a conventional system of signs.
ERNST CASSIRER

I love metaphor. It provides two loaves where there seems to be one. Sometimes it throws in a load of fish.
BERNARD MALAMUD

The English eighteenth-century poet William Blake says, "The tigers of wrath are wiser than the horses of instruction." We need no nudging to make us realize that these animals are not literally there. They are brought in by way of comparison. Reading such metaphors, we mentally fill in the possible connections: Righteous anger is fiery *like* a tiger and moves us to swift action. Compared with the powerful welling-up of passion, instruction is more plodding, like the horses pulling a brewery wagon. It makes us do what we are told, as horses do what pleases their masters. It is not likely to move us to generous or passionate endeavor.

Both an image on the literal level and a metaphor may appeal strongly to our visual imagination. The difference is that the metaphor makes us visualize something that we could not literally interact with or see. When the poet Adrien Stoutenburg says, "The strawberry's leaves / Are a green hand spread open," we are looking at real leaves but not at a real hand. We are looking at small leaves that together form a kind of hand holding up the ripening strawberry. The psalm says, "The Lord is my shepherd; / I shall not want. / He maketh me to lie down in green pastures: / He leadeth me beside the still waters." When we recite the psalm, the sheep and the caring, protecting shepherd are not literally there as part of our lives. *We* are there, and the psalm is about our relationship to the Lord.

Metaphor (from a Greek word meaning "to carry over") carries us over from the normal surface meaning of a word to something else. It exploits similarities and makes connections between things we might otherwise keep apart. A metaphor may be a single word: Blake uses the single word *tiger* to set up the metaphorical connection between righteous wrath and the fiery, ferocious, threatening animal. The richer the metaphor, the more it challenges our imagination to call up a full range of similarities. For instance, righteous anger is fiery and passionate. It is threatening to evildoers, and it would probably be futile to try to control.

Often, however, the poet will develop a metaphor beyond a single word. Such an **extended metaphor** traces the ramifications of the implied comparison, following up related similarities. Look at the extended (or **sustained**) metaphor in the following poem by a leading figure of the "Harlem Renaissance" of the thirties and forties.

C O U N T E E   C U L L E N   (1903–1946)

For My Grandmother   1927

This lovely flower fell to seed;
Work gently sun and rain;
She held it as her dying creed
That she would grow again.

The central metaphor in this poem compares the grandmother to a flower. But the poet extends the metaphor beyond the flower in bloom to its whole life cycle: The flower grows from a seed, helped by sun and rain; it then decays and in turn leaves a seed. We cherish it because of its loveliness, but it is also subject to death and decay. However, the seed the flower leaves behind carries the promise of renewed growth—of rebirth and new life.

THE RECEPTIVE READER

Are the sun and the rain in this poem literal or metaphorical or both? When speaking of renewed growth, was the poet thinking of resurrection and eternal life? Or was he thinking of the grandchildren that were the "seed" representing continued life?

When a single extended metaphor gives shape to a poem as a whole, it becomes an **organizing metaphor** (it is also called a **controlling metaphor**). More often, however, a poem moves through several related, interacting metaphors. The following poem is built around three related metaphors: the house, the horse, and the dog. Look at the way these metaphors work together. What do they make you see? What do they make you feel? How do they challenge more familiar ways of looking at our bodies?

MAY   SWENSON   (born 1919)

Question   1954

Body my house
my horse my hound
What will I do
When you are fallen

Where will I sleep   5
How will I ride
What will I hunt

Where can I go without my mount
all eager and quick
How will I know   10
in thicket ahead
is danger or treasure
When Body my good
bright dog is dead

How will it be   15
to lie in the sky
without roof or door
and wind for an eye

with cloud for shift°   *woman's shirt or chemise*
how will I hide?   20

In this poem, three interlocking, meshing metaphors make us reexamine the way we feel about our bodies. To judge from the way the poet develops or follows them up in the poem, these metaphors mean something like the following:

✧ The poet calls the body "my house," reminding us that it puts up the roof and walls giving us shelter and the doors barring intruders. It offers us a place to sleep, to hide. The word *house* is likely to make us think of a place that offers refuge and protection.

✧ The poet calls the body "my horse." Apparently we are asked to imagine not a tired nag but a spirited mount—"all eager and quick"—ready to carry us to adventure. We are not rooted like a tree. Life is movement, motion, activity—but only if we can depend on the body to carry us into action.

✧ The poet calls the body "my hound"—a "good bright dog" that like a hunting dog serves its master well. It alerts us to danger (lurking "in thicket ahead") or hunts down "treasure." We depend on our bodies to keep us alert, prepared to deal with the threats and promises of every day.

THE RECEPTIVE READER

1. How is the way this poem looks at the body different from other, more familiar ways of looking at our bodies? Do you share the feelings or sympathize with the attitudes that the metaphors in this poem suggest?

2. For you, what is the connecting *thread* that links the three metaphors? What do they have in common?

3. What tone does the *title* set for the poem? What is the poet's "question"? Does the poem suggest an answer?

THE CREATIVE DIMENSION

Explore your own possible metaphors for the body. Complete the line "My body my . . ." in your own way, writing your own body poem or passage about the body. How well does the central metaphor work in the following example?

Body

You ship of a fool!
Why do I worry about
   sprung planks
   leaky decks
   spent rigging
   peeling paint?
The rats left a long time ago,
and you're still afloat!

EXPLORATIONS ━━━━━

Understanding Metaphor

How do you explain the metaphors in the following lines? What do they make you see? What do they make you feel? What do they make you think? Compare your own responses with those of other readers.

1. We drive the same highways
   in the dark, not seeing each other,
         only the lights.
        Diane Wakoski, "Meeting an Astronomer"

2. Like any other man
   I was born with a knife
   in one hand
   and a wound in the other.
        Gregory Orr, "Like Any Other Man"

3. The heart has need of some deceit
    To make its pistons rise and fall;
    For less than this it would not beat,
    Nor flush the sluggish veins at all.
                    Countee Cullen, "Only the Polished Skeleton"

4.   One morning last March,
    I pressed against the new barbed and galvanized

    fence on the Boston Common. Behind their cage,
    yellow dinosaur steamshovels were grunting
    as they cropped up tons of mush and grass
    to gouge their underworld garage.
                    Robert Lowell, "For the Union Dead"

EXPLORATIONS

The Extended Metaphor

What is the central metaphor in the following poem? How does the poet develop it into an extended metaphor? Which of the similarities between hope and "the thing with feathers" seem most fitting? Which seem most strange? Which to you are most thought provoking or revealing?

EMILY DICKINSON   (1830–1886)

"Hope" is the thing with feathers   1861

"Hope" is the thing with feathers—
That perches in the soul—
And sings the tune without the words—
And never stops—at all—

And sweetest—in the Gale—is heard—   5
And sore must be the storm—
That could abash° the little Bird   *subdue and silence*
That kept so many warm—

I've heard it in the chillest land—
And on the strangest Sea—   10
Yet, never, in Extremity,°   *in extreme danger or adversity*
It asked a crumb—of Me.

THE RECEPTIVE READER

1. What, to the poet, makes a bird a good metaphor for hope? What related details or ramifications make this *extended metaphor* vivid or real for you?
2. Why would the song be heard "sweetest in the gale"? How does the song keep "so many warm"? What does it say about hope that the bird never "asked a crumb"?

THE CREATIVE DIMENSION

Cluster the word *hope*. What images, memories, or associations does the word call up? In your cluster, how do they branch out from the central stimulus word? What kind of pattern takes shape? Write a passage that pulls together the ideas and associations. How do your own associations with the word compare with those in Dickinson's poem?

CROSS-REFERENCES—For Discussion or Writing

Dickinson's "'Hope' is the thing with feathers" and Hardy's "The Darkling Thrush" (Chapter 2) are both poems about hope. Explore how one poet uses a bird as an image and the other uses a bird as a metaphor.

FIGURATIVE LANGUAGE: METAPHOR, SIMILE, PERSONIFICATION

Metaphor is one kind of nonliteral language under the larger umbrella heading of **figurative** language. Like a metaphor, a **simile** is a brief, compressed imaginative comparison. Unlike a metaphor, a simile uses the words *as* or *like* or *as if* to advertise that a comparison will follow. These signals alert us to look for the similarities that the poet had in mind: "My love is like a red, red rose"; "My love is like a silken tent." A simile says outright that something is like something else. Sometimes simile is considered merely a special kind of metaphor—a metaphor announced rather than implied.

Love poems through the centuries have used metaphor and simile to express feelings that might otherwise be hard to put into words. A famous simile opens the following poem by the Scottish poet Robert Burns. Look at what the two similes in the opening stanza (group of four related lines) do for the poem as a whole. Note that *fair* in this poem means "beautiful"—as in much early love poetry.

ROBERT BURNS   (1759–1796)
A Red, Red Rose   1796

O my luve's like a red, red rose
That's newly sprung in June;
O my luve's like the melodie
That's sweetly played in tune.

As fair art thou, my bonny lass,°   *my dear girl*   5
So deep in luve am I;
And I will luve thee still, my dear,
Till a'° the seas gang dry°—   *all / run (go) dry*

Till a' the seas gang dry, my dear,
And the rocks melt wi' the sun: 10

O I will luve thee still, my dear,
While the sands o' life shall run.

And fare thee weel, my only luve,
And fare thee weel awhile!
And I will come again, my luve,   15
Though it were a thousand mile.

The opening simile here draws on the rich traditional associations of the rose: For instance, its rich red color is pleasing to the eye (and it is often associated with passion). People who love roses treasure the delicate petals and the fresh scent on a June morning. The second simile likens the poet's love to a "melody sweetly played in tune"—soothing the nerves frazzled by the jangling noises of every day. The poet then tells his readers what many of them want to hear: A love like the poet's is not a casual, passing encounter. It will last forever, longer than the rocks and the sea. Any separation will be only for "awhile."

THE RECEPTIVE READER

1. How, or how well, do the two opening *similes* work together?
2. What explains the "sands of life" *metaphor*? Sand (on beaches) does not usually "run." What traditional device used sand to measure time?
3. Much traditional love poetry used *hyperbole*, or extreme exaggeration—for instance, to praise the beauty of the beloved to the skies. What instances of hyberbole can you find in this poem?

THE PERSONAL RESPONSE

To you, does Burns' love poem seem timeless or out of date? Would you consider sending it to someone? If someone sent it to you, what might be your response?

The bolder and the more original a poet's similes, the more they are likely to stimulate our imagination. The following poem focuses on the big bird— "the great gull"—that came from the sea. What images and feelings are brought into the poem by two key similes: "like a high priest" and "like a merchant prince"?

HOWARD NEMEROV   (born 1920)

The Great Gull   1951

Restless, rising at dawn
I saw the great gull come from the mist
To stand upon the lawn.
And there he shook his savage wing
To quiet, and stood like a high priest   5
Bird-masked, mantled in gray.
Before his fierce austerity

My thought bowed down, imagining
The wild sea-lanes he wandered by
And the wild waters where he slept   10
Still as a candle in the crypt.
Noble, and not courteous,
He stared upon my green concerns.
Then, like a merchant prince
Come to some poor province,   15
Who, looking all about, discerns
No spice, no treasure house,
Nothing that can be made
Delightful to his haughty trade,
And so spreads out his sail,   20
Leaving to savage men
Their miserable regimen;°   *rigidly ordered life*
So did he rise, making a gale
About him with his wings,
And fought his huge freight into air   25
And vanished seaward with a cry—
A strange tongue but the tone clear.

This poem focuses on the large seabird that came out of the ocean fog to stand on the lawn. The speaker in the poem is fascinated by the sight of the bird, from the time it lands and stashes its large wings for an at-rest position until it finally unfolds them again for takeoff. Concrete visual images help us imagine this fascinating bird: First, the bird "shook his savage wing / To quiet"; later, it spread out its wings like a sail, creating a miniature storm like a gale at sea, "fighting" its way into the air to lift the "huge freight" of its body. The poet's carefully trimmed lawn (his "green concerns") must seem petty and tame to this "savage," "fierce," and "haughty" bird from the "wild sea-lanes" and "wild waters."

The poet uses several similes to help us share his feelings about this majestic wild bird. For instance, he compares the bird to a high priest, wearing a bird mask and mantle of gray (like its coat of gray feathers), expecting us to bow down to it as to a priest in a strange pagan ritual. This simile should help us sense the bird's "fierce austerity": The bird is aloof, not wasting time on frivolous diversions; it is "not courteous"—not folksy like someone trying to sell us a used car.

THE RECEPTIVE READER

1. The second simile compares the bird to a "merchant prince." How would such a person be different from an ordinary merchant? What would such a merchant prince be looking for and where? What would be disappointing about the "poor province" the gull actually found? What does this second simile have in common with the first?

2. A third simile makes us imagine the bird sleeping on the waters "still as a candle in the crypt." What images and feelings does this simile bring into the poem? How is it related to the other two similes?

3. For you, what is the connecting thread that links the three similes? How do they work together; how are they related?

THE PERSONAL RESPONSE

What animal would *you* choose to represent untamed savage nature? Do you think a sea animal would be a better choice than a land animal? Why?

Personification is a metaphor or a simile that treats something nonhuman as if it were human. It is figurative language that makes things or animals behave as if they were human. The heavens are personified in the line "The heavens declare the glory of God" (as if they were preachers or apostles). Talking about a bird from the sea as if it were a high priest or a merchant prince exemplifies personification. Personification often serves to project personal human feelings onto a larger screen. It can make the world around us mirror our own state of mind. When a blues singer sings, "The sky is crying / Look at the tears roll down the street," the whole world seems to share the singer's sadness and loneliness.

Note: Students of poetry have often set up additional subcategories for figurative language. **Metonymy,** for instance, is a metaphor that does not rove far afield but lights on something closely related. It uses *Pentagon* for the Defense Department, *crown* for the monarchy, *laurels* (from the practice of honoring people with laurel wreaths) for fame. *Gown* (academic gown) comes to stand for university in the expression "town and gown." **Synecdoche** uses the part to stand for the whole: "give us a *hand*" (when we actually need the assistance of the whole person). Or it may use the whole to stand for the part: "Outraged *womanhood* called for his resignation" (actually only a group of outraged women). It may use the individual to stand for the species (or vice versa), as when we call every miser a Scrooge.

EXPLORATIONS

Understanding Similes

How do you explain each of the following similes?

1. I had even forgotten how married love
   is a territory more mysterious
   the more it is explored, like one of those terrains
   you read about, a garden in the desert
   where you stoop to drink, never knowing
   if your mouth will fill with water or sand.
   > Linda Pastan, "After an Absence"

2. A sentence starts out like a lone traveler
   Heading into a blizzard at midnight.
   > Billy Collins, "Winter Syntax"

3. If we have quarreled our bodies wait
   patient as horses for their owners' huffy
   departure. Those masters gone they turn,
   nuzzle, and flank to flank speak
   to each other all night long
   the eloquent touching language of the dumb.
                Nils Peterson, "Bedtime"

EXPLORATIONS

A Dream Deferred

In the thirties and forties, Langston Hughes came to be considered the "poet laureate" or unofficial voice of black America. Each simile in the following poem sets up a different scenario for what might happen if a dream is deferred or hope denied. Which similes fit exceptionally well? Which scenario can you most vividly imagine? Which seems to you most likely?

LANGSTON HUGHES   (1902–1967)

Dream Deferred   1951

What happens to a dream deferred?
Does it dry up
Like a raisin in the sun?
Or fester like a sore—
And then run?   5
Does it stink like rotten meat?
Or crust and sugar over—
like a syrupy sweet?

Maybe it just sags
like a heavy load.   10

Or does it explode?

THE RANGE OF METAPHOR

When I put myself out on a saucer
       in the sun
               or moonlight
                       of the back stoop

cats
in
the form of
images
come feeding
       DIANA CHANG, "CANNIBALISM"

Poetic metaphors range from the easily accessible to the more challenging. Many of the metaphors of ordinary speech are well established and familiar. We turn to a dog-eared page, watch tempers boil, or give someone a fish-eyed stare. When they have become overused, losing their tread like a bald tire, such metaphors turn into **clichés:** the tip of the iceberg, the bottom of the barrel, the window of opportunity. By contrast, poetic metaphors are often fresh and thought provoking. They forge new connections; they discover unexpected, revealing similarities. When the American poet Carl Sandburg asks us to

Remember all paydays of lilacs and songbirds

no familiar connection between paydays and songbirds guides us. We have to work out the implied equation ourselves. It sounds as if the poet had in mind the sense of reward and elation that workers might feel on payday. That elation corresponds to the joy brought by the rich blooms of the lilac and the song of birds.

Poets—and major styles in the history of poetry—vary in how boldly they explore new metaphorical connections. Love poems of earlier centuries featured fanciful extended metaphors called **conceits.** Although elaborately developed, they often moved along conventional or fairly predictable lines. A conceit sets up an analogy between what we are literally talking about (the beloved person, say) and what we are metaphorically calling it (the sun of our universe, for example). It then traces the analogy in careful detail. Such conceits were an expected ornament of the love sonnets written by the Italian fourteenth-century poet Petrarch and the many translators and followers he inspired. The **sonnet** is an elaborately crafted fourteen-line poem with an interlaced rhyme scheme and iambic meter. (See Chapter 7 for more on the formal features of the traditional sonnet.)

In the following sonnet by one of Petrarch's English translators, the lover's "enemy" steering the ship is also called "my lord." Both of these terms early love poets applied to the haughty, disdainful, "cruel" lady to whom they addressed their "plaints." (Note: Wyatt's editors are not sure whether he intended us to read as two syllables words like *charged* and *forced*—chargèd? forcèd?—which would then make for a more regular iambic beat.)

What is the central conceit or extended metaphor in the poem? How is it developed?

THOMAS WYATT (1503–1542)

My galley charged with forgetfulness   before 1540

My galley charged with forgetfulness	
Thorough° sharp seas in winter nights doth pass	*through*
'Tween rock and rock; and eke° mine enemy, alas,	*also*
That is my lord, steereth with cruelness;	
And every oar a thought in readiness,	5
As though that death were light in such a case.	
An endless wind doth tear the sail apace	
Of forced sighs and trusty fearfulness	
A rain of tears, a cloud of dark disdain,	
Hath done the wearied cords great hinderance;	10
Wreathed with error and eke with ignorance,	
The stars be hid° that led me to this pain;	*are hidden*
Drowned is reason that should me consort,°	*stay with me*
And I remain despairing of the port.	

THE RECEPTIVE READER

1. A conceit often follows the basic metaphor into every conceivable detail. (In this poem, once we are on the ship, we stay on the ship.) Why is it winter and night? What are the oars, the wind, the rain, the cloud, the harbor? Who or what drowned? What are the rocks?

2. What is the *keynote* of this poem? What are the prevailing emotions? Why do you think generations of readers related to this kind of love poetry (and still do)?

When conceits become too predictable, they may seem to hem in rather than stimulate the imagination. (The poet has to stay on the track prescribed by the dominating metaphor.) By contrast, the metaphors in a Shakespearean sonnet more often keep developing and shifting. They may start as elaborate conceits, but then they escalate, following up new and unexpected associations. What are the three key metaphors in the following sonnet? How do they develop; how do they mesh? (Note that the word *choir* in the fourth line stands for the part of a church reserved for the choir.)

WILLIAM SHAKESPEARE   (1564–1616)
Sonnet 73   before 1598

That time of year thou mayst in me behold
When yellow leaves, or none, or few, do hang
Upon those boughs which shake against the cold,
Bare ruined choirs, where late the sweet birds sang.
In me thou seest the twilight of such day   5
As after sunset fadeth in the west;
Which by and by° black night doth take away,   *gradually*
Death's second self, that seals up all in rest.
In me thou seest the glowing of such fire
That on the ashes of his youth doth lie,   10
As the deathbed whereon it must expire,
Consumed with that which it was nourished by.
This thou perceivest, which makes thy love more strong,
To love that well which thou must leave ere long.°   *before long*

The much-analyzed first metaphor in this sonnet makes us think of approaching age as the late autumn of the speaker's life, when we see the bare branches of the tree shaken by cold winds, with only a few last withered yellow leaves clinging to the boughs. But the metaphor shifts and develops: The bare wood of the branches apparently makes the poet think of the wooden pews where the choirboys or choristers used to sit in church (where they sang the way the "sweet birds" sang in the tree). Now the church is in ruins (like many of the great abbey churches of England after the Protestant reformation had shut down the monasteries). Both the tree and the church used to be filled with sweet song, but they are now fitting metaphors for the approaching decay and loneliness of age. They are likely to make us long for the rich growth and sweet bird song of summers past.

THE RECEPTIVE READER

1. What is the *second* major metaphor, developed in the second set of four lines (or quatrain) in the sonnet? What parallels or connections make it especially fitting or expressive? How does it shift to acquire a further dimension? (How is night "Death's second self"?)

2. What is the metaphor in the *third* set of four lines? (What was "consumed with that which it was nourished by," and how?) Can you see more than one parallel or connection between this third major metaphor and the other two?

3. Many Shakespearean sonnets provide a "turning" in the final couplet, or set of two lines—an answer to a central question, or a *counterpoint* to an earlier assertion. How does this sonnet fit this pattern?

POEMS FOR FURTHER STUDY

Pay special attention to the workings of metaphor, simile, and personification in the following poems.

ROSEMARY CATACALOS   (born 1944)

La Casa   1984

The house by the acequia,°   *irrigation canal*
its front porch dark and
cool with begonias,
an old house, always there,
always of the same adobe,   5
always full of the same lessons.
We would like to stop.
We know we belonged there once.
Our mothers are inside.
All the mothers are inside,   10
lighting candles, swaying
back and forth on their knees,
begging The Virgin's forgiveness
for having reeled us out
on such very weak string.   15
They are afraid for us.
They know we will not stop.
We will only wave as we pass by.
They will go on praying
that we might be simple again.   20

THE RECEPTIVE READER

In this poem by a bilingual Mexican American poet, what is the key metaphor for
parents' sending children into the outside world? What are the implications and ramifications of the metaphor? Is the speaker in the poem thinking of a literal house—a real
house she remembers from her childhood? How would you sum up the speaker's attitude toward the past?

WILLIAM SHAKESPEARE   (1564–1616)

Sonnet 29   before 1598

When, in disgrace with Fortune and men's eyes,
I all alone beweep my outcast state,
And trouble deaf heaven with my bootless° cries,   *useless*
And look upon myself and curse my fate,
Wishing me like to one more rich in hope,   5
Featured like him, like him with friends possessed,
Desiring this man's art and that man's scope,
With what I most enjoy contented least;
Yet in these thoughts myself almost despising,
Haply I think on thee, and then my state°   *condition*   10
(Like to the lark at break of day arising

From sullen earth) sings hymns at heaven's gate;
For thy sweet love remembered such wealth brings
That then I scorn to change my state with kings.

THE RECEPTIVE READER

1. In the first eight lines, or *octave,* of this sonnet, what is literal statement? What is metaphor? (What image or associations does the reference to Fortune bring to mind?)

2. Lines 11 and 12 combine simile, metaphor, and personification. How? As Shakespeare's use of figurative language often does, the lark simile seems to escalate, shifting to a further and bolder metaphor in midflight. How, and with what effect on the reader?

3. Sonnets often reach a turning point at the end of the octave; Shakespeare's sonnets especially often lead up to a concluding couplet that leaves us with a thought to remember. How does this sonnet illustrate both of these features?

LINDA PASTAN   (born 1932)
Anger   1985

You tell me
that it's all right
to let it out of its cage,
though it may claw someone,
even bite.   5
You say that letting it out
may tame it somehow.
But loose it may
turn on me, maul
my face, draw blood.   10
Ah, you think you know so much,
you whose anger is a pet dog,
its canines dull with disuse.
But mine is a rabid thing, sharpening its teeth
on my very bones,   15
and I will never let it go.

THE RECEPTIVE READER

1. What is the *central metaphor* in this poem? Into how many details can you trace this central organizing metaphor? Which details are especially graphic or concrete? Where and how does the metaphor branch out into two opposite variations?

2. Prepare a *paraphrase,* translating the poet's metaphorical language into plain literal prose. What is lost in the translation?

THE PERSONAL RESPONSE

Where do you stand on the question raised by this poem?

THE CREATIVE DIMENSION

Write an imaginative response to this poem, using your own central metaphor instead of the one used by the poet. Or do the same for another poem with a striking central metaphor. How do you react to the following student-written sample?

I watch you,
you who say,
"Be emotional; it's all right."
But you sit with the emotion
clamped to your leg
like a steel trap on a rabbit.
You struggle to get free
without chance of success.
I watch you
trying to gnaw it loose
as the rabbit would.

NIKKI GIOVANNI   (born 1943)

The Drum   1983

daddy says the world is
a drum tight and hard
and i told him
i'm gonna beat
out my own rhythm   5

THE RECEPTIVE READER

1. How does the central metaphor change its meaning or implications in this poem?

2. How would it change the poem if instead of "i'm gonna" the poet had written "I am going to" or "I shall"?

SYLVIA PLATH   (1932–1963)

Metaphors   1960

I'm a riddle in nine syllables,
An elephant, a ponderous° house,   *very weighty*
A melon strolling on two tendrils.
O red fruit, ivory, fine timbers!
This loaf's big with its yeasty rising.   5
Money's new-minted in this fat purse.
I'm a means, a stage, a cow in calf.
I've eaten a bag of green apples,
Boarded the train there's no getting off.

THE RECEPTIVE READER

1. Where in your reading of the poem did you first guess at the answer to the riddle? What in the poem did most to confirm your guess?

2. Why "nine syllables"? Why a poem of nine lines of nine syllables each? (The title has nine letters, but this may be just a coincidence.)

3. Why green apples? Which metaphors in the poem seem to be most expressive or to fit the speaker's condition best?

4. What are the speaker's feelings? Which of the metaphors do most to reveal her attitude? Is there humor in the poem, and what kind?

THE PERSONAL RESPONSE

The situation in which the speaker in this poem finds herself has often inspired mixed emotions or contradictory feelings. Have you observed or perhaps personally shared these? Write about the mixed emotions.

LAURA ST. MARTIN (born 1957)
The Ocean   1977

the ocean is a strange
midnight lover
skinny dipping when the beach patrol has left
she is a cool seduction
wrapping blue thunder around slick brown shoulders   5
raising great foam-fringed arms to a steel sky
rushing over us
sometimes tumbling us to the shore
licking the rocks passionately
only to retreat into swirling   10
indecision
tense always prancing
and the moon casts a furious gleam on the many-knuckled sea

THE RECEPTIVE READER

How does this poem go beyond routine and limited personification? What striking human qualities does this poem read into the ocean and the moon? Does the poet's use of personification make the ocean less or more real?

THE PERSONAL RESPONSE

How do you react to this poem? What does it do for you as the reader?

JOHN DONNE   (1572–1631)

A Valediction: Forbidding Mourning   1611

As virtuous men pass mildly away,
And whisper to their souls to go,
Whilst some of their sad friends do say
The breath goes now, and some say no:

So let us melt, and make no noise,   5
No tear floods, nor sigh-tempests move;
'Twere profanation° of our joys   *it would make something sacred common*
To tell the laity our love.

Moving of the earth° brings harms and fears;   *earthquakes*
Men reckon what it did and meant;   10
But trepidation of the spheres,°   *trembling of the heavenly spheres*
Though greater far, is innocent.

Dull sublunary° lovers' love   *below the moon, earthbound*
(Whose soul is sense) cannot admit
Absence, because it doth remove   15
Those things which elemented° it.   *gave it substance*

But we, by a love so much refined
That ourselves know not what it is,
Inter-assurèd° of the mind,   *mutually sure*
Care less eyes, lips, and hands to miss.   20

Our two souls, therefore, which are one,
Though I must go, endure not yet
A breach, but an expansion,
Like gold° to airy thinness beat.   *like gold leaf*

If they be two, they are two so   25
As stiff twin compasses are two:
Thy soul, the fixed foot, makes no show
To move, but doth if the other do.

And though it in the center sit,
Yet when the other far doth roam,   30
It leans and harkens after it,
And grows erect as that comes home.

Such wilt thou be to me, who must,
Like the other foot, obliquely° run;   *at a wide angle*
Thy firmness makes my circle just,°   *makes it perfect*   35
And makes me end where I begun.

THE RECEPTIVE READER

1. According to Izaak Walton, a contemporary biographer, Donne wrote this
farewell poem for his wife before leaving on a journey to France. What is the connection

between the parting of the spouses and the death scene described in the first stanza? (Why do you think Donne's contemporaries believed that good, virtuous people would have a "mild" or gentle death?)

2. If outsiders are the "laity," what does the implied comparison make the two people in love?

3. Donne's contemporaries believed that the heavens were perfect (reflecting the perfection of God). Everything "sublunary"—below the moon, on this earth—was *im*perfect, subject to decay and death. Furthermore, the planets moving in orbit around the earth in the geocentric, earth-centered Ptolemaic view of the universe were attached to spheres of crystal. At times these moved or shook, accounting for apparent irregularities in the astronomers' calculations. How does Donne draw on these contemporary beliefs in this poem?

4. Probably the best-known example of figurative language in English literature is the comparison of the two people in love to the pair of "twin compasses" used in geometry classes to draw a circle. What does this device look like? How does it work? How does Donne put it to work in this poem?

THE PERSONAL RESPONSE

Critics (and presumably lovers) have been divided on whether to welcome into love poetry comparisons drawn from areas like astronomy, geometry, and medicine. How would you vote on this issue, and why?

WRITING ABOUT LITERATURE

4. Interpreting Metaphor (Organizing the Paper)

The Writing Workshop   Reading a poem is different from scanning unemployment statistics. One key difference is that in reading a poem we have to be alert to metaphor and simile. We have to respond to imaginative comparisons that make us see one thing while making us think of another.

For instance, in John Donne's "A Valediction: Forbidding Mourning," we are asked to visualize "gold to airy thinness beat"—gold hammered incredibly thin by the goldsmith's art, so that an ounce or less of the metal will yield enough gold leaf to gild a whole column or an altar in a church. But in reading the poem, we are expected to make the connection between the gold leaf we see and the love uniting the speaker in the poem and his wife. Their love (precious like gold) also is infinitely malleable or "stretchable," so that instead of the journey causing a "breach" or break, their love will merely expand (enduring an "expansion") to bridge the distance.

When you prepare a paper that focuses on the workings of metaphor, consider the following guidelines:

◇ Look for imaginative comparisons *spelled out or implied*. Similes are easy to recognize because the *as* or *like* or *as if* is part of the text ("*As* virtuous men pass mildly away . . ."). Metaphors do not carry such a label; the *as if* is merely implied. They are easiest to recognize when something is clearly not literally true. "Tear-floods" and "sigh-tempests" are not literally floods and tempests.

✧ Look for *sustained or extended metaphors* that the poet traces into their ramifications. The poet comparing his love to a ship lost at sea is likely to show more than one way in which being in love is like being on a drifting ship.

✧ Look for *organizing metaphors* that play a central role in the poem as a whole. A poem may be built around the metaphor of the ice skaters, who are like people moving quickly across the surface of their lives, dancing on the ice. (Often a poem builds up to a culminating metaphor that stays with us after we finish reading.)

✧ Respond to the *range of associations* of key metaphors. With most poetic metaphors, there is no simple one-to-one relationship between figurative and literal meaning. Try to do justice to what is left out in a simple prose paraphrase of a metaphorical line. Explore the images it conjures up; respond to the emotions it brings into play.

✧ Look for the *connections* between the metaphors in a poem. For instance, they may be variations on a theme, reinforcing or driving home a central concern of the poet. Or they may reflect polarities that set up the basic tension or challenge in a poem. Or they may be part of an escalating series of metaphors that lead up to a new way of seeing or feeling.

Reading Notes   When writing a paper about a poem rich in metaphor and simile, you may want to start with reading notes that take stock of the imaginative comparisons in the poem. Here are sample reading notes for John Donne's "A Valediction: Forbidding Mourning":

> The parting of the lovers is compared to a death: "As virtuous men pass mildly away / . . . So let us melt, and make no noise." Virtuous people who are dying have nothing to fear in the afterlife and therefore die in peace. A journey separating the lovers is in some ways like the separation caused by death, but it should be like a virtuous person's death—without fear and emotional upheaval.

> The noisy mourning of others is compared to floods ("tear-floods") and tempests ("sigh-tempests").

> Telling others of the speaker's intimate, private love (through loud display of grief) would be like priests revealing the mysteries of their faith to "the laity," that is, to lay people—to unappreciative, unprepared outsiders. The lovers would then "profane" the mysteries of their love—desecrating something sacred by taking it down to the level of ordinary reality.

> The upheavals in the lives of ordinary lovers are earthquakes ("moving of the earth"). But any disturbance in the more refined loves of the two people in this poem is "a trepidation of the spheres"—it is like the far-off trembling in

the crystal spheres of the heavens, which is "innocent" or harmless as far as actual damage in the world around us is concerned.

The "souls" of ordinary clods are not really soul but sense—they stay on the level of sense perception and sensual feeling; they don't really have a "soul."

True love is like gold—it can be stretched incredibly thin like gold leaf without breaking.

The souls of the two lovers are joined like twin compasses. One leg, "the fixed foot," is planted firmly in the center. The other "travels," describing a perfect circle, returning to its point of origin. The farther the moving leg extends from the fixed center, the more the stationary leg needs to incline or lean toward it (it "harkens after it"). But at the same time the stationary leg keeps the moving leg from roaming too far, from going off on a tangent. In fact the firmness of the "fixed foot" (the person who stayed home) makes sure the absent lover comes full circle.

Organizing the Paper How would you organize this material? The metaphors and similes in Donne's poem are each bold and original in their own right. You often need to make the required mental leap from what you see to what it means. At the same time, the metaphors shift rapidly, and you need to be alert if you are not to be left behind. To write a unified paper, you will have to aim at working out an overall framework or perspective. You will have to try to fit the rapidly shifting individual metaphors into an overall pattern.

The student author of the following paper uses the idea of the journey—which is the subject of the poem—as the organizing principle for the paper.

SAMPLE STUDENT PAPER

Thou Shalt Not Cry When I Am Gone

In a favorite scene in yesterday's romantic movies, someone is boarding a train, going off to war or to some far-off assignment or tour of duty. The person left behind is fighting back tears as the train slowly pulls out of the station. The traveler is trying to stay calm, forestalling the "tear-floods" and "sigh-tempests" that John Donne dreads in his farewell poem, "A Valediction: Forbidding Mourning." Scheduled to leave on a journey to France, Donne pleads with his wife Anne More to accept his departure in a spirit of calm acceptance, confident that the strength of their love will triumph over their physical separation.

In arguing against mourning and emotional upheaval, Donne takes us on a journey through a sequence of bold unexpected images, each one a metaphor or a simile for the love between him and his wife. Finally we reach the circle drawn by the twin compasses in the final stanzas as the metaphor for a perfect love that will bring him back to the starting point of his journey, making "me end where I begun." The structure of the poem, a progression from one striking metaphor or simile to another, is the more appropriate when we consider that the poem was presented to his wife before he departed on a journey.

The journey begins with an unexpected analogy between the impending separation of the lovers and death. The poet says, "So let us melt"—go quietly, like snow that melts in the March sun, making "no noise" (5). The startling comparison is between their parting and the death of "virtuous men," who "pass mildly away / And whisper to their souls to go" (1–2). Virtuous men and their friends have no need to mourn unduly at their passing—after all, their virtue in this life has assured them of glory and reward in the life to come. Similarly, the poet and his love have no need for noise at their separation—"no tear-floods, nor sigh-tempests" (6). There is no need to weep and sigh, since the beauty and strength of their love will survive their separation.

Their love is in fact almost sacred. It would be profaned if it should be made known to others, who could not comprehend love on such a high spiritual plane. Since it is almost holy, the lovers should not cheapen or defile it through such ordinary demonstration of grief as weeping or lamenting. Like priests, they should guard their sacred mysteries from "profanation" by the laity (7–8).

We next move to a larger circle than the temple where love is protected from the uninitiated. Even the earth is not adequate to contain true love. For more common lovers, the earthquake of separation would bring "harms and fears" (9). But the love between the poet and his wife is above the reach of such earthly upheavals. It is as if their love resided in the heavens, among the crystal spheres of the Ptolemaic universe. Even when there is "trepidation" or trembling of the spheres, it is "innocent"—it will cause no harm here below. Donne remains in the Ptolemaic universe for another verse or two: Ordinary earth-bound lovers are caught up in the physical presence of the other person, which like all material things in this "sublunary" sphere below the moon is subject to change and decay. Their "soul is sense"; the only outlet for what soul they have is through the five senses. Their love hinges on the physical act of love, which cannot be consummated in the absence of the beloved. More refined lovers don't need the presence of the physical body; they "care less" if they have to miss "eyes, lips, and hands" (13–20).

The love of these two exceptional lovers is like gold—not just because it is precious, but because gold can be beaten into a layer of the thinnest gold leaf that stretches incredibly far—perhaps even from England to France without a "breach" or breaking. However, the culminating metaphor is that of the twin compasses, which "are two" only in the sense that there are two legs joined permanently at the top. The "fixed foot" of the stay-at-home "leans and harkens" after the other that "far doth roam" (25–30). As the foot that actually draws the circle travels around the stationary part, that part must incline at the right angle. (It cannot just forget about the "roaming" part.)

Together, the twin compasses create a circle, to Donne's contemporaries the most perfect shape in the universe. The firmness of the "other foot" enables the poet to come full circle; it makes his journey "end where I begun" (36).

QUESTIONS

1. How well does this paper read the metaphors in the poem? (In the poem, which are metaphors, and which are similes?) Where or how does the paper help you understand Donne's figurative language? Do you disagree with any of the interpretations? Did the student writer miss anything important?

2. Which of the metaphors or similes in this poem seem to you particularly unexpected or strange? Which make the most sense after the reader has a chance to think about them?

3. One reader thought the poem "terribly romantic," since the poet wants the love between him and his wife to be perfect, better than anyone else's. At the opposite end of the spectrum, another reader found the poet to be romantic on the surface but really insensitive, lecturing a silent, passive partner about what she should feel and think. Where do you stand? How do you respond to the poem?

5 SYMBOL
A World of Meanings

Symbols are the bridging language between the visible and the invisible world.

ANGELIS ARRIEN

FOCUS ON SYMBOLS

A **symbol** is something that we can see but that has acquired a meaning beyond itself. A plow was literally the peasant's most basic tool—needed to break the sod and start the planting cycle that would lead to the bounty of the harvest. Through the ages, the plow became a symbol for the steady anonymous toil required to feed humankind. Like other powerful symbols, the plow activates a rich network of associations. It reminds us to honor the labor that staves off famine. It serves as an admonition to the privileged who squander in thoughtless luxury what the workers in the fields gain toiling from sunup to sundown.

We all know the language of symbols: The dove of peace prevails when nations sheathe the sword of war. The red cross protects volunteers on missions of mercy. The daily bread stands for what we need to sustain life; it becomes "the staff of life." Posters used in political campaigns often speak a symbolic language: The raised fist calls to armed struggle. Hands joined in a handshake proclaim human brotherhood. Chains were used to shackle a prisoner; they became a symbol of slavery and oppression. A broken chain, in turn, became a powerful symbol of freedom.

Many such symbols are well established. We read them the way we read familiar gestures: the raised palm that says "Stop!" or the outstretched palm that says "Please give." Poets use or adapt traditional symbols, but they will also often give new symbolic significance to objects and events. Rather than bring the meaning of a symbol *into* the poem from the outside, we have to read the meaning of the symbol *out of* the poem.

The following poem focuses our attention on the rose and on water, which are both rich in symbolic overtones and associations. The rose, often a deep red or blood red, has long stood for passion or for beauty. The more arid the country, the more water is likely to be worshiped as the source of life, making the desert bloom, creating an oasis in a wasteland of rock or sand. What is the symbolic meaning of the rose and of water in this poem?

DENISE LEVERTOV   (born 1923)

To One Steeped in Bitterness   1964

Nail the rose
          to your mind's door
like a rat, a thwarted chickenhawk.
Yes, it has had its day.

And the water   5
          poured for you
which you disdain to drink,
yes, throw it away.

Yet the fierce rose
          stole nothing   10
from your cooped heart,
nor plucked your timid eye;

and from inviolate rock
          the liquid light
was drawn, that's dusty now   15
and your lips dry.

In this poem, we see a number of symbolic objects and symbolic gestures. We can imagine someone being offered a rose or a drink of water. We can also imagine the person turning these down. In the poem, as in real life, both of these gestures invite symbolic interpretation. Both the water and the disdainful gesture that throws it out are likely to mean something beyond themselves. They reveal an attitude, a state of mind. The gesture of pouring the water may mean friendship or hospitality. The gesture of refusing it may symbolize bitterness and hostility.

What is likely to be the symbolic meaning of the rose? We are asked to imagine it nailed to the "mind's door" by the bitter, hostile person being addressed in the poem. The person "steeped in bitterness," with a "cooped heart," would nail the rose to the barn door the way ranchers nail varmint they consider their natural enemies. The bitter person has become hostile to what would bring rich beauty like that of the rose into his or her starved life. The rose is "fierce"; its beauty is not meek (like that of a shrinking violet) but assertive, calling passionately for our attention. But it would take or steal nothing for offering its intense, challenging beauty to the beholder.

THE RECEPTIVE READER

What is likely to be the symbolic meaning of the water? The person steeped in bitterness disdainfully rejects the offered water, which is like "liquid light," and which would bring much-needed liquid to dry, parched lips. What would the parched soul be thirsting for? Love? Human contact?

What is the difference between symbol and metaphor?

✧ The water being offered a person is *literally* there. It could be provided impersonally the way a glass of water is routinely set down in front of a restaurant guest. But it can also become part of a symbolic gesture, the way we offer a drink to show hospitality, human interest. The water then becomes a symbol. It is literally there, but it has a meaning beyond itself.

✧ When in the poem the rose is nailed to the "mind's door," the mind does not literally have any doors. The mind resides in the gray matter of the brain, where there are no hinges or knobs, no doors. The door is not literally there; it is a metaphor. It is *as if* the mind had a door like a barn door, to which the embittered person could nail the offering like a trophy, the way a vengeful farmer might display there the pelt of a coyote. The metaphor acts out the rejecting person's anger and hostility, enabling us to visualize and share these emotions.

THE LANGUAGE OF SYMBOLS

What the bee knows
Tastes in the honey
Sweet and sunny.
JOHN FANDEL, "TRIBUTE."

Symbols, like metaphors, are close to the heart of the poet's language. Metaphor and symbol both connect what we see to something else, but they work differently. We use a metaphor when we call our planet "spaceship earth." We focus on the planet and compare it to a spaceship (which has limited resources and an uncertain destination). The spaceship is not literally there. We speak symbolically when we make the ill-fated *Titanic* a symbol of human pride. In this case, the ship was literally there and sank to the bottom of the sea. There was a real ship, which now makes us think of something beyond itself—shortsighted human pride brought low by a catastrophic event.

A poet will often center a poem on a unifying symbol. Often these symbols are rooted in age-old human experience, drawing on a community of shared meanings. They are often rich in overtones and associations. For instance, since the dawn of human history, the first budding green life of April, after the barrenness and ice of winter, has served as a symbol of the triumph of life over death. The earliest poets and storytellers told stories of the return of spring; Easter rites celebrated the faith of the tribe in rebirth and renewal. Green is a potently symbolic color: In the depth of winter, a sprig of evergreen (or a whole tree) can symbolize our defiant faith that burgeoning life will return to the barren, frozen land.

Poets draw on this common fund of symbolic meanings, shaping them to their own creative purposes. In reading the following poem, we soon realize that the frogs in the basement of the abandoned house are more than a strange footnote in the speaker's childhood memories. They make us wonder: Where do they come from? How can they survive in the wrecked ruin of the abandoned house? We are likely to conclude that they have a larger meaning: They become symbols of surviving and renewing life. The "green chorus" of the green frogs, who had "slept in an icy bed" all winter, comes back to life in the spring, "pouring / Out of their green throats."

DAVID WAGONER   (born 1926)

The Other House   1983

As a boy, I haunted an abandoned house
Whose basement was always full of dark-green water
Or dark-green ice in winter,
Where frogs came back to life and sang each spring.

On broken concrete under the skeleton   5
Of a roof, inside ribbed walls, I listened alone
Where the basement stairs went down
Under the water, down into their music.

During storms, our proper house would be flooded too.
The water would spout from drains, through the foundation   10
And climb the basement stairs
But silently, and would go away silently,

As silent as my father and mother were
All day and during dinner and after
And after the radio   15
With hardly a murmur all the way into sleep.

All winter, the frogs slept in an icy bed,
Remembering how to sing when it melted.
If I made a sound, they stopped
And listened to me sing nothing, singing nothing.   20

But gradually, finally April would come pouring
Out of their green throats in a green chorus
To chorus me home toward silence.
Theirs was the only home that sang all night.

THE RECEPTIVE READER

1. Would you call the sound the frogs make "music"? What makes the "other house" an unlikely or unpromising setting for songs celebrating the return of spring? Do the frogs and the setting undercut the symbolism of spring and renewal for you?

2. The poet does not take us to the boy's own "proper house" till the third stan-

za. Why? What is the key to the polar opposition of what the two houses stand for? How is this polarity central to the poem as a whole?

3. Is there anything symbolic about the frogs' falling silent when they heard the boy?

4. Do you think the boy has been permanently influenced by his parents? Do you agree with the following student reaction to the poem?

> There is no renewal in spring-green trees if it does not resonate on the inside. A soul that cannot sing at the melting of the snows is winter-cold, ice-hard, regardless of the sun's warmth. A dark mysterious center that sings without sunlight breathes more life than this proper emptiness. The coldness of the silent parent is visited upon the son, perhaps for always, so his soul can never vibrate with mysterious yearnings, never feel the spring-green trees.

THE PERSONAL RESPONSE

In your own growing up, how much "silence" has there been and how much "song"?

THE CREATIVE DIMENSION

When we read a poem that has a strong impact on us, a haunting image or central symbol may linger in our minds. Look at the way the following student-written passage re-creates the lasting impression the poem left in the student's mind. Then do your own re-creation of a lasting impression left in your mind by this poem, by the Levertov poem, or by a poem later in this chapter.

> In spring,
> after the ice melts
> and the drains fill
> the concrete cracks
> of the basement floor
> with green water,
> the frogs are born
> to keep me company
> and fill my silent nights
> with songs.

When the language of symbols threatens to become too conventional, poets—like painters, photographers, or journalists—help it evolve and refresh itself. In our modern world, the bulldozer and the oil-drenched seabird have become symbols in the confrontation between technological progress and ecological survival. In a newspaper photograph printed after an oil spill, we do not just see an individual bird, its plumage clotted with black goo. We see a symbol of both wildlife and human life endangered by a technology spinning out of control.

In the following poem, the poet seizes on a symbolic incident in order to enlist the readers' sympathies. How does the chain saw become a symbol for the machine age in the poem?

DONALD FINKEL (born 1929)

They   1975

are at the end of our street now cutting down trees
a scream like a seven foot locust
they have cut off another
neatly at the pavement
never again will the pin-oak threaten a taxi   5
will the ash lie in wait to fall on a child

it is a good time for this
the sun is bright
the plane° has only just begun   *sycamore*
to sprout little shoots from under her fingernails   10
never again will she dance
her terrible saraband° in the tornado   *stately court dance*
the sweet gum trembles
bristling with tiny mines like brown sea urchins
never again will he drop them on the walk   15
to menace the sensible shoes of mailmen

they have brought a machine that eats trees
and shits sawdust
they cut off limbs to feed it
snarling it chews the pale green fingers of the plane   20
the pin-oak's wrinkled elbows and knees
they fill truck after truck with the dust
in the schoolyard now they are cutting down the children
I hear their screams
first at the ankles   25
it is nothing then to sever
their soles from the asphalt
there is no danger their falling
on the school and crushing it

I have invented a machine that shoots words   30
I type faster and faster
I cannot keep up with them
in front of the house now they are cutting the rosebush
vainly she scratches their hands like a drowning kitten
they are cutting the grass   35
scythes in their wheels they race over our lawn
flashing in the sun like the chariots of the barbarians
the grass blades huddle whimpering
there is no place to go
it is spring and the street is alive   40
with the clamor of motors
the laughter of saws

THE RECEPTIVE READER

1. Where in the poem do we hear the voices approving of the tree-cutting operation? With what effect does the poet cite them?

2. How many examples can you find of pervasive *personification* in this poem—ascribing quasi-human features to the vegetation? What is the effect on the readers? How does it prepare them for what happens in the school yard? (Why is there no stanza break or transition before the school yard massacre?) What makes the cutting of the rose bush especially traumatic?

3. How does the chariot *simile* reinforce the prevailing perspective of the poem? Why does the poet keep reminding us that it is spring?

THE PERSONAL RESPONSE

What makes the machines in this poem frightening symbols of human technology? What side do you take in the confrontation conjured up by this poet?

The following poem is by a Chinese immigrant who came with his parents from Indonesia. Central to the poem is the meeting of two worlds: One of these worlds is symbolized by the scroll paintings that link the father to millennia of old-country tradition and by the fruit (the persimmon) that is a touch of home to the poet but a curiosity to his classmates. The other world is represented by the monolingual teacher questioning the intelligence of students learning to learn in a new language, learning to live in a new culture.

L I - Y O U N G   L E E   (born 1957)

Persimmons   1986

In sixth grade Mrs. Walker
slapped the back of my head
and made me stand in the corner
for not knowing the difference
between *persimmon* and precision.   5
How to choose

persimmons. This is precision.
Ripe ones are soft and brown-spotted.
Sniff the bottoms. The sweet one
will be fragrant. How to eat: 10
put the knife away, lay down newspaper.
Peel the skin tenderly, not to tear the meat.
Chew on the skin, suck it,
and swallow. Now, eat
the meat of the fruit,   15
so sweet
all of it, to the heart.

Dona undresses, her stomach is white.
In the yard, dewy and shivering
with crickets, we lie naked,   20
face-up, face-down.
I teach her Chinese. Crickets: *chiu chiu*. Dew: I've forgotten.
Naked: I've forgotten.
Ni, wo: you and me.
I part her legs,   25
remember to tell her
she is beautiful as the moon.

Other words
that got me into trouble were
fight and *fright, wren* and *yarn*.   30
Fight was what I did when I was frightened,
fright was what I felt when I was fighting.
Wrens are small, plain birds,
yarn is what one knits with.
Wrens are soft as yarn.   35
My mother made birds out of yarn.
I loved to watch her tie the stuff;
a bird, a rabbit, a wee man.

Mrs. Walker brought a persimmon to class
and cut it up   40
so everyone could taste
a *Chinese apple*. Knowing
it wasn't ripe or sweet, I didn't eat
but watched the other faces.

My mother said every persimmon has a sun   45
inside, something golden, glowing,
warm as my face.

Once, in the cellar, I found two wrapped in newspaper
forgotten and not yet ripe.
I took them and set them both on my bedroom windowsill,   50
where each morning a cardinal
sang. *The sun, the sun.*

Finally understanding
he was going blind,
my father would stay up all one night   55
waiting for a song, a ghost.
I gave him the persimmons,
swelled, heavy as sadness,
and sweet as love.

This year, in the muddy lighting   60
of my parents' cellar, I rummage, looking
for something I lost.
My father sits on the tired, wooden stairs,

black cane between his knees,
hand over hand, gripping the handle.   65

He's so happy that I've come home.
I ask how his eyes are, a stupid question.
All gone, he answers.

Under some blankets, I find a box.
Inside the box I find three scrolls.   70
I sit beside him and untie
three paintings by my father:
Hibiscus leaf and a white flower.
Two cats preening.
Two persimmons, so full they want to drop from the cloth.   75

He raises both hands to touch the cloth,
asks, *Which is this?*

This is persimmons, Father.

Oh, the feel of the wolftail on the silk,
the strength, the tense   80
precision in the wrist.
I painted them hundreds of times
eyes closed. These I painted blind.
Some things never leave a person:
scent of the hair of one you love,   85
the texture of persimmons,
in your palm, the ripe weight.

THE RECEPTIVE READER

1. From what angle are you looking at the bilingual student's learning in this poem? How is it different from what you might have expected? (How does the poem turn the tables on the teacher?)

2. The persimmon is first introduced in a casual or humorous way. (How and why?) It becomes a *central symbol,* providing a common strand for the poem as a whole. What different associations and memories cluster around the fruit? What role does it play in the poem as a whole?

3. What other details in this poem have a symbolic significance?

4. How close to or distant from the family's cultural roots is the speaker in the poem?

THE PERSONAL RESPONSE

What experience have you had with different cultural traditions or bilingual Americans? What have you learned about barriers to communication? Does this poem help you cross the barriers separating different cultures?

THE CREATIVE DIMENSION

Write about a symbolic object or incident that for you calls up memories of home, family, or the older generation. Choose a symbol that best sums up deep-seated feelings or vivid memories.

EXPLORATIONS

Understanding Symbols

The following poem was written by a famous English poet of the Romantic Age, an era of both revolution and reaction. The title of the poem names an Egyptian pharaoh who, like other early Egyptian rulers, commissioned colossal statues of himself. According to the poem, what did he want the statue he commissioned to symbolize? What does the statue symbolize for the poet? Shelley, like other Romantics, was a rebel against tyrannical authority. How does this commitment show in the poem?

PERCY BYSSHE SHELLEY (1792–1822)

Ozymandias 1818

I met a traveler from an antique land
Who said: "Two vast and trunkless legs of stone
Stand in the desert . . . Near them on the sand,
Half-sunk, a shattered visage° lies, whose frown, *face*
And wrinkled lip, and sneer of cold command, 5
Tell that its sculptor well those passsions read
Which yet survive, stamped on these lifeless things,
The hand that mocked them, and the heart that fed:
And on the pedestal these words appear:
'My name is Ozymandias, king of kings: 10
Look on my works, ye Mighty, and despair!'
Nothing beside remains. Round the decay
Of that colossal wreck, boundless and bare
The lone and level sands stretch far away."

PUBLIC AND PRIVATE SYMBOLS

Some poets develop a symbolic language of their own that may at first seem private or obscure. However, it gradually becomes more meaningful to us as we learn more about the poet or read several poems by the same poet. We learn the poet's symbolic language; we gradually feel less like strangers in the poet's world of meanings. The English poet William Blake was a precursor of the Romantic movement. For him, all experience was shot through with symbolic meanings—he was able "to see a world in a grain of sand / And a heaven in a wild flower." Breaking with eighteenth-century standards of rationality and restraint, he used bold, unusual symbols to celebrate the divine energies at work in the universe. He glorified exuberance and excess, using the lion, the tiger, and the eagle as symbols of the fierce, terrifying divine energy animating creation.

The following is Blake's most famous poem. What do you think would be the poet's answers to the questions he asks in this poem?

WILLIAM BLAKE   (1757–1827)

The Tyger   1794

Tyger! Tyger! burning bright
In the forests of the night,
What immortal hand or eye
Could frame thy fearful symmetry?

In what distant deeps or skies   5
Burnt the fire of thine eyes?
On what wings dare he aspire?
What the hand, dare° seize the fire?   *hand that dares*

And what shoulder, & what art,
Could twist the sinews of thy heart?   10
And when thy heart began to beat,
What dread hand? & what dread feet?

What the hammer? what the chain?
In what furnace was thy brain?
What the anvil? what dread grasp   15
Dare its deadly terrors clasp?

When the stars threw down their spears,
And water'd heaven with their tears,
Did he smile his work to see?
Did he who made the lamb make thee?   20

Tyger! Tyger! burning bright
In the forests of the night,
What immortal hand or eye
Dare frame thy fearful symmetry?

THE RECEPTIVE READER

1. How does Blake make us see the tiger as beautiful and terrifying at the same time?

2. How does Blake make us imagine the process of creation? (What associations do the images in the fourth stanza—the anvil, the furnace, the forge—bring into play?) How is his vision of the process different from what we might conventionally expect?

3. How has the lamb traditionally been used as a symbol of goodness? How has the tiger traditionally been used as a symbol of evil? How is Blake's use of these symbols different? Is the tiger evil or sinister in this poem?

4. What is the answer to the questions the poet asks in this poem?

In the twentieth century, the Irish poet William Butler Yeats stands out among poets using a highly individual symbolic language. In his earlier poetry, he had often drawn inspiration from the folklore and history of his native Ireland. In his later years, he repeatedly used symbols from the rich religious art of Byzantium (later Constantinople and now Istanbul), the fabled capital of the eastern part of the Roman Empire during the early Christian era. Byzantine art was famous for precious materials and finely crafted artifice. It was legendary for the ornamental patterns of its mosaics, for its carved ivory, its enamel work, and the work of its goldsmiths. Shortly before he wrote the following poem, Yeats had seen spectacular examples of Byzantine mosaics depicting saints and prophets (the "sages" mentioned in the third stanza) in a church at Ravenna in northern Italy.

In the poem, the poet takes us on a symbolic voyage. We travel from a country of the young that is "no country for old men" to a country of the mind more attuned to the spiritual needs of the aging speaker in the poem—"the holy city of Byzantium." What special fascination does the "artifice" of the Greek artists of Byzantium hold for the poet?

WILLIAM BUTLER YEATS   (1865–1939)
Sailing to Byzantium   1927

1
That is no country for old men. The young
In one another's arms, birds in the trees
—Those dying generations—at their song,
The salmon-falls, the mackerel-crowded seas,
Fish, flesh, or fowl, commend all summer long   5
Whatever is begotten, born, and dies.
Caught in that sensual music all neglect
Monuments of unaging intellect.

2
An aged man is but a paltry thing,
A tattered coat upon a stick, unless   10
Soul clap its hands and sing, and louder sing
For every tatter in its mortal dress,
Nor is there singing school but studying
Monuments of its own magnificence;
And therefore I have sailed the seas and come   15
To the holy city of Byzantium.

3
O sages standing in God's holy fire
As in the gold mosaic of a wall,
Come from the holy fire, perne in a gyre,°   *turn with a spiral motion*
And be the singing masters of my soul.   20
Consume my heart away, sick with desire
And fastened to a dying animal
It knows not what it is; and gather me
Into the artifice of eternity.

4

Once out of nature, I shall never take   25
My bodily form from any natural thing,
But such a form as Grecian° goldsmiths make   *Greek*
Of hammered gold and gold enameling
To keep a drowsy Emperor awake;
Or set upon a golden bough to sing   30
To lords and ladies of Byzantium
Of what is past, or passing, or to come.

    Much of the early part of the poem revolves around a polar opposition of youth and age. The speaker in the poem finds himself out of place in a country of the young that is full of "sensual music." Conditioned to think positively of youth and burgeoning nature, we have to read out of the poem what turns the speaker away from them: Paradoxically, the very fact that the lovers are young reminds us that they are part of the inevitable cycle of begetting, growth, and decay. Like the birds in the trees, they are "dying generations"—the script that dooms them to aging, decay, and death is already written.

    To the aging speaker in the poem, fastened to his decaying body as "to a dying animal" (line 22), there is no comfort in the surface vitality of a life caught up in the world of the senses. The second stanza focuses on the central paradox of the poem: The body decays, leaving the physical person little more than a scarecrow, "a tattered coat upon a stick." However, the intellect survives; the soul is still capable of song and artistic creation. Here is the answer to the decay of the body: The soul can metaphorically "clap its hands" and create immortal music. The "singing school" for the soul, teaching it to triumph over decay, is the work of artists that have gone before. In them, the human spirit has created "monuments of its own magnificence."

    It is the search for a "singing school" for the human spirit that makes us embark on the voyage to the mythical "holy city of Byzantium." In the third stanza, we get a glimpse of the art that flourishes there. It does not aim at imitating nature. Instead, it creates an alternative to nature—a world of art that will defy age, decay, and death. We prize precious metals because they do not turn to rust like common iron. The hammered gold leaf and the finely crafted products of the goldsmith's art triumph over corrosion. Mosaics and enamel inlays resist the ravages of time. For us today, the word *artifice* often carries negative connotations, suggesting artwork that is *too* artificial, too far removed from nature. But here the creation of "artifice" is the whole point of the artist's work. The art of Byzantium shows sages and prophets purged of mortality in "God's holy fire." The incorruptible gold of the Byzantine goldsmith's work becomes a symbol of eternity.

    In the fourth stanza, the speaker projects a state "out of nature," after death. Given a chance to assume a new shape, he would choose to be a bird made of hammered gold and gold enameling, set on a golden bough, singing "to lords and ladies of Byzantium." Art would leave nature behind. The creative spirit would triumph over the imperfections of the body. The conflict of youth and age would be resolved in the ageless permanence of art.

THE RECEPTIVE READER

1. Much of this poem revolves around related *polarities:* the opposition of youth and age, of intellect and the body, and of nature and art. What striking details help flesh out each of these polarities?

2. Why do the salmon fighting their way up the "salmon-falls" provide the poet with an especially appropriate *symbol* for life in the natural world?

3. In your own words, what vision of art or "artifice" is developed in the final two stanzas? How will "artifice" provide the answer to age and decay? What makes the artifacts of Byzantine art apt symbols for the poet's way of transcending or overcoming age?

4. In this poem, Yeats uses a finely crafted interlaced rhyme scheme called *ottava rima* (or "set of eight"). Why is it more appropriate to this poem than free-flowing free verse would be?

THE PERSONAL RESPONSE

Do you know or believe in a different view of the relationship between nature and art? How does it compare with the view developed in this poem?

CROSS-REFERENCES —For Discussion or Writing

Another famous exploration of the relation between life and art is John Keats' "Ode on a Grecian Urn" (p. 303). Compare and contrast the way the two poems deal with such central themes as youth and age, change and permanence, nature and art.

EXPLORATIONS

Crossing the Boundaries

The Russian poet Yevgeny Yevtushenko said, "Poetry is like a bird. It ignores all frontiers." How true is this statement of the language of symbols? How universal are they? Look at the use of a central but multifaceted symbol in the following poem by a Latin American poet. Gabriela Mistral grew up in poverty in Chile and left school at age eleven, but she became a teacher and was for many years the best-known woman writing in Latin America. She was the first Latin American to win the Nobel Prize (1945). She worked on educational reform in Mexico and later taught at Barnard, Vassar, Middlebury, and the University of Puerto Rico.

GABRIELA MISTRAL　(1889–1957)
To Drink　　　　　　　　　　　　　　　　　1938
TRANSLATED BY GUNDA KAISER

I remember gestures of infants
and they were gestures of giving me water.

In the valley of Rio Blanco
where the Aconcagua has its beginning,
I came to drink, I rushed to drink   5
in the fountain of a cascade,
which fell long and hard
and broke up rigid and white.
I held my mouth to the boiling spring
and the blessed water burned me,   10
and my mouth bled three days
from that sip from the valley of Aconcagua.

     In the fields of Mitla, a day
of harvest flies, of sun, of motion,
I bent down to a well and a native came   15
to hold me over the water,
and my head, like a fruit,
was within his palms.
I drank what he drank,
for his face was with my face,   20
and in a lightning flash I realized
I, too, was of the race of Mitla.

     On the Island of Puerto Rico,
During the slumber of full blue,
my body calm, the waves wild,   25
and the palms like a hundred mothers,
a child broke through skill
close to my mouth a coconut for water,
and I drank, like a daughter,
water from a mother, water from a palm.   30
And I have not partaken greater sweetness
with my body nor with my soul.

     At the house of my childhood
my mother brought me water.
From one sip to another sip   35
I saw her over the jug.
The more her head rose up
the more the jug was lowered.
I still have my valley,
     I have my thirst and her vision.   40
This will be eternity
for we still are as we were.

I remember gestures of infants
     and they were gestures of giving me water.

THE RECEPTIVE READER

     How does water serve as the central symbol in this poem? What are its widening circles of association and symbolic meaning? Which of the symbolic meanings and associations seem universal? Which seem specific to this poem or to this poet's experience?

THE CREATIVE DIMENSION

Water—like sun, earth, light, birth, or death—is one of the great constants of human experience. Cluster one of these. Then write a passage tracing the web of meanings that the term has for you.

SYMBOL AND ALLEGORY

In an **allegory,** symbols work together in a set pattern. Symbolic figures or objects play their roles like actors in a drama. In the following poem, the road, the hill, the inn, the darkness at end of day, the traveler, and the other wayfarers all play their assigned roles in the poet's allegorical vision of our journey through life. Each detail in the literal journey has its parallel in our spiritual journey to our final destination. The poet belonged to a group of painters and writers (the Pre-Raphaelites) who turned to medieval art and religion for inspiration, and her poem has the earnest, solemn tone of much English Victorian (mid-nineteenth-century) poetry.

CHRISTINA ROSSETTI (1830–1894)
Uphill   1858

Does the road wind uphill all the way?
    Yes, to the very end.
Will the day's journey take the whole long day?
    From morn to night, my friend.

But is there for the night a resting place?   5
    A roof for when the slow dark hours begin.
May not the darkness hide it from my face?
    You cannot miss that inn.

Shall I meet other wayfarers at night?
    Those who have gone before.   10
Then must I knock, or call when just in sight?
    They will not keep you standing at that door.

Shall I find comfort, travel-sore and weak?
    Of labor you shall find the sum.
Will there be beds for me and all who seek?   15
    Yea, beds for all who come.

THE RECEPTIVE READER

Who are the two speakers in this poem? What is the meaning of each of the symbolic details in this allegory? What makes this poem earnest and uplifting in the Victorian nineteenth-century manner?

EXPLORATIONS ══════════

Understanding Allegory

In the following short allegorical poem, what is the meaning of the symbolic details? What role does each play in the allegory?

WILLIAM BLAKE (1757–1827)

A Poison Tree 1794

I was angry with my friend:
I told my wrath, my wrath did end.
I was angry with my foe:
I told it not, my wrath did grow.

And I watered it in fears, 5
Night and morning with my tears:
And I sunnèd° it with smiles, *gave it sunlight*
And with soft deceitful wiles.

And it grew both day and night,
Till it bore an apple bright. 10
And my foe beheld it shine,
And he knew that it was mine.

And into my garden stole
When the night had veiled the pole:
In the morning glad I sce 15
My foe outstretched beneath the tree.

THE RECEPTIVE READER

1. Much medieval poetry preached against wrath as one of the seven deadly sins. Is this poem a warning against wrath?
2. What makes this poem simple and almost childlike in its form and its symbolism? Does the simple form undercut the serious question the poem raises?

THE PERSONAL RESPONSE

Are you aware of any trends in pop psychology that relate to the issue of whether to hold in or release negative emotions?

EXPLORATIONS ══════════

Interacting Symbols

What is the relationship between the three key symbols in the following poem by Mexico's best-known poet? Octavio Paz, who won a Nobel Prize for literature in 1991, has lectured to large audiences in the United States. He served as Mexico's ambassador to India but resigned in 1968 in protest over the bloody repression of student demonstrators before the Olympic Games in Mexico City. He has thought and written much about the dialogue between the North American and Latin American cultures. He has said, "The vision of Latin America as part of the Third World is oversimple. . . . It's enough to reflect that we are Christians, we are Spanish and Portuguese and gained our independence with the tools of French and English ideas."

OCTAVIO PAZ   (born 1914)

Wind and Water and Stone   1979

TRANSLATED BY MARK STRAND

The water hollowed the stone,
the wind dispersed the water,
the stone stopped the wind.
Water and wind and stone.

The wind sculpted the stone.   5
the stone is a cup of water,
the water runs off and is wind.
Stone and wind and water.

The wind sings in its turnings,
the water murmurs as it goes,   10
the motionless stone is quiet.
Wind and water and stone.

One is the other, and is neither:
among their empty names
they pass and disappear,   15
water and stone and wind.

THE RECEPTIVE READER

In this poem, what is the relationship of water, wind, and stone? What is their possible symbolic significance? Why does the order of the three vary in the last line of each stanza?

POEMS FOR FURTHER STUDY

In reading the following poems, pay special attention to objects or figures that may have symbolic significance. How does the poet use or change familiar symbols? What images, emotions, or ideas does the symbol bring into play? What role does a symbol play in the poem as a whole?

LORNA DEE CERVANTES   (born 1954)

Refugee Ship   1981

Like wet cornstarch, I slide
past my grandmother's eyes. Bible
at her side, she removes her glasses.
The pudding thickens.
Mama raised me without language,   5

I'm orphaned from my Spanish name.
The words are foreign, stumbling
on my tongue. I see in the mirror
My reflection: bronzed skin, black hair.

I feel I am a captive   10
aboard the refugee ship.
The ship that will never dock.
El barco que nunca atraca.

THE RECEPTIVE READER

1. Do the cornstarch and the Bible in this poem have possible *symbolic* meanings?
2. How could the speaker in the poem have been raised "without language" and
be "orphaned" from her Spanish name?
3. What did the mirror tell her?
4. The last line repeats in Spanish the previous line about the refugee ship "that
will never dock." Why are some refugee ships not allowed to dock or their passengers
not allowed to reach land? What makes the refugee ship a symbol of the speaker's own
journey? What makes it a symbol of the experience of untold millions of refugees in the
modern world?

THE CREATIVE DIMENSION

Sometimes a poem is for us like a mirror in which we see our own faces. Look at
what one student saw in the mirror of the Cervantes poem. Then write your own response to a poem that seems like a mirror for a part of yourself.

> The refugee ship reminds me of the girl I see in the mirror every day.
> The speaker feels left out of the culture in which she grew up. In the Hispan-
> ic culture, there is a certain pressure from the family to retain one's culture.
> Maybe the poet is a refugee because she forgot all her tradition. Now she
> sees the Hispanic only in her appearance, not in her head.

MATTHEW ARNOLD   (1822–1888)

Dover Beach   1867

The sea is calm tonight.
The tide is full, the moon lies fair
Upon the straits; on the French coast the light

Gleams and is gone; the cliffs of England stand,
Glimmering and vast, out in the tranquil bay.   5
Come to the window, sweet is the night-air!
Only, from the long line of spray
Where the sea meets the moon-blanched° land,   *pale under the moon*
Listen! you hear the grating roar
Of pebbles which the waves draw back, and fling,   10
At their return, up the high strand,
Begin, and cease, and then again begin,
With tremulous cadence° slow, and bring   *regular rhythm*
The eternal note of sadness in.

Sophocles° long ago   *Greek playwright*   15
Heard it on the Aegean,° and it brought   *sea circling Greece*
Into his mind the turbid° ebb and flow   *murky*
Of human misery; we
Find also in the sound a thought,
Hearing it by this distant northern sea.   20

The Sea of Faith
Was once, too, at the full, and round° earth's shore   *around*
Lay like the folds of a bright girdle° furled.   *sash circling waist*
But now I only hear
Its melancholy, long, withdrawing roar,   25
Retreating, to the breath
Of the night-wind, down the vast edges drear
And naked shingles° of the world.   *pebble-strewn beaches*

Ah, love, let us be true
To one another! for the world, which seems   30
To lie before us like a land of dreams,
So various, so beautiful, so new,
Hath really neither joy, nor love, nor light,
Nor certitude, nor peace, nor help for pain;
And we are here as on a darkling plain   35
Swept with confused alarms of struggle and flight,
Where ignorant armies clash by night.

THE RECEPTIVE READER

Matthew Arnold, influential Victorian lecturer and critic, was part of an idealistic generation beset by religious doubts. What is the *central symbol* in this poem? What gives it its special power or hold on the imagination? How is it followed up or reinforced in the poem? What is the poet's answer to the religious soul-searching of his time?

JOHN KEATS   (1795–1821)
Bright Star   1819

Bright star, would I° were steadfast as thou art—   *I wish*
   Not in lone splendor hung aloft the night°   *high in night sky*

And watching, with eternal lids apart,
  Like nature's patient, sleepless Eremite,°   *religious hermit*
The moving waters at their priestlike task   5
  Of pure ablution° round earth's human shores,   *cleansing*
Or gazing on the new soft fallen mask
  Of snow upon the mountains and the moors—
No—yet still steadfast, still unchangeable,
  Pillowed upon my fair love's ripening breast,   10
To feel forever its soft fall and swell.
  Awake forever in a sweet unrest,
Still, still to hear her tender-taken breath,
And so live ever—or else swoon to death.

THE RECEPTIVE READER

1. Like the other Romantic poets of his generation, Keats intuitively and naturally imbued the physical universe around us with quasi-human life and feeling, at the same time endowing it with divine qualities inspiring religious awe. How does *personification* help Keats achieve these ends in this poem? (What is striking about images like the "eternal lids apart" or ebb and tide attending to their task of "pure ablution"?)

2. The first eight lines (or octave) of this sonnet develop one set of symbolic associations for the star, and then the next six lines (sestet) *reject* these. Why? What is the basic symbolic meaning of the star in this poem? Why is it strange or unexpected when applied to human love?

L U C I L L E   C L I F T O N   (born 1936)
My Mama Moved among the Days   1969

My Mama moved among the days
like a dreamwalker in a field;
seemed like what she touched was hers
seemed like what touched her couldn't hold,
she got us almost through the high grass   5
then seemed like she turned around and ran
right back in
right back on in

THE RECEPTIVE READER

What is the symbolic meaning of the high grass? Why does the poet repeat the last line?

A D R I E N N E   R I C H   (born 1929)
Aunt Jennifer's Tigers   1951

Aunt Jennifer's tigers prance across a screen,
Bright topaz denizens of a world of green.

They do not fear the men beneath the tree;
They pace in sleek chivalric certainty.

Aunt Jennifer's fingers fluttering through her wool   5
Find even the ivory needle hard to pull.
The massive weight of Uncle's wedding band
Sits heavily upon Aunt Jennifer's hand.

When Aunt is dead, her terrified hands will lie
Still ringed with ordeals she was mastered by.   10
The tigers in the panel that she made
Will go on prancing, proud and unafraid.

THE RECEPTIVE READER

1. What do the tigers represent in Aunt Jennifer's world? What does the wedding
band represent? How do these two symbols function as *polar opposites* in this poem?
2. What is the range of meaning your dictionary gives for words like *topaz*,
denizen, chivalric, ordeal? What do these words mean in the context of this poem?
3. In a later reprinting of this poem, the poet changed the words *prance* (line 1)
and *prancing* (line 12) to *stride* and *striding*. What difference does the change make?
Why do you think the poet might have wanted to change the words?

WRITING ABOUT LITERATURE

5. *Seeing Symbols in Context (Focus on Prewriting)*

> *A short poem is like a cricket; it rubs parts of its small body
> together to produce a sound that is magnified far above
> that of larger bodies and leaves a loud, chirping sound
> reverberating in the ears of a listener, saying, "I am small,
> but I am alive."*
>
> STUDENT PAPER

The Writing Workshop   When you write about symbolic meanings, you
soon learn to steer your course between two extremes. Some readers are too
literal-minded to respond to symbolic overtones and associations. To them,
water is always just water. They need to become more perceptive, more alert to
possible symbolic overtones. Water, for instance, may become the symbol of
spiritual regeneration in a wasteland of dried-up feeling, where a poet might
say: "In the desert of the heart / Let the healing fountain start" (W. H.
Auden).

At the other extreme, some readers free-associate *too freely,* stopping only
briefly to take a partial clue from the poem and leaving it behind too soon. If
you do not keep an eye on how a symbol works in the poem, the danger is
that anything may come to mean anything else. Look for reinforcement of
possible symbolic meanings in the **context** of the poem as a whole. Green, a

color that in one poem may symbolize envy, may in another poem be a symbol of growth, standing for the bright untamed vitality of nature. Ask yourself:

❖ Does a poem focus on *recurrent* elements with symbolic meanings? In Adrienne Rich's poem "Aunt Jennifer's Tigers," the proud, unafraid tigers keep prancing and pacing throughout the poem.

❖ Does the poem play off symbolic elements against their *opposites*, the way Rich plays off the untamed tigers against the restraining heavy wedding band symbolizing an oppressive marriage?

❖ Does the poem *build up* to the poet's introduction of a central symbol?

Focus on Prewriting

The following might be part of your prewriting as you work up a paper on Adrienne Rich's "Aunt Jennifer's Tigers."

Reading Notes   Here is a partial record of one student's close attention to key words and phrases:

> "Aunt Jennifer's *tigers* prance across a screen"
>   Rich uses the tigers to represent Aunt Jennifer's free and true spirit, that part of her which is suppressed by her marriage to Uncle. This symbol is close to Blake's "Tyger," which represents divine energy that animates all creation. In Rich, the tiger represents that same energy within Aunt Jennifer, and ultimately in all women. The tiger is feared but not despised. Its ferocity is tempered because of its feline, catlike grace that makes it seem both beautiful and terrible at the same time.

> "Bright *topaz* denizens of a world of green. . .
> They pace in sleek *chivalric* certainty."
>   The word *topaz* stands for a jewel, implying that the tigers are precious to the aunt. *Denizen* means "native inhabitant." These tigers are in their natural element, just as Aunt Jennifer wishes to be her true self. *Chivalric* seems to imply that like knights in armor the tigers are proud and sure in their role, not afraid of the men in their native territory.

> "The *massive* weight of Uncle's *wedding band*
> Sits *heavily* upon Aunt Jennifer's hand."
>   The wedding ring, traditionally a symbol of love, honor, and protection, is transformed by words like *massive* and *heavily*. We get a mental picture of shackles and chains, not of wedding bells and love tokens.

Clustering   **Clustering** is a way of exploring the associations and connections of key words or concepts. In the more linear kind of free association, you jot ideas down more or less in the order in which they come to mind. Clustering instead allows you to branch out from a common core, pursuing different lines of association that soon form a web of meaning. Clustering is more suited to sketching possible *connections* than other kinds of brainstorming and prewriting.

Since many related associations tend to cluster around a central symbol, clustering may prove a good way to map the possible range of associations of a symbol that you mean to focus on in a paper. Here is one student's cluster of the key word *green:*

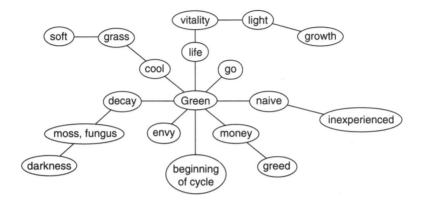

Here is the student writing up the results of the cluster:

> The word *green* has many positive associations; in fact, I listed all of my positive ones before the negative ones. Green makes us think of grass, rich in color, soft to the touch. Green vegetation signifies life—a plant thriving with water and sunlight. Plants are green at the beginning of their life cycle. (They fall into the "sear and yellow leaf" at the end—see *Macbeth.*) With this comes vitality. On the possibly negative side, green represents envy, as well as the greed associated with money. Green can be found in moss and fungus, a note of contrast with the green grass. Green, because of its use with unripe early vegetation, also represents inexperience (one who "just fell off the turnip truck," one who is not street-smart).

Background Notes   The tiger poem is one of the poet's earlier poems (Rich wrote it while she was a student). She wrote about Aunt Jennifer "with deliberate detachment" as a woman of a different generation, keeping a "cool" distance. In hindsight, she realized that she was weaving into this poem a part of herself she did not yet fully understand or recognize—her own role as a woman in a man's world. One student writer found the following illuminating statement by the poet in a collection of her essays:

> In writing this poem, composed and apparently cool as it is, I thought I was creating a portrait of an imaginary woman. But this woman suffers from the opposition of her imagination, worked out in

tapestry, and her life-style, "ringed with ordeals she was mastered by." It was important to me that Aunt Jennifer was a person as distinct from myself as possible—distanced by the formalism of the poem, by its objective, observant tone—even by putting the woman in a different generation.

From *On Lies, Secrets, and Silence*

A paper has a good chance of success when the writer at the beginning of the process of shaping and organizing has this kind of prewriting material at hand—a rich array of notes and tentative ideas to sort out and pull into shape.

SAMPLE STUDENT PAPER

Tigers and Terrified Hands

"When Aunt is dead, her terrified hands will lie / Still ringed with ordeals she was mastered by. / The tigers in the panel that she made / Will go on prancing, proud and unafraid." So ends the lush and very focused poem "Aunt Jennifer's Tigers" by Adrienne Rich. With memorable symbolism, the poet illuminates the tragedy of a woman who has lived the greater part of her life as the subordinate member in an unbalanced marriage.

The tiger has been symbolically used many times, and readers may assume that the presence of a tiger represents evil or darkness. In this poem, however, the tigers have an entirely different symbolic meaning. Aunt Jennifer's tigers, those "topaz denizens of a world of green" (2), are the brilliant jewel-like embodiments of the faded shadows hiding in their creator's spirit. Their world of green, bursting with life, vitality, regeneration, receives its life-force from the crushed stirrings in Aunt Jennifer's defeated soul. Any shred of hope or victory or joy that somehow remains within her flows unconsciously through her fluttering fingers into the tapestry she so painfully sews. These wonderful tigers do not sidle or sneak or skulk; they stride "proud and unafraid" (12). With the natural confidence of knighthood, they "pace in sleek chivalric certainty" (4). And, perhaps most importantly, they "do not fear the men beneath the tree" (3). Aunt Jennifer stitches her defiance the only way she can, unconscious of her own vision.

Aunt Jennifer is the perfect foil for her creations, the gorgeous tigers. She is so fraught with anxiety, nervous confusion, exhausted resignation, fear, and defeat, that her fingers, which can only "flutter" through her wool (5), "find even the ivory needle hard to pull" (6). This shade of woman is still weighed down by the "massive weight of Uncle's wedding band," which has doubtlessly drained her of any capacity for joy, celebration of life, or even peace. She is feeble, afraid, and "mastered." Even in death her "terrified hands will lie / Still ringed with ordeals she was mastered by" (9–10). She cannot escape the "ordeals" that were thrust upon her by her partner in marriage; the dominance and oppression that were her lot in marriage will always be part of who she was.

However, she has left a legacy. She has stitched a panel of glittering tigers that will "go on prancing, proud and unafraid" (12). Other women will come after Aunt Jennifer, and they may be inspired by her tigers to hold their heads up proudly and assume their rightful places as equals, rejecting any subordinate or humiliating roles. The tigers, often symbols of vitality, power, pride, fearlessness, here are those and more: They are the irrepressible human spirit and symbols of hope for woman's future.

The readers are not told of the particular ordeals in her marriage that defeated Aunt Jennifer. But they can make guesses and poke around for possibilities. The word *mastered* itself, used to describe Aunt Jennifer's situation, implies a "master." It is not a wild or unlikely conjecture that Aunt Jennifer's husband resembled other males who played the role of "master of the house," such as the poet's own father. Rich has said about her father: "After your death I met you again as the face of patriarchy, could name at last precisely the principle you embodied; there was an ideology at last which let me dispose of you, identify the suffering you caused, hate you righteously as part of a system, the kingdom of the fathers." Aunt Jennifer's husband, in the poet's mind, represents the traditional power of the male. And as one who has stated that "the search for justice and compassion is the great wellspring for poetry in our time," Rich is drawing from that wellspring in her poem "Aunt Jennifer's Tigers."

QUESTIONS

1. How does the initial quotation bring the two central interacting symbols in the poem into focus? What sentence in the introduction serves as the *thesis* spelling out the aunt's role in her marriage?

2. The body of the paper has a clear *plan;* it is laid out in accordance with a simple design. We look first at the tigers and their symbolic implications: What, according to this paper, do they symbolize? We then look at the symbolic meaning of the wedding ring: For what does it serve as a symbol? We then *return* to the tigers and look at them as the aunt's legacy: How does it point forward to the life of a future generation?

3. The flow of the paper owes much to *transitions* that point up an organic or dynamic rather than mechanical sequence. (The writer does not start major sections by saying, "The first symbol means . . ." and "The second symbol means. . . .") What major links highlight logical connections between key sections of the paper?

4. Major paragraphs of this paper have a rich *texture* of brief quotations interwoven with explanation and interpretation. For instance, how does the writer spell out shades of meanings or overtones and associations when looking at the role key words like *prance* or *chivalric* play in the poem?

5. Having finished the close reading of the poem, the writer addresses a question in the minds of many readers: "What is the connection between this poem and the poet's own life?" How does the *conclusion* of the paper answer this question?

6. Where do you agree and where do you want to take issue with this writer?

6 WORDS
The Web of Language

Humans are animals suspended in webs of significance
they themselves have spun.

CLIFFORD GEERTZ

After many years as a writer, I find myself falling in love
with words. Maybe this is strange, like a carpenter
suddenly discovering how much he likes wood.

J. RUTH GENDLER

Stripped
day by day of all my garments,
dry naked tree,
in my solitary withered mouth
fresh words
will still blossom

ALAÍDE FOPPA, "WORDS"

FOCUS ON WORDS

Poets are in love with words. Language is their tool, but it is a tool that fascinates and challenges them. They wrestle with words and meanings. They are sticklers for the right word. They may spend hours and days fine-tuning a poem—trading an almost-right word for a word with the exact shade of meaning. As readers, we have to be prepared to slow down and respond fully to a single word, taking in its full meaning, savoring its overtones and associations. We have to see how an important word echoes or interacts with other words in a poem. A key word may have widening circles of associations that spread from a center like the ripples when a rock has been dropped in a pond.

The following poem is by a nineteenth-century Catholic priest. His intense and difficult poetry remained unpublished in his lifetime, but he delighted twentieth-century readers with his bold, unconventional use of language. How does the poet's diction go beyond ordinary language?

GERARD MANLEY HOPKINS (1844–1889)
Pied Beauty   1877

Glory be to God for dappled things—
    For skies of couple-color as a brinded° cow;   *streaked, flecked*
        For rose-moles all in stipple upon trout that swim;
Fresh firecoal chestnut-falls; finches' wings;
    Landscape plotted and pieced—fold,° fallow, and plow;   *pasture*   5
        And áll trádes, their gear and tackle and trim.
All things counter, original, spare, strange;
    Whatever is fickle, freckled (who knows how?)
        With swift, slow; sweet, sour; adazzle, dim;
He fathers-forth whose beauty is past change: 10
        Praise him.

This poem, in the words of one reader, is about "all the lovely dappled, alternating, changing and shifting things in the world" that come from God (J. R. Watson). Several points about the use of language in this poem stand out:

◆ First, the poet draws on a *range* of words for the "pied beauty" that he loves—and that he prefers to whatever is too smooth, too simple, too much of one piece. The word *pied* itself means showing two or more colors in blotches or splotches, like the hide of a horse. Then we have *dappled, stipple, plotted* (for land laid out in small strips and plots that alternate pasture, land lying fallow, and land under the plow). We have *pieced* (together), *freckled.* All these words work together to show the poet's preference for what goes "counter" to boring smoothness and simplicity—the same preference that makes the poet value sweet-and-sour over either cloying sweet or mouth-puckering sour.

◆ Second, the wording is often *compressed,* with much meaning packed into a compact phrase. For instance, "Fresh firecoal chestnut-falls" asks us to visualize chestnuts that have freshly fallen from the tree. They have split open their thick green covering on hitting the ground, revealing the intense reddish-brown of their skins. These seem to glow like coals on fire.

◆ Third, the poet's vocabulary is rooted in common speech. A cow is a cow, and a finch a finch. *Plow, trade, gear,* and *tackle* are all part of our everyday vocabulary. However, the poet's language easily moves *beyond* common speech: With "swift, slow," we might expect "bright, dim" as a parallel pairing of opposites. However, the poet uses "*adazzle,* dim" instead—heightening the contrast, making it more dazzling.

THE RECEPTIVE READER

1. What in the *wording* of this poem is most difficult for you? What are skies of "couple-color"? What do you make of the compressed phrase "fathers-forth"?

2. How would the gear and tackle of different trades meet Hopkins' criteria of beauty? Can you give examples of what he might have had in mind? What, for you, would be examples of things "counter, original, spare, strange"?

3. Is it strange that an unchanging God would create beauty that is variable and made up of contradictory elements?

4. How does the language of this poem live up to the poet's own standard of what is beautiful?

THE PERSONAL RESPONSE

The poet Richard Wilbur called this poem a "celebration of the rich and quirky particularity of all things whatever." Can you relate to this taste for the "quirky" and irregular, or do you prefer beauty that is smooth and harmonious?

When we concentrate on a poet's choice of words, we focus on the poet's **diction.** At times, prevailing fashion made poets adopt a special **poetic diction,** more elevated and more refined than ordinary speech. Poets went out of their way to widen the distance between common language and the language of poetry. The deer being hunted in the forest became the "beasts of chase" and the antlered trophies in the hunter's lodge became the "horny spoils that grace the walls." A phrase that takes the long way around, like *primary residence* for home, is called a **circumlocution.** In the eighteenth century, a fashionable poet might have called the finches in Hopkins' poem "members of the feathered tribe" or the plow "the plowman's humble tool." Modern poets have generally thought of common language and poetic language as a continuum. The poet uses our common mother tongue, making us hear in poetry the echo of the natural human voice. But the poet makes fuller and better use of it, going beyond the limited register of everyday talk. The poet uses *more* of language than we ordinarily do.

THE WILLING EAR

I wanted to write poetry in the beginning because I had fallen in love with words. The first poems I knew were nursery rhymes, and before I could read them for myself I had come to love them just for the words of them, the words alone.

DYLAN THOMAS

Although poems speak to the heart and the mind, they first of all please the ear. Words have a shape and texture of their own, and they combine in patterns that please (or grate upon) our ears. Children first fall in love with poetry not because of its meaning but because of its sound. (What is the meaning of "Hickory-dickory-dock / The mouse ran up the clock"?) The following poem makes us see the nighttime setting and share in night thoughts. However, it asks us first of all to relish the words and revel in the way they echo and play off one another in the poem. (How should the poem sound when read aloud?)

REUEL DENNEY (born 1913)

Fixer of Midnight 1961

He went to fix the awning,
Fix the roping,
In the middle of the night,
On the porch;
He went to fix the awning, 5
In pajamas went to fix it,
Fix the awning,
In the middle of the moonlight,
On the porch;
He went to fix it yawning; 10
The yawning of this awning
In the moonlight
Was his problem of the night;
It was knocking,
And he went to fix its flight. 15
He went to meet the moonlight
In the porch-night
Where the awning was up dreaming
Dark and light.
It was shadowy and seeming; 20
In the night the unfixed awning,
In his nightmare,
Had been knocking dark and bright.
It seemed late
To stop it in its deep careening. 25
The yawner went to meet it,
Meet the awning,
By the moon of middle night,
On his porch;
And he went to fix it right. 30

The sounds in this poem echo and run together without a full stop till the
end. We can listen to the sound the way we can listen to the comings and go-
ings of the surf as it washes over rocks by the shore. However, even with this
poem, we do not just let the sounds wash over us. We delight in the interplay
of sound and meaning. We can imagine the wide-open mouth of the sleepy
"yawner" as the words y-A-A-W-W-n-i-n-g and A-A-W-W-*ning* echo through the
poem. We can almost hear the "fixer" tiptoeing "in the middle of the night."
We seem to hear the repeated KNOCK-KNOCK-KNOCKing of the careening
awning echoing through the nightmare of the sleeper by the moon of middle
night.

THE RECEPTIVE READER

Listen to more than one classmate read this poem aloud. How close do they come
to how you think the poem is meant to sound?

When sound and sense intertwine as they do in "Fixer of Midnight," the sound seems to dance out the meaning. Sound echoes sense just as strongly in the following poem, inspired by a painting by the sixteenth-century Flemish painter Pieter Breughel. Breughel delighted in painting down-to-earth scenes of rural life, showing the peasants cavorting at weddings or at a country fair (the traditional Kermess). Look for the words that help you hear the sounds of the peasant music. Look for the words that help you see the peasants dance.

WILLIAM CARLOS WILLIAMS (1883–1963)
The Dance 1944

In Breughel's great picture, The Kermess,
the dancers go round, they go round and
around, the squeal and the blare and the
tweedle of bagpipes, a bugle and fiddles
tipping their bellies (round as the thick-   5
sided glasses whose wash they impound)
their hips and their bellies off balance
to turn them. Kicking and rolling about
The Fair Grounds, swinging their butts, those
shanks must be sound to bear up under such   10
rollicking measures, prance as they dance
in Breughel's great picture, The Kermess

Many of the words here seem exactly right for what they stand for. Blunt words like *bellies* (thick as the thick-sided glasses) and *butts* and *shanks* seem more right than would squeamish words when applied to the anatomy of these very physical, unpolished merrymakers. *Squeal* and *blare* and *tweedle* make us hear the rustic instruments (it's not the New York Philharmonic!). The word *squeal* seems to sound out the penetrating, high-pitched sound that pigs make when in distress; *blare* blares forth like a trumpet; *tweedle* seems to tootle like a bagpipe that forever runs over the same limited range of sounds. The words for movements seem to roll and rollick just as the peasants do. *Prance* is indeed a prancing word, quite different from *slink* or *shuffle* or *slouch*. (To prance, we need room to high-step and half-lift our arms, proud of ourselves, feeling our oats.)

THE RECEPTIVE READER

1. Can you read this poem with the right rolling, rollicking rhythm? Can you read it so that your listeners can hear the underlying drumbeat of the peasant music? (Your class may want to audition several readings of this poem and vote for the best rendition.)

2. What is the difference between violins and fiddles, between belly and abdomen? (Where does the poet show that he is not *limited* to blunt down-to-earth language?)

THE PERSONAL RESPONSE

What kind of readers would love this poem? What kind of readers might get little out of it?

When words seem to sound out the sounds they describe, we call them **onomatopoeic,** or sound-mirroring, words. The *pop* in "Pop! goes the weasel" is onomatopoeic, as are the meow of the cat, the cockadoodledo of the rooster, and the ta-ra-ra-boom-diay of the marching band. We hear the same sound-mirroring effect in the hisssing of snakes, the buzzzing of bees, the rUMBLing of thunder, and the C-R-A-C-K of a whip. Although sound seldom echoes sense this closely, the right word in a poem is often a word that sounds right. When G. M. Hopkins says that "generations have TROD, have TROD," we seem to hear the heavy, slow, monotonous tread of successive generations. The same poet asks us to imagine a plowshare being made shiny by the friction of the plowed-up earth as the plodding horse pulls the plow through the furrow: "sheer PLOD makes PLOW down sillion [furrow] / Shine." The repeated initial *pl-* sound (which seems to offer more resistance than a simple *l*), together with the sequence of single syllables that each seem to require almost equal stress, seems to slow down the reader. It attunes the reader's ear to the slow plodding movement the passage describes. In a successful poem, there seems to be a wedding of words and meaning, of sound and sense.

EXPLORATIONS

The Sound of the Poem

What makes the following poem appeal to the ear as much as to the eye and the mind?

A L Y O U N G   (born 1939)

For Poets   1968

Stay beautiful
but don't stay down underground too long
Dont turn into a mole
or a worm
or a root   5
or a stone

Come on out into the sunlight
Breathe in trees
Knock out mountains
Commune with snakes   10
& be the very hero of birds

Dont forget to poke your head up
& blink
think
Walk all around   15
Swim upstream

Dont forget to fly

THE RECEPTIVE READER

1. How should this poem sound when read aloud? How does this poet use rhyme, repetition, and parallel phrasing? How do you think they should guide the reader?

2. Where does this poem go counter to what is conventional or expected? Where does a counterrhythm seem to mirror the poet's determination to "swim upstream"?

THE RIGHT WORD

A poet is, before anything else, a person who is passionately in love with language.
                                                                W. H. AUDEN

I try to make each and every word carry its full measure and not just its meaning defined.
                                                                LUCILLE CLIFTON

*I have a lot to say,
but no words to use.
I have problems to release,
but no release valve.
HELP ME!*
                STUDENT POEM

Poets wrestle with both the sounds of words and their meanings. A short poem is a message that says much in little. In the days before direct long-distance dialing, fax, and Federal Express, people sent important messages by telegram. The hitch was that the telegraph office charged by the word, so the sender had to make every word count. Poets are not charged by the word, but they feel a similar need to make every word count. Instead of three words that blur the point, poets try to find the one word that has the right shade of meaning. The following poem, though very short, has long been a favorite of readers.

WILLIAM CARLOS WILLIAMS (1883–1963)
The Red Wheelbarrow 1923

so much depends
upon

a red wheel
barrow

glazed with rain
water

beside the white
chickens.

5

In a poem addressed to Williams and titled "So Much Depends," William Coles, psychiatrist and writer, talked about "so many things / the rest of us would never / have seen except for you." How does rainwater look on a surface like that of the wheelbarrow? If we said the water "coated" the surface, the objection might be that often a coat covers up what is underneath. "*Glazed* with rain / water" is right because it means coated with a shiny, transparent cover not hiding what is underneath. When another poet refers to the "distant glitter / of the January sun," *glitter* is a better word than *blaze* or *glare* because it is colder, more frigid, less blinding, though bright.

THE CREATIVE DIMENSION

Write your own "So much depends" passage or poem.

Poets have a *range* of vocabulary that enables them to make the right choices. The following poem stays especially close to the tangible details that make up firsthand experience. In much of this poem, the poet's language serves as a mirror of "what was there." Many of the words are specific, accurate words that give a faithful accounting of sights and events. (Others bring in striking imaginative comparisons, like the simile that compares the pink swim bladder of the fish to a big peony.)

ELIZABETH BISHOP (1911–1979)
The Fish 1946

I caught a tremendous fish
and held him beside the boat
half out of water, with my hook
fast in a corner of his mouth.
He didn't fight.
He hadn't fought at all.
He hung a grunting weight,

5

battered and venerable
and homely. Here and there
his brown skin hung in strips   10
like ancient wall-paper,
and its pattern of darker brown
was like wall-paper:
shapes like full-blown roses
stained and lost through age.   15
He was speckled with barnacles,
fine rosettes of lime,
and infested
with tiny white sea-lice,
and underneath two or three   20
rags of green weed hung down.
While his gills were breathing in
the terrible oxygen
—the frightening gills,
fresh and crisp with blood,   25
that can cut so badly—
I thought of the coarse white flesh
packed in like feathers,
the big bones and the little bones,
the dramatic reds and blacks   30
of his shiny entrails,
and the pink swim-bladder
like a big peony.
I looked into his eyes
which were far larger than mine   35
but shallower, and yellowed,
the irises backed and packed
with tarnished tinfoil
seen through the lenses
of old scratched isinglass.°   *fish gelatin*   40
They shifted a little, but not
to return my stare.
—It was more like the tipping
of an object toward the light.
I admired his sullen face,   45
the mechanism of his jaw,
and then I saw
that from his lower lip
—if you would call it a lip—
grim, wet, and weapon-like,   50
hung five old pieces of fish-line,
or four and a wire leader
with the swivel still attached,
with all their five big hooks
grown firmly in his mouth.   55
A green line, frayed at the end
where he broke it, two heavier lines,

and a fine black thread
still crimped from the strain and snap
when it broke and he got away.   60
Like medals with their ribbons
frayed and wavering,
a five-haired beard of wisdom
trailing from his aching jaw.
I stared and stared   65
and victory filled up the little rented boat,
from the pool of bilge
where oil had spread a rainbow
around the rusted engine
to the bailer rusted orange,   70
the sun-cracked thwarts,
the oarlocks on their strings,
the gunnels—until everything
was rainbow, rainbow, rainbow!
And I let the fish go.   75

The poet has the language resources to give us not just a distant, blurry picture of the fish and the boat but to close in on the specifics that call the scene up before our eyes in vivid detail. Many of the words in this poem are *specific* words—*barnacles, gills*—that the poet uses to call things by their right names. Many are **concrete** words that bring our senses into play, calling up for us things we can see, hear, or touch. We can almost see the fish "speckled with barnacles" and "infested / with tiny white sea-lice." We get a vivid picture of the brown skin that "hung in strips." We feel its "grunting weight" as the fish hangs half out of water with a "hook / fast in the corner of his mouth."

Without words like *speckled, barnacles, strips, gills, bilge,* or *bailer,* the poem could not make us share as completely in the experience the speaker in the poem relives here. Without these and the striking similes—the wall-paper, the "tarnished tinfoil" of the irises, the "beard of wisdom"—we could not put ourselves as completely in her shoes when at the end she makes the decision that otherwise might seem strange or irrational. The fish, with its yellowed eyes and its "beard" of broken fish lines, becomes overpoweringly real—indeed a "tremendous fish."

THE RECEPTIVE READER

1. How familiar are you with the *special language* of boaters and anglers? What are thwarts, oarlocks, gunnels?

2. How and where does the speaker in the poem show her *feelings* about the fish? Which details make the fish seem near-human? Which remind you that it is a fish?

3. What was the *rainbow* that the speaker saw spreading in the bilge at the bottom of the boat?

4. Were you ready for the *ending*? Were you prepared for what happened in the last line of the poem? Why or why not?

DENOTATION AND CONNOTATION

[Poets] must learn to strum that colossal and resonant
harp, the English language, a temperamental instrument
that calls for practiced fingering.

X. J. KENNEDY

You may as well think of pushing a brick out of a wall
with your forefinger as attempt to remove a word out of
any of their finished passages.

SAMUEL TAYLOR COLERIDGE ABOUT SHAKESPEARE AND MILTON

Poets have a keen ear for the emotional quality of words. Language does not just describe or report; it is alive with threat, warning, pleading, rejection, and regret. Words do not simply point—they point with pride; they point the finger. A demagogue was once literally a "leader of the people," but today we use the word to point the finger at a leader who leads the people by the nose. A paramour (a word using the French word for love) is more than a bedmate; medieval poets used the word for a lover cherished in defiance of a censorious society. Language is not like the Morse code, where a dot and a dash and two dots always stand for the letter *l*—no more and no less. Language is more like the icons on road signs that say "Slippery" (so look out!) or "Vista Point" (good place to stop and rest!).

Fews words are void of preference or emotion; many carry built-in attitudes, preferences, and feelings. We call the emotional overtones and attitudes that words carry the **connotations** of a word. In plain fact, the word *candle* stands for an old-fashioned lighting device that gives a limited, flickering light. But the word has romantic connotations, since candles light tender moments (or expensive meals in elegant restaurants). We call the stripped-down, bare-fact meaning of a word its **denotation.** The denotation of *hound* is dog, but there may be more to a hound than nondescript ordinary doggishness. Traditionally, *hound* has often stood for a special kind of dog, more sleek or alert, a valuable hunting dog or the like.

The following lines glow with the magic of words that have favorable, pleasing connotations—*slender, roses, music, blooms, flares, candle*—the more so since they are played off against the drab "grey streets":

When I with you so wholly disappear
into the mirror of your slender hand
grey streets of the city grow roses
and daisies, the music of flowers
blooms in our voices, the eye of
the grocer flares like a candle
Peter Meinke, "When I with You"

Connotations range over the whole spectrum from the most positive or flattering to the most negative and condemning. The word *sword* often has connotations of valor and chivalry, but the word *dagger* connotes treachery, making us expect to be stabbed in the back. Poets use words with the right connotations to steer our reactions, to guide our emotions. The following short poem makes us feel the contradictory emotions of first getting up in the morning.

CHARLES SIMIC (born 1938)
Poem   1971

Every morning I forget how it is.
I watch the smoke mount
In great strides above the city.
I belong to no one.

Then, I remember my shoes,   5
How I have to put them on,
How, bending over to tie them up,
I will look into the earth.

As many readers read this poem, the central polarity in it opposes the sensation of looking up into the morning sky and feeling free ("I belong to no one") to the feeling of bending over to put on shoes, a move that brings us down to earth. The two key words at the opposite poles of this poem are *strides* and *earth*. *Stride* is a very different word from *slink, trudge,* or *shuffle* (let alone *crawl* or *creep*). When we stride, we walk with fresh energy and a sense of purpose, as if certain of our destination. The connotations of *stride* are just right to help us share the early-morning feeling of being ready to meet the opportunities of the new day.

Earth has the right connotations to convey the opposite feeling. The poet could have said *floor*, because that is literally what people look at when putting on shoes. But much of the emotional impact of the poem would have been lost, since the floor is simply the part of the building that keeps us from falling through the ceiling of the apartment below. Earth represents what is heavy, tied down, and grubby about our existence. It keeps us from soaring.

THE RECEPTIVE READER

1. *Earth* is a richly *connotative* word that has different associations in different contexts. What other connotations could the word have in other contexts? (Cluster the word to explore the personal meanings and associations it has for you.)

2. Some readers see the *polarity* in this poem differently. The first stanza to them has negative connotations. It makes them feel disconnected and lost, like the smoke that rises and dissipates, dooming them "to belong to no one." Could you argue in favor of this alternative reading? And do you think there is a way to read the second stanza positively—finding security and safety in our bonds to the earth?

THE PERSONAL RESPONSE

How well did the student who wrote the following response get into the spirit of the poem? How do *you* respond to the poem?

> Every morning I wake up like Charles Simic and forget how the city is. I watch the smoke mount in vaporous strides over city roof tops. In the morning, the smoke and I belong to no one. Then I remember that the hard lines of schedules wait for me to put my shoes on and walk those lines. How I hate putting them on; the bending stiffens me. I tie the leather on the stumps of my feet, locking myself to the earth.

JUXTAPOSITIONS ━━━━━━━━━━━

Cityscapes

In the following poems (written within ten years of each other), two English poets look at the city of London. However, they use language to steer the reader's reactions in very different directions. In reading these poems, explore especially the connotations of words—their emotional impact, overtones, and associations.

WILLIAM WORDSWORTH   (1770–1850)

Composed upon Westminster Bridge, September 3, 1802   1802

Earth has not anything to show more fair:°	*more beautiful*
Dull would he be of soul who could pass by	
A sight so touching in its majesty;	
This City now doth, like a garment, wear	
The beauty of the morning; silent, bare,	5
Ships, towers, domes, theaters, and temples lie	
Open unto the fields, and to the sky;	
All bright and glittering in the smokeless air.	
Never did sun more beautifully steep	
In his first splendor, valley, rock, or hill;	10
Never saw I, never felt, a calm so deep!	
The river glideth at his own sweet will:	
Dear God! the very houses seem asleep;	
And all that mighty heart is lying still!	

THE RECEPTIVE READER

Explore the associations and overtones of the many connotative words in this poem. What would be missing from the poem if the poet had said, "Dull would he be of brain" rather than "of soul"? What if he had said, "doth, like a coat, wear" instead of "like a garment" wear? What makes the words *domes* and *temples* different from the word *churches*? What if the poet had said, "With his first rays" rather than "In his first splendor"? What would be different if the poet had said at the end, "that mighty nerve center" rather than "that mighty heart"?

WILLIAM BLAKE (1757–1827)
London 1794

I wander through each chartered° street,   *legally set up*
Near where the chartered Thames does flow,
And mark in every face I meet
Marks of weakness, marks of woe.

In every cry of every man,   5
In every Infant's cry of fear,
In every voice, in every ban,°   *announcement*
The mind-forged manacles I hear.

How the chimney-sweeper's cry
Every blackening church appalls;   10
And the hapless soldier's sigh
Runs in blood down Palace walls.

But most through midnight streets I hear
How the youthful Harlot's curse
Blasts the new-born Infant's tear,   15
And blights with plagues the Marriage hearse.

THE RECEPTIVE READER

1. What words most directly describe the speaker's *emotions* when contemplating a city with maimed or penniless veterans, young prostitutes, and soot-covered churches? What would be different if the poet had used "mind-made bonds" rather than "mind-forged manacles"? What would be missing in the last line if he had said "damages" rather than "blights"? What gives metaphors like "Runs in blood down Palace walls" and the "Marriage hearse" their special force?

2. How would you pinpoint the difference in *perspective* between this and Wordsworth's poem?

THE PERSONAL RESPONSE

If you were to write out your feelings about one of today's cities, would your point of view be closer to Wordsworth's or to Blake's?

THE CREATIVE DIMENSION

Try your hand at a modern *rewrite* or update of one of these poems. How might a modern poet looking at the identical sights describe them—in what language?

THE LIMITS OF LANGUAGE

The reader must not sit back and expect the poet to do all the work.

EDITH SITWELL

Everything which opens out to us a new world is bound to appear strange at first.

EDITH SITWELL

Poets vary greatly in how far they will stretch the limits of language. Difficult but rewarding poets use language in original or intensely personal ways. First of all, the poet's vocabulary may include exotic gleanings brought back from excursions into ancient history, legend, or fabled places. The following poem delights readers who cherish words that, like rare coins, seldom see the light of common day.

JOHN MASEFIELD   (1878–1967)

Cargoes

1902

Quinquereme of Nineveh from distant Ophir,
Rowing home to haven in sunny Palestine,
With a cargo of ivory,
And apes and peacocks,
Sandalwood, cedarwood, and sweet white wine.   5

Stately Spanish galleon coming from the Isthmus,
Dipping through the Tropics by the palm-green shores,
With a cargo of diamonds,
Emeralds, amethysts,
Topazes, and cinnamon, and gold moidores.   10

Dirty British coaster with a salt-caked smoke-stack,
Butting through the Channel in the mad March days,
With a cargo of Tyne coal,
Road-rails, pig-lead,
Firewood, iron-ware, and cheap tin trays.   15

What is a quinquereme? The context of the poem tells us that it is an ancient ship being rowed to its home harbor, carrying rich exotic cargo. (Some readers may remember the triremes of ancient Rome, with three banks of galley slaves plying *three* levels of oars. The legendary ship in this poem then would have *five* levels of oars.) Nineveh is clearly a city in ancient Palestine, wealthy enough to outfit magnificent trading ships. (It is mentioned in the Bible as a great city.) Ophir sounds like a legendary faraway city of great wealth. (Poets mention it: "More than all of Ophir's gold / does the fleeting second hold.")

The second of the three ships in this poem—the elaborately ornamented Spanish galleon carrying rich loot from tropical Central America back to the Old World—takes us closer to what we know about history and geography. The "Isthmus" is likely to be the isthmus of Panama—a thin strip of land that kept ships from reaching the Pacific from the Atlantic until the Panama Canal saved them the trouble of going around the southernmost tip of South America.

Although not likely to be able to afford emeralds, amethysts, and topazes, we can at least revel in the marvelous exotic names of these priceless gems. If *quinquereme* has not sent us to the dictionary, *moidores* will—although our knowledge that the Spanish conquistadores melted down the golden artifacts of the Aztecs and Incas in their greed for gold might make us conclude that these would be gold coins (actually "money of gold" minted in Portugal and Brazil).

By the third stanza, finally, we are within range of a more everyday vocabulary: The coal is from Newcastle-upon-Tyne ("carrying coals to Newcastle" was for a long time the equivalent of shipping hogs to Missouri).

THE RECEPTIVE READER

1. One student reader called this poem a "three-sided prism," with each stanza reflecting a different view of the cargo ships that since time immemorial have plied the seas. How would you label the three different cargoes?

2. Which words in this poem are rich in *connotation*—in overtones or personal association—for you? For instance, what ideas or feelings do words like *Palestine, ivory, peacock, galleon,* or *emerald* bring to mind?

THE RANGE OF INTERPRETATION

Where do you stand on the issue raised in the following excerpt from a student paper about this poem? What in the poem helps you make up your mind one way or the other?

> The last stanza is particularly intriguing in its contrast with the other two. The "dirty British coaster" brings us forward in time to the grimy industrial age. The sooty words and leaden cargo describe a harshly realistic working vessel, whereas the other two ships were romanticized, idealized, and seen through a nostalgic haze. We could easily argue that the harshness of the final stanza gives us a negative view of the modern world. We get a glimpse here of the sordid materialism of our age.
>
> However, we might easily argue the opposite as well. If the poet had cast the same realistic eye on the past as he did on the present, he might have picked slave ships or cattle boats, quite common in the ancient days, or he might have shown us the chained galley slaves rowing the splendid ancient ship. The dirty British coaster then would not come off so badly after all. In any case, Masefield suggests strength and power and working muscle in his description of the coaster "butting" stubbornly through the English Channel in ugly weather. This ship carries no glittering booty from "palm-green shores." It is a workaday mule of the seas. Its cargo represents the

everyday needs served by the economy of an industrial nation. We should not look down on it but accept it as part of living everyday reality.

Poets whose work is especially challenging may not only extend the reaches of language but also use language resources in provocative creative ways. They may use words that combine familiar building blocks in strange new patterns. They may yoke words together that do not usually work together. They may employ strange telescopings or foreshortenings. They may use reversals or transposings that pull words out of their usual order for special attention.

Some of the poet's creative innovations may take us only one step beyond ordinary language. In a poem about a lonely dark winter setting, the poet may not use the familiar word *absent-minded* but *absent-spirited* instead. Apparently the word *absent-minded* was not strong enough, because the speaker was not just temporarily thinking about something else. Instead, the speaker's *spirit* was too heavy with wintery thoughts and feelings to attend to trivial tasks at hand.

Some of the poetry most admired by modern readers goes farther in testing the boundaries of language. The following poem shows the word play and wrenchings of normal word order that we expect to find in the tense religious poetry of Gerard Manley Hopkins. The poem centers on the dove as a familiar symbol of peace. But here the bird is a "wild wooddove," shyly "roaming" around the poet. As a wild bird of the forest, it is hard to entice it to settle down with the speaker in the poem, who would, like a tree, spread for it protective "boughs."

GERARD MANLEY HOPKINS (1844–1889)

Peace   1887

When will you ever, Peace, wild wooddove, shy wings shut,
Your round me roaming end, and under be my boughs?
When, when, Peace, will you, Peace? I'll not play hypocrite
To own my heart: I yield° you do come sometimes; but   *I admit*
That piecemeal peace is poor peace. What pure peace allows   5
Alarms of wars, the daunting wars, the death of it?

O surely, reaving° Peace, my Lord should leave in lieu   *taking away*
Some good! And so he does leave Patience exquisite,
That plumes° to Peace thereafter. And when Peace does here house *spreads plumage*
He comes with work to do, he does not come to coo,   10
     He comes to brood and sit.

Where does the text of the poem run counter to what you are prepared to read? What changes does the poet ring on the central word *peace*?

The phrase "Your round me roaming end" would normally be "end your roaming around me." The poet's reordering of the words pulls the key word out for emphasis: "Your ROUND me roaming end" (the bird keeps away, roaming *around* the speaker). At the same time, the reshuffling sets up a strong counterpull or counterrhythm (part of what the poet called **sprung rhythm**). The result is a jostling effect in keeping with the restless, "peaceless" feelings of someone whose strong faith has yet left him strangely restless, with only "sometimes" a feeling of inner peace.

That word—*peace*—echoes through the poem like a plea for something intensely desired. The poet uses two **puns** to keep the word ringing in our ears. We use a pun when we play on the different meanings of words that sound or look alike. We want *peace* that is all of a *piece*. Instead, we get *piecemeal* peace that comes in small unsatisfactory pieces. That makes the peace we obtain poor peace when what we desire is *pure* peace. As one student reader said, "Hopkins must make his own peace with the piecemeal bits of faith that come to him."

THE RECEPTIVE READER

1. Could you argue that the changed *word order* in "under be my boughs" and "to own my heart" also pulls a key word to the front of a phrase?

2. What does the *metaphor* make you visualize when the poet says that patience "plumes to Peace thereafter"?

3. What kind of *work* does the poet seem to have in mind at the end? (What kind of brooding is productive rather than counterproductive?)

Less dramatic or experimental departures from the kind of language we expect may nevertheless seriously change the **tone** of a poem—the attitude it suggests (toward the subject or toward the reader) or its emotional coloring. A poet may branch out beyond current standard English in one of several directions:

✦ Language that is no longer in common use is **archaic.** Examples are *brethren* for brothers, *fain* or *lief* for gladly, and *ere* for before. (When words have gone out of use altogether, they are **obsolete.**) *Thou*, *thy*, and *thine*—and the special verb forms that go with *thou* ("thou liest")—were still current in Shakespeare's time, used in exchanges between people who, as we would say today, were on a first-name basis. "Hamlet, thou hast thy father much offended," says Queen Gertrude to her son. As these forms became archaic, poets used them to strike a special solemn, elevated note: "Dust thou art, to dust returnest, / Was not spoken of the soul" (Henry Wadsworth Longfellow).

✦ A poet may move beyond the standard English of office, school, and media to echo the **folk speech** of factory, pool hall, or down-home neighborhood. "We real cool" begins a famous poem by Gwendolyn Brooks. Shifts from formal to informal English or **slang** can make for brash, humorous effects: "My telephone rang in the middle of the night, / but I didn't answer it. It rang and rang / and rang and SHUT UP! and rang as if it were possessed" (Richard Brautigan).

✦ For a time, observers of language habits assumed that radio, television, and cheap paperbacks would average out regional differences. However, recent years have seen a renewed pride in traditional **dialects,** which help their speakers assert a regional identity separate from that promoted by a central government, synchronized school system, and official national language. Dialects are regional variations of a common language that are still mutually intelligible—but some are actually on the borderline of becoming separate languages. How much do you understand of the Scots, or Scottish dialect, in the following lines?

HUGH MACDIARMID (1892–1978)
Weep and Wail No More   1948

Stop killin' the deid. Gi'e owre
Your weepin' and wailin'.
    You maun keep quiet
If you want to hear them still
And no' blur their image in your mind.   5

For they've only a faint wee whisperin' voice
Makin' nae mair noise ava'
Than the growin' of the grass
That flourishes whaur naebody walks.

EXPLORATIONS
The Range of Reference

In the following poem, the English Romantic poet John Keats moves beyond everyday language to create a rich overlay of associations taking us beyond the ordinary. He compares his awe and excitement at discovering Chapman's sixteenth-century translation of Homer's *Iliad* with the excitement the Spanish conquerors of Mexico must have felt when they first saw the Pacific Ocean from Darien in Panama. Which words are unfamiliar or difficult for you? Which would you have to check in a dictionary?

JOHN KEATS (1795–1821)
On First Looking into Chapman's Homer   1816

Much have I traveled in the realms of gold,
    And many goodly states and kingdoms seen;
    Round many western islands have I been
Which bards in fealty to Apollo hold.
Oft of one wide expanse had I been told   5
    That deep-browed Homer ruled as his demesne;
    Yet did I never breathe its pure serene
Till I heard Chapman speak out loud and bold:

Then felt I like some watcher of the skies
   When a new planet swims into his ken;   10
Or like stout Cortez when with eagle eyes
   He stared at the Pacific—and all his men
Looked at each other with a wild surmise—
   Silent, upon a peak in Darien.

THE RECEPTIVE READER

1. Each of the following is a simpler or more familiar word for a richer, *more connotative* word used by the poet. Parentheses enclose the overtones or associations added by the word Keats actually chose in the poem. Which word in the poem matches each of the following: (ancient, venerable) kingdom; (ancient, honored) poets; loyalty (to a feudal medieval overlord); (brilliant, divine) patron of poetry; (a lord's) lands; expanse (of calm, pure sky or sea); (sharply perceived) field of vision?

2. What features make you recognize this poem as a *sonnet*? Where is its turning point? Can you argue that the poem follows a cumulative or climactic order?

EXPLORATIONS

Testing the Boundaries

When we call a poem difficult, it is often because the poet has trusted us to read the right meanings out of apparent shortcuts and shifts. Dylan Thomas, a Welsh poet, often seems impatient with plodding ordinary language, leaping ahead instead to make new connections. One reader said of him that he "strips from words their old, dull, used sleepiness, and gives them a refreshed and awakened meaning."

Read the following poem the first time without puzzling over difficult phrases. Allow yourself to be carried along by the chanting rhythm. Then go back over the poem, trying to see connections and meanings in Thomas' plays on words and in his strange telescopings or juxtapositions. (Fern Hill is the name of a farm that Thomas' uncle and aunt rented as tenant farmers.)

DYLAN THOMAS   (1914–1953)
Fern Hill   1946

Now as I was young and easy under the apple boughs
About the lilting house and happy as the grass was green,
   The night above the dingle° starry,   *wooded valley*
      Time let me hail and climb
   Golden in the heydays of his eyes,   5
And honored among wagons I was prince of the apple towns
And once below a time I lordly had the trees and leaves

Trail with daisies and barley
Down the rivers of the windfall light.

And as I was green and carefree, famous among the barns   10
About the happy yard and singing as the farm was home,
    In the sun that is young once only,
        Time let me play and be
    Golden in the mercy of his means,
And green and golden I was huntsman and herdsman, the calves   15
Sang to my horn, the foxes on the hills barked clear and cold,
        And the sabbath rang slowly
    In the pebbles of the holy streams.

All the sun long it was running, it was lovely, the hay
Fields high as the house, the tunes from the chimneys, it was air   20
    And playing, lovely and watery
        And fire green as grass.
    And nightly under the simple stars
As I rode to sleep the owls were bearing the farm away,
All the moon long I heard, blessed among stables, the night-jars°   *night birds*   25
Flying with the ricks,° and the horses   *haystacks*
        Flashing into the dark.

And then to awake, and the farm, like a wanderer white
With the dew, come back, the cock on his shoulder: it was all
    Shining, it was Adam and maiden,   30
        The sky gathered again
    And the sun grew round that very day.
So it must have been after the birth of the simple light
In the first, spinning place, the spellbound horses walking warm   .
    Out of the whinnying green stable   35
        On to the fields of praise.

And honored among foxes and pheasants by the gay house
Under the new made clouds and happy as the heart was long,
    In the sun born over and over,
        I ran my heedless ways,   40
    My wishes raced through the house high hay
And nothing I cared, at my sky blue trades, that time allows
In all his tuneful turning so few and such morning songs
    Before the children green and golden
        Follow him out of grace,   45

Nothing I cared, in the lamb white days, that time would take me
Up to the swallow thronged loft by the shadow of my hand,
    In the moon that is always rising,
        Nor that riding to sleep
    I should hear him fly with the high fields   50
And wake to the farm forever fled from the childless land.
Oh as I was young and easy in the mercy of his means,
        Time held me green and dying
    Though I sang in my chains like the sea.

THE RECEPTIVE READER

1. Try to puzzle out possible connections that explain telescoped phrases or strange juxtapositions in the early stanzas. For instance, what could have been "lilting" about the house? How did the child "hail and climb / Golden" in the heydays of Time? How was he "prince of the apple towns"? What is the connection between light and "rivers" and a "windfall"? Why in this poem is the sun "young once only"?

2. What is the *symbolic* meaning of the colors "green and golden," whose names echo through this poem?

3. What are key *images* and prevailing feelings in the poet's account of the first days after Creation? What is borrowed from and what is different from the account in Genesis?

4. What are the "chains" at the conclusion of the poem? Assuming the words are not meant literally, in what sense did Time hold the child "green and dying"?

POEMS FOR FURTHER STUDY

In reading the following poems, pay special attention to the poet's word choice, or diction. Where does the sound of words seem to mirror sense? Which words seem particularly accurate or fitting? Which seem to have just the right connotations, overtones, or associations? Where does the poet seem to stretch the limits of ordinary language?

MARGARET ATWOOD   (born 1939)

Dreams of the Animals   1970

Mostly the animals dream
of other animals   each
according to its kind

       (though certain mice and small rodents
       have nightmares of a huge pink   5
       shape with five claws descending)

: moles dream of darkness and delicate
mole smells

frogs dream of green and golden
frogs   10
sparkling like wet suns
among the lilies

red and black
striped fish, their eyes open
have red and black striped   15
dreams   defense, attack, meaningful
patterns

birds dream of territories
enclosed by singing.

Sometimes the animals dream of evil 20
in the form of soap and metal
but mostly the animals dream
of other animals.

There are exceptions:

       the silver fox in the roadside zoo 25
       dreams of digging out
       and of baby foxes, their necks bitten

       the caged armadillo
       near the train
       station, which runs 30
       all day in figure eights
       its piglet feet pattering,
       no longer dreams
       but is insane when waking;

       the iguana 35
       in the petshop window on St. Catherine Street
       crested, royal-eyed, ruling
       its kingdom of water-dish and sawdust

       dreams of sawdust

THE RECEPTIVE READER

1. What are the usual associations of the animals in this poem? How does the poem transform these associations or leave them behind? Look at the words that cluster around the names of the animals here. Which of the words have positive connotations, showing the poet's empathy or fellow feeling? (Which of these words are especially *unusual* or unexpected?)

2. In this poem, what is the difference between the animals in the wild and those in captivity? What words especially drive home the contrast between the animals in the wild and their caged cousins?

THE PERSONAL RESPONSE

Disney cartoons have often made animals seem cute, harmless, and lovable. Disney wildlife films, however, have often taken an uncompromisingly honest look at life in the wild. Does Atwood make animals seem too lovable and human?

GERARD MANLEY HOPKINS (1844–1889)

The Windhover 1877

To Christ Our Lord

I caught this morning morning's minion,° king-   *beloved*
    dom of daylight's dauphin,° dapple-dawn-drawn Falcon, in his riding   *crown prince*
    Of the rolling level underneath him steady air, and striding

High there, how he rung upon the rein of a wimpling° wing   *rippling*
In his ecstasy! then off, off forth on swing,   5
    As a skate's heel sweeps smooth on a bow-bend: the hurl and gliding
    Rebuffed the big wind. My heart in hiding
Stirred for a bird,— the achieve of, the mastery of the thing!

Brute beauty and valor and act, oh, air, pride, plume, here
    Buckle! AND the fire that breaks from thee then, a billion   10
Times told lovelier, more dangerous, O my chevalier!°   *knight*

    No wonder of it: shéer plód makes plow down sillion°   *furrow*
Shine, and black-blue embers, ah my dear,
    Fall, gall themselves, and gash gold-vermilion.

THE RECEPTIVE READER

1. Several of the words Hopkins applies to the falcon and to Christ suggest the glamor and pageantry of chivalry: a *minion* is a cherished, beloved court favorite; the *dauphin* was the crown prince of medieval France; a *chevalier* is a knight who represents the chivalric virtues (*chevalier* and *chivalry* come from the same root). Where in the poem does Hopkins spell out the *connotations* that these words suggest?

2. When the poet celebrates the masterful, ecstatic flight of the falcon, what do *concrete* words like *riding, striding, sweep, hurl,* and *gliding* add to the meaning of the generic term *fly?* (What does each make you visualize? What associations or feelings does it carry with it?) What makes *rebuff* different from *resist?*

3. In the pivotal word *buckle,* not only do the inspiring qualities of the falcon "come together" or are welded together (as the two ends of a belt are buckled or fastened). The two parts of the poem also meet: the splendor of God's creation and the billionfold "lovelier, more dangerous" splendor of "Our Lord." How do the two concluding images in the last three lines of the poem mirror the relationship between the "brute" creature and its creator?

4. In addition to the end rhyme that is traditional in a sonnet like this one, Hopkins uses *alliteration*—the repetition of the same sound at the beginning of several words in the same line ("this MORNing MORNing's MINion"). The telescoped phrase "dapple-dawn-drawn" allows the poet to complete the alliteration started by "DAYlight's DAUPHin." How would you spell out the meaning of the telescoped phrase in more ordinary language?

THE RANGE OF INTERPRETATION

According to a recent introduction to Hopkins' poetry, some critics "have seen the poem as one of frustration and sadness." The poem is "concerned with the unbridgeable distance between the hawk, flying so freely and beautifully, and the poet, whose heart is 'in hiding'; the heart is hidden away as if afraid, locked up by the severe discipline of the priesthood and the demands of self-sacrifice which it makes." To other readers, the poem "does not seem to be a poem of frustration so much as a poem of enthusiasm and exultation. . . . The excitement is conveyed in the way in which the heart, while it may have been 'in hiding,' that is, inactive, now 'Stirred for a bird'; as if the heart moved and leaped at the sight of the hawk" (J. R. Watson, *The Poetry of Gerard Manley Hopkins*). Which of these two interpretations would you be inclined to support? (What do *you* make of the phrase "my heart in hiding"?)

WOLE SOYINKA   (born 1934)

Nobel Prize winner Wole Soyinka—playwright, poet, and novelist—is one of the African writers best known in the West. After the end of British colonial rule, his native Nigeria went through a phase of tribal conflict, with an unsuccessful war of secession fought by the Ibo. Soyinka, a Yoruba, wrote some of his poems while imprisoned during the civil war. He has written with biting satire about discrimination based on color and about the political maneuverings of leaders, whether in the Western imperialist, the Eastern socialist, or the Third World camp.

Lost Tribe   1988

Ants disturbed by every passing tread,
The wandering tribe still scurries round
In search of lost community. Love by rote,
Care by inscription. Incantations without magic.
Straws outstretched to suck at every passing broth,   5
Incessant tongues pretend to a way of thought—
Where language mints are private franchise,
The coins prove counterfeit on open markets.

Hard-sell pharmacies dispense all social pills:
"Have a nice day now." "Touch someone."   10
There's premium on the verb imperative—some
Instant fame psychologist pronounced it on TV—
He's now forgotten like tomorrow's guru,
Instant cult, disposable as paper diaper—
Firm commands denote sincerity;   15
The wish is wishy-washy, lacks "contact
Positive." The waiter barks: "Enjoy your meal,"
Or crisper still "Enjoy!" You feel you'd better!
Buses, subway, park seats push the gospel,
Slogans like tickertapes emblazon foreheads—   20
"Talk it over with someone—now, not later!"
"Take down fences, not mend them."
"Give a nice smile to someone." But, a tear-duct
Variant: "Have you hugged your child today?"

THE RECEPTIVE READER

1. Soyinka has a marvelous quick ear for how language reveals (or betrays) who we are. How does this poem show him to be a good listener?

2. What has happened to the magic of language according to this poem? Who or what is to blame?

3. This poem is rich in provocative metaphor. What are the figurative meanings of the ants, the straws, the coins, the pharmacies, the paper diaper? Look at the lines referring to the tickertapes and to the tear ducts. Can you translate what they say into more ordinary language? What is the difference between the ordinary-language version and the poet's use of language?

4. To judge from the poet's examples, what is the imperative form of a verb? What kind of question concludes the poem?

5. In what sense were the original lost tribes of Israel lost, and what use does the poem make of this biblical allusion?

THE PERSONAL RESPONSE

Do you share the poet's allergy to the kind of language he focuses on in this poem? Can you think of other examples? Is there something to be said in defense of this kind of language?

JOHN HEAVISIDE
A Gathering of Deafs 1989

By the turnstiles
in the station
where the L train greets
the downtown six there was
a congregation of deafs 5
passing forth
a jive wild
and purely physical
in a world dislocated
from the subway howling 10
hard sole shoe stampede
punk rock blasted radio
screaming, pounding, honking
they gather in community
lively and serene, engaging 15
in a dexterous conversation

An old woman
of her dead husband tells
caressing the air
with wrinkled fingers that demonstrate the story with 20
delicate, mellifluous motion
she places gentle configurations before the faces of the group

A young Puerto Rican
describes a fight with his mother emphasizing each word
with abrupt, staccato movements jerking his elbows 25
and twisting his wrists
teeth clenched and lips pressed
he concluded the story
by pounding his fist
into his palm 30

By the newsstand
two lovers express emotion

caressing the air
with syllables
graceful and slow   35
joining their thoughts
by the flow of fingertips

THE RECEPTIVE READER

1. In this student-written poem, what is right about words like *congregation, jive, community, dexterous, configuration?* How effective or expressive are the words setting up the contrast between the punk rock and the silent conversation of the deaf?

2. What is the difference between *mellifluous* and *staccato?* What words clustering around each of these help a reader unfamiliar with them?

3. What statement is the student poet making about the sign language of the deaf?

WRITING ABOUT LITERATURE

6. Responding to Connotation (Interpreting the Evidence)

The Writing Workshop   When studying a poem rich in connotative language, you will be paying special attention to emotional overtones and implied attitudes. How do emotionally charged words steer the reactions of the reader? (Remember that dictionaries tend to concentrate on the denotations of words, though they may include hints on possible connotations.)

✧ You may want to start your paper by defining your *key term*. You may want to get the subject of connotative language clearly into focus, using brief striking illustrations.

✧ Show evidence of close, careful reading. Show that you have read carefully for *implications*—you have gone through the poem line by line, paying special attention to key words or to recurrent words that echo in the poem.

✧ Do not take words out of *context*. Is a word part of a network of similar or related terms? Are its associations or implications reinforced by what goes with it in the poem? Or are unusual associations negated or overruled by other words that strongly affect the tone or emotional quality of the poem?

✧ Work out a clear overall *plan*. For instance, you may want to follow the overall pattern of the poem. (Is there perhaps an initial set of words with very similar connotations but then a turning, with the poem moving in a different or opposed direction?) Or you may sort out different kinds of connotative language or different effects of connotative language on the reader.

Study the model student paper examining connotative language in the following poem. How carefully has the writer read the poem? What use does she make of evidence from the poem? Are any of the connotations she traces private or personal rather than widely shared associations? How convincing are her conclusions?

JEFFREY HARRISON
Bathtubs, Three Varieties 1975

First the old-fashioned kind, standing on paws,
like a domesticated animal—
I once had a whole flock of these
(seven—for good luck? I never asked
the landlord) under a walnut tree 5
in my backyard, like sheep in shade.
They collected walnuts in the fall then filled up with snow, like thickening wool.

Modern tubs are more like ancient tombs.
And it is a kind of death we ask for
in the bath. Nothing theatrical 10
like Marat with his arm hanging out—
just that the boundary between the body
and the world dissolve, that we forget
ourselves, and that the tub become
the sarcophagus of dreams. 15

My bathtub in Japan was square, and deep.
You sat cross-legged like a Zen
monk in meditation, up to your neck
in water always a little too hot,
relaxed and yet attentive to the moment 20
(relaxation as a discipline)—
staring through a rising cloud of steam
at the blank wall in front of you.

SAMPLE STUDENT PAPER

Connotative Language: Harrison's Three Bathtubs

Dictionary meanings are usually denotative meanings; they give us exact, objective, limited definitions. When words take us beyond objective labeling to expand our associations, when they carry an overlay of emotional association, they have connotative meaning. For example, the word *house* denotes a structure with walls, floors, ceilings, and doors, and including bedrooms and a kitchen; *house* does not have the emotional overlay that the word *home* suggests. *Home* may recall the warmth of a featherbed in winter or the smell of newly-mown grass in summer. It suggests a place that provides security and protection, an anchor in an uncertain world.

Connotative meanings may be personal and private. Abigail may be a beautiful name to many, but if we have known an Abigail who was cross and domineering, the word will have unpleasant associations for us. To work for the poet, a word must usually have more broadly shared layers of meaning. When Romeo calls Juliet's balcony the east and Juliet the sun, we know he is suggesting that, like the rising sun, Juliet is new, fresh, bright, warm, and central in his life.

In Jeffrey Harrison's "Bathtubs, Three Varieties," the poet relies on both the denotative and connotative meanings of words. In three stanzas, he describes three kinds of bathtubs: "an old-fashioned kind," "modern tubs," and his "bathtub in Japan." He does not flatly state his preference for one kind of bathtub over another, but if we focus on his word choices and the connotations of certain words, we may conclude that he does indeed have a preference.

In the first stanza, the speaker in the poem surprises us with not one but seven old-fashioned tubs under a walnut tree in his backyard. Parenthetically, he adds that he has not asked his landlord why they are there, but he associates seven with "good luck." Interior decorators call old-fashioned tubs claw-footed or lion-footed, but the speaker chooses to see this kind of tub as standing on "paws, / like a domesticated animal." Unlike lions' claws, paws are non-threatening and connote the softness of a cat's paws. Another reference to a domesticated animal, tame and trusting, reinforces this kind of feeling: Seven of these tubs make a "whole flock" of "sheep in shade"; the connotation here is of a gathering of domesticated animals in a pleasant, pastoral scene. When cold weather comes, the tubs fill with snow—normally cold and forbidding, but here compared to the thickening wool of the sheep; thus the snow sounds paradoxically warm and protecting. Earlier, the tubs were collecting walnuts, reminding us of the rich bounty of harvest time.

The second stanza, on modern tubs, presents a startling contrast. Here we have tubs "like ancient tombs," a bath that is a "kind of death," and a tub that becomes a "sarcophagus," or massive stone coffin. Our tub death is not even "theatrical," like the dramatic death in the French painter David's portrait of Marat, the French revolutionary hero stabbed in his bath.

In the third stanza, we find ourselves in a Japanese tub described as "square"— without the welcoming comfort of a circular or oval shape. We do not stretch out in this tub but sit "cross-legged like a Zen / monk in meditation." We sit up to our necks in deep water "always a little too hot." We hear an echo here of the expressions "up to our necks in something" and "being in hot water," both of which have negative implications. This is a strange mixture of relaxation with "discipline," as we find ourselves staring "at the blank wall." This tub sounds uninviting for any but those stoic people who like a strenuous life.

For me, at least, the tubs in the first stanza suggest memories of peaceful contentment. There is something bleak and forbidding about the modern tomblike tub. And it would probably take special training in Zen to maintain the proper half-relaxed, half-disciplined attitude proper to the over-hot, steamy Japanese variety.

QUESTIONS

Do you agree with this student's reading of the poem? Why or why not? Did she overlook any significant details? Does she bring in personal associations that you would question? What parts of the paper are for you especially instructive or convincing?

7 FORM
Rhyme, Meter, and Stanza

Remember: Our deepest perceptions are a waste if we have no sense of form.

THEODORE ROETHKE

Let chaos storm!
Let cloud shapes swarm!
I wait for form.
ROBERT FROST, "PERTINAX"

FOCUS ON FORM

Poetry today moves between the two poles of traditional form and the **open form** that is second nature to many modern poets. Traditional form is shaped by such features as rhyme, meter, and stanza. Open form in varying degrees modifies or abandons these, allowing the poet to give each poem its own unique pattern and rhythm.

For centuries, strongly metrical lines of verse ("With HOW | sad STEPS, | O MOON, | thou CLIMB'ST | the SKIES") were often marked off by rhyme (SKIES / TRIES). They were often arranged in stanzas of similar shape. These traditional formal features long helped make the difference between poetry and prose. When handled too mechanically, they make a poem jingle, lulling us to sleep rather than sharpening our attention. However, for first-rate poets traditional form has been (and is) a challenge, stimulating their imagination and creative abilities.

The following poem is a traditional sonnet, written by a leading poet of the English Romantic movement. As sonnets have for over five hundred years, the poem has fourteen lines. Like many other sonnets, it has an interlaced rhyme scheme: "free—Nun—sun—(tranquili)ty; Sea—(a)wake—make—(everlasting)ly" (abbaabba). It has the traditional underlying five-beat meter (iambic pentameter): "The HO | ly TIME | is QUI | et AS | a NUN." However, its pattern, rhythm, and tone make it memorable and unique. It is different from any other sonnet. Look at the interplay of traditional form and creative freedom in this poem. Like several other Wordsworth poems, this poem addresses a younger sister, who lived with him and shared his love of nature.

170

WILLIAM WORDSWORTH   (1770–1850)

It Is a Beauteous Evening   1807

It is a beauteous° evening, calm and free,	*beautiful*
The holy time is quiet as a Nun	
Breathless with adoration; the broad sun	
Is sinking down in its tranquility;	
The gentleness of heaven broods o'er the Sea:	5
Listen! the Mighty Being is awake,	
And doth with his eternal motion make	
A sound like thunder—everlastingly.	
Dear Child! dear Girl! that walkest with me here,	
If thou appear untouched by solemn thought,	10
Thy nature is not therefore less divine:	
Thou liest in Abraham's bosom all the year,	
And worship'st at the Temple's inner shrine,	
God being with thee when we know it not.	

What keeps this poem from being predictable in its use of traditional form?

✧ First, the poem has a strong metrical pattern, but it is not monotonous: At several key points, the poem reverses the iambic (DeTROIT—DeTROIT) pattern to stress the first rather than the second syllable of a line: "BREATHless with adoration"; "LISten! the Mighty Being is awake"; "GOD being with thee." This variation does more than introduce variety. It emphasizes key words; it sets off key stages in how the poem as a whole takes shape. Sound and sense, form and meaning, blend.

✧ Second, rhyme words do not neatly mark off sentences or clauses. At the end of the second line, we are pulled over into the third with only a minor pause. But then we come to a major break *within* the line, setting up a strong counterrhythm: "The holy time is quiet as a Nun / Breathless with adoration; || the broad sun. . . ." Strong breaks vary the rhythm when the speaker turns to the person addressed: "Listen! || the Mighty Being . . ."; "Dear Child! || dear Girl! || that walkest with me here. . . ." Again, these breaks are not just pleasing variations of a pattern. They at the same time make us stop and listen; they help make the listener pay solemn attention to the words of the speaker.

THE RECEPTIVE READER

1. How should this poem *sound* when read aloud? How much should the reading make the listener aware of the meter—and of the line breaks following the rhyme words? At what point would overemphasis on these formal features begin to make the poem sound mechanical?

2. What is the *rhyme* scheme in the concluding six lines (sestet) of this sonnet? Which of the lines in the sestet are closest to illustrating regular iambic *meter*?

3. How many *images* in this poem help the poet create and maintain a feeling of religious awe?

4. What is the attitude of the speaker in the poem toward the person listening?

Form, traditional or modern, is a large umbrella heading for features that determine the texture and shape of a poem. Form is what makes a poem more deliberate, more crafted, than the effortless flow of ordinary language. Poetic form intertwines in fascinating ways with meaning. When a poem is truly of one piece, formal features do not seem imposed on meaning from without, like the ornaments hung on a Christmas tree. A successful poem does not have a prior prose meaning that could have been separately expressed by other means. We expect form to be organic. We expect the texture and shape of a poem to evolve from within. *What* the poem means and *how* the poem means blend and become one.

RHYME, ALLITERATION, FREE VERSE

Like meter, rhyme is a highly formal device. It is a signal that language is going to be used in an unusual, often a serious and memorable, way. . . . Because it is out of the ordinary, rhyme attracts our attention and prepares us for a completely organized and unusually expressive language.

KARL SHAPIRO

Why **rhyme?** Rhyme bonds two or more lines by final syllables that start out differently but end alike. Children—and adults who have kept children's gift for finding inexpensive, wholehearted pleasures—delight in the echo effects of rhyme: "Celery, RAW, / Develops the JAW, / But celery, STEWED, / Is more quietly CHEWED" (Ogden Nash). Beyond this simple pleasure, as elementary as the pleasure of hopping and skipping, rhyme can serve as the most visible external sign that the poem we are reading is going to have a shape, a pattern. It is going to be more patterned, more ordered, than ordinary fragmented and disjointed life, not to mention life at its chaotic, nerve-jarring worst.

Rhyme helps the poet measure off lengths of verse; it sets up recurrent points of rest. It thus helps the poet set up a basic rhythm, as different from disjointed chatter as purposeful walking is from scurrying hither and yon. We can see this measuring-off effect of rhyme well in song lyrics like the following.

AMERICAN FOLK SONG   (Anonymous)

Black Is the Color   traditional

Black, black, black is the color of my true love's hair.	a
His lips are something wond'rous fair,	a
The purest eyes and the bravest hands,	b
I love the ground whereon he stands.	b
Black, black, black is the color of my true love's hair.	a

5

I love my love and well he knows	c
I love the ground whereon he goes.	c
And if my love no more I see,	d
My life would quickly fade away.	d
Black, black, black is the color of my true love's hair.	a 10

Lines like "I love the ground whereon he stands," marked off by the rhyme word *stands,* stand out from the stream of audio input that reaches our ears and linger in the memory. At the same time, rhyme has a bonding effect, giving a sense of continuity, of meaningful forward movement. This effect of pulling things together or keeping them headed in the same direction is especially strong with **multiple** rhymes—more than two lines rhyming—as in the following opening lines of a Bob Dylan song:

Darkness at the break of noon	a
Shadows even the silver spoon	a
The hand made blade, the child's balloon	a
Eclipses both the sun and moon	a 5
To understand you know too soon,	a
There is no sense in trying.	b

Bob Dylan, "It's Alright Ma (I'm Only Bleeding)"

Rhymes that are too predictable (*love/dove*) make a poem sound slight and pat. At the opposite extreme, farfetched or forced rhymes can have a humorous effect—sometimes unintentional but often, as in the last two lines of the following excerpt, intentional:

I shall be sweet and crafty, soft and sly;
You will not catch me reading any more:
I shall be called a wife to pattern by;
And some day when you knock and push the door,
Some sane day, not too bright and not too stormy,
I shall be gone, and you may whistle for me.

Edna St. Vincent Millay, "Oh, oh, you will be sorry for that word"

Some poets have relied more strongly on the segmenting effect of rhyme than others. In the eighteenth century, when prevailing fashion encouraged the tidy packaging of ideas, rhyme helped seal off sets of two rhyming lines in self-contained **closed couplets.** In the following eighteenth-century poem, rhyme helps the poet frame snapshots of city sights in two neatly boxed lines. Most of the couplets give us a capsule portrait of one of the city people—from the apprentice cleaning up the employer's premises to the prison "turnkey" letting out his jailbirds at night for apparently most irregular purposes.

JONATHAN SWIFT　(1667–1745)

A Description of the Morning　　　　　　　　　1709

Now hardly here and there a hackney-coach	a
Appearing, showed the ruddy morn's approach.	a
Now Betty from her master's bed had flown,	b
And softly stole to discompose her own;	b
The slip-shod 'prentice from his master's door	c
Had pared the dirt and sprinkled round the floor.	c
Now Moll had whirled her mop with dexterous airs,	d
Prepared to scrub the entry and the stairs.	d
The youth with broomy stumps began to trace	e
The kennel-edge, where wheels had worn the place.	e
The small-coal man was heard with cadence deep,	f
Till drowned in shriller notes of chimney-sweep:	f
Duns at his lordship's gate began to meet;	g
And brickdust Moll had screamed through half the street.	g
The turnkey now his flock returning sees,	h
Duly let out a-nights to steal for fees:	h
The watchful bailiffs take their silent stand,	i
And schoolboys lag with satchels in their hands.	i

(line numbers: 5, 10, 15)

THE RECEPTIVE READER

1. Which of the *couplets* strike you as exceptionally neatly packaged?

2. Swift had a sharp *satirical* eye. What are some of the seedier sights you see in this poem? (What are duns, and why is their appearance at the lord's gate one of Swift's satirical touches?) Do the more positive elements in this "description of the morning" counterbalance the negative ones?

Later poets moved away from neatly packaged rhymed couplets. We see fewer boxed-in lines where rhyme routinely signals both the end of a sentence and the end of a line. Instead, we see more of the fluid spillover effect that results when the unfinished sense pulls us beyond what might have been a full stop into the next line. Then the sentence may come to an end halfway through the next line, causing a strong break that works counter to the prevailing pattern of strong breaks *between* rather than *within* lines:

> We are as clouds that veil the midnight moon; ||
> How restlessly they speed, and gleam, and quiver, →
> Streaking the darkness radiantly! || Yet soon →
> Night closes round, and they are lost forever.
> > Percy Bysshe Shelley, "Mutability"

We call the spillover from one line to the next **enjambment,** with the same sentence straddling two lines. We call the strong break that comes *within* a line—contrary to the prevailing pattern—a **caesura** (literally, a "cut" that divides the line). The straddling effect of enjambment partly counteracts the segmenting effect of rhyme. It sometimes helps weave a long series of lines into a kind of verse paragraph.

Like songbirds, rhymes are easier to listen to and enjoy than to classify. Rhyme watchers note many variations from the simple *love/dove, moon/soon* pattern:

❖ Most rhymes are **end rhymes,** marking off a line of verse. **Internal rhymes** multiply the echo effect of rhyme *within* a line:

> All is SEARED with trade; BLEARED, SMEARED with toil.
> Gerard Manley Hopkins, "God's Grandeur"

❖ **Single** (or **masculine**) **rhymes** are the prevailing single-syllable rhymes. Only the opening consonant (or consonant cluster) varies, while the rest of the syllable stays the same: *high/sky, leave/grieve, stone/own.* **Double** (or **feminine**) **rhymes** match two-syllable words (or parts of words) with the first syllable stressed and the second unstressed: *ocean/motion, started/parted, (re)peated/(de)feated.* **Triple rhymes** are three-syllable rhymes, with stress on the first of the three (*beautiful/dutiful*). The following stanza uses all three kinds of rhyme:

Now Donna Inez had, with all her merit,	a	double
A great opinion of her own good qualities;	b	triple
Neglect, indeed, requires a saint to bear it,	a	double
And such, indeed, she was in her moralities;	b	triple
But then she had a devil of a spirit,	a	double
And sometimes mixed up fancies with realities,	b	triple
And let few opportunities escape	c	single
Of getting her liege lord into a scrape.	c	single

Lord Byron, "Don Juan"

❖ In the stanza from "Don Juan," the double rhymes are actually only **half-rhymes,** since the vowel sounds in the first syllables of *merit/bear it/spirit* are only similar, not alike. Byron here uses them tongue-in-cheek. However, for poets who came to consider traditional rhyme too conventional and predictable, such **slant rhymes** were a step toward a greater range of choice. (Words that coincide in spelling but not in sound, like *come* and *home,* are called **sight rhymes.**)

In the following poem, which rhymes are slant rhymes?

EMILY DICKINSON   (1830–1886)

The Soul selects her own Society

about 1862

The Soul selects her own Society—
Then—shuts the Door—

To her divine Majority—
Present no more—

Unmoved—she notes the Chariots—pausing   5
At her low Gate—
Unmoved—an Emperor be kneeling
Upon her Mat—

I've known her—from an ample nation—
Choose One—   10
Then—close the Valves of her attention—
Like Stone—

THE RECEPTIVE READER

1. Which are conventional *full* rhymes? Which are slant rhymes?
2. A literal *paraphrase* of this poem might run like this:

> The human soul chooses friends or soulmates carefully and then shuts
> out any others, allowing no one else to join in. It will not be moved by others
> humbly asking to be admitted. I have known her to select only one from a
> large group and then pay absolutely no attention to anyone else.

How do the metaphors in the poem go beyond this bare-bones paraphrase? What
do they make you see? What do they make you feel? What do they make you think?

❖ When only the internal vowel sounds of final syllables are similar or
alike, the result is **assonance,** again a more distant echo than full rhyme. Assonance is a partial sound echo, as in *break/fade* or *mice/fight.*

❖ Occasionally, a poet goes back to a very different kind of rhyme. **Alliteration** is an echo effect that was once a key feature of poetry and that is still
active in popular speech: "<u>s</u>afe and <u>s</u>ound," "<u>sp</u>ick and <u>sp</u>an," "<u>k</u>it and <u>c</u>aboo-
dle." Alliteration was the precursor and the opposite of end rhyme. Tradition-
ally, three or more stressed syllables in a line *started* with the same sound: "A
<u>w</u>onder on the <u>w</u>ave—<u>w</u>ater turned bone" (from a riddle whose answer is
"ice"). The words that alliterated started either with the same consonant or
else with any vowel. The earliest recorded poems in English used an alliterating four-beat line, approximated in the following modernized passage:

> Leave <u>s</u>orrow a<u>s</u>ide | for it <u>s</u>eems more <u>w</u>ise
> To <u>f</u>ight for a <u>fr</u>iend | than to <u>fr</u>et and <u>m</u>ourn.
> We <u>a</u>ll in the <u>e</u>nd | go <u>o</u>ut of this <u>w</u>orld.
> Let us <u>d</u>o great <u>d</u>eeds | before <u>d</u>eath <u>t</u>akes us.
> That is <u>b</u>est for the <u>br</u>ave | who are <u>b</u>orn to <u>d</u>ie.
>   From *Beowulf*

In later times, partial alliteration, not following a regular pattern and
sometimes stretching over more than one line, has served to enrich the texture
of both rhymed and unrhymed verse. Shakespeare at times uses alliteration to
accentuate the often highly individualized rhythm of his sonnets. Look for the
repetition of initial consonants in the following example.

WILLIAM SHAKESPEARE (1564–1616)

Sonnet 30

before 1598

When to the sessions of sweet silent thought
I summon up remembrance of things past,
I sigh the lack of many a thing I sought,
And with old woes new wail° my dear time's waste: *newly mourn*
Then can I drown an eye (unused to flow)   5
For precious friends hid in death's dateless° night,   *endless*
And weep afresh love's long since canceled woe,
And moan the expense° of many a vanished sight.   *the loss*
Then can I grieve at grievances foregone,°   *griefs long past*
And heavily from woe to woe tell o'er   10
The sad account of fore-bemoanèd moan,
Which I new pay as if not paid before.
But if the while I think on thee, dear friend,
All losses are restored and sorrows end.

THE RECEPTIVE READER

1. Look at the repetition of the initial *s* in the first three lines. In reading the poem aloud, how much would you make the alliterating syllables stand out?

WHEN to | the SESS | ions of | SWEET SI | lent THOUGHT
I SUMM | on UP | ReMEM | brance of | things PAST,
I SIGH | the LACK | of MAN | y a THING | I SOUGHT.

2. How many other examples of repeated initial consonants can you find? How important are the alliterating words in the poem?

3. Where is the *turning point* in this sonnet? How does the poem lead up to it?

As part of the changing outward shape of poetry during the last century, rhyme became increasingly optional. Today, some poets rely on rhyme; many more don't; and some use it when it suits their purpose. Instead of making every line, or every second line, rhyme, they may use rhyme, if at all, at irregular intervals. The decline of rhyme, together with the appeal of rhythms freer and more variable than traditional meter, made possible the rise of **free verse**—poetry less governed by formal conventions—as the dominant mode of poetry.

EXPLORATIONS ══════════════════════════

Understanding Rhyme

Point out any examples of full rhyme, single and double rhyme, half-rhyme, internal rhyme, assonance, or alliteration.

1. Durable bird pulls interminable worm,
   Coiled in subterranean caverns;
   Feeds on fossils of ferns and monsters.
   Beatrice Janosco, "To a Tidelands Oil Pump"

2. My last defense
   Is the present tense.

   It little hurts me to know
   I shall not go

   Cathedral-hunting in Spain
   Nor cherrying in Michigan or Maine.
   Gwendolyn Brooks, "Old Mary"

3. Last night I saw the savage world
   And heard the blood beat up the stair;
   The fox's bark, the owl's shrewd pounce,
   The crying creatures—all were there,
   And men in bed with love and fear.
   Elizabeth Jennings, "Song for a Birth or a Death"

4. I bring fresh showers for the thirsting flowers,
   From the seas and the streams;
   I bear light shade for the leaves when laid
   In their noonday dreams.
   From my wings are shaken the dews that waken
   The sweet buds every one,
   When rocked to rest on their mother's breast,
   As she dances about the sun.
   Percy Bysshe Shelley, "The Cloud"

RHYTHM AND METER

*Poetry is oral; it is not words, but words performed. . . .
the "real" poem is not the scratches on the paper, but the
sounds those scratches stand for.*

JUDSON JEROME

*In a poem, the words charm the ear as much as what is
said charms the mind.*

WILLIAM J. MARTZ

*The line will have the more charm for not being
mechanically straight. We enjoy the straight crookedness of
a good walking stick.*

ROBERT FROST

Meter regularizes the natural rhythms of speech. Poetry is rhythmic, like breathing, walking, dancing. When the rhythm of successive lines is regular enough to become predictable, we call it meter. The poet enters into a metrical contract with the reader, setting up an underlying recurring beat over which the actual poem plays variations. The meter is the steadying beat of the metronome over which longer and shorter notes dance out the actual music of the verse. The metrical pattern creates expectations that please us when they are satisfied and that keep us from being lulled to sleep when they are denied.

Meter regularizes the natural ups and downs that make live language different from the drone of computerized speech. In natural speech, **stress,** or accent, makes us raise our voices slightly and makes us seem to linger briefly over the accented syllable or word. Stress makes one syllable stand out from the others in words like reMAIN and dePART; or LIsten and SUMmon; or PEDigree and destiNAtion. In a sentence as a whole, stressed words (or stressed parts of words) stand out in phrases like "in the WOODS," "under the SUN," or "have to aGREE." Meter results when we lay words and phrases end to end in such a way that the stressed syllables set up a regular beat, as in the opening lines of the Beatles song:

> PICture yourSELF on a BOAT in a RIVer,
> With TANgerine TREES and MARmalade SKIES,
> SOMEbody CALLS you, you ANswer quite SLOWly,
> A GIRL with kaLEIdoscope EYES.
>> "Lucy in the Skies with Diamonds"

Meter is rhythm regular enough to be measured, or scanned. **Scansion** charts the underlying beat and its variations, the way a cardiogram charts the heartbeat and any irregularities. In the actual poem, of course, meter is not noted or transcribed as part of the written text; we need to listen for it with the inner ear. We have to sense it as the eye moves over successive lines. To make meter visible, we can use a special notation for stressed and unstressed syllables: a sharp accent (´) for strong stress; a flat accent (`) for weaker stress; no mark (or often a small half-circle resting on its curved side) for an unstressed syllable.

Read the following short poem first with exaggerated emphasis on the underlying beat ("The WAY a CROW / Shook DOWN on ME"). Then try to read it with enough variation in the *degree* of stress to bring your reading closer to the natural rhythms of speech. Note weaker or secondary stress alternating with strong stress in the first two lines.

R O B E R T   F R O S T   (1874–1963)

Dust of Snow

1923

The wày a crów
Shook dówn on mè
The dúst of snów
From a hémlock trée

Has gíven my héart
A chánge of móod
And sáved some párt
Of a dáy I had rúed.°   5

                                            viewed with regret

     The basic unit of our metrical currency is the **foot**—one stressed syllable
with one or more unstressed ones. Several feet together make up a line of
verse. The Frost poem uses an unusually short line with only two feet: "The
dúst | of snów." The traditional line of verse most commonly used is a four-
beat or five-beat line; in other words, it is made up of four or five feet:

> Wórds are | like léaves; | and whére | they móst | abóund,
> Much frúit | of sénse | benéath | is ráre | ly fóund.
>   Alexander Pope, "Essay on Criticism"

     ✧ The most common meter of English poetry has for centuries been
iambic—a basic "one-TWO | one-TWO | one-TWO" rhythm akin to the rhythm
of walking. The iamb is a foot made up of two syllables, with the stressed one
last: DeTROIT—DeTROIT—DeTROIT—DeTROIT. (The Greek name originally
labeled a lame-footed person, whose gimpy gait made one foot come down
harder than the other.) The following lines set up a prevailing iambic beat.
Notice that words spill over from one foot to the next, preventing the meter
from cutting the lines mechanically like slices of cheese:

> I képt | my án | swers smáll | and képt | them néar;
> Big qués | tions brúised | my mínd | but stíll | I lét
> Small án | swers bé | a búl | wark tò | my féar.
>   Elizabeth Jennings, "Answers"

     ✧ The first line in the Pope couplet shows a common reversal (or **in-
version**): "WORDS are | like leaves. . . . " The stress has shifted to the first
syllable; the result is a **trochaic** foot, or trochee, on the "BOSton—BOSton—
BOSton" model. A line of trochaic feet changes the metrical pattern from "clip-
CLOP | clip-CLOP | clip-CLOP" to "CLIP-clop | CLIP-clop | CLIP-clop." Poems
with an underlying trochaic beat throughout are rare. The most common assignment of the trochaic foot is to bring variation into a prevailing iambic pattern. A trochaic foot, starting out strong, can serve as an attention getter. (Is it
only an accident that in Pope's couplet the most important word—namely,
Words—is pulled to the front of the first line by trochaic inversion?)
     Here is an example of a predominantly trochaic poem. The seventh and
eighth lines fall back on the more common iambic pattern. (In reading this
poem aloud, can you make the listener aware of the trochaic pattern—without
making it sound mechanical?)

PERCY BYSSHE SHELLEY   (1792–1822)

To ——— 1824

Músic, I whèn soft I vóices I díe,	trochaic
Víbrates I ìn the I mémo I r`y.	trochaic
Odors, I whèn sweet I víolets I sícken,	trochaic
Líve with I ín the I sénse they I quícken.	trochaic
Róse leaves, I whèn the I róse is I déad,	trochaic
Are héaped I for the I belóv I ed's béd.	iambic
And só I thy thóughts, I when thóu I are góne,	iambic
Lóve it I sélf shall I slúmber I ón.	trochaic

❖ A third kind of foot also serves mainly as a bit player introducing variation into an iambic line. The **anapest** doubles up two unstressed syllables to lead up to the third and stressed syllable, on the "New ROCHELLE—New ROCHELLE—New ROCHELLE" model. The added unstressed syllable can have a "hurry UP I hurry UP I hurry UP" effect. A predominantly anapestic line would look like this:

> *But his* wíngs I *will not* rést I *and his* féet I *will not* stáy I for us.
>   Algernon Charles Swinburne, "At Parting"

More common is anapestic variation in an otherwise iambic line:

> The wóods I *are prep*ár I *ing to* wáit I out wínter.
> Gusts blów I *with an* éarn I *est of* áll I there ís I *to be* dóne
>   Charles Tomlinson, "The View"

❖ A fourth kind of foot, reversing the pattern of the anapest, was familiar to readers of classical Greek but is nearly extinct in English. The **dactyl** doubles up two unstressed syllables after a stressed one, on the "BALtimore—BALtimore—BALtimore" model. A hundred years ago, there was a large popular audience for dactylic verse like the following. Listen for the doubling up of the unstressed syllables in Longfellow's six-beat line:

> Thís *is the* I fórest prim I éval; *but* I whére *are the* I héarts *that be* I néath it,
> Léaped *like the* I róe, *when he* I héars *in the* I wóod*land the* I vóice *of the* I
>   húntsman?
>   Henry Wadsworth Longfellow, "Evangeline"

In discussions of meter, one further term labels a variation that can strongly emphasize part of a line. The **spondee** is *all* emphasis—it juxtaposes *two* stressed syllables, slowing down the reader and calling special attention. (This is the way many people pronounce HONG KONG.) A spondee often follows or comes before a set of two *un*stressed syllables, so that the total number of beats in a line need not change. The following are the opening lines of a sonnet John Milton wrote in 1655 about his blindness. The spondee in the second line propels us into the world of darkness in which he already lived when he dictated his most ambitious poems:

When I | consíd | er hòw | my líght | is spént
Ere hálf | my dáys | *in this* | DARK WORLD | and wíde . . .

Even in verse that is alive with variations and pauses, exceptionally regular lines are likely to help establish or maintain the basic underlying beat. Meter is the combined product of the chosen kind of foot multiplied by the *number* of feet per line. To label different kinds of meter, we identify the kind of foot (iambic or trochaic, for instance) and then show the number of feet (for instance, pentameter—a five-beat line). Meters with four or five feet to the line are by far the most common.

✧   Three-beat or four-beat lines make up many songs and songlike poems. As a trilogy is a set of three books (or plays), so **trimeter** is meter with three stressed syllables to the line. **Tetrameter** is meter with four stressed syllables to the line. In folk song and ballad, tetrameter and trimeter often alternate in a four-line stanza:

They líghted dówn to táke a drínk	tetrameter
Of the spríng that rán so cléar,	trimeter
And dówn the spríng ran his góod heart's blóod,	tetrameter
And sóre she begán to féar.	trimeter
"Hold úp, hold úp, Lord Wílliam," she sáys,	tetrameter
"For I féar that yòu are sláin."	trimeter
"Tis nóthing but the shádow of my scárlet clóak,	tetrameter
That shínes in the wáter so pláin."	trimeter

(Anonymous) "The Douglas Tragedy"

✧   The five-beat line is by far the most common in English poetry, whether rhymed as in the sonnet, or unrhymed as in the **blank verse** of Shakespeare's plays. As the pentagon is a building with five sides, so **pentameter** is a meter with five stressed syllables to the line. A five-foot line using predominantly iambic feet is in iambic pentameter. The iambic pentameter line often sounds natural and unforced; it seems to stay especially close to the natural speech patterns of English. ("By dáy the bát is cóusin tò the móuse. / He líkes the áttic òf an áging hóuse"—Theodore Roethke.)

✧   A six-beat line, or **hexameter,** was the line of Homer's epics. Later, English poets who knew Greek sometimes slowed down their verse by following the usual pentameter lines with a hexameter line "thát, like a wóunded snáke, drágs its slow léngth alóng" (Alexander Pope). In the following lines, as often with hexameter, a slight break, marked here by a slash, divides the long lines into half-lines. (A noticeable break *within* a line is called a **caesura**.) How would you read these lines?

I would that we were, my beloved, / white birds on the foam of the sea!
We tire of the flame of the meteor, / before it can fade and flee;

And the flame of the blue star of twilight, / hung low on the rim of the sky,
Has awaked in our hearts, my beloved, / a sadness that may not die.
        William Butler Yeats, "The White Birds"

When poetry started to break loose from traditional meter, poets like Walt Whitman for a time wrote poems with irregular length of line and with a harder-to-chart but nevertheless strongly felt rhythm. In most of the free-flowing, metrically irregular **free verse** of the twentieth century, the rhythmic beat has been less pronounced—more understated and "cool." Commenting on long-prevailing critical trends, one recent observer said, "The cooler the voice, the warmer the reception" (Alicia Ostriker).

The following poem is in its own way insistent and cumulative, but its beat does not become chanting. (The opening lines allude to the beginning of a sonnet by William Wordsworth: "The world is too much with us.")

DENISE LEVERTOV   (born 1923)

O Taste and See   1962

The world is
not with us enough.
O taste and see

the subway Bible poster said,
meaning The Lord, meaning   5
if anything all that lives
to the imagination's tongue,

grief, mercy, language,
tangerine, weather, to
breathe them, bite,   10
savor, chew, swallow, transform

into our flesh our
deaths, crossing the street, plum, quince,
living in the orchard and being
                                                                    15
hungry, and plucking
the fruit.

THE RECEPTIVE READER

1. How noticeable should the *line breaks* be when the poem is read aloud?
2. This poem owes its insistent rhythm in part to its repeated use of a *series*—several items of the same kind, separated by commas and juxtaposed in a sequence that allows us to dwell briefly on each. Which series can you identify? Which string together items that are clearly related? Which contain items that seem oddly matched?
3. How is what the speaker in the poem says about the imagination analogous to what the Bible poster said about God?
4. How does the poem as a whole lead up to the last few lines?

EXPLORATIONS

Understanding Meter

What is the dominant meter in each of the following passages as a whole or in individual lines? What variations are there? Which are lines of free verse, difficult or impossible to scan along traditional lines?

1. Double, double, toil and trouble;
   Fire burn and caldron bubble.
   > Shakespeare, *Macbeth*

2. My wife and I lived all alone,
   contention was our only bone.
   I fought with her, she fought with me,
   and things went on right merrily.
   > Robert Creeley, "Ballad of the Despairing Husband"

3. It was many and many a year ago,
   In a kingdom by the sea,
   That a maiden there lived whom you may know
   By the name of Annabel Lee.
   > Edgar Allan Poe, "Annabel Lee"

4. But yesterday the word of Caesar might
   Have stood against the world. Now lies he here,
   And none so poor to do him reverence.
   > Shakespeare, *Julius Caesar*

5. Poplars are standing there still as death.
   > Arna Bontemps, "Southern Mansion"

6. last week
   my mother died/
   & the most often asked question
   at the funeral
   was not of her death
   or of her life before death
   > but
   why was i present
   with/out
   a
   tie on.
   > Don L. Lee, "Last Week"

THE CREATIVE DIMENSION

Eighteenth-century writers delighted in using the *closed couplet* (two self-contained rhymed lines, usually in iambic pentameter) to sum up a striking thought in pointed, quotable form. You are likely to appreciate the polish and sparkle of these couplets more if you have tried your hand at a few of them. See how close you can come to the form and spirit of the original couplets.

ORIGINAL: Good nature and good sense must ever join;
To err is human; to forgive, divine.
Alexander Pope, "Essay on Criticism"

SAMPLE IMITATION: Use witty sayings once, and then no more—
First time, it's wit; the second time, a bore.

TRADITIONAL STANZA FORM

Scorn not the sonnet: Critic, you have frowned
Mindless of its just honors; with this key
Shakespeare unlocked his heart.
WILLIAM WORDSWORTH

Much traditional poetry is laid out in **stanzas.** It is fashioned into sets of lines similar in shape. Traditional stanzas may repeat the same rhyme scheme, as if programed to make lines rhyme according to the same formula. They may show the same alternation of longer and shorter lines, making lines expand or contract in the same sequence. As each stanza leads us through the familiar established pattern, we experience the pleasure of recognition.

Familiar stanza form harks back to a time when the history of song and poem was still one. We expect a songlike poem to have stanzas the way we expect a song to have successive verses, all sung to the same melody. Some of the golden moments in Shakespeare's comedies come when the jester and assorted revelers take time out to sing haunting, bittersweet songs of innocent young love, simple country life, or cruel death. Look at the rhyme scheme that is shared by both stanzas in each of the following songs. Look at how the final lines of the stanza come back in the second song.

WILLIAM SHAKESPEARE   (1564–1616)

O Mistress Mine   1602

O mistress mine, where are you roaming?	a
O, stay and hear; your true love's coming	a
That can sing both high and low.	b
Trip no further, pretty sweeting,	c
Journeys end in lovers meeting,	c
Every wise man's son doth know.	b

5

What is love? 'Tis not hereafter;
Present mirth hath present laughter;
What's to come is still unsure.
In delay there lies no plenty;
Then come kiss me, sweet and twenty,
Youth's a stuff will not endure.

10

Under the Greenwood Tree   1599

Under the greenwood tree	a
Who loves to lie with me,	a
And turn his merry note	b
Unto the sweet bird's throat,	b
Come hither, come hither, come hither!	c 5
Here shall he see	a
No enemy	a
But winter and rough weather.	c

Who doth ambition shun,
And loves to live i' the sun,   10
Seeking the food he eats,
And pleased with what he gets,
Come hither, come hither, come hither!
Here shall he see
No enemy   15
But winter and rough weather.
                    From *As You Like It*

The interlaced, intertwining rhyme schemes (such as aabccb) help knit each stanza together. They help give it a distinctive shape, or configuration, that imprints itself easily on our memory. (A configuration is a pattern with a distinctive outline—like the New York City skyline—that human minds, and computers, can easily pick up and recognize.) In the second song, the configuration of the stanza is especially distinctive: the line length contracts from a three-beat line to a two-beat line (in the sixth and seventh lines of each stanza) and then expands again in the last line. The second poem has a **refrain**—a line, or set of lines, that comes back in each stanza—usually at the end. A refrain sounds a keynote that comes back like the tolling of a bell.

CROSS-REFERENCES—For Discussion or Writing

Do you know any current popular songs that are in form and content in some way similar to these Shakespearean songs? Do you know any that are strikingly different? Compare or contrast the lyrics of one or several current favorites with these Shakespeare lyrics.

Refrains that come back and drive home a prevailing mood or idea are also a feature of another kind of songlike poem—the **popular ballads.** These anonymous folk ballads (many of them going back to the Middle Ages) were originally sung as the record of a notable exploit or calamity, often presented in stark outline, hitting home without frivolous embellishment.

Some of the best-known early ballads repeat a question-and-answer format in a pattern of **cumulative** repetition. The questioner persists in asking questions until the horrible truth is revealed. "Why does your brand (sword) so drip with blood?" asks the mother of her son in one of the best-known Scottish ballads. "I have killed my hawk," answers the son at the end of the first stanza; and then, "I have killed my steed" at the end of the second stanza; and finally, "I have killed my father" at the end of the third.

Poets of later ages have often re-created the ballad style. The following **literary ballad** picks up the question-and-answer style of many earlier ballads. Here, the question-and-answer pattern is repeated three times. Once we become attuned to the pattern, we wait for the next question—and the next answer, as the poem builds up to its grim conclusion. (Make sure you read this poem—or hear the poem read—aloud.)

MELVIN WALKER LA FOLLETTE   (born 1930)
The Ballad of Red Fox   1959

Yellow sun yellow
Sun yellow sun,
When, oh, when
Will red fox run?

When the hollow horn shall sound,   5
When the hunter lifts his gun
And liberates the wicked hound,
Then, oh, then shall red fox run.

Yellow sun yellow
Sun yellow sun,   10
Where, oh, where
Will red fox run?

Through meadows hot as sulphur,
Through forests cool as clay,
Through hedges crisp as morning   15
And grasses limp as day.

Yellow sky yellow
Sky yellow sky,
How, oh, how
Will red fox die?   20

With a bullet in his belly,
A dagger in his eye,
And blood upon his red red brush
Shall red fox die.

THE RECEPTIVE READER

1. The questions in this poem provide a variable rather than completely identical *refrain*. How does it change?

2. To what extent do the answers in this poem follow the *rhyme* scheme of the traditional ballad stanza—a four-liner (or quatrain) rhyming abcb? A rhyming pattern can place special emphasis on key words in a poem. What rhymes make key words echo throughout this poem?

3. What do you think accounts for the continuing appeal of the old ballad style?

THE PERSONAL RESPONSE

In the battle between the hunter and the hunted, on which side is the poet? On which side are you?

Many of the more elaborately crafted traditional stanza patterns go back to the love poetry of the Middle Ages and the Renaissance. The word *artificial* then did not yet mean unnatural or insincere. Rather, it meant artfully done, finely crafted, pleasing to the eye and ear. An example of such an artfully crafted form is the **villanelle** (originally a song in a country setting). Intermeshing rhymes link the three-line stanzas (or **tercets**) until the poem slows down and comes to a stop in the final four-line stanza (or **quatrain**). Rhymes and whole lines keep coming back. What is the pattern?

E L I Z A B E T H   B I S H O P   (1911–1979)

One Art   1976

The art of losing isn't hard to master;
so many things seem filled with the intent
to be lost that their loss is no disaster.

Lose something every day. Accept the fluster
of lost door keys, the hour badly spent.   5
The art of losing isn't hard to master.

Then practice losing farther, losing faster:
places, and names, and where it was you meant
to travel. None of these will bring disaster.

I lost my mother's watch. And look! my last, or   10
next-to-last, of three loved houses went.
The art of losing isn't hard to master.

I lost two cities, lovely ones. And, vaster,
some realms I owned, two rivers, a continent.
I miss them, but it wasn't a disaster.   15

—Even losing you (the joking voice, a gesture
I love) I shan't have lied. It's evident
the art of losing's not too hard to master
though it may look like (Write it!) like disaster.

THE RECEPTIVE READER

1. What is the *rhyme* scheme of this typical villanelle? Where does the poet stretch it by slant rhyme or by a playful forced rhyme?

2. The villanelle uses a double *refrain*. How does it work?

3. The highly-patterned villanelle, like other highly patterned traditional forms, can be half playful and half serious. What are the serious and the playful parts in this poem?

The best known and most widely practiced of traditional stanza forms is the **sonnet.** The sonnet is a single, self-contained stanza of fourteen lines (although the best known of the early sonneteers repeated the same form again and again in sonnet sequences of over a hundred poems). During the height of the sonneteering vogue in the sixteenth century, sonnets were poems of unrequited love, with the mournful, humble lover forever replaying his "plaint" to the conventionally cruel, disdainful lady-on-the-pedestal. Soon, however, poets extended the form to other personal, political, and religious subjects.

Traditionally, the sonnet works with a five-beat iambic line; it therefore often has ten or eleven syllables to the line. Sonneteers following the model of the Italian poet Petrarch rhyme the first eight lines (the **octave**) in an interlaced pattern: abbaabba. The remaining six lines (the **sestet**) may rhyme cdcdee or cdecde. Sonneteers imitating the Shakespearean sonnet group the fourteen lines somewhat differently: They generally have alternating rhymes in the first three **quatrains,** or groups of four (abab/cdcd/efef), followed by a concluding couplet (gg).

In a Petrarchan sonnet, a turning in the flow of thought may start at or near the break after the first eight lines. The remaining six lines then represent a kind of countertide. (Robert Frost said that "a true sonnet goes eight lines and then takes a turn for better or worse.") Where is the turn in the flow of ideas in John Milton's poem on his blindness?

JOHN MILTON   (1608–1674)
When I consider how my light is spent   1655

When I consider how my light is spent	
Ere° half my days, in this dark world and wide,	*before*
And that one talent which is death to hide	
Lodged with me useless, though my soul more bent	
To serve therewith my Maker, and present	5
My true account, lest he° returning chide;	*so he won't*
"Doth God exact day-labor, light denied?"°	*with sight denied*
I fondly° ask; but Patience to prevent	*foolishly*
That murmur, soon replies, "God doth not need	
Either man's work or his own gifts; who best	10
Bear his mild yoke, they serve him best. His state	
Is kingly. Thousands at his bidding speed	
And post° o'er land and ocean without rest:	*carry messages*
They also serve who only stand and wait."	

Milton's sonnet illustrates the tremendous variety of rhythm and effect possible with traditional form when sentences are not neatly packaged into lines or couplets. In Milton's sonnet, the magnificent long first sentence runs through all but the last three lines of the fourteen-line poem. It elaborates on a train of thought whose underlying pattern is "When I think about my blindness . . . I ask a foolish rebellious question (does God expect a blind poet to continue his work?) . . . but Patience replies that God does not depend on any one person's labor or gifts." This long elaborate sentence puts the poet's whole situation—both the question it raises and the answer the poet has reached—before us. But after the first period, which comes almost at the end of the eleventh line, we stop short at a terse sentence that goes to the opposite extreme. It has four words. It makes us take in and ponder the essence of the lesson the poet has learned: the majesty of God. "His state / Is kingly." His glory does not depend on our praise or service, however dedicated.

THE RECEPTIVE READER

1. What *rhyme* words fill in the typical Petrarchan rhyme scheme?
2. What lines come closest to perfect *iambic pentameter?* Where do you see clear examples of trochaic inversion at the beginning of a line?
3. What are some striking examples of *enjambment,* with the sense spilling over into the next line to give the poem a characteristically Miltonic sense of flow—of long, rich sentences moving forward regardless of line boundaries? (Where does a subsequent *caesura,* or cut within a line, help to set up a syncopating counterrhythm?)
4. How does the poem as a whole lead up to its famous last line?

EXPLORATIONS

An Unconventional Sonnet

Conventionally, sonnets looked at love from the perspective of the lover yearning for a love that often seemed unattainable. How does the author of the following sonnet depart from this convention?

EDNA ST. VINCENT MILLAY (1892–1950)

I, being born a woman and distressed   1923

I, being born a woman and distressed
By all the needs and notions of my kind,
Am urged by your propinquity° to find   *nearness*
Your person fair, and feel a certain zest
To bear your body's weight upon my breast: 5
So subtle is the fume of life designed
To clarify the pulse and cloud the mind,
And leave me once again undone, possessed.
Think not for this, however, the poor treason
Of my stout blood against my staggering brain,   10
I shall remember you with love, or season
My scorn with pity,—let me make it plain:
I find this frenzy insufficient reason
For conversation when we meet again.

THE RECEPTIVE READER

1. What *formal* features of the traditional sonnet does this poem illustrate? (What is the rhyme scheme?)

2. What basic *polarities* help organize this poem? Where in this sonnet is there a turning or countertide, and what makes it central to the poem as a whole?

THE PERSONAL RESPONSE

Millay has been called "very much a revolutionary in all her sympathies, and a whole-hearted Feminist" (Floyd Dell). In most of the sonnet tradition, the woman was the silent audience and the silent partner in the love relationship. How do you react as the woman in this poem speaks up and talks back?

CROSS-REFERENCES—For Discussion or Writing

Compare and contrast the perspective on love in this sonnet with the perspective on love in sonnets in the Petrarchan tradition—sonnets by Wyatt (p. 103), Petrarch (p. 260), and Shakespeare (p. 177).

TRADITIONAL   FORM   AND   OPEN   FORM

Of all the possible distinctions between verse and prose, the
simplest, and most objective, is that verse uses the line as a
unit. Prose goes right on. . . . Verse turns.

JUDSON JEROME

As rhyme, meter, and stanza become optional, a more basic definition of poetic form remains: Poetry is lines of verse, laid out in a pattern on a page. The individual lines slow down the hasty reader; they encourage full attention to the individual image and to each phase in the flow of thought. This laying out of the text is a signal that even modern **open form** is not formless. It is merely less obvious, harder to chart and to schematize. However, like traditional form, open form (or free verse) makes for a richer, denser texture than that of ordinary language. It still uses patterns of repetition, the echoing of sounds and of words, the playing off of opposites, the interplay of sound and meaning.

For a time, champions of modernism did battle with defenders of tradition, who scorned poets playing "tennis with the net down" (Robert Frost). However, widely admired twentieth-century poets have written poems in either vein—some poems with a stricter traditional pattern, and some in a more open modern style. Study the following two examples, both by poets who move easily between traditional formal discipline and modern creative freedom. What can traditional form do that might be hard to achieve in a more open modern format? What is possible with open form that traditional form might make it hard for the poet to do?

ANNE SEXTON (1928–1974)

Her Kind
1960

I have gone out, a possessed witch,
haunting the black air, braver at night;
dreaming evil, I have done my hitch
over the plain houses, light by light:
lonely thing, twelve-fingered, out of mind.   5
A woman like that is not a woman, quite.
I have been her kind.

I have found the warm caves in the woods,
filled them with skillets, carvings, shelves,
closets, silks, innumerable goods;   10
fixed the suppers for the worms and the elves:
whining, rearranging the disaligned.
A woman like that is misunderstood.
I have been her kind.

I have ridden in your cart, driver,   15
waved my nude arms at villages going by,
learning the last bright routes, survivor
where your flames still bite my thigh
and my ribs crack where your wheels wind.
A woman like that is not ashamed to die.   20
I have been her kind.

How do the formal features of this poem serve the poet's purpose? The poem is intense, concentrated, deliberate. The patterns of repetition and the refrains give it a ritualistic quality. It is like an incantation—the poem, as it were, puts a spell (or a hex, if you wish) on the reader. The poem is elaborately crafted, using major features of traditional form:

◇ The poem is divided into three stanzas of identical shape, each following the same rhyme scheme, each laid out according to the same plan. This poet deals with a disturbing subject—which she has brought fully under *control*. The poem has a finished, definitive quality—as if the poet had earlier worked through her horror and anguish and is now ready to give us, for the time being, her final word on the subject.

◇ Each stanza, clearly marked off in the traditional fashion, frames a striking, haunting picture. The stanza brings that picture into sharp *focus*, allowing us to ponder it as the stanza is brought to a close and the picture becomes etched into memory. Within each stanza, the interlacing rhyme scheme knits the material together, as if all distracting detail had been left out.

◇ The threefold repetition of the elaborately crafted stanza form makes us expect that each of the three will indeed be part of the same story. This expectation is strongly reinforced by **parallelism,** that is, closely similar sentence structure or wording. The opening lines are parallel in sentence pattern: "I have gone . . ."; "I have found . . ."; "I have ridden. . . ." So is the last-but-one line in each stanza ("A woman like that is . . ."). The poem has the impact that comes from exceptional *unity* and concentration. We sense that the perspective will remain the same: The speaker will continue to look at the witch not from the point of view of her persecutors but of someone who identifies with the outcast: "I have been her kind."

✧ The last line, affirming the speaker's human solidarity with "her kind," returns at the end of each stanza and thus serves as a refrain. But this refrain does more than repeat. Each time it comes back, it gains in force, until the *cumulative* pattern of the poem reaches its climax in martyrdom and final defiance.

THE RECEPTIVE READER

1. How does the *rhyme scheme* bond the two weighty final lines of each stanza to the earlier lines? How does the rhyme scheme link stanza to stanza?

2. What *details* give this poem the intensity of a nightmare?

3. Women accused of being witches were for centuries the target of persecution and lynch justice. How does the poet want you to think of the women behind the caricatures and stereotypes?

THE CREATIVE DIMENSION

Have you ever identified with the outcast, the outsider, the underdog? Write a poem or passage in which the refrain might be "I have been her (his) kind."

In the following poem, what gives shape to the poem as a whole—in the absence of such traditional features as rhyme, meter, and stanza?

SHARON OLDS   (born 1942)

I Go Back to May 1937   1987

I see them standing at the formal gates of their colleges,
I see my father strolling out
under the ochre sandstone arch, the
red tiles glinting like bent
plates of blood behind his head, I   5
see my mother with a few light books at her hip
standing at the pillar made of tiny bricks with the
wrought-iron gate still open behind her, its
sword-tips black in the May air,
they are about to graduate, they are about to get married,   10
they are kids, they are dumb, all they know is they are
innocent, they would never hurt anybody.
I want to go up to them and say Stop,
don't do it—she's the wrong woman,
he's the wrong man, you are going to do things   15
you cannot imagine you would ever do,

you are going to do bad things to children,
you are going to suffer in ways you never heard of,
you are going to want to die. I want to go
up to them there in the late May sunlight and say it,   20
her hungry pretty blank face turning to me,
her pitiful beautiful untouched body,
his arrogant handsome blind face turning to me,
his pitiful beautiful untouched body,
but I don't do it. I   25
want to live. I take them up like the male and female
paper dolls and bang them together
at the hips like chips of flint as if to
strike sparks from them. I say
Do what you are going to do, and I will tell about it.   30

What makes this second poem an example of open form?

Some differences meet the eye (and ear): There is no rhyme (although there are some echo effects like "at the *hips* like *chips*"). The lines are of irregular, unpredictable length, and the line breaks often come at strange points in the middle of a phrase (the / red tiles), making it hard for the poet to rhyme lines even if she had wanted to. There is no steady underlying drumbeat of meter. No stanzas segment the poem, pleasing us with the recurrence of a characteristic pattern. These differences in the formal features of the two poems prepare us for differences in the way they affect the reader:

⬦ Compared with the Sexton poem, this poem seems more *open-ended*. We have the sense that the story of the speaker's parents, and her attempt to come to terms with it, are still in progress. As the flashback to a time before the speaker's birth continues, we can still share in the impulse to tell her parents No! but then resolve to let human nature take its course. Key phrases like "I want to live" are not pulled out, set off, and dramatized. Instead, they appear as natural stages in the flow of thought.

⬦ **Parallelism** in this poem sets up open frames allowing the poet *free scope* to multiply the striking lifelike details that well up from her active imagination. Open-ended parallel structure ("I see . . ."; "I see . . ."; "I see . . .") allows the poet to build up the details that make the imagined campus scene come hauntingly to life, from the sandstone arch and glinting red tiles to the "few light books" at the mother's hip and the black "sword-tips" of the wrought-iron gate. The same kind of open frame allows her to keep sounding the note of urgent warning that builds up in intensity in the middle of the poem ("you are going to . . ."; "you are going to . . ."; "you are going to . . .").

THE RECEPTIVE READER

1. What *line breaks* come at an unexpected place in a sentence or in the middle of a phrase, partly counteracting the pause traditionally signaled by the end of a line?

2. How does *parallel structure* serve for emphasis in tne lines, making us look at the faces and bodies of the parents? How do these lines sum up the mixed emotions of the speaker?

3. How does this poem achieve *closure*, leaving us with a satisfying sense of completeness?

THE PERSONAL RESPONSE

In recent years, the concern of (grown) children with the quality of the parenting they received has become a major focus in the media and in popular psychology. How would you sum up the attitude of the speaker in this poem toward her parents? How does it compare with your own attitudes?

JUXTAPOSITIONS

Close and Free Translation

Translators of poetry have to decide how far they will go to reproduce features of form, such as meter and rhyme. It is often very difficult to approximate the origanic blend of form and meaning in the original, so that many translations use a more open form than the original poet did.

The two following translations are different versions of a much-translated poem by a widely translated German poet. The first translation hews close to the regular iambic pentameter and the end rhymes of the original stanzas. (In the original, the first and third lines of each stanza also rhyme.) The second translation aims at getting close to the spirit of the original while abandoning the more traditional formal features of the original. How does the difference in form affect your response to the poem?

RAINER MARIA RILKE   (1875–1926)

The Panther   1927

TRANSLATED BY HANS P. GUTH

Jardin des Plantes, Paris

From pacing past the barriers of his cage
His tired gaze no longer seems to see.
All that exists: a thousand iron bars.
The world beyond the bars has ceased to be.

The supple tread of sinuous steps revolves   5
In circles of benumbing narrowness,
Like power dancing round a pedestal
Where a majestic will stands powerless.

And yet, at times, the veil that blunts his eye
Moves stealthily aside—an image enters,   10
Glides through the silence of his tautened limbs—
And ceases where his being centers.

Many translators of poetry are poets in their own right. They bring to the translator's task a special empathy, a special ability to get into the spirit of a fellow poet. This affinity shows when Robert Bly translates and comments on the same Rilke poem.

The Panther   1927

TRANSLATED BY ROBERT BLY

From seeing and seeing the seeing has become so exhausted
it no longer sees anything anymore.
The world is made of bars, a hundred thousand
bars, and behind the bars, nothing.

The lithe swinging of that rhythmical easy stride   5
that slowly circles down to a single point
is like a dance of energy around a hub,
in which a great will stands stunned and numbed.

At times the curtains of the eye lift
without a sound—then a shape enters,   10
slips through the tightened silence of the shoulders,
reaches the heart and dies.

The poet translator said about this much-reprinted poem:

Rilke . . . watched a panther at the zoo, and his German lines, in rhythm and sound, embody movingly the repetitive, desperate walk of the panther. By the end of the poem he is somehow inside the panther's body. Each time the panther glimpses a shape, say a dog or a child, the image goes to the body's center, the place from which a leap begins; but no leap can take place. A leap can't take place, and so the image "reaches the heart, and dies."

THE RECEPTIVE READER

Where do the two translations seem very close, reflecting the common original? Where do they diverge and with what effect? What difference does the difference in form make to your response? What do you think is the key to the fascination this poem has had for readers and translators around the world?

POEMS FOR FURTHER STUDY

In reading the following poems, pay special attention to the way they use or modify traditional formal features, such as rhyme, meter, and stanza form.

POPULAR BALLAD   (Anonymous)
Lord Randal   traditional

"O where have you been, Lord Randal, my son?
And where have you been, my handsome young man?"
"I have been at the greenwood; mother, make my bed soon,
For I'm wearied with hunting, and fain° would lie down."   *gladly*

"And who met you there, Lord Randal, my son?   5
And who met you there, my handsome young man?"
"O I met with my true-love; mother, make my bed soon,
For I'm wearied with hunting, and fain would lie down."

"And what did she give you, Lord Randal, my son?
And what did she give you, my handsome young man?"   10
"Eels fried in a pan; mother, make my bed soon,
For I'm wearied with hunting, and fain would like down."

"And who got your leavings, Lord Randal, my son?
And what became of them, my handsome young man?"
"My hawks and my hounds; mother, make my bed soon,   15
For I'm wearied with hunting, and fain would lie down."

"And what became of them, Lord Randal, my son?
And what became of them, my handsome young man?"
"They stretched their legs out and died; mother, make my bed soon,
For I'm wearied with hunting, and fain would lie down."   20

"O I fear you are poisoned, Lord Randal, my son!
I fear you are poisoned, my handsome young man!"
"O yes, I am poisoned; mother, make my bed soon,
For I'm sick at heart, and fain would lie down."

"What d' you leave to your mother, Lord Randal, my son?
What d' you leave to your mother, my handsome young man?"   25
"Four and twenty milk kine;° mother, make my bed soon,   *cattle*
For I'm sick at heart, and fain would lie down."

"What d' you leave to your sister, Lord Randal, my son?
What d' you leave to your sister, my handsome young man?"   30
"My gold and my silver; mother, make my bed soon,
For I'm sick at heart, and fain would lie down."

"What d' you leave to your brother, Lord Randal, my son?
What d' you leave to your brother, my handsome young man?"
"My houses and my lands; mother, make my bed soon,   35
For I'm sick at heart, and fain would lie down."

"What d' you leave to your true-love, Lord Randal, my son?
What d' you leave to your true-love, my handsome young man?"
"I leave her hell and fire; mother, make my bed soon,
For I'm sick at heart, and fain would lie down."   40

THE RECEPTIVE READER

When does the often-repeated *refrain* first turn ominous? How does this ballad use the pattern of *cumulative repetition* twice? How does the ballad strip the story down to *essentials*? What do you think made this story survive through the centuries?

CHRISTINE DE PISAN   (1363–1430)

Marriage Is a Lovely Thing   before 1400

TRANSLATED BY JOANNA BANKIER

Marriage is a lovely thing
—my own example proves it—
for her whose husband is as kind
as he whom God has found for me.
Since day by day he has sustained me,   5
praised be He who guards his life
and keeps him safe for me,
          and surely my gentle one loves me well.

On the night of our union,
the first time we slept together   10
I could see how kind he was.
Nothing did that could have hurt me
and before the rising sun
had kissed me, oh a hundred times
but never urged against my will,   15
          and surely my gentle one loves me well.

And how sweet the words he spoke;
"Dearest Friend, God led me to you
to serve you courteously and well
as if he wished to raise me up."   20
Thus he mused all through the night
and his manner never faltered
but stayed the same, unwaveringly,
          and surely my gentle one loves me well.

                                                                          25
O Prince, his love can drive me to distraction
when he assures me he's all mine
and of sweetness makes me burst.

THE RECEPTIVE READER

1. Like many other love poems of the Middle Ages, this poem has a *refrain* and a "send-off" (or *envoi*) of three lines. (The modern translator has not attempted to reproduce the rhymes of the original French poem.) What gives the refrain in this poem its special appeal or special force? How does the poem as a whole lead up to the send-off?

2. Christine de Pisan, a native of Italy living in France, was happily married for a few short years. After her husband's death, she became one of the first women in Eu-

rope to support herself by her writing. How is the treatment of love in this poem different from that in other early love lyrics you have read?

WILLIAM WORDSWORTH   (1770–1850)

I Wandered Lonely as a Cloud   1807

I wandered lonely as a cloud
    That floats on high o'er vales and hills,
When all at once I saw a crowd,
    A host,° of golden daffodils;   *massed ranks*
Beside the lake, beneath the trees,   5
Fluttering and dancing in the breeze.

Continuous as the stars that shine
    And twinkle on the milky way,
They stretched in never-ending line
    Along the margin of a bay: 10
Ten thousand saw I at a glance,
Tossing their heads in sprightly dance.

The waves beside them danced; but they
    Outdid the sparkling waves in glee;
A poet could not but be gay,   15
    In such a jocund° company;   *joyful*
I gazed—and gazed—but little thought
What wealth the show to me had brought:

For oft, when on my couch I lie
    In vacant or in pensive° mood,   *thoughtful*   20
They flash upon that inward eye
    Which is the bliss of solitude;
And then my heart with pleasure fills,
And dances with the daffodils.

THE RECEPTIVE READER

How does the poet use rhyme, meter, and stanza form? Does the poet make the
experience reenacted in this poem come to life for you as the reader? Can you follow,
and sympathize with, the train of thought in the last stanza?

CROSS-REFERENCES—For Discussion or Writing

During the years when Wordsworth wrote much of his best-known nature poetry,
his sister Dorothy kept her *Journals,* in which she recorded many of the activities they
shared: their long nature walks, their observation of the rapidly changing moods of nature, their observation of the country people at work in the fields or on the road in
search of work or a place to live. The following is Dorothy Wordsworth's journal account of the same (or same kind of) experience that inspired her brother's poem. What
are the major differences in the way the prose and the poem affect the reader? What
does the poem do that the prose journal does not? What does the journal have that the
poem does not?

The wind seized our breath; the lake was rough. There was a boat by itself floating in the middle of the bay below Water Millock. . . . When we were in the woods beyond Gowbarrow park we saw a few daffodils close to the water-side. We fancied that the lake had floated the seeds ashore and that a little colony had sprung up. But as we went along, there were more and yet more; and at last under the boughs of the trees, we saw that there was a long belt of them along the shore, about the breadth of a country turnpike road. I never saw daffodils so beautiful. They grew among the mossy stones and about them, some rested their heads upon these stones as on a pillow for weariness, and the rest tossed and reeled and danced and seemed as if they verily laughed. The wind blew upon them over the lake; they looked so gay ever glancing ever changing.

THOMAS NASHE (1567–1601)
A Litany in Time of Plague 1592

Adieu, farewell, earth's bliss;
This world uncertain is;
Fond° are life's lustful joys; *foolish*
Death proves them all but toys;
None from his darts can fly; 5
I am sick, I must die.
      Lord, have mercy on us!

Rich men, trust not in wealth,
Gold cannot buy you health:
Physic° himself must fade; *the physician's art* 10
All things to end are made;
The plague full swift goes by.
I am sick, I must die.
      Lord, have mercy on us!

Beauty is but a flower 15
Which wrinkles will devour;
Brightness falls from the air;
Queens have died young and fair;
Dust hath closed Helen's° eye. *Helen of Troy*
I am sick, I must die. 20
      Lord, have mercy on us!

Strength stoops unto the grave,
Worms feed on Hector° brave; *Trojan prince*
Swords may not fight with fate;
Earth still holds ope° her gate; *open* 25
Come, come, the bells do cry.
I am sick, I must die.
      Lord, have mercy on us!

Wit with his wantonness
Tastes death's bitterness; 30
Hell's executioner

Hath no ears for to hear
What vain art can reply.
I am sick, I must die.
        Lord, have mercy on us!   35

Haste, therefore, each degree,°   *rank*
To welcome destiny;
Heaven is our heritage,
Earth but a player's stage;
Mount we° unto the sky;   *let us mount*   40
I am sick, I must die.
        Lord, have mercy on us!

THE RECEPTIVE READER

1. A litany is a chantlike prayer with much *repetition*. What use does this prayer make of outright repetition? What use does it make of parallel structure?

2. What is the *rhyme scheme*? How does rhyme carry over from one stanza to the next? What is the central word to which the carryover rhyme directs attention?

3. What is the underlying *meter* in the first five lines of each stanza? In what lines does it show most clearly? What is the major recurrent variation on this metrical pattern? How does the meter change in the refrain? How does the change in meter affect your reading of the poem?

THE PERSONAL RESPONSE

How remote or how understandable are the sentiments expressed in this poem for you as a modern reader?

THEODORE ROETHKE   (1908–1963)

The Waking   1953

I wake to sleep, and take my waking slow.
I feel my fate in what I cannot fear.
I learn by going where I have to go.

We think by feeling. What is there to know?
I hear my being dance from ear to ear.   5
I wake to sleep, and take my waking slow.

Of those so close beside me, which are you?
God bless the ground! I shall walk softly there,
And learn by going where I have to go.

Light takes the Tree; but who can tell us how?   10
The lowly worm climbs up a winding stair;
I wake to sleep, and take my waking slow.

Great Nature has another thing to do
To you and me; so take the lively air,
And, lovely, learn by going where to go.   15

This shaking keeps me steady. I should know
What falls away is always. And is near.
I wake to sleep, and take my waking slow.
I learn by going where I have to go.

THE RECEPTIVE READER

1. How does this poem illustrate the traditional formal features of the *villanelle*? Where does it modify the traditional rhyme scheme by the use of half-rhymes?

2. What is the meaning of some of the *recurrent phrases* to which the circular pattern of the villanelle keeps returning? How does the poem as a whole lead up to the two concluding lines?

WRITING ABOUT LITERATURE

7. Relating Form to Meaning (First and Second Draft)

The Writing Workshop Much writing about poetry aims at showing the connection between form and meaning. It tries to trace the relationship between technical formal features and what the poem as a whole does for the reader. Writing about form and meaning is an ambitious undertaking. In the first place, you obviously need to be able to recognize traditional formal features. You then need to look at how they work in a poem. You need to study the interplay between what is said and how is it said. Furthermore, you need to recognize how formal features are modified or replaced in much modern poetry.

Remember the following guidelines:

✧ See what use the poem makes of *rhyme*. Does it use traditional full rhymes throughout? part of the time? in strategic places? Is there an alternating rhyme scheme or other pattern that bonds a series of lines? Does the poem make use of half-rhymes or internal rhymes? Does rhyme serve to highlight important words? Does it help to segment the poem neatly into lines, or does the sense of a line frequently spill over into the next line (enjambment)?

✧ Check if the poem sets up a strong underlying beat, or *meter*. (Be sure to read lines aloud.) Does it use the common iambic pentameter line? How regular are the lines? Is there much variation—with what effect? Is variation used for emphasis, or to speed up or slow down a line? If the poem uses free verse, is it strongly rhythmic—and does the rhythm give the lines an eloquent or hypnotic effect? Or is the rhythm of the lines closer to the casual pattern of ordinary speech? Is the poet's treatment of the subject or attitude toward the reader also casual?

✧ Check whether the poem is divided into *stanzas*. Does the poet use a traditional stanza such as the four-line ballad stanza or the fourteen-line sonnet? If the first, does the poem have a songlike quality? Does it keep commentary out, ballad-style? Does it use a refrain—with what effect? If the second, does the poem have the ceremonial, carefully crafted quality of the traditional sonnet?

✧ If the poem uses modern *open form,* check for features that help organize or structure the poem. Look for deliberate repetition for emphasis, parallel sentence structure tying together closely related parts of the poem, the echoing of words or phrases, the playing off of opposites.

The following are key sections from the first draft of a student paper that focuses on form and meaning. The comments are feedback from an instructor; they are designed to guide the writer in revising and strengthening the paper. Study the comments, and then see how the student writer has responded to them in the second draft of the paper.

FIRST DRAFT

New England Discipline

COMMENT: Title too dry or uninformative? Use a title that conveys the spirit of the poem in more dramatic fashion?

In his sonnet "New England," Edwin Arlington Robinson skillfully employs the powers of form and sound to intensify the meaning of the poem. Robinson fittingly uses the most demanding of poetic forms, the Petrarchan or Italian sonnet, to frame his objection to the New England tradition of emphasizing discipline and self-denial at the expense of love and joy. Robinson himself observes the strict discipline of the traditional fourteen lines, subdivided into octet (first eight lines) and sestet (remaining six lines). . . .

COMMENT: Excellent focus on the central concern of the poem and on its overall intention. To introduce your thesis more effectively, replace the somewhat interchangeable first sentence (it could fit many different poems)? Perhaps start with a striking quotation instead?

The first word of the poem appropriately forms an inversion of the iambic rhythm, a trochee: "Here where the wind is always north-north-east," focusing the reader's attention quite forcibly on cold New England. The "always north-north-east" wind, and the children in the next line who "learn to walk on frozen toes," start out the poem on a distinctly chilly note. New England is cold in more ways than one. Here it is so cold that "joy shivers in the corner where she knits." Note that in this line the word *joy* forms a spondee with the following word, *shivers,* adding emphasis. . . .

COMMENT: Good here and later on how formal features emphasize or highlight meaning. Try to explain more—and demonstrate the workings of the technical features a little more graphically?

Lines three to eight introduce a major contrast. They are like a simmering stew of lush, hothouse words that describe the opposite of traditional New England values—"those / Who boil elsewhere with such a lyric yeast / Of love that you will hear them at a feast / Where demons would appeal for some repose, / Still clamoring where the chalice overflows / And crying wildest who have drunk the least." Here all the bars are down—the words rush by and knock down the structure that contained them. The reader is flooded with a rush of passionate warmth and feeling, which the New Englander can only regard with "wonder [that] begets . . . envy." Robinson has used enjambment to create this effect. . . .

> COMMENT: A good paragraph. Set off the group of five lines as a block quotation for easier reading (and for added emphasis). Use partial quotes to avoid awkward use of square brackets?

At the end of line eight, the sonnet takes its traditional turn in direction. The excursion into passion ends. The sestet, or concluding six lines, sums up the poet's rebellion against the traditional New England attitude toward life: "Passion here is a soilure of the wits, / We're told, and Love a cross for them to bear," it begins. . . .

Edwin Arlington Robinson, himself a New Englander with deep roots in the Puritan tradition, has written a memorable poem that utilized traditional form very effectively to deepen its message.

> COMMENT: Your conclusion, like your introduction, seems too perfunctory and interchangeable. Develop the key point about the poet's own New England roots?

SECOND DRAFT

Shivering Joy, Comfortable Conscience

"Joy shivers in the corner where she knits / And Conscience always has the rocking-chair" (11–12). With such vivid images, Edwin Arlington Robinson in his sonnet "New England" explores the New England values of hard work, moral uprightness, and distrust of emotion. Robinson skillfully employs form and sound to enhance the meaning of the poem.

Fittingly, he uses the most highly disciplined and demanding of poetic forms, the sonnet, to explore and question the New England tradition of rigorous discipline and self-denial at the expense of such human passions as love and joy. Robinson's sonnet observes the traditional discipline of fourteen lines; a variation of the traditional Petrarchan rhyme scheme (abba/abba/cdcdcd); and the traditional iambic pentameter. Ironically, however, the traditional sonnet form here becomes a vehicle for questioning traditional attitudes that restrict the free development of the human spirit.

The very first word of the poem causes an inversion of the iambic rhythm, shifting the stress from the second syllable of the line to the first (a trochee). The first line reads: "*Here* where I the wind I is al I ways north- I north-east," focusing the reader's attention forcibly on cold New England. The "always north-north-east" wind and the children in the next line who "learn to walk on frozen toes" start out the poem on a distinctly chilly note. The poet's native New England is cold in more ways than one, we are soon to learn. Here it is so cold that "Joy shivers in the corner where she knits" (11). In this line, the word *Joy*, stressed at the beginning of the line, forms a spondee with what would normally be the second and accented syllable of the first iambic foot: "*Joy shiv* I ers in I the cor I ner where I she knits." Several words in that line—*shivers, in, knits*—have the short *i* sound, suggesting smallness or diminution, which is apparently what the strict New Englanders, apprehensive that joy might get out of hand, would desire. And even joy must not sit idly wasting time—she sits in her designated cold corner, knitting, probably warm mittens or woollen socks needed for survival in the chill outdoors.

And now for the polar opposite: Lines three to eight are a simmering stew of lush, hothouse words, describing those

> Who boil elsewhere with such a lyric yeast
> Of love that you will hear them at a feast
> Where demons would appeal for some repose,
> Still clamoring where the chalice overflows
> And crying wildest who have drunk the least. (4–8)

Here all the bars are down: The words rush unrestrainedly, seemingly of their own volition, and knock down the structure that has been carefully erected to contain them. The lines spill over (enjambment), as in "a lyric yeast / Of love" (4–5). The reader is flooded with a rush of passionate warmth and feeling, which the New Englander can only regard with wonder that "begets an envy" (3).

At the end of line eight, however, the sonnet takes the traditional turn in direction. The excursion into passion ends. The sestet, or concluding six lines, reaffirms the dominance of a more restrictive view of life. "Passion here is a soilure of the wits, / We're told, and Love a cross for them to bear" (9–10). The key word at the beginning of these lines again is emphasized by trochaic inversion: "*Passion* I here is." In these final six lines, everything is again under control, with the thoughts arranged in neat rhyming couplets. Here we see Joy shivering in her corner, while the mistress of the house, Conscience, "always has the rocking-chair." Conscience is perversely "cheerful"—note again the emphasis on this unexpected word through trochaic inversion: "*Cheer*ful I as when . . ." (13). She was apparently equally cheerful when she caused the death of the first cat to be killed not, as in the familiar saying, by curiosity but, New England style, by too much worry and care.

Edward Arlington Robinson was himself a New Englander with deep roots in the Puritan tradition. He was related through his mother to Anne Bradstreet, Puritan New England's first poet. In this poem, he uses the traditional sonnet form effectively to explore the New England tradition of stressing discipline and distrusting emotion.

QUESTIONS

1. Where and how does this student writer show examples of outward form serving as "a mirror to the sense"? How convincing are the examples in this paper?

2. Does this paper seem to capture Robinson's attitude toward the New England tradition? Does the paper seem prejudiced or too negative?

3. Why does the poet's use of traditional form seem ironic to the student writer?

4. When confronted with the polarity explored in this paper, where would you take your stand?

8 PERSONA
Masks and Faces

All writing is the assumption of a mask, a persona,
an implied author.

DAVID W. SMIT

I write in the first person because I have always
wanted to make my life more interesting than it was.

DIANE WAKOSKI

This is my daily mask
daughter, sister
wife, mother
poet, teacher
grandmother.

My mask is control
concealment
endurance
my mask is escape
from my
self.

MITSUYE YAMADA, "MASKS OF WOMAN"

FOCUS ON PERSONA

The **persona** is the voice speaking to us in a poem. This voice may be different from that of the poet as a person. In reading a poem, we often need to ask: "Who is speaking? And to whom?" We may need to distinguish between the poet as a biographical person (whom we could interview and question about the poem) and the "I" addressing us in the poem—the persona.

The distance between the poet and the persona speaking in the poem varies greatly from poem to poem. A poet may share with us real-life experiences and personal feelings. We then hear the voice of the poet speaking to us as a person, taking us into his or her confidence, the way someone might speak to us in a frank personal letter. However, the poet may be revealing to us only one part of his or her personality—perhaps a side that is often hidden from view. Or else the voice speaking in the poem may be an idealized version of the actual poet-as-a-person. The poet may then be speaking to us in a public role, living up to a public image or speaking to us as the voice of a group or a movement. Finally, the persona speaking in the poem may be a disguise, a mask—designed to shield the real poet from prying eyes.

Sometimes the persona is a historical personage or an imaginary character very different from the poet. Listen to the voice you hear in the following poem. Who is speaking? To whom?

C. K. WILLIAMS   (born 1936)
Hood   1969

Remember me? I was the one
In high school you were always afraid of.
I kept cigarettes in my sleeve, wore
engineer's boots, long hair, my collar
up in back and there were always   5
girls with me in the hallways.
You were nothing. I had it in for you—
when I peeled rubber at the lights
you cringed like a teacher.
And when I crashed and broke both lungs   10
on the wheel, you were so relieved
that you stroked the hard Ford paint
And your hands shook.

In this poem, we are exceptionally aware of the speaker. We are listening to the "hood" of the title, who is speaking to a third person. If we remember being bullied ourselves, we are likely to sympathize with the victim. We are likely to share the cringing—and the guilty feeling of relief when the bully crashed. Where is the poet in this poem? Maybe the poet is somewhat of a bully, but more likely the bully's role is an assumed identity.

THE RECEPTIVE READER

1. Does the "hood" of this poem become a believable bully? Why or why not? Can you identify with the listener? What details help make the situation real for you?

2. In this brief confrontation, where is the poet? As a person, is the poet likely to resemble the speaker or the listener? What do you think made the poet write this poem?

THE CREATIVE DIMENSION

Write a passage or poem in which you re-create the persona of a childhood bully or other person who teased or tormented you in earlier years.

THE AUTOBIOGRAPHICAL "I"

All poetry is confession.
JOHANN WOLFGANG VON GOETHE

I hadn't found the courage yet to do without authorities,
or even to use the pronoun "I."
ADRIENNE RICH

I am not a metaphor or symbol.
This you hear is not the wind in the trees,
Nor a cat being maimed in the street.
It is I being maimed in the street.
CALVIN C. HERNTON, "THE DISTANT DRUM"

Poems using the **autobiographical "I"** share with us their personal experiences and feelings. Such poetry is sometimes called **confessional poetry,** as if the poet were sharing secrets never before revealed. The poet takes us into his or her confidence, revealing part of the self that may normally be hidden behind a noncommittal façade. We are privileged to look beyond the outer shell that shields people from prying or ridicule. The more autobiographical the poem, the more the person speaking in the poem and the poet who wrote the poem become identical in the reader's mind.

Some poems are occasioned by actual events in the poet's life. A poet-playwright and contemporary of Shakespeare wrote the following poem about an actual son who was named Benjamin (literally "child of the right hand") and who died at age seven.

BEN JONSON   (1572–1637)
On My First Son   1616

Farewell, thou child of my right hand, and joy;
My sin was too much hope of thee, loved boy:
Seven years thou wert lent to me, and thee I pay,°   *pay back*
Exacted° by thy fate, on the just day.   *when billed*
O could I lose all father° now! For why   *fatherly thoughts*   5
Will man lament the state he should envy—
To have so soon escaped world's and flesh's rage
And, if no other misery, yet age?
Rest in soft peace and, asked,° say, "Here doth lie   *when asked*
Ben Jonson his° best piece of poetry."   *Jonson's*   10
For whose sake henceforth all° his vows be such   *may all*
As what he loves may never° like too much.   *may he never*

THE RECEPTIVE READER

1. The father's feelings in this poem are in keeping with traditional religious attitudes toward death. How? Are these attitudes still meaningful to the modern reader? Why or why not?

2. Where in the poem do you think the father's personal feelings show most strongly? Where do his thoughts and feelings seem different or unexpected to you?

Poets take a risk when they remove the mask that usually hides private feelings from the outside world. However, they also set up a special human contact with the sympathetic, responsive reader. Poetry in the "I" mode often records a part of the poet's spiritual history. We embark with the poet on an exploration of inner space, which may take us to childhood scenes or to way stations in the poet's later life. We watch a fellow human being fitting together the pieces of the puzzle that together make up a person.

How well do you come to know or understand the persons behind the two following poems?

MAXINE KUMIN   (born 1925)
Nurture   1976

From a documentary on marsupials I learn
that a pillowcase makes a fine
substitute pouch for an orphaned kangaroo.

I am drawn to such dramas of animal rescue.
They are warm in the throat. I suffer, the critic proclaims,   5
from an overabundance of maternal genes.

Bring me your fallen fledgling, your bummer lamb,
lead the abused, the starvelings, into my barn.
Advise the hunted deer to leap into my corn.

And had there been a wild child—   10
filthy and fierce as a ferret, he is called
in one nineteenth-century account—

a wild child to love, it is safe to assume,
given my fireside inked with paw prints,
there would have been room.   15

Think of the language we two, same and not-same,
Might have constructed from sign,
scratch, grimace, grunt, vowel:

Laughter our first noun, and our long verb, howl.

THE RECEPTIVE READER

1. What *tone* does the poet set by her opening reference to kangaroos and other marsupials?
2. What in this poem strikes you as autobiographical fact and what as imaginative *what if*?
3. What is the special fascination of stories about abandoned children growing up wild without human nurture or language? What is the special fascination of such stories for the poet?

4. What is the perspective on *language* in this poem? What poet's-eye view does the poem give you of the origin or basic functions of language?

5. What kind of *person* would you expect the poet to be? Where would you expect to encounter her? What would you expect her to do?

THE PERSONAL RESPONSE

Is a nurturing, caring attitude toward life a gender-specific quality? Is nurturing the special province of women? What are some practical or political implications of the debate—what difference does it make? What side would you take?

In classical Greece, the Nine Muses were quasi-divine beings who inspired poets, musicians, historians, and followers of the other arts and sciences. The philosopher Plato called Sappho "the tenth Muse," and many Greeks considered her their most outstanding lyric poet. She lived on the island of Lesbos and is thought to have run a school for women there. Book burners of a later age destroyed most of her poems (but not her legendary reputation). A few whole poems and fragments of others survive. Gay women still call themselves lesbians in her honor.

SAPPHO   (about 620–550 B.C.)

Letter to Anaktoria   sixth century B.C.

TRANSLATED BY RICHMOND LATTIMORE

Like the very gods in my sight is he who
sits where he can look in your eyes, who listens
close to you, to hear the soft voice, its sweetness
          murmur in love and

laughter, all for him. But it breaks my spirit;   5
underneath my breath all the heart is shaken.
Let me only glance where you are, the voice dies,
          I can say nothing,

but my lips are stricken to silence, under-
neath my skin the tenuous flame suffuses;   10
nothing shows in front of my eyes, my ears are
          muted in thunder.

And the sweat running upon me, fever
shakes my body, paler I turn than grass is;
I can feel that I have been changed, I feel that   15
          death has come near me.

THE RECEPTIVE READER

What kind of person is speaking in this poem? What is the situation? What are the mixed emotions the speaker feels toward the two people in this poem? Do her feelings seem strange or familiar? How would you expect to react to a poem written 2,500 years ago? How *do* you react to this poem?

THE CREATIVE DIMENSION

Write a poem or prose passage that re-creates what for you is the dominant emotion in this poem.

Intensely personal poetry often seems like a catharsis—a cleansing or purifying of painful memories or passionate grievances. In recent decades, minority authors have made the majority listen to the voices of those that Martin Luther King, Jr., called the "unheard." The following poem speaks for young native Americans taken from their families to be made over in the white man's image. Of German and Chippewa heritage, the poet relives her experience with the forced assimilation of young people denied pride in their own past.

LOUISE ERDRICH   (born 1954)

Indian Boarding School: The Runaways   1984

Home's the place we head for in our sleep.
Boxcars stumbling north in dreams
don't wait for us. We catch them on the run.
The rails, old lacerations that we love,
soot parallel across the face and break   5
just under Turtle Mountains. Riding scars
you can't get lost. Home is the place they cross.

The lame guard strikes a match and makes the dark
less tolerant. We watch through cracks in boards
as the land starts rolling, rolling till it hurts   10
to be here, cold in regulation clothes.
We know the sheriff's waiting at midrun
to take us back. His car is dumb and warm.
The highway doesn't rock, it only hums
like a wing of long insults. The worn-down welts   15
of ancient punishments lead back and forth.

All runaways wear dresses, long green ones,
the color you would think shame was. We scrub
the sidewalks down because it's shameful work.
Our brushes cut the stone in watered arcs   20
and in the soak frail outlines shiver clear
a moment, things us kids pressed on the dark
face before it hardened, pale, remembering
delicate old injuries, the spines of names and leaves.

THE RECEPTIVE READER

1. To you, does the poem seem like intensely felt *personal experience* or like an imaginary situation vividly imagined? If pressed to explain your answer, what would you say?

2. What *assumptions* about reservation life and Indian schools do you bring to this poem? How does this poem change or challenge them?

3. What is the *situation* of the runaways? What do they think, feel, and remember?

4. In this poem, much of what you see—the railroad tracks, the highway, work, a color—takes on *symbolic* significance. Where and how?

THE PERSONAL RESPONSE

When you read this poem, are you looking at the young runaways from the outside? Do you identify with the "we" speaking in the poem? Why or why not?

JUXTAPOSITIONS ===========

Variations of "I"

Even when using the autobiographical "I," poets differ widely in how completely they bare their souls. (Mitsuye Yamada has said that to discover our real selves we have to peel away our masks "like the used skin / of a growing reptile.") In much nineteenth-century poetry, even personal emotions went dressed in a high-minded vocabulary, with anything low or disturbing locked away in the private recesses of the mind. In the twentieth century, candor gradually drove out Victorian uplift and decorum. Compare the two following examples. The first is one of a series of sonnets that Elizabeth Barrett addressed to the poet Robert Browning when they were about to be married. The second was written more than a hundred years later in a more modern vein.

ELIZABETH BARRETT BROWNING   (1806–1861)

How do I love thee? Let me count the ways   1845

How do I love thee? Let me count the ways.
I love thee to the depth and breadth and height
My soul can reach, when feeling out of sight
For the ends of Being and ideal Grace.
I love thee to the level of every day's   5
Most quiet need, by sun and candle-light.
I love thee freely, as men strive for right;
I love thee purely, as they turn from Praise.
I love thee with the passion put to use
In my old griefs, and with my childhood's faith.   10
I love thee with a love I seemed to lose
With my lost saints—I love thee with the breath,
Smiles, tears, of all my life!—and, if God choose,
I shall but love thee better after death.

THE RECEPTIVE READER

1. What kind of person is speaking in this poem? What kind of voice do you hear? Do you think of the person speaking as the poet herself or as a public *persona*?

2. What feelings voiced in this sonnet seem *old-fashioned* to you? How do you explain that this poem still appears in almost every major collection of favorite poems? What about it might still speak strongly to a modern reader?

3. How does the poet use a pattern of insistent *repetition* building up to a climactic ending?

What part of the poet's personality is uppermost in the following poem?

GWENDOLYN BROOKS (born 1917)
A Song in the Front Yard   1945

I've stayed in the front yard all my life.
I want to peek at the back
Where it's rough and untended and hungry weeds grow.
A girl gets sick of a rose.

I want to go in the back yard now   5
And maybe down the alley,
To where the charity children play.
I want a good time today.

They do some wonderful things.
They have some wonderful fun.   10
My mother sneers, but I say it's fine
How they don't have to go in at quarter to nine.
My mother, she tells me that Johnnie Mae
Will grow up to be a bad woman.
That George will be taken to Jail soon or late   15
(On account of last winter he sold our back gate).

But I say it's fine. Honest, I do.
And I'd like to be a bad woman, too,
And wear the black stockings of night-black lace
And strut down the street with paint on my face.   20

THE RECEPTIVE READER

1. What is the *symbolic* meaning of the front yard, the back yard, the alley, and the street? Does it matter that the song is about the back yard but is sung in the front yard?

2. Brooks published this poem when she was an adult. What *identity* is she assuming in this poem? (What is the persona?) What kind of voice are you hearing? What kind of person does it make you imagine? (How is the person talking?)

3. Often a single *metaphor* carries much meaning, with various implications and associations. What is the full meaning of the line "A girl gets sick of a rose"? (Does it make a difference that this is one of the shortest lines in a poem of longer lines?)

THE PERSONAL RESPONSE

How well do the following student reactions get into the spirit of the poem? Write your own personal response to the poem.

1. I've always been a good boy. I've done what my parents say. I want to see how the others live. I want to throw a rock through a window and get chased by the cops. I want to knock on a door and run and hide. I want to be bad, just for a day.

2. How can a girl get sick of a rose? A rose has everything. It has beauty and ugliness; it grows and dies. A rose is well-balanced: If you are sick of a rose, try its thorns.

CROSS-REFERENCES—For Discussion or Writing

Which of the two poets do you think you come to know better as a person, and why? Which style of voicing personal emotions appeals to you more, and why?

THE PUBLIC PERSONA

> *The age*
> *requires this task:*
> *create*
> *a different image;*
> *re-animate*
> *the mask.*
>   DUDLEY RANDALL

The "I" we hear in a poem may be speaking to us as the voice of a group, a commitment, or a cause. The plural *we* (like the editorial *we* or the royal *we*) may replace the singular *I*. It is as if the poet were speaking to us in an official capacity, assuming a public persona. Dylan Thomas was a Welsh poet whose chanting voice and powerful cryptic poems converted a generation of listeners and readers to the cause of poetry. In the following poem, he speaks of his mission as a poet with a grand sweep, without diffidence or self-doubt. The persona he assumes in the poem is that of the charismatic bard, mesmerizing his audience with his hypnotic voice, dramatizing and glorifying the poet's calling.

DYLAN THOMAS   (1914–1953)

In My Craft or Sullen Art   1946

In my craft or sullen art
Exercised in the still night
When only the moon rages
And the lovers lie abed
With all their griefs in their arms,   5
I labor by singing light
Not for ambition or bread
Or the strut and trade of charms
On the ivory stages
But for the common wages   10
Of their most secret heart.

Not for the proud man apart
From the raging moon I write
On these spindrift° pages   *sea spray*
Nor for the towering dead   15
With their nightingales and psalms
But for the lovers, their arms
Round the griefs of the ages,
Who pay no praise or wages
Nor heed my craft or art.   20

THE RECEPTIVE READER

1. Dylan Thomas' poetry was shot through with bold, provocative *metaphors*. Why or how could his art be "sullen," and what could he mean by "singing light"? How does he use metaphorically *bread, strut, ivory, common wages, spindrift pages, towering dead*?

2. Where and how often does the central word *art* appear in the poem, and with what effect? What other key word rhymes with it, and where in the poem? Why is *wages* also a key word in the poem? Where does it appear, and how many rhymes help it echo through the poem?

3. What is the *symbolic* role of the moon in this poem?

4. With what *tone* should this poem be read? What kind of person do you imagine the poet to be?

Among poets who have seen themselves as the conscience of their time, Walt Whitman created for himself a persona as the voice of a new continent and a new nation. In many of his poems, he is speaking to us as the prophet of the new American democracy. The following poem, a part of his *Song of Myself*, shows the kind of **empathy**—sharing the feelings of others—that could make him say, "I am the hounded slave," and, "I do not ask the wounded person how he feels, I myself become the wounded person."

WALT WHITMAN   (1819–1892)
I Understand the Large Hearts of Heroes   1855

I understand the large hearts of heroes.
The courage of present times and all times,
How the skipper saw the crowded and rudderless wreck of the steamship, and Death
    chasing it up and down the storm,
How he knuckled tight and gave not back an inch, and was faithful of days and faithful
    of nights,
And chalked in large letters on a board, "Be of good cheer, we will not desert you";   5
How he followed with them and tacked with them three days and would not give it up,
How he saved the drifting company at last,
How the lank loose-gowned women looked when boated from the side of their
    prepared graves,
How the silent old-faced infants and the lifted sick, and the sharp-lipped unshaved men;
All this I swallow, it tastes good, I like it well, it becomes mine,   10
I am the man, I suffered, I was there.

THE RECEPTIVE READER

1. Whitman was fascinated with *people*—how they looked and talked and moved, whether in developing the continent or in the agonies of civil war. What striking, revealing details make this account of shipwreck and rescue come to life for the reader?

2. What kind of *person* is speaking to you in this poem? Whitman has at times been accused of striking heroic poses. Do you think he is sincere in this poem? Why or why not?

THE PERSONAL RESPONSE

How do you react to the following *journal entry* by a fellow student?

"All this I swallow, it tastes good, I like it well, it becomes mine, / I am the man, I suffered, I was there." Whitman here boldy proclaims the glorious things that common people only sense in a confused, ambiguous way while thinking to themselves. At achieving this grand persona, few have matched the grandeur of Whitman. In this poem, Whitman rises to the level of a great and heroic event. The sea captain is the kind of person who will not deviate from a cause once the course is set. With absolute determination, "he knuckled tight and gave not back an inch, and was faithful of days and . . . nights." Whitman makes himself the spokesperson that commemorates and celebrates this courage and heroism: "I understand the large heart of heroes / The courage of present times and all times." Today, a poet might view the state of our nation as slipping into chaos one notch at a time. Every time an oil tanker spills its load or someone is gunned down in the streets, America loses another piece of its soul. In Whitman's time, this country was taking gigantic leaps forward. He had ample subject-matter for such heart-swelling subjects as this.

Today, some of the most eloquent voices we hear speak to us in the name of a larger group. They help formulate a changed consciousness, a new sense of group identity. They may speak for women in search of a new self-image. They may speak for minority groups proud of their heritage. The following poem is by an American poet of West Indian descent who has said that she speaks not only for the woman who inhabits her physical self but "for all those feisty incorrigible black women who insist on standing up and saying, 'I *am* and you cannot wipe me out, no matter how irritating I am, how much you fear what I might represent.' "

A U D R E   L O R D E   (born 1934)

Coal   1976

I
is the total black, being spoken
from the earth's inside.
There are many kinds of open
how a diamond comes into a knot of flame
how sound comes into a word, colored
by who pays what for speaking.

5

Some words are open like a diamond
on glass windows
singing out within the passing crash of sun.   10
Then there are words like stapled wagers
in a perforated book,—buy and sign and tear apart—
and come whatever wills all chances
the stub remains
an ill-pulled tooth with a ragged edge.   15
Some words live in my throat
breeding like adders. Others know sun
seeking like gypsies over my tongue
to explode through my lips
like young sparrows bursting from shell.   20
Some words
bedevil me.

Love is a word, another kind of open.
As the diamond comes into a knot of flame
I am Black because I come from the earth's inside   25
now take my word for jewel in the open light.

THE RECEPTIVE READER

1. Look at the bold provocative *metaphors* and *similes* in this poem. What is their meaning? What role do they play in the poem?

2. The word *open* becomes a key word in this poem. What role does it play? What meanings and associations cluster around it?

3. Some earlier black poets used a formal literary language, avoiding all echoes of *Black English*. How is this poem different? What is the effect on the reader?

4. Who is the collective *I* speaking in this poem? What kind of collective self-image takes shape in this poem?

CROSS-REFERENCES—For Discussion or Writing

Compare and contrast the two poems by Whitman and Lorde. How do the two poets compare as voices of social awareness? How do they shape our self-image as members of society, as socially responsible beings?

IMAGINED SELVES

Aye! I am a poet and upon my tomb
Shall maidens scatter rose leaves
And men myrtles, ere the night
Slays day with her dark sword.
                    EZRA POUND

Sometimes the voice speaking in a poem is clearly distant or separate from the poet's autobiographical self. The "I" speaking may be an imaginary or historical character to whom both we and the poet are listening. Poems by the author of the following poem have appeared in collections of science fiction poetry. What is the fictitious identity of the person speaking in the poem?

EDWARD LUCIE-SMITH (born 1933)

Afterwards

1964

Inhospitable.
        Another bald
Barren lump spinning in a thin shawl
Of unbreathable gas. I see it
From my narrow window, from what these   5
Hovering needles tell me in their
Too truthful gauges. I might descend,
Opening the airlock, adjusting my
Cumbersome helmet, hands gloved thick
Against the cold, or heat, or acid,   10
Strapping upon my back the light slim
Canister of my own atmosphere—
And each breath links me again with what,
The further I travel seems stranger:
Greenness, water, movement, a sphere not   15
Sufficient unto itself, but once
Happy to feed and lodge an itchy
Parasite.
        Now inhospitable.

THE RECEPTIVE READER

1. Where are we in this poem, and when? Who is speaking? What is the *persona*?
2. What is the *key word* in what the speaker says, and what is its effect on the reader? What details in the poem follow it up or make it come to life? What changes the impact of the word when it is repeated at the end of the poem?
3. What is the poet's attitude toward the human species and its prospects?
4. How is this poem different from other previews of a catastrophic future?

The speaker in a first-person poem is often a character from history or legend who has a special fascination for the poet. We may sense a special affinity or attraction, as we do in the following poem about Cassandra, the mad Trojan princess and priestess, who in the ancient Greek poems and plays about the siege of Troy speaks as the voice of impending doom. In her prophetic visions, Cassandra saw her native city in flames, with its towers crashing down. She also prophesied that Agamemnon, the Greek commander who carried her off as part of the spoils of war, would be murdered on his return to Greece by his wife and her lover.

LOUISE BOGAN (1897–1970)

Cassandra

1968

To me, one silly task is like another.
I bare the shambling tricks of lust and pride.
This flesh will never give a child its mother—

Song, like a wing, tears through my breast, my side,
And madness chooses out my voice again,   5
Again. I am the chosen no hand saves:
The shrieking heaven lifted over men,
Not the dumb earth, wherein they set their graves.

THE RECEPTIVE READER

1. What do you think is the special attraction the character of Cassandra had for
the author as a woman and as a poet? What might make the legendary character a kind
of *alter ego* for her—a "second self" or counterpart?

2. Why is it strange or contradictory that this poem should have a neat regular
rhyme scheme and underlying iambic meter? Is it a coincidence that the word *again,*
repeated at the beginning of the sixth line, breaks up the pattern of neatly marked off
lines as it pulls us over into the new line?

What is the role the poet imagines for herself in the following poem?
When Hitler drove many German artists and writers into exile, others, including this poet, went through a period of "emigration to the interior"—staying
in Germany while trying to live intellectually and spiritually outside the mentality of the Nazi era. She was much honored by the West German literary es-
tablishment after the war. The following poem shows her affinity with an
active women's movement in Germany.

MARIE LUISE KASCHNITZ   (1901–1974)

Women's Program   1972

TRANSLATED BY LISEL MÜLLER

I give a talk on the radio
Toward morning when no one is listening
I offer my recipes

Pour milk into the telephone
Let your cats sleep   5
In the dishwashers
Smash the clocks in your washing machines
Leave your shoes behind

Season your peaches with paprika
And your soup meat with honey   10

Teach your children the alphabet of foxes
Turn the leaves in your gardens silver side up
Take the advice of the owl

When summer arrives put on your furs
Go meet the ones with the bagpipes   15
Who come from inside the mountains
Leave your shoes behind

Don't be too sure
Evening will come
Don't be too sure   20
That God loves you.

THE RECEPTIVE READER

1. What kind of person is speaking in this poem? (How close do you think the poet's personality is to the *persona* in the poem?)

2. What is the point and the motivation of the subversive advice given in this poem? (Does any of it seem particularly strange or particularly sensible?)

3. Where and how does the poet *allude* to the story of the Pied Piper of Hamlin? How does her use of the story depart from what you might expect?

EXPLORATIONS

The Dramatic Monologue

In some poems, we listen to a **dramatic monologue,** or lengthy first-person speech, as it might be delivered by a character in a play. The best-known author of dramatic monologues is the English nineteenth-century poet Robert Browning, who lived for a time in Italy after eloping with his fellow poet Elizabeth Barrett, the semi-invalid daughter of a domineering father. In many of his monologues, we listen as artists, scholars, church dignitaries, or aristocrats of the Italian Renaissance reveal to us their ambitions and aspirations—or, as in the following poem, their passions and hidden motives. In the poem that follows, we listen to a sixteenth-century Duke of Ferrara whose last duchess died young and who is now talking to a representative of another aristocratic family about a second marriage.

ROBERT BROWNING   (1812–1889)

My Last Duchess   1842

Ferrara

That's my last duchess painted on the wall,
Looking as if she were alive. I call
That piece a wonder, now: Frà Pandolf's° hands   *Brother Pandolf (a monk or friar)*
Worked busily a day, and there she stands.
Will 't please you sit and look at her? I said   5
"Frà Pandolf" by design,° for never read   *on purpose*
Strangers like you that pictured countenance,°   *face*
The depth and passion of its earnest glance,
But to myself they turned (since none puts by
The curtain I have drawn for you, but I)   10
And seemed as they would ask me, if they durst,°   *dared*
How such a glance came there; so, not the first

Are you to turn and ask thus. Sir, 't was not
Her husband's presence only, called° that spot   *that called*
Of joy into the Duchess' cheek: perhaps   15
Frà Pandolf chanced to say "Her mantle laps
Over my lady's wrist too much," or "Paint
Must never hope to reproduce the faint
Half-flush that dies along her throat": such stuff
Was courtesy, she thought, and cause enough   20
For calling up that spot of joy. She had
A heart—how shall I·say?—too soon made glad,
Too easily impressed; she liked whate'er
She looked on, and her looks went everywhere.
Sir, 't was all one! My favor° at her breast,   *love token*   25
The dropping of the daylight in the west,
The bough of cherries some officious° fool   *eager to serve*
Broke in the orchard for her, the white mule
She rode with round the terrace—all and each
Would draw from her alike the approving speech,   30
Or blush, at least. She thanked men—good! but thanked
Somehow—I know not how—as if she ranked
My gift of a nine-hundred-years-old name
With anybody's gift. Who'd stoop to blame
This sort of trifling? Even had you° skill   *if you had*   35
In speech—which I have not—to make your will
Quite clear to such an one, and say, "Just this
Or that in you disgusts me; here you miss,
Or there exceed the mark"—and if she let
Herself be lessoned so, nor plainly set   40
Her wit to yours, forsooth,° and made excuse   *in truth*
—E'en then would be some stooping; and I choose
Never to stoop. Oh sir, she smiled, no doubt,
Whene'er I passed her, but who passed without
Much the same smile? This grew; I gave commands;   45
Then all smiles stopped together. There she stands
As if alive. Will 't please you rise? We'll meet
The company below, then. I repeat,
The Count your master's known munificence°   *generosity*
Is ample warrant° that no just pretense   *guarantee, demand* 50
Of mine for dowry will be disallowed;
Though his fair daughter's self, as I avowed
At starting, is my object. Nay, we'll go
Together down, sir. Notice Neptune, though,
Taming a sea-horse, thought a rarity,   55
Which Claus of Innsbruck cast in bronze for me.

THE RECEPTIVE READER

1. What is the *situation*? Where in the poem did you first suspect what happened to the duchess? When were you sure?

2. To judge from this monologue by her husband, what was the duchess like as a *person*? What was her offense? Do you consider her a frivolous or superficial person?

3. What is the key to the *persona* created by Browning in this poem? What is the duke's problem? Why didn't he explain how he felt to the duchess?

4. What is strange about the duke's speaking in a relaxed, polite conversational *tone*? Is it in keeping with his character? Many of his sentences start in the middle of a line and spill over into the next. (The technical term for this effect is *enjambment*— from the French word for "straddling.") How does the straddling effect contribute to the conversational tone?

5. What public persona has the duke created for himself—what *image* does he present to the world? (The Italian Renaissance was a golden age of the creative arts. What is the role of art in this poem?)

THE PERSONAL RESPONSE

Has the duke's mentality become extinct with the passing of the aristocratic society of his time? Do you think there could be any modern parallels to his mind set and behavior?

POEMS FOR FURTHER STUDY

In reading the following poems, pay special attention to questions like the following: Who is speaking? What kind of voice do you hear in the poem? What is the persona or assumed identity? How much distance do you think there is between the persona and the person behind the poem?

COUNTEE CULLEN (1903–1946)
Saturday's Child　　　　　　　　　　　　　　　　　　1925

Some are teethed on a silver spoon,
With the stars strung for a rattle;
I cut my teeth as the black raccoon—
For implements of battle.

Some are swaddled in silk and down,   5
And heralded by a star;
They swathed my limbs in a sackcloth gown
On a night that was black as tar.

For some godfather and goddame°   *godmother*
The opulent° fairies be;   *living richly* 10
Dame Poverty gave me my name,
And Pain godfathered me.

For I was born on Saturday—
"Bad time for planting a seed,"
Was all my father had to say,   15
And, "One more mouth to feed."

Death cut the strings that gave me life,
And handed me to Sorrow,
The only kind of middle wife
My folks could beg or borrow. 20

THE RECEPTIVE READER

1. How do the stanza form and rhyme scheme help the poet line up the *opposites* that give shape to the poem as a whole?

2. What is the role of *personified abstractions* in this poem? (How did "Death cut the strings that gave me life"?)

3. What is the *persona* the poet creates for himself in this poem? How close do you think it is to the poet's real-life personality?

DENISE LEVERTOV (born 1923)

In Mind 1964

There's in my mind a woman
of innocence, unadorned but

fair-featured, and smelling of
apples or grass. She wears

a utopian smock or shift, her hair 5
is light brown and smooth, and she
is kind and very clean without
ostentation—
    but she has
no imagination. 10
        And there's a
turbulent moon-ridden girl

or old woman or both
dressed in opals and rags, feathers

and torn taffeta. 15
and who knows strange songs—

but she is not kind.

THE RECEPTIVE READER

Do you recognize the two different personalities in this poem? What are their virtues and shortcomings? (Are they polar opposites?) Do you think two such different personalities could dwell in the same mind?

CROSS-REFERENCES—For Discussion or Writing

Compare the treatment of two sides of the same personality in this poem and in Gwendolyn Brooks' "A Song in the Front Yard" earlier in this chapter.

NIKKI GIOVANNI (born 1943)

Legacies 1972

her grandmother called her from the playground
    "yes, ma'am"
    "i want chu to learn how to make rolls," said the old
woman proudly
but the little girl didn't want 5
to learn how because she knew
even if she couldn't say it that
that would mean when the old one died she would be less
dependent on her spirit so
she said 10
    "i don't want to know how to make no rolls" with her lips poked out
and the old woman wiped her hands on
her apron saying "lord
    these children"
and neither of them ever 15
said what they meant
and i guess nobody ever does

THE RECEPTIVE READER

    1. The poet says that both the grandmother and the girl in this poem never said what they really meant. What did the grandmother mean—what did she really think and feel? What did the girl mean—what did she really "know" without being able to put it into words?

    2. Which of the two persons in this poem is closer to the poet as a person? Does she identify or sympathize more with the one or the other? (With which of the two do *you* identify or sympathize?)

SYLVIA PLATH (1932–1963)

Mirror 1961

I am silver and exact. I have no preconceptions.
Whatever I see I swallow immediately
Just as it is, unmisted by love or dislike.
I am not cruel, only truthful—
The eye of a little god, four-cornered. 5
Most of the time I meditate on the opposite wall.
It is pink, with speckles. I have looked at it so long
I think it is a part of my heart. But it flickers.
Faces and darkness separate us over and over.

Now I am a lake. A woman bends over me, 10
Searching my reaches for what she really is.
Then she turns to those liars, the candles or the moon.

I see her back, and reflect it faithfully.
She rewards me with tears and an agitation of hands.
I am important to her. She comes and goes.   15
Each morning it is her face that replaces the darkness.
In me she has drowned a young girl, and in me an old woman
Rises toward her like a terrible fish.

THE RECEPTIVE READER

1. What touches early in the poem might make the mirror sound like a curious observer—with a limited or even naive perspective and no evil intentions? (How is the mirror like the eye of a god—and why of "a little god"?)

2. How does the lake metaphor make the mirror seem more knowing and more threatening? Why or how would "candles or the moon" be more likely to prove liars than the mirror?

3. Do you think the mirror is cruel? Do you think the poet is being cruel? Where is the poet in this poem?

THE CREATIVE DIMENSION

What story would your own mirror tell if it could speak?

CROSS-REFERENCES—For Discussion or Writing

Several poems in this chapter (as well as in other parts of this book) are the record of a poet exploring her identity as a woman or embarked in the search of self. Study several such poems, looking for shared themes, recurrent issues, or similar perspectives.

WRITING ABOUT LITERATURE

8. Playing the Role (Imitation and Parody)

The Writing Workshop   We like to think that creative spirits burst upon the scene with the clear marks of genius. However, many poets passed through phases where they idolized a mentor or role model, and often the experience strongly influenced their attempts to find a style of their own. They often learned their craft by conscious *imitation* of what was famous, fashionable, or new. Adrienne Rich has said that at age sixteen she spent months memorizing and writing imitations of the sonnets of Edna St. Vincent Millay ("in notebooks of that period I find what are obviously attempts to imitate Dickinson's metrics and verbal compression").

As readers, we can learn as much from creative imitation as practicing poets do. Imitation or re-creation (like translation from another language) makes us enter into a poet's world of imagination more fully than a passive reading can. It alerts us to distinctive features of the poet's style, making us look at them from the performer's rather than the spectator's point of view.

Study the following attempts to re-create the persona of a poem in this chapter, and then try your hand at a similar imitation or re-creation of a poem of your choice. The first poem in this chapter is C. K. Williams' "Hood." The student who wrote the following personal re-creation of the "Hood" poem tried to create a similar persona. Compare the original and this student's response. How successful was the student poet?

Bully

Remember me?
I'm the one who calls you Chinaman.
I laugh at you all the time
and throw balls at you
when you don't know how to play.
I play jokes around you with my friends.
I took your lunch money in the restroom.
I'm the one you hate and fear the most.
When Teacher yelled at me,
you felt good.
When I am absent,
You feel safe.

Poets with an especially unmistakable style seem to invite imitation. Their poems seem to cry out for **parody**—an imitation that lovingly or mockingly exaggerates characteristic traits. The poetry of Robert Browning has been much imitated and much parodied. What features of the original did the student capture who wrote the following dramatic monologue?

My Last Essay

That's my last essay pinned up on the wall,
Looking as if it's not survived. I call
That piece a wonder, now! Jim Bello's hand
Worked busily an hour, and thus its state.
Will 't please you stay and read of it? I said
"Jim Bello" by design, for never saw
Strangers like you such tattered manuscript
But to myself they turned in stunned surprise
And seemed as they would ask me, if they durst,
How such red marks came there; so not the first
Are you to turn and ask thus. Nay, 't was not
Just split infinitives that roused his ire—
"Support unclear," he muttered through his teeth
In reference to my cherished prose. He had
A mind—how shall I say?—too soon made mad,
Too easily overcome; he slashed what words
He looked on, and his looks went everywhere!
Yes, 't was all one. My pronoun reference fault,
Verb disagreement, too—and "Comma splice!"

So, friend you see my tattered work displayed,
Defiled with red disgracefully, I know.
But I retyped it, and the ms sold
To Murdoch's tabloid for an even thou'.
You caught that issue? Thanks!

A parody is a close imitation with a humorous twist, achieving comic effects by exaggerating characteristic features of the original. A parody may be affectionate, gently spoofing mannerisms that are like quirks of someone we love. But a parody may also be cruel, holding up to ridicule what is overdone or outdated in its target.

To parody something well takes time and careful attention. Poets who write successful parody need a quick ear and a gift for patient observation. The following stanza is from a flip poem (written in 1601) by a would-be lover eager to dispense with the tedious preliminaries of courtship. The next stanza is from a student-written parody written almost four hundred years later.

I care not for these ladies,
That must be wooed and prayed:
Give me kind Amaryllis,
The wanton country maid.
   Her when we court and kiss,
   She cries, "Forsooth, let go!"
   But when we come where comfort is,
   She never will say no.
                    Thomas Campion

The student who wrote the following rejoinder had a good ear, and she gets well into the spirit of the original poem:

They care not for us ladies
That want to be loved and pursued.
They care for Amaryllis
Who is impure and crude.
   'Cause when men seek a kiss,
   Her cries have just begun.
   No longer can she resist;
   She pleads for more than one.
                    Sharee Pearson, "Ladies"

9 TONE
The Human Voice

Poetry is the revelation of a feeling that the poet believes to be interior and personal but which the readers recognize as their own.

SALVATORE QUASIMODO

The poet sheds his blood in the ring and calls the pools poems.

GEORGE BARKER

this is important enough:
to get your feelings down.
it is better than shaving
or cooking beans with garlic.

CHARLES BUKOWSKI, "COOKING BEANS WITH GARLIC"

FOCUS ON TONE

In the poet's language, as in ordinary language, much of the message is in the **tone.** Live language has a human coloring that conveys the feelings, attitudes, and intentions of the speaker. Live language does not pass on neutral information; it tells us much about the likes, dislikes, private agendas, and ulterior motives of a breathing human being. "It's you again!" may be said in a tone of welcome—but also in a tone of barely concealed disappointment. "Thanks!" may be said in a tone of warm gratitude or of a cold "thank-you-for-nothing."

Facing a speaker, we read the speaker's body language; we respond to the knowing wink or defiant gesture. We respond to the sweet or harsh music of the voice; we flinch at the raised volume; we perk up our ears at a whispered aside. When looking at a poem on the printed page, we have to read for tone the way an actor reads a script for clues to gesture and movement. The poet's words convey tone without the raised eyebrows, the shrug of the shoulders, or the raised decibels. To respond to tone, we need to become sensitive to tender or harsh and angry words. We need to respond to how a poet lets passion build up—or plays down an emotion-charged situation. We need to sense when the poet is being serious and when speaking tongue-in-cheek.

Tone in poetry runs the gamut of human attitudes and emotions. The poet may set a *mournful* tone, as Walt Whitman does in the opening lines of his elegy on the death of President Lincoln:

> When lilacs last in the dooryard bloomed,
> And the great star early drooped in the western sky in the night,
> I mourned, and yet shall mourn with ever-returning spring.

The poet may speak in a tone of *religious awe,* as the seventeenth-century poet Henry Vaughan does in the opening lines of his poem "The World":

> I saw eternity the other night
> Like a great ring of pure and endless light,
>   All calm as it was bright;
> And round beneath it, Time, in hours, days, years,
>   Driven by the spheres,
> Like a vast shadow moved, in which the world
>   And all her train were hurled.

Toward the other end of the religious spectrum, the tone of a poem may be *irreverent,* as in these rebellious lines from Maxine Kumin's "Address to the Angels":

> Angels, where were you when
> my best friend did herself in?
> Were you lunching beside us
> that final noon, did you catch
> some nuance that went past my ear?
> Did you ease my father out
> of his cardiac arrest that wet
> fall day I sat at the high crib bed
> holding his hand? And when
> my black-eyed susan-child ran
> off with her European lover
> and has been ever since an unbelonger,
> were you whirligiging over
> the suitcases?

A poem may be playful in tone or gently spoofing, or it may be scornful, bitter, charged with contempt. To become sensitive to tone, remember that in reading a poem you are listening to a human voice. The printed poem on the page is to the heard and felt poem as the sheet music is to Beethoven's Moonlight Sonata. Reading aloud and hearing others read aloud is your best insurance against proving tone deaf to the human voice speaking to you in a poem.

THE REGISTER OF EMOTIONS

Forgive me that I pitch your praise too low.
Such reticence my reverence demands.
For silence falls with laying on of hands.
Forgive me that my words come thin and slow.
    JOHN WAIN, "APOLOGY FOR UNDERSTATEMENT"

the voice of your eyes is deeper than all roses
nobody, not even the rain, has such small hands
    E. E. CUMMINGS, "SOMEWHERE I HAVE NEVER TRAVELLED"

Poems vary greatly in emotional intensity. Traditionally, poetry has been the voice of passion: the joy of mutual love and the sorrow of separation, the fear of death and the joyful certainty of resurrection. Homer's warriors wept for their dead comrades; religious poetry through the ages has sung the grandeur of God. Much twentieth-century poetry has been more sparing in its expression of emotions. Modern poets have often been wary of anything that might seem gushy or maudlin. They have tended to understate rather than to overstate their feelings.

In much traditional love poetry, the poet's emotional thermostat is set high, with the poem giving voice to yearning, ecstasy, or despair. Romantic love celebrates love as an overwhelming passion, giving meaning to otherwise meaningless lives, promising fulfillment to frustrated, anxiety-ridden people. Poets in this tradition were given to **hyperbole**—frank overstatement praising the angelic beauty of the beloved, idealizing the devotion of the lover. "O she doth teach the torches to burn bright!" says Shakespeare's Romeo when discovering the loveliness of Juliet—"Beauty too rich for use, for earth too dear!" Shakespeare, like other poets of his time, occasionally rebelled against the convention of hyperbolical praise. ("My mistress' eyes are nothing like the sun; / Coral is far more red than her lips' red; / If snow be white, why then her breasts are dun.") But many of his sonnets use the traditional heightened, exalted language of idealized love.

WILLIAM SHAKESPEARE (1564–1616)
Sonnet 18   before 1598

Shall I compare thee to a summer's day?	
Thou art more lovely and more temperate:	
Rough winds do shake the darling buds of May,	
And summer's lease° hath all too short a date:	*time span*
Sometimes too hot the eye of heaven shines,	5
And often is his gold complexion dimmed;	
And every fair° from fair sometimes declines,	*everything lovely*
By chance or nature's changing course untrimmed;°	*undone*

But thy eternal summer shall not fade,
Nor lose possession of that fair thou ow'st;°   *you own*   10
Nor shall death brag thou wander'st in his shade,
When in eternal lines° to time thou grow'st: *lines of verse*
So long as men can breathe, or eyes can see,
So long lives this, and this gives life to thee.

THE RECEPTIVE READER

1. How does this sonnet employ *hyperbole*? (How, in fact, does it go hyperbole one better?) Normally, to compare the beloved to the days of early summer or to the dazzling beauty of the glorious sun would be considered high praise. Why does the poet consider these comparisons inadequate?

2. Sometimes the final six lines (the *sestet*) and sometimes the final couplet provide a major "turning" in a sonnet. Which is it here? What answer does this poem give to the questions raised earlier?

Early in the twentieth century, the prevailing tone of poetry began to change from the richer chords of much traditional poetry to the sparer, understated tone that became the modern idiom. **Understatement** makes the poet play down personal feelings, letting the images of a poem speak for themselves. This does not mean that the poem is devoid of feeling. It often means that the poet trusts images and incidents faithfully rendered to call up the emotions and attitudes in the reader.

In many a modern poem, the emotional thermostat seems set lower than it might have been in an earlier day. The following is an understated modern poem that lets a thought-provoking, disturbing incident speak for itself.

WILLIAM STAFFORD (born 1914)

Traveling through the Dark   1960

Traveling through the dark I found a deer
dead on the edge of the Wilson River road.
It is usually best to roll them into the canyon:
that road is narrow; to swerve might make more dead.

By glow of the tail-light I stumbled back of the car   5
and stood by the heap, a doe, a recent killing;
she had stiffened already, almost cold.
I dragged her off; she was large in the belly.

My fingers touching the side brought me the reason—
her side was warm; her fawn lay there waiting,   10
alive, still, never to be born.
Beside that mountain road I hesitated.

The car aimed ahead its lowered parking lights;
under the hood purred the steady engine.
I stood in the glare of the warm exhaust turning red;   15
around our group I could hear the wilderness listen.

I thought hard for us all—my only swerving—
then pushed her over the edge into the river.

The poem starts on a dry, matter-of-fact note: The deer is dead; the road is narrow; best "to roll them into the canyon" to prevent further accidents. The speaker in the poem unceremoniously calls the dead deer a "heap"; he notes that it is "a recent killing." But he soon makes it hard for us as readers to maintain a matter-of-fact attitude: The side of the killed deer is still warm; she is large with a fawn,"alive, still, never to be born." The speaker in the poem hesitates, but only for a time. Then he does the right thing.

What are the poet's feelings? Maybe the poet is sick at heart at the thought of a mindless machine barreling down the highway to destroy one of God's creatures. Maybe the poet is sickened at the thought of the budding life in the doe's belly dumped into the river like garbage. However, the poem does not say. We can "hear the wilderness listen," and we also listen. But we hear no expressions of protest or grief; the only sound we hear is the motor of the automobile "purring" steadily in the background. Whatever he may feel, the speaker in the poem does the practical and necessary thing. He does not wave his arms or shout "I hate you!" at the universe. We know he "thought hard for us all." As one student reader said, "for a brief moment, he makes us think of the impossible task of saving the fawn." He hesitates for a time—that was his "only swerving" from acting businesslike and sensible. We as readers are left to wrestle with the traumatic event.

THE RECEPTIVE READER

1. Some readers have found the title of the poem to have more than a simple descriptive or factual significance. What could be its *symbolic* meaning?

2. What details or phrases for you do most to *set the tone* of the poem?

3. Do you think the poet felt emotions that the poem does not express? Do you think he *should have* expressed them?

THE PERSONAL RESPONSE

Do you think different readers would react differently to this poem? How much depends on the reader's experience with similar situations and on the reader's mind set or personality?

Rather than emote for the reader, most modern poets re-create for the reader's eyes emotion-charged images. Such is the practice of the Latino poet (North American of Puerto Rican ancestry) who wrote the following poem. One of his readers said of him that he "brings to life his love for his people while etching haunting pictures that create lasting images" for his readers.

MARTIN ESPADA   (born 1957)

Latin Night at the Pawnshop   1987

Chelsea, Massachusetts
Christmas, 1987

The apparition of a salsa band
gleaming in the Liberty Loan
pawnshop window:

Golden trumpet.
silver trombone,   5
congas, maracas, tambourine,
all with price tags dangling
like the city morgue ticket
on a dead man's toe.

THE RECEPTIVE READER

What thoughts and feelings do you think were in the poet's mind in front of the
pawnshop window? (What is sad about the name of the pawnshop? What are the emotions created by the concluding simile?)

Some poems build up emotional intensity by concentrating on a single
overwhelming passion. Others, however, do justice to mixed feelings or contradictory emotions. Modern poets especially have often been fascinated by the
crosscurrents and subtexts that complicate conventionally expected feelings.
The following is a modern poem of mourning that does not focus on the sadness of the bereaved. What are the memories and emotions in the mourners'
minds?

JOHN CROWE RANSOM   (1888–1974)

Bells for John Whiteside's Daughter   1924

There was such speed in her little body,
And such lightness in her footfall,
It is no wonder her brown study
Astonishes us all.

Her wars were bruited° in our high window,   *were heard of*   5
We looked among orchard trees and beyond
Where she took arms against her shadow,
Or harried unto the pond

The lazy geese like a snow cloud
Dripping their snow on the green grass,   10
Tricking and stopping, sleepy and proud,
Who cried in goose, Alas,

For the tireless heart within the little
Lady with rod that made them rise
From their noon apple-dreams and scuttle   15
Goose-fashion under the skies!

But now go the bells, and we are ready,
In one house we are sternly stopped
To say we are vexed at her brown study,
Lying so primly propped.   20

In this understated modern poem, the speaker does not pour forth his grief at the untimely death of a child. Instead, much of the poem helps us relive the speaker's delight in the remembered quickness and light footfall of the young girl. We flash back to the girl who used to play tirelessly in the orchard, conducting shadow wars with her own shadow or harrying the lazy, sleepy geese, driving them toward the pond. Now, as the bells call the mourners to pay their last respects to the body, they are "astonished" to see the child, who used to be so full of life, at rest as if in a "brown study"—as if she were absorbed in deciphering a difficult passage in a book. They are "vexed" or annoyed to see her once so speedy little body "lying so primly propped."

THE RECEPTIVE READER

1. Is there any hint of the mourners' emotions beyond their being "vexed"?
2. What is witty about the geese crying out "in goose"?
3. Do you feel mixed emotions in reading this poem?

THE RANGE OF INTERPRETATION

Critics have interpreted this poem in very different ways. Which of the two following ways of reading this poem seems more persuasive to you?

1. In this poem, the remembered delight in a child full of innocent life and the bitter disappointment at her death make us experience mixed emotions. The poet's feelings are ambivalent (from a Latin word meaning "marching in two directions at once"). For a parent or friend of the family, the loss of a young innocent child, full of life, is a shattering blow. But it is as if the vivid memory of the "tireless" child, carrying on her mock "wars" with the geese, and our "astonishment" at her transformation could for a time fend off the bitter irony of her death. We protect ourselves against the harsh, merciless reality of death by dwelling on our memory of the living child and by pretending to be "astonished" and not fully understand what has happened to her.

2. The speakers in the poem (the "we" in the poem) can recall the child's vitality in astonishment because it is not their child; it is "John Whiteside's Daughter." The speakers have watched the girl from their "high window," suggesting that the girl without a name of her own is a servant's child. (Ransom was a Southern poet.) The poem is not one of grief or bereavement as much as it is a poem of shock, of vexation. The speakers are not weeping or mourning; they are "sternly stopped." They are troubled more by the unpredictability of death's indifference to youth and vitality than they are grieving, as parents would.

EXPLORATIONS

The Poet's Voice

What is the prevailing tone in each of the following poems? How do they compare in emotional intensity? How overt is each poem in expressing the poet's attitudes and emotions? What kind of voice do you hear in each poem?

ROBERT HASS   (born 1941)

Song   1973

Afternoon cooking in the fall sun—
who is more naked
          than the man
yelling, "Hey, I'm home!"
          to an empty house?   5
thinking because the bay is clear,
the hills in yellow heat,
& scrub oak red in gullies
         that great crowds of family
should tumble from the rooms   10
         to throw their bodies on the Papa-body,
         I-am-loved.

Cat sleeps in the windowgleam,
         dust motes.
         On the oak table   15
    filets of sole
stewing in the juice of tangerines,
    slices of green pepper
        on a bone-white dish.

THE RECEPTIVE READER

1. What is the *underlying emotion* in this poem? For you, what images or phrases come closest to bringing it to the surface?

2. Would you call the poem as a whole *understated*? (Are the filets of sole and the bone-white dish in the poem by accident? How do the many short lines or half-lines affect the tone of the poem?)

LOUISE BOGAN   (1897–1970)

The Dream   1941

O God, in the dream the terrible horse began
To paw at the air, and make for me with his blows.
Fear kept for thirty-five years poured through his mane,
And retribution equally old, or nearly, breathed through his nose.

Coward complete, I lay and wept on the ground 5
When some strong creature appeared, and leapt for the rein.
Another woman, as I lay half in a swound°   *fainting fit*
Leapt in the air, and clutched at the leather and chain.

Give him, she said, something of yours as a charm.
Throw him, she said, some poor thing you alone claim. 10
No, no, I cried, he hates me; he's out for harm,
And whether I yield or not, it is all the same.

But, like a lion in a legend, when I flung the glove
Pulled from my sweating, my cold right hand,
The terrible beast, that no one may understand, 15
Came to my side, and put down his head in love.

THE RECEPTIVE READER

1. What is the *prevailing tone* in this poem? What kind of a dream are we asked to share? What words and phrases openly label emotion? What images help project it? How many words refer to violent motion?

2. How is this poem like a legend or *fairy tale*?

3. How did you expect the poem to *end*? How did you react to the ending?

4. Why are the *long, flowing* lines of this poem more appropriate here than the short, choppy lines of the preceding poem?

THE PERSONAL RESPONSE

What nightmares, if any, do you have? Have they changed over the years?

COUNTEE CULLEN (1903–1946)

Incident 1925

Once riding in old Baltimore,
    Heart-filled, head-filled with glee,
I saw a Baltimorean
    Keep looking straight at me.

Now I was eight and very small, 5
    And he was no whit° bigger,   *not a bit*
And so I smiled, but he poked out
    His tongue and called me "Nigger."

I saw the whole of Baltimore
    From May until December; 10
Of all the things that happened there
    That's all that I remember.

THE RECEPTIVE READER

1. What is the prevailing tone of this poem? Is it hostile, angry, outraged, aggressive, militant? How would you have reacted to this "incident"?

2. What makes the poem an example of *understatement*?

3. Why do you think many readers remember this poem—even though they may have forgotten other, more emotional indictments of racial prejudice?

THE PERSONAL RESPONSE

What has been your own experience with racial or ethnic slurs or with other kinds of prejudiced language? How do you react to them?

DYLAN THOMAS (1914–1953)

Do Not Go Gentle into That Good Night   1952

Do not go gentle into that good night,
Old age should burn and rave at close of day;
Rage, rage against the dying of the light.

Though wise men at their end know dark is right,
Because their words had forked no lightning they   5
Do not go gentle into that good night.

Good men, the last wave by, crying how bright
Their frail deeds might have danced in a green bay,
Rage, rage against the dying of the light.

10

Wild men who caught and sang the sun in flight,
And learn too late, they grieved it on its way,
Do not go gentle into that good night.

Grave men, near death, who see with blinding sight
Blind eyes could blaze like meteors and be gay,
Rage, rage against the dying of the light.   15

And you, my father, there on the sad height,
Curse, bless, me now with your fierce tears, I pray.
Do not go gentle into that good night.
Rage, rage against the dying of the light.

THE RECEPTIVE READER

1. What is the prevailing tone in this poem by the Welsh poet Dylan Thomas? How is the tone different from what you might expect in a poem about death?

2. The speaker in the poem does not address his own father directly till the *last stanza* of the poem. How does this last stanza affect your response to the poem? (How do you think your response to the poem might have been different if the father had been brought into the poem at the beginning?)

3. Thomas attracted a large following in the thirties and forties by writing with passionate intensity about the experiences of *ordinary people*. In this poem, what are striking examples of his writing about ordinary experience in heightened, intensely emotional language? How much of the heightened, passionate quality of his verse results from the playing off of extreme *opposites*?

4. This poem uses the traditional form of the *villanelle,* a set of three-line stanzas repeating the same rhyme scheme (aba), which is further reinforced by a fourth line added to the concluding stanza (rhyming abaa). What are the two opposed key words in the poem that the rhyme scheme keeps driving home? Two final lines alternate in the stanzas till they are juxtaposed in the concluding couplet. Why is this kind of insistent *repetition* more appropriate to Thomas' poem than it would be to a poem written in a more understated style?

THE PERSONAL RESPONSE

If wise men know that in the end "dark is right," is the "rage" the poet calls up futile? (Is it impious?)

JUXTAPOSITIONS ═══════════════

Poems of Mourning

Poems cover the emotional spectrum; they sensitize us to the feelings of others and educate the emotions. Some of the earliest known poems are **elegies,** or poems of mourning and lamentation. Compare the following more recent poems striking a mournful, elegiac note. The speaker in the first poem is "rueful"—filled with sadness and regret.

A. E. HOUSMAN   (1859–1936)

With Rue My Heart Is Laden   1896

With rue my heart is laden
    For golden friends I had,
For many a rose-lipped maiden
    And many a lightfoot lad.

By brooks too broad for leaping   5
    The lightfoot boys are laid;
The rose-lipped girls are sleeping
    In fields where roses fade.

THE RECEPTIVE READER

Why does the poet say that the "lightfoot lads" are laid "by brooks too broad for leaping"? Housman's sad poems were for a time immensely popular. Why do readers enjoy sad poems such as this one?

Traditional elegies do not always maintain the same note of bitterness to the end. They often work their way through bitter grief to calm acceptance or to the joyful certainty of resurrection. How does the following poem come to terms with loss?

N. SCOTT MOMADAY   (born 1934)

Earth and I Gave You Turquoise   1974

Earth and I gave you turquoise
    when you walked singing
We lived laughing in my house
    and told old stories
You grew ill when the owl cried   5
We will meet on Black Mountain

I will bring corn for planting
    and we will make fire
Children will come to your breast
    You will heal my heart   10
I speak your name many times
The wild cane remembers you

My young brother's house is filled
    I go there to sing
We have not spoken of you   15
    but our songs are sad
When Moon Woman goes to you
I will follow her white way

Tonight they dance near Chinle
    by the seven elms   20
There your loom whispered beauty
    They will eat mutton
and drink coffee till morning
You and I will not be there

I saw a crow by Red Rock   25
    standing on one leg
It was the black of your hair
    The years are heavy
I will ride the swiftest horse
You will hear the drumming hooves   30

THE RECEPTIVE READER

Although Momaday places his poem in the setting of the tribal past, it speaks a language that transcends time and place. Which of the images and statements in the poem do most to help you share the speaker's emotions? Which do most to help you place yourself in the speaker's place? How does the speaker deal with his grief?

THE PERSONAL RESPONSE

As you look back over these two poems, which of the two ways of dealing with loss and mourning appeals to you more? Why?

THE CREATIVE DIMENSION

The following re-creation captures the elegiac tone of Momaday's poem. For this or another poem in this chapter, do a similar re-creation that captures the tone of the original.

> We walked the earth together
> In my house we danced and drank coffee till morning
> I planted corn
> You wanted children
> But you became ill
> I thought love could heal you
> The years drag
> I'll dance no more
> But one day I'll speak your name
> And you'll come on a swift horse

THE USES OF WIT

> *Tsars,*
>   *Kings,*
>   *Emperors,*
> *sovereigns of all the earth,*
> *have commanded many a parade,*
> *but they could not command*
>   *humor.*
>
> YEVGENY YEVTUSHENKO

> *The human mind is kind of like a piñata. When it breaks open, there's a lot of surprises inside.*
>
> LILY TOMLIN

In our psychological armory, humor is a prize weapon for survival. It ranges from the inspired clowning that deflates pompousness to the dark humor that makes the unbearable bearable. When other means of attack seem unavailing, humor becomes the weapon of the satirist, using ridicule to cut an opponent down to size. Much humor deflates; we laugh when it punctures the balloon (while we may regret the loss of the balloon). What familiar daydreams are the target of the poet's wit in the following poem?

ISHMAEL REED   (born 1938)

.05   1973

If i had a nickel
For all the women who've
Rejected me in my life

I would be the head of the
World Bank with a flunkie   5
To hold my derby as i
Prepare to fly chartered
Jet to sign a check
Giving India a new lease
On life   10

If i had a nickel for
All the women who've loved
Me in my life i would be
The World Bank's assistant
Janitor and wouldn't need   15
To wear a derby
All i'd think about would
Be going home

In this poem, the soul of wit is **incongruity:** Things are mismatched, the way Charlie Chaplin's bowler hat and bow tie were mismatched with the king of silent screen comedy's baggy pants. A person thinking in terms of nickels is not likely to realize the impossible daydream of being a World Bank executive in a chartered jet—even if his money-raising scheme were based on something less pitiable than his failures in love. And if he did indeed achieve such status, he would likely call the person assisting him something more dignified than a "flunkie." We are likely to smile again when the neatly parallel second stanza juxtaposes our need for love, glorified by generations of poets, with an achievement record comparable to that of an assistant janitor.

THE RECEPTIVE READER

1. What details or phrases in this poem strike you as funny?
2. What is the connection between the daydream in this poem and current versions of the "American Dream"?

THE CREATIVE DIMENSION

Write your own "If-I-had-a-nickel" poem or prose passage.

Poems become more aggressive or bitter in tone when **satire** wields humor as a weapon. Satire employs ridicule to jab at callousness, pomposity, hypocrisy, false prophets, rip-off artists, and the law's delay. Some satirists flail out at miscellaneous abuses, but much effective satire takes clear aim at its target. It measures offenders against an implied standard of righteous or humane behavior and finds them wanting. What is the target in the following satirical poem?

EVE MERRIAM   (born 1916)
Robin Hood   1970

has returned
to Sherwood Forest
as
Secretary of the Interior

And the greenery   5
is to be preserved
for the public good

directly alongside
the parts reserved
for Hood enterprises   10

for Sherwood Homesites
Shop-and-Sher Parking Plaza
and
Sherburger Franchises.

THE RECEPTIVE READER

What accounts for the mocking tone of this poem? What is the target of the poet's *satire*? Where and how does the poem show the poet's wicked sense of humor?

What does the following poem imitate? What satirical points does it score?

DAVID WAGONER   (born 1927)
Breath Test   1983

He isn't going to stand for it sitting down
As far as he can from the unshaded glare
And the TV camera where he isn't breathing
In no machine no thanks because no way
Being sober as a matter of fact his body   5
Without a warrant is nobody's damn business
And to a republic for which he isn't
Putting that thing in his mouth as a citizen
Who voted he has a right to disobey
The Laws of Supply and Demand by running short   10
Of supplies and they can all go take a walk
On their own straight line all night if they feel like it.

THE RECEPTIVE READER

What garbled sayings and mixed clichés do you recognize in this monologue? What kind of person is talking? What is the *target* of the poet's satire?

EXPLORATIONS

Parodies Regained

Modern writers have often felt the urge to update traditional stories with comic effect. Often their retellings make us think both about the traditional story and the writer's modern slant on it.

A. D. HOPE   (born 1907)

Coup de Grâce   1970

Just at the moment the Wolf,
Shag jaws and slavering grin,
Steps from the property wood,
Oh, what a gorge, what a gulf
Opens to gobble her in,   5
Little Red Riding Hood!

O, what a face full of fangs!
Eyes like saucers at least
Roll to seduce and beguile.
Miss, with her dimples and bangs,   10
Thinks him a handsome beast;
Flashes the Riding Hood Smile;

Stands her ground like a queen,
Velvet red of the rose
Framing each little milk-tooth   15
Pink tongue peeping between.
Then, wider than anyone knows,
Opens her minikin mouth

Swallows up Wolf in a trice;
Tail going down gives a flick,   20
Caught as she closes her jaws.
Bows, all sugar and spice.
O, what a lady-like trick!
O, what a round of applause!

THE RECEPTIVE READER

1. What do you think moved the poet to retell this familiar classic? What about the old story needed updating and why?

2. What twists to the retelling seem to you particularly *modern*? What touches seem particularly comic and why? (What makes this poet a good storyteller?)

THE CREATIVE DIMENSION

Do your own modern retelling (in verse or prose) of a fairy tale that seems in need of updating.

POEMS FOR FURTHER STUDY

When reading the following poems, pay special attention to tone. What is the prevailing tone in each poem? What kind of voice is speaking to you in the poem?

SIR JOHN SUCKLING (1609–1642)

Song   1638

Why so pale and wan, fond° lover?   *foolish*
    Prithee,° why so pale?   *please*
Will, when looking well can't move her,
    Looking ill prevail?
    Prithee, why so pale?   5

Why so dull and mute, young sinner?
    Prithee, why so mute?
Will, when speaking well can't win her,
    Saying nothing do 't?

Quit, quit, for shame; this will not move,°   *persuade*   10
    This cannot take her.
If of herself she will not love,
    Nothing can make her:
    The devil take her!

RICHARD LOVELACE (1618–1658)

To Lucasta, Going to the Wars   1649

Tell me not, sweet, I am unkind
That from the nunnery
Of thy chaste breast and quiet mind,
To war and arms I fly.°   *hurry*

True, a new mistress now I chase,   5
The first foe in the field;
And with a stronger faith embrace
A sword, a horse, a shield.

Yet this inconstancy is such
As you too shall adore;   10
I could not love thee, dear, so much,
Loved I not° honor more.   *if I did not*

THE RECEPTIVE READER

What is the central metaphor the poet chooses for going away to war? What makes it playful or humorous? How does the poet play on words in the final two lines?

SHARON OLDS   (born 1942)

Quake Theory

1980

When two plates of earth scrape along each other
like a mother and daughter
it is called a fault.

There are faults that slip smoothly past each other
an inch a year, with just a faint rasp   5
like a man running his hand over his chin,
that man between us,

and there are faults that get stuck at a bend for twenty years.
The ridge bulges up like a father's sarcastic forehead
and the whole thing freezes in place, the man between us.   10

When this happens, there will be heavy damage
to industrial areas and leisure residences
when the deep plates
finally jerk past
the terrible pressure of their contact.   15

                              The earth cracks
and innocent people slip gently in like swimmers.

THE RECEPTIVE READER

How does the earthquake metaphor affect the tone of this poem? In developing
the implications of this central metaphor, how does the poet start in a low key and
build up to a climax? (Where is the high point? How does the poet make it stand out?)
What is the speaker's attitude toward the daughter? What is the speaker's attitude toward the father? Who are the "innocent people"?

CLAUDE MCKAY   (1890–1948)

If We Must Die

1919

If we must die, let it not be like hogs
Hunted and penned in an inglorious spot,
While round us bark the mad and hungry dogs,
Making their mock at our accursèd lot.
If we must die, O let us nobly die,   5
So that our precious blood may not be shed
In vain; then even the monsters we defy
Shall be constrained to honor us though dead!
O kinsmen we must meet the common foe!
Though far outnumbered let us show us brave,   10
And for their thousand blows deal one deathblow!
What though before us lies the open grave?
Like men we'll face the murderous, cowardly pack
Pressed to the wall, dying, but fighting back!

THE RECEPTIVE READER

1. How should this poem be read? What is the *stance* of the speaker in the poem? What words and images most strongly convey his feelings?

2. The language of protest and of race relations has changed since McKay's day. If you had been a contemporary of the poet, do you think you would have been moved by McKay's defiant rhetoric? Why or why not?

WRITING ABOUT LITERATURE
9. Responding to Tone (Reading the Clues)

The Writing Workshop   When you write about tone, you need to read between the lines. You need to have your antenna out for the emotional quality of a poem. Modern poets are not likely to establish the tone of a poem by announcement ("Ah, how I suffer!"). Neither can you simply infer the tone of a poem from its apparent subject matter. For instance, you might expect a poem about a funeral to be sad and solemn. However, you cannot take the tone for granted. The poem may have been written in a tone of stern moralizing about the shortcomings of the deceased. Or it may dwell on bittersweet memories of happier hours.

Make your paper show that you have read for clues to the attitudes and feelings that seem built into a poem:

❖ Pay special attention to the *connotations* of words. *Vexed, angry,* and *furious* are different points on a continuing scale. They go from a low-key state of annoyance and perplexity (or "vexation") through ordinary anger to furious uncontrolled rage. Look for a network of related words that might help set the tone of a poem. A poet might create a careless, joyful mood by the repeated use of synonyms or near-synonyms like *mirth, merry, jocund, revelry, good cheer, fiesta, frolic, joyous.* (A poem in which words like these echo is not likely to be a solemn ode in praise of the Puritan work ethic.)

❖ Listen to the *rhythm* of the poem as it is read out loud. Is the poem slow-moving, deliberate, earnest? Is it skipping and cheerful? Is it urgent, insistent, driven by passionate indignation?

❖ Take into account the attitude the poem adopts toward the *reader* or listener: Is the tone defiant, challenging? Does the poem take you into the speaker's confidence as if in a conspiratorial whisper? Does it treat you like a boon companion?

❖ Try to become sensitive to *nuances.* Unconditional love or hate or admiration is rare. A poet may admire something "this side idolatry" (as Ben Jonson did his fellow poet and playwright William Shakespeare).

❖ Look for signs of humorous intention or irreverent *wit.* When Lord Byron says about the high-toned philosophical speculations of a fellow poet, "I wish he would explain his explanations," we know that Byron's attitude will be less than worshipful. Watch especially for irreverent slangy expressions that undercut serious pretentions ("thus Milton's universe *went to smash*"). Read for revealing metaphors or similes ("Thus in his head / science and ignorance were kneaded like a sticky dough together").

❖ Look for *shifts* in tone that may help shape a poem as a whole. A poem may move from a tone of bitterness and indignation to a more understanding and forgiving tone. A Christian elegy may start with notes of deep mourning but is likely to work its way to the joyful certainty of resurrection. It will not just project grief but try to come to terms with it, leaving us at the end cleansed and calm, ready to move on "to fresh woods, and pastures new."

How does the following student paper read the clues that help the poet set the tone?

SAMPLE STUDENT PAPER

"Quake Theory," or Whose Fault Is It?

There is nothing quite as much fun as a punning wit. To utilize one word to mean two different things creates an effect like those optical illusions where we can see an old woman or a young girl . . . or again an old woman—this tickles the brain. And, tickled, we smile until, as in Sharon Olds' poem "Quake Theory," the serious message sinks in, and we realize this isn't fun anymore.

An initial metaphor is developed in the first stanza; it also sets up the pun: "When two plates of earth scrape along each other / like a mother and daughter / it is called a fault." The word *fault* does double-time here as a description of a fracture in the earth and as a key word to alert us to the distance between a mother and her daughter. That distance can best be summed up in the question: "Whose fault is it?" What is the *it* that isn't working?

The poem does not enlighten us immediately. Instead it sounds for a moment as though it might drone along in a professorial manner, informing us of two different kinds of fault in two stanzas. ("There are faults that slip smoothly past each other / an inch a year.") We read along, smiling in anticipation of further developments in what may prove an extended joke. The tone is dry, almost too dry, but we have been trained by generations of deadpan comedians to expect lurking underneath the surface dryness the levity of a joke. Sharon Olds lures us in but then abruptly shifts gears to refer to "that man between us."

Just who is this man? The man, as Sharon Olds intended, is a discordant note in this poem. Not only does his introduction into the poem upset the flow of the poem, but he himself is an upsetting influence in the relationship between mother and daughter.

We read in the second stanza that a fault can be trouble-free with only a bit of friction—friction likened to what results when a man rubs his five-o'clock shadow (not just any man, but "that man between us"). However, in the third stanza, we read that a fault may also be blocked and build up tension "like a father's sarcastic forehead," and "the whole thing freezes in place, the man between us." With this ominous note, the poem no longer seems to point toward a humorous conclusion. The repeated references to "that man," ending each of the two stanzas, remind us that the central metaphor in this poem is the earthquake.

The point of view is that of the mother speaking to the daughter (or perhaps vice-versa). The speaker is trying to describe their relationship, which remains in constant motion, "scraping" at times, building up tension at others. But there is also a third dynamic, "that man," the father. He is there benignly or as an active threat, but he is certainly there.

What is the result when the tension builds up between the two locked bodies? "There will be heavy damage / . . . when the deep plates / finally jerk past / the terrible pressure of their contact." In keeping with the metaphor of the earthquake, the poem itself fractures at this point, skips a line, and then resumes:

> The earth cracks
> and innocent people slip gently in like swimmers.

What an odd analogy! We may assume that in a clash of wills or land masses, some who are bystanders will suffer, perhaps even be swallowed, but this image seems both deadly and harmless at the same time. To "slip gently in like swimmers" seems to belie the violence just described. But this is perhaps as it should be: In any family upset there are not necessarily bleeding victims left lying around afterwards. People are sucked under without a surface struggle or disturbance.

In this poem, we are carried along at first amused, then puzzled or disturbed, and then saddened at the end. We sense that things might have been different; there is regret here. But whose "fault" is it? It is neither the mother's nor the daughter's but, as in plate tectonics, the fault of the rift between them, the father.

QUESTIONS

1. How does this paper trace the shifts in tone in this poem? Does it discover nuances that you might have missed?

2. This student writer was especially sensitive to the relation between form and meaning, sound and sense. Where and how does the paper show the connection between meaning and outward shape or form?

3. How close is this writer's reaction to the poem to your own reaction?

10 IRONY AND PARADOX
Marrying Contraries

Although life is an affair of light and shadow, we never accept it as such. We are always reaching toward the light. From childhood we are given values which correspond only to an ideal world. The shadowy side of real life is ignored. Thus, we are unable to deal with the mixture of light and shadow of which life really consists.

MIGUEL SERRAN

Life is bounded by wonder on one side and terror on the other.

SAM KEEN

FOCUS ON IRONY AND PARADOX

Some art and poetry filter out what is ugly or disappointing in life. Their patrons adorn living room walls with paintings of sunsets or of stags posed in forest clearings. They like poems about children playing in a garden or about offspring honoring their elders. Filtered poetry is like a portrait photographer who airbrushes blemishes, frowns, and signs of age. We are flattered by the re-touched picture, but we know it tells only part of the truth. Most modern poets (like many poets of earlier ages) resist the temptation to make the world unconvincingly beautiful. They resist the impulse to oversimplify. They take naturally to irony and paradox as ways of doing justice to the undercurrents and countercurrents of life.

Irony and paradox are the poet's way of bringing in a neglected or ignored part of the story:

◇ **Irony** produces a wry humorous effect by bringing in a part of the truth that we might have preferred to hide. Irony knows that the idol has feet of clay, and may tell us so with glee. It often has the last word, undercutting the more flattering or idealizing hypothesis. The truth irony discovers may be unexpected or unwelcome, but it may be true nevertheless.

◇ A **paradox** is an apparent contradiction that begins to make sense on second thought. Something at first does not seem true, but when we think

249

about it we see how it might be. Like irony, paradox is aware of the discrepancy between the rest of the idol and its feet, but it is more likely to make us try to resolve the contradiction. We may begin to see the point of it: Life itself is neither all clay or all gold. What is beautiful in our world is ultimately rooted in common clay.

Many observers have noted a special affinity between irony and the modern temper. Much of the best-known modern poetry has an ironic tone. Whenever something seems too beautiful to be true, we seem prepared for the ironic counterpoint. We seem ready for the kind of irony that is the revenge of reality on rosy projections. The following concluding stanza from a poem by Sylvia Plath is attuned to the modern temper.

SYLVIA PLATH (1932–1963)

From *Watercolor of Grantchester Meadows* 1959

Droll, vegetarian, the water rat
Saws down a reed and swims from his limber grove,
While the students stroll or sit,
Hands laced, in a moony indolence° of love— *carefree laziness*
Black-gowned, but unaware 5
How in such mild air
The owl shall stoop from his turret,° the rat cry out. *small tower jutting from a castle*

The first few words of this stanza hint at an unusual perspective: The water rat (which we might expect to be repulsive) is described as "droll"—amusing in a harmless eccentric way—and "vegetarian," as if watching its health like a fellow human. The rat provides an ironic underside to the idyllic collegiate setting where students stroll lazily in the "mild air," absorbed in moony thoughts of young love. They are ironically unaware of the life-and-death drama played out as the owl swoops down on the harmless-seeming amusing rat.

Ironically, the students' sense of security is only an illusion. When we least suspect it, evil lurks, ready to strike and make us "cry out." The poet's sense of irony makes her bring into the poem the kind of knowledge we like to push to the back of our minds.

THE RECEPTIVE READER

1. Why did the poet make this minidrama take place in "mild air" rather than in threatening weather? Is there any point in her mentioning the black academic gowns? (Why are they being worn?)
2. Do you identify with the students? the rat? the owl?
3. In this excerpt, does irony have the *last word?* Why or why not?

THE PERSONAL RESPONSE

Does your own campus have an idyllic atmosphere? Is it ever threatened or disrupted?

THE USES OF IRONY

*Neatness, madam has
nothing to do
with the Truth.
The Truth
is quite messy
like
a wind blown room.*
        WILLIAM J. HARRIS

*Snowy egrets stand
graceful, majestic, serene
among the beer cans*
        STUDENT HAIKU

Irony makes us smile, but with a wry rather than a happy smile. It may leave us with a bitter aftertaste as we say to ourselves: "I should have known." It is ironic when a crusader for family values gets divorced. Such ironies may make us smile with a knowing smile, but they do not make us glad. What is the irony in the following poem by a master ironist among American poets?

STEPHEN CRANE   (1871–1900)

A Man Saw a Ball of Gold   1895

A man saw a ball of gold in the sky;
He climbed for it,
And eventually he achieved it—
It was clay.
Now this is the strange part: 5
When the man went to earth
And looked again,
Lo, there was the ball of gold.
Now this is the strange part:
It was a ball of gold.   10
Ay, by heavens, it was a ball of gold.

There is a double irony in this poem: Something golden we worship from afar may turn out to be made of common clay when we come closer. (An admired leader may turn out to be corrupt. A person we adore may turn out to be petty or totally unresponsive to our love.) This sad and funny defeat of our human expectations is the essence of irony. But such disillusionment may not destroy our capacity for illusion: When we have barely returned to reality, our capacity for being fooled is already activated again. The larger irony is that we are protected against facing the truth as by an armored vest. We stubbornly refuse to learn from experience.

THE RECEPTIVE READER

1. What is the effect of the poet's abrupt, very brief presentation of the ironic counterpoint in line 4?

2. Why is there so much repetition in this poem? (Why do you think the poet considered it necessary? What effect does it have on the reader?)

THE PERSONAL RESPONSE

Have you had any experience with a "ball of gold" turning into common clay?

Irony ranges in tone from playful to bitter or desperate. It ranges from gently teasing to aggressive and slashing, turning into **sarcasm.** In the following poem, a master of the more playful and indulgent kind of irony points to the ironic discrepancy between our dignified, self-important self-image and our odd behavior.

OGDEN NASH   (1902–1971)

The Hunter

1949

The hunter crouches in his blind
'Neath camouflage of every kind,
And conjures up a quacking noise
To lend allure to his decoys.
This grown-up man, with pluck and luck,   5
Is hoping to outwit a duck.

THE RECEPTIVE READER

In how many ways does Nash heighten the ironic contrast between the hunter and the target?

Ogden Nash delighted in the spectacle of a grown man pretending to be a duck. As the heavyweight of light verse, his mission was to help us take ourselves less seriously. Much modern poetry has gravitated to the opposite end of the spectrum, asking us to be more serious when we might be thoughtless or uncaring. The following bitterly ironic poem looks at the exploitation of the Indian past as a tourist attraction from the point of view of a native American poet. nila northSun was born in Nevada and is of Shoshoni-Chippewa heritage. What is the irony in this poem?

NILA NORTHSUN   (born 1951)

Moving Camp Too Far   1984

i can't speak of
    many moons
    moving camp on travois
i can't tell of
    the last great battle   5
    counting coup or
    taking scalp
i don't know what it
    was to hunt buffalo
    or do the ghost dance   10
but
i can see an eagle
    almost extinct
    on slurpee plastic cups
i can travel to powwows   15
    in campers & winnebagos
i can eat buffalo meat
    at the tourist burger stand
i can dance to indian music
    rock-n-roll hey-a-hey-o   20
i can
    & unfortunately
    i do

THE RECEPTIVE READER

1. What's the meaning of *travois* and *counting coup*? What does the title mean?

2. An editor reprinting this poem said, "This poem is a mourning song, as it is one of a stunted and trivialized vision made to fit a pop-culture conception of the Indian. . . . it highlights some of the more enraging aspects of American culture" as they can appear only to native Americans. What did she mean?

THE PERSONAL RESPONSE

Have you ever experienced feelings similar to those expressed in this poem?

We use the term *irony* in at least two major ways. A contrast between what we expect and what really happens makes for **irony of situation.** When the ocean liner *Titanic,* touted as unsinkable, went down on her maiden voyage with a terrible loss of life, the English poet Thomas Hardy pondered the ironic contrast between human "vaingloriousness" and the ship's inglorious end. A deliberate contrast between what we say and what we really mean makes for **verbal irony**—intentional irony in our use of language. The following poem, by a British-born poet who became an American citizen, is an extended exercise in verbal irony, starting with the title. Monuments to the Unknown Soldier were meant to commemorate the heroic war dead by honoring the remains of an unidentified soldier killed in action. As we read the following poem, we find that there is nothing heroic about the "unknown citizen," and it is not the poet's intention to honor him. (What *is* the poet's intention?)

W. H. AUDEN   (1907–1973)

The Unknown Citizen   1940

(To JS/O7/M/378
This Marble Monument
Is Erected by the State)

He was found by the Bureau of Statistics to be
One against whom there was no official complaint,
And all the reports of his conduct agree
That in the modern sense of an old-fashioned word, he was a saint,
For in everything he did he served the Greater Community.   5
Except for the War till the day he retired
He worked in a factory and never got fired,
But satisfied his employers, Fudge Motors Inc.
Yet he wasn't a scab° or odd in his views,   *strikebreaker*
For his Union reports that he paid his dues,   10
(Our report on his Union shows it was sound)
And our Social Psychology workers found
That he was popular with his mates° and liked a drink.   *his friends*
The Press are convinced that he bought a paper every day
And that his reactions to advertisements were normal in every way.   15
Policies taken out in his name prove that he was fully insured,
And his Health-card shows he was once in a hospital but left it cured.
Both Producers Research and High-Grade Living declare
He was fully sensible to the advantages of the Installment Plan
And had everything necessary to the Modern Man,   20
A phonograph, a radio, a car and a frigidaire.
Our researchers into Public Opinion are content
That he held the proper opinions for the time of year;
When there was peace, he was for peace; when there was war he went.
He was married and added five children to the population,   25
Which our Eugenist° says was the right number for a parent of his generation, *population*
And our teachers report that he never interfered with their education.   *planner*
Was he free? Was he happy? The question is absurd:
Had anything been wrong, we should certainly have heard.

THE RECEPTIVE READER

1. The Unknown Soldier was anonymous because the remains could not be identified. Why does Auden give his Unknown Citizen no name but only a number?

2. What clues in the poem remind us that the poet is speaking ironically? For instance, what is wrong with holding "the proper opinions for the time of year"? What is ironic about the citizen's attitude toward war? Why is what the teachers say about him a

left-handed compliment? (Can you find other examples of mock compliments that are examples of verbal irony?)

3. Many of the institutions keeping tab on the citizenry apparently regarded JS/07/M/378 as a model citizen, if not a "saint." What is the poet's basic criticism of him? (What is the poet's basic criticism of the state?)

THE CREATIVE DIMENSION

Auden wrote this poem in 1940. What would you include in an updated portrait of the Unknown Citizen or the Unknown Consumer? Write your own ironic portrait of today's Unknown Citizen.

Much twentieth-century poetry has focused on the ironic contrast between official war propaganda and the horrible realities of war. The following poem is by Wilfred Owen, a British officer who wrote about the "sorrowful dark hell" of the Great War—World War I—and who was killed on the western front a week before the armistice ended the war in 1918. The motto he quotes in the title of the poem (and again at the end) is a quotation from the Roman poet Horace. It was known to every British schoolboy of Owen's generation: *Dulce et decorum est pro patria mori*—"How sweet and fitting it is to die for one's country." Owen once said, "My subject is war and the pity of war. The poetry is in the pity."

WILFRED OWEN   (1893–1918)

Dulce et Decorum Est   1918

Bent double, like old beggars under sacks,
Knock-kneed, coughing like hags, we cursed through sludge,
Till on the haunting flares we turned our backs
And toward our distant rest began to trudge.
Men marched asleep. Many had lost their boots   5
But limped on, blood-shod. All went lame; all blind;
Drunk with fatigue; deaf even to the hoots
Of tired, outstripped Five-Nines° that dropped behind.   *gas shells*

Gas! Gas! Quick, boys!—An ecstasy of fumbling,
Fitting the clumsy helmets just in time;   10
But someone still was yelling out and stumbling,
And floundering like a man in fire or lime . . .
Dim, through the misty panes and thick green light,
As under a green sea, I saw him drowning.
In all my dreams, before my helpless sight,   15
He plunges at me, guttering, choking, drowning.

If in some smothering dreams you too could pace
Behind the wagon that we flung him in,
And watch the white eyes writhing in his face,
His hanging face, like a devil's sick of sin;   20

If you could hear, at every jolt, the blood
Come gargling from his froth-corrupted lungs,
Obscene as cancer, bitter as the cud
Of vile, incurable sores on innocent tongues,—
My friend, you would not tell with such high zest   25
To children ardent for some desperate glory,
The old Lie: Dulce et decorum est
Pro patria mori.

THE RECEPTIVE READER

1. How does the picture the first stanza paints of the troops being withdrawn from the front lines for "rest" differ from the one you would expect to encounter on propaganda posters or in patriotic speeches? Why is there a bitter irony in the *timing* of the gas attack in this poem?

2. Many people have read about the use of poison gas by the belligerents in World War I. How does Owen drive the realities of chemical warfare home? From what *perspectives*—when and how—do you see the victim? What is the effect on you as the reader?

3. How and with what effect is the word *drowning* repeated in this poem? What gives the word *innocent* toward the end of the poem its special power? Who is guilty in this poem?

4. This poem owes its eloquence in part to the insistent piling on of related words and similar, *parallel* structures. Where and how?

5. What is the basic irony in this poem?

THE PERSONAL RESPONSE

Are we today too removed from the realities of war to share feelings like those expressed in this poem? Are our feelings too blunted from overexposure? How does the treatment of war in the media affect our feelings about war?

JUXTAPOSITIONS ⊂══════════════════

Modern Parables

> A man said to the universe:
> "Sir, I exist!"
> "However," replied the universe,
> "The fact has not created in me
> A sense of obligation."
>   STEPHEN CRANE

A **parable** is a brief story with a weighty meaning, which the listeners or readers are left to ponder and make out for themselves. Study the workings of irony in the following short monologues and dialogues. Is there a common thread or a shared underlying attitude?

STEPHEN CRANE (1871–1900)

The Wayfarer   1895

The wayfarer,
Perceiving the pathway to truth,
Was struck with astonishment.
It was thickly grown with weeds.
"Ha," he said,   5
"I see that none has passed here
In a long time."
Later he saw that each weed was a singular knife.
"Well," he mumbled at last,
"Doubtless there are other roads."   10

There Was Crimson Clash of War   1895

There was crimson clash of war.
Lands turned black and bare;
Women wept;
Babes ran, wondering.
There came one who understood not these things.   5
He said: "Why is this?"
Whereupon a million strove to answer him.
There was such intricate clamor° of tongues,   *confused outcry*
That still the reason was not.

THE RECEPTIVE READER

What is Crane's ironic comment on the pursuit of truth? What is his ironic comment on the causes of war?

BRUCE BENNETT (born 1940)

Leader   1984

A man shot himself
in the foot.

"OW!" he howled,
hopping this way and
that. "Do something!   5
Do something!"

"We are! We are!"
shouted those around
him. "We're hopping!
We're hopping!"   10

THE RECEPTIVE READER

How closely does this poem follow the pattern of Stephen Crane's "A-man-did-such-and-such" poems? What is the poet's ironic comment on leaders and followers?

THE CREATIVE DIMENSION

Write your own updated "A-person-did-such-and-such" poem.

THE USES OF PARADOX

Whatever it is, it must have
A stomach that can digest
Rubber, coal, uranium, moons, poems.
Like the shark, it contains a shoe.
It must swim for miles through the desert
Uttering cries that are almost human.
LOUIS SIMPSON ON AMERICAN POETRY

One must live in the middle of contradiction because if all
contradiction were eliminated at once life would collapse.
There are simply no answers to some of the great pressing
questions. You continue to live them out, making your life
a worthy expression of leaning into the light.
BARRY LOPEZ

Be patient with all that is unsolved in your heart.
RAINER MARIA RILKE

A **paradox** is a seeming contradiction that begins to make sense on second thought. Like irony, a paradox challenges us to keep more than one idea in mind at the same time. We are confronted with a paradox when we realize that many feel lonely in a crowd, that many are alone in the midst of our crowded, congested cities. When we think about it, however, this apparent contradiction begins to make sense: The physical presence of others is not enough; we need to be with people who understand and who care.

Poets have found love a paradoxical emotion, fraught with attraction and rejection, joy and pain, hope and despair. What makes the following poem about love paradoxical?

NELLE FERTIG   (born 1919)

I Have Come to the Conclusion   1974

I have come to the conclusion
          she said
that when we fall in love

we really fall in love with ourselves—
that we choose particular people
because they provide
the particular mirrors
in which we wish to see.

And when did you discover
this surprising bit of knowledge?
      he asked.

After I had broken a few
very fine mirrors
      she said.

5

10

What the woman in this poem says is paradoxical because at first glance it doesn't seem to be true. Supposedly, when we fall in love, we go beyond our usual self-love to make someone else more important than we are to ourselves. Isn't the beauty of love that it lifts us out of our petty needs and complaints? It makes us care for somebody else. But, on second thought, we may begin to see the point: We may well be prone to fall in love with people who think that we are in some way special or wonderful. We are moved when we ask the mirror on the wall, "Who's the fairest of them all?" and the mirror replies, "You are." We may get angry when the mirror replies, "Someone else is." (To judge from the poem, some "very fine mirrors" are broken this way.)

What then is the difference between irony and paradox? Both bring in a part of the truth that simpleminded people tend to ignore. But irony tends to have the last word. When we discover that the idol has feet of clay, we may cease to worship the idol. A paradox asks us to puzzle over the apparent contradiction and to balance off the conflicting points of view. We may have to live with both parts of the paradox. When we look for someone to admire, we may have to settle for someone who has human imperfections.

THE CREATIVE DIMENSION

Cluster the word *mirror*. What images, associations, or memories does the word bring to mind? Are any of them related to the role mirrors play in Fertig's poem?

Love poetry in the Western world long followed the lead of the Italian fourteenth-century poet Petrarch. In the Petrarchan tradition, love was a paradoxical mixture of joy and sorrow. Love was a source of much joy, but it was often disappointed and therefore also the cause of much suffering. The following is a modern translation of a sonnet by Petrarch. (Trace the interlaced rhyme scheme of the traditional fourteen-line poem, and listen for the underlying iambic meter.) What makes this poem paradoxical? How much of it makes sense on second thought?

FRANCESCO PETRARCA   (1304–1374)

Or Che 'l Ciel e la Terra e 'l Vento Tace   1369

TRANSLATED BY HANS P. GUTH

Calm now are heaven and earth, and the winds asleep.
No birds now stir; wild beasts in slumber lie.
Night guides her chariot across the starry sky.
No wave now moves the waters of the deep.
I only keep vigil—I think, I burn, I weep.   5
She who destroys me dazzles my mind's eye.
At war with myself, raging and grieving , I
Long for the peace that's hers to give or keep.
From the same single fountain of life
Rise the bitter and sweet that feed my soul.   10
I am caressed and slashed by the same hand.
A martyr in a world of ceaseless strife,
I have died and risen a thousandfold.
So far am I from reaching the promised land.

THE RECEPTIVE READER

1. What is fitting, and what is *paradoxical,* about the nighttime setting?
2. What examples can you find of *opposed* concepts, clashing images, and mixed emotions?
3. Poets who made love into a religion often used the vocabulary of religious devotion. Where and how does this poem use *religious imagery?* What makes the religious images paradoxical?

In the following Shakespeare sonnet, a central paradox sets up many of the apparent contradictions in the poem. At first, the time of year seems to be winter—freezing, bare, and barren. A loved person is away, and everything seems dark and empty. But here is the paradox: It's actually summer, the season of bird song and abundance. Why then is the speaker in the poem shivering and freezing? The answer is that it is summer outside but winter in the poet's soul. Our true mental climate is not determined by the outside temperature but by the built-in thermostats in our minds.

WILLIAM SHAKESPEARE   (1564–1616)

Sonnet 97   before 1598

How like a winter hath my absence been
From thee, the pleasure of the fleeting° year!   *quickly passing*
What freezings have I felt, what dark days seen!
What old December's bareness everywhere!

And yet this time removed° was summer's time   *with you absent*   5
The teeming autumn, big with rich increase,°   *full of new life*
Bearing the wanton burthen of the prime,°   *giving birth to spring's luxurious offspring*
Like widowed wombs after their lords' decease:
Yet this abundant issue seemed to me
But hope of orphans and unfathered fruit;   10
For summer and his pleasures wait on thee,
And, thou away,° the very birds are mute.   *with you away*
Or, if they sing, 'tis with so dull a cheer
That leaves look pale, dreading the winter's near.

THE RECEPTIVE READER

1. As one student reader said, "In this poem, summer comes only when the loved person is there." In how many different ways is this *central paradox* followed up or echoed in this poem?

2. Where and how does the central metaphor shift from autumn to widowhood? What is the connection? What paradoxical emotions does the orphan metaphor bring into the poem?

3. How do the leaves in the last line illustrate *personification*—reading human qualities into the inanimate world? Where else does the poem show the power of personification to turn the world around us into a mirror of our emotions?

EXPLORATIONS

Understanding Paradox

Explain the paradoxes in the following lines. What makes them strange or contradictory? How do they make sense on second thought?

1. I am the dove
   Whose wings are murder.
   My name is love.
   > Charles Causley, "Envoi"

2. The reverse side also has a reverse side.
   > Japanese proverb

3. Sprayed with strong poison
   my roses are crisp this year
   In the crystal vase
   > Paul Goodman, "Haiku"

4. All poems say the same thing, and each poem is unique.
   > Octavio Paz

EXPLORATIONS ═══════════════════

Paradoxes of Faith

> *This, in its essence, is a description of the metaphysical poet who thinks with his body: an idea for him can be as real as the smell of a flower or a blow on the head. And those so lucky as to bring their whole sensory equipment to bear on the process of thought grow faster, jump more frequently from one plateau to another more often.*
>
> THEODORE ROETHKE

The **metaphysical** poets of the early seventeenth century are known for their love of paradox. They are fond of yoking together things from widely different areas of experience. In their religious poetry, they translate the mysteries of faith into language borrowed from science, medicine, mechanics, or war. They deal with the central paradoxes of religious doctrine: the certainty of death but yet the belief in life after death; our yearning for God's love and yet our stubborn attachment to sin.

The title of the following religious poem refers not to altars or incense but to a mechanical device made of wheels, blocks, and rope. A pulley was used to multiply human strength and lift heavy weights in the days before steam-powered or electricity-driven winches. One of Herbert's editors has said that the secret of Herbert's poetry is "the recovery of fresh feeling" from old formulas. What is different or unexpected about the relationship between God and humanity in the poem? What is the central paradox in this poem?

GEORGE HERBERT   (1593–1633)

The Pulley   1633

When God at first made man,
Having a glass of blessings standing by,
"Let us," he said, "pour on him all we can:
Let the world's riches, which dispersèd° lie,   *lie scattered*
　　Contract into a span."°   *short space*   5

So strength first made a way;
Then beauty flowed, then wisdom, honor, pleasure.
When almost all was out, God made a stay,°   *paused*
Perceiving that, alone of all his treasure,
　　Rest in the bottom lay.   10

"For if I should," said he,
"Bestow° this jewel also on my creature,   *pass on*
He would adore my gifts instead of me,
And rest in Nature, not the God of Nature;
　　So both should losers be.   15

"Yet let him keep the rest,
But keep them with repining° restlessness: *yearning*
Let him be rich and weary, that at least,
If goodness lead him not, yet weariness
    May toss him to my breast."   20

THE RECEPTIVE READER

1. Admirers have praised Herbert and the other metaphysical poets for their *wit*, in the more general sense of a quick mind or intellectual alertness. Part of this mental quickness is their willingness to use a play on words, or *pun*, even when writing about solemn subjects. What does the word *rest* mean when "*Rest* in the bottom lay"? (*Restlessness* later appears as its opposite.) What does the word mean when God's creature is likely to "*rest* in Nature, not the God of Nature"? How does the poet pun, or play on the word, when God decides to let us "keep the *rest*"—everything except *rest*? (How does the poet make this key word stand out in the poem?)

2. What is paradoxical about richly blessed creatures suffering from "repining restlessness"? Do you think it is true?

3. One student wrote that in this poem humanity is "deprived rather than depraved." What did she mean?

The second metaphysical poem in this group focuses on a key paradox of Christian doctrine: Central to the believer's religious awakening is the realization of mortality, the fear of death. But ultimately the hope of resurrection makes death lose its sting. In the words of the poem, death has no reason to "swell" with pride. We are afraid of death, and yet we are not afraid of death.

JOHN DONNE   (1572–1631)
Holy Sonnet 10   about 1609

Death, be not proud, though some have callèd thee
Mighty and dreadful, for thou are not so;
For those whom thou thinkst thou dost overthrow
Die not, poor Death, nor yet canst thou kill me.
From rest and sleep, which but thy pictures be,°   *are your lookalikes*   5
Much pleasure—then from thee much more must flow,
And soonest our best men with thee do go,
Rest of their bones, and soul's delivery.°   *release of their souls*
Thou art slave to fate, chance, kings, and desperate men,
And dost with poison, war, and sickness dwell,   10
And poppy or charm can make us sleep as well
And better than thy stroke; why swellst thou then?
One short sleep past, we wake eternally
And death shall be no more; Death, thou shalt die.

THE RECEPTIVE READER

1. In his religious poems, as in his earlier love poetry, Donne projects his personal feelings onto a large screen. He acts out his personal soul-searching on a large cosmic stage. What makes this poem a striking example?

2. How is death a "slave" to "fate, chance, kings, and desperate men"? How would he do their bidding? The poet refers to sleep once literally and once figuratively—where and how?

3. Donne often structures his poem like a set of arguments—the *rhetoric* of a lawyer pleading a case in front of a jury, for instance. Can you outline the arguments he uses to devalue "poor Death"?

4. What is the meaning of the *play on words* in the last half of the last line? How has the poem as a whole led up to it?

JUXTAPOSITIONS

Convention and Originality

> *No surprise for the writer, no surprise for the reader; we want the poem to change our way of seeing.*
> MICHAEL RYAN

The following two early-seventeenth-century poems are among the ten most widely reprinted poems in the English language. Both echo the familiar plea of the lover to a reluctant (or "coy") partner: "Seize the day; make use of the passing day" (**carpe diem** in the original Latin). The first poem follows a well-established convention: The too-soon-fading rose "smiles today," but if we do not enjoy it now, it will have wilted by tomorrow. Therefore, "gather ye rosebuds while ye may." The second poem, this one in the metaphysical vein, is Andrew Marvell's "To His Coy Mistress" (meaning "To His Reluctant Lady," without the current negative connotations of *mistress*). This poem has no rosebuds, no songbirds, and no conventional springtime setting in the English countryside. As you read these two poems, compare Herrick's pleasing conventional metaphors with the bold and jostling metaphors in Marvell's poem. Then read a poem by the Countess of Dia, a French poet of the twelfth century, who looks at love and courtship from a female rather than the conventional male perspective.

ROBERT HERRICK   (1591–1674)

To the Virgins, to Make Much of Time   1648

Gather ye rosebuds while ye may,
    Old time is still a-flying,
And this same flower that smiles today
    Tomorrow will be dying.

The glorious lamp of heaven, the sun,   5
    The higher he's a-getting,
The sooner will his race be run,
    And nearer he's to setting.

That age is best which is the first,
    When youth and blood are warmer;   10
But being spent, the worse, and worst
    Times still succeed the former.

Then be not coy, but use your time,
    And while ye may go marry,
For, having lost but once your prime,°   *best season*   15
    You may forever tarry.°   *stay behind*

THE RECEPTIVE READER

How much in this poem merely confirmed what you already knew? Did any part of it surprise you?

Marvell's poem goes beyond the convention. Its bold and paradoxical images roam from the Humber River in northern England to the river Ganges in India (then famous for its jewels and spices) and from there to "deserts of vast eternity." The poem ranges over vast stretches of time, from Noah's flood to the "conversion of the Jews," then not expected till the end of time. Paradoxically, the metaphors and similes in this poem are drawn from geography, biblical history, and botany—areas not conventionally associated with love.

ANDREW MARVELL   (1621–1678)

To His Coy Mistress   before 1678

    Had we but world enough, and time,
This coyness, lady, were° no crime.   *would be*
We would sit down and think which way
To walk and pass our long love's day.
Thou by the Indian Ganges' side   5
Shouldst rubies find; I by the tide
Of Humber would complain.° I would   *write plaintive love songs*
Love you ten years before the flood,
And you should, if you please, refuse
Till the conversion of the Jews.   10
My vegetable love should grow
Vaster than empires and more slow;
An hundred years should go to praise
Thine eyes and on thy forehead gaze,
Two hundred to adore each breast,   15
But thirty thousand to the rest,
An age at least to every part,

And the last age should show your heart.
For, lady, you deserve this state,°   *this high station*
Nor would I love at lower rate.   20
    But at my back I always hear
Time's wingèd chariot hurrying near,
And yonder all before us lie
Deserts of vast eternity.
Thy beauty shall no more be found,   25
Nor, in thy marble vault, shall sound
My echoing song; then worms shall try
That long-preserved virginity,
And your quaint honor° turn to dust,   *deliberate virtue*
And into ashes all my lust.   30
The grave's a fine and private place,
But none, I think, do there embrace.
    Now therefore, while the youthful hue
Sits on thy skin like morning dew,
And while thy willing soul transpires°   *breathes forth*   35
At every pore with instant fires,
Now let us sport us while we may,
And now, like amorous birds of prey,
Rather at once our time devour
Than languish in his slow-chapped° power.   *chewing with slow-moving jaws*   40
Let us roll all our strength and all
Our sweetness up into one ball,
And tear our pleasures with rough strife
Thorough° the iron gates of life.   *through*
Thus, though we cannot make our sun   45
Stand still, yet we will make him run.

THE RECEPTIVE READER

1. Where and how does Marvell carry *hyperbole,* or poetic exaggeration, to new extremes?

2. What is paradoxical about a "vegetable love" growing slowly to vast size like a giant cabbage? On second thought, what might be desirable or welcome about the idea?

3. What images and associations do time and eternity usually bring to your mind? How are the metaphors Marvell uses different? (What were the original uses of a chariot?)

4. What is the effect of the poet's bringing graveyard imagery into a love poem? (Can you find a good example of *verbal irony* in this passage?)

5. When Marvell replaces the conventional songbirds with birds of prey, what is the effect on the way we think about love and lovers? How do these birds help him turn the tables on all-devouring time? Why does he make us imagine "the iron gates of life" rather than a meadow with spring flowers?

6. How does Marvell's use of the sun differ from Herrick's? (Why would lovers want to make the sun "stand still"? How would they make the sun "run" to keep up with them?)

THE CREATIVE DIMENSION

A student poet wrote in her "Reply of Your Coy Mistress":

We have the world, and we have the time;
To wait a while longer would be no crime.

Write your own personal reply or response to either Herrick or Marvell.

We tend to think of the early love poets, or troubadours, of southern France as male. However, the poems of several women troubadours have come down to us. How does the following poem depart from the conventions of much male-oriented love poetry?

COUNTESS OF DIA   (born about 1140)
I Sing of That Which I Would Rather Hide   before 1200

TRANSLATED BY HANS P. GUTH

I sing of that which I would rather hide:
Where is the one who should be at my side
And whom I dearly love, come ebb or tide?
My kindness and sweet grace he has denied,
My beauty and good sense and goodly show.   5
I am betrayed, deceived, my love defied,
As if I were the lowest of the low.

Yet I take heart: I never brought you shame
Nor ever did the least to hurt your name.
My love surpasses loves of greater fame,   10
And I am pleased I beat you at love's game—
Outscored you when devotion was the test.
Your cold words and your slights all speak the same—
And yet you play the charmer with the rest.

THE RECEPTIVE READER

1. How is the *perspective* of the speaker in this poem different from that in traditional male-oriented poems of love and courtship? How much of this poem seems to belong to a different time, a different world? How much seems relevant or intelligible in our own time?

2. Modern translators of the southern French, or Provençal, poetry of the early Middle Ages often do not attempt to reproduce the finely crafted *stanza forms* and the intricate rhyme schemes of the originals. How do you think the rhyme scheme and the stanza form re-created here affect the reader's reactions to the poem?

CROSS-REFERENCES—For Discussion or Writing

In traditional *carpe diem* poetry, the woman who is admonished to make the most of time remains silent. What she thinks while the speaker in the poem makes his plea is not recorded. For an indication of possible unconventional responses, look at a modern poem like Edna St. Vincent Millay's "I, being born a woman and distressed" (p. 586).

POEMS FOR FURTHER STUDY

Pay special attention to the role of irony or paradox in the following poems. What is different, strange, or unexpected in each poem? If the poem uses irony, is it gentle and teasing or bitter and sarcastic? Does it have the last word? If the poem uses paradox, what is the basic contradiction? How does it begin to make sense on second thought?

ANNE SEXTON (1928–1975)

Ringing the Bells

1960

And this is the way they ring
the bells in Bedlam
and this is the bell-lady
who comes each Tuesday morning
to give us a music lesson 5
and because the attendants make you go
and because we mind by instinct,
like bees caught in the wrong hive,
we are the circle of the crazy ladies
who sit in the lounge of the mental house 10
and smile at the smiling woman
who passes us each a bell,
who points at my hand
that holds my bell, E flat,
and this is the gray dress next to me 15
who grumbles as if it were special
to be old, to be old,
and this is the small hunched squirrel girl
on the other side of me
who picks at the hair over her lip, 20
who picks at the hairs over her lip all day,
and this is how the bells really sound,
as untroubled and clean
as a workable kitchen,
and this is always my bell responding 25
to my hand that responds to the lady
who points at me, E flat;
and although we are no better for it,
they tell you to go. And you do.

THE RECEPTIVE READER

Bedlam was the name of a notorious London insane asylum. In the dark ages of mental health care, people came there to gawk at the antics of the inmates. What is the irony in the poet's use of this name? What is ironic about the music therapy she describes? What is ironic about the smiles in this poem? What is ironic about the sound of the bells? (How are the patients like "bees caught in the wrong hive"?) Why is there so much repetition, with everything running together without proper punctuation?

WILLIAM SHAKESPEARE   (1564–1616)

Sonnet 130   before 1598

My mistress' eyes are nothing like the sun;	
Coral is far more red than her lips' red;	
If snow be white, why then her breasts are dun;°	*grayish brown*
If hairs be wires, black wires grow on her head.	
I have seen roses damasked,° red and white,	*multicolored* 5
But no such roses see I in her cheeks;	
And in some perfumes there is more delight	
Than in the breath that from my mistress reeks.	
I love to hear her speak, yet well I know	
That music hath a far more pleasing sound;	10
I grant I never saw a goddess go;	
My mistress, when she walks, treads on the ground.	
And yet, by heaven, I think my love as rare°	*marvelous*
As any she belied° with false compare.	*any woman misrepresented*

THE RECEPTIVE READER

1. How does this poem illustrate the idea that irony is the revenge of reality on poetic exaggeration?

2. Readers hostile to irony accuse it of undercutting our capacity for sincere emotion. Do you think it does so in this sonnet?

PABLO NERUDA   (1904–1973)

The Fickle One   1972

TRANSLATED BY DONALD D. WALSH

My eyes went away from me
Following a dark girl
who went by.

She was made of black mother-of-pearl,
Made of dark-purple grapes,   5
and she lashed my blood
with her tail of fire.

After them all
I go.

A pale blonde went by   10
like a golden plant
swaying her gifts.
And my mouth went
like a wave
discharging on her breast   15
lightningbolts of blood.

After them all
I go.

But to you, without my moving,
without seeing you, distant you,   20
go my blood and my kisses,
my dark one and my fair one,
my tall one and my little one,
my broad one and my slender one,
my ugly one, my beauty,   25
made of all the gold
and of all the silver,
made of all the wheat
and of all the earth,
made of all the water   30
of the sea waves,
made for my arms,
made for my kisses,
made for my soul.

THE RECEPTIVE READER

What is strange or paradoxical about the imagery in the early parts of the poem? How do you explain the yoking of contraries in the last part of the poem? Do you think the speaker in the poem can be sincere in the last part of the poem after what he said in the earlier parts? What is your personal reaction to the poem?

WRITING ABOUT LITERATURE

10. Exploring Irony and Paradox (Using Quotations)

The Writing Workshop   Writing a paper focused on irony and paradox will remind you of the need to pay close attention to the poet's language. Poets are more   aware than others of shades of meaning and the range of associations that connotative words activate. (To respond fully to the language of a poem, you have to be sensitive to the connotations of words like *prance, stride, pace*— they are very different from *slink, trudge, traipse*.) Poets are especially sensitive to the way words interact or form a web of meaning. We know, for instance, that a poet has a lively sense of paradox if we encounter contradictory, apparently self-canceling phrases like *aching joys, living death, sweet foe, angelic fiend*. (Such pairings are **oxymorons**—phrases that at the same time run hot and cold.)

Study the way the following sample paper pays close attention to the poet's language. Notice how close the paper stays to the actual text of the poem. Study the way the student writer weaves quotations into the texture of the paper.

SAMPLE STUDENT PAPER

Herbert's Pulley

"When God at first made man," begins George Herbert's original contribution to the creation myth. The poem, twenty lines divided neatly into four stanzas, is called "The Pulley." This is the first puzzle. The poet uses the name of a mechanical device, similar to a winch or other such mechanism, to title a poem that, on the surface and indeed on second and maybe even on third reading, does not appear to ever mention or explain a pulley.

In this very personal reinterpretation of Genesis, there is no mention of the creation of Eve or of original sin. Instead, the poem focuses on our paradoxical human reluctance to come to God. That reluctance is strange because Herbert's God speaks royally, like a magnanimous, loving sovereign bestowing gifts on his subject. "'Let us,' he said, 'pour on him all we can: / Let the world's riches, which dispersed lie, / Contract into a span.'" Herbert's God anticipates the magnanimous bearing of the Sun King, Louis XIV of France, surrounded by courtiers who depend on his liberality. But at the same time, paradoxically, this divine sovereign is very human—a being who craves adoration, who needs others to admire and worship him.

Looking at the last blessing in the "glass of blessings," God says that if he should "bestow this jewel also on my creature, / He would adore my gifts instead of me." This "jewel" is another puzzle, a pun. The word *rest* refers at the same time to the "rest" or remainder of God's gifts that we will be allowed to keep—and to the "rest" that God is going to deny his human subjects. This second punning use of the word *rest* refers not so much to restful sleep as to the concept of peace, of contentment (setting our minds at rest). God did desire all good things for His creature. Starting with strength, then "beauty flowed, then wisdom, honor, pleasure." Yet God felt that if everything was given to his human creation, they would want for nothing and would "rest in Nature, not the God of Nature; / So both should losers be."

Into such a short poem, Herbert packs ambiguous and punful words requiring the reader to do doubletakes. *Rest* can be the remainder ("let him keep the rest"); it can be serenity or peace ("alone of all his treasure, / Rest in the bottom lay"); and *rest* can mean to stay in place ("rest in Nature"). If we as human beings were too content to stay in our place in the natural world, we would never feel the need to come to God.

To prevent both himself and us from losing out, God has decided to keep the gift of rest or contentment from us. He reasons about his creature, "Let him be rich and weary, that at least / If goodness lead him not, yet weariness / May toss him to my breast." God appears to need a plan or device to prevent human beings from being caught up in this world. And so we sense the logic of calling the poem "The Pulley." A pulley is a device used in hoisting heavy objects that are hard to move. Our human restlessness is what God sees as his pulley, which will "toss" us to his breast.

And this is the ultimate paradox—that although God has given us many blessings and riches, yet he denies us the capacity to enjoy them and find lasting happiness in them. This is the way it had to be to keep us from turning away and forgetting our debt to our Maker.

QUESTIONS

How sensitive is the student writer to overtones or implications and to double meanings? Where does this paper clarify or illuminate parts of the poem that you found difficult or confusing? Do you anywhere part company with the writer's interpretation?

11 THEME
The Making of Meaning

*For me the real issues of our time are the issues of
every time—the hurt and wonder of loving; making
in all its forms, children, loaves of bread, paintings,
building; and the conservation of life of all people and
all places, the jeopardizing of which no abstract
doubletalk of "peace" or "implacable foes" can excuse.*

SYLVIA PLATH

*A goal I think you can find in all my poems is to plead
with the world, with the reader, with the person the poem is
addressed to, to be kinder, more compassionate, more
understanding, more intelligent. My poems are often
about the pain I feel and they are a plea to the world to
relieve it.*

DIANE WAKOSKI

*When I landed in the republic of conscience
it was so noiseless when the engines stopped
I could hear a curlew high above the runway.*

SEAMUS HEANEY, "FROM THE REPUBLIC OF CONSCIENCE"

FOCUS ON THEME

Poetry helps us find meanings in the bewildering flow of experience.
Poems make us think: Often a poem asks us to look at familiar ideas in a new
light. It may challenge familiar rutted ways of thinking. It may nudge us into
trying a new route to the solution of a familiar problem. When we focus on
the **theme** of a poem, we try to sum up its meaning. We try to put into words
what makes the poem thought provoking: We look at the issues a poem seems
to raise and the possible answers it suggests. We try to formulate the idea or
insights that the poem as a whole seems to leave us with, for us to ponder and
remember.

How close do poets come to spelling out in so many words the theme or
central idea of a poem? Some poets leave larger meanings implied, hinted at,
suggested only. Most twentieth-century poets have been wary of large abstrac-

tions: happiness, alienation, growth, patriotism, love. **Abstractions** are labels for large areas of human experience. In themselves, they are neither good nor bad. However, they do "abstract"—they draw us away, from specifics and individuals. They extrapolate the larger patterns that help us chart our way. Many modern poets have steered clear of them, afraid they might become *mere* abstractions, mere labels that remove us from flesh-and-blood realities.

Other poets are less shy about spelling out key ideas in so many words. Poets of earlier ages, and some in our own time, draw explicit conclusions; they formulate their insights. Even so, you have to remember an important caution: Ideas in poetry are live ideas—anchored to what you can see and hear and feel. You cannot take them out of a poem the way you take candy out of a wrapper. The poet's ideas take shape before your eyes—embedded in graphic images, acted out in scenes and events that stir your emotions.

The Polish poet Czeslaw Milosz, who resigned from the post–World War II Communist Polish government in protest against political repression, is an eloquent voice of human solidarity, of shared values crossing the borders of race, sex, and creed. What is the central idea or dominant theme in the following poem? How does the interplay of large abstractions and striking images give shape to the poem?

CZESLAW   MILOSZ   (born 1911)

Incantation   1968

TRANSLATED BY ROBERT PINSKY AND CZESLAW MILOSZ

Human reason is beautiful and invincible.
No bars, no barbed wire, no pulping of books,
No sentence of banishment can prevail against it.
It establishes the universal ideas in language,
And guides our hand so we write Truth and Justice   5
With capital letters, lie and oppression with small.
It puts what should be above things as they are,
Is an enemy of despair and a friend of hope.
It does not know Jew from Greek or slave from master,
Giving us the estate of the world to manage.   10
It saves austere and transparent phrases
From the filthy discord of tortured words.
It says that everything is new under the sun,
Opens the congealed fist of the past.
Beautiful and very young are Philo-Sophia   15
And poetry, her ally in the service of the good.
As late as yesterday Nature celebrated their birth,
The news was brought to the mountains by a unicorn and an echo.
Their friendship will be glorious; their time has no limit.
Their enemies have delivered themselves to destruction.   20

By modern standards, this poem has a high abstraction count. It invokes (with capital letters) ideas like Truth, Justice, and Nature. These abstractions are easy to abuse, and they have often been on poets' mental checklists of words to handle with care. ("Go in fear of abstractions," said the American poet Ezra Pound.) But the concern with the abuse of abstractions turns out to be exactly the impetus behind this poem. The poet's agenda is to cleanse "austere and transparent" words like *reason* and *justice* of the verbal pollution they have suffered. The agenda is to rescue them from dishonest use by timeservers, party hacks, and oppressors.

This work of verbal renewal and reconstruction Milosz accomplishes with the tools of the poet. He employs the eloquent image: the undesirable books being pulled off the shelves to be shredded and reduced to pulp. He uses the potent metaphor: Reason is "guiding our hand" as we write Truth and Justice; reason is helping us "open the congealed fist of the past." He uses words with a witty twist, as when he starts *oppression* with a lowercase letter, while capitalizing *Truth* and *Justice*. Finally, he restores jaded words to their full meaning (such as *philosophy*—"Philo-Sophia"—the "love of wisdom"). The unicorn bringing the good news to the mountains is a lovely symbol for the triumph of the imagination over its literal-minded enemies.

The theme or central idea that animates this poem is spelled out, stated explicitly in the first line: "Human reason is beautiful and invincible." The rest of the poem acts it out, translates it into memorable images, traces its ramifications and implications.

THE RECEPTIVE READER

1. Why is it witty that the poem starts *oppression* with a lowercase letter? What familiar saying does the poet play on when he says "everything is new under the sun"? What does he mean?

2. In your own words, what does this poem say about the large abstractions—Reason, Truth, and Justice? What does it say about the abuse of language? What is this poet's perspective on oppression?

3. When a poet's political agenda becomes overt, poetry shades over into political advocacy and finally into political propaganda. How overt is the poet's political agenda in this poem? Where would you place this poem on a spectrum ranging from disinterested poetry cutting across party lines through strong political commitment to political propaganda?

THE PERSONAL RESPONSE

Are any lines or phrases especially eloquent for you? Do any of them raise questions in your mind? In what ways does this poem connect with your own experience?

IDEA AND IMAGE

Poems are like dreams; in them you put what you don't know you know.

ADRIENNE RICH

Poetry doesn't just come from the mind. Art is not just a thing of the intellect, but of the spirit.

LUCILLE CLIFTON

Poets and critics use the word *theme* in two different but related ways: Sometimes the term simply points to the general **subject,** to a general area of concern. A collection may sort poems out under such large thematic headings as Love, Family, Identity, Alienation, and Dissent. Such themes are large umbrella headings, under which individual poems will offer different perspectives. Under the heading of Family, one poem might be mourning the lost golden world of childhood. Another poem might focus on the need for breaking the fetters the family clamps on the individual.

However, often the term *theme* (as in this chapter) stands for the statement that a poem as a whole makes *about* a subject. The theme then is what the poem as a whole says about identity, alienation, or dissent. The theme is the recurrent message, insistent plea, or fresh insight that stays with us as we leave the poem behind. To use an analogy from the fine arts, the Spanish painter Francisco José de Goya (1746–1828) did a series of etchings about Spanish resistance fighters being hunted down by Napoleon's armies. His general subject he summed up in his title for the series: "The Disasters of War." But his theme in the sense of a central idea he summed up in the legend that appears with his stark visions of repression and executions. This recurrent statement, or indictment, reads "There is no remedy." Whereas other results of human callousness and folly can be corrected or remedied, the carnage of war cannot be made good.

Poets vary greatly in how explicitly they verbalize the ideas implied in or acted out in their poems. Some poets largely let their images speak for themselves. (These are the poets who tell readers looking for a message to call Western Union.) Other poets speak for their images, serving as guides or interpreters, spelling out more or less fully the message embedded in metaphor or symbol.

The following is a famous poetic manifesto embodying the modern distrust of mere words. Its title, meaning "A Guide to the Art of Poetry," is borrowed from a work by the Roman poet Horace, who lived from 65 to 8 B.C. (One of the familiar catchphrases from Horace's treatise is the admonition that poetry should both "teach and delight.")

ARCHIBALD MACLEISH (1892–1982)

Ars Poetica

1926

A poem should be palpable and mute
As a globed fruit,

Dumb
As old medallions to the thumb

Silent as the sleeve-worn stone
Of casement ledges where the moss has grown—

5

A poem should be wordless
As the flight of birds.

     *

A poem should be motionless in time
As the moon climbs,   10

Leaving, as the moon releases
Twig by twig the night-entangled trees,

Leaving, as the moon behind the winter leaves,
Memory by memory the mind—

A poem should be motionless in time   15
As the moon climbs.

     *

A poem should be equal to:
Not true.

For all the history of grief
An empty doorway and a maple leaf.   20

For love,
The leaning grasses and two lights above the sea—

A poem should not mean
But be.

    The subtext, or implied message, of this poem is that poets should not use words lightly. There should be no showy displays of grief, no gushing about love. Since language is the poet's medium, what explains MacLeish's paradoxical preference for silence? In part, the answer lies in the historical context of the poem. The poet wrote it when the horrors of World War I had alienated many poets and artists from the oratory of flag-waving politicians. To MacLeish's generation, speeches eulogizing the "grateful dead" who had died in the trenches seemed impious. What was real was the grass growing over the graves in the military cemeteries, the bones in the sandy soil, and the wind and rain. Better to remain silent than to use words dishonestly.

    But of course poems, including this one, are not literally silent. They are not literally "mute," "dumb," or "wordless." They use words, but, according to the speaker in this poem, they should use words to create images that speak for themselves. They should create for us something we can touch (something that is "palpable"), like the "globed fruit," over whose curved outline we can run our fingers, reading its texture and shape. Poems should give us something concrete to see and contemplate, like the "flight of birds" or the "empty doorway."

    A central paradox of the poem is that "silent" sights can be more eloquent than preachings or editorializings. The grief of separation sinks in as we contemplate the "empty doorway" where friends or lovers used to linger while bidding each other good night. In the context of a poem, the deserted doorway becomes "equal to" our experience of grief; it becomes its concrete embodiment. The central idea of the poem is summed up in the often-quoted final lines: "A poem should not mean / But be." We should first of all let a poem exist, we should let it speak to our senses and emotions, before we interrogate it about what it means.

THE RECEPTIVE READER

1. Why do people finger (or thumb) "old medallions"? What emotions do you think you would feel when contemplating a "casement ledge" or windowsill worn smooth by people's sleeves resting on it but now overgrown with moss?

2. Why does the moon seem "motionless" while it is climbing at the same time? If we prefer poems without much overt motion (apparently preferring the still frames capturing the moon rising slowly behind the bare twigs of the wintery trees), what kinds of poetry would we seem to rule out?

3. Is it paradoxical that MacLeish himself spelled out the central idea of his poem in his concluding lines?

THE PERSONAL RESPONSE

Are you resistant or allergic to preaching, editorializing, lecturing?

Poets before and after MacLeish have often opted intuitively for concrete images over theory and explicit assertion. The following poem by the American poet Walt Whitman clearly "makes a statement" about the speaker's alienation from coldly analytical science, but it does so without verbalizing the poet's implied attitude.

WALT WHITMAN   (1819–1892)
When I Heard the Learn'd Astronomer   1865

When I heard the learn'd astronomer,
When the proofs, the figures, were ranged in columns before me,
When I was shown the charts and diagrams, to add, divide, and measure them,
When I sitting heard the astronomer where he lectured with much applause in the
    lecture room,
How soon unaccountable I became tired and sick,   5
Till rising and gliding out I wandered off by myself,
In the mystical moist night air, and from time to time,
Looked up in perfect silence at the stars.

What is the theme of Whitman's poem? The poem does not make an explicit assertion about the scientific as against the poetic temperament. But we can infer the poet's attitude from the brief scenario we see acted out. The speaker in the poem attended an astronomy lecture that showed modern science at its most methodical and analytical, with its toolbox of charts, diagrams, logical proofs, and mathematical calculations. Feeling "tired and sick," the speaker wandered off by himself. Once outside the lecture room, he found the antidote: Instead of feeling oppressed or stifled by figures and charts and columns, he could commune "in perfect silence" with the stars, soothed by the "mystical moist night air." The poem as a whole implies or points to a unifying central idea: Paradoxically, astronomy, when taught in a drily analytical mode, does not help us find wonder and inspiration in the stars.

THE PERSONAL RESPONSE

Do you sympathize with the poet's reponse to the astronomy lecture? Do you feel there is something to be said on the other side?

In the following poem, what is the relation between idea and image? How does the poet take a large abstraction to the level of firsthand experience?

WILLIAM STAFFORD   (born 1914)

Freedom   1969

Freedom is not following a river.
Freedom is following a river
   though, if you want to.
It is deciding now by what happens now.
It is knowing that luck makes a difference.   5

No leader is free; no follower is free—
   the rest of us can often be free.
Most of the world are living by
creeds too odd, chancy, and habit-forming
   to be worth arguing about by reason.   10

If you are oppressed, wake up about
four in the morning; most places
you can usually be free some of the time
   if you wake up before other people.

Several recurrent notes are struck in this poem that together may help us formulate an overall perspective on freedom. First, much in our lives restricts our freedom. Apparently, being a leader and being a follower are both incompatible with making free choices. (Both leader and follower march with the main body of troops.) To be caught up in habitual creeds, to make today's decisions bound by yesterday's precedents, to be oppressed—all these limit the sphere of free choice. (The guardians of religious and legal doctrine do not encourage bold departures from received truth.) Nevertheless, there is a margin of freedom—if only in the margins of our existence—such as in the early morning hours, before the mechanisms that constrain us kick in.

THE RECEPTIVE READER

1. What do you make of the concrete *images* in this poem? When or how would someone want to follow a river? What does freedom have to do with following or not following it? What does freedom have to do with getting up early?

2. Why do you think the speaker claims that part of freedom is "deciding now by what happens now"? What makes the speaker in the poem say that neither a "leader" nor a "follower" can be free? What is "habit-forming" about "creeds" (and how do they limit your freedom)?

3. Does the poem provide any hints or guidelines on how to enlarge your margin of freedom?

4. How would you sum up in a sentence or two the *theme* of this poem—the statement the poem as a whole makes about freedom?

THE PERSONAL RESPONSE

How does the statement about freedom that the poem makes as a whole compare with the ideas you yourself associate with the word?

EXPLORATIONS ══════════════════

Religion and Poetry

John Donne's *Holy Sonnets,* like the religious poetry of some of his contemporaries, centered on the basic doctrines of traditional faith. However, Donne, like the other metaphysical poets, did not simply restate traditional beliefs. His poems are not **didactic** in the sense of teaching ideas already accepted and approved. Instead, the poet asks basic questions and then works his way toward the answers. How does the following poem reveal the poet's own religious temperament and the workings of the poet's imagination?

JOHN DONNE (1573–1631)

Holy Sonnet 5   1635

I am a little world made cunningly°	*skillfully*
Of elements and an angelic sprite,°	*angel-like spirit*
But black sin hath betrayed to endless night	
My world's both parts, and O, both parts must die.	
You which° beyond that heaven which was most high	*you who* 5
Have found new spheres and of new lands can write,	
Pour new seas in mine eyes, that so I might	
Drown my world with my weeping earnestly,	
Or wash it if it must be drowned no more.°	*(God's promise to Noah)*
But O, it must be burnt! Alas, the fire	10
Of lust and envy have burnt it heretofore,	
And made it fouler; let their flames retire,	
And burn me, O Lord, with a fiery zeal	
Of Thee and Thy house, which doth in eating heal.	

THE RECEPTIVE READER

1. The poet starts from a basic shared assumption: the duality of body and soul. Where and how does this idea enter into the poem? What other *polarities* help organize this poem?

2. One familiar feature of Donne's poetry is the *paradoxical* intermingling of scientific and biblical lore. Where or how do science and faith meet in this poem?

3. Donne's *metaphors*, like Shakespeare's, are not static; they develop and shift in unexpected ways as the poem takes shape. How do both water and fire change their significance in the course of the poem?

THE PERSONAL RESPONSE

The following is one student's record of a close reading of the poem. How familiar or strange are Donne's religious ideas to a reader of your generation?

Water and Fire

Donne's Holy Sonnet 5 deals with the basic theme of sin and redemption. However, this poem is not a dry lecture on the subject of salvation. The poet is "weeping earnestly" for his sins and looking forward to redemption with "fiery zeal." In his search for his soul's salvation, he ranges from the waters that drowned the earth during Noah's flood to the reaches of outer space discovered by the new astronomy. His tears of repentance must be like oceans; or, alternatively, his repentance must be like a fire that cleanses and heals as it consumes the sins it feeds on.

What are the basic doctrines assumed by the poem? The poet tells us that he is a world cunningly, skillfully made of two parts: body and soul. This "little world" or microcosm, like the larger universe that it mirrors, houses both matter and spirit. The body is made up of the elements of the world of matter (such as earth and water). The soul is the "angelic sprite," a spirit made of the same substance as the angels.

The crucial "But" comes at the beginning of the third line of the sonnet: As the serpent entered the Garden of Eden, so sin has entered "my world's both parts" and "betrayed" them. As a result, both parts must die and face the "endless night" of damnation.

What is the answer? Donne, ranging far beyond our everyday world, turns to the astronomers who in his time were beginning to find new worlds beyond our own solar system. (These are the "new spheres" beyond the traditional heaven.) He invokes the explorers who, traveling across the uncharted oceans, were finding "new lands" or new continents. Between them, can the stargazers and navigators find new oceans to replenish his tears, so that his weeping can drown out his sinful world with a flood of tears? Or, since God promised after Noah's flood that he would drown humanity no more, the poet's tears could wash him clean of sin.

He feels that if he repents for his sins, he will be saved. Actually, however, the world will end not by water but by fire, as flames consume the world on the Day of Judgment. Before then, the flames of lust and envy (which turn the world foul) have to die out, and the flames of a "fiery" religious zeal have to cleanse the sinner. The poet knows he has to repent in time, because he knows what will happen if his heart is not with God at the point of death.

THE COMMITTED POET

The galleries are full of music, the pianist is storming the keys,
the great cellist is crucified over his instrument,
That none may hear the ejaculations of the sentinels,
Nor the sighs of the most numerous and the most poor;
the thud of their falling bodies.

W. H. AUDEN

I am a poet
who yearns to dance on rooftops,
to whisper delicate lines about joy
and the blessings of human understanding.
I try. I go to my land, my tower of words and
bolt the door, but the typewriter doesn't fade out
the sounds of blasting and muffled outrage.

LORNA DEE CERVANTES,
"POEM FOR THE YOUNG WHITE MAN"

Bear in mind
that after the great destruction
one and all will prove
they were innocent.

GÜNTER EICH

Should poems take sides? When we explore the ideas embedded in poems, we face the question of the poet's engagement or commitment. Should poets take a stand on the social and political issues of their time? Can they afford to testify on behalf of causes? Can poets serve party, ideology, or country?

Poets have often been warned to speak for neither their class nor their kind nor their trade: "Wrap the bard in a flag or a school and they'll jimmy his / door down and be thick in his bed—for a month" (Archibald MacLeish). When art becomes propaganda, when poets write poems "for daily political use," their art becomes disposable, fading like the campaign posters of yesteryear. When poets follow a party line, they may seem to cease speaking to us in their own right as one human being to another. Nevertheless, in practice, poets from William Shakespeare and John Milton to Gwendolyn Brooks and Adrienne Rich have found it hard to stay aloof from the political and ideological struggles of their time. When the British suppressed the Easter Rebellion in Ireland in 1916 and executed the leading rebels, William Butler Yeats, who was to become a leading poet of the Irish Renaissance, wrote:

We know their dream; enough
To know they dreamed and are dead . . .

I write it out in a verse—
MacDonagh and MacBride
And Connolly and Pearse
Now and in time to be,
Wherever green is worn,
Are changed, changed utterly:
A terrible beauty is born.
"Easter 1916"

Two world wars, the rise of fascism and communism, the struggle against colonialism, the Vietnam War—these made it hard for poets to stay on the fence. Many found they could not remain Rapunzel in the tower, never letting her hair down to ground level to help the real world climb in. Much modern poetry has been poetry of protest and of warning. At the same time, a poet's keeping *silent* about the political issues of the time has also often been seen as a political statement. By not confronting the issues, a poem might seem to be signaling acceptance of, or at least resignation to, oppression or abuses.

The German playwright Bertolt Brecht wrote the following poem when the rising tide of Nazism was driving writers and artists into exile.

BERTOLT BRECHT   (1898–1956)
On the Burning of Books   1936
TRANSLATED BY HANS P. GUTH

When the new masters announced that books full of harmful knowledge
Were to be publicly burned and when here and yonder
Oxen were made to draw carts full of books
To the stake, a poet, hunted from home (he was one of the best)
Discovered aghast, when reading the list of those burned,   5
His own books had been forgotten. He rushed to his desk,
Furious, and wrote to the rulers:

Burn me at once! he wrote with a frantic pen.
You cannot do this to me! How can you spare me?
Have I not always   10
Recorded the truth in my books? And now
you class me with liars!

              This is an order:
Burn me!

Our response to the work of a committed poet like Brecht is shaped at least in part by our own commitments. Readers used to be told that their personal like or dislike of lobsters should not affect their reading of a poem about lobsters. But this detached stance is hard to maintain when, as Brecht would say, the lobsters wear helmets and boots. Readers will rejoice in the satirical barbs of Brecht's poem if they are inclined to share the poet's contempt for censors of "harmful knowledge." (Apparently censors do not tend to persecute harmful ignorance.) As often in his poetry and plays, Brecht strips a situation to its essentials. The ox-drawn carts probably make us imagine a simpler world than Hitler's Germany in the thirties. In such a world, books would be more rare and precious than they were later. The poet speaking in the poem also is a somewhat simpler and less complicated person than his modern counterparts: He rushes to defy the powers-that-be without a second thought. He turns the enemies' list of the "new masters" into an honor roll, from which he is "aghast" and "furious" to be excluded. We can relish his mimicking of people married not to the language of dialogue but to the language of command: "This is an order!" We can be proud to takes sides with those who have "always / Recorded the truth" against timeserving liars.

THE PERSONAL RESPONSE

What experiences with censorship have shaped your own attitudes toward censorship and censors? Do you find Brecht's poem eloquent or effective? Why or why not?

Poetry can be timely and timeless at the same time if readers sense that the poet's long-range solidarity with suffering and deluded humanity is as strong as the commitment to the current struggle. Does the following poem take sides? Whose?

DENISE LEVERTOV   (born 1923)

What Were They Like?   1966

1) Did the people of Vietnam
   use lanterns of stone?
2) Did they hold ceremonies
   to reverence the opening of buds?
3) Were they inclined to quiet laughter?   5
4) Did they use bone and ivory,
   jade and silver, for ornament?
5) Had they an epic poem?
6) Did they distinguish between speech and singing?

1) Sir, their light hearts turned to stone.   10
   It is not remembered whether in gardens
   stone lanterns illumined pleasant ways.
2) Perhaps they gathered once to delight in blossom,
   but after the children were killed
   there were no more buds.   15
3) Sir, laughter is bitter to the burned mouth.
4) A dream ago, perhaps. Ornament is for joy.
   All the bones were charred.
5) It is not remembered. Remember,
   most were peasants; their life   20
   was in rice and bamboo.
   When peaceful clouds were reflected in the paddies
   and the water buffalo stepped surely along terraces,
   maybe fathers told their sons old tales.
   When bombs smashed those mirrors   25
   there was time only to scream.
6) There is an echo yet
   of their speech which was like a song.
   It was reported their singing resembled
   the flight of moths in moonlight.   30
   Who can say? It is silent now.

THE RECEPTIVE READER

1. Who are the two speakers in this poem? What is the difference in their *points of view*? What kind of person is asking the questions? What kind of person is giving the answers?

2. Why do you think the poet used a *question-and-answer* format? What effect does it have on the reader?

3. The poem shifts easily from the factual questionnaire mode to the metaphorical language of the poet. What are memorable *metaphors,* and what role do they play in the poem?

THE PERSONAL RESPONSE

What for you is the message of this poem? What is your personal response to this poem?

The following poem by a twentieth-century black writer is a tribute to Frederick Douglass, who in his autobiography told the story of his rebellion against and escape from slavery. As a journalist and public speaker, Douglass became a leader of the antislavery movement in the United States. What makes the following poem in his honor eloquent?

ROBERT HAYDEN   (1913–1980)

Frederick Douglass   1966

When it is finally ours, this freedom, this liberty, this beautiful
and terrible thing, needful to man as air,
usable as earth; when it belongs at last to all,
when it is truly instinct, brain matter, diastole, systole,°   *phases of the heartbeat*
reflex action; when it is finally won, when it is more   5
than the gaudy mumbo jumbo of politicians:
this man, this Douglass, this former slave, this Negro
beaten to his knees, exiled, visioning a world
where none is lonely, none hunted, alien,
this man, superb in love and logic, this man   10
shall be remembered. Oh, not with statues' rhetoric,
nor with legends and poems and wreaths of bronze alone,
but with the lives grown out of his life, the lives
fleshing his dream of the beautiful, needful thing.

THE RECEPTIVE READER

1. What in this poem is different from the "gaudy mumbo jumbo of politicians" and conventional rhetoric in praise of liberty? What is strange or unexpected in the poet's description of freedom?

2. Is the poet speaking for a limited group? Is he speaking to a limited group? Do you think the poem would speak eloquently to a white audience? Why or why not?

THE PERSONAL RESPONSE

We are often told that modern audiences have few heroes. Write a tribute (poem or prose passage) to someone you admire, trying to make it convincing for the skeptical modern reader.

JUXTAPOSITIONS ━━━━━

Poems of War

   Much modern poetry has dealt with the subject of war. From what point of view are you asked to look at war in each of the following poems? Does the poet spell out the ideas or attitudes implied or embedded in the poem? What does the poem as a whole say about war?

HENRY REED   (born 1914)

Naming of Parts   1946

Today we have naming of parts. Yesterday,
We had daily cleaning. And tomorrow morning,
We shall have what to do after firing. But today,
Today we have naming of parts. Japonica
Glistens like coral in all of the neighboring gardens,   5
      And today we have naming of parts.

This is the lower sling swivel. And this
Is the upper sling swivel, whose use you will see,
When you are given your slings. And this is the piling swivel,
Which in your case you have not got. The branches   10
Hold in the gardens their silent, eloquent gestures,
      Which in our case we have not got.

This is the safety-catch, which is always released
With an easy flick of the thumb. And please do not let me
See anyone using his finger. You can do it quite easy   15
If you have any strength in your thumb. The blossoms
Are fragile and motionless, never letting anyone see
      Any of them using their finger.

And this you can see is the bolt. The purpose of this
Is to open the breech, as you see. We can slide it   20
Rapidly backwards and forwards: we call this
Easing the spring. And rapidly backwards and forwards
The early bees are assaulting and fumbling the flowers:
      They call it easing the Spring.

They call it easing the Spring: it is perfectly easy   25
If you have any strength in your thumb: like the bolt,
And the breech, and the cocking-piece, and the point of balance,
Which in our case we have not got; and the almond-blossom
Silent in all of the gardens and the bees going backwards and forwards,
      For today we have naming of parts.   30

THE RECEPTIVE READER

1. Much of the talking in this poem is done by the drill instructor. Is what he says a *caricature*—a comic distortion exaggerating key traits to make them ridiculous? Or does it sound to you like a fairly accurate rendering of what an instructor might say?

2. The technology of war and the world of nature provide a steady play of *point and counterpoint* in this poem. How? With what effect? What does the poem as a whole say about technology and nature?

3. What is this poet's attitude toward war?

RICHARD EBERHART   (born 1904)

The Fury of Aerial Bombardment   1947

You would think the fury of aerial bombardment
Would rouse God to relent; the infinite spaces
Are still silent. He looks on shock-pried faces.
History, even, does not know what is meant.

You would feel that after so many centuries   5
God would give man to repent; yet he can kill
As Cain could, but with multitudinous will,
No farther advanced than in his ancient furies.

Was man made stupid to see his own stupidity?
Is God by definition indifferent, beyond us all?   10
Is the eternal truth man's fighting soul
Wherein the Beast ravens° in its own avidity?   *prowls*

Of Van Wettering I speak, and Averill,
Names on a list, whose faces I do not recall
But they are gone to early death, who late in school   15
Distinguished the belt feed lever from the belt holding pawl.

THE RECEPTIVE READER

1. What questions does this poem raise about God's intentions? What questions does it raise about our human responsibilities? Why does the poet bring the *allusion* to Cain into the poem?

2. Like Reed's poem, this poem takes us to the schoolrooms of military training. (Eberhart himself was for a time an aerial gunnery instructor in World War II.) How is Eberhart's use of the training experience similar to or different from Reed's?

3. Does this poem answer the questions it raises?

POEMS FOR FURTHER STUDY

In reading the following poems, pay special attention to theme. What ideas or attitudes are expressed or implied in the poem? What statement does the poem as a whole have for the reader? Does the poem spell it out in so many words? How does the poem as a whole carry its message?

DENISE LEVERTOV   (born 1923)

The Mutes   1966

Those groans men use
passing a woman on the street
or on the steps of the subway
to tell her she is a female
and their flesh knows it,   5

are they a sort of tune,
an ugly enough song, sung
by a bird with a slit tongue

but meant for music?

Or are they the muffled roaring   10
of deafmutes trapped in a building that is
slowly filling with smoke?

Perhaps both.

Such men most often
look as if groan were all they could do,   15
yet a woman, in spite of herself,

knows it's a tribute:
if she were lacking all grace
they'd pass her in silence:

so it's not only to say she's   20
a warm hole. It's a word

in grief-language, nothing to do with
primitive, not an ur-language;°   *earliest human language*
language stricken, sickened, cast down

in decrepitude.° She wants to   *deterioration*   25
throw the tribute away, dis-
gusted, and can't,

it goes on buzzing in her ear,
it changes the pace of her walk,
the torn posters in echoing corridors   30

spell it out, it
quakes and gnashes as the train comes in.
Her pulse sullenly

had picked up speed,
but the cars slow down and   35
jar to a stop while her understanding

keeps on translating:
"Life after life after life goes by
without poetry
without seemliness   40
without love."

THE RECEPTIVE READER

1. What is the role in the poem of the bird metaphor? Why is the deaf-mute metaphor central to the poem? What kind of counterpoint does the subway provide in the poem?

2. What, in your own words, is the theme the poet spells out in the last stanza? How does the poem as a whole lead up to it?

3. Does this poem express hostility toward men?

THE PERSONAL RESPONSE

What attitudes about sexual harassment are widespread among women? What reactions to current concerns about sexual harassment are widespread among men? How does the poem relate to either?

PHILIP LARKIN (1922–1985)

Born Yesterday

1955

Tightly folded bud,
I have wished you something
None of the others would:
Not the usual stuff
About being beautiful,   5
Or running off a spring
Of innocence or love—
They all wish you that.
And should it prove possible,
Well, you're a lucky girl.   10

But if it shouldn't, then
May you be ordinary;
Have like other women
An average of talents:
Not ugly, not good-looking,   15
Nothing uncustomary
To pull you off your balance,
That, unworkable in itself,
Stops all the rest from working.
In fact, may you be dull—   20
If that is what a skilled,
Vigilant, flexible,
Unemphasized, enthralled
Catching of happiness is called.

THE RECEPTIVE READER

1. What is the meaning and effect of the *metaphor* in the first line?

2. One of the oldest temptations is for the older generation to make wishes or chart directions for the next. How does this poet try to steer clear of the "usual stuff"? What are his best wishes for the child's future?

THE PERSONAL RESPONSE

How would you react if someone told you, "May you be ordinary" and "May you be dull"?

ALICE WALKER   (born 1944)

Women   1970

They were women then
My mamma's generation
Husky of voice—Stout of
Step
With fists as well as   5
Hands
How they battered down
Doors
And ironed
Starched white   10
Shirts
How they led
Armies
Headragged Generals
Across mined   15
Fields
Booby-trapped
Ditches
To discover books
Desks   20
A place for us
How they knew what we
Must know
Without knowing a page
Of it   25
Themselves.

THE RECEPTIVE READER

1. What is the role of the *military metaphor* in this poem? (Why "headragged" generals?) What was the campaign in which the women of the mother's generation participated? (What clue is provided by the shirts?)

2. What is the paradox that concludes the poem?

3. What, for you, is the prevailing *mood* or emotion in this poem?

WRITING ABOUT LITERATURE

11. Tracing a Common Theme (Comparing and Contrasting)

The Writing Workshop   Comparison is a good teacher. It can alert us to what otherwise might go unnoticed; it can make us take a fresh look at what we took for granted. We value what we have when we look at what might take its place. We question what we have come to accept when someone shows us a viable alternative.

A **comparison-and-contrast** paper presents a special challenge to your ability to organize material. You will have to develop a strategy for laying out your material in such a way that your reader can see the points of comparison. The reader has to see important connections—whether unsuspected similarities or striking differences setting apart things that seem similar on the surface. Consider some familiar strategies for organizing a comparison and contrast of two poems:

❖ *You may want to develop a* **point-by-point** *comparison.* For instance, you may want to begin by showing how two poets share a distrust of "big words." This idea then provides the starting point both for your paper and for their poetic technique. You may go on to show how both poets rely on startling, thought-provoking images. Here you come to the heart of both your paper and of their way of writing poetry. You may conclude by showing how both nevertheless in the end spell out the kind of thought that serves as an *earned* conclusion, a generalization that the poem as a whole has worked out. Simplified, the scheme for such a point-by-point comparison might look like this:

    Point 1—poem A and then B
    Point 2—poem A and then B
    Point 3—poem A and then B

❖ *You may want to develop a* **parallel-order** *comparison.* You show first the distrust of abstractions, then the bold, provocative images, and finally the poet's spelling out of the theme in poem A. You then take these three points up again in the same, or parallel, order for poem B. This way you may be able to give your reader a better sense of how each poem works on its own terms, as a self-contained whole. However, you will have to make a special effort to remind your readers of what in the second poem is parallel to or different from what you showed in the first.

❖ *You may want to start from a common base.* You may want to emphasize similarities first. You may then want to go on to the significant differences. You might vary this strategy by starting with surface similarities that might deceive the casual observer. You then go on to essential distinctions.

How does the following student paper use or adapt these organizing strategies?

SAMPLE STUDENT PAPER

Today We Have Naming of Parts

Disillusioned by the experience of World War II, Henry Reed in "Naming of Parts" and Richard Eberhart in "The Fury of Aerial Bombardment" condemn and reject the horror of war. Both poems condemn our failure to see war as it is, attack our indifference, and reflect postwar antiwar feeling. We shall see that Eberhart's poem takes the attack on indifference one step further than Reed's poem does.

Henry Reed's "Naming of Parts" satirically attacks the callousness of the military. By using impersonal, neutral words and phrases ("Today we have naming of parts. Yesterday / We had daily cleaning"), the speaker satirizes how precise and impersonal these lessons are. The trainee learns a process, without being taught or made aware how terrible and ugly practicing that process is. References to "the lower sling swivel," "the upper sling swivel," and the "slings" describe machinery. Such references to mechanical parts evoke neutral or even positive feelings, since most machines are used for the good of humanity. This technical language conceals the horror of using this particular machinery. Saying that "you can do it quite easy / If you have any strength in your thumb" obscures the possibility that it might be difficult emotionally to gun down a fellow human being.

Reed uses a comparison to nature at the end of each stanza. Jumping from the mechanics of the gun to the beauty of the garden in consecutive sentences presents a contrast between the gun and the flower, the one a symbol of death and the other a symbol of life. The references in the first two stanzas stress the innocence of nature. The line "Japonica / Glistens like coral in all of the neighboring gardens" evokes an image of serenity and peace. The branches with "their silent, eloquent gestures" paint another image of bliss. The sterile descriptions of the gun and the beautiful descriptions of nature proceed in a point-counterpoint fashion.

Richard Eberhart's "The Fury of Aerial Bombardment" shares the theme of "Naming of Parts" in that both poems attack indifference to violence and suffering. By saying that "history, even, does not know what is meant," the poet seems to lament that even painful experience does not teach us to prevent the senselessness of war. We are "no farther advanced," making the poet ask: "Was man made stupid?" Here again, as in Reed's poem, technical, impersonal references to the "belt feed lever" and the "belt holding pawl" imply a criticism of the callousness with which people handle the subject of war. A lesson about a belt feed lever might be more instructive if the part were named the genocide lever, for instance.

However, "The Fury of Aerial Bombardment" contrasts with "Naming of Parts" because Eberhart goes beyond attacking human indifference by attacking divine indifference to the horrors of war. The poet questions why God has not intervened to stop the aerial bombardment. The answer, that "the infinite spaces / Are still silent," is a criticism of God's looking passively upon "shock-pried faces." These are the faces of the people who have witnessed the horror of the bombing but to whom God offers no respite. The poet seems to expect a thinking, feeling entity to intervene, but no such intervention takes place. Men still kill with "multitudinous will." In the third stanza, the poet asks: "Is God by definition indifferent, beyond us all?"

Both of these poems were written half a century ago, yet their relevance remains undiminished today. In an age when we read daily of war and death, indifference is commonplace. The way in which a news reporter casually reads death tolls from current conflicts is reminiscent of the cold, sterile wording of "Naming of Parts." The casual and callous projections of the cost in human lives of "winning" a nuclear war are another example of what is under attack in these poems. And people who ponder such atrocities as Auschwitz and Hiroshima have cause to question divine indifference, for the earth is long on suffering.

QUESTIONS

How convincing do the parallels between the two poems become in this paper? What are striking examples? How, according to this student writer, does the second poem go beyond the first? For you, do the two poems seem dated, or do they seem still relevant today?

12 MYTH AND ALLUSION
Twice-Told Tales

*The capacity to personify, mythologize, imagine,
harmonize, improvise, is one of the great mercies granted
in human life.*

STEPHEN NACHMANOVITCH

*Myths are public dreams; dreams are private myths. Myths
are vehicles of communication between the conscious and
the unconscious just as dreams are.*

JOSEPH CAMPBELL

The mythic journey is as ancient as the human race itself.

JOHN A. ALLEN

FOCUS ON MYTH

Myths (from *mythos,* the Greek word for tale) are stories about gods, monsters, and heroes. Myths are rooted in prehistoric oral tradition. People heard them in a spirit of religious awe, listening for clues to the nature of the mysterious universe in which they lived. Creation myths celebrated genesis— the creation of the earth, of man and woman, or of the alternation of sun and moon. In the dark of winter, myths of rebirth kept alive the faith in renewal, in the return of spring. In the prehistoric past, our ancestors listened to stories about how death entered the world or about the titanic struggle between good and evil. Often myths were embedded in **rituals** that acted out a mythical story or celebrated a godlike champion or redeemer.

In literal-minded times, the word *myth* has meant "superstition," to be swept away by the march of science. (In the language of politics, *myth* is a fancy word for a lie concocted by a self-serving opponent.) However, our modern world has seen a resurgence of interest in myth as a mirror—often obscure and tantalizing—of deep-seated human needs and feelings. What fascinates modern scholars is that many ancient myths have parallels in diverse cultures. It is as if recurrent mythical patterns were part of our collective consciousness, wired into the collective memory of the human race.

The American poet Stanley Kunitz said, "Old myths, old gods, old heroes have never died. They are only sleeping at the bottom of our minds, waiting for our call." Some of the myths "sleeping at the bottom of our minds" have had a special fascination for moderns. For instance, in traditions from many sources, we see a mythical god-king undergo a ritual of death and mourning, followed by rebirth or resurrection. We witness a cycle of defeat, death, and triumphant return. In the words of Joseph Campbell, we see different incarnations of "a hero with a thousand faces." Students of myth, from nineteenth-century anthropologists to today's feminist scholars, have reconstructed myths about the earth goddess that echo in the earliest lore of the Middle East, cradle of Western civilization. These myths give a voice to the need for bonding and nurturing essential for human survival. The Babylonian Ishtar and the Greek Demeter, goddess of the harvest, may hark back to a phase of human culture centered on the worship of a life-giving and life-preserving feminine principle.

Myth detects the long, slow rhythms of human experience that drum beneath the short staccato beats of short-range events. Many myths focus on **archetypal** experiences and needs that are constants in the lives of people from different cultures. Many cultures, for instance, have myths about the fire bringer—who brings the fire that symbolizes warmth, the hearth, survival, permanence, the light of knowledge. The fire bringer in Greek mythology was Prometheus, who defied the king of the gods by returning to humanity the fire that Zeus had meant to deny them. To poets and artists of later generations, Prometheus became a symbol of aspiration, of rebellion, of determination "to defy power, which seems omnipotent" (Percy Bysshe Shelley, *Prometheus Unbound*). We still call people Promethean who are willing to test the boundaries, to reach for what was thought unattainable.

Poets and artists discovered in myth and legend rich sources of symbol and allusion. An **allusion** is a brief mention that calls up a whole story, rich in overtones and associations. A single word, a single name, may activate a whole network of memories. When a poet alludes to Cassandra, we see with the mind's eye the Trojan princess to whom the god Apollo had given the gift of foreseeing the future—and the curse of not being believed. In her mad ravings, she foresaw the death of Hector, the Trojan champion; she saw Troy in flames, the towers falling down, the men killed, the women sold into slavery. But no one believed her. As Robinson Jeffers says in his poem "Cassandra," people truly "hate the truth"; they would sooner

Meet a tiger on the road.
Therefore the poets honey their truth with lying.

The following example shows the central role allusion can play in a poem. The central figure in the poem is a balloon vendor who is literally lame. But the poet calls him "goat-footed"—a hint that we may be watching a half-human, half-animal mythic creature.

E. E. CUMMINGS (1894–1963)   1923

in Just-

in Just-
spring   when the world is mud-
luscious the little
lame balloonman

whistles   far   and wee   5

and eddieandbill come
running from marbles and
piracies and it's
spring

when the world is puddle-wonderful   10

the queer
old balloonman whistles
far   and   wee
and bettyandisbel come dancing

from hop-scotch and jump-rope and   15

it's
spring
and
    the

        goat-footed   20

balloonMan   whistles
far
and
wee

     Who has goat's feet and whistles? Pan, Greek god of flocks and shepherds, often appears in works of art as a sensual being with horns, a snub nose, and goat's feet. He is often shown dancing or playing the shepherd's flute, which he had invented. Often, he is leading the dances of the nymphs, or female woodland creatures. In later times, he is often shown as one of a group of goat-footed satyrs, fond of wine and sensual pleasures.

     In short, Pan is one of the many lesser semidivine beings who, in Greek mythology, populate nature. They turn it from an alien, savage place into a world full of breathing, sensitive life. For cummings, Pan became a fitting symbol of spring—of the spirit of joy, mirth, frolic, holiday, or fiesta. It is a time of children dancing and skipping—as the poem itself skips over the printed page. The goat-footed balloonman (Pan in a modern disguise) becomes a symbol of innocent pleasure that children enjoy but that grownups seem to lose as they become neurotic, frustrated adults.

THE RECEPTIVE READER

1. What is "luscious" about mud or "wonderful" about puddles?

2. How should the poem *sound* when read aloud? How does it "dance out" the dancing and skipping it describes?

3. How does the poet use *repetition* and pauses to highlight, to focus our attention?

4. Do you think this poem would work for readers who have never heard of Pan? Why or why not?

THE RANGE OF ALLUSION

People do gossip
And they say about
Leda, that she
Once found an egg
hidden under
wild hyacinths
SAPPHO

Allusion is a kind of shorthand. What, in so many words, does a writer mean when saying, "We are all Custer"? The short, cryptic statement encloses layers of meaning that we can peel away like the layers of an onion. Some of the meaning is close to the surface: George Armstrong Custer was an American general in command of the U.S. Seventh Cavalry. He attacked a large encampment of the Sioux or Lakota on the Little Big Horn in 1876. He was killed with most of his men in the last desperate battle the Lakota fought against the invaders. The allusion here, however, says more: As Americans, it suggests, we are all implicated in a history that pitted the U.S. Cavalry against the native American tribes, ravaged by the starvation and disease the white settlers had brought. We share the guilt for the massacre at Wounded Knee, where men, women, and children were gunned down.

Richly allusive poetry assumes a shared cultural tradition that allows the poet to play on a common knowledge of myth, legend, and history. The language of allusion is as much a shared language as the language of the computer age—and it similarly challenges the uninitiated. One large source of allusion is **Greek mythology**—the body of myths and legends poets inherited from the civilization of ancient, classical Greece. What kind of cultural literacy does the poet assume in the following poem? What is the poet's range of allusion?

WILLIAM BUTLER YEATS   (1865–1939)

Leda and the Swan   1923

A sudden blow: the great wings beating still
Above the staggering girl, her thighs caressed
By the dark webs, her nape caught in his bill,
He holds her helpless breast upon his breast.

How can those terrified vague fingers push   5
The feathered glory from her loosening thighs?
And how can body, laid in that white rush,
But feel the strange heart beating where it lies?

A shudder in the loins engenders there
The broken wall, the burning roof and tower   10
And Agamemnon dead.

                        Being so caught up,
So mastered by the brute blood of the air,
Did she put on his knowledge with his power
Before the indifferent beak could let her drop?   15

The terrifying swan is a mythic creature: Zeus, the king of the Olympian gods (the Greek gods, residing on Mount Olympus) has assumed the shape of an animal. The offspring of his union with Leda is going to be Helen, whose abduction by the Trojan prince Paris will launch the "thousand ships" of the Greek war against Troy. The "broken wall, the burning roof and tower" call up before our eyes the city of Troy being reduced to rubble and ashes in defeat. In the aftermath of the war, Agamemnon, the leader of the Greek forces, will return home after years of absence, to be murdered by his wife Clytemnestra and her lover Aegisthus.

THE RECEPTIVE READER

Through the centuries, the world of Greek myth has offered artists and poets an alternative universe, where imaginings repressed in ordinary society could be enacted and explored. In the world of Greek myth, animals often do not have derogatory connotations. What are the connotations of the animal in Yeats' poem? Is the swan mostly beast? human? divine?

Helen of Troy—the daughter of Zeus, who had made love to Leda in the shape of a swan—was often blamed for the bloody conflict between Greece and Troy. Helen had married Menelaus, king of Sparta, and she incurred the hatred of her fellow Greeks when she allowed the "firebrand" Trojan prince Paris to carry her away to Troy, thus causing the bloody Trojan war. What two different ways of viewing Helen contend in the following poem?

H. D. (HILDA DOOLITTLE) (1886–1961)
Helen   1924

All Greece hates
the still eyes in the white face,
the luster as of olives
where she stands,
And the white hands.   5

All Greece reviles
the wan face when she smiles,
hating it deeper still
when it grows wan and white,
remembering past enchantments   10
And past ills.

Greece sees unmoved,
God's daughter, born of love,
the beauty of cool feet
and slenderest knees,   15
could love indeed the maid,
only if she were laid,
white ash amid funereal cypresses.

THE RECEPTIVE READER

1. How does the poet emphasize and drive home the unrelenting hate felt for
Helen by her countrymen and countrywomen?

2. What labels that the poet applies to Helen and what descriptive details *counteract*
these powerful negative feelings, and how? Explore as fully as you can the connotations—
associations, implications—of words like *luster, enchantments, maid,* and of phrases like
"God's daughter, born of love" and "beauty of cool feet / and slenderest knees."

3. Is the poet herself taking sides? As you read the poem, are you?

EXPLORATIONS ════════════════════════

Understanding Allusions

In a dictionary or other reference work, look up the allusions in the following lines. What does a reader have to know to catch the allusion? What network of meanings and associations is the allusion supposed to activate? How
might these associations vary for different readers?

1. Janus writes books for women's liberation;
   His wife types up the scripts from his dictation.
               Laurence Perrine, "Janus"

2. But Ariadne's eyes are lakes
   Beside the maze's starwhite wall:
   For in the Caribbean midnight
   Of her wild and gentle wisdom, she foreknows
   And solves the maze's cruel algebra.
               Thomas Merton, "Ariadne"

3. Something is always approaching; every day
   Till then we say,
   Watching from a bluff the tiny, clear,
   Sparkling armada of promises draw near,
   How slow they are! And how much time they waste,
   Refusing to make haste!
               Philip Larkin, "Next, Please"

JUXTAPOSITIONS ═══════════════════════════════

The Sacrifice of Isaac

For many centuries, allusions to the Bible have been woven into the language of poets and artists. Old Testament themes like Cain's fratricide, Noah's flood, or David slaying Goliath are part of our collective memory bank of archetypes and symbols. New Testament parables like those of the Good Samaritan help shape our thinking on subjects like charity. The sacrifice of Isaac as the Lord's test of Abraham's obedience has long been a favorite subject for artists. Compare the Old Testament story with its use by a twentieth-century poet.

GENESIS (22:1–13)

And it came to pass after these things that God did tempt Abraham and said unto him, Abraham: and he said, Behold, here I am.

And he said, Take now thy son, thine only son Isaac, whom thou lovest, and get thee into the land of Moriah; and offer him there for a burnt offering upon one of the mountains which I will tell thee of.

And Abraham rose up early in the morning, and saddled his ass, and took two of his young men with him, and Isaac his son, and clave the wood for the burnt offering, and rose up, and went unto the place of which God had told him.

Then on the third day Abraham lifted up his eyes, and saw the place afar off.

And Abraham said unto his young men, Abide ye here with the ass; and I and the lad will go yonder and worship, and come again to you.

And Abraham took the wood of the burnt offering, and laid it upon Isaac his son; and he took the fire in his hand, and a knife; and they went both of them together.

And Isaac spake unto Abraham his father, and said, My father: and he said, Here am I, my son. And he said, Behold the fire and the wood: but where is the lamb for a burnt offering?

And Abraham said, My son, God will provide himself a lamb for a burnt offering: so they went both of them together.

And they came to the place which God had told him of; and Abraham built an altar there, and laid the wood in order, and bound Isaac his son, and laid him on the altar upon the wood.

And Abraham stretched forth his hand, and took the knife to slay his son.

And the angel of the Lord called unto him out of heaven, and said, Abraham, Abraham: and he said, Here am I.

And he said, Lay not thine hand upon the lad, neither do thou anything unto him: for now I know that thou fearest God, seeing thou hast not withheld thy son, thine only son from me.

And Abraham lifted up his eyes, and looked, and behold behind him a ram caught in a thicket by his horns: and Abraham went and took the ram, and offered him up for a burnt offering in the stead of his son.

Wilfred Owen wrote his adaptation of the biblical story during the years of trench warfare in World War I, when Britain, France, and Germany were sacrificing the lives of hundreds of thousands of young men. How far and how closely does the poet follow the biblical story? When do you first realize that Owen has transposed the story from its ancient setting? How does he change the climactic ending of the story?

WILFRED OWEN (1893–1918)
The Parable of the Old Men and the Young   1918

So Abram rose, and clave the wood, and went,
And took the fire with him, and a knife.
And as they journeyed both of them together,
Isaac the first-born spake and said, My Father,
Behold the preparations, fire and iron,   5
But where the lamb for this burnt-offering?
Then Abram bound the youth with belts and straps,
And builded parapets and trenches there,
And stretched forth the knife to slay his son.
When lo! an angel called him out of heaven,   10
Saying, Lay not thy hand upon the lad,
Neither do anything to him. Behold,
A ram caught in a thicket by its horns;
Offer the Ram of Pride instead of him.
But the old man would not so, but slew his son—   15
And half the seed of Europe, one by one.

THE RECEPTIVE READER

1. What are the *common* elements in both versions of the story?

2. How has the poet *changed* the meaning of the test undergone by Abraham? What does the "Ram of Pride" stand for? Who or what is the target of Owen's indictment?

3. What biblical *parables* do you know? How is this poem like a parable? Why does the poet's use of the biblical story give his indictment special force?

THE LANGUAGE OF MYTH

. . . *still the heart doth need a language, still*
Doth the old instinct bring back the old names.
SAMUEL TAYLOR COLERIDGE

Man today, stripped of myth, stands famished among all
his pasts and must dig frantically for roots, even if among
the most remote antiquities.
FRIEDRICH NIETZSCHE

Often a myth seems to find an echo deep in our minds and feelings. It seems to act out for us deep-rooted patterns in human experience. To many modern readers, myths have seemed, in the words of the psychoanalyst Carl Jung, "still fresh and living" in the hidden recesses of their minds. Anthropologists and psychoanalysts have probed recurrent **archetypes**—symbolic embodiments of vital forces and life cycles that we encounter in many disguises and variations. The earliest religions may have centered on mother goddesses associated with the development of agriculture and worshiped in fertility cults. Such earth goddesses were Ishtar of Mesopotamia (now Iraq) or Cybele of Asia Minor (now Turkey). To some contemporary feminist poets, they symbolize the human need for bonding and for living in harmony with the generative forces in nature.

J U D Y   G R A H N   (born 1940)

They Say She Is Veiled   1982

They say she is veiled
and a mystery. That is
one way of looking.
Another
is that she is where   5
she has always been,
exactly in place,
and it is we,
we who are mystified,
we who are veiled   10
and without faces.

THE RECEPTIVE READER

How does the poet play on the words *mystery* and *mystified*? What are the two ways "of looking" in this poem?

In Greek myth, the earth mother or "grain mother" is Demeter, the goddess of the harvest, who sustains and nourishes all that lives on land, in the sea, and in the air. When her daughter Persephone was abducted by Hades, the king of the netherworld, the distraught mother wandered in search of her, and warmth and light left the earth, ice and snow covered the land, and the fields turned barren. (Roman poets later called mother and daughter by their Latin names, Ceres and Proserpina.)

When Demeter finally found her daughter, she appealed to Zeus, the king of the gods, to let Persephone return to the light. However, once visitors to the world below had shared food with the dead, they were doomed to stay. Persephone had eaten only four of the juicy red seeds that make up the rich meaty center of the pomegranate fruit. So Zeus ruled that she would be able to rejoin her mother for part of the year but that she would have to spend four months each year with Hades in the regions of hell. When she returns to earth in the spring, grass sprouts on the hills, and flowers break through the earth's crust. To celebrate her daughter's return, Demeter causes the wheat to turn rich and golden on its stalks; clusters of grapes swell on the vines. Sheep and cattle turn plump and sleek, ready for sacrifice. The people raise their voices in thanksgiving to the

> Sacred Goddess, Mother Earth,
> Thou from whose immortal bosom
> Gods, and men, and beasts have birth.
> > Percy Bysshe Shelley, "Song of Proserpine"

At times, poets have immersed themselves in Greek myth as a world more attuned than grey reality to their needs as imaginative, passionate human beings. English Romantic poets like John Keats and Percy Bysshe Shelley take us to classical Greece (of the sixth or fifth century B.C.) as the ideal homeland of the artistic imagination. In his "Ode on a Grecian Urn," Keats calls up before our eyes mythological scenes of the kind he may have seen sculpted in marble or as vase paintings on ancient Greek amphoras (literally vases with two handles).

The **ode** is a Greek form with elaborately crafted stanzas fit for solemn subjects. As we read the stanzas of the ode, Keats makes us see the scenes we would see pictured on the urn as we slowly turn it. In the first three stanzas, we see young men (or gods?) pursuing young women in a forest setting. In the third stanza, we see a musician playing a shepherd's flute in a springtime setting of fresh leaves and flowers. In the fourth stanza, we see a religious procession leading an animal to the altar for sacrifice. Contemplating these scenes, Keats re-creates for us a mythical world closer to the heart's desire than inadequate reality. Here, gods and mortals intermingle, the music of flutes and drums resounds in forest glades, and the rich ceremonial of a religious holiday satisfies our yearning for dignity, grace, and beauty.

Like other poems taking us to the world of Greek mythology, the poem assumes a reader steeped in classical tradition. The setting is Greek: *Tempe* is a beautiful valley in Greece; *Arcady* (or Arcadia) is a Greek mountain region symbolic of idyllic, carefree country life. An *Attic* shape is from Attica, the region around Athens. Keats calls the urn a cold (that is, not moving or breathing) *pastoral* because, like traditional pastoral poetry, it takes us to fields and meadows, where *pastors,* or shepherds, tend their sheep. The *pipes* and *timbrels* are the simple flutes and small drums of early Greek times.

JOHN KEATS (1795–1821)

Ode on a Grecian Urn

1819

1

Thou still unravished bride of quietness,
   Thou foster-child of silence and slow time,
Sylvan° historian, who canst thus express   *of the woods*
   A flowery tale more sweetly than our rhyme:
What leaf-fringed legend haunts about thy shape   5

Of deities or mortals, or of both,
     In Tempe or the dales° of Arcady?   *valleys*
  What men or gods are these? What maidens loth?°   *unwilling*
What mad pursuit? What struggle to escape?
     What pipes and timbrels? What wild ecstasy?   10

2

Heard melodies are sweet, but those unheard
     Are sweeter; therefore, ye soft pipes, play on;
Not to the sensual ear, but, more endeared,
     Pipe to the spirit ditties° of no tone: *songs*
Fair youth, beneath the trees, thou canst not leave   15
     Thy song, nor ever can those trees be bare;
          Bold Lover, never, never canst thou kiss,
Though winning near the goal—yet, do not grieve;
          She cannot fade, though thou hast not thy bliss,
     For ever wilt thou love, and she be fair!   20

3

Ah, happy, happy boughs! that cannot shed
     Your leaves, nor ever bid the Spring adieu;°   *farewell*
And, happy melodist,° unwearièd,   *musician*
     For ever piping songs for ever new;
More happy love! more happy, happy love!   25
     For ever warm and still to be enjoyed,
          For ever panting, and for ever young;
All breathing human passion far above,
     That leaves a heart high-sorrowful and cloyed,
          A burning forehead, and a parching tongue.   30

4

Who are these coming to the sacrifice?
     To what green altar, O mysterious priest,
Lead'st thou that heifer° lowing at the skies,   *young cow*
     And all her silken flanks with garlands dressed?
What little town by river or sea shore,   35
     Or mountain-built with peaceful citadel,°   *fortress*
          Is emptied of this folk, this pious morn?
And, little town, thy streets for evermore
     Will silent be; and not a soul to tell
          Why thou art desolate, can e'er° return.   *ever*   40

5

O Attic shape! Fair attitude! with brede°   *interwoven pattern*
     Of marble men and maidens overwrought,
With forest branches and the trodden weed;
     Thou, silent form, dost tease us out of thought
As doth eternity: Cold Pastoral!   45
     When old age shall this generation waste,
          Thou shalt remain, in midst of other woe
          Than ours, a friend to man, to whom thou say'st,
"Beauty is truth, truth beauty,"— that is all
     Ye know on earth, and all ye need to know.   50

In this poem, the language of myth provides the medium for the Romantic rebellion against the ordinary. The silent shape of the urn is able to "tease us out of" our ordinary dejected thoughts. The time travel of the poetic imagination takes us from the grimy city to a forest setting where lovers experience passion and "wild ecstasy." Later, instead of going about our dull routine chores, we participate with the priest and pious worshipers in the procession that takes the heifer bedecked with garlands to the sacrifice.

Paradoxically, however, we see nature here not face to face but in the mirror of art. The lovers are not flesh and blood; the music ("the spirit ditties of no tone") remains "unheard." The urn freezes a moment in time and preserves it for future generations. We may think these cold, frozen images inferior to warm breathing life, but they are really superior, because they are not corruptible, not subject to corruption and change. Living and "breathing human passion" leaves the heart "high-sorrowful and cloyed." Therefore, the unheard melodies are "sweeter." In the context of timeless art, beauty cannot fade, and love cannot fade, into the light of common day. The lovers in the poem, stopped in mid-course, will never attain the object of their quest—but they will therefore never lose it either. Art—whether the poet's, the sculptor's, or the potter's art—triumphs over decay and outlasts the ravages of time.

The poem culminates in the credo of the poet starved for beauty and passion in an unimaginative society: "Beauty is truth, truth beauty." That is all we need to know. This conclusion gives trouble to skeptical readers: Beauty is only skin deep, they say. Surface beauty may be a thin varnish covering ugly truths. But the speaker in the poem seems certain of the beauty of truth and the truth of beauty. This, for him, is the message of the urn. As Keats said in one of his letters, "I am certain of the heart's affection and the truth of imagination—What the imagination seizes as beauty must be truth." Art and poetry celebrate not surface prettiness but an indwelling unity and harmony that make life meaningful and the world livable.

THE RECEPTIVE READER

1. In your own words, how or why is the vase the "still unravished bride of quietness"?

2. What is the poet's view of "breathing human passion" in the real world?

3. Why are the "unheard" melodies of the vase sweeter than heard ones? What is the advantage that art has over nature?

THE PERSONAL RESPONSE

As you see it, is the truth ever beautiful? Or is it more likely to be ugly? Does the phrase "Beauty is truth" in some way have meaning for you?

THE CREATIVE DIMENSION

Museum-goers and gallery-goers (and readers of art books) experience thoughts and feelings that they often do not put into words. Verbalize the thoughts and feelings passing through your mind as you look at a work of art (or architecture) that your readers might recognize. For instance, write about the Mona Lisa, a Chagall painting, Michelangelo's "Creation of Adam" from the Sistine Chapel, the Lincoln Memorial, or the New York World Trade Center.

JUXTAPOSITIONS

The Icarus Myth

A universally known Greek myth is the story of Daedalus and Icarus. Daedalus fashioned wings for himself and his son Icarus, but as Icarus flew too close to the sun, the wax gluing the feathers in his wings melted and he perished in the sea. We know the Icarus story best in the version of the Roman poet Ovid (43 B.C.–A.D. 18), who in his *Metamorphoses* rewrote many of the ancient stories. The myth is part of a web of stories taking place on the island of Crete, where Pasiphaë, the queen of King Minos, had been consumed by tormented longing for a beautiful white bull and given birth to monstrous off-spring, half man, half bull—the Minotaur. Daedalus was the Athenian inventor employed by King Minos to build the maze, or labyrinth, designed to pen in the Minotaur. Afterwards, when Minos refused Daedalus' request to let him and his son return to Athens, Daedalus constructed wings from feathers and wax so that father and son could make their escape through the air. Ovid concludes his retelling of the myth as follows:

> When the boy, too bold, too young, too ambitious in daring,
> Forced his way too high, leaving his father below,
> So the bonds of the wings were loosened, the fastenings melted,
> Nor could the moving arms hold in the desert of air.
> Panic seized him: he stared from heaven's height at the water;
> In the rush of his fear, darkness brimmed in his eyes.
> All of the wax was gone: his arms were bare as he struggled
> Beating the void of the air, unsupported, unstayed.
> "Father!" he cried as he fell, "Oh, father, father, I'm falling!"
> Till the green of the wave closed on the agonized cry,
> While the father, alas, a father no longer, was calling,
> "Icarus, where do you fly, Icarus, where in the sky?
> Icarus!" he would call—and saw the wings on the water.
> Now earth covers his bones; now that sea has his name.
> Translated by Rolfe Humphries

Different readers have used the traditional story as a prompt to construct their own private myths. Here are some of the readings:

✧ The myth acts out the age-old archetypes of impetuous, headstrong, ambitious youth and cautious, prudent, shell-shocked age.

✧ The myth focuses on the theme of overreaching, of overambitious, heedless pride that goes before a fall. In the words of a student reader, "Each time we dare, we taunt the gods a little." The Greeks called arrogant human pride *hubris,* and they expected it to provoke the wrath of the gods.

✧ The myth glorifies the human capacity for aspiration, for "testing the boundaries." Flight has long been a symbol for our human capacity to struggle up from the mud and clay, even at the risk of failure.

✧ The myth drives home the tragic irony of gallant effort coming to grief. It focuses on the agony of "almost-was"—we come close to triumph; we can see success within reach, yet it eludes our grasp.

✧ The myth focuses on the strongest kind of human love—the love of a parent for a child.

Look at the treatment of the Icarus myth in the following modern poems. What is the meaning of the myth for each poet?

ANNE SEXTON   (1928–1974)

To a Friend Whose Work Has Come to Triumph   1962

Consider Icarus, pasting those sticky wings on,
testing that strange little tug at his shoulder blade,
and think of that first flawless moment over the lawn
of the labyrinth. Think of the difference it made!
There below are the trees, as awkward as camels;   5
and here are the shocked starlings pumping past
and think of innocent Icarus who is doing quite well;
larger than a sail, over the fog and blast
of the plushy ocean he goes. Admire his wings!
Feel the fire at his neck and see how casually   10
he glances up and is caught, wondrously tunneling
into that hot eye. Who cares that he fell back into the sea?
See him acclaiming the sun and come plunging down
while his sensible daddy goes straight into town.

THE RECEPTIVE READER

1. Traditionally, people have listened to myths with grave attention. What details and imaginative comparisons give this poem a more irreverent or *ironic* modern twist?

2. What in the poem could lead a reader to conclude that nevertheless the myth has a serious meaning for the modern poet? What is the *theme* of this poem?

3. Both form and content of this poem play modern variations on traditional patterns. How does this fourteen-line poem live up to the requirements of the traditional *sonnet*? How does it depart from them?

The poem that follows gives us a retelling that takes us "down to earth" in its search for the reality behind the mythical tradition. The poem thus becomes a modern countermyth in which the ancient story becomes demythologized and the original heroes become modern antiheroes. The tone is irreverent toward both gods and human beings. How much does the poem preserve of the spirit or appeal of the original myth?

DAVID WAGONER   (born 1926)
The Return of Icarus   1958

He showed up decades later, crook-necked and hip-sprung,
Not looking for work but cadging food and wine as artfully
As a king, while our dogs barked themselves inside out
At the sight of his hump and a whiff of his goatskin.

We told him Daedalus was dead, worn out with honors   5
(Some of them fabulous), but especially for making
Wings for the two of them and getting them off the ground.
He said he remembered that time, but being too young a mooncalf,

He hadn't cared about those labyrinthine double-dealings
Except for the scary parts, the snorting and bellowing.   10
He'd simply let the wax be smeared over his arms
And suffered handfuls of half-stuck second-hand chicken feathers

And flapped and flapped, getting the heft of them, and taken
Off (to both their amazements), listening for his father's
Endless, garbled, and finally inaudible instructions   15
From further and further below, and then swooping

And banking and trying to hover without a tail and stalling
While the old man, a slow learner, got the hang of it.
At last, with the weight of his years and his genius,
Daedalus thrashed aloft and was gawkily airborne.   20

And they went zigzagging crosswing and downwind over the water,
Half-baked by the sirocco,° with Daedalus explaining   *hot wind*
Everything now: which way was up, how to keep your mouth
Shut for the purpose of breathing and listening,

How to fly low (having no choice himself) in case of Harpies,°   *monstrous birds*   25
And how to keep Helios° beaming at a comfortable distance   *the sun*
By going no higher than the absolute dangling minimum
To avoid kicking Poseidon,° the old salt, square in the froth.   *god of the sea*

But Icarus saw the wax at his skinny quill-tips sagging,
And he couldn't get a word in edgewise or otherwise,   30
So he strained even higher, searching for ships or landfalls
While he still had time to enjoy his share of the view,

And in the bright, high-spirited silence, he took comfort
From his father's lack of advice, and Helios turned
Cool, not hot as Icarus rose, joining a wedge of geese   35
For an embarrassing, exhilarating moment northward,

And then he grew cold till the wax turned brittle as marble,
Stiffening his elbows and suddenly breaking
Away, leaving him wingless, clawing at nothing, then falling
Headfirst with a panoramic, panchromatic vista   40

Of the indifferent sun, the indifferent ocean, and a blurred
Father passing sideways, still chugging and flailing away

With rows of eagle feathers. When Icarus hit the water,
He took its salt as deeply as his own.

He didn't tell us how he'd paddled ashore or where   45
He'd been keeping himself or what in the world he'd been doing
For a living, yet he didn't seem bitter. "Too bad
You weren't around," we said, "there'd have been something in it

For you, probably—an apartment straddling an aqueduct,
Orchards, invitations, hecatombs° of women."   *crowds (as in communal tombs)*   50
"No hard feelings," he said. "Wings weren't my idea."
And he told odd crooked stories to children for hours

About what lived under water, what lived under the earth,
And what still lived in the air, and why. A few days later
He slouched off on his game leg and didn't come back.   55
He didn't steal any chickens or girls' hearts

Or ask after his father's grave or his father's money
Or even kick the dogs. But he showed us calluses
Thicker than hooves on his soles and palms, and told us
That's how he'd stay in touch, keeping his feet on the ground.   60

THE RECEPTIVE READER

1. How does the first stanza signal that the ancient story is again being retold with a modern twist? How does it realign your perspective?

2. How does this retelling redraw the portrait of the father? How does it change your image of the father and your image of the young son? How does it reinterpret or refashion the relationship between father and son?

3. In the retelling of the flight, which parts of it are *humorous;* which seem serious?

4. For you, does the last line of the poem spell out the *theme* of the poem? Does it point a moral? Does it strike the keynote for the poem as a whole?

5. What is witty about the *allusion* in the father's "labyrinthine double-dealings" and the "snorting and bellowing"? What other references remind you that we are in the world of Greek mythology?

THE PERSONAL RESPONSE

Do this poet's changes in the story make the myth more believable or less?

The following modern sonnet strips the Icarus myth of many of its traditional trappings. There is no literal flight in this poem—no flying with false feathers like the original Icarus, nor flying in a metal bird that shears the clouds and becomes a menace to real birds. Perhaps we thus get to the mythic core of the ancient story. The flight of Icarus here becomes a central extended metaphor: The flights here are "imaged" flights, journeys of the mind. Although our bodies are earthbound, our minds are capable of tremendous flights of the imagination, making us outsoar the highest reaches of heaven and making us plummet to deepest hell.

VASSAR MILLER   (born 1924)

The New Icarus   1956

Slip off the husk of gravity to lie
Bedded with wind; float on a whimsy, lift
Upon a wish: your bow's own arrow, rift
Newton's decorum—only when you fly.
But naked. No false-feathered fool, you try   5
Dalliance with heights, nor, plumed with metal, shift
And shear the clouds, imperiling lark and swift
And all birds bridal-bowered in the sky.
Your wreck of bone, barred their delight's dominions,
Lacking their formula for flight, holds imaged   10
Those alps of air no eagle's wing can quell.
With arms flung crosswise, pinioned to wooden pinions,
You in one motion, plucked and crimson-plumaged,
Outsoar all Heaven, plummeting all Hell.

THE RECEPTIVE READER

1. Examine the poet's graphic *metaphors*. What is exceptionally appropriate or fitting about the image she creates by the phrase "Slip off the husk of gravity"?

2. Look at the *paradoxical* metaphors—metaphors that at first glance seem contradictory or physically impossible: How could the person addressed be told to be "your bow's own arrow"? (We propel our imaginary selves on the imagined voyage with the force of our own will and desire; these serve as the bow shooting forth ourselves as the arrow.) What do you make of the paradoxical "plumed with metal" or "alps of air"? What sense do they make on second thought?

3. The *allusion* to Newton, master physicist and mathematician of the eighteenth century, makes us think of Newtonian science. We are expected to think of a mechanistic model of the universe, where everything behaves according to the strict laws of physics—as if in accordance with strict etiquette or "decorum." How would the new Icarus "rift / Newton's decorum"?

4. The *pun* in the phrase "pinioned [fastened, shackled] to wooden pinions [wings]" makes us imagine a person with arms flung wide and fastened to the wooden wings as to a cross. Are you prepared to agree with the student who wrote the following passage about the possible religious implications of the poem?

> The new Icarus is Christ, whose "wreck of bone" finds salvation through suffering. Christ "pinioned to wooden pinions" and "crimson-plumaged" reaches heights of love that ancient humanity (Icarus) or modern humanity, "plumed with metal" of modern airplanes, will never outsoar. Living the life of the spirit incurs a great risk, since it can bring suffering , a "plummeting" to "all Hell." However, although Christ lacks the birds' "formula for flight," he can go the eagle one better. He can rise from his "plucked" "wreck of bone" to "those alps of air no eagle's wing can quell." Despite being nailed to the cross, "pinioned to wooden pinions," he can "in one motion . . . Outsoar all Heaven."

The following poem is one of several commenting on the painting "The Fall of Icarus" by the Flemish painter Pieter Breughel (about 1525–1569). How does the poem put the mythical story in perspective?

WILLIAM CARLOS WILLIAMS   (1883–1963)
Landscape with the Fall of Icarus   1960

According to Breughel
when Icarus fell
it was spring

a farmer was plowing
his field   5
the whole pageantry

of the year was
awake tingling
near

the edge of the sea   10
concerned with itself
sweating in the sun
that melted the wings' wax

unsignificantly
off the coast   15
there was

a splash quite unnoticed
this was
Icarus drowning

CROSS-REFERENCES—For Discussion or Writing

Explore the versions of the Icarus myth found in these poems. What do they show about the perennial or universal appeal of the myth? What do they show about the difference between more traditional and more modern perspectives? Which of the poems do you find most congenial or personally appealing and why?

THE CREATIVE DIMENSION

Write your own personal version of the Icarus myth or of another myth that you have known for some time.

MODERN MYTHS

goddess of the silver screen
the only original American queen
JUDY GRAHN, "HELEN IN HOLLYWOOD"

Although many myths are age-old, we can see the mythmaking faculty at work in our own time. The lone rider of the American frontier assumed mythical proportions in the cowboy myth that is at the heart of our popular culture. Its central figure, like the mythical heroes of the past, appears in countless permutations, from Buffalo Bill to space-age cowboys like Captain Kirk. To city-dwellers hemmed in by the restrictions and annoyances of city life, the cowboy seems to stimulate a collective memory of wide-open spaces, of depending on oneself, of being able to move on.

The Hollywood dream factory created mythical sex goddesses. Norma Jean Baker was turned into Marilyn Monroe, who became the daydream of every immature male: "Marilyn, who was every man's love affair . . . who was blonde and beautiful and had a little rinky-dink of a voice . . . which carried such ripe overtones of erotic excitement and yet was the voice of a little child" (Norman Mailer, *Marilyn*). After her death, admirers and defenders created the countermyth of the actress rebelling against the stereotype of the dumb screen blonde that denied her her own humanity—Marilyn "who tried, I believe, to help us see that beauty has a mind of its own" (Judy Grahn).

SHARON OLDS   (born 1942)
The Death of Marilyn Monroe   1983

The ambulance men touched her cold
body, lifted it, heavy as iron,
onto the stretcher, tried to close the
mouth, closed the eyes, tied the
arms to the sides, moved a caught   5
strand of hair, as if it mattered,
saw the shape of her breasts, flattened by
gravity, under the sheet,
carried her, as if it were she,
down the steps.   10

These men were never the same. They went out
afterwards, as they always did,
for a drink or two, but they could not meet
each other's eyes.

                Their lives took   15
a turn—one had nightmares, strange
pains, impotence, depression. One did not
like his work, his wife looked
different, his kids. Even death
seemed different to him—a place where she   20
would be waiting,

And one found himself standing at night
in the doorway to a room of sleep, listening to
a woman breathing, just an ordinary
woman   25
breathing.

THE RECEPTIVE READER

1. What was the cause of Marilyn Monroe's death?
2. Why were the men in the poem "never the same"? What is the *mythic* or symbolic significance of Monroe in this poem?
3. Has popular entertainment left the *stereotype* of the Hollywood blonde behind?
4. Is the Marilyn Monroe myth alive?

THE CREATIVE DIMENSION

What is the keynote of this poem for you? What lasting impression does it leave in your mind? Look at the following re-creation by a fellow student, and then write your own.

Those ambulance men
shocked into recognition of death and tenuous life
shifted the body
prepared her for the journey
The body wasn't going anywhere special
they were
One to nightmares, strangeness
Another to dislike, to fear
The last to listening.

How does the following poem rewrite the cowboy myth?

E. E. C U M M I N G S   (1894–1963)
Portrait   1923

Buffalo Bill's
defunct
        who used to
        ride a watersmooth-silver
                                        stallion   5
and break onetwothreefourfive pigeonsjustlikethat
                                Jesus
he was a handsome man
                        and what i want to know is
how do you like your blueeyed boy   10
Mister Death

THE RECEPTIVE READER

Who was Buffalo Bill? What was his claim to fame? In what ways is he a symbol of his period in American history? What is the attitude toward him in this poem?

THE CREATIVE DIMENSION

A student wrote the following tribute shortly after e. e. cummings had died. How well did the student writer get into the spirit of the original? Try your hand at a similar portrait of someone more recently defunct.

Portrait II

e. e. someone
buried by busy ones,
        used to
        wish yes aprils with a you
              and a me
and write onetwothreefourfive poemsjustlikethat
                by dong and ding
he was a perceptive man
          and what i want to know is
where is he now when we need him
Mister Death

POEMS FOR FURTHER STUDY

In reading the following poems, pay special attention to the poet's use of myth and allusion. What knowledge of myth, legend, or history does the poet assume? What is the role of an allusion in a poem as a whole?

WILLIAM WORDSWORTH (1770–1850)

The World Is Too Much with Us   1807

The world is too much with us; late and soon,
Getting and spending, we lay waste our powers;
Little we see in Nature that is ours;
We have given our hearts away, a sordid boon.
This Sea that bares her bosom to the moon,   5
The winds that will be howling at all hours,
And are up-gathered now like sleeping flowers,
For this, for everything, we are out of tune;
It moves us not.—Great God! I'd rather be
A Pagan suckled in a creed outworn;   10
So might I, standing on this pleasant lea,°   *grassland*
Have glimpses that would make me less forlorn;
Have sight of Proteus rising from the sea;
Or hear old Triton blow his wreathèd horn.

THE RECEPTIVE READER

From a dictionary or other reference work, what can you find out about Proteus and Triton? What role do they play in the poem? What does the world of Greek myth mean to the speaker in this sonnet?

EDNA ST. VINCENT MILLAY   (1892–1950)
An Ancient Gesture   1931

I thought, as I wiped my eyes on the corner of my apron:
Penelope did this too.
And more than once: you can't keep weaving all day
And undoing it all through the night;
Your arms get tired, and the back of your neck gets tight;   5
And along towards morning, when you think it will never be light,
And your husband has been gone, and you don't know where, for years,
Suddenly you burst into tears;
There is simply nothing else to do.

And I thought, as I wiped my eyes on the corner of my apron: 10
This is an ancient gesture, authentic, antique,
In the very best tradition, classic, Greek;
Ulysses did this too.
But only as a gesture,—a gesture which implied
To the assembled throng that he was much too moved to speak.   15
He learned it from Penelope . . .
Penelope, who really cried.

THE RECEPTIVE READER

1. What is the story of Penelope and Ulysses?
2. In Homer, men weep over their slain comrades. What makes this poet suspicious of Ulysses' tears?

WILLIAM DICKEY   (born 1928)
Exploration over the Rim   1959

Beyond that sandbar is the river's turning.
There a new country opens up to sight,
Safe from the fond researches of our learning.
Here it is day; there it is always night.

Around this corner is a certain danger.   5
The streets are streets of hell from here on in.
The Anthropophagi° and beings stranger   *man-eaters*
Roast in the fire and meditate on sin.

After this kiss will I know who I'm kissing?
Will I have reached the point of no return?   10
What happened to those others who are missing?
Oh, well, to hell with it. If we burn, we burn.

THE RECEPTIVE READER

What echoes of mythic voyages do you hear in this poem? Does the irreverent ending undercut the rest of the poem?

DONALD FINKEL   (born 1929)
The Sirens   1959

The news lapped at us out of all
Horizons: the ticking night full
Of gods; sensed, heard the tactile

Sea turn in his bed, prickling
Among derelicts. When the song   5
Was clear enough, we spread our hair,

Caught it. Under the comb the strands
Whipped into fresh harmonies, untangled
Again. The wind took it, and he heard.

The droll ship swung leeward;   10
Caught sight of him (rather, could
Have seen, busy with the fugue)

Yanking his bonds, the strings of his wide
Neck drawn like shrouds, his scream
Caught in the sail.   15
            Now in a sea

Of wheat he rows, reconstructing.
In his ridiculous, lovely mouth the strains
Tumble into place. Do you think
Wax could have stopped us, or chains?   20

THE RECEPTIVE READER

The sirens were mythical women whose song was so irresistible that mariners would steer their ships into the rocks of the sirens' island and perish. This poem alludes to the story of a famous traveler who passed by the island during his far-flung voyages. What is the story of Ulysses and the sirens? How does this poem reverse the usual perspective from which we see this story—and with what effect?

WRITING ABOUT LITERATURE

12. Reinterpreting Myth (Focus on Peer Review)

The Writing Workshop   Writers don't write in a vacuum. They live with feedback from friends, family, colleagues, editors, reviewers—or just plain readers. In a classroom, you can simulate such input by having your peers react to your writing as individuals or in a group. Such feedback helps make you more audience conscious; it strengthens your sense of what happens when your writing reaches the reader.

In turn, when you act as a peer reviewer for others, you help alert other writers to the reader's needs. You help them see their writing through the reader's eyes. Remember that critics and reviewers easily lapse into a faultfinding mode. Although it is important to identify weaknesses and mistakes, it is just as important to help writers develop what is promising and to help them build on their strengths. Try to balance negative criticism with constructive suggestions. The key question in your mind should be: What can the writer do to improve, to make the writing more instructive, more effective?

Here are sample passages with comments that might help a writer develop the full potential of a paper:

> Ovid, David Wagoner, and Vassar Miller offer vastly different interpretations of the classic myth. However, we are also able to see a few similarities.

COMMENT: What *are* these differences and similarities? Give us a hint to keep us interested? Give us more of a preview?

> In the biblical account, Abraham "bound Isaak his son, and laid him on the altar upon the wood." Owen's poem says that "Abram bound the youth with belts and straps, / And builded parapets and trenches." Belts and straps, parapets and trenches are surely alien to people of biblical times who herded sheep for a living. These words denote the military.

COMMENT: Follow up and explain? Why does the poet use these "military" references? What kind of warfare and what war does he have in mind?

> The first thing that must be taken into consideration about this poem is its basis in the traditional biblical story. . . . Once the element of war and sacrifice has been introduced, the whole concept of sacrifice is looked at in respect to the ones that do the sacrificing as well as the ones being sacrificed. . . . Owen has successfully conveyed the personalities and situations involved with war and sacrifice.

COMMENT: Rewrite to avoid the wooden, impersonal passive? "The element of war and sacrifice *has been introduced*"—by whom? Try "Once the poet *has introduced* . . . he *looks* at this theme . . ."? Cut down on jargony words like *basis, element, concept, situation*? Rewrite chunky passages like "looked at in respect to the ones that"?

STUDENT PAPER FOR PEER REVIEW

Monroe: Quest of Beauty

Marilyn Monroe became something more than human even before her suicide in the early 60s. Her image—celluloid clips, photo stills—keeps appearing in sometimes unlikely places. Sometimes her image reappears in another embodiment, such as Madonna, and the casual observer will still think "Monroe" before recognition sets in. We know who she is, or was. Or at least we think we do.

Norman Mailer in *Marilyn,* one of a never-ending stream of books about the "goddess of the silver screen," said, "She was not the dark contract of the passionate brunette depths that speak of blood, vows taken for life, and the furies of vengeance. . . . no, Marilyn suggested sex might be difficult or dangerous with others, but ice cream with her." Mailer said, "We think of Marilyn, who was every man's love affair" and whose "little rinky-dink voice" carried "ripe overtones of erotic excitement and yet was the voice of a little child."

In her poem "The Death of Marilyn Monroe," Sharon Olds describes the impact that Marilyn's death had on the ambulance attendants who carried "her cold / body" to the ambulance. "These men were never the same." One had nightmares, became impotent, suffered depression. One did not "like his work, his wife looked / different, his kids." Death became a place "where she / would be waiting." Another

> found himself standing at night
> in the doorway to a room of sleep, listening to
> a woman breathing, just an ordinary
> woman
> breathing.

For these men, and all men and women, the death of Marilyn meant far more than the tragedy of an individual; it was the death of a modern goddess, of a mythical being.

To Judy Grahn, a feminist poet, Monroe, like Harlowe, Holiday, or Taylor, represents an older myth, that of Helen of Troy. In her poem "Helen in Hollywood," she says, "'That's the one,' we say in instant recognition, / because our breath is taken away by her beauty, / or what we call her beauty." Helen herself, to Judy Grahn, is merely the human incarnation of a deity humanity has almost forgotten. This deity goes by many names and lives in many cultures and is represented in our world by the Hollywood star who

> writes in red red lipstick
> on the window of her body,
> long for me, oh need me!

We, her fans, crowd around her to share in her "luminescent glow," and we may destroy her in the process:

> We adore her. we imitate and rob her
> adulate   envy
> admire   neglect
> scorn.   leave alone
> invade, fill
> ourselves with her.
> we love her, we say
> and if she isn't careful
> we may even kill her.

She is our "leaping, laughing leading lady," who "sweeps eternally / down the steps / in her long round gown." But it is also she "who lies strangled / in the belltower"; it is she "who is monumentally drunk and suicidal." It is she who when "locked waiting in the hightower . . . leaps from her blue window."

For years after Marilyn's death, men would say (and women, too): "If only she had met me, I could have saved her!" Something in her flawed beauty, in her vulnerability, made her personal to millions of people. She became the best celluloid representation of the goddess of beauty, approachable and accepting of everyone's gifts. She taught us the power of sexual awareness, the power of our sexual selves. Everyone was welcome at her well. To Sharon Olds, not to have Marilyn as a symbol in our lives is the price the ambulance crew paid. It is not to have connection; it is not to have sexual, social, or family bonds. It is to stand alone in the dark, doubting and seeking reaffirmation of the reality of a loved person in our lives, "listening to / a woman breathing, just an ordinary / woman / breathing."

QUESTIONS

1. Should the writer have brought out her *thesis* earlier or more clearly in the paper? What would you suggest as a possible thesis statement early in the paper? Compare your suggestions with those of your classmates.

2. Could the relation between Mailer, Olds, and Grahn have been clarified more to make the overall *pattern* or drift of the paper clearer to the reader? What is the connection? What is the overall pattern?

3. Do you feel anywhere in the essay a need for additional *explanation* or discussion of the quoted passages?

4. Do you need additional *quotations*? Do you need more of a sense of the overall *intention* and pattern of a source? Where or why?

5. Do you have suggestions for strengthening *beginning and end*—title, introduction, conclusion?

6. What is your personal *reaction* to this writer's interpretation of the Monroe myth? Does it need more explanation or justification? How do you think other readers will react?

7. "Helen in Hollywood" appears in Judy Grahn's *Queen of Wands,* along with other Helen poems. Does this paper make you want to read the whole poem by Judy Grahn or more of her poetry? Why or why not?

13 THREE POETS IN DEPTH
Dickinson, Frost, Brooks

*In our age, and typically in a large, mobile industrial
society . . . people tend to become indifferent about their
ability to think or feel for themselves. . . . the poet's voice
is needed now more than ever before—that voice which
celebrates the difficult, joyous, imaginative process by which
the individual discovers and enacts selfhood.*

EDWIN HONIG

*Experiment escorts us last—
His pungent company
Will not allow an Axiom
An Opportunity*

EMILY DICKINSON

FOCUS ON THE POET

When reading a poet like Emily Dickinson, Robert Frost, or Gwendolyn
Brooks, we treasure the poet's personal voice. We recognize it with pleasure,
the way we welcome a cherished face or honor a signature. For a time, the
New Critics (originally "new" in the forties and fifties) asked that we treat each
individual poem as a self-contained whole. We were to read each poem on its
own terms, regardless of what we might know about the poet or the setting.
This way, we could attend to what the poem actually said rather than what we
expected it to say—because we knew the author, the time, or the party line. In
practice, however, we do not read an anonymous poem and then discover with
surprise that it is by Walt Whitman. There is name recognition in poets as
there is in singers or composers. The memory of past pleasure attracts us. As
we read, we are already attuned to the poet's way of looking at the world. Our
previous acquaintance with the poet shapes our expectations—although of
course a poem by a favorite poet may surprise us, taking a turn we find puzzling or strange.

In the poet's work, the individual poem is part of a larger whole. (We call
the accumulated work of a poet the **canon** when it is formidable enough to be

inventoried by critics and scholars.) Moving from one poem to the next, we recognize themes, preoccupations, obsessions. One poem helps us understand another. We interpret a difficult passage by way of cross-reference to a similar passage elsewhere. In addition, we may test our interpretation against statements made by the poet or by people in the poet's confidence.

Looking at the work of three poets in depth, this chapter will ask you to focus in turn on three kinds of investigation that can enhance your understanding of an individual poem.

The Personal Voice   The best-loved poets have an unmistakable personal idiom or **style.** They have an inimitable, personal way of looking at the world and sharing with us what they see. We do not mistake Emily Dickinson for e. e. cummings. (Beginning poets, by contrast, often find it difficult not to sound like clones of their fashionable predecessors.)

The Poet as a Person   Ever since Samuel Johnson wrote his *Lives of the Poets* (1779–1781), **author biography** has been a thriving branch of literary scholarship. It is fueled by investigators who agree with Johnson that "the biographical part of literature is what I love most." Who is the biographical person behind the persona speaking in a poem? Who is the person behind the masks and disguises particular poems may create? How does a poem become more meaningful when we see it in the context of the poet's life?

The Poet's Commitment   In the work of an **engaged,** that is, politically committed, poet, individual poems may be bulletins from an ongoing struggle. To relate to recurrent themes, we may have to understand the poet's sense of mission. We may have to understand the poet's social conscience, class consciousness, or solidarity with the oppressed.

EMILY DICKINSON: THE POET'S VOICE

*In Amherst Emily lived on
though the world forgot
moving with calm coiled hair through tidy days.
Her face shrank to a locket. She explored
miniaturized worlds known only to moths and angels
walked to the far side of a raindrop—
trespassed
on Infinity.*

OLGA CABRAL

*Maybe that is one of the most valuable things about the
poetry of Emily Dickinson: to teach that there is something
in poetry that cannot be handled, cannot be studied
scientifically.*

LINDA GREGG

Surgeons must be very careful
When they take the knife!
Underneath their fine incisions
Stirs the culprit,—Life!
                    EMILY DICKINSON

Emily Dickinson (1830–1886) is the supreme example of a poet with a distinctive voice—a voice that seemed willfully strange to her contemporaries but that gradually came to be recognized and cherished by lovers of poetry everywhere. She led a withdrawn life and found practically no recognition in her day. She thought about success and fame ("Fame is a bee. / It has a song— / It has a sting— / Ah, too it has a wing"), but she ultimately had to settle for "fame of my mind"—recognition in her own mind. It was for posterity to discover her

                    sheer sanity
        of vision, the serious mischief
        language, the economy of pain.
                    Linda Pastan, "Emily Dickinson"

Although she sent over a hundred poems to editors and corresponded with an editor of the *Atlantic Monthly* for years, only a handful of her poems found their way into print in her lifetime. Magazines then published much conventionally uplifting poetry in dutifully regular meter and rhyme. To the editors, the bold experimental features of her poetry seemed "technical imperfections"; her work, like the work of other great innovators, was considered uncontrolled and eccentric. When they did publish her poems, editors conventionalized them. They changed bold metaphorical words to uninteresting ones; they changed her dashes to commas and periods; they made her off-rhymes and half-rhymes rhyme.

A collection of over a hundred poems published shortly after Dickinson's death astonished her publishers by running through eleven editions in two years. Almost two thousand of her poems have since been found and published. (Several times that number may have been lost.) Twentieth-century readers discovered in her a great precursor of the modern temper. They cherished her for her gift for provocative metaphor, her searching paradoxical intelligence, and her intensely personal point of view. Today, with her poems everywhere known and anthologized, and "with feminist considerations of her work abounding" (Leslie Camhi), she is widely recognized as America's greatest poet.

Much ink has flowed to create, embroider, and question the legend of Emily Dickinson as the mysterious lady dressed in white and living secluded in her father's house, embarked on her own private "journey into the interior." Who was the biographical person behind the persona—which she called the "supposed person"—that speaks to us in her poetry?

Dickinson "was born into a family that did everything for her but understand her" (Richard B. Sewall). Her grandfather had been a founder of

Amherst College. Her father—a lawyer, judge, and member of Congress—practiced a stern Puritanical religion in the New England tradition. He led morning prayers for family and servants, reading scripture in what his daughter Emily called a "militant accent." At a time when questioning even minor points of doctrine was scandalous, Dickinson developed serious doubts about original sin. She stopped going to church by the time she was thirty. She decided to keep the Sabbath at home, where, in her words, a "noted clergyman" (namely God) preached better and shorter sermons.

Her father was suspicious of books that "joggle the mind"; he banned novels, which young Emily and her brother Austin had to smuggle into the house while the father was "too busy with his briefs to notice what we do." She read and admired the great woman writers of her day, from the Brontë sisters to Elizabeth Barrett Browning. In addition to the Bible, Shakespeare, and theological works, her reading included Charlotte Brontë's *Jane Eyre* and George Eliot's *Middlemarch,* each the record of the spiritual pilgrimage of a woman in search of an identity other than the roles presented ready-made by society. In a poem she wrote a few years after the death of Charlotte Brontë, the poet said:

Soft fall the sounds of Eden
Upon her puzzled ear—
Oh what an afternoon for Heaven,
When "Brontë " entered there!

Dickinson attended Amherst Academy and for a year Mount Holyoke Female Seminary, one of the first women's colleges. Letters she wrote as a student show a young woman in love with exuberant word play and fired by youthful enthusiasm. Her quick wit and lively sense of irony never deserted her—in a poem written many years later, she said about a pompous fraud that "he preached upon 'Breadth' till it argued him narrow." However, she gradually withdrew from the outside world. One of her best-known poems begins "The Soul selects her own Society— / Then—shuts the door— / To her divine Majority— / Present no more."

She stayed in touch by letter with the few people who provided her with feedback for her poetry, including her sister-in-law Susan Gilbert Dickinson and Thomas Wentworth Higginson, the *Atlantic Monthly* editor whom she addressed as her mentor or "preceptor." Although Higginson had advanced ideas for his time, he was unable to come to terms with the strange and "wayward" poems she sent him. She in turn could not conform to the demands of the literary marketplace—to auction off "the Mind of Man" and to merchandise "Heavenly Grace" and the "Human Spirit."

As friends of earlier days drifted away, Dickinson, in the words of a biographer, increasingly withdrew to "her garden, her conservatory, the kitchen (where she baked bread for her father), but especially her room where, often far into the night, . . . she could explore her own 'real life' and write her poems in peace" (Richard B. Sewall).

Much detective work has probed possible psychological, social, or medical reasons for her increasing isolation. In poems and letters, she hints at intense emotional attachments that ended in anguish and disappointment. Passionate, yearning letters to an unknown recipient survive, possibly addressed to a married minister. Women writers today stress the fact that outlets for the creative energies of a fiercely independent woman were limited if not nonexistent in Dickinson's day. Thwarted in her early visions of fame, she was forced into resignation. Alternatively, psychoanalysts have searched her relationship with an authoritarian father, an invalid mother, or an uncomprehending brother and sister for clues to the intense, disturbed emotions in some of her poems. She may have suffered from agoraphobia, a debilitating fear of public places.

What is certain is that she found in the everyday routines of the household and in the enclosed natural life of her garden plot the food for far-flung questionings and explorations. In the words of one of her recent editors,

> From a life narrow by conventional standards, and from the household tasks that women have performed silently for generations, Dickinson drew the material for metaphysical speculation. Baking, sweeping, caring for the ill, mourning the dead, and observing the quiet nature of a garden were the occasions for sudden mysteries. . . . Ambivalent religious attitudes, together with the themes of death, immortality, and eternity, permeate her work. The Puritan sense of spiritual mystery inhabiting the circumstances of everyday life informs her minute observations of nature. Her meter is adapted from eighteenth-century hymns. But hers was "that religion / That doubts as fervently as it believes" (poem 1144).
>
> Leslie Camhi, "Emily Dickinson," in Marian Arkin and Barbara Shollar, eds., *Longman Anthology of World Literature by Women, 1875–1975*

What is the distinctive voice that makes her poems unmistakably hers? First of all, her poems remain fresh because of their intensely personal, often startling *perspective*. Her poems typically make us look at the world from an unexpected angle, thus forcing us to see something anew as if for the first time. She summed up her poetic credo in the following poem. (Numbers of poems refer to the numbering in Thomas H. Johnson's *The Collected Poems of Emily Dickinson*.)

Tell all the Truth but tell it slant
about 1868

J. 1129

Tell all the Truth but tell it slant—
Success in circuit lies
Too bright for our infirm Delight
The Truth's superb surprise

As Lightning to the Children eased   5
With explanation kind
The truth must dazzle gradually
Or every man be blind—

The truth is a "superb surprise," and it is too bright and dazzling for our infirm and weak capacity to absorb it. It must be presented "in circuit"—in a roundabout way. It must be allowed to dazzle and delight us "gradually." The way to tell the truth, therefore, is to tell it "slant"—not directly but aslant, so that it can approach us not head-on but from a slanted, nonthreatening angle. (We do not tell children straight-on about the awesome power of lightning to kill in a flash. Instead, we make the truth easy on them with "kind" explanation.)

CROSS-REFERENCES—For Discussion or Writing

What is the connection between this poem and Gwendolyn Brooks' poem "Truth" (p. 20)?

The way Dickinson tells the truth "slant" is not to preach at us but to speak to us through startling graphic *images* and eye-opening metaphors. She looks at the world with a special alertness, marveling at what she finds, keeping alive in us the art of wondering. For people who notice birds only in passing, the following poem presents a series of striking visual images designed to surprise them into paying attention.

A Bird came down the Walk   about 1862
J. 328

A Bird came down the Walk—
He did not know I saw—
He bit an Angleworm in halves
And ate the fellow, raw,

And then he drank a Dew   5
From a convenient Grass—
And then hopped sidewise to the Wall
To let a Beetle pass—

He glanced with rapid eyes
That hurried all around—   10
They looked like frightened Beads, I thought—
He stirred his Velvet Head

Like one in danger. Cautious,
I offered him a Crumb
And he unrolled his feathers   15
And rowed him softer home—

Than Oars divide the Ocean,
Too silver for a seam—
Or Butterflies, off Banks of Noon
Leap, plashless° as they swim.   *without a splash*   20

The opening lines zero in on the bird without much ado. They give us a startling close-up view of the visitor that has come down from its natural element the air to go about essential bird business: We see the angleworm being bitten "in halves," then eaten raw, and washed down with dew drunk from a conveniently close blade of grass. We keep watching as the bird hops sidewise to get out of the way of a beetle. We get a glimpse of the beadlike eyes that are forever hurriedly glancing and shifting, looking for lurking danger.

At the approach of the human observer (who means no harm and offers a crumb), the bird returns to its natural airborne habitat, where he "rowed him softer home" than an oar-propelled boat does in the ocean. We watch the striking transition from the comically hopping, restless, and anxious earthbound bird to the bird at home and at ease in the seamless air where it effortlessly glides. Indeed, the flight of the bird seems smoother, less slowed down by resistance, than the fluttering of butterflies as they "leap" into the air from their noontime resting place without making a splash and then "swim" in it.

Does the transformation (or metamorphosis) of the bird from its awkwardly hopping, frightened grounded state to its serenely floating skyborne state have a symbolic meaning? Are our bodies stumbling awkwardly through life in our present earthbound existence? Will our souls float serenely upward, returning to their spiritual home, during a future state? The poem does not say. If this is the larger truth hinted at in the poem, the poet tells it "slant."

THE RECEPTIVE READER

1. Dickinson's *wording* is often cryptic—compressing or telescoping meaning into short, puzzling phrases. When she talks about the "ocean" of air, what is the meaning of "too silver for a seam"? What is it about silver that keeps us from expecting to see seams? How would butterflies leap "off Banks of Noon"?

2. Many people lay out money for photographs, paintings, or figurines of pretty birds. Is the bird in this poem pretty? Why or why not?

3. What words and images in this poem make the natural creatures seem almost human? Which remind us that they are not? One student said after reading this poem, "We like to humanize animals, but we cannot communicate with them. Sometimes we feel kinship with animals, and at other times we don't." How would you sum up the poet's perspective on the animal world in this poem?

Dickinson's *metaphors* are often startling and thought provoking because they connect mundane details of every day with the most troubling questions about life, death, and immortality. In the following poem, household chores become a solemn metaphor for the housekeeping of the heart.

The Bustle in a House   about 1866
J. 1078

The Bustle in a House
The Morning after Death
Is solemnest of industries
Enacted upon Earth—

The Sweeping up the Heart   5
And putting Love away
We shall not want to use again
Until Eternity.

The solid ground floor of the metaphorical structure of this poem is the
bustling of activity in the house after someone beloved has died. Literally, the
diligent or industrious activity (the "solemnest of industries") involves tidying
up—sweeping the house and putting things away that with the deceased gone
may not be used again for a long time, if ever. But metaphorically these commonplace activities come to stand for the wrenching adjustments we have to
make in our hearts. We try to purge our hearts of cluttered, destructive emotions; we try to put everything in order. We realize we can no longer put our
love to its accustomed daily uses; we can only keep it on a back shelf until the
distant day of resurrection.

A third feature of Dickinson's poetry is the deceptive *simplicity* of her
style. There are no lush rhythms and elaborate rhymes to call attention to
themselves. Her basic line is a sparse, irregular three-beat or four-beat line.
Lines are usually held loosely together by slant rhyme or half-rhyme in a four-
line stanza, reminding us of simple popular forms like hymns and ballads. No
outward ornament comes between the poet and the reader. This very absence
of extraneous adornment highlights the importance of the individual word, the
individual metaphor. In one of her last letters, she wrote, "I hesitate which
word to take, as I can take but a few and each must be the chiefest."

EXPLORATIONS

The Poet's Voice

What features of the following poem seem to illustrate the distinctive
Dickinson style? For instance, does it show her way of looking at the world
from a startling new perspective? Does it show her way of giving concrete
shape to abstract ideas? Does it seem simple on the surface?

Because I could not stop for Death   about 1863
J. 712

Because I could not stop for Death—
He kindly stopped for me—
The Carriage held but just Ourselves—
And Immortality.

We slowly drove—He knew no haste   5
And I had put away
My labor and my leisure too,
For His Civility—

We passed the School, where Children strove
At Recess—in the Ring—
We passed the Fields of Gazing Grain—
We passed the Setting Sun—

10

Or rather—He passed Us—
The Dews drew quivering and chill—
For only Gossamer, my Gown—
My Tippet°—only Tulle—

15

scarf (of lacelike material)

We paused before a House that seemed
A Swelling of the Ground—
The Roof was scarcely visible—
The Cornice—in the Ground—

20

Since then—'tis Centuries—and yet
Feels shorter than the Day
I first surmised the Horses' Heads
Were toward Eternity—

THE RECEPTIVE READER

1. What is strange or different about the attitude toward *death* reflected in this poem? Can you sympathize with or relate to the feelings that seem to be mirrored in this poem?

2. What is the *symbolism* of the school, the fields, the setting sun, the house "that seemed / A Swelling of the Ground"?

EXPLORATIONS

The Range of Interpretation

Dickinson was an intensely personal poet, looking at the world from a highly individual perspective. In turn, critics have looked at her poetry from distinct, highly individual points of view. Study the following poem and the quotations that follow it. How do you react to them? Which do you tend to agree with and why?

I heard a Fly buzz—when I died
J. 465

about 1862

I heard a Fly buzz—when I died—
The Stillness in the Room
Was like the Stillness in the Air—
Between the Heaves of Storm—

The Eyes around—had wrung them dry—
And Breaths were gathering firm
For that last Onset—when the King
Be witnessed—in the Room—

5

I willed my Keepsakes—Signed away
What portion of me be   10
Assignable—and then it was
There interposed a Fly—

With Blue—uncertain stumbling Buzz—
Between the light—and me—
And then the Windows failed—and then   15
I could not see to see—

1. The buzzing fly, so familiar a part of the natural order of persistent household discomfort, is brought in at the last to give the touch of petty irritabilities that are concomitant with living—and indeed with dying. (Thomas Johnson)

2. The dying person does in fact not merely suffer an unwelcome external interruption of an otherwise resolute expectancy but falls from a higher consciousness, from liberating insight, from faith, into an intensely skeptical mood. . . . To the dying person, the buzzing fly would thus become a timely, untimely reminder of man's final, cadaverous condition and putrefaction. (Gerhard Friedrich)

3. I understand that fly to be the last kiss of the world . . . think of the fly not as a distraction taking Emily's thoughts from glory and blocking the divine light . . . but a last dear sound from the world as the light of consciousness sank from her. (John Ciardi)

4. The only sound of heavenly music, or of wings taking flight, was the "Blue—uncertain stumbling buzz" of a fly that filled her dying ear. Instead of a final vision of the hereafter, this world simply faded from her eyes. (Ruth Miller)

5. And what kind of fly? A fly "With Blue—uncertain stumbling Buzz"—a blowfly. . . . She was a practical housewife, and every housewife abhors a blowfly. It pollutes everything it touches. Its eggs are maggots. . . . What we know of Emily Dickinson gives us assurance that just as she would abhor the blowfly she would abhor the deathbed scene. (Caroline Hogue)

CROSS-REFERENCES—For Discussion or Writing

Other poems by Emily Dickinson included earlier in this volume are "Apparently with no surprise" (p. 91), "'Hope' is the thing with feathers" (p. 96), and "The Soul selects her own Society" (p. 175). Do these poems illustrate such characteristic features as a startling different perspective, bold metaphors, or a deceptive simplicity?

POEMS FOR FURTHER STUDY

The following selection includes many of the most widely read of Dickinson's poems. What in each poem helps you recognize her unmistakable personal voice? What are themes she returns to again and again? What is her characteristic way of treating them?

J. 67   about 1859

Success is counted sweetest
By those who ne'er succeed
To comprehend a nectar

Requires sorest need.

Not one of all the purple Host   5
Who took the Flag today
Can tell the definition
So clear of Victory

As he defeated—dying—
On whose forbidden ear   10
The distant strains of triumph
Burst agonized and clear!

J. 214   about 1860

I taste a liquor never brewed—
From Tankards scooped in Pearl—
Not all the Vats upon the Rhine
Yield such an Alcohol!

Inebriate of Air—am I—   5
And Debauchee of Dew—
Reeling—thro endless summer days—
From inns of Molten Blue—

When "Landlords" turn the drunken Bee
Out of the Foxglove's door—   10
When Butterflies—renounce their "drams"—
I shall but drink the more!

Till Seraphs swing their snowy Hats—
And Saints—to windows run—
To see the little Tippler   15
Leaning against the—Sun—

J. 249   about 1861

Wild Nights—Wild Nights!
Were I with thee
Wild Nights should be
Our luxury!

Futile—the Winds—   5
To a Heart in port—
Done with the Compass—
Done with the Chart!

Rowing in Eden—
Ah, the Sea!   10
Might I but moor—Tonight—
In Thee!

J. 258

about 1861

There's a certain Slant of light,
Winter Afternoons—
That oppresses, like the Heft
Of Cathedral Tunes—

Heavenly Hurt, it gives us—   5
We can find no scar,
But internal difference,
Where the Meanings, are—

None may teach it—Any—
'Tis the Seal Despair—   10
An imperial affliction
Sent us of the Air—

When it comes, the Landscape listens—
Shadows—hold their breath—
When it goes, 'tis like the Distance   15
On the look of Death—

J. 288

about 1861

I'm Nobody! Who are you?
Are you—Nobody—Too?
Then there's a pair of us?
Don't tell! They'd advertise—you know!

How dreary—to be—Somebody!   5
How public—like a Frog—
To tell one's name—the livelong June—
To an admiring Bog!

J. 341

about 1862

After great pain, a formal feeling comes—
The Nerves sit ceremonious, like Tombs—
The stiff Heart questions was it He, that bore,
And Yesterday, or Centuries before?

The Feet, mechanical, go round—   5
Of Ground, or Air, or Ought—
A Wooden way
Regardless grown,
A Quartz contentment, like a stone—

This is the Hour of Lead—   10
Remembered, if outlived,
As Freezing persons, recollect the Snow—
First—Chill—then Stupor—then the letting go—

J. 435

about 1862

Much Madness is divinest Sense—
To a discerning Eye—
Much Sense—the starkest Madness—
'Tis the Majority
In this, as All, prevail—
Assent—and you are sane—
Demur—you're straightway dangerous—
And handled with a Chain—

5

Facsimile of Emily Dickinson's original manuscript. Courtesy The Houghton Library, Harvard University, Cambridge.

J. 449

about 1862

I died for Beauty—but was scarce
Adjusted in the Tomb
When One who died for Truth, was lain
In an adjoining Room—

He questioned softly "Why I failed"?   5
"For Beauty," I replied—
"And I—for Truth—Themself Are One—
We Brethren, are," He said—

And so, as Kinsmen, met a Night—   10
We talked between the Rooms—
Until the Moss had reached our lips—
And covered up—our names—

J. 526   about 1862

To hear an Oriole sing
May be a common thing—
Or only a divine.

It is not of the Bird
Who sings the same, unheard,   5
As unto Crowd—

The Fashion of the Ear
Attireth that it hear
In Dun, or fair—

So whether it be Rune,   10
Or whether it be none
Is of within.

The "Tune is in the Tree—"
The Skeptic—showeth me—
"No Sir! In Thee!"   15

J. 579   about 1862

I had been hungry, all the Years—
My Noon had Come—to dine—
I trembling drew the Table near—
And touched the Curious Wine—

'Twas this on Tables I had seen—   5
When turning, hungry, Home
I looked in Windows, for the Wealth
I could not hope—for Mine—

I did not know the ample Bread—
'Twas so unlike the Crumb   10
The Birds and I, had often shared
In Nature's—Dining Room—

The Plenty hurt me—'twas so new—
Myself felt ill—and odd—

                                                                      15

As Berry—of a Mountain Bush—
Transplanted—to the Road—

Nor was I hungry—so I found
That Hunger—was a way
Of Persons outside Windows—
The Entering—takes away—   20

J. 986   about 1865

A narrow fellow in the Grass
Occasionally rides—
You may have met Him—did you not
His notice sudden is—

The grass divides as with a Comb—   5
A spotted shaft is seen—
And then it closes at your feet
And opens further on—

He likes a Boggy Acre°   *swampy ground*
A Floor too cool for Corn—   10
Yet when a Boy, and Barefoot—
I more than once at Noon

Have passed, I thought, a Whiplash
Unbraiding in the Sun
When stooping to secure it   15
It wrinkled, and was gone—

Several of Nature's People
I know, and they know me—
I feel for them a transport°   *sudden impulsive feeling*
Of cordiality—   20

But never met this Fellow
Attended, or alone
Without a tighter breathing
And Zero at the Bone—

J. 1052   about 1865

I never saw a Moor—
I never saw the Sea—
Yet know I how the Heather looks
And what a Billow be.

I never spoke with God   5
Nor visited in Heaven—
Yet certain am I of the spot
As if the Checks were given—

J. 1263

There is no Frigate like a Book
To take us Lands away
Nor any Coursers like a Page
Of prancing Poetry—
This Traverse may the poorest take   5
Without oppress of Toll—
How frugal is the Chariot
That bears the Human soul.

J. 1732

My life closed twice before its close—
It yet remains to see
If Immortality unveil
A third event to me
So huge, so hopeless to conceive   5
As these that twice befell
Parting is all we know of heaven,
And all we need of hell.

THE CREATIVE DIMENSION

From the poems by Dickinson you have read, choose a haunting image or a striking, puzzling detail that left a lasting impression. Write a passage in which you re-create the image or impression and follow the train of associations—of images, thoughts, or feelings—that it sets in motion in your mind.

CROSS-REFERENCES—For Discussion or Writing

For a library research project, search for books and articles that would provide material for a treatment of one of the following topics:

✦ A range of critical interpretations of the same Dickinson poem. How does the same poem look when read by different readers? Are there major areas of agreement? What are major differences in interpretation, and what might explain them?

✦ Several critics' treatment of a recurrent theme in Dickinson's poetry. What do different critics say about the poet's treatment of a central recurrent theme like death, nature, love, faith, or immortality?

✦ Several critics' discussion of a key feature of her style or personal voice.

Book-length sources you may be able to consult may include the following:

Charles R. Anderson, *Emily Dickinson's Poetry: Stairway to Surprise* (1960)
Richard B. Sewall, ed., *Emily Dickinson: A Collection of Critical Essays* (1963)
Albert Gelpi, *Emily Dickinson: The Mind of the Poet* (1965)
Ruth Miller, *The Poetry of Emily Dickinson* (1974)
Richard B. Sewall, *The Life of Emily Dickinson* (1974)
Robert Weisbuch, *Emily Dickinson's Poetry* (1975)

Sharon Cameron, *Lyric Time: Dickinson and the Limits of Genre* (1980)
David Porter, *Dickinson: The Modern Idiom* (1981)
Joanne F. Diehl, *Dickinson and the Romantic Imagination* (1981)
Antonina Clarke Mossberg, *Emily Dickinson: When a Writer Is a Daughter* (1982)
Susan Juhasz, *The Undiscovered Continent: Emily Dickinson and the Space of the Mind* (1983)
Susan Juhasz, ed., *Feminist Critics Read Emily Dickinson* (1983)
Jerome Loving, *Emily Dickinson: The Poet on the Second Story* (1986)
Helen McNeil, *Emily Dickinson* (1986)
Cynthia Griffin Wolff, *Emily Dickinson* (1986)
Christanne Miller, *Emily Dickinson: A Poet's Grammar* (1987)

Numberless discussions of Dickinson's poetry have appeared in periodicals ranging from the *Explicator* to *New Literary History*.

ROBERT FROST: POET AND PERSONA

We are all toadies to the fashionable metaphor of the hour.
Great is he who imposes the metaphor.

ROBERT FROST

If Robert Frost was much honored in his lifetime, it was
because a good many preferred to ignore his darker truths.

JOHN F. KENNEDY

The figure a poem makes . . . begins in delight and ends
in wisdom.

ROBERT FROST

Robert Frost (1874–1963) became a living legend. He is the closest that twentieth-century America came to having a national poet who meant to the popular imagination what Whitman had meant to the new American nation in the nineteenth century. As with other legendary literary figures, biographers and critics have vested much effort in searching for the real-life person behind the legend. They have probed the paradoxical relationship between the public persona of the adored poet-sage and the personal difficulties and private demons of the poet's life.

In the early years, Frost struggled to make a living for himself and his family—as a farmer, a part-time teacher, a poet. Although he is commonly associated with the New England setting, he was born in San Francisco and spent his boyhood years in California. Frost's father, a Southerner who had named the boy Robert Lee, died when Frost was eleven years old. His Scottish mother then took him to New England, where she had relatives. Frost attended Lawrence High School in Massachusetts, where the curriculum was heavy on Greek and Roman history and literature. He later married Elinor White, who had been his covaledictorian there. He attended first Dartmouth and then

Harvard, but, as he put it later, he walked out of both of them, deciding to learn not from teachers but from "writers who had written before me."

With help from his grandfather, Frost bought a farm in New Hampshire, the setting of many of his early poems. Unable to make a living as a farmer and part-time teacher, unable to get more than a few poems accepted for publication, Frost and his wife took their growing family to England, where he made friends with other aspiring young poets. He was first recognized as a poet while in England, where he published two volumes: *A Boy's Will* (1913) and *North of Boston* (1914). When he returned to the United States, he was almost forty years old. Magazines started to print his poems, and he gradually became widely known as a poet and lecturer. His reading tours attracted large audiences. He helped found the Bread Loaf School of English at Middlebury College in Vermont. Honors multiplied: four Pulitzer Prizes, honorary degrees from Oxford and Cambridge, travel abroad as a government-sponsored ambassador of good will. Prestigious teaching appointments included stints as "poet in residence" at Amherst College and later at the University of Michigan in Ann Arbor. (He returned to Ann Arbor late in his life for the kind of poetry reading where he was adored and lionized by thousands of students.)

In his eighty-eighth year, Frost was asked to read one of his poems at the inauguration of President Kennedy. Eleven million television viewers saw the aged, white-maned poet struggle with his notes as the wind (or, in a different version of the story, the glaring sun) kept him from reading his prepared comments. He finally recited from memory "The Gift Outright," leaving his many admirers with the unforgettable memory of the poet's voice rising above the din and the hype of the nation's capital.

As a poet, performer, and public figure, Frost played the role of the New England sage. He appeared "wide shouldered, craggy, tough in texture, solid as New Hampshire granite" (Louis Untermeyer). He spoke as the voice of homely truths, distrusting science, progress, and professors. He maintained the image of someone staying close to the grass roots, keeping in touch with the simple realities of rural living, distancing himself from movements and trends. ("I never dared be radical when young / For fear it would make me conservative when old.") He was wary of large abstractions and sweeping historical generalizations. He was impatient with talk that our period was particularly bad or the worst in the world's history. He said in a famous letter to the *Amherst Student,*

> Ages may vary a little. One may be a little worse than another. But it's not possible to get outside the age you are in to judge it exactly. Indeed it is as dangerous to try to get outside of anything as large as an age as it would be to try to engorge a donkey. Witness the many who in the attempt have suffered a dilation from which the tissues and muscles of the mind have never been able to recover natural shape. They can't pick up anything delicate or small anymore.

In the following poem, Frost assumes the characteristic stance of the country sage: Something ordinary happens, related to the familiar chores of the country dweller. Some small happening raises a question in the poet's mind. Two different ways of looking at the issue suggest themselves. The speaker in the poem weighs simple alternatives, honestly thinking the matter through. On reflection, what seemed a simple matter turns out to have a serious significance for how we think of ourselves or shape our lives. There is no waving of arms, no getting up on a soapbox to make a speech. The tone is one of New England understatement. There is something here worth thinking about, without getting all bothered and excited.

The Tuft of Flowers   1906

I went to turn the grass once after one
Who mowed it in the dew before the sun.

The dew was gone that made his blade so keen
Before I came to view the leveled scene.

I looked for him behind an isle of trees;   5
I listened for his whetstone on the breeze.

But he had gone his way, the grass all mown,
And I must be, as he had been—alone.

"As all must be," I said within my heart,
"Whether they work together or apart."   10

But as I said it, swift there passed me by
On noiseless wing a bewildered butterfly,

Seeking with memories grown dim o'er night
Some resting flower of yesterday's delight.

And once I marked his flight go round and round,   15
As where some flower lay withering on the ground.

And then he flew as far as eye could see,
And then on tremulous wing came back to me.

I thought of questions that have no reply,
And would have turned to toss the grass to dry;   20

But he turned first, and led my eye to look
At a tall tuft of flowers beside a brook,

A leaping tongue of bloom the scythe had spared
Beside a reedy brook the scythe had bared.

The mower in the dew had loved them thus,   25
By leaving them to flourish, not for us,

Nor yet to draw one thought of ours to him,
But from sheer morning gladness at the brim.

The butterfly and I had lit upon,
Nevertheless, a message from the dawn,   30

That made me hear the wakening birds around,
And hear his long scythe whispering to the ground,

And feel a spirit kindred to my own;
So that henceforth I worked no more alone,

But glad with him, I worked as with his aid,   35
And weary, sought at noon with him the shade;

And dreaming, as it were, held brotherly speech
With one whose thought I had not hoped to reach.

"Men work together," I told him from the heart,
"Whether they work together or apart."   40

In form, this poem has an almost childlike simplicity. Most of the stanzas are self-contained couplets in iambic pentameter, with little metrical variation. The most noticeable variation occurs early and is repeated in the last stanza. Initial trochaic inversion ("WHETHer | they WORK") serves to alerts us to the key issue and then accentuates the pronouncement to which the poem as a whole has built up. The stanzas tell the story step by step in simple "and-then" fashion, with no poetic frills. The speaker in the poem sees the grass that had been mown before and that is to be turned so it will dry in the sun. The mower is nowhere to be seen. The speaker in the poem thinks about the lonely fellow worker's morning labor. Later he notices first the butterfly, then the flowers by the brook that had been spared by the blade of the mower's scythe.

Yet in spite of this simple natural progression, the poem is not artless. Looking in vain for the mower who had worked early in the morning but is already gone, we are ready for the tentative initial thought about how all workers work essentially alone, doing their jobs whether recognized and supported by others or not. But the fluttering butterfly appears at the right time to guide us to the counterevidence: the tall tuft of flowers, the "leaping tongue of bloom," that the mower has left standing. The mower apparently did not intentionally spare the flowers for the sake of other human observers. Nevertheless, we become aware of a kindred spirit, who also took a special pleasure in the tuft of flowers and decided not to turn them into hay. The speaker in the poem neatly reverses his earlier conclusion: He "worked no more alone." The two contrasting points of view on whether we work alone or together are stated in exactly parallel form, with the last lines of the two related couplets serving as an identical refrain: "Whether they work together or apart" (lines 10 and 40).

Although many of Frost's best-loved poems are simple on the surface, they may turn out to be puzzlers; they remain open-ended. Frost once said that his poems "are set to trip the reader head foremost into the boundless." They trip us up, disturbing our smug set ways of thinking, making us ponder first one way of looking at things, then another. On another occasion, he said that he liked to write poems that seem "altogether obvious" to the casual reader but that turn out to be subtle in unexpected ways. We may want to reduce them to a simple formula, but we don't quite succeed.

Some of Frost's most famous poems have been interpreted in radically different ways. For instance, different readers have read diametrically opposed meanings into the poem "Mending Wall." Is it true that "Good fences make good neighbors"? Or is this kind of territorial thinking the product of an obsolete Stone Age mentality?

Mending Wall

1914

Something there is that doesn't love a wall,
That sends the frozen-ground-swell under it
And spills the upper boulders in the sun,
And makes gaps even two can pass abreast.
The work of hunters is another thing: 5
I have come after them and made repair
Where they have left not one stone on a stone,
But they would have the rabbit out of hiding,
To please the yelping dogs. The gaps I mean,
No one has seen them made or heard them made, 10
But at spring mending-time we find them there.
I let my neighbor know beyond the hill;
And on a day we meet to walk the line
And set the wall between us once again.
We keep the wall between us as we go. 15
To each the boulders that have fallen to each.
And some are loaves and some so nearly balls
We have to use a spell to make them balance:
"Stay where you are until our backs are turned!"
We wear our fingers rough with handling them. 20
Oh, just another kind of outdoor game,
One on a side. It comes to little more:
There where it is we do not need the wall:
He is all pine and I am apple orchard.
My apple trees will never get across 25
And eat the cones under his pines, I tell him.
He only says, "Good fences make good neighbors."
Spring is the michief in me, and I wonder
If I could put a notion in his head:
"Why do they make good neighbors? Isn't it 30
Where there are cows? But here there are no cows.
Before I built a wall I'd ask to know
What I was walling in or walling out,
And to whom I was like to give offense.
Something there is that doesn't love a wall, 35
That wants it down." I could say "Elves" to him,
But it's not elves exactly, and I'd rather
He said it for himself. I see him there,
Bringing a stone grasped firmly by the top
In each hand, like an old-stone savage armed. 40
He moves in darkness as it seems to me,

Not of woods only and the shade of trees.
He will not go behind his father's saying,
And he likes having thought of it so well
He says again, "Good fences make good neighbors."   45

The two critical excerpts that follow continue the dialogue between the speaker in the poem and his neighbor. The first reader, reading the poet's meanings out of the poem, agrees with the speaker: "Something there is that doesn't love a wall." (Even the first reader, however, reserves an escape clause, well aware that the poet might be up to "mischief.")

Much of the public knows Frost by the phrase "Good fences make good neighbors." But the speaker in "Mending Wall" is saying just the opposite: that there is some mysterious force at work to break down barriers between human beings. "Elves," he calls it, in contrast to the matter-of-fact damage done by hunters (lines 5–11). But this is only a hint of what each person must discover for himself—companionship, respect, love, or the mystical togetherness of men who work.

The speaker's description of his neighbor makes the point even clearer (lines 38–42). The man and his ideas still belong to stone-age savagery. The darkness which surrounds him is not simply the natural darkness of the woods, but the primordial destructiveness in the heart of man. There is darkness also in the conventional mentality that makes a man repeat "Good fences make good neighbors" simply because his father said it (lines 43–44), when it does not fit the new situation at all (lines 30–31).

The poem, however, illustrates the difficulty of making a definite statement about any of Frost's ideas. The speaker does not agree with his neighbor in theory (lines 23–36); but, in the fact of his labor, he is doing the same thing his neighbor is doing.

From David A. Sohn and Richard H. Tyre, *Frost: The Poet and His Poetry*

The second reader reaches the opposite conclusion. He brings into the poem **external evidence,** drawing on his previous knowledge of the poet's characteristic attitudes and themes. He thus illustrates to what extent the reader's reponse is often shaped by what the reader *brings to* the poem. Here, we are not reading the poem in isolation. We bring to bear our assumptions about the poet as the voice of traditional "Yankee individualist" values.

Many general readers—and doubtless some stray sophisticated ones too—still see the poem as an argument against walls of all sorts, be they literal or metaphorical. To them walls are the divisive creations of selfish or short-sighted men who erect barriers to keep other people away. If only you will do away with useless, outmoded walls, they say, you will bring about a closer bond of fellowship—a deeper sense of community—among neighbors, in society at large, even among nations.

Generally, however, careful readers regard such views as hostile to the themes and attitudes they characteristically find in Frost. To them "Mending Wall" is Frost's finest expression of concern that in a world which doesn't seem to love a wall the individual may somehow get lost. To them the Yankee farmer, despite the scoffing questions that he puts to his neighbor, is the symbol of all those who love their privacy and their independence, and are resentful of those people—individuals or social planners—who would intrude upon that privacy. Or he is any individual who resents the levelers who would destroy walls and thus let others, even if friend or neighbor, infringe upon his right to be alone and to think his own thoughts after his own fashion. In short, despite the obvious warm appeal of the good neighborliness that wants walls down—even for the Yankee individualist resentful of intrusions—walls are nonetheless the essential barriers that must exist between man and man if the individual is to preserve his own soul, and mutual understanding and respect are to survive and flourish. . . .

A wall is something more than the means for walling something visible in or out. If apple trees and pine cones were the only concern, then good fences would scarcely be worth the trouble it takes to keep them repaired. But in spite of all his scoffing the narrator knows that this is the least of the purposes that are served by good fences. This is why each spring it is he who takes the initiative and lets his neighbor know beyond the hill that once again it's time for mending wall. Good fences make good neighbors.

From William S. Ward, "Lifted Pot Lids and Unmended Walls," *College English*, February 1966

THE RECEPTIVE READER

1. Cluster or free-associate the word *wall*. What images, associations, or memories does it bring to mind?

2. Which of the two readings do you agree with and why? Which of the two competing attitudes toward walls do you sympathize with and why?

3. Pressed in an interview to say where he stood on the issue of fences, Frost once said: "Maybe I was *both* fellows in the poem." What do you think he meant?

Honoring a poetic tradition that goes back to ancient Greece and Rome, Frost took his readers from the neuroses of city living to a simpler rural world. In the words of Babette Deutsch in *Poetry in Our Time,* he wrote about the commonplace subjects of country life: "the steady caring for crops and creatures"; the "homely details of barn and farmhouse, orchard, pasture and wood lot"; apple-picking, haymaking, repairing orchard walls of loosely piled stones. He celebrated "the jeweled vision of blueberries in rain-wet leaves"; no one wrote "more tenderly of the young life on and about the farm, be it a runaway colt, a young orchard threatened by false spring, a nestful of fledglings exposed by the cultivator."

Frost did not ignore the harsher or bleaker side of farm life: the "drudgery and isolation," ghastly accidents caused by machinery. However, only rarely do his best-known poems show the poet's darker and more pessimistic side. Donald Hall adored the older man when Hall himself was an aspiring young poet, and he befriended the aging poet toward the end of his career. Hall wrote about the anguish and sense of guilt that lay behind the public image of the "twinkling Yankee" of the Frost legend:

> To him—I learned over the years—his family background seemed precarious, dangerous; and his adult life cursed with tragedy, for which he took responsibility. His father was a sometime drunk, dead at an early age; his mother endured a bad marriage, was widowed young, and failed as a schoolteacher when she returned to her native Massachusetts; yet she was a fond mother, kind to her children—and she wrote poems. Her son felt dangerously

close to her, and followed that fondness into devotion to one young woman, Elinor White, whom he courted extravagantly, romantically, and doggedly. Apparently losing her, he considered suicide; at least, he later dropped hints to friends that he had considered suicide. When Elinor and Robert finally married, they settled in Derry, New Hampshire, and lived in poverty, enduring an extraordinary series of family misfortunes: their firstborn child, a son named Elliott, died of cholera infantum at the age of three; in later years, warning or bragging about his "badness," Frost said that the doctor who attended Elliott blamed him for the death, for not having called a doctor sooner. The next child was Lesley, daughter and eldest survivor, celebrator and denouncer of her father. Then there was Irma, mad in middle life and institutionalized; Frost's only sister had been insane, he himself frequently fearful of madness; he blamed himself and his genes for his daughter's insanity. Then came Carroll, his son, who killed himself at the age of thirty-eight. Youngest was Marjorie, dead after childbirth at twenty-nine.

The following late sonnet is the best known of the poems in which Frost confronted "the anguish of existence and the presence of the malign" (Babette Deutsch).

Design   1922

I found a dimpled spider, fat and white,
On a white heal-all, holding up a moth
Like a white piece of rigid satin cloth—
Assorted characters of death and blight
Mixed ready to begin the morning right,   5
Like the ingredients of a witches' broth—
A snow-drop spider, a flower like a froth,
And dead wings carried like a paper kite.

What had that flower to do with being white,
The wayside blue and innocent heal-all?   10
What brought the kindred spider to that height,
Then steered the white moth thither in the night?
What but design of darkness to appall?—
If design govern in a thing so small.

This poem is a finely crafted sonnet, with an underlying iambic pentameter beat, and with the interlaced rhyme scheme in the Petrarchan manner. The almost casual and at times playful tone sets up an ironic contrast with the miniature scene of death and blight:

> Frost achieves utter horror in this poem, which many consider his most terrifying work, by juxtaposing pleasant images with disgusting ones: the fat spider is "dimpled" and "white" like a baby; "dead wings" become a "paper kite": "death and blight" are cheerfully "mixed ready to begin the morning right," as in an ad for breakfast food. An air of abnormality pervades the entire poem. The flower, ironically called the "heal-all," is usually blue, but this is a mutant. The spider is at a height where it would not normally be found. Moths are ordinarily attracted by light, but this one has been "steered" to its death in

the night. And all the "characters of death" share the same ghastly whiteness.

Can we escape the conclusion that a dark design in nature plotted against the moth? The last line may not offer the ray of light its tone suggests. What would be better—that darkness terrorize by design, or that all the little evils in the world operate without design?

Consider also the game Frost plays with the reader by calling this sonnet "Design." A sonnet is a very small, yet intricately designed, poetic form of 14 lines; yet the speaker asks at the end if design really governs in very small things.

> From David A. Sohn and Richard H. Tyre, *Frost: The Poet and His Poetry*

THE RECEPTIVE READER

Do you agree with these two editors on the "utter horror" and on the "air of abnormality" that they say pervades the poem? Do you tend to answer the final question raised by the poem the same way they do?

Robert Frost achieved the difficult feat of being admired (sometimes grudgingly) by critics and his poetic peers while at the same time reaching a large popular audience. Critics and fellow poets acclaimed him even though he was at odds with poetic fashions in the first half of the twentieth century. The most influential and most widely imitated poets of his time were poets like T. S. Eliot and Ezra Pound. They wrote difficult poems, filled with shifting images and obscure allusions, that to some readers made Frost's more accessible, simple-on-the-surface poems seem unsophisticated by comparison. Furthermore, Frost made himself the advocate of traditional form when the modern tendency was to reject traditional meter and rhyme as artificial, confining, or extraneous. He said on the role of form in our lives and in the world,

> Any psychiatrist will tell you that making a basket, or making a horseshoe, or giving anything form gives you a confidence in the universe. . . that it has form, see. When you talk about your troubles and go to somebody about them, you're just a fool. The best way to settle them is to make something that has form, because all you want to do is get a sense of form.

CROSS-REFERENCES—For Discussion or Writing

✧ Other poems by Robert Frost printed earlier in this volume include "Stopping by Woods" (p. 6) and "Fire and Ice" (p. 62). Do they illustrate some of the features characteristic of the poems you have just read?

✧ Compare and contrast Frost's "Design" with Whitman's "A Noiseless Patient Spider"—another poem in which a spider serves as the central symbol (p. 17).

POEMS FOR FURTHER STUDY

In reading these poems by Robert Frost, keep in mind questions like the following: Does the poem conform to the pattern of making a natural scene or an event real for you and then making you share in the reflections it inspires?

Does the poem play off two different ways of looking at things? Which prevails and how? Is the poem in the "cool" New England voice? Or do you hear a more bitter, passionate, or questioning voice?

After Apple-Picking   1914

My long two-pointed ladder's sticking through a tree
Toward heaven still,
And there's a barrel that I didn't fill
Beside it, and there may be two or three
Apples I didn't pick upon some bough.   5
But I am done with apple-picking now.
Essence of winter sleep is on the night,
The scent of apples: I am drowsing off.
I cannot rub the strangeness from my sight
I got from looking through a pane of glass   10
I skimmed this morning from the drinking trough
And held against the world of hoary grass.
It melted, and I let it fall and break.
But I was well
Upon my way to sleep before it fell,   15
And I could tell
What form my dreaming was about to take.
Magnified apples appear and disappear,
Stem end and blossom end,
And every fleck of russet showing clear.   20
My instep arch not only keeps the ache,
It keeps the pressure of a ladder-round.
I feel the ladder sway as the boughs bend.
And I keep hearing from the cellar bin
The rumbling sound   25
Of load on load of apples coming in.
For I have had too much
Of apple-picking: I am overtired
Of the great harvest I myself desired.
There were ten thousand thousand fruit to touch,   30
Cherish in hand, lift down, and not let fall.
For all
That struck the earth,
No matter if not bruised or spiked with stubble,
Went surely to the cider-apple heap   35
As of no worth.
One can see what will trouble
This sleep of mine, whatever sleep it is.
Were he not gone,
The woodchuck could say whether it's like his   40
Long sleep, as I describe its coming on,
Or just some human sleep.

The Road Not Taken   1915

Two roads diverged in a yellow wood,
And sorry I could not travel both
And be one traveler, long I stood
And looked down one as far as I could
To where it bent in the undergrowth;   5

Then took the other, as just as fair,
And having perhaps the better claim,
Because it was grassy and wanted wear;
Though as for that the passing there
Had worn them really about the same,   10

And both that morning equally lay
In leaves no step had trodden black.
Oh, I kept the first for another day!
Yet knowing how way leads on to way,
I doubted if I should ever come back.   15

I shall be telling this with a sigh
Somewhere ages and ages hence:
Two roads diverged in a wood, and I—
I took the one less traveled by,
And that has made all the difference.   20

The Oven Bird   1916

There is a singer everyone has heard,
Loud, a mid-summer and a mid-wood bird,
Who makes the solid tree trunks sound again.
He says that leaves are old and that for flowers
Mid-summer is to spring as one to ten.   5
He says the early petal-fall is past,
When pear and cherry bloom went down in showers
On sunny days a moment overcast;
And comes that other fall we name the fall.
He says the highway dust is over all.   10
The bird would cease and be as other birds
But that he knows in singing not to sing.
The question that he frames in all but words
Is what to make of a diminished thing.

Acquainted with the Night   1928

I have been one acquainted with the night.
I have walked out in rain—and back in rain.
I have outwalked the furthest city light.

I have looked down the saddest city lane.
I have passed by the watchman on his beat   5

And dropped my eyes, unwilling to explain.

I have stood still and stopped the sound of feet
When far away an interrupted cry
Came over houses from another street,

But not to call me back or say good-by;   10
And further still at an unearthly height,
One luminary clock against the sky

Proclaimed the time was neither wrong nor right.
I have been one acquainted with the night.

Neither Out Far Nor In Deep   1936

The people along the sand
All turn and look one way.
They turn their back on the land.
They look at the sea all day.

As long as it takes to pass   5
A ship keeps raising its hull;
The wetter ground like glass
Reflects a standing gull.

The land may vary more;
But wherever the truth may be—   10
The water comes ashore,
And the people look at the sea.

They cannot look out far.
They cannot look in deep.
But when was that ever a bar   15
To any watch they keep?

The Silken Tent   1939

She is as in a field a silken tent
At midday when a sunny summer breeze
Has dried the dew and all its ropes relent,
So that in guys it gently sways at ease,
And its supporting central cedar pole,   5
That is its pinnacle to heavenward
And signifies the sureness of the soul,
Seems to owe naught to any single cord,
But strictly held by none, is loosely bound
By countless silken ties of love and thought   10
To everything on earth the compass round,
And only by one's going slightly taut
In the capriciousness of summer air
Is of the slightest bondage made aware.

Once by the Pacific

1928

The shattered water made a misty din.
Great waves looked over others coming in,
And thought of doing something to the shore
That water never did to land before.
The clouds were low and hairy in the skies, 5
Like locks blown forward in the gleam of eyes.
You could not tell, and yet it looked as if
The shore was lucky in being backed by cliff,
The cliff in being backed by continent;
It looked as if a night of dark intent 10
Was coming, and not only a night, an age.
Someone had better be prepared for rage.
There would be more than ocean-water broken
Before God's last *Put out the Light* was spoken.

Facsimile of Robert Frost's original manuscript. Courtesy Robert Frost Collection, Clifton Waller Barrett Library, Special Collections Department, Manuscripts, University of Virginia Library.

The Night Light

1947

She always had to burn a light
Beside her attic bed at night.
It gave bad dreams and broken sleep,
But helped the Lord her soul to keep.
Good gloom on her was thrown away.   5
It is on me by night or day,
Who have, as I suppose, ahead
The darkest of it still to dread.

On Being Idolized

1947

The wave sucks back and with the last of water
It wraps a wisp of seaweed round my legs,
And with the swift rush of its sandy dregs
So undermines my barefoot stand I totter
And did I not take steps would be tipped over   5
Like the ideal of some mistaken lover.

Nothing Gold Can Stay

1923

Nature's first green is gold,
Her hardest hue to hold.
Her early leaf's a flower;
But only so an hour.
Then leaf subsides to leaf.   5
So Eden sank to grief,
So dawn goes down to day.
Nothing gold can stay.

CROSS-REFERENCES—For Discussion or Writing

For a library research project, search for books and articles that would provide material for the treatment of one of the following topics:

♦ Several critical discussions of the same poem by Robert Frost. How does the poem look from different critical perspectives? How much common ground is there? What are significant differences, and how do you explain them?

♦ Several different perspectives on the private person behind the public legend. Books and articles have been written to defend Frost against what friends and biographers considered unjustified attacks on the poet. What was involved in these controversies?

Books you may be able to consult may include the following:

Reuben Brower, *The Poetry of Robert Frost* (1963)
Radcliffe Squires, *The Major Themes of Robert Frost* (1963)
J. F. Lynan, *The Pastoral Art of Robert Frost* (1964)

Philip L. Gerber, *Robert Frost* (1966)
Reginald L. Cook, *Robert Frost: A Living Voice* (1975)
Richard Poirier, *Robert Frost: The Work of Knowing* (1977)
John C. Kemp, *Robert Frost and New England: The Poet as Regionalist* (1979)
James L. Potter, *The Robert Frost Handbook* (1980)
William Pritchard, *Frost: A Literary Life Reconsidered* (1984)
John Evangelist Walsh, *Into My Own: The English Years of Robert Frost* (1988)

GWENDOLYN BROOKS: COMMITMENT AND UNIVERSALITY

Gwendolyn Brooks has never denied her engagement in the contemporary situation or been over-obsessed by it.
HARVEY CURTIS WEBSTER

Art hurts. Art urges voyages—
and it is easier to stay at home,
the nice beer ready.
GWENDOLYN BROOKS, "THE CHICAGO PICASSO"

I am absolutely free of what any white critic might say because I feel that it's going to be amazing if any of them understand the true significance of the struggle that's going on.
GWENDOLYN BROOKS

Gwendolyn Brooks (born 1917) is the most powerful and most widely respected of contemporary African-American poets. Many of her poems deal uncompromisingly with the bleak realities of poverty and racism. At the same time, they often bring tremendous empathy to representative lives and people in the black community, especially the old and the very young. (She has written many poems for or about children.) In the late sixties and early seventies, she became part of the movement that explored sources of strength in the black heritage and in solidarity with fellow artists exploring the African past. During an age of passionate but often short-lived rhetoric, she has written poems of understated eloquence and harsh beauty.

Gwendolyn Brooks was born in Topeka, Kansas, but she lived most of her life in Chicago, and she became poet laureate of the state of Illinois. She grew up in a closely knit, loving, traditional family ("no child abuse, no prostitution, no Mafia membership," she said in a 1984 self-interview). The Brooks' house was filled with poetry, story, music, and song; she grew up in a "family-oriented" world with much visiting by and of relatives, traditional holiday feasts, family and church picnics. Her parents, she says, "subscribed to duty, decency, dignity, industry—*kindness.*" Her first poem was published in a children's magazine when she was ten; when in high school, she published several poems in the *Defender,* a black newspaper in Chicago. She received a Pulitzer Prize for poetry in 1950, the first and only African-American woman to receive the award until Alice Walker won a Pulitzer for *The Color Purple* in 1983. In 1987, Brooks was the first black woman to be elected an honorary fellow of the Modern Language Association. She has spent much of her time working with young people in colleges and schools and promoting workshops and awards for young poets.

The constant in Brooks' poetry has been her loyalty to characters who find themselves trapped in an environment scarred by racial discrimination, poverty, and violence. She populated the imaginary community of Bronzeville with a haunting array of the living human beings behind the stereotypes and government statistics. She chronicled their grey daily lives, their disillusionment and self-doubts, their defiance and futile rebellions. She observed with icy scorn the charitable rich who, from winters in Palm Beach and their world of "hostess gowns, and sunburst clocks, / Turtle soup, Chippendale," venture forth in search of the "worthy poor," only to be appalled by the squalor of the slums. Her most famous poem is a poem of doomed youth— jaunty, defiant, lost.

We Real Cool   1960

The Pool Players.
Seven at the Golden Shovel.

We real cool. We
Left school. We

Lurk late. We
Strike straight. We

Sing sin. We   5
Thin gin. We

Jazz June. We
Die soon.

This poem, with its broken, syncopated, beboppy counterrhythm ("We real cool. We / Left school"), is an anthem for doomed youth who act "cool" as a defensive armor. They have dropped out and find themselves in the slow lane to a dead end. They jazz up, or live up, June and will be dead soon after.

THE RECEPTIVE READER

Do you think you recognize the young people in the poem? What do you think is the poet's attitude toward them? How does she relate to them? How do you?

Brooks writes with special affection of young people who rebel against the narrow boundaries of their lives, adopting a stance of defiance or escaping into an intensely imagined fantasy world. The sense of being trapped and intensely imagined dreams of escape become recurrent themes in poems like "Hunchback Girl."

Hunchback Girl: She Thinks of Heaven   1945

My Father, it is surely a blue place
And straight. Right. Regular. Where I shall find
No need for scholarly nonchalance or looks
A little to the left or guards upon the
Heart to halt love that runs without crookedness   5
Along its crooked corridors. My Father,
It is a planned place surely. Out of coils,
Unscrewed, released, no more to be marvelous,
I shall walk straightly through most proper halls
Proper myself, princess of properness.   10

The poem is in the form of a passionate prayer, with the girl addressing "My Father" twice. The hunchbacked girl thinks of a future state where her burden will be lifted. In heaven ("surely a blue place / And straight"), she will no longer be stared or marveled at ("no more to be marvelous"). Everything that is crooked or coiled will there be straightened out, made right and regular and proper. She will walk "straightly through most proper halls," a very "princess of properness." She will no longer have to try hard to look nonchalant when being stared at; she will no longer have to avoid people's eyes. So desperately needed is this release, so insistently wished for and imagined, so firmly believed in, that no one, inside the poem or out, could have the heart to call it merely a dream.

THE RECEPTIVE READER

1. To judge from the poem, what is the girl's usual way of coping with her disability?

2. Some critics have noted the *ambiguity* of the words *marvel* and *marvelous*. These words may refer to something to be stared at in fear but also to something arousing wonder or to be contemplated in awe. Does the poem bring into play either or both of these meanings?

3. Is it *paradoxical* that in the girl's heart love runs "without crookedness"—but that the corridors of the heart (hers? ours?) are themselves crooked? What did the poet have in mind? How do you explain the paradox?

4. One reader said that the irony underlying this poem is that "nothing in life is without its crookedness." What did she mean?

THE PERSONAL RESPONSE

Would you call the feelings expressed in this poem a mere dream? Have you or has someone you know well ever experienced similar feelings?

Brooks seems to speak most directly in her personal voice in poems of buried emotion, of humanity defeated by harsh reality. In the following sonnet, the "glory" of the pianist's music and the feeling of "proud delight" it calls up prevail for a time until they are drowned out by the unheard phantom cries of bitter men killed in war.

Piano after War   1945

On a snug evening I shall watch her fingers,
Cleverly ringed, declining to clever pink,
Beg glory from the willing keys. Old hungers
Will break their coffins, rise to eat and thank.
And music, warily, like the golden rose   5
That sometimes after sunset warms the west,
Will warm that room, persuasively suffuse
That room and me, rejuvenate a past.
But suddenly, across my climbing fever
Of proud delight—a multiplying cry.   10
A cry of bitter dead men who will never
Attend a gentle maker of musical joy.
Then my thawed eye will go again to ice.
And stone will shove the softness from my face.

The music in this poem unfolds like a "golden rose," wakening long since-buried capacities for joy. "Old hungers" break their coffins. The glow thaws the icy heart—but only for a time. Suddenly, the memory of the dead undercuts the feeling of gentleness and joy; their fate makes the glories of culture an unkept promise. However tempting, the blessings of traditional culture cannot really soften the bitterness left behind by disappointed hopes.

THE RECEPTIVE READER

1. What do you think are the "old hungers" aroused from "their coffins" in this poem?

2. How does this sonnet follow the traditional pattern of a *turning point* in the middle of a poem and of a concluding *couplet* that leaves the reader with a strong final impression?

3. Were you *surprised* by the turn the poem takes? Does the poem early strike a note of wariness, of ironic detachment?

Brooks writes with special empathy and understated tenderness about children, like the two girls in the following poem from *Bronzeville Boys and Girls*.

Mexie and Bridie   1945

A tiny tea-party
Is happening today.
Pink cakes, and nuts and bon-bons on
A tiny, shiny tray.

It's out within the weather,   5
Beneath the clouds and sun.
And pausing ants have peeked upon,
As birds and gods have done.

Mexie's in her white dress,
And Bridie's in her brown.   10
There are no finer ladies
Tea-ing in the town.

In the words of Gary Smith, the children in Brooks' poems confront the essential dilemma of "how to find meaning and purpose in a world that denies their very existence." They live in a world of enclosed space—"alleyways, front and back yards, vacant lots, and back rooms"—symbolizing the restrictions that prevent their physical and mental growth. "Although trees, flowers, and grass poke through the concrete blocks of the urban environment, they are only reminders of a forbidden Eden." Not surprisingly,

> the overwhelming desire for many of her children is the need to escape, to flee, the various forms of socioeconomic and psychological oppression that thwart self-fulfillment and threaten to destroy their lives. Because it is to a world free of adults where most of her children wish to escape, their unique ability to imagine this world—albeit on the wings of fantasy—distinguishes them from adults and creates some sense of hope.
>
> From Gary Smith, "Paradise Regained: The Children of Gwendolyn Brooks' *Bronzeville*," in Marie Mootry and Gary Smith, eds., *A Life Distilled: Gwendolyn Brooks, Her Poetry and Fiction*

Many of Brooks' poems were milestones in the spiritual journey of the black community from the goal of assimilation to the defiant acceptance of one's own identity. For her, as for many other black artists and writers, the years from 1967 to 1972 were years of awakening as the movement toward black pride and self-respect, in her words, "italicized black identity, solidarity, self-possession" and "vitally acknowledged African roots." In these years of "hot-breathing hope," when "the air was heavy with logic, illogic, zeal, construction," she read books about the black experience from W. E. Burghardt Du Bois' *The Souls of Black Folk* to the novels of Zora Neale Hurston. She exchanged views with black writers from James Baldwin to Don L. Lee. As she said later, "We talked, we walked, we read our work in taverns and churches and jail." She started to organize workshops for young poets and future teachers.

During these years, Brooks found her way to the self-affirmation and positive self-image needed to break the hold of negative stereotypes on one's own mind. She said,

> Black woman . . . must remember that her personhood precedes her female-hood; that sweet as sex may be, she cannot endlessly brood on Black man's blondes, blues, blunders. She is a person in the world—with wrongs to right, stupidities to outwit, with her man if possible, on her own when not. And she is also here to enjoy. She will be here, like any other, once only. Therefore she must, in the midst of tragedy and hatred and neglect, in the midst of her own efforts to purify, mightily enjoy the readily available: sunshine and pets and children and conversation and games and travel (tiny or large) and books and walks and chocolate cake.

During the years of the civil rights movement, Brooks' work, like the work of many African-American writers and artists, became more committed and more political. In her poems on major events in the struggle, she speaks both as a "seer and sayer" for the black experience and as the voice of conscience for the larger community. One of her best-known poems takes stock of a reporter's foray to Little Rock, Arkansas, during the desegregation battle fought over the admission of the first nine black students to Central High. Backed by the Supreme Court's *Brown* decision outlawing segregated public schools, protected by federal troops called in by President Eisenhower, the students prevailed against the governor of the state, spitting and jeering mobs, and harassment and abuse from fellow students. (For a year, in a last-ditch stand, the governor closed all public schools.)

The Chicago Defender *Sends a Man to Little Rock*   1960
Fall, 1957

In Little Rock the people bear
Babes, and comb and part their hair
And watch the want ads, put repair
To roof and latch. While wheat toast burns
A woman waters multiferns.   5

Time upholds or overturns
The many, tight, and small concerns.

In Little Rock the people sing
Sunday hymns like anything,
Through Sunday pomp and polishing.   10

And after testament and tunes,
Some soften Sunday afternoons
With lemon tea and Lorna Doones.

I forecast
And I believe   15

Come Christmas Little Rock will cleave
To Christmas tree and trifle, weave,
From laugh and tinsel, texture fast.

In Little Rock is baseball; Barcarolle.
That hotness in July . . . the uniformed figures raw and implacable   20
And not intellectual,
Batting the hotness or clawing the suffering dust.
The Open Air Concert, on the special twilight green. . . .
When Beethoven is brutal or whispers to lady-like air.
Blanket-sitters are solemn, as Johann troubles to lean   25
To tell them what to mean. . . .

There is love, too, in Little Rock. Soft women softly
Opening themselves in kindness,
Or, pitying one's blindness,
Awaiting one's pleasure   30
In azure
Glory with anguished rose at the root. . . .
To wash away old semi-discomfitures.
They re-teach purple and unsullen blue.
The wispy soils go. And uncertain   35
Half-havings have they clarified to sures.

In Little Rock they know
Not answering the telephone is a way of rejecting life,
That it is our business to be bothered, is our business
To cherish bores or boredom, be polite   40
To lies and love and many-faceted fuzziness.

I scratch my head, massage the hate-I-had.
I blink across my prim and pencilled pad.
The saga I was sent for is not down.
Because there is a puzzle in this town.   45
The biggest News I do not dare
Telegraph to the Editor's chair:
"They are like people everywhere."

The angry Editor would reply
In hundred harryings of Why.   50

And true, they are hurling spittle, rock,
Garbage and fruit in Little Rock.
And I saw coiling storm a-writhe
On bright madonnas. And a scythe
Of men harassing brownish girls.   55
(The bows and barrettes in the curls
And braids declined away from joy.)

I saw a bleeding brownish boy. . . .

The lariat lynch-wish I deplored.

The loveliest lynchee was our Lord.   60

The people in this poem attend to their many large and small concerns—giving birth, baking, grooming, watering, tinkering, answering the telephone. They listen to operatic favorites (Offenbach's "Barcarolle") and Beethoven; sitting on blankets, they solemnly listen at the open-air concert to Johann (Sebastian Bach). They sing Sunday hymns "like anything," and come Christmas they will do it justice, tree and tinsel and all. They are capable of love, politeness, and boredom. The problem is that all this ordinariness is not what the editor of the *Defender* sent the reporter to Little Rock to find.

The dramatic discovery in this poem is what the German-Jewish writer Hannah Arendt has called the "banality of evil." The reporter from the *Chicago Defender* was ready to hate and revile melodramatic villains. But the "biggest news" is: Evil here is committed in a city of everyday people. The rock-throwing, spittle-hurling mob disperses to return to everyday homes. This discovery makes us rethink our usual assumption that people who do evil are monstrous creatures very different from ourselves. The people throwing the rocks and spitting on the "bright madonnas" are someone's Uncle Joe or Cousin Roy. Jesus was crucified in a city full of ordinary people. The poet encourages us to look for the sources of evil not outside among alien intruders but inside the human heart.

THE RECEPTIVE READER

1. How do you think the people trying to block desegregation were seen by the civil rights workers at the time? How do you think the segregationists saw themselves? How is the poet's perspective different from either?

2. What use does she make of *religious references* at the end of the poem? With what effect?

3. Do you think the stand the poet takes on the events of the time is too strong or not strong enough?

CROSS-REFERENCES—For Discusssion or Writing

Other poems by Gwendolyn Brooks included earlier in this volume are "Truth" (p. 20) and "A Song in the Front Yard" (p. 213). Do you recognize in them the poet's characteristic voice or a characteristic way of looking at the world?

POEMS FOR FURTHER STUDY

An editor and fellow poet said about Gwendolyn Brooks that she is "a woman who cannot live without her art, but who has never put her art above or before the people she writes about." In reading the following poems, pay special attention to the relation between content and form, between the poet's subject matter and her use of language.

When You Have Forgotten Sunday: The Love Story   1945

——And when you have forgotten the bright bedclothes on a Wednesday and a
    Saturday,
And most especially when you have forgotten Sunday—
When you have forgotten Sunday halves in bed,
Or me sitting on the front-room radiator in the limping afternoon
Looking off down the long street   5
To nowhere,
Hugged by my plain old wrapper of no-expectation
And nothing-I-have-to-do and I'm-happy-why?
And if-Monday-never-had-to-come—
When you have forgotten that, I say,   10
And how you swore, if somebody beeped the bell,
And how my heart played hopscotch if the telephone rang;
And how we finally went in to Sunday dinner,
That is to say, went across the front-room floor to the ink-spotted table in the
    southwest corner
To Sunday dinner, which was always chicken and noodles   15
Or chicken and rice
And salad and rye bread and tea
And chocolate chip cookies—
I say, when you have forgotten that,
When you have forgotten my little presentiment   20
That the war would be over before they got to you;
And how we finally undressed and whipped out the light and flowed into bed,
And lay loose-limbed for a moment in the week-end
Bright bedclothes,
Then gently folded into each other—   25
When you have, I say, forgotten all that,
Then you may tell,
Then I may believe
You have forgotten me well.

The Chicago Picasso, August 15, 1967   1967

*Mayor Daley tugged a white ribon, loosing the blue percale
wrap. A hearty cheer went up as the covering slipped off
the big steel sculpture that looks at once like a bird and a
woman.*
                    CHICAGO *SUN-TIMES*

*(Seiji Ozawa leads the Symphony.
The Mayor smiles.
And 50,000 See.)*

Does man love Art? Man visits Art, but squirms.
Art hurts. Art urges voyages—
and it is easier to stay at home,

the nice beer ready.
    In commonrooms
we belch, or sniff, or scratch.
Are raw.

But we must cook ourselves and style ourselves for Art, who
is a requiring courtesan.
We squirm.
We do not hug the Mona Lisa.
We
may touch or tolerate
an astounding fountain, or a horse-and-rider.
At most, another Lion.

Observe the tall cold of a Flower
which is as innocent and as guilty,
as meaningful and as meaningless as any
other flower in the western field.

Pablo Picasso, "Chicago Civic Center." David H. Hamilton / The
Image Bank.

The Preacher Ruminates behind the Sermon   1945

I think it must be lonely to be God.
Nobody loves a master. No. Despite
the bright hosannas, bright dear-Lords, and bright
Determined reverence of Sunday eyes.

Picture Jehovah striding through the hall   5
Of His importance, creatures running out
From servant-corners to acclaim, to shout
Appreciation of his merit's glare.

But who walks with Him?—dares to take His arm,
To slap him on the shoulder, tweak His ear,   10
Buy Him a Coca-Cola or a beer,
Pooh-pooh his politics, call Him a fool?

Perhaps—who knows?—He tires of looking down.
Those eyes are never lifted. Never straight.
Perhaps sometimes he tires of being great   15
In solitude. Without a hand to hold.

The Ballad of the Light-Eyed Little Girl   1949

Sweet Sally took a cardboard box,
And in went pigeon poor.
Whom she had starved to death but not
For lack of love, be sure.

The wind it harped as twenty men.   5
The wind it harped like hate.
It whipped our light-eyed little girl,
It made her wince and wait.

It screeched a hundred elegies
As it punished her light eyes   10
(Though only kindness covered these)
And it made her eyebrows rise.

"Now bury your bird," the wind it bawled,
"And bury him down and down
Who had to put his trust in one   15
So light-eyed and so brown.

"So light-eyed and so villainous,
Who whooped and who could hum
But could not find the time to toss
Confederate his crumb."   20

She has taken her passive pigeon poor,
She has buried him down and down.

He never shall sally to Sally
Nor soil any roofs of the town.

She has sprinkled nail polish on dead dandelions.   25
And children have gathered around
Funeral for him whose epitaph
Is "PIGEON—Under the ground."

The Bean Eaters   1960

They eat beans mostly, this old yellow pair.
Dinner is a casual affair.
Plain chipware on a plain and creaking wood,
Tin flatware.
Two who are Mostly Good.   5
Two who have lived their day,
But keep on putting on their clothes
And putting things away.

And remembering . . .
Remembering, with twinklings and twinges,   10
As they lean over the beans in their rented back room that is full of beads and receipts
        and dolls and cloths, tobacco crumbs, vases and fringes.

The Boy Died in My Alley   1975

Without my having known.
Policeman said, next morning,
"Apparently died Alone."
"You heard a shot?" Policeman said.
Shots I hear and Shots I hear.   5
I never see the dead.

The Shot that killed him yes I heard
as I heard the Thousand shots before;
careening tinnily down the nights
across my years and arteries.   10

Policeman pounded on my door.
"Who is it?" "POLICE!" Policeman yelled.
"A boy was dying in your alley.
A boy is dead, and in your alley.
And have you known this Boy before?"   15

I have known this Boy before.
I have known this Boy before, who

ornaments my alley.
I never saw his face at all.
I never saw his futurefall.
But I have known this Boy.

20

I have always heard him deal with death.
I have always heard the shout, the volley.
I have closed my heart-ears late and early.
And I have killed him ever.
I joined the Wild and killed him
with knowledgeable unknowing.
I saw where he was going.
I saw him Crossed. And seeing,
I did not take him down.

25

30

He cried not only "Father!"
but "Mother!
Sister!
Brother!"
The cry climbed up the alley.
It went up to the wind.
It hung upon the heaven
for a long
stretch-strain of Moment.

35

The red floor of my alley
is a special speech to me.

40

CROSS-REFERENCES—For Discussion or Writing

For a library research project, search for books and articles that would provide material on one of the following topics:

❖ Gwendolyn Brooks' view of the social responsibility of the writer. What is the relationship between protest and poetry in her work? What are her views on the political responsibilities of the poet?

❖ Gwendolyn Brooks' relationship with or influence on other black writers. What black writer or writers did most to help shape her poetry or her views? What has been her influence on other black poets?

❖ What has been the treatment of black men in her poetry? Has it changed over the years?

Books you may be able to consult may include the following:

Harry B. Shaw, *Gwendolyn Brooks* (1980)
Claudia Tate, *Black Women Writers at Work* (1983)
Mari Evans, ed., *Black Women Writers (1950–80): A Critical Evaluation* (1984)
R. Baxter Miller, ed., *Black American Poets between Worlds, 1940–60* (1986)
Marie Mootry and Gary Smith, eds., *A Life Distilled: Gwendolyn Brooks, Her Poetry and Fiction* (1987)
Haki Madhubuti (Don L. Lee), *Say That the River Turns: The Impact of Gwendolyn Brooks* (1987)
D. H. Melhem, *Gwendolyn Brooks: Poetry and the Heroic Voice* (1987)
George E. Kent, *A Life of Gwendolyn Brooks* (1990)

WRITING ABOUT LITERATURE

13. The Poet and the Critics (Documented Paper)

The Writing Workshop   For the projects outlined earlier in this chapter, you will have to develop your own efficient, productive way of using library resources. Your finished paper will differ from other papers you have written in two major ways: First, you will be *integrating* material from a range of different sources. (Make sure that your paper will not appear to be made up of large chunks of undigested quotation.) Second, you will be *documenting* your sources, giving full information about the books and articles you have used.

Finding Promising Leads   To work up material for your paper, begin by checking in electronic or printed indexes for books, collections of critical articles, and individual articles in periodicals. For a writer like Dickinson, Frost, or Brooks, most college libraries will have a wide range of critical and scholarly sources. Often critical studies will include bibliographies alerting you to other promising leads.

Taking Notes   During your exploratory reading, you need to look sources over quickly, deciding whether they will be helpful. But you also have to slow down and close in when you hit upon promising materials. Remember:

♦ *Be a stickler for accuracy.* Copy direct quotations accurately, word for word. Enclose all quoted material in quotation marks to show material copied verbatim. (Include the *closing* quotation mark to show where the quotation ends.)

♦ *Tag your notes.* Start your notes with a tag or descriptor. (Indicate the subtopic or section of your paper where a quotation or piece of information will be useful.)

♦ *Record publishing information.* On your first entry for any one source (or in a separate bibliography entry), record all data you will need later when you identify your source in a documented paper. Include exact page numbers for your quotations. (Also note inclusive page numbers for a whole article or story.) Sample notes might look like this:

self-contained quotation

DICKINSON—SEXUAL IMAGERY

"Like her nature poetry, her use of female sexual imagery suggests . . . not the 'subversion' of an existing male tradition, nor the 'theft' of male power—but rather the assertion of a concept of female sexuality and female creativity."

Paula Bennett, *Emily Dickinson: Woman Poet* (Iowa City: U of Iowa P, 1990) 180.

paraphrase with partial direct quotation

DICKINSON—FREUDIAN PERSPECTIVE

The prime motive in D.'s life and poetry was fear created by a "bad child-parent relationship," specifically with her "cold and forbidding father." This relationship shaped her view of men, love, marriage, and religion. She viewed God as a forbidding father-figure who spurned her.

Clark Griffith, *The Long Shadow: Emily Dickinson's Tragic Poetry* (Princeton: Princeton UP, 1964) 78.

Distinguish clearly between **paraphrase** and direct quotation. When you paraphrase, you put someone else's ideas in your own words, highlighting what seems most important and condensing other parts. Even when you paraphrase, be sure to use quotation marks for striking phrases that you keep in the exact wording of the author.

Note finer points: Use **single quotation marks** for a phrase that appears as a quote-within-a-quote. Use the **ellipsis**—three spaced periods—to show an omission (see Bennett quotation above). Use four periods when the periods include the period at the end of a sentence. **Square brackets** show that you have inserted material into the original quotation: "In this poem, based on the Emmett Till murder [1955], Brooks creates a surreal aura of hysteria and violence underlying an ostensibly calm domestic scene."

Pushing toward a Thesis   Your note taking becomes productive when you begin to follow up tentative patterns and promising connections that you discover in your reading. Even during your preliminary reading and note taking, you will be looking for a unifying thread. Avoid a stitched-together pattern that goes from "one critic said this" to "another critic said that." Look for recurrent issues; look for a note that in your materials is struck again and again.

Suppose you are moving toward a paper showing how different critics have answered the question of Emily Dickinson's religious faith. The following might be a tentative thesis:

TRIAL THESIS: Emily Dickinson was not a believer or a skeptic but a poet always in search of the truth.

Using a Working Outline   To give direction to your reading and writing, sketch out a **working outline** as soon as you have a rough idea how your material is shaping up. At first, your plan might be very tentative. A working outline is not a final blueprint; its purpose is to help you visualize a possible pattern and to help you refine it as you go along. At an early stage, your working outline for the paper about Dickinson's faith might look like this:

WORKING OUTLINE: —poems of faith
　　　　　　　　　　—poems of despair
　　　　　　　　　　—poems of alienation
　　　　　　　　　　—poems of rebellion

Drafting and Revising   In your first draft, you are likely to concentrate on feeding into your paper the evidence you have collected. As always, feel free to work on later sections of the paper first—perhaps concentrating on key segments and filling in the connecting threads later. In your first draft, quotations are likely to be chunky, to be woven into the paper more tightly or more smoothly during revision. Often you will need to read a first draft back to yourself to see where major changes in strategy would be advisable. A reordering of major sections might be necessary to correct awkward backtrackings. You might need to strengthen the evidence for major points and play down material that tends to distract from your major arguments.

Documenting the Paper   When you draw on a range of sources—for instance, a range of critical interpretations of a poem—you may be asked to provide **documentation.** Remember that in a documented paper you fully identify your sources, furnishing complete publishing information and exact page numbers. Accurate documentation shows that your readers are welcome to go to the sources you have drawn on—to check your use of them and to get further information from them if they wish. As with other documented papers, follow the current style of the Modern Language Association (MLA) unless instructed otherwise. This current style no longer uses footnotes (though it still allows for **explanatory notes** at the end of a paper).

Remember three key features of the current MLA style:

❖ *Identify your sources briefly in your text.* Generally, introduce a quotation by saying something like the following:

> Mary Jo Salter says in her article "Puns and Accordions: Emily Dickinson and the Unsaid" that Dickinson "has inspired a massive critical industry rivaling that devoted to Shakespeare and Milton."

❖ *Give page references in parentheses in your text.* Usually, they will go at the end of the sentence and before the final period, for instance (89) or (89–90). If you have not mentioned the author, give his or her last name (Salter 192–93). If you are using more than one source by the same author, you may also have to specify briefly which one (Salter, "Puns" 192–93). Remember to tag author or title in parentheses only if you have *not* already given the information in your running text.

❖ *Describe each source fully in a final alphabetical listing of Works Cited.* Originally a bibliography (literally the "book list"), it now often includes nonprint sources—interviews, lectures, PBS broadcasts, videotapes, computer software. Here is a typical entry for an article in a critical journal. This entry includes volume number (a volume usually covers all issues for one year), year, and the complete page numbers for the whole article (not just the material you have quoted):

> Morris, Timothy. "The Development of Dickinson's Style." American Literature 60 (1988): 26–42.

Study sample entries for your alphabetical listing of Works Cited. Remember a few pointers:

⬦ Use *italics* (or <u>underlining</u> on a typewriter) for the title of a whole publication—whether a book-length study, a collection or anthology of stories or essays, a periodical that prints critical articles, or a newspaper that prints reviews. However, use quotation marks for titles of poems or critical articles that are *part* of a collection.

⬦ Leave *two* spaces after periods marking off chunks of information in the entry. Indent the second and following lines of each entry *five* spaces.

⬦ Use *ed.* for editor; *trans.* for translator.

⬦ Abbreviate the names of publishing houses (Prentice for Prentice-Hall, Inc; Southern Illinois UP for Southern Illinois University Press). Abbreviate the names of the months: Dec., Apr., Mar. Abbreviate the names of states when needed to locate a little-known place of publication: CA, NY, NJ.

Primary sources: listing of poems, lectures, or interviews

Brooks, Gwendolyn. *The World of Gwendolyn Brooks.* New York: Harper, 1971.
[Collected poems of the author. The publisher's name is short for Harper & Row.]

Colman, Cathy. "After Swimming in the Pacific." *New Poets: Women.* Ed. Terri Whetherby. Millbrae, CA: Les Femmes, 1976. 13.
[A poem printed in an anthology, with editor's name and with page number for the poem.]

Johnson, Thomas H., ed. *The Complete Poems of Emily Dickinson.* Boston: Little, Brown, 1960.
[Editor's name first when editor's work of compiling or establishing texts is important.]

Lorde, Audre. Interview. *Black Women Writers at Work.* Ed. Claudia Tate. Harpenden, Herts.: Oldcastle, 1985. 100–16.
[An interview with the poet, published in a collection of interviews.]

Clifton, Lucille. Lecture. Visiting Poets Series. Tucson, 23 Feb. 1992.
[Talk by a poet as part of a lecture series.]

Olsen, Tillie. Foreword. *Black Women Writers at Work.* Ed. Claudia Tate. Harpenden, Herts.: Oldcastle, 1985. ix–xxvi.
[Foreword by other than editor, with page numbers in small roman numerals for introductory material.]

Secondary sources: listing of critical studies, articles, or reviews

Johnson, Thomas H. *Emily Dickinson: An Interpretive Biography.* Cambridge: Harvard UP, 1966.
[Biography with subtitle, published by a university press.]

Rich, Adrienne. *On Lies, Secrets, and Silence: Selected Prose 1966–1978.* New York: Norton, 1975.
[Book with subtitle, with critical essays by the author.]

Spillers, Hortense J. "Gwendolyn the Terrible: Propositions on Eleven Poems." *A Life Distilled: Gwendolyn Brooks, Her Poetry and Fiction.* Ed. Maria K. Mootry and Gary Smith. Urbana: U of Illinois P, 1987. 224–35.
[Article in a collection, with inclusive page numbers. Note "Ed." for the editors who assembled the collection.]

Morris, Timothy. "The Development of Dickinson's Style." *American Litera-ture* 60 (1988): 26–42.
[Journal article, with volume number and inclusive page numbers. Note quotation marks for title of article; italics for title of publication.]

Monteiro, George. "Dickinson's 'We Thirst at First.'" *The Explicator* 48 (1990): 193–94.
[Title of poem (with single quotation marks) is cited in title of article (with double quotation marks).]

Jones, Rowena Revis. "'A Royal Seal': Emily Dickinson's Rite of Baptism." *Religion and Literature* 18.3 (1986): 29–51.
[Periodical with number of volume *and* issue. Number of issue may be needed when pages are not numbered consecutively throughout a single volume.]

Montgomery, Karen. "Today's Minimalist Poets." *New York Times* 22 Feb. 1992, late ed. , sec. 2: 1+.
[Newspaper article, with edition and section specified. Article starts on page 1 and continues not on the next page but later in the newspaper.]

Rev. of *The Penguin Book of Women Poets,* ed. Carol Cosman, Joan Keefe, and Kathleen Weaver. *Arts and Books Forum* May 1990: 17–19.
[Untitled, unsigned review.]

Poets of Protest. Narr. Joan Moreno. Writ. and prod. Lorna Herold. KSBM, Los Angeles. 8 Feb. 1992.
[A television program with names of narrator and writer-producer. To be listed alphabetically under "Poets."]

Study the following example of a documented paper. How well does the paper bring its subject into focus? How well does it support its main points? How clear and effective is its use of quotations from the poet and from the critics? Study the use of parenthetical documentation and the entries in the Works Cited; pay special attention to unusual situations or entries.

SAMPLE DOCUMENTED PAPER

Emily Dickinson's Strange Irreverence

Religion in one guise or another pervades many of Dickinson's poems. It appears in the form of tender and not so tender prayers, skeptical questionings, and bitter confrontations. Critics have constructed a whole range of interpretations designed to provide a key to her changing, ambivalent religious attitudes. Some have cast her in the role of the rebel, rescuing her readers from the harshness of a rigid, constricted religious tradition, erecting for them a "citadel of art" and cultivating "the ego or consciousness" (Burbick 62). Others, however, see her as a "lone pilgrim" in the tradition of Puritan austerity and asceticism. She could not "allow herself the long luxury" of the evangelical movement of her own day, which was turning away from earlier, harsher versions of the Christian faith and promoting a sentimental attitude toward God as a "creature of caring, even motherly generosity" (Wolff 260). Still others attribute Dickinson's ambivalent, shifting religious attitudes to her need to keep her friends, to her "preoccupation with attachment" (Burbick 65). Some of Dickinson's dearest friends, to whom she wrote about her cherished hope for "one unbroken company in heaven," had experienced a religious conversion at Mt. Holyoke Seminary, and she felt she had to follow their example so that the bonds of friendship that were so precious to her would not be dissolved.

Perhaps the closest to a connecting thread is Denis Donoghue's discussion of her as a truth-seeker, who in life as in poetry was *looking for* the truth. As Donoghue says, "In a blunt paraphrase, many of her peoms would contradict one another; but her answers are always provisional." Her answers are tentative; "only her questions are definitive" (13). Although there are in her poems many references to the Old and New Testaments, "nothing is necessarily believed" but may be entertained only as a poetic or symbolic truth (17).

Because of the elusive, ambivalent nature of Dickinson's relation to religion, each poem must be interpreted individually in the quest to plumb her heart. Several of her poems are direct affirmations of her faith in Christ. In poem 698 in the Johnson edition ("Life—is what we make it"), she calls Christ a "tender pioneer," who blazed the trail of life and death for his "little Fellowmen":

> He—would trust no stranger—
> Others—could betray—
> Just his own endorsement—
> That—sufficeth me.
>
> All the other Distance
> He hath traversed first—
> No new mile remaineth—
> Far as Paradise—
>
> His sure foot preceding—
> Tender Pioneer—
> Base must be the Coward—
> Dare not venture—now—   (333–34)

In other poems, however, the faith that is supposed to provide a bridge to the hereafter proves a bridge with "mouldering" or "brittle" piers. In a famous poem, "I heard a Funeral in my Brain" (280 in the Johnson edition), the promise of faith seems unable to counteract the sense of the nothingness at the end of life. The Christian teachings of resurrection and an afterlife here do not seem to avail against the "plunge" into despair:

> And then I heard them lift a Box
> And creak across my Soul
> With those same Boots of Lead, again,
> Then Space—began to toll,
>
> As all the Heavens were a Bell,
> And Being, but an Ear,
> And I, and Silence, some strange Race
> Wrecked, solitary, here—
>
> And then a Plank in Reason, broke,
> And I dropped down, and down—
> And hit a World, at every plunge,
> And Finished knowing—then   (128–29)

Other poems seem to protest against the "ambiguous silence maintained by God" (Griffith 273). The following are the opening lines of poem 376 in Johnson's edition:

> Of course—I prayed—
> And did God Care?

He cared as much as on the Air
A Bird—had stamped her foot—
And cried "Give Me"—   (179)

Many of her poems seem to mourn the absence of God, as does the following stanza from poem 502 in Johnson:

Thou settest Earthquake in the South—
And Maelstrom, In the Sea—
Say, Jesus Christ of Nazareth—
Hast thou no Arm for Me?   (244)

In her most rebellious poems, she openly expresses defiance. She protests against the "tyranny" of God that forced Abraham to consent to offer his own son Isaac in sacrifice (Johnson 571). She rebels against commandments that keep us within a "magic prison," a limited and "constricted life," while we are within sight of the feast of happiness that is earthly pleasure—as if God were jealous of "the heaven on earth that is human happiness" (McNeil 60).

To read Emily Dickinson's poems is to see a poet's struggle for finding a meaning in her existence, rebelling at times against blind faith but also shrinking from complete doubt. She looked for evidence of the divine not in traditional revealed faith but in our earthly human existence. In a letter written several years before her death, she wrote: "To be human is more than to be divine . . . when Christ was divine he was uncontented until he had been human" (qtd. in Wolff 519).

Works Cited

Burbick, Joan. "'One Unbroken Company': Religion and Emily Dickinson." *New England Quarterly* 53 (1980): 62–75.

Donoghue, Denis. *Emily Dickinson.* U of Minnesota Pamphlets on American Writers No. 81. 1969.

Griffith, Clark. *The Long Shadow: Emily Dickinson's Tragic Poetry.* Princeton: Princeton UP, 1964.

Johnson, Thomas H., ed. *The Complete Poems of Emily Dickinson.* Boston: Little, Brown, 1960.

McNeil, Helen. *Emily Dickinson.* New York: Pantheon, 1986.

Wolff, Cynthia Griffin. *Emily Dickinson.* Menlo Park, CA: Addison, 1988.

QUESTIONS

1. How does the writer succeed or fail in bringing the topic to life for you? Does she spell out her *thesis* early in the paper? Does a key term or key concept help sum up her point of view?

2. What are the major way stations in her overall *plan*? How convincing are the major points the writer makes? At what points in the paper would you have liked more explanation or support?

3. Does the *conclusion* merely recapitulate points already made?

4. Does the writer use a *range* of sources? Do her parenthetical documentation and her list of works cited show any major variations from routine identification or standard entries?

14 PERSPECTIVES
Poets and Critics

Scholars and artists thrown together are often annoyed at the puzzle of where they differ. Both work from knowledge, but I suspect they differ most importantly in the way their knowledge is come by. Scholars get theirs with conscientious thoroughness along projected lines of logic; poets theirs cavalierly and as it happens in and out of books. They stick to nothing deliberately, but let what will stick to them like burrs where they walk in the fields.

ROBERT FROST

FOCUS ON CRITICISM

The critic is often the third party at the interaction between poet and audience. Critics help explain and defend difficult new work. They sit in judgment, making and breaking reputations. As trend makers, they help shape movements and countermovements. On the one hand, they help establish critical orthodoxies—approved or right ways of thinking. On the other hand, they foment rebellions against current fashion. For us as readers of poetry, those critics are most relevant and valuable who circle back to questions that arise in our minds as we read:

✧ What is the link between the poet's personal *experience* and the poet's art? How much of a poem is personal revelation? How much is impersonal art?

✧ What is the relationship between intellect and the poetic *imagination*? How much in poetic creation is conscious control; how much is intuitive or subconscious?

✧ What kind of shaping or *control* is needed to keep poetry from being a mere "turning loose of emotion" (T. S. Eliot)?

✧ How much of the *reader's response* is shaped by the poem? How much depends on what we as readers bring to the poem?

✧ What is the difference between *good and bad* poetry? Who decides, and on what grounds?

POETS ON POETRY

*A poet writes always of his personal life, in his finest work
out of its tragedy, whatever it be, remorse, lost love, or mere
loneliness.*

WILLIAM BUTLER YEATS

*I was early in life sick to my very pit with order that cuts
off the crab's feelers to make it fit into the box.*

WILLIAM CARLOS WILLIAMS

*I have never been one to write by rule, even by my own
rules.*

T. S. ELIOT

Today we see everywhere poets writing and lecturing about poetry—defending their art, explaining their work, or reminiscing about way stations in their poetic careers. Poetry, like other kinds of imaginative literature, has become very much self-aware, self-conscious, "self-reflective."

Some of the most influential poets have been poet-critics, publishing critical manifestos that chart new directions. One of the earliest of such poet-critics was Alexander Pope, who published his verse-essay on criticism in 1711 at the age of twenty-three. The following excerpts touch on some of the major tenets of the **neoclassical** thinking of his time: Sound *judgment* should guide and restrain the poetic imagination. The poet's language should observe *decorum*—it should be suitable to the purpose. Poetic language and form are the vehicle for the poet's ideas (frequently ideas already often thought "but ne'er so well expressed").

ALEXANDER POPE   (1688–1744)
From *An Essay on Criticism*   1711

First follow nature, and your judgment frame		
By her just standard, which is still the same.		
Unerring nature, still divinely bright—		
One clear, unchanged, and universal light—		
Life, force, and beauty, must to all impart,°	*must give life . . . to all*	5
At once the source, and end, and test of art.		
. . . .		
Some, to whom Heaven in wit has been profuse,		
Want° as much more, to turn it to its use;	*need*	
For wit and judgment often are at strife,		
Though meant each other's aid, like man and wife.		10
'Tis more to guide than spur the Muse's steed;		
Restrain his fury, than provoke his speed;		
The wingèd courser, like a generous horse,		
Shows most true mettle when you check° his course.	*restrain*	
. . . .		

True wit is nature to advantage dressed,   15
What oft was thought, but ne'er so well expressed;
Something, whose truth convinced at sight we find,
That gives us back the image of our mind.

. . . .

Expression is the dress of thought, and still
Appears more decent, as more suitable.   20
A vile conceit° in pompous words expressed   *concept*
Is like a clown in regal purple dressed;
For different styles with different subjects sort°   *agree with*
As several garbs with country, town, and court.

QUESTIONS

1. A favorite topic of neoclassical writers was the relationship between *art and nature.* How is this relationship viewed in these excerpts?

2. *Wit* here does not just mean a capacity for witty remarks but more generally a quick, fertile intelligence. How would it be different from judgment?

3. What role does *Pegasus,* the winged horse that symbolizes poetic creation, play here?

4. What is the *recurrent metaphor* Pope uses for ideas and the way they are expressed?

5. How is the *closed couplet* "suitable" for the ideas Pope expresses here?

Much **Romantic** writing about poetry was part of a rebellion against the eighteenth-century overemphasis on reason and judgment. Like other Romantic poets, John Keats believed in the supremacy of the creative imagination over the reasoning intellect. He placed spontaneous feeling over deliberate control, believing, with his fellow Romantics, that what we feel deeply and sincerely cannot be wrong. In the following excerpt from a famous letter, he champions the passions and sensation, or sense experience, as against "consecutive reasoning."

JOHN KEATS   (1795–1821)
Letter to John Bailey   1817

. . . I am certain of nothing but of the holiness of the Heart's affections and the truth of Imagination—What the Imagination seizes as Beauty must be truth—whether it existed before or not—for I have the same Idea of all our Passions as of Love: they are all in their sublime creative of essential Beauty. . . . I am the more zealous in this affair because I have never yet been able to perceive how anything can be known for truth by consecutive reasoning—and yet it must be—Can it be that even the greatest Philosopher ever arrived at his goal without putting aside numerous objections—However it may be, O for a Life of Sensations rather than of Thoughts!

QUESTIONS

In this excerpt, what is the relation between beauty, passion, and truth? What is the relation between the words *beautiful* and *sublime*?

CROSS-REFERENCES—For Discussion or Writing

How is the point of view expressed in this letter related to Keats' "Ode on a Grecian Urn" (p. 303)?

Poets vary greatly in their writing habits and in how they explain their motives and procedures in writing poetry. Dylan Thomas is a Welsh poet who did more than other poets to make his readers sense some of the sheer inspired exuberance of the creative act. The following excerpt is from "Notes on the Art of Poetry," which he wrote in response to a student's questions. A crowd-pleasing performer, he insisted that "a poem on a page is only half a poem," with the actual shared reading of a poem serving as the culminating acting out and interpretation of the written text.

DYLAN THOMAS   (1914–1953)
Notes on the Art of Poetry   1951

I wanted to write poetry in the beginning because I had fallen in love with words. The first poems I knew were nursery rhymes, and before I could read them for myself I had come to love just the words of them, the words alone. What the words stand for, symbolized, or meant was of very secondary importance. What mattered was the sound of them as I heard them for the first time on the lips of the remote and incomprehensible grown-ups who seemed, for some reason, to be living in my world. And these words were, to me, as the notes of bells, the sounds of musical instruments, the noises of wind, sea, and rain, the rattle of milkcarts, the clopping of hooves on cobbles, the fingering of branches on a window pane, might be to someone, deaf from birth, who has miraculously found his hearing. I did not care what the words said, overmuch, nor what happened to Jack and Jill and the Mother Goose rest of them; I cared for the shapes of sound that their names, and the words describing their actions, made in my ears; I cared for the colors the words cast on my eyes. I realize that I may be, as I think all that way, romanticizing my reactions to the simple and beautiful words of those pure poems; but that is all I can honestly remember, however much time might have falsified my memory. I fell in love—that is the only expression I can think of—at once, and am still at the mercy of words, though sometimes now, knowing a little of their behavior very well, I think I can influence them slightly and have even learned to beat them now and then, which they appear to enjoy. I tumbled for words at once. And, when I began to read the nursery rhymes for myself, and, later, to read other verses and ballads, I knew that I had discovered the most important thing to me, that could be ever. There they were, seemingly lifeless, made only of black and white, but out of them, out of their own being, came love and terror and pity and pain and wonder and all the other vague abstractions that make our ephemeral lives dangerous, great, and bearable. Out of them came the gusts and grunts and hiccups and heehaws of common fun on the earth; and though what the words meant was, in its own way, often deliciously funny enough, so much funnier seemed to me, at that almost forgotten time, the shape and shade and size and noise of the words as they hummed, strummed, jugged and galloped along.

From *Modern Poetics*, edited by James Scully

QUESTIONS

How would you describe this poet's relationship with words? In this selection, what are striking examples of Thomas' own wildly imaginative use of words?

CROSS-REFERENCES—For Discussion or Writing

Poems by Dylan Thomas reprinted in this volume include "In My Craft or Sullen Art" (p. 214), "Do Not Go Gentle into That Good Night" (p. 237), and "Fern Hill" (p. 160). How do they show the poet's love of language?

For many women who are part of the women's movement, poetry has become a means of self-definition and self-assertion. Audre Lorde is a black American poet of West Indian heritage. What does she mean when she says that "poems are not luxuries"?

A U D R E   L O R D E   (born 1934)

*A new generation of women poets is already working out
of the psychic energy released when women begin to move
out toward what the feminist philosopher Mary Daly has
described as the "new space" in the boundaries of
patriarchy. Women are speaking to and of women in these
poems, out of a newly released courage to name, to love
each other, to share risk and grief and celebration.*

ADRIENNE RICH

Poems Are Not Luxuries   1977

For each of us as women, there is a dark place within where hidden and growing our true spirit rises, "Beautiful and tough as chestnut / Stanchions against our nightmare of weakness" and of impotence. These places of possibility within ourselves are dark because they are ancient and hidden; they have survived and grown strong through darkness. Within these deep places, each one of us holds an incredible reserve of creativity and power, storehouse of unexamined and unrecorded emotion and feeling. The woman's place of power within each of us is neither white nor surface; it is dark, it is ancient, and it is deep.

When we view living, in the european mode, only as a problem to be solved, we rely solely upon our ideas to make us free, for these were what the white fathers told us were precious. But as we become more in touch with our own ancient, black, noneuropean view of living as a situation to be experienced and interacted with, we learn more and more to cherish our feelings, to respect those hidden sources of our power from where true knowledge and therefore lasting action comes. At this point in time, I believe that women carry within ourselves the possibility for fusion of these two approaches as a keystone for survival, and we come closest to this combination in our poetry. I speak here of poetry as the revelation or distillation of experience, not the sterile word play that, too often, the white fathers distorted the word *poetry* to mean—in order to cover their desperate wish for imagination without insight.

For women, then, poetry is not a luxury. It is a vital necessity of our existence. It forms the quality of the light within which we predicate our hopes and dreams toward survival and change, first made into language, then into idea, then into more tangible action. Poetry is the way we help give name to the nameless so it can be thought. The farthest external horizons of our hopes and fears are cobbled by our poems, carved from the rock experiences of our daily lives.

As they become known and accepted to ourselves, our feelings, and the honest exploration of them, become sanctuaries and fortresses and spawning ground for the most radical and daring of ideas, the house of difference so necessary to change and the conceptualization of any meaningful action. Right now, I could name at least ten ideas I would once have found intolerable or incomprehensible and frightening, except as they came after dreams and poems. This is not idle fantasy, but the true meaning of "It feels right to me." We can train ourselves to respect our feelings and to discipline (transpose) them into a language that catches those feelings so they can be shared.

From *Claims for Poetry*, edited by Donald Hall

QUESTIONS

According to this poet, what is the role of poetry in women's struggle for change and survival? What is the difference between the European and the non-European mode?

CROSS-REFERENCES—For Discussion or Writing

Audre Lorde's poem "Coal" appears on page 216 of this volume. How does it live up to the program sketched out in this selection?

JUXTAPOSITIONS ━━━━━

The Poet's Motives

In the following selections, two poets speak with exceptional candor about what makes them write. What inspired or motivated them as poets?

DIANE WAKOSKI   (born 1937)
On Experience and Imagination   1974

It has always been a premise of mine in writing poetry that the poet has the same experiences everybody else does, but the technical challenge is to invent some imaginative way of talking about these problems, these realities so that they can be taken seriously. It does not really seem like a big deal to anyone else when you say a man or woman you loved betrayed you. So what? Everyone sometimes feels betrayed. However, that's precisely why it is so important for the poet to find a way to say it. I believe in the use of extravagant surrealist imagery, like the girl riding naked on a zebra wearing only diamonds, as a way of making the reader accept the specialness of the feelings of the speaker in the poem.

I write in the first person because I have always wanted to make my life more interesting than it was. So I created a Diane whose real experiences were dramatized and exaggerated, were presented as surrealist experiences or metaphysical ones, who involved herself with imaginary people who often had the characteristics of real people but were more interesting and mysterious. Perhaps I have always been the isolated lonely person living around dull or sad people, and the poems were a way of inventing myself into a new life. I do feel a strange connection with the worlds I have created and the people in them, though I do not feel they are me or my world. It had been my obsession to try to see and understand the world truly, but that means seeing it over and over again, with all its changes, its attendant contradictions. I am never satisfied with anything I see but must keep inventing and reinventing ways to understand it.

From "Introduction" to *Trilogy*

QUESTIONS

What, for Wakoski, is the relationship between common shared experience and imaginative creation? What, for her, is the relationship between "realism" and "surrealism"? What do you learn about the persona in those of her poems she likes best?

PABLO NERUDA   (1904–1973)
Childhood and Poetry   1954

One time, investigating in the backyard of our house in Temuco the tiny objects and miniscule beings of my world, I came upon a hole in one of the boards of the fence. I looked through the hole and saw a landscape like that behind our house, uncared for, and wild. I moved back a few steps, because I sensed vaguely that something was about to happen. All of a sudden a hand appeared—a tiny hand of a boy about my own age. By the time I came close again, the hand was gone, and in its place there was a marvelous white sheep.

The sheep's wool was faded. Its wheels had escaped. All of this only made it more authentic. I had never seen such a wonderful sheep. I looked back through the hole but the boy had disappeared. I went into the house and brought out a treasure of my own: a pinecone, opened, full of odor and resin, which I adored. I set it down in the same spot and went off with the sheep.

I never saw either the hand or the boy again. And I have never again seen a sheep like that either. The toy I lost finally in a fire. But even now, in 1954, almost fifty years old, whenever I pass a toy shop, I look furtively into the window, but it's no use. They don't make sheep like that anymore.

I have been a lucky man. To feel the intimacy of brothers is a marvelous thing in life. To feel the love of people whom we love is a fire that feeds our life. But to feel the affection that comes from those whom we do not know, from those unknown to us, who are watching over our sleep and solitude, over our dangers and our weaknesses—that is something still greater and more beautiful because it widens out the boundaries of our being, and unites all living things.

That exchange brought home to me for the first time a precious idea: that all of humanity is somehow together. That experience came to me again much later; this time it stood out strikingly against a background of trouble and persecution.

It won't surprise you then that I attempted to give something resiny, earthlike, and fragrant in exchange for human brotherhood. Just as I once left the pinecone by the fence, I have since left my words on the door of so many people who were unknown to me, people in prison, or hunted, or alone.

From *Neruda and Vallejo: Selected Poems,* edited by Robert Bly

QUESTIONS

What was the significance of the childhood incident for the poet? In what way did it become a motivating force for his poetry?

EXPLICATION: SOUND AND SENSE

'Tis not enough no harshness gives offense;
The sound must seem an echo to the sense.
ALEXANDER POPE

Some poems are simple, but many are rich in concentrated meaning. Critics can help meanings reach the reader. A good critic can serve as a guide, explaining and interpreting, taking us step by step through a close reading of the poem. We call such patient line-by-line explanation **explication.** The critic who explicates a poem for us becomes our senior partner in the business of reading. The critic's function then is to make us pay attention, to defog our windshield, to alert us to missed clues, to fill in missed links.

The critic can be our guide to unsuspected shades and layers of meaning, our interpreter of metaphorical and symbolical significance. In particular, critics can alert us to the interplay of sound and sense, of form and meaning, that may escape the literal-minded reader. Critics in the modern tradition tend to ask not just *what* a poem means but *how* it means. In the following poem by G. M. Hopkins, sound and rhythm blend with the assertions made and questions asked by the poet in one of the great poems of English literature. The line-by-line explication by an experienced reader helps us clear up difficulties and helps us respond more fully to the richness of the poem.

GERARD MANLEY HOPKINS   (1844–1889)
God's Grandeur   1877

The world is charged with the grandeur of God.
　　It will flame out, like shining from shook foil;
　　It gathers to a greatness, like the ooze of oil
Crushed. Why do men then now not reck his rod?
Generations have trod, have trod, have trod;

And all is seared with trade; bleared, smeared with toil;
   And wears man's smudge and shares man's smell: the soil
Is bare now, nor can foot feel, being shod.

And for all this, nature is never spent;
   There lives the dearest freshness deep down things;   10
And though the last lights off the black West went
   Oh, morning, at the brown brink eastward, springs—
Because the Holy Ghost over the bent
   World broods with warm breast and with ah! bright wings.

J. R. WATSON
"God's Grandeur"   1987

The world is charged with the grandeur of God.

As a first line this is uncompromising. Its rhythm is confident and assured, and the full stop at the end of the line seems to emphasize the completeness and finality of the statement. The world is charged with God's grandeur, and that is that. Hopkins was so careful with line-endings and rhythms that this sentence within a line is evidently there for a purpose, to make the claim as strongly as possible. It does so especially because of the emphatic word "charged," which usefully has two meanings: "loaded," and "full of electricity" as a battery is when it has been charged. The world is therefore electric with God's grandeur, and loaded with it (which suggests that the grandeur is heavy and substantial): the image of electricity is carried on in the second line, when he senses that the grandeur of God will "flame out, like shining from shook foil." As foil, when shaken, gives off shining light, so the world, when looked at carefully, is full of the shining light of God Himself, leaping out like flames or sparks. Hopkins described it to Bridges as "I mean foil in its sense of leaf or tinsel. . . . Shaken gold foil gives off broad glares like sheet lightning, and this is true of nothing else, owing to its zigzag dints and creasings and network of small many cornered facets, a sort of fork lightning too"(L B 169). Its fullness is indicated by the next image

It gathers to a greatness, like the ooze of oil
Crushed.

Hopkins is here thinking of an olive press, with the oil oozing from the pressed fruit. It oozes from every part of the press, in a fine film, and then the trickles gather together to form a jar of oil. In the same way the grandeur of God is found everywhere, trickling from every simple thing in the created universe and accumulating to form a greatness, a grandeur that is perceived by the discerning mind of the Christian and poet. This is made clear in the lines that follow, which are a lament for the neglect and indifference shown by mankind. Once again the poetry is dense with metaphors: instead of saying "why do men take no notice?" Hopkins writes

Why do men then now not reck his rod?

The rhythms and sounds are themselves awkward, like the question: "men then," "now not" and "reck his rod" (care for his rule: "reck" means "heed," occurring in ordinary speech in the word "reckless"). And these sounds continue, as if Hopkins is using the vocabulary and rhythms of his verse to act out, as well as describe, the situation:

> Generations have trod, have trod, have trod;
>> And all is seared with trade; bleared, smeared with toil;
>> And wears man's smudge and shares man's smell: the soil
> Is bare now, nor can foot feel, being shod.

Here the mechanical forces are captured in verse by the heavy accents. What is sometimes called the "daily grind" is a repetitive thump in which the feet of generations march on; and the "trod . . . trod . . . trod" sets up the three-beat rhythm of the next line: "seared . . . bleared . . . smeared." The verbs themselves sprawl across the line, preventing any delicacy of feeling or perception. "Seared," for instance, means "dried up" or it can mean "rendered incapable of feeling": it is accomplished by "bleared" (blurred inflammation of the eyes) and "smeared" (rubbed over with dirt). When we think of the minute attention to detail of Hopkins' drawings, these adjectives take on yet more force: they are part of the process of treading down, smudging, and generally spoiling nature. Because of this the soil is barren, and feet, being both shod with boots, cannot feel it. For Hopkins, the "foot feel" is but a part of the whole process of insensitivity: as a man's feet are encased in boots, so his whole soul is bound up, unfree. . . .

It is then that the sestet throws into the equation another mysterious force, the feeling of freshness and growth of nature that causes it to live on, to survive against all the neglect and exploitation of man. Its nature is in this way to be itself: to go on growing each year with its own process of generation and renewed life, so that against the unfeeling energies of man there is placed something greater, the inexhaustible forces of nature. Its spirit of growth is everywhere: it is as natural and inevitable as the coming of morning after nightfall. It is the "dearest freshness" deep down in things which ensures that "nature is never spent"; and in the final lines this inexhaustible quality is associated with the working of the Holy Ghost, the spirit of God who created all things and sustains them:

> Because the Holy Ghost over the bent
>> World broods with warm breast and with ah! bright wings.

From J. R. Watson, *The Poetry of Gerard Manley Hopkins*

QUESTIONS

How does the critic show that the word *charged* is charged with meaning? What inside information does he use from the poet himself? Where and how does the critic show the meshing of content and form? What difficulties did this reading clear up for you? How did this explication change your understanding of and response to the poem?

EVALUATION: POEMS   GOOD   AND   BAD

There is something wrong
with this poem. Can you
*   find it?*
RICHARD BRAUTIGAN, "CRITICAL CAN OPENER"

A poem on cabbages, if we like cabbages, may seem better
than a poem on kings, if we dislike kings.
JOSEPHINE MILES

Critics are not content to explain and interpret. They judge. They set standards; they rank the first-rate and the second-rate. In our time, however, movements and countermovements have made it difficult to set up generally binding standards for what makes good contemporary poetry. Nevertheless, some basic requirements underlie many of the critical judgments you may encounter:

✧ Critics look in good poetry for *freshness* of language. They look for phrases that make us pay attention, that recharge our power of vision, that startle us into taking a new look.

✧ Critics look in good poetry for more than raw experience. They look for some kind of *control*. They look for evidence of the sifting and shaping that take a poem beyond the expression of raw emotion. They expect poets to put some distance between themselves and whatever pain or grievance or joy might have been the original impetus of a poem. In more traditional terms, the poet needs to transform the raw stuff of life into art.

✧ Critics look in good poetry for a challenge. They look for some degree of *complexity*. Poetry that is too regular, too smooth, too uncomplicated, will seem to them undemanding and simpleminded. They expect the poet to do more than to indulge in a single mood, however pleasing. Whatever ordering or shaping takes place should make us sense that jostling reality has been brought under control. Modern critics look for the tensions, the paradoxes, or the ironies that enable poets to do justice to mixed emotions and divided loyalties. They look for attempts to face and resolve ambiguities. They delight in the play of polarities. They look for the inversions and breaks or counter-rhythms that break up the tedúm-tedúm-tedúm patterns of "jingle-poets." Complexity of form became for the modern critic one manifestation of a poem's "maturity or sophistication or richness or depth, and hence its value" (W. K. Wimsatt).

✧ Critics look for an *organic* relation between substance and form. They stress the interconnectedness of a poem's parts. Meter, rhyme, pleasing sounds—these should not be embellishments, added like ornaments on a Christmas tree. Stanza form should not be like an empty container, to be filled by interchangeable content. A rhymed stanza should not be like "a jug into which the syrup of verse is poured." Instead, modern critics have looked for the "interaction of every element—image, statement, rhythm, rhyme—every element that goes to make up the whole poem" (Louis Martz).

❖ Critics insist that emotion be appropriate to the subject or justified by the context. Modern critics have been wary of overindulgence in emotion. They disapprove of **sentimentality.** Sentimentality allows readers to bask in a glow of self-approving emotions. It does not challenge them to examine their thoughts and actions. The following poem is often criticized as an example of sentimentality or excessive emotion.

R O D   M C K U E N   (born 1933)

Thoughts on Capital Punishment   1954

There ought to be capital punishment for cars
that run over rabbits and drive into dogs
and commit the unspeakable, unpardonable crime
of killing a kitty cat still in his prime.

Purgatory, at the very least   5
                    should await the driver
          driving over a beast.

Those hurrying headlights coming out of the dark
that scatter the scampering squirrels in the park
should await the best jury that one might compose   10
of fatherless chipmunks and husbandless does

And then found guilty, after too fair a trial
should be caged in a cage with a hyena's smile
or maybe an elephant with an elephant gun
should shoot out his eyes when the verdict is done.   15

There ought to be something, something that's fair
to avenge Mrs. Badger as she waits in her lair
for her husband who lies with his guts spilling out
cause he didn't know what automobiles are about.

Hell on the highway, at the very least   20
should await the driver
driving over a beast.

The following is a short sample from one representative discussion of this poem:

> Sentimentality is the evocation of a greater amount of feeling or emotion than is justified by the subject. . . . The poet who adopts a sentimental tone becomes more tearful or more ecstatic over his subject than it deserves. The sentimentalist is addicted to worn-out baby shoes, gray-haired mothers, and small animals—subjects certain to evoke an automatic response in a particular kind of reader. But sentimentality is not so much a matter of subject as it is a matter of treatment. . . .
>
> The chief defect of this poem is its sentimentality; the feelings it expresses are wholly disproportionate to the subject matter. No person with decent feel-

ings, of course, takes pleasure in the deaths of animals on the road; and if it is our own pet that is killed we may be genuinely grieved. But to call such accidents unspeakable, unpardonable crimes seems rather excessive. Unfortunately there is no evidence that the speaker's maudlin language is redeemed by irony. "Kitty cat" is baby talk; and chipmunks with fathers, does with husbands, and Mrs. Badger and her husband belong to the world of children's animal stories. (Such sentimentality also yields failures in logic. Would the crime be more pardonable if the kitty cat were not in its prime? Are the cars or the drivers who steer them to be punished?) A little reflection leads us to the conclusion that there are worse evils in this world than the accidental deaths of animals on the road.

From C. F. Main and Peter J. Seng, *Poems,* 4th ed.

QUESTIONS

What is the key to the definition of sentimentality in this passage? How do the authors apply it to the poem? Do you agree with them? Can you give your own examples of "excessive" emotion? (Is there more to this poem than these critics seem to acknowledge?)

CROSS-REFERENCES—For Discussion or Writing

Compare and contrast McKuen's poem with two other road-kill poems: William Stafford's "Traveling through the Dark" (p. 231) and Mary Oliver's "The Black Snake" (p. 71).

To some readers, the term *criticism* implies negative criticism. However, if critics castigate clichés, glib abstractions, and jingling verse, they also praise with equal fervor what they consider authentic and challenging. The following is a modern poem in a style valued by many contemporary critics. Much modern criticism modeled its standards on the practice of the seventeenth-century **metaphysical** poets: John Donne, Andrew Marvell, and George Herbert in England; Edward Taylor in America. Modern critics prized in the metaphysicals their yoking of intellect and passion, their love of paradox and irony, their use of complex, demanding form.

ANNE HALLEY   (born 1928)

Dear God, the Day Is Grey   1960

Dear God, the day is grey. My house
is not in order. Lord, the dust
sifts through my rooms and with my fear,
I sweep mortality, outwear
my brooms, but not this leaning floor   5
which lasts and groans. I, walking here,
still loathe the labors I would love
and hate the self I cannot move,
And God, I know the unshined boards,

the flaking ceiling, various stains 10
that mottle these distempered goods,
the greasy cloths, the jagged tins,
the dog that paws the garbage cans.
I know what laborings, love, and pains,
my blood would will, yet will not give: 15
the knot of hair that clogs the drains
clots in my throat. My dyings thrive.

The refuse, Lord, that I put out
burns in vast pits incessantly.
All piecemeal deaths, trash, undevout 20
and sullen sacrifice, to thee.

LAURENCE PERRINE
On "Dear God, the Day Is Grey"   1966

Three aspects of this poem strike one immediately. First, the quality of the religious devotion. The self-questioning, the struggling with the infirm will, the fear of unworthiness, the desire to be worthy—all express an intensity of religious feeling that takes us back to the seventeenth century. We can find counterparts of the feeling, to be sure, in T. S. Eliot and Gerard Manley Hopkins in more recent times, but the spirit of the poem finds its real reflection in Edward Taylor, George Herbert, and John Donne. Here, as in them, are expressed the burning desire to be found worthy in God's sight, full consciousness of the difficulty of performing the tasks imposed on one not only faithfully but with love, distress at the enormous impossibility of fulfilling the commandment "Be ye therefore perfect, even as your Father which is in heaven is perfect."

Then, secondly, the boldness with which the devotional feeling is coupled with the commonest, most daily domestic imagery. The sifting dust in a house, the brooms, "the flaking ceiling," the stains, "the knot of hair that clogs the drains"—these images bespeak a boldness of imagination that literary scholars have named "metaphysical"—denoting, in the words of Dr. Johnson, "a kind of *discordia concors,* a combination of dissimilar images, or discovery of occult resemblances in things apparently unlike." And yet the linking of love, sin, contrition, and the glory of God in this poem with greasy cloths, trash, and garbage cans does not strike us as bizarre or sacrilegious, but natural and devout. The tone of the poem is established early. When the poet says, "My house / is not in order," we know at once that she is speaking metaphorically and refers not to a house built of bricks and boards but to a life filled with strivings and failures, devout wishes, struggle with temptation, broken resolutions—in short, the problems of mortality.

Third, its modernity. In its religious devotion and in its bold domestic imagery, the poem reminds us of the seventeenth century. But it is not a seventeenth-century poem, as the imagery tells us. The jagged tins, the garbage cans, and the drains are part of the modern scene and could not have been found in a poem before this century. With all its seventeenth-century quality of subject and imagination, what gives the poem quality is its originality. That flaking ceiling and the knot of hair clogging the drain, we feel, have not been found in poetry before. The religious feeling of the poem is not faked, or imitated, but felt.

QUESTIONS

What qualities does this reader value in Halley's poem? Which of them do you consider most valuable (or least valuable) yourself?

CROSS-REFERENCES—For Discussion or Writing

Compare and contrast Halley's modern "metaphysical" poem with a poem by one of the seventeenth-century metaphysical poets printed earlier in this volume. Choose a religious poem by John Donne or George Herbert. What features of style and perspective do the two poems share?

EXPLORATIONS

Judging the Poem

Study the following poem and the two critical reactions that were published in *Poet and Critics*. Do you share the critics' reactions? Are they too harsh? Or too lenient? Write a short critical reaction of your own. Feel free to express your likes and dislikes, but support them by pointing to specific things in the poem.

DANIEL ORT

Can a Merry-Go-Round Horse Gallop in a Straight Line?   1966

As a kid on a merry-go-round
you could point at the whole
world by sticking one finger
out. Rings must have been
on rich kids' merry-go-rounds,   5
but there was lots of sky,
and mom's wave of new courage
always followed the popcorn
stand. The blind man would
squeeze your last ticket   10
into his brown hand while
Sousa's "Stars and Stripes
Forever" would come around
again like a red and white
goose after a blue elk and   15
you came to expect things.
Like the popcorn stand and mom.
Will a policeman who is used
to waving stop and go at anonymous
cars let a green and blue horse   20
on a yellow pole run a red light
on its way to the rainbow?

1. No: this doesn't work for me at all. . . . this is labored and heavy: cotton-candy stuffed with lead. For me, it never gets past cuteness, never gets past prose. And it's filled with sloganized nonsense: the "brown hand" of the ticket-taker (God: the thing might just as well be "weather-beaten"); the Sousa-music (for Colorful Nostalgia); and —egh—Mom, mom. Stuffed down a tuba, I hope.

No. My sympathies are all with the cop, who ought to take that green and blue little teensy horse and break both its legs. (Stanley Cooperman)

2. A poem is nothing for me unless it purges my sensitivities. Once it accomplishes this I give it an automatic ear-notch for having quality. Then I go back to the work and single out finer aspects, but keeping in mind that the poem has already done its job.

"Can a Merry-Go-Round Horse Gallop in a Straight Line?" has the ear-notch. It brings back a sensitivity of my youth. It is the excitement and wonder and mouth-gaping curiosity found at a carnival. It is wild imagination bounded by mother's pessimism and the authority of the traffic cop.

The poem is lacking in craft. A close examination reveals mulberry stains on the quilt. The sentence beginning "The blind man would . . ." is very awkward. "Would" is a vague verb and using it twice in the same sentence to show simultaneous actions weakens the structure. Going from the blind man's squeeze through the "Stars and Stripes Forever" and "like a red and white goose after a blue elk" is too much to swallow in one gulp.

Just one more thing. I can understand why a kid who has spent his last nickel for a ride on the merry-go-round is jealous of the rich kids, but where can I see one of these "rich kids' merry-go-rounds"? (Tom E. Knowlton)

WRITING ABOUT LITERATURE

14. Writing the Essay (Preparing for Tests)

The Writing Workshop   When you write about poetry as part of an essay exam, you need to be a quick, alert reader, and you need to think on your feet (metaphorically speaking). Common types of essay questions will ask you to

❖ interpret a poem without detailed questions to guide you. You are on your own, applying the critical skills you have learned.

❖ do a close reading of a poem, responding to detailed questions focused on the formal features of the poem.

❖ compare and contrast two poems, mapping similarities but also striking differences in such areas as form, theme, or point of view.

❖ respond to the thematic implications of a poem. You may, for instance, be asked to compare the way a common theme is treated in a poem and in a related prose passage.

Study the following sample exam. How would you answer the questions? Compare your answers with the student responses that follow the questions.

INSTRUCTIONS

Study the following poem, one of John Donne's *Holy Sonnets* (Number 5). Then answer the questions that follow it.

I am a little world made cunningly°   *skillfully*
Of elements and an angelic sprite;°   *spirit*
But black sin hath betrayed to endless night
My world's both parts, and O, both parts must die.
You which° beyond that heaven which was most high   *you who*   5
Have found new spheres and of new lands can write,
Pour new seas in mine eyes, that so I might
Drown my world with my weeping earnestly,
Or wash it if it must be drowned no more.
But O, it must be burned! Alas, the fire   10
Of lust and envy have burnt it heretofore
And made it fouler; let their flames retire,
And burn me, O Lord, with a fiery zeal
Of thee and thy house, which doth in eating heal.

QUESTIONS

1. What is the sustained or organizing metaphor in the first four lines?

2. By Donne's time, the new science of astronomy had made people think of new reaches of space beyond the traditional heavenly spheres. Explorers and navigators like Columbus had discovered new worlds. What use does Donne make of these developments in this poem?

3. After Noah's flood, God had promised not ever to send floods again to drown sinful humanity. Where and how does the poet allude to this promise?

4. Sonnets often reach a turning point at or near the division between the opening octet and the concluding sestet. Does this sonnet follow this pattern?

5. The final lines of the poem make us imagine three different kinds of fire or flame. What are they?

6. What is paradoxical about the concluding couplet?

7. What is the prevailing tone of this sonnet? What are the dominant emotions? What kind of speaker does it make you imagine?

8. How does the poem as a whole develop or take shape? What is the overall movement or pattern that gives shape to the poem as a whole?

Compare your own answers with the following sample student responses:

SAMPLE STUDENT RESPONSES

1. The sustained opening metaphor compares the speaker in the poem to the larger universe in which we live. A human being is a "little world" (a microcosm) made by the same creator that created the larger world outside. A human being is composed of earthly elements and an angelic, heavenly soul, just as the universe is composed of the earth and the heavens, inhabited by spirits or angels. Both the "little world" of the individual and the larger world (the macrocosm) will eventually be destroyed—the one at the end of our natural lives, the other on the eve of eternity.

2. Donne seems fascinated with geography, astronomy, and the other sciences. The opening up of new vistas in geography and astronomy gave his hyperbolical mind new areas in which to wander. In lines 5 and 6, he is turning to the new astronomers (who "have found new spheres") and to the discoverers of new continents (who can write "of new lands"). He asks them hyperbolically about newly discovered oceans that might replenish the reservoir of tears he has shed in weeping for his sins.

3. The speaker in the poem wants to "drown" his sinful "little world" with weeping, submerging it in tears. But God had promised Noah that He would not again allow humanity to be drowned; therefore, the speaker will use his tears merely to "wash" and cleanse rather than to drown (line 9).

4. There is a turning signaled by the word *but,* not exactly at the end of the octave but at the beginning of line 10. The tears of repentance alone will not be enough; the whole world will have to be destroyed by fire before we can enter into communion with God (no more floods—"the fire next time").

5. The first kind of fire is the physical fire that will destroy the world at the end. The second is the "fire of lust and envy" that leaves everything "foul" or scorched and besmirched. The third is the "fiery zeal" that cleanses us of sin.

6. It is paradoxical that Donne asks to be destroyed in order to be saved. The idea of a healing fire is paradoxical because the fire eats or devours what it consumes. But this fire "heals" by consuming only the infected part—it burns out sin.

7. The tone is paradoxical. The poem is somber and full of passionate remorse and despair, but it ends on a note of reaffirming the poet's faith . The speaker is a very intense person, passionately introspective, constantly dramatizing his own emotions.

8. The poem develops beautifully by first making us admire God's handiwork (the little world of the human body, "made cunningly" by God). But the poet almost immediately mourns its desperate condition after it has been "betrayed" by sin. The poet then asks for cleansing by water, then corrects himself in a rush of passion by asking for all-consuming fire. The poem proceeds by playing off polar opposites: the angelic spirit and the dark night of sin, water and fire.

OTHER VOICES/OTHER VISIONS
Poems for Further Reading

ANONYMOUS

Edward

(traditional Scottish ballad)

1
"Why does your brand sae drap wi' bluid,°   *sword so drip with blood*
    Edward, Edward,
Why does your brand sae drap wi' bluid,
    And why sae sad gang° ye, O?"   *so sad go*
"O I ha'e killed my hawk sae guid,°   *good*   5
    Mither, mither,
O I ha'e killed my hawk sae guid,
    And I had nae mair but he, O."

2
"Your hawke's bluid was never sae reid,°   *red*
    Edward, Edward,   10
Your hawke's bluid was never sae reid,
    My dear son I tell thee, O."
"O I ha'e killed my reid-roan steed,
    Mither, mither,
O I ha'e killed my reid-roan steed,   15
    That erst was° sae fair and free, O."   *that once was*

3
"Your steed was auld, and ye ha'e gat mair,°   *more*
    Edward, Edward,
Your steed was auld, and ye ha'e gat mair,
    Some other dule ye drie,° O."   *other grief you suffer*   20
"O I ha'e killed my fader dear,
    Mither, mither,
O I ha'e killed my fader dear,
    Alas, and wae° is me, O!"   *woe*

4
"And whatten° penance wul ye drie for that,   *what sort of*   25
    Edward, Edward?
And whatten penance wul ye drie for that,

My dear son, now tell me, O?"
"I'll set my feet in yonder boat,
    Mither, mither,   30
I'll set my feet in yonder boat,
    And I'll fare over the sea, O."

5
"And what wul ye do wi' your towers and your ha',°   *hall*
    Edward, Edward?
And what wul ye do wi' your towers and your ha',   35
    That were sae fair to see, O?"
"I'll let them stand tul they down fa',°   *fall*
    Mither, mither,
I'll let them stand tul they down fa',
    For here never mair maun° I be, O."   *never more must* 40

6
"And what wul ye leave to your bairns° and your wife,   *children*
    Edward, Edward?
And what wul ye leave to your bairns and your wife,
    Whan ye gang over the sea, O?"
"The warlde's° room, let them beg thrae° life,   *world's/through* 45
    Mither, mither,
The warlde's room, let them beg thrae life,
    For them never mair wul I see, O."

7
"And what wul ye leave to your ain mither dear,
    Edward, Edward?   50
And what wul ye leave to your ain mither dear,
    My dear son, now tell me, O?"
"The curse of hell frae me sall° ye bear,   *from me shall*
    Mither, mither,
The curse of hell frae me sall ye bear,   55
    Sic° counsels ye gave to me, O."   *such*

ANONYMOUS

Sir Patrick Spens   thirteenth century

1
The king sits in Dumferling town,
    Drinking the blude-reid° wine: *blood-red*
"O whar will I get guid° sailor,   *good*
    To sail this ship of mine?"

2
Up and spak an eldern knicht,°   *spoke an elderly knight* 5
    Sat at the king's richt° knee: *right*
"Sir Patrick Spens is the best sailor
    That sails upon the sea."

3
The king has written a braid° letter   *broad*
    And signed it wi' his hand,   10
And sent it to Sir Patrick Spens,
    Was walking on the sand.

4
The first line that Sir Patrick read,
    A loud lauch° lauched he;   *laugh*
The next line that Sir Patrick read,   15
    The tear blinded his ee.°   *eye*

5
"O wha is this has done this deed,
    This ill deed done to me,
To send me out this time o' the year,
    To sail upon the sea?   20

6
"Mak haste, mak haste, my mirry men all,
    Our guid ship sails the morn."
"O say na sae,° my master dear,   *not so*
    For I fear a deadly storm.

7
"Late, late yestre'en I saw the new moon   25
    Wi' the auld moon in hir arm,
And I fear, I fear, my dear master,
    That we will come to harm."

8
O our Scots nobles were richt laith°   *loath*
    To weet their cork-heeled shoon,°   *wet their cork-heeled shoes*   30
But lang or° a' the play were played   *before*
    Their hats they swam aboon.°   *above*

9
O lang, lang may their ladies sit,
    Wi' their fans into their hand,
Or ere they see Sir Patrick Spens   35
    Come sailing to the land.

10
O lang, lang may the ladies stand
    Wi' their gold kems° in their hair,   *combs*
Waiting for their ain° dear lords,   *own*
    For they'll see them na mair.   40

11
Half o'er, half o'er to Aberdour
    It's fifty fadom deep,
And there lies guid Sir Patrick Spens
    Wi' the Scots lords at his feet.

W . H . A U D E N   (1907–1973)
Musée des Beaux Arts   1940

About suffering they were never wrong,
The Old Masters:° how well they understood   *traditional European painters*
Its human position; how it takes place   *in Paris Museum of Fine Arts*
While someone else is eating or opening a window or just
    walking dully along;
How, when the aged are reverently, passionately waiting   5
For the miraculous birth, there always must be
Children who did not specially want it to happen, skating
On a pond at the edge of the wood:
They never forgot
That even the dreadful martyrdom must run its course   10
Anyhow in a corner, some untidy spot
Where the dogs go on with their doggy life and the torturer's horse
Scratches its innocent behind on a tree.

In Breughel's *Icarus*,° for instance: how everything turns away   *The Fall of Icarus, painted*
Quite leisurely from the disaster; the ploughman may   *by Pieter Breughel (16th c.)*   15
Have heard the splash, the forsaken cry,
But for him it was not an important failure; the sun shone
As it had to on the white legs disappearing into the green
Water; and the expensive delicate ship that must have seen
Something amazing, a boy falling out of the sky,   20
Had somewhere to get to and sailed calmly on.

I M A M U   A M I R I   B A R A K A   (L E R O I   J O N E S)   (born 1934)
The Turncoat   1961

The steel fibrous slant & ribboned glint
of water. The Sea. Even my secret speech is moist
with it. When I am alone & brooding, locked in
with dull memories & self hate, & the terrible disorder
of a young man.   5

I move slowly. My cape spread stiff & pressing cautiously
in the first night wind off the Hudson. I glide down
onto my own roof, peering in at the pitiful shadow of myself.

How can it mean anything? The stop & spout, the
wind's dumb shift. Creak of the house & wet smells   10
coming in. Night forms on my left. The blind still
up to admit a sun that no longer exists. Sea move.

I dream long bays & towers . . . & soft steps on moist sand.
I become them, sometimes. Pure fight. Pure fantasy. Lean.

APHRA BEHN   (1640–1689)

Song   1676

Love in fantastic triumph° sat,   *celebration of victory*
Whilst bleeding hearts around him flowed,
For whom fresh pains he did create,
And strange tyrannic power he showed.
From thy bright eyes he took his fire,   5
Which round about, in sport he hurled;
But 't was from mine he took desire,
Enough to undo the amorous° world.   *filled with love*

From me he took his sighs and tears,
From thee his pride and cruelty;   10
From me his languishments and fears,
And every killing dart from thee.
Thus thou and I, the god have armed,
And set him up a deity;°   *as a deity*
But my poor heart alone is harmed,   15
Whilst thine the victor is, and free.

JOHN BERRYMAN   (1914–1972)

The Ball Poem   1948

What is the boy now, who has lost his ball,
What, what is he to do? I saw it go
Merrily bouncing, down the street, and then
Merrily over—there it is in the water!
No use to say "O there are other balls":   5
An ultimate shaking grief fixes the boy
As he stands rigid, trembling, staring down
All his young days into the harbor where
His ball went. I would not intrude on him,
A dime, another ball, is worthless. Now   10
He senses first responsibility
In a world of possessions. People will take balls,
Balls will be lost always, little boy,
And no one buys a ball back. Money is external.
He is learning, well behind his desperate eyes,   15
The epistemology° of loss, how to stand up   *philosophical questioning*
Knowing what every man must one day know   *about the nature of knowledge*
And most know many days, how to stand up.
And gradually light returns to the street,
A whistle blows, the ball is out of sight,   20
Soon part of me will explore the deep and dark
Floor of the harbor . . . I am everywhere,
I suffer and move, my mind and my heart move
With all that move me, under the water
Or whistling, I am not a little boy.   25

JOHN BERRYMAN (1914–1972)

Dream Song 14

1964

Life, friends, is boring. We must not say so.
After all, the sky flashes, the great sea yearns,
we ourselves flash and yearn,
and moreover my mother told me as a boy
(repeatedly) "Ever to confess you're bored   5
means you have no

Inner Resources." I conclude now I have no
inner resources, because I am heavy bored.
Peoples bore me,
literature bores me, especially great literature,   10
Henry bores me, with his plights & gripes
as bad as achilles,°   *mythical Greek warrior invulnerable*
                                        except in the heel

who loves people and valiant art, which bores me.
And the tranquil hills, & gin, look like a drag
and somehow a dog   15
has taken itself & its tail considerably away
into mountains or sea or sky, leaving
behind: me, wag.

WILLIAM BLAKE (1757–1827)

The Chimney Sweeper

1789

When my mother died I was very young,
And my father sold me while yet my tongue
Could scarcely cry weep weep weep weep.°   *child's pronunciation of "sweep sweep"?*
So your chimneys I sweep & in soot I sleep.

Theres little Tom Dacre, who cried when his head   5
That curl'd like a lambs back, was shav'd, so I said
Hush Tom never mind it, for when your head's bare,
You know that the soot cannot spoil your white hair.

And so he was quiet, & that very night,
As Tom was a sleeping he had such a sight,   10
That thousands of sweepers Dick, Joe Ned & Jack
Were all of them lock'd up in coffins of black°   *due to lung diseases*

And by came an Angel who had a bright key,
And he open'd the coffins & set them all free.
Then down a green plain leaping laughing they run   15
And wash in a river and shine in the Sun.

Then naked & white, all their bags left behind,
They rise upon clouds, and sport in the wind.
And the Angel told Tom if he'd be a good boy,
He'd have God for his father & never want° joy.   *lack*   20

And so Tom awoke and we rose in the dark
And got with our bags & our brushes to work.
Tho' the morning was cold, Tom was happy & warm,
So if all do their duty, they need not fear harm.

WILLIAM BLAKE   (1757–1827)

The Garden of Love   1794

I went to the Garden of Love,
And saw what I never had seen:
A Chapel was built in the midst,
Where I used to play on the green.

And the gates of this Chapel were shut,   5
And "Thou shalt not" writ over the door;
So I turn'd to the Garden of Love,
That so many sweet flowers bore,

And I saw it was filled with graves,
And tomb-stones where flowers should be: 10
And Priests in black gowns were walking their rounds,
And binding with briars my joys & desires.

WILLIAM BLAKE   (1757–1827)

The Lamb   1789

    Little Lamb, who made thee?
    Dost thou know who made thee?
Gave thee life & bid thee feed,
By the stream & o'er the mead;
Gave thee clothing of delight,   5
Softest clothing wooly bright;
Gave thee such a tender voice,
Making all the vales° rejoice!   *valleys*
    Little Lamb who made thee?
    Dost thou know who made thee?   10

    Little Lamb I'll tell thee,
    Little Lamb I'll tell thee!
He is callèd by thy name,
For he calls himself a Lamb:
He is meek & he is mild,   15
He became a little child:
I a child & thou a lamb,
We are callèd by his name.
    Little Lamb God bless thee.
    Little Lamb God bless thee.   20

R O B E R T   B L Y   (born 1926)

Snowfall in the Afternoon   1962

1
The grass is half-covered with snow.
It was the sort of snowfall that starts in late afternoon,
And now the little houses of the grass are growing dark.

2
If I reached my hands down, near the earth,
I could take handfuls of darkness!   5
A darkness was always there, which we never noticed.

3
As the snow grows heavier, the cornstalks fade farther away,
And the barn moves nearer to the house.
The barn moves all alone in the growing storm.

4
The barn is full of corn, and moving toward us now,   10
Like a hulk blown toward us in a storm at sea;
All the sailors on deck have been blind for many years.

L O U I S E   B O G A N   (1897–1970)

Women   1923

Women have no wilderness in them,
They are provident° instead,   *frugal*
Content in the tight hot cell of their hearts
To eat dusty bread.

They do not see cattle cropping red winter grass,   5
They do not hear
Snow water going down under culverts
Shallow and clear.

They wait, when they should turn to journeys,
They stiffen, when they should bend.   10
They use against themselves that benevolence°   *good will*
To which no man is friend.

They cannot think of so many crops to a field
Or of clean wood cleft by° an axe.   *split by*
Their love is an eager meaninglessness   15
Too tense, or too lax.

They hear in every whisper that speaks to them
A shout and a cry.
As like as not, when they take life over their door-sills
They should let it go by.   20

RUPERT BROOKE   (1887–1915)
The Soldier   1915

If I should die, think only this of me:
    That there's some corner of a foreign field
That is for ever England. There shall be
    In that rich earth a richer dust concealed;
A dust whom England bore, shaped, made aware,   5
    Gave, once, her flowers to love, her ways to roam,
A body of England's, breathing English air,
    Washed by the rivers, blest by suns of home.

And think, this heart, all evil shed away,
    A pulse in the eternal mind, no less   10
        Gives somewhere back the thoughts by England given;
Her sights and sounds; dreams happy as her day;
    And laughter, learnt of friends; and gentleness,
        In hearts at peace, under an English heaven.

ROBERT BROWNING   (1812–1889)
Fra Lippo Lippi   1855

I am poor brother Lippo,° by your leave!   *Florentine painter (ca. 1406–1469)*
You need not clap your torches to my face.
Zooks, what's to blame? you think you see a monk!
What, 'tis past midnight, and you go the rounds,
And here you catch me at an alley's end   5
Where sportive ladies leave their doors ajar?
The Carmine's° my cloister: hunt it up,   *Carmelite monastery*
Do—harry out, if you must show your zeal,
Whatever rat, there, haps on his wrong hole,
And nip each softling of a wee white mouse,   10
Weke, weke, that's crept to keep him company!
Aha, you know your betters! Then, you'll take
Your hand away that's fiddling on my throat,
And please to know me likewise. Who am I?
Why, one, sir, who is lodging with a friend   15
Three streets off—he's a certain . . . how d'ye call?
Master—a . . . Cosimo of the Medici,°   *a politically powerful patron of the arts*
I' the house that caps the corner. Boh! you were best!
Remember and tell me, the day you're hanged,
How you affected such a gullet's-gripe!°   *throat-grip*   20
But you, sir, it concerns you that your knaves
Pick up a manner nor discredit you:
Zooks, are we pilchards,° that they sweep the streets   *fish*
And count fair prize what comes into their net?
He's Judas to a tittle,° that man is!   *just like Judas, the apostle who betrayed Jesus*   25
Just such a face! Why, sir, you make amends.

Lord, I'm not angry! Bid your hangdogs go
Drink out this quarter-florin to the health
Of the munificent° House that harbors me   *generous*
(And many more beside, lads! more beside!)   30
And all's come square again. I'd like his face—
His, elbowing on his comrade in the door
With the pike and lantern—for the slave that holds
John Baptist's head a-dangle by the hair°   *John the Baptist, beheaded by Herod*
With one hand ("Look you, now," as who should say)   35
And his weapon in the other, yet unwiped!
It's not your chance to have a bit of chalk,
A wood-coal or the like? or you should see!
Yes, I'm the painter, since you style me so.
What, brother Lippo's doings, up and down,   40
You know them and they take you? like enough!
I saw the proper twinkle in your eye—
'Tell you, I liked your looks at very first.
Let's sit and set things straight now, hip to haunch.
Here's spring come, and the nights one makes up bands   45
To roam the town and sing out carnival,
And I've been three weeks shut within my mew,°   *narrow quarters*
A-painting for the great man, saints and saints
And saints again. I could not paint all night—
Ouf! I leaned out of window for fresh air.   50
There came a hurry of feet and little feet,
A sweep of lute-strings, laughs, and whiffs of song—
Flower o' the broom,
Take away love, and our earth is a tomb!
Flower o' the quince,   55
I let Lisa go, and what good in life since?
Flower o' the thyme—and so on. Round they went.
Scarce had they turned the corner when a titter
Like the skipping of rabbits by moonlight—three slim shapes,
And a face that looked up . . . zooks, sir, flesh and blood,   60
That's all I'm made of! Into shreds it went,
Curtain and counterpane and coverlet,
All the bed-furniture—a dozen knots,
There was a ladder! Down I let myself,
Hands and feet, scrambling somehow, and so dropped,   65
And after them. I came up with the fun
Hard by Saint Laurence,° hail fellow, well met—   *Church of San Lorenzo*
Flower o' the rose,
If I've been merry, what matter who knows?
And so as I was stealing back again   70
To get to bed and have a bit of sleep
Ere I rise up to-morrow and go work
On Jerome knocking at his poor old breast°   *on a painting of St. Jerome in the desert*
With his great round stone to subdue the flesh,
You snap me of the sudden. Ah, I see!   75
Though your eye twinkles still, you shake your head—
Mine's shaved—a monk, you say—the sting's in that!

If Master Cosimo announced himself,
Mum's the word naturally; but a monk!
Come, what am I a beast for? tell us, now!   80
I was a baby when my mother died
And father died and left me in the street.
I starved there, God knows how, a year or two
On fig-skins, melon-parings, rinds and shucks,
Refuse and rubbish. One fine frosty day,   85
My stomach being empty as your hat,
The wind doubled me up and down I went.
Old Aunt Lapaccia trussed me with one hand,
(Its fellow was a stinger as I knew)
And so along the wall, over the bridge,   90
By the straight cut to the convent. Six words there,
While I stood munching my first bread that month:
"So, boy, you're minded," quoth the good fat father
Wiping his own mouth, 't was reflection-time—°   *meal time*
"To quit this very miserable world?   95
"Will you renounce" . . . "the mouthful of bread?" thought I;
By no means! Brief, they made a monk of me;
I did renounce the world, its pride and greed,
Palace, farm, villa, shop and banking-house,
Trash, such as these poor devils of Medici   100
Have given their hearts to—all at eight years old.
Well, sir, I found in time, you may be sure,
'T was not for nothing—the good bellyful,
The warm serge and the rope that goes all round,
And day-long blessed idleness beside!   105
"Let's see what the urchin's fit for"—that came next.
Not overmuch their way, I must confess.
Such a to-do! They tried me with their books:
Lord, they'd have taught me Latin in pure waste!
Flower o' the clove,   110
All the Latin I construe is, "amo" I love!
But, mind you, when a boy starves in the streets
Eight years together, as my fortune was,
Watching folk's faces to know who will fling
The bit of half-stripped grape-bunch he desires,   115
And who will curse or kick him for his pains—
Which gentleman processional and fine,
Holding a candle to the Sacrament,
Will wink and let him lift a plate and catch
The droppings of the wax to sell again,   120
Or holla for the Eight° and have him whipped—   *the Florentine magistrates*
How say I? nay, which dog bites, which lets drop
His bone from the heap of offal° in the street—   *waste*
Why, soul and sense of him grow sharp alike,
He learns the look of things, and none the less   125
For admonition from the hunger-pinch.
I had a store of such remarks, be sure,
Which, after I found leisure, turned to use.

I drew men's faces on my copy-books,
Scrawled them within the antiphonary's marge,°   *margin of a religious book*   130
Joined legs and arms to the long music-notes,
Found eyes and nose and chin for A's and B's,
And made a string of pictures of the world
Betwixt the ins and outs of verb and noun,
On the wall, the bench, the door. The monks looked black.   135
"Nay," quoth the Prior, "turn him out, d'ye say?
"In no wise. Lose a crow and catch a lark.
"What if at last we get our man of parts,
"We Carmelites, like those Camaldolese°   *members of a religious order at Camaldoli*
"And Preaching Friars,° to do our church up fine   *Dominicans*   140
"And put the front on it that ought to be!"
And hereupon he bade me daub away.
Thank you! my head being crammed, the walls a blank,
Never was such prompt disemburdening.
First, every sort of monk, the black and white,   145
I drew them, fat and lean: then, folk at church,
From good old gossips waiting to confess
Their cribs of barrel-droppings, candle-ends—
To the breathless fellow at the altar-foot,
Fresh from his murder, safe and sitting there   150
For that white anger of his victim's son
Shaking a fist at him with one fierce arm,
Signing° himself with the other because of Christ   *making the sign of the cross*
(Whose sad face on the cross sees only this
After the passion of a thousand years)   155
Till some poor girl, her apron o'er her head,
(Which the intense eyes looked through) came at eve
On tiptoe, said a word, dropped in a loaf,
Her pair of earrings and a bunch of flowers
(The brute took growling), prayed, and so was gone.   160
I painted all, then cried "'Tis ask and have;
"Choose, for more's ready!"—laid the ladder flat,
And showed my covered bit of cloister-wall.
The monks closed in a circle and praised loud
Till checked, taught what to see and not to see,   165
Being simple bodies—"That's the very man!
"Look at the boy who stoops to pat the dog!
"That woman's like the Prior's niece who comes
"To care about his asthma: it's the life!"
But there my triumph's straw-fire flared and funked;   170
Their betters took their turn to see and say:
The Prior and the learned pulled a face
And stopped all that in no time. "How? what's here?
"Quite from the mark of painting, bless us all!
"Faces, arms, legs and bodies like the true   175
"As much as pea and pea! it's devil's-game!
"Your business is not to catch men with show,
"With homage to the perishable clay,
"But lift them over it, ignore it all,

"Make them forget there's such a thing as flesh.   180
"Your business is to paint the souls of men—
"Man's soul, and it's a fire, smoke . . . no, it's not . . .
"It's vapor done up like a new-born babe—
"(In that shape when you die it leaves your mouth)
"It's . . . well, what matters talking, it's the soul!   185
"Give us no more of body than shows soul!
"Here's Giotto,° with his Saint a-praising God,   *Florentine painter (1267–1337)*
"That sets us praising—why not stop with him?
"Why put all thoughts of praise out of our head
"With wonder at lines, colors, and what not?   190
"Paint the soul, never mind the legs and arms!
"Rub all out, try at it a second time.
"Oh, that white smallish female with the breasts,
"She's just my niece . . . Herodias,° I would say—   *Herod's sister-in-law, instrumental*
"Who went and danced and got men's heads cut off!   *in beheading of John the Baptist*   195
"Have it all out!" Now, is this sense, I ask?
A fine way to paint soul, by painting body
So ill, the eye can't stop there, must go further
And can't fare worse! Thus, yellow does for white
When what you put for yellow's simply black,   200
And any sort of meaning looks intense
When all beside itself means and looks nought.
Why can't a painter lift each foot in turn,
Left foot and right foot, go a double step,
Make his flesh liker and his soul more like,   205
Both in their order? Take the prettiest face,
The Prior's niece . . . patron-saint—is it so pretty
You can't discover if it means hope, fear,
Sorrow or joy? won't beauty go with these?
Suppose I've made her eyes all right and blue,   210
Can't I take breath and try to add life's flash,
And then add soul and heighten them threefold?
Or say there's beauty with no soul at all—
(I never saw it—put the case the same—)
If you get simple beauty and nought else,   215
You get about the best thing God invents:
That's somewhat: and you'll find the soul you have missed,
Within yourself, when you return him thanks.
"Rub all out!" Well, well, there's my life, in short,
And so the thing has gone on ever since.   220
I'm grown a man no doubt, I've broken bounds:
You should not take a fellow eight years old
And make him swear to never kiss the girls.
I'm my own master, paint now as I please—
Having a friend, you see, in the Corner-house!°   *the Medici palace*   225
Lord, it's fast holding by the rings in front—
Those great rings serve more purposes than just
To plant a flag in, or tie up a horse!
And yet the old schooling sticks, the old grave eyes
Are peeping o'er my shoulder as I work,   230

The heads shake still—"It's art's decline, my son!
"You're not of the true painters, great and old;
"Brother Angelico's the man, you'll find;
"Brother Lorenzo stands his single peer:
"Fag on at flesh, you'll never make the third!"   235
Flower o' the pine,
You keep your mistr . . . manners, and I'll stick to mine!
I'm not the third, then: bless us, they must know!
Don't you think they're the likeliest to know,
They with their Latin? So, I swallow my rage,   240
Clench my teeth, suck my lips in tight, and paint
To please them—sometimes do and sometimes don't;
For, doing most, there's pretty sure to come
A turn, some warm eve finds me at my saints—
A laugh, a cry, the business of the world—   245
(*Flower o' the peach,*
Death for us all, and his own life for each!)
And my whole soul revolves, the cup runs over,
The world and life's too big to pass for a dream,
And I do these wild things in sheer despite,   250
And play the fooleries you catch me at,
In pure rage! The old mill-horse, out at grass
After hard years, throws up his stiff heels so,
Although the miller does not preach to him
The only good of grass is to make chaff.   255
What would men have? Do they like grass or no—
May they or mayn't they? all I want's the thing
Settled for ever one way. As it is,
You tell too many lies and hurt yourself:
You don't like what you only like too much,   260
You do like what, if given you at your word,
You find abundantly detestable.
For me, I think I speak as I was taught;
I always see the garden and God there
A-making man's wife: and, my lesson learned,   265
The value and significance of flesh,
I can't unlearn ten minutes afterwards.

　　　You understand me: I'm a beast, I know.
But see, now—why, I see as certainly
As that the morning-star's about to shine,   270
What will hap some day. We've a youngster here
Comes to our convent, studies what I do,
Slouches and stares and lets no atom drop:
His name is Guidi—he'll not mind the monks—
They call him Hulking Tom, he lets them talk—   275
He picks my practice up—he'll paint apace,
I hope so—though I never live so long,
I know what's sure to follow. You be judge!
You speak no Latin more than I, belike;
However, you're my man, you've seen the world   280
—The beauty and the wonder and the power,

The shapes of things, their colors, lights and shades,
Changes, surprises—and God made it all!
—For what? Do you feel thankful, ay or no,
For this fair town's face, yonder river's line,   285
The mountain round it and the sky above,
Much more the figures of man, woman, child,
These are the frame to? What's it all about?
To be passed over, despised? or dwelt upon,
Wondered at? oh, this last of course!—you say.   290
But why not do as well as say, paint these
Just as they are, careless what comes of it?
God's works—paint anyone, and count it crime
To let a truth slip. Don't object, "His works
"Are here already; nature is complete: 295
"Suppose you reproduce her (which you can't)
"There's no advantage! you must beat her, then."
For, don't you mark? we're made so that we love
First when we see them painted, things we have passed
Perhaps a hundred times nor cared to see;   300
And so they are better, painted—better to us,
Which is the same thing. Art was given for that;
God uses us to help each other so,
Lending our minds out. Have you noticed, now,
Your cullion's° hanging face? A bit of chalk,   *sad person's* 305
And trust me but you should, though! How much more,
If I drew higher things with the same truth!
That were to take the Prior's pulpit-place,
Interpret God to all of you! Oh, oh,
It makes me mad to see what men shall do   310
And we in our graves! This world's no blot for us,
Nor blank; it means intensely, and means good:
To find its meaning is my meat and drink.
"Ay, but you don't so instigate to prayer!"
Strikes in the Prior: "when your meaning's plain   315
"It does not say to folk—remember matins,°   *morning prayers*
"Or, mind you fast next Friday!" Why, for this
What need of art at all? A skull and bones,
Two bits of stick nailed crosswise, or, what's best,
A bell to chime the hour with, does as well.   320
I painted a Saint Laurence six months since
At Prato,° splashed the fresco in fine style: *town near Florence*
"How looks my painting, now the scaffold's down?"
I ask a brother: "Hugely," he returns—
"Already not one phiz° of your three slaves   *facial expression* 325
"Who turn the Deacon off his toasted side,°   *St. Lawrence was burned to death*
"But's scratched and prodded to our heart's content,   *on a gridiron*
"The pious people have so eased their own
"With coming to say prayers there in a rage:
"We get on fast to see the bricks beneath.   330
"Expect another job this time next year,
"For pity and religion grow i' the crowd—

"Your painting serves its purpose!" Hang the fools!

—That is—you'll not mistake an idle word
Spoke in a huff by a poor monk, God wot,°   *knows*   335
Tasting the air this spicy night which turns
The unaccustomed head like Chianti wine!
Oh, the church knows! don't misreport me, now!
It's natural a poor monk out of bounds
Should have his apt word to excuse himself: 340
And hearken how I plot to make amends.
I have bethought me: I shall paint a piece
. . . There's for you! Give me six months, then go, see
Something in Sant' Ambrogio's!° Bless the nuns!   *St. Ambrose's church in Florence*
They want a cast o' my office. I shall paint   345
God in the midst, Madonna and her babe,
Ringed by a bowery flowery angel-brood,
Lilies and vestments and white faces, sweet
As puff on puff of grated orris-root
When ladies crowd to Church at midsummer.   350
And then i' the front, of course a saint or two—
Saint John, because he saves the Florentines,°   *San Giovanni is the patron saint of Florence*
Saint Ambrose, who puts down in black and white
The convent's friends and gives them a long day,
And Job, I must have him there past mistake,   355
The man of Uz (and Us without the z,
Painters who need his patience). Well, all these
Secured at their devotion, up shall come
Out of a corner when you least expect,
As one by a dark stair into a great light,   360
Music and talking, who but Lippo! I!
Mazed, motionless and moonstruck—I'm the man!
Back I shrink—what is this I see and hear?
I, caught up with my monk's-things by mistake,
My old serge gown and rope that goes all round,   365
I, in this presence, this pure company!
Where's a hole, where's a corner for escape?
Then steps a sweet angelic slip of a thing
Forward, puts out a soft palm—"Not so fast!"
—Addresses the celestial presence, "nay—   370
"He made you and devised you, after all,
"Though he's none of you! Could Saint John there draw—
"His camel-hair° make up a painting-brush?   *camel-hair robe*
"We come to brother Lippo for all that,
"*Iste perfecit opus!*"° So, all smile—   *"This man accomplished the work!"*   375
I shuffle sideways with my blushing face
Under the cover of a hundred wings
Thrown like a spread of kirtles° when you're gay   *skirts*
And play hot cockles,° all the doors being shut,   *a game*
Till, wholly unexpected, in there pops   380
The hothead husband! Thus I scuttle off
To some safe bench behind, not letting go

The palm of her, the little lily thing
That spoke the good word for me in the nick,
Like the Prior's niece . . . Saint Lucy, I would say,   385
And so all's saved for me, and for the church
A pretty picture gained. Go, six months hence!
Your hand, sir, and good-bye: no lights, no lights!
The street's hushed, and I know my own way back,
Don't fear me! there's the gray beginning. Zooks!   390

GEORGE GORDON, LORD BYRON   (1788–1824)
She Walks in Beauty   1815

1
She walks in beauty, like the night
    Of cloudless climes° and starry skies;   *climates*
And all that's best of dark and bright
    Meet in her aspect and her eyes:
Thus mellowed to that tender light   5
    Which heaven to gaudy day denies.

2
One shade the more, one ray the less,
    Had half impaired the nameless grace
Which waves in every raven tress,
    Or softly lightens o'er her face;   10
Where thoughts serenely sweet express
    How pure, how dear their dwelling place.

3
And on that cheek, and o'er that brow,
    So soft, so calm, yet eloquent,
The smiles that win, the tints that glow,   15
    But tell of days in goodness spent,
A mind at peace with all below,
    A heart whose love is innocent!

SAMUEL TAYLOR COLERIDGE   (1772–1834)
Kubla Khan   1798
or a vision in a dream, a fragment

In Xanadu did Kubla Khan°   *13th-century Chinese ruler*
A stately pleasure dome decree:
Where Alph, the sacred river, ran
Through caverns measureless to man
    Down to a sunless sea.   5

So twice five miles of fertile ground
With walls and towers were girdled round:
And there were gardens bright with sinuous rills,°   *winding brooks*
Where blossomed many an incense-bearing tree;
And here were forests ancient as the hills,   10
Enfolding sunny spots of greenery.

But oh! that deep romantic chasm which slanted
Down the green hill athwart a cedarn cover!
A savage place! as holy and enchanted
As e'er beneath a waning moon was haunted   15
By woman wailing for her demon lover!
And from this chasm, with ceaseless turmoil seething,
As if this earth in fast thick pants were breathing,
A mighty fountain momently° was forced: *moment by moment*
Amid whose swift half-intermitted burst   20
Huge fragments vaulted like rebounding hail,
Or chaffy grain beneath the thresher's flail:
And 'mid these dancing rocks at once and ever
It flung up momently the sacred river.
Five miles meandering with a mazy motion   25
Through wood and dale the sacred river ran,
Then reached the caverns measureless to man,
And sank in tumult to a lifeless ocean:
And 'mid this tumult Kubla heard from far
Ancestral voices prophesying war!   30
      The shadow of the dome of pleasure
      Floated midway on the waves;
      Where was heard the mingled measure
      From the fountain and the caves.
It was a miracle of rare device,   35
A sunny pleasure dome with caves of ice!

      A damsel with a dulcimer°   *a stringed musical instrument*
      In a vision once I saw:
      It was an Abyssinian° maid,   *Ethiopian*
      And on her dulcimer she played,   40
      Singing of Mount Abora.
      Could I revive within me
      Her symphony and song,
      To such a deep delight 'twould win me,
That with music loud and long,   45
I would build that dome in air,
That sunny dome! those caves of ice!
And all who heard should see them there,
And all should cry, Beware! Beware!
His flashing eyes, his floating hair!   50
Weave a circle round him thrice,
And close your eyes with holy dread,
For he on honey-dew hath fed,
And drunk the milk of Paradise.

MICHAEL COLLIER (born 1952)

The Problem 1989

Awake in the dark, I counted the planes
that hung by thumbtacks and string from the ceiling.

I brought them out of their shadows with their names:
Hellcat, Spitfire, Messerschmitt and Zero.

They were part of a problem that made death fair. 5

Part promise, part gamble, the problem went like this:
How old must I be before I am old enough for my father to die?

The answer was always twenty-one—
a number impossible to imagine.

It made the world fair enough for sleep. 10

My father didn't die when I was twenty-one.
I didn't blame him. He didn't know that night after night

I had bargained his life away for sleep.

Now to calm my fear of my father's death,
I remember the delicate plastic landing gear 15

of those airplanes, their sharp axles protruding
from the hard gray tires. You had to be careful

with the noxious glue. You had to put one drop
of it on a difficult place and then blow lightly

until the tire began to spin. 20

ROBERT CREELEY (born 1926)

Fathers 1986

Scattered, aslant
faded faces a column
a rise of the packed
peculiar place to a
modest height makes 5
a view of common lots
in winter then, a ground
of battered snow crusted
at the edges under
it all, there under 10
my fathers their
faded women, friends,
the family all echoed,
names trees more tangible
physical place more tangible 15
the air of this place the road

going past to Watertown
or down to my mother's
grave, my father's grave, not
now this resonance of   20
each other one was his, his
survival only, his curious
reticence, his dead state,
his emptiness, his acerbic
edge cuts the hands to   25
hold him, hold on, wants
the ground, *wants* this frozen ground.

ROBERT CREELEY   (born 1926)
Four   1973

This number for me
is comfort, a secure
fact of things. The

table stands on
all fours. The dog   5
walks comfortably,

and two by two
is not an army
but friends who love

one another. Four   10
is a square,
or peaceful circle,

celebrating return,
reunion,
love's triumph.   15

E. E. CUMMINGS   (1894–1963)
All in green went my love riding   1923

All in green went my love riding
on a great horse of gold
into the silver dawn.

four lean hounds crouched low and smiling
the merry deer ran before.   5

Fleeter be they than dappled dreams
the swift sweet deer
the red rare deer.

Four red roebuck at a white water
the cruel bugle sang before.   10

Horn at hip went my love riding
riding the echo down
into the silver dawn.

four lean hounds crouched low and smiling
the level meadows ran before.   15

Softer be they than slippered sleep
the lean lithe deer
the fleet flown deer.

Four fleet does at a gold valley
the famished arrow sang before.   20

Bow at belt went my love riding
riding the mountain down
into the silver dawn.

four lean hounds crouched low and smiling
the sheer peaks ran before.   25

Paler be they than daunting death
the sleek slim deer
the tall tense deer.

Four tall stags at a green mountain
the lucky hunter sang before.   30

All in green went my love riding
on a great horse of gold
into the silver dawn.

four lean hounds crouched low and smiling
my heart fell dead before.   35

E. E. CUMMINGS   (1894–1963)

it is so long since my heart has been with yours   1926

it is so long since my heart has been with yours

shut by our mingling arms through
a darkness where new lights begin and
increase,
since your mind has walked into   5
my kiss as a stranger
into the streets and colors of a town—

that i have perhaps forgotten
how, always (from
these hurrying crudities   10
of blood and flesh) Love
coins His most gradual gesture,

and whittles life to eternity

—after which our separating selves become museums
filled with skilfully stuffed memories   15

E. E. CUMMINGS   (1894–1963)
my sweet old etcetera   1926

my sweet old etcetera
aunt lucy during the recent

war could and what
is more did tell you just
what everybody was fighting   5

for,
my sister

isabel created hundreds
(and
hundreds) of socks not to   10
mention shirts fleaproof earwarmers

etcetera wristers etcetera, my
mother hoped that

i would die etcetera
bravely of course my father used   15
to become hoarse talking about how it was
a privilege and if only he
could meanwhile my

self etcetera lay quietly
in the deep mud et   20

cetera
(dreaming,
et

    cetera, of
Your smile   25
eyes knees and of your Etcetera)

EMILY DICKINSON   (1830–1886)
I like to see it lap the Miles   about 1862

I like to see it lap the Miles
And lick the Valleys up—
And stop to feed itself at Tanks—
And then—prodigious° step   *huge and making us stare in wonder*

Around a Pile of Mountains—   5
And supercilious° peer   *with raised eyebrows*
In Shanties—by the sides of Roads—
And then a Quarry pare

To fit its sides
And crawl between   10
Complaining all the while
In horrid-hooting stanza—
Then chase itself down Hill—

And neigh like Boanerges°—   *a (biblical) loudmouth preacher or orator*
Then—prompter than a Star   15
Stop—docile and omnipotent°   *all-powerful*
At its own stable door.

JOHN DONNE   (1572–1631)

The Flea   1633

Mark° but this flea, and mark in this   *note*
How little that which thou deny'st me is;
Me it sucked first, and now sucks thee,
And in this flea our two bloods mingled be;
Thou know'st that this cannot be said   5
A sin, nor shame, nor loss of maidenhead,°   *virginity*
    Yet this enjoys before it woo,
    And pampered swells with one blood made of two,
    And this, alas, is more than we would do.

Oh stay, three lives in one flea spare,   10
Where we almost, yea more than married are.
This flea is you and I, and this
Our marriage bed, and marriage temple is;
Though parents grudge, and you, we're met
And cloistered in these living walls of jet.°   *black*   15
    Though use° make you apt to kill me,   *although habit*
    Let not to that, self-murder added be,
    And sacrilege, three sins in killing three.

Cruel and sudden, hast thou since
Purpled thy nail in blood of innocence?   20
Wherein could this flea guilty be,
Except in that drop which it sucked from thee?
Yet thou triumph'st, and say'st that thou
Find'st not thyself, nor me, the weaker now;
    'Tis true; then learn how false, fears be;   25
    Just so much honor, when thou yield'st to me,
    Will waste, as this flea's death took life from thee.

JOHN DONNE   (1572–1631)
The Good-Morrow   1633

I wonder, by my troth, what thou and I
Did, till we loved? were we not weaned till then?
But sucked on country pleasures, childishly?
Or snorted° we in the Seven Sleepers'° den?   *snored/they slept 230 years in a cave*
'Twas so; but this,° all pleasures fancies be.   *except for this*   5
If ever any beauty I did see,
Which I desired, and got, 'twas but a dream of thee.

And now good-morrow to our waking souls,
Which watch not one another out of fear;
For love, all love of other sights controls,   10
And makes one little room an everywhere.
Let sea-discoverers to new worlds have gone,
Let maps° to others, worlds on worlds have shown,   *maps of the heavens*
Let us possess our world, each hath one, and is one.

My face in thine eye, thine in mine appears,   15
And true plain hearts do in the faces rest;
Where can we find two better hemispheres,
Without sharp north, without declining west?
Whatever dies was not mixed equally;°   *dies as a result of bodily imbalance*
If our two loves be one, or, thou and I   20
Love so alike that none do slacken, none can die.

JOHN DONNE   (1572–1631)
Holy Sonnet 14   1633

Batter my heart, three-personed God; for You
As yet but knock, breathe, shine, and seek to mend;
That I may rise and stand, o'erthrow me, and bend
Your force to break, blow, burn, and make me new.
I, like an usurped town, to another due,   5
Labor to admit You, but Oh, to no end.
Reason, Your viceroy in me, me should defend,
But is captived, and proves weak or untrue.
Yet dearly I love You, and would be loved fain,°   *gladly*
But am betrothed unto Your enemy: 10
Divorce me, untie or break that knot again,
Take me to You, imprison me, for I,
Except You enthrall me, never shall be free,
Nor ever chaste, except You ravish me.

R I T A   D O V E   (born 1952)

Daystar

1986

She wanted a little room for thinking:
but she saw diapers steaming on the line,
a doll slumped behind the door.
So she lugged a chair behind the garage
to sit out the children's naps.   5

Sometimes there were things to watch—
the pinched armor of a vanished cricket,
a floating maple leaf. Other days
she stared until she was assured
when she closed her eyes   10
she'd see only her own vivid blood.

She had an hour, at best, before Liza appeared
pouting from the top of the stairs.
And just *what* was mother doing
out back with the field mice? Why,   15

building a palace. Later
that night when Thomas rolled over and
lurched into her, she would open her eyes
and think of the place that was hers
for an hour—where   20
she was nothing,
pure nothing, in the middle of the day.

T .   S .   E L I O T   (1888–1965)

The Love Song of J. Alfred Prufrock

1917

S'io credesse che mia risposta fosse
A persona che mai tornasse al mondo,
Questa fiamma staria senza piu scosse.
Ma perciocche giammai di questo fondo
Non torno vivo alcun, s'i'odo il vero,
Senza tema d'infamia ti rispondo.

[From Dante's *Inferno*: "If I thought my answer were given / to anyone who
would ever return to the world, / this flame would stand still without moving
any further. / But since never from this abyss has anyone ever returned alive,
if what I hear is true, / without fear of infamy I answer thee."]

Let us go then, you and I,
When the evening is spread out against the sky
Like a patient etherized upon a table;
Let us go, through certain half-deserted streets,
The muttering retreats   5
Of restless nights in one-night cheap hotels

And sawdust restaurants with oyster-shells:
Streets that follow like a tedious argument
Of insidious intent
To lead you to an overwhelming question . . .
Oh, do not ask, "What is it?"
Let us go and make our visit.

In the room the women come and go
Talking of Michelangelo.

The yellow fog that rubs its back upon the window-panes
The yellow smoke that rubs its muzzle on the window-panes
Licked its tongue into the corners of the evening,
Lingered upon the pools that stand in drains,
Let fall upon its back the soot that falls from chimneys,
Slipped by the terrace, made a sudden leap,
And seeing that it was a soft October night,
Curled once about the house, and fell asleep.

And indeed there will be time
For the yellow smoke that slides along the street,
Rubbing its back upon the window-panes;
There will be time, there will be time
To prepare a face to meet the faces that you meet;
There will be time to murder and create,
And time for all the works and days of hands
That lift and drop a question on your plate;
Time for you and time for me,
And time yet for a hundred indecisions,
And for a hundred visions and revisions,
Before the taking of a toast and tea.

In the room the women come and go
Talking of Michelangelo.

And indeed there will be time
To wonder, "Do I dare?" and, "Do I dare?"
Time to turn back and descend the stair,
With a bald spot in the middle of my hair—
[They will say: "How his hair is growing thin!"]
My morning coat, my collar mounting firmly to the chin,
My necktie rich and modest, but asserted by a simple pin—
[They will say: "But how his arms and legs are thin!"]
Do I dare
Disturb the universe?
In a minute there is time
For decisions and revisions which a minute will reverse.

For I have known them all already, known them all:
Have known the evenings, mornings, afternoons,
I have measured out my life with coffee spoons;
I know the voices dying with a dying fall
Beneath the music from a farther room.
    So how should I presume?

10

15

20

25

30

35

40

45

50

55

And I have known the eyes already, known them all—
The eyes that fix you in a formulated phrase,
And when I am formulated, sprawling on a pin,
When I am pinned and wriggling on the wall,
Then how should I begin
To spit out all the butt-ends of my days and ways?   60
    And how should I presume?

And I have known the arms already, known them all—
Arms that are braceleted and white and bare
[But in the lamplight, downed with light brown hair!]
Is it perfume from a dress   65
That makes me so digress?
Arms that lie along a table, or wrap about a shawl.
    And should I then presume?
    And how should I begin?

          . . . . .

Shall I say, I have gone at dusk through narrow streets   70
And watched the smoke that rises from the pipes
Of lonely men in shirt-sleeves, leaning out of windows? . . .

I should have been a pair of ragged claws
Scuttling across the floors of silent seas.

          . . . . .

And the afternoon, the evening, sleeps so peacefully!   75
Smoothed by long fingers,
Asleep . . . tired . . . or it malingers,
Stretched on the floor, here beside you and me.
Should I, after tea and cakes and ices,
Have the strength to force the moment to its crisis?   80
But though I have wept and fasted, wept and prayed,
Though I have seen my head [grown slightly bald] brought in upon a platter,
I am no prophet—and here's no great matter;
I have seen the moment of my greatness flicker,
And I have seen the eternal Footman hold my coat, and snicker,   85
And in short, I was afraid.

And would it have been worth it, after all,
After the cups, the marmalade, the tea,
Among the porcelain, among some talk of you and me,
Would it have been worth while,   90
To have bitten off the matter with a smile,
To have squeezed the universe into a ball
To roll it toward some overwhelming question,
To say: "I am Lazarus,° come from the dead,   *whom Jesus raised from the dead*
Come back to tell you all, I shall tell you all"—   95
If one, settling a pillow by her head,
    Should say: "That is not what I meant at all.
    That is not it, at all."

And would it have been worth it, after all,
Would it have been worth while,   100

After the sunsets and the dooryards and the sprinkled streets,
After the novels, after the teacups, after the skirts that trail along the floor—
And this, and so much more?—
It is impossible to say just what I mean!
But as if a magic lantern threw the nerves in patterns on a screen: 105
Would it have been worth while
If one, settling a pillow or throwing off a shawl,
And turning toward the window, should say:
        "That is not it at all,
        That is not what I meant, at all."   110

                        . . . . .

No! I am not Prince Hamlet, nor was meant to be;
Am an attendant lord, one that will do
To swell a progress, start a scene or two,
Advise the prince; no doubt, an easy tool,
Deferential, glad to be of use,   115
Politic, cautious, and meticulous;
Full of high sentence, but a bit obtuse;
At times, indeed, almost ridiculous—
Almost, at times, the Fool.

I grow old . . . I grow old . . .   120
I shall wear the bottoms of my trousers rolled.

Shall I part my hair behind? Do I dare to eat a peach?
I shall wear white flannel trousers, and walk upon the beach.
I have heard the mermaids singing, each to each.

I do not think that they will sing to me.   125

I have seen them riding seaward on the waves
Combing the white hair of the waves blown back
When the wind blows the water white and black.

We have lingered in the chambers of the sea
By sea-girls wreathed with seaweed red and brown   130
Till human voices wake us, and we drown.

LAWRENCE FERLINGHETTI   (born 1919)
Constantly risking absurdity   1958

            Constantly risking absurdity
                            and death
                whenever he performs
                        above the heads
                            of his audience   5
        the poet like an acrobat
                climbs on rime
                        to a high wire of his own making
and balancing on eyebeams

                        above a sea of faces   10
            paces his way
                              to the other side of day
        performing *entrechats*°   *ballet leaps*
                        and sleight-of-foot tricks
and other high theatrics   15
                and all without mistaking
            any thing
                    for what it may not be
        For he's the super realist
                        who must perforce perceive   20
            taut truth
                        before the taking of each stance or step
        in his supposed advance
                        toward that still higher perch
where Beauty stands and waits   25
                        with gravity
                    to start her death-defying leap
        And he
                a little charleychaplin man
                              who may or may not catch   30
                her fair eternal form
                        spreadeagled in the empty air
            of existence

CAROLYN FORCHÉ   (born 1950)

Selective Service   1977

We rise from the snow where we've
lain on our backs and flown like children,
from the imprint of perfect wings and cold gowns,
and we stagger together wine-breathed into town
where our people are building   5
their armies again, short years after
body bags, after burnings. There is a man
I've come to love after thirty, and we have
our rituals of coffee, of airports, regret.
After love we smoke and sleep   10
with magazines, two shot glasses
and the black and white collapse of hours.
In what time do we live that it is too late
to have children? In what place
that we consider the various ways to leave?   15
There is no list long enough
for a selective service card shriveling
under a match, the prison that comes of it,
a flag in the wind eaten from its pole
and boys sent back in trash bags.   20

We'll tell you. You were at that time
learning fractions. We'll tell you
about fractions. Half of us are dead or quiet
or lost. Let them speak for themselves.
We lie down in the fields and leave behind   25
the corpses of angels.

TESS GALLAGHER   (born 1943)

The Hug   1987

A woman is reading a poem on the street
and another woman stops to listen. We stop too,
with our arms around each other. The poem
is being read and listened to out here
in the open. Behind us   5
no one is entering or leaving the houses.

Suddenly a hug comes over me and I'm
giving it to you, like a variable star shooting light
off to make itself comfortable, then
subsiding. I finish but keep on holding   10
you. A man walks up to us and we know he hasn't
come out of nowhere, but if he could, he
would have. He looks homeless because of how
he needs. "Can I have one of those?" he asks you,
and I feel you nod. I'm surprised,   15
surprised you don't tell him how
it is—that I'm yours, only
yours, etc., exclusive as a nose to
its face. Love—that's what we're talking about, love
that nabs you with "for me   20
only" and holds on.

So I walk over to him and put my
arms around him and try to
hug him like I mean it. He's got an overcoat on
so thick I can't feel   25
him past it. I'm starting the hug
and thinking, "How big a hug is this supposed to be?
How long shall I hold this hug?" Already
we could be eternal, his arms falling over my
shoulders, my hands not   30
meeting behind his back, he is so big!

I put my head into his chest and snuggle
in. I lean into him. I lean my blood and my wishes
into him. He stands for it. This is his
and he's starting to give it back so well I know he's   35
getting it. This hug. So truly, so tenderly

we stop having arms and I don't know if
my lover has walked away or what, or
if the woman is still reading the poem, or the houses—
what about them?—the houses.   40

Clearly, a little permission is a dangerous thing.
But when you hug someone you want it
to be a masterpiece of connection, the way the button
on his coat will leave the imprint of
a planet in my cheek   45
when I walk away. When I try to find some place
to go back to.

ALLEN GINSBERG   (born 1926)

A Supermarket in California   1956

What thoughts I have of you tonight, Walt Whitman, for I walked down the sidestreets under the trees with a headache self-conscious looking at the full moon.

In my hungry fatigue, and shopping for images, I went into the neon fruit supermarket, dreaming of your enumerations!°   *cataloging of data*

partial shadows

What peaches and what penumbras!° Whole families shopping at night! Aisles full of husbands! Wives in the avocados, babies in the tomatoes—and you, Garcia Lorca,° what were you doing down by the watermelons?   *Spanish poet*

I saw you, Walt Whitman, childless, lonely old grubber, poking among the meats in the refrigerator and eyeing the grocery boys.

I heard you asking questions of each: Who killed the pork chops? What price bananas? Are you my Angel?   5

I wandered in and out of the brilliant stacks of cans following you, and followed in my imagination by the store detective.

We strode down the open corridors together in our solitary fancy tasting artichokes, possessing every frozen delicacy, and never passing the cashier.

Where are we going, Walt Whitman? The doors close in an hour. Which way does your beard point tonight?

(I touch your book and dream of our odyssey in the supermarket and feel absurd.)

Will we walk all night through solitary streets? The trees add shade to shade, lights out in the houses, we'll both be lonely.   10

Will we stroll dreaming of the lost America of love past blue automobiles in driveways, home to our silent cottage?

Ah, dear father, graybeard, lonely old courage-teacher,
what America did you have when Charon° quit poling his
ferry and you got out on a smoking bank and stood watching the boat disappear on the black waters of Lethe?°

*mythical ferryman conveying
souls across River Styx to Hades*

*mythical underworld river of
forgetfulness*

NIKKI GIOVANNI   (born 1943)
Nikki-Rosa   1968

childhood remembrances are always a drag
if you're Black
you always remember things like living in Woodlawn
with no inside toilet
and if you become famous or something   5
they never talk about how happy you were to have your mother
all to yourself and
how good the water felt when you got your bath from one of those
big tubs that folk in chicago barbecue in
and somehow when you talk about home   10
it never gets across how much you
understood their feelings
as the whole family attended meetings about Hollydale
and even though you remember
your biographers never understand   15
your father's pain as he sells his stock
and another dream goes
and though you're poor it isn't poverty that
concerns you
and though they fought a lot   20
it isn't your father's drinking that makes any difference
but only that everybody is together and you
and your sister have happy birthdays and very good christmasses
and I really hope no white person ever has cause to write about me
because they never understand Black love is Black wealth and they'll   25
probably talk about my hard childhood and never understand that
all the while I was quite happy

LOUISE GLÜCK   (born 1943)
The School Children   1975

The children go forward with their little satchels.
And all morning the mothers have labored
to gather the late apples, red and gold,
like words of another language.

And on the other shore   5
are those who wait behind great desks
to receive these offerings.

How orderly they are—the nails
on which the children hang
their overcoats of blue or yellow wool.   10

And the teachers shall instruct them in silence
and the mothers shall scour the orchards for a way out,
drawing to themselves the gray limbs of the fruit trees
bearing so little ammunition.

ROBERT GRAVES   (born 1895)

The Frog and the Golden Ball   1965

She let her golden ball fall down the well
        And begged a cold frog to retrieve it;
For which she kissed his ugly, gaping mouth—
        Indeed, he could scarce believe it.

And seeing him transformed to his princely shape,   5
        Who had been by hags enchanted,
She knew she could never love another man
        Nor by any fate be daunted.

But what would her royal father and mother say?
        They had promised her in marriage   10
To a cousin whose wide kingdom marched with theirs,
        Who rode in a jeweled carriage.

"Our plight, dear heart, would appear past human hope
        To all except you and me: to all
Who have never swum as a frog in a dark well   15
        Or have lost a golden ball."

"What then shall we do now?" she asked her lover.
        He kissed her again, and said:
"Is magic of love less powerful at your Court
        Than at this green well-head?"   20

DONALD HALL   (born 1928)

My Son, My Executioner   1955

My son, my executioner,
        I take you in my arms,
Quiet and small and just astir,
        And whom my body warms.

Sweet death, small son, our instrument   5
    Of immortality,
Your cries and hungers document
    Our bodily decay.

We twenty-five and twenty-two,
    Who seemed to live forever,   10
Observe enduring life in you
    And start to die together.

DANIEL HALPERN   (born 1945)

How to Eat Alone   1975

While it's still light out
set the table for one:
a red linen tablecloth,
one white plate, a bowl
for the salad   5
and the proper silverware.
Take out a three-pound leg of lamb,
rub it with salt, pepper and cumin,
then push in two cloves
of garlic splinters.   10
Place it in a 325-degree oven
and set the timer for an hour.
Put freshly cut vegetables
into a pot with some herbs
and the crudest olive oil   15
you can find.
Heat on a low flame.
Clean the salad.
Be sure the dressing is made
with fresh dill, mustard   20
and the juice of hard lemons.
Open a bottle of good late harvest zinfandel
and let it breathe on the table.
Pour yourself a glass
of cold California chardonnay   25
and go to your study and read.
As the story unfolds
you will smell the lamb
and the vegetables.
This is the best part of the evening: 30
the food cooking, the armchair,
the book and bright flavor
of the chilled wine.
When the timer goes off
toss the salad   35

and prepare the vegetables
and the lamb. Bring them out
to the table. Light the candles
and pour the red wine
into your glass.   40
Before you begin to eat,
raise your glass in honor
of yourself.
The company is the best you'll ever have.

THOMAS HARDY   (1840–1928)

Hap   1866

If but some vengeful god would call to me
From up the sky, and laugh: "Thou suffering thing,
Know that thy sorrow is my ecstasy,
That thy love's loss is my hate's profiting!"

Then would I bear it, clench myself, and die,   5
Steeled by the sense of ire° unmerited;   *anger*
Half-eased in that a Powerfuller than I
Had willed and meted° me the tears I shed.   *allotted*

But not so. How arrives it joy lies slain,
And why unblooms the best hope ever sown?   10
—Crass Casualty° obstructs the sun and rain,   *chance, happenstance*
And dicing Time for gladness casts a moan. . . .
These purblind° Doomsters had as readily strown   *partly blind*
Blisses about my pilgrimage as pain.

THOMAS HARDY   (1840–1928)

In Time of "The Breaking of Nations"   1915

Only a man harrowing clods°   *breaking up lumps (thrown up*
    In a slow silent walk   *by the plow)*
With an old horse that stumbles and nods
    Half asleep as they stalk.

Only thin smoke without flame   5
    From the heaps of couch-grass;°   *creeping grassy weed*
Yet this will go onward the same
    Though dynasties pass.

Yonder a maid and her wight°   *young male*
    Come whispering by: 10
War's annals will cloud into night
    Ere° their story die.   *before*

SEAMUS HEANEY   (born 1939)

The Forge   1969

All I know is a door into the dark.
Outside, old axles and iron hoops rusting;
Inside, the hammered anvil's short-pitched ring,
The unpredictable fantail of sparks
Or hiss when a new shoe toughens in water.   5
The anvil must be somewhere in the center.
Horned as a unicorn, at one end square,
Set there immovable: an altar
Where he expends himself in shape and music.
Sometimes, leather-aproned, hairs in his nose,   10
He leans out on the jamb, recalls a clatter
Of hoofs where traffic is flashing in rows;
Then grunts and goes in, with a slam and flick
To beat real iron out, to work the bellows.

GEORGE HERBERT   (1593–1633)

The Collar   1633

I struck the board° and cried, "No more;   *table*
    I will abroad!
What? shall I ever sigh and pine?
My lines and life are free, free as the road,
    Loose as the wind, as large as store.°   *abundance*   5
        Shall I be still in suit?°   *begging favors*
    Have I no harvest but a thorn
    To let me blood, and not restore
What I have lost with cordial° fruit?   *life-giving*
        Sure there was wine   10
Before my sighs did dry it; there was corn
Before my tears did drown it.
Is the year only lost to me?
    Have I no bays° to crown it,   *laurel wreaths symbolizing honor*
No flowers, no garlands gay? All blasted?   15
        All wasted?
    Not so, my heart; but there is fruit,
        And thou hast hands.
    Recover all thy sigh-blown age
On double pleasures: leave thy cold dispute   20
Of what is fit and not. Forsake thy cage,
        Thy rope of sands,
Which petty thoughts have made, and made to thee
    Good cable, to enforce and draw,
        And be thy law,   25

While thou didst wink and wouldst not see.
        Away! take heed;
        I will abroad.
Call in thy death's-head° there; tie up thy fears.   *skull*
        He that forbears   30
      To suit and serve his need,
        Deserves his load."
But as I raved and grew more fierce and wild
        At every word,
Methought I heard one calling, *Child!*   35
      And I replied, *My Lord.*

GEORGE HERBERT   (1593–1633)

Easter Wings   1633

Lord, who createdst man in wealth and store,°   *abundance*
    Though foolishly he lost the same,
        Decaying more and more
            Till he became
              Most poor.   5
              With thee
            O let me rise
        As larks, harmoniously,
      And sing this day thy victories:
Then shall the fall further the flight in me.   10

    My tender age in sorrow did begin:
    And still with sicknesses and shame
        Thou didst so punish sin,
            That I became
              Most thin.   15
              With thee
            Let me combine,
      And feel this day thy victory;
    For, if I imp° my wing on thine,   *graft*
Affliction shall advance the flight in me.   20

GERARD MANLEY HOPKINS   (1844–1889)

Spring and Fall   1880

to a young child

Márgarét, áre you gríeving
Over Goldengrove unleaving?°   *losing its leaves*
Leáves, líke the things of man, you
With your fresh thoughts care for, can you?

Áh! ás the heart grows older
It will come to such sights colder
By and by, nor spare a sigh
Though worlds of wanwood leafmeal lie;°   *leaves of pale trees lie piecemeal (scattered)*
And yet you *will* weep and know why.
Now no matter, child, the name: 10
Sórrow's spríngs áre the same.
Nor mouth had, no nor mind, expressed
What heart heard of, ghost° guessed: *soul*
It ís the blight man was born for,
It is Margaret you mourn for.   15

A. E. HOUSMAN   (1859–1936)

To an Athlete Dying Young   1896

The time you won your town the race
We chaired you through the market-place;
Man and boy stood cheering by,
And home we brought you shoulder-high.

Today, the road all runners come,   5
Shoulder-high we bring you home,
And set you at your threshold down,
Townsman of a stiller town.

Smart lad, to slip betimes away
From fields where glory does not stay   10
And early though the laurel grows
It withers quicker than the rose.

Eyes the shady night has shut
Cannot see the record cut,
And silence sounds no worse than cheers   15
After earth has stopped the ears:

Now you will not swell the rout
Of lads that wore their honors out,
Runners whom renown outran
And the name died before the man.   20

So set, before its echoes fade,
The fleet foot on the sill of shade,
And hold to the low lintel° up   *low beam*
The still-defended challenge-cup.

And round that early-laureled head   25
Will flock to gaze the strengthless dead,
And find unwithered on its curls
The garland briefer than a girl's.

LANGSTON HUGHES   (1902–1967)

End   1959

There are
No clocks on the wall,
And no time,
No shadows that move
From dawn to dusk   5
Across the floor.

There is neither light
Nor dark
Outside the door.

There is no door!   10

TED HUGHES   (born 1930)

Hawk Roosting   1959

I sit in the top of the wood, my eyes closed.
Inaction, no falsifying dream
Between my hooked head and hooked feet:
Or in sleep rehearse perfect kills and eat.

The convenience of the high trees!   5
The air's buoyancy and the sun's ray
Are of advantage to me;
And the earth's face upward for my inspection.

My feet are locked upon the rough bark.
It took the whole of Creation   10
To produce my foot, my each feather:
Now I hold Creation in my foot

Or fly up, and revolve it all slowly—
I kill where I please because it is all mine.

There is no sophistry° in my body: *plausible but fallacious argument*   15
My manners are tearing off heads—

The allotment of death.
For the one path of my flight is direct
Through the bones of the living.
No arguments assert my right: 20

The sun is behind me.
Nothing has changed since I began.
My eye has permitted no change.
I am going to keep things like this.

VICENTE HUIDOBRO   (1892–1948)

Ars Poetica

TRANSLATED BY DAVID M. GUSS

Let poetry be like a key
Opening a thousand doors.
A leaf falls; something flies by;
Let all the eye sees be created
And the soul of the listener tremble.   5

Invent new worlds and watch your word;
The adjective, when it doesn't give life, kills it.

We are in the age of nerves.
The muscle hangs,
Like a memory, in museums;   10
But we are not the weaker for it:
True vigor
Resides in the head.

Oh Poets, why sing of roses!
Let them flower in your poems;   15

For us alone
Do all things live beneath the Sun.

The poet is a little God.

BEN JONSON   (1572–1637)

Song: To Celia   1616

Drink to me only with thine eyes,
And I will pledge with mine;
Or leave a kiss but in the cup,
And I'll not look for wine.
The thirst that from the soul doth rise,   5
Doth ask a drink divine:
But might I of Jove's° nectar sup,   *Roman name of Zeus*
I would not change for thine.

I sent thee late a rosy wreath,
Not so much honoring thee,   10
As giving it a hope, that there
It could not withered be.
But thou thereon did'st only breathe,
And sent'st it back to me;
Since when it grows and smells, I swear,   15
Not of itself, but thee.

JUNE JORDAN (born 1936)

Lullaby

1973

as suddenly as love

the evening burns a low
red
line occasional with golden glass
across the sky   5

i celebrate the color of the heat
you fill me with
the bloodbeat
you instill me with

as suddenly as love   10

DONALD JUSTICE (born 1925)

Time and the Weather

1967

Time and the weather wear away
The houses that our fathers built.
Their ghostly furniture remains—
All the sad sofas we have stained
With tears of boredom and of guilt,   5

The fraying mottoes, the stopped clocks . . .
And still sometimes these tired shapes
Haunt the damp parlors of the heart.
What Sunday prisons they recall!
And what miraculous escapes!   10

JOHN KEATS (1795–1821)

La Belle Dame sans Merci

1819

O what can ail thee, Knight at arms,
    Alone and palely loitering?
The sedge° has withered from the Lake   *grassy plants*
    And no birds sing!

O what can ail thee, Knight at arms,   5
    So haggard, and so woebegone?
The squirrel's granary is full
    And the harvest's done.

I see a lily on thy brow
    With anguish moist and fever dew,   10
And on thy cheeks a fading rose
    Fast withereth too.

"I met a Lady in the Meads,°   *meadows*
    Full beautiful, a faery's child,
Her hair was long, her foot was light   15
    And her eyes were wild.

"I made a Garland for her head,
    And bracelets too, and fragrant Zone;°   *belt of sweet-smelling flowers*
She looked at me as she did love
    And made sweet moan.   20

"I set her on my pacing steed
    And nothing else saw all day long,
For sidelong would she bend and sing
    A faery's song.

"She found me roots of relish sweet,   25
    And honey wild, and manna° dew,   *a miraculous food*
And sure in language strange she said
    'I love thee true.'

"She took me to her elfin grot°   *cave*
    And there she wept and sighed full sore,   30
And there I shut her wild wild eyes
    With kisses four.

"And there she lullèd me asleep,
    And there I dreamed, Ah Woe betide!
The latest dream I ever dreamt   35
    On the cold hill side.

"I saw pale Kings, and Princes too,
    Pale warriors, death-pale were they all;
They cried, 'La belle dame sans merci°   *lovely lady without pity*
    Thee hath in thrall!'°   *in bondage*   40

"I saw their starved lips in the gloom°   *in the twilight*
    With horrid warning gapèd wide,
And I awoke, and found me here
    On the cold hill's side.

"And this is why I sojourn here,   45
    Alone and palely loitering;
Though the sedge is withered from the Lake
    And no birds sing."

JOHN KEATS   (1795–1821)

Ode to a Nightingale   1820

1
My heart aches, and a drowsy numbness pains
    My sense, as though of hemlock° I had drunk,   *poison*
Or emptied some dull opiate to the drains

One minute past, and Lethe-wards° had sunk: *toward Lethe, mythical underworld*
'Tis not through envy of thy happy lot,   *river of forgetfulness*   5
    But being too happy in thine happiness—
        That thou, light-wingèd Dryad° of the trees,   *wood nymph*
            In some melodious plot
Of beechen green, and shadows numberless,
        Singest of summer in full-throated ease.   10

2
O, for a draught of vintage!° that hath been   *drink of wine*
    Cooled a long age in the deep-delvèd earth,
Tasting of Flora° and the country green,   *Roman goddess of flowers*
    Dance, and Provençal song,° and sunburnt mirth!   *songs of Provence, in southern France*
O for a beaker full of the warm South,   15
    Full of the true, the blushful Hippocrene,°   *fountain of the Muses in Greece*
        With beaded bubbles winking at the brim,
            And purple-stainèd mouth;
    That I might drink, and leave the world unseen,
        And with thee fade away into the forest dim: 20

3
Fade far away, dissolve, and quite forget
    What thou among the leaves hast never known,
The weariness, the fever, and the fret
    Here, where men sit and hear each other groan;
Where palsy shakes a few, sad, last gray hairs,   25
    Where youth grows pale, and specter-thin, and dies,
        Where but to think is to be full of sorrow
            And leaden-eyed despairs,
    Where Beauty cannot keep her lustrous eyes,
        Or new Love pine at them beyond tomorrow.   30

4
Away! away! for I will fly to thee,
    Not charioted by Bacchus and his pards,°   *god of wine and his leopards*
But on the viewless° wings of Poesy,   *invisible*
    Though the dull brain perplexes and retards:
Already with thee! tender is the night,   35
    And haply the Queen-Moon is on her throne,
        Clustered around by all her starry Fays;°   *fairies*
            But here there is no light,
    Save what from heaven is with the breezes blown
        Through verdurous glooms and winding mossy ways.   40

5
I cannot see what flowers are at my feet,
    Nor what soft incense hangs upon the boughs,
But, in embalmèd° darkness, guess each sweet   *perfumed*
    Wherewith the seasonable month endows
The grass, the thicket, and the fruit tree wild;   45
    White hawthorn, and the pastoral eglantine:°   *wood roses*
        Fast fading violets covered up in leaves;

And mid-May's eldest child,
   The coming musk-rose, full of dewy wine,
      The murmurous haunt of flies on summer eves.   50

6
Darkling° I listen; and for many a time   *in darkness*
   I have been half in love with easeful Death,
Called him soft names in many a musèd rhyme,
   To take into the air my quiet breath;
Now more than ever seems it rich to die,   55
   To cease upon the midnight with no pain,
      While thou art pouring forth thy soul abroad
         In such an ecstasy!
   Still wouldst thou sing, and I have ears in vain—
      To thy high requiem become a sod.   60

7
Thou wast not born for death, immortal Bird!
   No hungry generations tread thee down;
The voice I hear this passing night was heard
   In ancient days by emperor and clown:
Perhaps the selfsame song that found a path   65
   Through the sad heart of Ruth,° when, sick for home,   *of the biblical Book of Ruth*
      She stood in tears amid the alien corn;
         The same that ofttimes hath
   Charmed magic casements, opening on the foam
      Of perilous seas, in faery lands forlorn.   70

8
Forlorn! the very word is like a bell
   To toll me back from thee to my sole self!
Adieu! the fancy cannot cheat so well
   As she is famed to do, deceiving elf.
Adieu! adieu! thy plaintive anthem fades   75
   Past the near meadows, over the still stream,
      Up the hill side; and now 'tis buried deep
         In the next valley-glades:
   Was it a vision, or a waking dream?
      Fled is that music:—Do I wake or sleep?   80

JOHN KEATS   (1795–1821)

When I Have Fears   1818

When I have fears that I may cease to be
   Before my pen has gleaned my teeming brain,
Before high-pilèd books, in charact'ry,°   *written symbols*
   Hold like rich garners the full-ripened grain;
When I behold, upon the night's starred face,   5
   Huge cloudy symbols of a high romance,

And think that I may never live to trace
      Their shadows, with the magic hand of chance;
And when I feel, fair creature of an hour,
      That I shall never look upon thee more,   10
Never have relish in the faery° power   *magical*
      Of unreflecting love!—then on the shore
Of the wide world I stand alone, and think
Till Love and Fame to nothingness do sink.

GALWAY KINNELL   (born 1927)

Blackberry Eating   1980

I love to go out in late September
among the fat, overripe, icy, black blackberries
to eat blackberries for breakfast,
the stalks very prickly, a penalty
they earn for knowing the black art   5
of blackberry-making; and as I stand among them
lifting the stalks to my mouth, the ripest berries
fall almost unbidden to my tongue,
as words sometimes do, certain peculiar words
like *strengths* or *squinched,*   10
many-lettered, one-syllabled lumps,
which I squeeze, squinch open, and splurge well
in the silent, startled, icy, black language
of blackberry-eating in late September.

GALWAY KINNELL   (born 1927)

For William Carlos Williams   1960

When you came and you talked and you read with your
Private zest from the varicose marble
Of the podium, the lovers of literature
Paid you the tribute of their almost total
Inattention, although someone when you spoke of a pig   5
Did squirm, and it is only fair to report another gig-

gled. But you didn't even care. You seemed
Above remarking we were not your friends.
You hung around inside the rimmed
Circles of your heavy glasses and smiled and   10
So passed a lonely evening. In an hour
Of talking your honesty built you a tower.

When it was over and you sat down and the chair-
man got up and smiled and congratulated
You and shook your hand, I watched a professor   15
In neat bow tie and enormous tweeds, who patted

A faint praise of the sufficiently damned,
Drained spittle from his pipe, then scrammed.

ETHRIDGE KNIGHT   (born 1933)

He Sees through Stone   1968

He sees through stone
he has the secret
eyes this old black one
who under prison skies
sits pressed by the sun   5
against the western wall
his pipe between purple gums

the years fall
like overripe plums
bursting red flesh   10
on the dark earth

his time is not my time
but I have known him
in a time gone

he led me trembling cold   15
into the dark forest
taught me the secret rites
to take a woman
to be true to my brothers
to make my spear drink   20
the blood
of my enemies

now black cats circle him
flash white teeth
snarl at the air   25
mashing green grass beneath
shining muscles
ears peeling his words
he smiles
he knows   30
the hunt the enemy
he has the secret eyes
he sees through stone

MAXINE KUMIN   (born 1925)

The Retrieval System   1975

It begins with my dog, now dead, who all his long life
carried about in his head the brown eyes of my father,

keen, loving, accepting, sorrowful, whatever;
they were Daddy's all right, handed on, except
for their phosphorescent gleam tunneling the night   5
which I have to concede was a separate gift.

Uncannily when I'm alone these features
come up to link my lost people
with the patient domestic beasts of my life. For example,
the wethered° goat who runs free in pasture and stable   *gelded*   10
with his flecked, agate eyes and his minus-sign pupils
blats in the tiny voice of my former piano teacher

whose bones beat time in my dreams and whose terrible breath
soured *Country Gardens, Humoresque,* and unplayable Bach.
My elderly aunts, wearing the heads of willful   15
intelligent ponies, stand at the fence begging apples.
The sister who died at three has my cat's faint chin,
my cat's inscrutable squint, and cried catlike in pain.

I remember the funeral. *The Lord is my shepherd,*
we said. I don't want to brood. Fact: it is people who fade,   20
it is animals that retrieve them. A boy
I loved once keeps coming back as my yearling colt,
cocksure at the gallop, racing his shadow
for the hell of it. He runs merely to be.
A boy who was lost in the war thirty years ago   25
and buried at sea.

Here, it's forty degrees and raining. The weatherman
who looks like my resident owl, the one who goes out and in
by the open haymow, appears on the TV screen.
With his heart-shaped face, he is also my late dentist's double,   30
donnish,° bifocaled, kind. Going a little gray,   *bookish*
advising this wisdom tooth will have to come out someday,
meanwhile filling it as a favor. Another save.
It outlasted him. The forecast is nothing but trouble.
It will snow fiercely enough to fill all these open graves.   35

PHILIP LARKIN   (1922–1985)

Poetry of Departures   1955

Sometimes you hear, fifth-hand,
As epitaph:
He chucked up everything
And just cleared off,
And always the voice will sound   5
Certain you approve
This audacious,° purifying   *bold*
Elemental move.

And they are right, I think.
We all hate home   10
And having to be there:
I detest my room,
Its specially-chosen junk,
The good books, the good bed,
And my life, in perfect order: 15
So to hear it said

He walked out on the whole crowd
Leaves me flushed and stirred,
Like *Then she undid her dress*
Or *Take that you bastard;*   20
Surely I can, if he did?
And that helps me stay
Sober and industrious.
But I'd go today,

Yes, swagger the nut-strewn roads,   25
Crouch in the fo'c'sle°   section of a ship
Stubbly with goodness, if
It weren't so artificial,
Such a deliberate step backwards
To create an object: 30
Books; china; a life
Reprehensibly perfect.

D. H. LAWRENCE   (1885–1930)

Snake   1923

A snake came to my water-trough
On a hot, hot day, and I in pajamas for the heat,
To drink there.

In the deep, strange-scented shade of the great dark carob-tree°   *tree common in Italy*
I came down the steps with my pitcher   5
And must wait, must stand and wait, for there he was at the trough before me.

He reached down from a fissure in the earth-wall in the gloom
And trailed his yellow-brown slackness soft-bellied down, over the edge of the stone
    trough

And rested his throat upon the stone bottom,
And where the water had dripped from the tap, in a small clearness,   10
He sipped with his straight mouth,
Softly drank through his straight gums, into his slack long body,
Silently.

Someone was before me at my water-trough,
And I, like a second-comer, waiting.   15

He lifted his head from his drinking, as cattle do,
And looked at me vaguely, as drinking cattle do,
And flickered his two-forked tongue from his lips, and mused a moment,
And stooped and drank a little more,
Being earth-brown, earth-golden from the burning bowels of the earth   20
On the day of Sicilian July, with Etna° smoking.   *volcano in Italy*

The voice of my education said to me
He must be killed,
For in Sicily the black, black snakes are innocent, the gold are venomous.

And voices in me said, If you were a man   25
You would take a stick and break him now, and finish him off.

But must I confess how I liked him,
How glad I was he had come like a guest in quiet, to drink at my water-trough

And depart peaceful, pacified, and thankless,
Into the burning bowels of this earth.   30

Was it cowardice, that I dared not kill him?
Was it perversity, that I longed to talk to him?
Was it humility, to feel so honored?
I felt so honored.

And yet those voices: 35
If you were not afraid, you would kill him!

And truly I was afraid, I was most afraid,
But even so, honored still more
That he should seek my hospitality
From out the dark door of the secret earth.   40

He drank enough
And lifted his head, dreamily, as one who has drunken,
And flickered his tongue like a forked night on the air, so black,

Seeming to lick his lips,
And looked around like a god, unseeing, into the air,   45
And slowly turned his head,
And slowly, very slowly, as if thrice adream,
Proceeded to draw his slow length curving round
And climb again the broken bank of my wall-face.

And as he put his head into that dreadful hole,   50
And as he slowly drew up, snake-easing his shoulders, and entered farther,
A sort of horror, a sort of protest against his withdrawing into that horrid black hole,
Deliberately going into the blackness, and slowly drawing himself after,
Overcame me now his back was turned.

I looked round, I put down my pitcher,   55
I picked up a clumsy log
And threw it at the water-trough with a clatter.

I think it did not hit him,
But suddenly that part of him that was left behind convulsed in undignified haste,
Writhed like lightning, and was gone   60

Into the black hole, the earth-lipped fissure in the wall-front,
At which, in the intense still noon, I stared with fascination.

And immediately I regretted it.
I thought how paltry, how vulgar, what a mean act!
I despised myself and the voices of my accursed human education.   65

And I thought of the albatross°   *the bird shot by Coleridge's*
And I wished he would come back, my snake.   *Ancient Mariner*

For he seemed to me again like a king,   .
Like a king in exile, uncrowned in the underworld,
Now due to be crowned again.   70

And so, I missed my chance with one of the lords
Of life.
And I have something to expiate;°   *atone for*
A pettiness.

DENISE LEVERTOV   (born 1923)

The Ache of Marriage   1964

The ache of marriage:

thigh and tongue, beloved,
are heavy with it,
it throbs in the teeth

We look for communion   5
and are turned away, beloved,
each and each

It is leviathan° and we   *monstrous sea creature that swallowed the prophet Jonah*
in its belly
looking for joy, some joy   10
not to be known outside it

two by two in the ark of
the ache of it.

AUDRE LORDE   (born 1934)

Sister Outsider   1978

We were born in a poor time
never touching
each other's hunger
never
sharing our crusts   5
in fear
the bread became enemy.

Now we raise our children
to respect themselves
as well as each other.   10

Now you have made loneliness
holy and useful
and no longer needed
now
your light shines very brightly   15
but I want you
to know
your darkness also
rich
and beyond fear.   20

ROBERT LOWELL   (1917–1977)

Skunk Hour   1959
(for Elizabeth Bishop)

Nautilus Island's° hermit   *in Castine, Maine*
heiress still lives through winter in her Spartan cottage;
her sheep still graze above the sea.
Her son's a bishop. Her farmer
is first selectman° in our village;   *elected official*   5
she's in her dotage.°   *second childhood*

Thirsting for
the hierarchic privacy
of Queen Victoria's century,
she buys up all
the eyesores facing her shore,   10
and lets them fall.

The season's ill—
we've lost our summer millionaire,
who seemed to leap from an L. L. Bean°   *sporting goods company*   15
catalogue. His nine-knot yawl°   *boat*
was auctioned off to lobstermen.
A red fox stain covers Blue Hill.

And now our fairy
decorator brightens his shop for fall;   20
his fishnet's filled with orange cork,
orange, his cobbler's bench and awl;
there is no money in his work,
he'd rather marry.

One dark night,   25
my Tudor Ford climbed the hill's skull;
I watched for love-cars. Lights turned down,

they lay together, hull to hull,
where the graveyard shelves on the town. . . .
My mind's not right.   30

A car radio bleats,
"Love, O careless Love. . . ." I hear
my ill-spirit sob in each blood cell,
as if my hand were at its throat. . . .
I myself am hell;   35
nobody's here—

only skunks, that search
in the moonlight for a bite to eat.
They march on their soles up Main Street:
white stripes, moonstruck eyes' red fire   40
under the chalk-dry and spar spire°   *pole used as a mast*
of the Trinitarian Church.

I stand on top
of our back steps and breathe the rich air—
a mother skunk with her column of kittens swills the garbage pail.   45
She jabs her wedge-head in a cup
of sour cream, drops her ostrich tail,
and will not scare.

MARY MACKEY   (born 1945)

When I Was a Child I Played with the Boys   1974

when I was a child
I played with the boys
and (because I was only a girl)
they made me
be   5
the Indians

my name was Fox Woman
and they hunted me
like dogs

my name was   10
White Bird
and I flew to escape them

my name was
Last Star
the last   15
of my people

my name was
Sunset
for they caught me
and burned me   20

my name was
Won't Talk
for I never
betrayed us

time after time   25
the boys shot me down
and I came back
Red Witch
wild and chanting

came back   30
Ghost Dance
came back
Can't Forget
and Crazy-With-Grief

I know where they went   35
those boys with their guns
they're still hunting Indians

look
you can see
their names are   40
Spills Blood
and Kills-Without-Mercy

CHRISTOPHER MARLOWE   (1564–1593)

The Passionate Shepherd to His Love   1600

Come live with me and be my love,
And we will all the pleasures prove°   *try*
That valleys, groves, hills, and fields,
Woods, or steepy mountain yields.

And we will sit upon the rocks,   5
Seeing the shepherds feed their flocks,
By shallow rivers to whose falls
Melodious birds sing madrigals.°   *harmonic songs*

And I will make thee beds of roses
And a thousand fragrant posies,   10
A cap of flowers, and a kirtle°   *skirt*
Embroidered all with leaves of myrtle;

A gown made of the finest wool
Which from our pretty lambs we pull;
Fair lined slippers for the cold,   15
With buckles of the purest gold;

A belt of straw and ivy buds,
With coral clasps and amber studs:

And if these pleasures may thee move,
Come live with me, and be my love.   20

The shepherds' swains° shall dance and sing   *lovers*
For thy delight each May morning:
If these delights thy mind may move,
Then live with me and be my love.

ANDREW MARVELL   (1621–1678)

The Definition of Love   before 1678

My Love is of a birth as rare
As 'tis, for object, strange and high;
It was begotten by Despair
Upon Impossibility.

Magnanimous Despair alone   5
Could show me so divine a thing,
Where feeble Hope could ne'er have flown
But vainly flapped its tinsel wing.

And yet I quickly might arrive
Where my extended soul is fixed;   10
But Fate does iron wedges drive,
And always crowds itself betwixt.

For Fate with jealous eye does see
Two perfect loves, nor lets them close;°   *unite*
Their union would her ruin be,   15
And her tyrannic power depose.

And therefore her decrees of steel
Us as the distant poles have placed
(Though Love's whole world on us doth wheel),
Not by themselves to be embraced,   20

Unless the giddy heaven fall,
And earth some new convulsion tear,
And, us to join, the world should all
Be cramped into a planisphere.°   *sphere projected on a plane surface*

As lines, so loves oblique may well   25
Themselves in every angle greet;°   *may converge*
But ours, so truly parallel,
Though infinite, can never meet.

Therefore the love which us doth bind,
But Fate so enviously debars,°   *prevents*   30
Is the conjunction of the mind,
And opposition of the stars.

PETER MEINKE   (born 1932)

Advice to My Son

1981

The trick is, to live your days,
as if each one may be your last
(for they go fast, and young men lose their lives
in strange and unimaginable ways)
but at the same time, plan long range   5
(for they go slow: if you survive
the shattered windshield and the bursting shell
you will arrive
at your approximation here below
of heaven or hell).   10

To be specific, between the peony and the rose
plant squash and spinach, turnips and tomatoes;
beauty is nectar
and nectar in a desert, saves—
but the stomach craves stronger sustenance   15
than the honied vine.

Therefore, marry a pretty girl
after seeing her mother;
show your soul to one man,
work with another,   20
and always serve bread with your wine.

But, son,
always serve wine.

W. S. MERWIN   (born 1927)

For the Anniversary of My Death

1967

Every year without knowing it I have passed the day
When the last fires will wave to me
And the silence will set out
Tireless traveler
Like the beam of a lightless star   5

Then I will no longer
Find myself in life as in a strange garment
Surprised at the earth
And the love of one woman
And the shamelessness of men   10
As today writing after three days of rain
Hearing the wren sing and the falling cease
And bowing not knowing to what

JOHN MILTON   (1608–1674)
How Soon Hath Time   1631

How soon hath Time, the subtle thief of youth,
   Stoln on his wing my three and twentieth year!
   My hasting days fly on with full career,
   But my late spring no bud or blossom shew'th.°   *shows*
Perhaps my semblance might deceive the truth,   5
   That I to manhood am arrived so near,
   And inward ripeness doth much less appear,
   That some more timely-happy spirits endu'th.°   *endow*
Yet be it less or more, or soon or slow,
   It shall be still in strictest measure even   10
   To that same lot, however mean or high,
Toward which Time leads me, and the will of Heaven;
   All is, if I have grace to use it so,
   As ever in my great Taskmaster's eye.

MARIANNE MOORE   (1887–1972)
The Mind Is an Enchanting Thing   1944

is an enchanted thing
   like the glaze on a
katydid-wing
      subdivided by sun
      till the nettings are legion.   5
Like Gieseking playing Scarlatti;°   *pianist (1895–1956) and Italian composer (1685–1757)*

like the apteryx-awl
   as a beak,° or the   *beak like a pointed tool*
kiwi's rain-shawl
      of haired feathers, the mind   10
      feeling its way as though blind,
walks along with its eyes on the ground.

It has memory's ear
   that can hear without
having to hear.   15
      Like the gyroscope's fall,
      truly unequivocal
because trued by regnant° certainty,   *ruling*

it is a power of
   strong enchantment. It   20
is like the dove-
      neck animated by
      sun; it is memory's eye;
it's conscientious inconsistency.

It tears off the veil; tears   25
    the temptation, the
mist the heart wears,
        from its eyes—if the heart
        has a face; it takes apart
dejection. It's fire in the dove-neck's   30

iridescence; in the
    inconsistencies
of Scarlatti.
        Unconfusion submits
        its confusion to proof; it's   35
not a Herod's oath° that cannot change.   *ruler's promise to behead John the Baptist*

HOWARD NEMEROV   (born 1920)

Lobsters   1977

Here at the Super Duper, in a glass tank
Supplied by a rill of cold fresh water
Running down a glass washboard at one end
And siphoned off at the other, and so
Perpetually renewed, a herd of lobster   5
Is made available to the customer
Who may choose whichever one he wants
To carry home and drop into boiling water
And serve with a sauce of melted butter.

Meanwhile, the beauty of strangeness marks   10
These creatures, who move (when they do)
With a slow, vague wavering of claws,
The somnambulist's° effortless clambering   *sleepwalker's*
As he crawls over the shell of a dream
Resembling himself. Their velvet colors,   15
Mud red, bruise purple, cadaver green
Speckled with black, their camouflage at home,
Make them conspicuous here in the strong
Day-imitating light, the incommensurable°   *immeasurable*
Philosophers and at the same time victims   20
Herded together in the marketplace, asleep
Except for certain tentative gestures
Of their antennae, or their imperial claws
Pegged shut with a whittled stick at the wrist.

We inlanders, buying our needful food,   25
Pause over these slow, gigantic spiders
That spin not. We pause and are bemused,
And sometimes it happens that a mind sinks down
To the blind abyss in a swirl of sand, goes cold
And archaic in a carapace of horn°   *lobster shell* 30
Thinking: There's something underneath the world. . . .

The flame beneath the pot that boils the water.

S H A R O N   O L D S   (born 1942)

The Promise   1989

With the second drink, at the restaurant,
holding hands on the bare table
we are at it again, renewing our promise
to kill each other. You are drinking gin,
night-blue juniper berry   5
dissolving in your body, I am drinking Fumé,
chewing its fragrant dirt and smoke, we are
taking on earth, we are part soil already,
and always, wherever we are, we are also in our
bed, fitted naked closely   10
along each other, half passed out
after love, drifting back and
forth across the border of consciousness, our
bodies buoyant, clasped. Your hand
tightens on the table. You're a little afraid   15
I'll chicken out. What you do not want
is to lie in a hospital bed for a year
after a stroke, without being able to
think or die, you do not want
to be tied to a chair like my prim grandmother,   20
cursing. The room is dim around us,
ivory globes, pink curtains
bound at the waist, and outside
a weightless bright lifted-up
summer twilight. I tell you you don't   25
know me if you think I will not
kill you. Think how we have floated together
eye to eye, nipple to nipple,
sex to sex, the halves of a single creature
drifting up to the lip of matter   30
and over it—you know me from the bright, blood-
flecked delivery room, if a beast
had you in its jaws I would attack it, if the ropes
binding your soul are your own wrists I will cut them.

W I L F R E D   O W E N   (1893–1918)

Anthem for Doomed Youth   1920

What passing-bells for these who die as cattle?
    Only the monstrous anger of the guns.
    Only the stuttering rifles' rapid rattle
Can patter out their hasty orisons.°   *prayers*
No mockeries now for them; no prayers nor bells,   5
    Nor any voice of mourning save the choirs—
The shrill, demented choirs of wailing shells;
    And bugles calling for them from sad shires.°   *shire horses*

What candles may be held to speed them all?
    Not in the hands of boys, but in their eyes   10
Shall shine the holy glimmers of good-byes.
    The pallor of girls' brows shall be their pall;
Their flowers the tenderness of patient minds,
And each slow dusk a drawing-down of blinds.

LINDA PASTAN   (born 1932)
1932–   1991

I saw my name in print the other day
with 1932 and then a blank
and knew that even now some grassy bank
just waited for my grave. And somewhere a gray

slab of marble existed already   5
on which the final number would be carved—
as if the stone itself were somehow starved
for definition. When I went steady

in high school years ago, my boyfriend's name
was what I tried out, hearing how it fit   10
with mine; then names of film stars in some hit.
My husband was anonymous as rain.

There is a number out there, odd or even
that will become familiar to my sons
and daughter. (They are the living ones   15
I think of now: Peter, Rachel, Stephen.)

I picture it, four integers in a row
5 or 7, 6 or 2 or 9:
a period; silence; an end-stopped line;
a hammer poised . . . delivering its blow.   20

LINDA PASTAN   (born 1932)
Posterity   1991

For every newborn child
We planted one live tree,
A green posterity,°   *future generation*
So death could be beguiled°   *deluded or diverted*
By root and branch and flower   5
To abdicate° some power.   *relinquish*
And we were reconciled.

Now we must move away
Leaving the trees behind

For anyone to climb. 10
The gold-rimmed sky goes gray.
Snow, as we turn our backs,
Obliterates our tracks.
Not even leaves can stay.

ROBERT PHILLIPS (born 1938)

Running on Empty 1981

As a teenager I would drive Father's
Chevrolet cross-county, given me

reluctantly: "Always keep the tank
half full, boy, half full, ya hear?"

The fuel gauge dipping, dipping 5
toward Empty, hitting Empty, then

—thrilling—'way below Empty,
myself driving cross-county

mile after mile, faster and faster,
all night long, this crazy kid driving 10

the earth's rolling surface,
against all laws, defying chemistry,

rules, and time, riding on nothing
but fumes, pushing luck harder

than anyone pushed before, the wind 15
screaming past like the Furies° . . . *Greek deities who pursue evildoers*

I stranded myself only once, a white
night with no gas station open, ninety miles

from nowhere. Panicked for a while,
at standstill, myself stalled. 20

At dawn the car and I both refilled. But,
Father, I am running on empty still.

SYLVIA PLATH (1932–1963)

Daddy 1965

You do not do, you do not do
Any more, black shoe
In which I have lived like a foot
For thirty years, poor and white,
Barely daring to breathe or Achoo. 5

Daddy, I have had to kill you.
You died before I had time—
Marble-heavy, a bag full of God,
Ghastly statue with one gray toe
Big as a Frisco seal   10

And a head in the freakish Atlantic
Where it pours bean green over blue
In the waters off beautiful Nauset.
I used to pray to recover you.
Ach, du.°   *O, you (German)*   15

In the German tongue, in the Polish town°   *Granbow, Otto Plath's birthplace*
Scraped flat by the roller
Of wars, wars, wars.
But the name of the town is common.
My Polack friend   20

Says there are a dozen or two.
So I never could tell where you
Put your foot, your root,
I never could talk to you.
The tongue stuck in my jaw.   25

It stuck in a barb wire snare.
Ich, ich, ich, ich,°   *I, I, I, I (German)*
I could hardly speak.
I thought every German was you.
And the language obscene   30

An engine, an engine
Chuffing me off like a Jew.
A Jew to Dachau, Auschwitz, Belsen.
I began to talk like a Jew.
I think I may well be a Jew.   35

The snows of the Tyrol, the clear beer of Vienna
Are not very pure or true.
With my gipsy ancestress and my weird luck
And my Taroc pack and my Taroc pack°   *Tarot cards used to tell the future*
I may be a bit of a Jew.   40

I have always been scared of *you,*
With your Luftwaffe,° your gobbledygoo.   *German air force*
And your neat mustache
And your Aryan eye, bright blue.
Panzer-man,° panzer-man, O You—   *member of tank crew*   45

Not God but a swastika
So black no sky could squeak through.
Every woman adores a Fascist,
The boot in the face, the brute
Brute heart of a brute like you.   50

You stand at the blackboard, daddy,
In the picture I have of you,

A cleft in your chin instead of your foot
But no less a devil for that, no not
Any less the black man who   55

Bit my pretty red heart in two.
I was ten when they buried you.
At twenty I tried to die
And get back, back, back to you.
I thought even the bones would do.   60

But they pulled me out of the sack,
And they stuck me together with glue.
And then I knew what to do.
I made a model of you,
A man in black with a Meinkampf° look   My Battle, *Adolf Hitler's autobiography*   65

And a love of the rack and the screw.
And I said I do, I do.
So daddy, I'm finally through.
The black telephone's off at the root,
The voices just can't worm through.   70

If I've killed one man, I've killed two—
The vampire who said he was you
And drank my blood for a year,
Seven years, if you want to know.
Daddy, you can lie back now.   75

There's a stake in your fat black heart
And the villagers never liked you.
They are dancing and stamping on you.
They always *knew* it was you.
Daddy, daddy, you bastard, I'm through.   80

EZRA POUND   (1885–1972)

In a Station of the Metro   1916

The apparition of these faces in the crowd;
Petals on a wet, black bough.

EZRA POUND   (1885–1972)

A Pact   1926

I make a pact with you, Walt Whitman—
I have detested you long enough.
I come to you as a grown child
Who has had a pig-headed father;

I am old enough now to make friends.   5
It was you that broke the new wood,

Now is a time for carving.
We have one sap and one root—
Let there be commerce between us.

EZRA POUND   (1885–1972)

The River-Merchant's Wife: A Letter   1915

(after Rihaku)°   *Japanese name for Li Po,*
                                            an 8th-century Chinese poet

While my hair was still cut straight across my forehead
I played about the front gate, pulling flowers.
You came by on bamboo stilts, playing horse,
You walked about my seat, playing with blue plums.
And we went on living in the village of Chokan: 5
Two small people, without dislike or suspicion.

At fourteen I married My Lord you.
I never laughed, being bashful.
Lowering my head, I looked at the wall.
Called to, a thousand times, I never looked back.   10

At fifteen I stopped scowling,
I desired my dust to be mingled with yours
For ever and for ever and for ever.
Why should I climb the look out?

At sixteen you departed,   15
You went into far Ku-to-yen, by river of swirling eddies,
And you have been gone five months.
The monkeys make sorrowful noise overhead.

You dragged your feet when you went out.
By the gate now, the moss is grown, the different mosses,   20
Too deep to clear them away!
The leaves fall early this autumn, in wind.
The paired butterflies are already yellow with August
Over the grass in the West garden;
They hurt me. I grow older,   25
If you are coming down through the narrows of the river Kiang,
Please let me know beforehand,
And I will come out to meet you
      As far as Cho-fu-Sa.

SIR WALTER RALEIGH   (1552–1618)

The Nymph's Reply to the Shepherd   1600

(A reply to Marlowe's "The Passionate Shepherd to His Love")

If all the world and love were young,
And truth in every shepherd's tongue,
These pretty pleasures might me move
To live with thee and be thy love.

Time drives the flocks from field to fold   5
When rivers rage and rocks grow cold,
And Philomel° becometh dumb;   *the nightingale*
The rest complains of cares to come.

The flowers do fade, and wanton fields
To wayward winter reckoning yields;   10
A honey tongue, a heart of gall,°   *bitter heart*
Is fancy's spring, but sorrow's fall.

Thy gowns, thy shoes, thy beds of roses,
Thy cap, thy kirtle,° and thy posies   *dress*
Soon break, soon wither, soon forgotten—   15
In folly ripe, in reason rotten.

Thy belt of straw and ivy buds,
Thy coral clasps and amber studs,
All these in me no means can move
To come to thee and be thy love.   20

But could youth last and love still breed,
Had joys no date° nor age no need,   *no end*
Then these delights my mind might move
To live with thee and be thy love.

DUDLEY RANDALL   (born 1914)

Ballad of Birmingham   1969
(On the bombing of a church in Birmingham, Alabama, 1963)

"Mother dear, may I go downtown
Instead of out to play,
And march the streets of Birmingham
In a Freedom March today?"

"No, baby, no, you may not go,   5
For the dogs are fierce and wild,
And clubs and hoses, guns and jails
Aren't good for a little child."

"But, mother, I won't be alone.
Other children will go with me,   10
And march the streets of Birmingham
To make our country free."

"No, baby, no, you may not go,
For I fear those guns will fire.
But you may go to church instead   15
And sing in the children's choir."

She has combed and brushed her night-dark hair,
And bathed rose petal sweet.
And drawn white gloves on her small brown hands,
And white shoes on her feet.   20

The mother smiled to know her child
Was in the sacred place,
But that smile was the last smile
To come upon her face.

For when she heard the explosion,   25
Her eyes grew wet and wild.
She raced through the streets of Birmingham
Calling for her child.

She clawed through bits of glass and brick,
Then lifted out a shoe.   30
"Oh, here's the shoe my baby wore,
But, baby, where are you?"

JOHN CROWE RANSOM   (1888–1974)

Janet Waking   1927

Beautifully Janet slept
Till it was deeply morning. She woke then
And thought about her dainty-feathered hen,
To see how it had kept.

One kiss she gave her mother.   5
Only a small one gave she to her daddy
Who would have kissed each curl of his shining baby;
No kiss at all for her brother.

"Old Chucky, old Chucky!" she cried,
Running across the world upon the grass   10
To Chucky's house, and listening. But alas,
Her Chucky had died.

It was a transmogrifying° bee   *transforming*
Came droning down on Chucky's old bald head
And sat and put the poison. It scarcely bled,   15
But how exceedingly

And purply did the knot
Swell with the venom and communicate
Its rigor! Now the poor comb stood up straight
But Chucky did not.   20

So there was Janet
Kneeling on the wet grass, crying her brown hen
(Translated far beyond the daughters of men)
To rise and walk upon it.

And weeping fast as she had breath   25
Janet implored us, "Wake her from her sleep!"
And would not be instructed in how deep
Was the forgetful kingdom of death.

ADRIENNE RICH   (born 1929)

Bears   1969

Wonderful bears that walked my room all night,
Where have you gone, your sleek and fairy fur,
Your eyes' veiled and imperious light?

Brown bears as rich as mocha or as musk,
White opalescent bears whose fur stood out   5
Electric in the deepening dusk,

And great black bears that seemed more blue than black,
More violet than blue against the dark—
Where are you now? Upon what track

Mutter your muffled paws that used to tread   10
So softly, surely, up the creakless stair
While I lay listening in bed?

When did I lose you? Whose have you become?
Why do I wait and wait and never hear
Your thick nocturnal pacing in my room?   15
My bears, who keeps you now, in pride and fear?

ADRIENNE RICH   (born 1929)

Dissolve in Slow Motion   about 1965

When you watch a marriage
Dissolve, in slow motion,
Like a film, there is a point
Early on when the astute
Observer understands nothing   5
Can prevent the undesired
End, not shrinks, or friends,
Or how-to-love books,
Or the decency or the will
Of the two protagonists   10
Who struggle gamely like lab
Mice dropped in a jar
Of something viscous:° the   *gluey*
Observer would rather snap
The marriage like a twig,   15
Speed the suffering up, but
The rules of the lab forbid.

Other rules govern decay
From within; so she just watches.

The little paws claw   20
Then cease, the furred

Bubbles of lungs stop.
The creatures get rigid.
Has something been measured?
It all gets thrown away.   25

ADRIENNE RICH   (born 1929)

Diving into the Wreck   1973

First having read the book of myths,
and loaded the camera,
and checked the edge of the knife-blade,
I put on
the body-armor of black rubber   5
the absurd flippers
the grave and awkward mask.
I am having to do this
not like Cousteau with his
assiduous° team   *diligent*   10
aboard the sun-flooded schooner
but here alone.

There is a ladder.
The ladder is always there
hanging innocently   15
close to the side of the schooner.
We know what it is for,
we who have used it.
otherwise
it is a piece of maritime floss   20
some sundry° equipment.   *miscellaneous*

I go down.
Rung after rung and still
the oxygen immerses me
the blue light   25
the clear atoms
of our human air.
I go down.
My flippers cripple me,
I crawl like an insect down the ladder   30
and there is no one
to tell me when the ocean
will begin.

First the air is blue and then
it is bluer and then green and then   35
black I am blacking out and yet
my mask is powerful
it pumps my blood with power

the sea is another story
the sea is not a question of power   40
I have to learn alone
to turn my body without force
in the deep element.

And now: it is easy to forget
what I came for   45
among so many who have always
lived here
swaying their crenellated° fans   *indented, scalloped*
between the reefs
and besides   50
you breathe differently down here.

I came to explore the wreck.
The words are purposes.
The words are maps.
I came to see the damage that was done   55
and the treasures that prevail.
I stroke the beam of my lamp
slowly along the flank
of something more permanent
than fish or weed   60

the thing I came for:
the wreck and not the story of the wreck
the thing itself and not the myth
the drowned face always staring
toward the sun   65
the evidence of damage
worn by salt and sway into this threadbare beauty
the ribs of the disaster
curving their assertion
among the tentative haunters.   70

This is the place.
And I am here, the mermaid whose dark hair
streams black, the merman in his armored body.
We circle silently
about the wreck   75
we dive into the hold.
I am she: I am he

whose drowned face sleeps with open eyes
whose breasts still bear the stress
whose silver, copper, vermeil° cargo lies   *red*   80
obscurely inside barrels
half-wedged and left to rot
we are the half-destroyed instruments
that once held to a course
the water-eaten log   85
the fouled compass

We are, I am, you are
by cowardice or courage
the one who find our way
back to this scene   90
carrying a knife, a camera
a book of myths
in which
our names do not appear.

EDWIN ARLINGTON ROBINSON   (1869–1935)
Miniver Cheevy   1910

Miniver Cheevy, child of scorn,
    Grew lean while he assailed the seasons;
He wept that he was ever born,
    And he had reasons.

Miniver loved the days of old   5
    When swords were bright and steeds were prancing;
The vision of a warrior bold
    Would set him dancing.

Miniver sighed for what was not,
    And dreamed, and rested from his labors;   10
He dreamed of Thebes° and Camelot,°   *Greek city/King Arthur's court*
    And Priam's° neighbors.   *king of Troy*

Miniver mourned the ripe renown
    That made so many a name so fragrant;
He mourned Romance, now on the town,   15
    And Art, a vagrant.

Miniver loved the Medici,°   *ruling family of Renaissance Florence*
    Albeit he had never seen one;
He would have sinned incessantly
    Could he have been one.   20

Miniver cursed the commonplace
    And eyed a khaki suit with loathing;
He missed the medieval grace
    Of iron clothing.

Miniver scorned the gold he sought,   25
    But sore annoyed was he without it;
Miniver thought, and thought, and thought,
    And thought about it.

Miniver Cheevy, born too late,
    Scratched his head and kept on thinking;   30
Miniver coughed, and called it fate,
    And kept on drinking.

EDWIN ARLINGTON ROBINSON   (1869–1935)
Richard Cory   1897

Whenever Richard Cory went down town,
We people on the pavement looked at him:
He was a gentleman from sole to crown,
Clean favored, and imperially slim.

And he was always quietly arrayed,   5
And he was always human when he talked;
But still he fluttered pulses when he said,
"Good-morning," and he glittered when he walked.

And he was rich—yes, richer than a king—
And admirably schooled in every grace: 10
In fine, we thought that he was everything
To make us wish that we were in his place.

So on we worked, and waited for the light,
And went without the meat, and cursed the bread;
And Richard Cory, one calm summer night,   15
Went home and put a bullet through his head.

THEODORE ROETHKE   (1908–1963)
I Knew a Woman   1958

I knew a woman, lovely in her bones,
When small birds sighed, she would sigh back at them;
Ah, when she moved, she moved more ways than one:
The shapes a bright container can contain!
Of her choice virtues only gods should speak,   5
Or English poets who grew up on Greek
(I'd have them sing in chorus, cheek to cheek).

How well her wishes went! She stroked my chin,
She taught me Turn, and Counter-turn, and Stand;°   *dance moves of chorus in Greek plays*
She taught me Touch, that undulant white skin;   10
I nibbled meekly from her proffered hand;
She was the sickle; I, poor I, the rake,
Coming behind her for her pretty sake
(But what prodigious mowing we did make).

Love likes a gander, and adores a goose: 15
Her full lips pursed, the errant° note to seize;   *straying*
She played it quick, she played it light and loose,
My eyes, they dazzled at her flowing knees;
Her several parts could keep a pure repose,
Or one hip quiver with a mobile nose   20
(She moved in circles, and those circles moved).

Let seed be grass, and grass turn into hay:
I'm martyr to a motion not my own;
What's freedom for? To know eternity.
I swear she cast a shadow white as stone.   25
But who would count eternity in days?
These old bones live to learn her wanton ways:
(I measure time by how a body sways).

THEODORE ROETHKE   (1908–1963)

The Meadow Mouse   1954

In a shoe box stuffed in an old nylon stocking
Sleeps the baby mouse I found in the meadow,
Where he trembled and shook beneath a stick
Till I caught him up by the tail and brought him in,
Cradled in my hand.   5
A little quaker, the whole body of him trembling,
His absurd whiskers sticking out like a cartoon mouse,
His feet like small leaves,
Little lizard-feet,
Whitish and spread wide when he tries to struggle away,   10
Wriggling like a miniscule° puppy.   *very small*

Now he's eaten his three kinds of cheese and drunk from his bottle-cap watering
      trough—
So much he just lies in one corner,
His tail curled under him, his belly big
As his head; his batlike ears   15
Twitching, tilting toward the least sound.

Do I imagine he no longer trembles
When I come close to him?
He seems no longer to tremble.

But this morning the shoe-box house on the back porch is empty.   20
Where has he gone, my meadow mouse,
My thumb of a child that nuzzled in my palm?—
To run under the hawk's wing,
Under the eye of the great owl watching from the elm-tree,
To live by courtesy of the shrike,° the snake, the tomcat.   *a bird of prey* 25

CARL SANDBURG   (1878–1967)

Grass   1918

Pile the bodies high at Austerlitz and Waterloo.°   *battles in Napoleon's wars*
Shovel them under and let me work—
            I am the grass; I cover all.

And pile them high at Gettysburg
And pile them high at Ypres and Verdun.°   *World War I battles*   5
Shovel them under and let me work.
Two years, ten years, and passengers ask the conductor:
        What place is this?
        Where are we now?

        I am the grass.   10
        Let me work.

ANNE SEXTON   (1928–1974)

The Truth the Dead Know   1961

For my mother, born March 1902, died March 1959
and my father, born February 1900, died June 1959

Gone, I say and walk from church,
refusing the stiff procession to the grave,
letting the dead ride alone in the hearse.
It is June. I am tired of being brave.

We drive to the Cape. I cultivate   5
myself where the sun gutters from the sky,
where the sea swings in like an iron gate
and we touch. In another country people die.

My darling, the wind falls in like stones
from the whitehearted water and when we touch   10
we enter touch entirely. No one's alone.
Men kill for this, or for as much.

And what of the dead? They lie without shoes
in their stone boats. They are more like stone
than the sea would be if it stopped. They refuse   15
to be blessed, throat, eye and knucklebone.

ANNE SEXTON   (1928–1974)

Two Hands   before 1974

From the sea came a hand,
ignorant as a penny,
troubled with the salt of its mother,
mute with the silence of the fishes,
quick with the altars of the tides,   5
and God reached out of His mouth
and called it man.
Up came the other hand
and God called it woman.

The hands applauded.   10
And this was no sin.
It was as it was meant to be.

I see them roaming the streets:
Levi complaining about his mattress,
Sarah studying a beetle,   15
Mandrake holding his coffee mug,
Sally playing the drum at a football game,
John closing the eyes of the dying woman,
and some who are in prison,
even the prison of their bodies,   20
as Christ was prisoned in His body
until the triumph came.

Unwind, hands,
you angel webs,
unwind like the coil of a jumping jack,   25
cup together and let yourselves fill up with sun
and applaud, world,
applaud.

WILLIAM SHAKESPEARE (1564–1616)
Full Fathom Five   1611

Full fathom five thy father lies;
    Of his bones are coral made;
Those are pearls that were his eyes:
    Nothing of him that doth fade,
But doth suffer a sea change   5
Into something rich and strange.
Sea nymphs hourly ring his knell:
    Ding-dong.
Hark! now I hear them—Ding-dong, bell.

WILLIAM SHAKESPEARE (1564–1616)
Sonnet 116   1609

Let me not to the marriage of true minds
Admit impediments. Love is not love
Which alters when it alteration finds,
Or bends with the remover to remove:°   *responds to inconstancy with inconstancy*
Oh, no! it is an ever-fixèd mark,   5
That looks on tempests and is never shaken;
It is the star to every wandering bark,°   *boat*
Whose worth's unknown, although his height be taken.°   *although its elevation can be measured*

Love's not Time's fool, though rosy lips and cheeks
Within his bending sickle's compass come;   10
Love alters not with his brief hours and weeks,
But bears it out even to the edge of doom.°   *Day of Judgment*
If this be error and upon me proved,
I never writ, nor no man ever loved.

PERCY BYSSHE SHELLEY (1792–1822)

To a Skylark   1820

    Hail to thee, blithe Spirit!
        Bird thou never wert,
  That from Heaven, or near it,
        Pourest thy full heart
In profuse strains of unpremeditated art.   5

    Higher still and higher
        From the earth thou springest
  Like a cloud of fire;
        The blue deep thou wingest,
And singing still dost soar, and soaring ever singest.   10

    In the golden lightning
        Of the sunken sun,
  O'er which clouds are bright'ning,
        Thou dost float and run;
Like an unbodied joy whose race is just begun.   15

    The pale purple even
        Melts around thy flight;
  Like a star of Heaven,
        In the broad daylight
Thou art unseen, but yet I hear thy shrill delight,   20

    Keen as are the arrows
        Of that silver sphere,°   *star*
  Whose intense lamp narrows
        In the white dawn clear
Until we hardly see—we feel that it is there.   25

    All the earth and air
        With thy voice is loud,
  As, when night is bare,
        From one lonely cloud
The moon rains out her beams, and Heaven is overflowed.   30

    What thou art we know not;
        What is most like thee?
  From rainbow clouds there flow not
        Drops so bright to see
As from thy presence showers a rain of melody.   35

Like a Poet hidden
    In the light of thought,
Singing hymns unbidden,
    Till the world is wrought
To sympathy with hopes and fears it heeded not: 40

Like a high-born maiden
    In a palace tower,
Soothing her love-laden
    Soul in secret hour
With music sweet as love, which overflows her bower:°   *private chamber*   45

Like a glowworm golden
    In a dell of dew,
Scattering unbeholden
    Its aërial hue
Among the flowers and grass, which screen it from the view!   50

Like a rose embowered
    In its own green leaves,
By warm winds deflowered,
    Till the scent it gives
Makes faint with too much sweet those heavy-wingèd thieves: 55

Sound of vernal° showers   *spring*
    On the twinkling grass,
Rain-awakened flowers,
    All that ever was
Joyous, and clear, and fresh, thy music doth surpass: 60

Teach us, Sprite° or Bird,   *spirit*
    What sweet thoughts are thine:
I have never heard
    Praise of love or wine
That panted forth a flood of rapture so divine.   65

Chorus Hymeneal°   *as for a wedding*
    Or triumphal chant,
Matched with thine would be all
    But an empty vaunt,°   *boast*
A thing wherein we feel there is some hidden want.   70

What objects are the fountains
    Of thy happy strain?
What fields, or waves, or mountains?
    What shapes of sky or plain?
What love of thine own kind? what ignorance of pain?   75

With thy clear keen joyance
    Languor° cannot be: *sluggishness*
Shadow of annoyance
    Never came near thee:
Thou lovest—but ne'er knew love's sad satiety.   80

Waking or asleep,
    Thou of death must deem
Things more true and deep
    Than we mortals dream,
Or how could thy notes flow in such a crystal stream?   85

We look before and after,
    And pine for what is not:
Our sincerest laughter
    With some pain is fraught;
Our sweetest songs are those that tell of saddest thought.   90

Yet if we could scorn
    Hate, and pride, and fear;
If we were things born
    Not to shed a tear,
I know not how thy joy we ever should come near.   95

Better than all measures
    Of delightful sound,
Better than all treasures
    That in books are found,
Thy skill to poet were, thou scorner of the ground!   100

Teach me half the gladness
    That thy brain must know,
Such harmonious madness
    From my lips would flow
The world should listen then—as I am listening now.   105

SIR PHILIP SIDNEY   (1554–1586)

Sonnet 108   1582

When Sorrow, using mine own fire's might,
Melts down his lead into my boiling breast,
Through that dark furnace to my heart oppressed
There shines a joy from thee my only light;
But soon as thought of thee breeds my delight,   5
And my young soul flutters to thee his nest,
Most rude despair, my daily unbidden guest,
Clips straight my wings, straight wraps me in his night,
And makes me then bow down my head and say:
"Ah, what does Phoebus'° gold that wretch avail   *the sun god's* 10
Whom iron doors do keep from use of day?"
So strangely, alas, thy works in me prevail,
That in my woes for thee thou art my joy,
And in my joys for thee my only annoy.°   *grief*

GARY SNYDER   (born 1930)

After Work   1959

The shack and a few trees
float in the blowing fog

I pull out your blouse,
warm my cold hands
        on your breasts.   5
you laugh and shudder
peeling garlic by the
        hot iron stove.
bring in the axe, the rake,
the wood   10

we'll lean on the wall
against each other
stew simmering on the fire
as it grows dark
                drinking wine.   15

GARY SNYDER   (born 1930)

Hay for the Horses   1966

He had driven half the night
From far down San Joaquin
Through Mariposa, up the
Dangerous mountain roads,
And pulled in at eight a.m.   5
With his big truckload of hay
        behind the barn.
With winch and ropes and hooks
We stacked the bales up clean
To splintery redwood rafters   10
High in the dark, flecks of alfalfa
Whirling through shingle-cracks of light,
Itch of haydust in the
        sweaty shirt and shoes.
At lunchtime under black oak   15
Out in the hot corral,
—The old mare nosing lunchpails,
Grasshoppers crackling in the weeds—
"I'm sixty-eight" he said,
"I first bucked hay when I was seventeen.   20
I thought, that day I started,
I sure would hate to do this all my life.
And dammit, that's just what
I've gone and done."

GARY SNYDER   (born 1930)

Old Woman Nature   1983

Old Woman Nature
naturally has a bag of bones
            tucked away somewhere.
            a whole room full of bones!

A scattering of hair and cartilage   5
        bits in the woods.

A fox scat° with hair and a tooth in it.   *animal dropping*
        a shellmound
            a bone flake in a streambank.

A purring cat, crunching   10
        the mouse head first,
            eating on down toward the tail—

The sweet old woman
        calmly gathering firewood in the
                    moon . . .   15

Don't be shocked,
She's heating you some soup.

CATHY SONG   (born 1955)

Lost Sister   1983

1
In China,
even the peasants
named their first daughters
Jade—
the stone that in the far fields   5
could moisten the dry season,
could make men move mountains
for the healing green of the inner hills
glistening like slices of winter melon.

And the daughters were grateful: 10
They never left home.
To move freely was a luxury
stolen from them at birth.
Instead, they gathered patience;
learning to walk in shoes   15
the size of teacups,
without breaking—
the arc of their movements
as dormant as the rooted willow,
as redundant as the farmyard hens.   20

But they traveled far
in surviving,
learning to stretch the family rice,
to quiet the demons,
the noisy stomachs.   25

2
There is a sister
across the ocean,
who relinquished her name,
diluting jade green
with the blue of the Pacific.   30
Rising with a tide of locusts,
she swarmed with others
to inundate another shore.
In America,
there are many roads   35
and women can stride along with men.

But in another wilderness,
the possibilities,
the loneliness,
can strangulate like jungle vines.   40
The meager provisions and sentiments
of once belonging—
fermented roots, Mah-Jong° tiles and firecrackers—set but   *Oriental game*
a flimsy household
in a forest of nightless cities.   45
A giant snake rattles above,
spewing black clouds into your kitchen.
Dough-faced landlords
slip in and out of your keyholes,
making claims you don't understand,   50
tapping into your communication systems
of laundry lines and restaurant chains.

You find you need China:
your one fragile identification,
a jade link   55
handcuffed to your wrist.
You remember your mother
who walked for centuries,
footless—
and like her,   60
you have left no footprints,
but only because
there is an ocean in between,
the unremitting space of your rebellion.

WALLACE STEVENS   (1879–1955)

Anecdote of the Jar   1923

I placed a jar in Tennessee,
And round it was, upon a hill.
It made the slovenly wilderness
Surround that hill.

The wilderness rose up to it,   5
And sprawled around, no longer wild.
The jar was round upon the ground
And tall and of a port in air.

It took dominion everywhere.
The jar was gray and bare.   10
It did not give of bird or bush,
Like nothing else in Tennessee.

WALLACE STEVENS   (1879–1955)

Domination of Black   1923

At night, by the fire,
The colors of the bushes
And of the fallen leaves,
Repeating themselves,
Turned in the room,   5
Like the leaves themselves
Turning in the wind.
Yes: but the color of the heavy hemlocks
Came striding.
And I remembered the cry of the peacocks.   10

The colors of their tails
Were like the leaves themselves
Turning in the wind,
In the twilight wind.
They swept over the room,   15
Just as they flew from the boughs of the hemlocks

Down to the ground.
I heard them cry—the peacocks.
Was it a cry against the twilight
Or against the leaves themselves   20
Turning in the wind,
Turning as the flames
Turned in the fire,
Turning as the tails of the peacocks
Turned in the loud fire,   25

Loud as the hemlocks
Full of the cry of the peacocks?
Or was it a cry against the hemlocks?

Out of the window,
I saw how the planets gathered   30
Like the leaves themselves
Turning in the wind.
I saw how the night came,
Came striding like the color of the heavy hemlocks
I felt afraid.   35
And I remembered the cry of the peacocks.

WALLACE STEVENS (1879–1955)
The Emperor of Ice-Cream   1923

Call the roller of big cigars,
The muscular one, and bid him whip
In kitchen cups concupiscent° curds.   *stirring desire*
Let the wenches dawdle in such dress
As they are used to wear, and let the boys   5
Bring flowers in last month's newspapers.
Let be be finale of seem.
The only emperor is the emperor of ice-cream.

Take from the dresser of deal,°   *pinewood*
Lacking the three glass knobs, that sheet   10
On which she embroidered fantails° once   *fantail pigeons*
And spread it so as to cover her face.
If her horny feet protrude, they come
To show how cold she is, and dumb.
Let the lamp affix its beam.   15
The only emperor is the emperor of ice-cream.

WALLACE STEVENS (1879–1955)
Thirteen Ways of Looking at a Blackbird   1923

1
Among twenty snowy mountains,
The only moving thing
Was the eye of the blackbird.

2
I was of three minds,
Like a tree   5
In which there are three blackbirds.

3
The blackbird whirled in the autumn winds.
It was a small part of the pantomime.

4
A man and a woman
Are one.   10
A man and a woman and a blackbird
Are one.

5
I do not know which to prefer,
The beauty of inflections
Or the beauty of innuendoes,   15
The blackbird whistling
Or just after.

6
Icicles filled the long window
With barbaric glass.
The shadow of the blackbird   20
Crossed it, to and fro.
The mood
Traced in the shadow
An indecipherable cause.

7
O thin men of Haddam,°   *an industrial Connecticut town*   25
Why do you imagine golden birds?
Do you not see how the blackbird
Walks around the feet
Of the women about you?

8
I know noble accents   30
And lucid,° inescapable rhythms;   *clear*
But I know, too,
That the blackbird is involved
In what I know.

9
When the blackbird flew out of sight,   35
It marked the edge
Of one of many circles.

10
At the sight of blackbirds
Flying in a green light,
Even the bawds of euphony°   *those who prostitute themselves to beautiful sounds*   40
Would cry out sharply.

11
He rode over Connecticut
In a glass coach.

Once, a fear pierced him,
In that he mistook
The shadow of his equipage   45
For blackbirds.

12
The river is moving.
The blackbird must be flying.

13
It was evening all afternoon.   50
It was snowing.
And it was going to snow.
The blackbird sat
In the cedar-limbs.

MARK STRAND   (born 1934)

Eating Poetry   1967

Ink runs from the corners of my mouth.
There is no happiness like mine.
I have been eating poetry.

The librarian does not believe what she sees.
Her eyes are sad   5
and she walks with her hands in her dress.

The poems are gone.
The light is dim.
The dogs are on the basement stairs and coming up.

Their eyeballs roll,   10
their blond legs burn like brush.
The poor librarian begins to stamp her feet and weep.

She does not understand.
When I get on my knees and lick her hand,
she screams.   15

I am a new man.
I snarl at her and bark.
I romp with joy in the bookish dark.

ALFRED, LORD TENNYSON   (1809–1892)

Ulysses   1833

It little profits that an idle king,
By this still hearth, among these barren crags,
Matched with an agèd wife, I mete and dole

Unequal laws unto a savage race,
That hoard, and sleep, and feed, and know not me.   5
I cannot rest from travel; I will drain
Life to the lees. All times I have enjoy'd
Greatly, have suffer'd greatly, both with those
That love me, and alone; on shore, and when
Thro' scudding drifts the rainy Hyades   10
Vexed the dim sea. I am become a name;
For always roaming with a hungry heart
Much have I seen and known,—cities of men
And manners, climates, councils, governments,
Myself not least, but honored of them all,—   15
And drunk delight of battle with my peers,
Far on the ringing plains of windy Troy.
I am a part of all that I have met;
Yet all experience is an arch wherethrough
Gleams that untravelled world whose margin fades   20
For ever and for ever when I move.
How dull it is to pause, to make an end,
To rust unburnished, not to shine in use!
As though to breathe were life! Life piled on life
Were all too little, and of one to me   25
Little remains; but every hour is saved
From that eternal silence, something more,
A bringer of new things; and vile it were
For some three suns to store and hoard myself,
And this gray spirit yearning in desire   30
To follow knowledge like a sinking star,
Beyond the utmost bound of human thought.
      This is my son, mine own Telemachus,
To whom I leave the scepter and the isle,—
Well-loved of me, discerning to fulfill   35
This labor, by slow prudence to make mild
A rugged people, and through soft degrees
Subdue them to the useful and the good.
Most blameless is he, centered in the sphere
Of common duties, decent not to fail   40
In offices of tenderness, and pay
Meet adoration to my household gods,
When I am gone. He works his work, I mine.
      There lies the port; the vessel puffs her sail;
There gloom the dark, broad seas. My mariners,   45
Souls that have toiled, and wrought, and thought with me,—
That ever with a frolic° welcome took   *cheerful*
The thunder and the sunshine, and opposed
Free hearts, free foreheads,—you and I are old;
Old age hath yet his honor and his toil.   50
Death closes all; but something ere the end,
Some work of noble note, may yet be done,
Not unbecoming men that strove with Gods.
The lights begin to twinkle from the rocks;

The long day wanes; the slow moon climbs; the deep   55
Moans round with many voices. Come, friends,
'Tis not too late to seek a newer world.
Push off, and sitting well in order smite
The sounding furrows; for my purpose holds
To sail beyond the sunset, and the baths   60
Of all the western stars, until I die.
It may be that the gulfs will wash us down;
It may be we shall touch the Happy Isles,
And see the great Achilles, whom we knew.
Though much is taken, much abides;° and though   *remains*   65
We are not now that strength which in old days
Moved earth and heaven, that which we are, we are,—
One equal temper of heroic hearts,
Made weak by time and fate, but strong in will
To strive, to seek, to find, and not to yield.   70

DYLAN THOMAS   (1914–1953)

The Force That through the Green Fuse Drives the Flower   1934

The force that through the green fuse drives the flower
Drives my green age; that blasts the roots of trees
Is my destroyer.
And I am dumb to tell the crooked rose°   *I have no way of telling the rose*
My youth is bent by the same wintry fever.   5

The force that drives the water through the rocks
Drives my red blood; that dries the mouthing streams
Turns mine to wax.
And I am dumb to mouth unto my veins
How at the mountain spring the same mouth sucks.   10

The hand that whirls the water in the pool
Stirs the quicksand; that ropes the blowing wind
Hauls my shroud sail.
And I am dumb to tell the hanging man
How of my clay is made the hangman's lime.°   *hangman's tree*   15

The lips of time leech to the fountain head;
Love drips and gathers, but the fallen blood
Shall calm her sores.
And I am dumb to tell a weather's wind
How time has ticked a heaven round the stars.   20

And I am dumb to tell the lover's tomb
How at my sheet goes the same crooked worm.

DAVID WAGONER   (born 1926)

The Old Words

This is hard to say
Simply, because the words
Have grown so old together:
Lips and eyes and tears,
Touch and fingers   5
And love, out of love's language,
Are hard and smooth as stones
Laid bare in a streambed,
Not failing or fading
Like the halting speech of the body   10
Which will turn too suddenly
To ominous silence,
But like your lips and mine
Slow to separate, our fingers
Reluctant to come apart,   15
Our eyes and their slow tears
Reviving like these words
Springing to life again
And again, taken to heart,
To touch, love, to begin.   20

EDMUND WALLER   (1606–1687)

Go, Lovely Rose   1645

  Go, lovely rose,
Tell her that wastes her time and me
  That now she knows,
When I resemble° her to thee,   *compare*
  How sweet and fair she seems to be.   5

  Tell her that's young,
And shuns to have her graces spied,
  That hadst thou sprung
In deserts, where no men abide,
  Thou must have uncommended died.   10

  Small is the worth
Of beauty from the light retired;
  Bid her come forth,
Suffer herself to be desired,
  And not blush so to be admired.   15

Then die, that she
The common fate of all things rare
   May read in thee:
How small a part of time they share,
   That are so wondrous sweet and fair.   20

KAREN WHITEHILL   (born 1947)

Morning in Gainesville   1976

Here the whitest birds
Learn to stalk cattle for flies

Against the brilliant hard sky
clouds billow and drift
like sheets hung up to dry   5

Wandering in fields
students gather magic
mushrooms sprung up after rain

Black lovebugs are all over now
stuck together in twos   10
sucked into every closing door

In the distance
the skeleton of a live oak
licked clean by beards of moss
gleams in the sun   15

WALT WHITMAN   (1819–1892)

There Was a Child Went Forth   1855

There was a child went forth every day,
And the first object he looked upon, that object he became,
And that object became part of him for the day or a certain
    part of the day,
Or for many years or stretching cycles of years.

The early lilacs became part of this child,   5
And grass and white and red morning-glories, and white and
    red clover, and the song of the phoebe-bird,
And the Third-month° lambs and the sow's pink-faint litter,   *March*
    and the mare's foal and the cow's calf,
And the noisy brood of the barnyard or by the mire of the
    pond-side,
And the fish suspending themselves so curiously below there,
    and the beautiful curious liquid,
And the water-plants with their graceful flat heads, all be-
    came part of him.   10

The field-sprouts of Fourth-month and Fifth-month became
    part of him,

Winter-grain sprouts and those of the light-yellow corn, and
    the esculent° roots of the garden,   *edible*

And the apple-trees covered with blossoms and the fruit af-
    terward, and wood-berries, and the commonest weeds
    by the road,

And the old drunkard staggering home from the outhouse
    of the tavern whence he had lately risen,

And the schoolmistress that passed on her way to the school,   15

And the friendly boys that passed, and the quarrelsome boys,

And the tidy and fresh-cheeked girls, and the barefoot negro
    boy and girl,

And all the changes of city and country wherever he went.

His own parents, he that had fathered him and she that had
    conceived him in her womb and birthed him,

They gave this child more of themselves than that,   20

They gave him afterward every day, they became part of him.

The mother at home quietly placing the dishes on the sup-
    per-table,

The mother with mild words, clean her cap and gown, a
    wholesome odor falling off her person and clothes as
    she walks by,

The father, strong, self-sufficient, manly, mean, angered, un-
    just,

The blow, the quick loud word, the tight bargain, the crafty
    lure,   25

The family usages, the language, the company, the furniture,
    the yearning and swelling heart,

Affection that will not be gainsayed,° the sense of what is   *denied*
    real, the thought if after all it should prove unreal,

The doubts of day-time and the doubts of night-time, the
    curious whether and how,

Whether that which appears so is so, or is it all flashes and
    specks?

Men and women crowding fast in the streets, if they are not
    flashes and specks what are they?   30

The streets themselves and the façades of houses, and goods
    in the windows,

Vehicles, teams, the heavy-planked wharves, the huge cross-
    ing at the ferries,

The village on the highland seen from afar at sunset, the
    river between,

Shadows, aureola° and mist, the light falling on roofs and   *bands of light*
    gables of white or brown two miles off,

The schooner near by sleepily dropping down the tide, the
    little boat slack-towed astern,   35

The hurrying tumbling waves, quick-broken crests, slapping,

The strata of colored clouds, the long bar of maroon-tint
    away solitary by itself, the spread of purity it lies mo-
    tionless in,
The horizon's edge, the flying sea-crow, the fragrance of salt
    marsh and shore mud,
These became part of that child who went forth every day,
    and who now goes, and will always go forth every day.

RICHARD WILBUR   (born 1921)

Boy at the Window   1956

Seeing the snowman standing all alone
In dusk and cold is more than he can bear.
The small boy weeps to hear the wind prepare
A night of gnashings and enormous moan.
His tearful sight can hardly reach to where   5
The pale-faced figure with bitumen° eyes   *carbon, coal*
Returns him such a god-forsaken stare
As outcast Adam gave to Paradise.
The man of snow is, nonetheless, content,
Having no wish to go inside and die.   10
Still, he is moved to see the youngster cry.
Though frozen water is his element,
He melts enough to drop from one soft eye
A trickle of purest rain, a tear
For the child at the bright pane surrounded by   15
Such warmth, such light, such love, and so much fear.

RICHARD WILBUR   (born 1921)

The Writer   1976

In her room at the prow of the house
Where light breaks, and the windows are tossed with linden,°   *shade trees with*
My daughter is writing a story.   *heart-shaped leaves*

I pause in the stairwell, hearing
From her shut door a commotion of typewriter-keys   5
Like a chain hauled over a gunwale.°   *boat's rail*

Young as she is, the stuff
Of her life is a great cargo, and some of it heavy:
I wish her a lucky passage.

But now it is she who pauses,   10
As if to reject my thought and its easy figure.
A stillness greatens, in which

The whole house seems to be thinking,
And then she is at it again with a bunched clamor
Of strokes, and again is silent.   15

I remember the dazed starling°   *bird*
Which was trapped in that very room, two years ago,
How we stole in, lifted a sash

And retreated, not to affright it;
And how for a helpless hour, through the crack of the door,   20
We watched the sleek, wild, dark

And iridescent creature
Batter against the brilliance, drop like a glove
To the hard floor, or the desk-top,

And wait then, humped and bloody,   25
For the wits to try it again; and how our spirits
Rose when, suddenly sure,

It lifted off from a chair-back,
Beating a smooth course for the right window
And clearing the sill of the world.   30

It is always a matter, my darling,
Of life or death, as I had forgotten. I wish
What I wished you before, but harder.

WILLIAM CARLOS WILLIAMS   (1883–1963)

Spring and All   1923

By the road to the contagious hospital
under the surge of the blue
mottled clouds driven from the
northeast—a cold wind. Beyond, the
waste of broad, muddy fields   5
brown with dried weeds, standing and fallen

patches of standing water
the scattering of tall trees

All along the road the reddish
purplish, forked, upstanding, twiggy   10
stuff of bushes and small trees
with dead, brown leaves under them
leafless vines—

Lifeless in appearance, sluggish
dazed spring approaches—   15

They enter the new world naked,
cold, uncertain of all
save that they enter. All about them
the cold, familiar wind—

Now the grass, tomorrow   20
the stiff curl of wildcarrot leaf
One by one objects are defined—
It quickens: clarity, outline of leaf

But now the stark dignity of
entrance—Still, the profound change   25
has come upon them: rooted, they
grip down and begin to awaken

WILLIAM WORDSWORTH   (1770–1850)

A Slumber Did My Spirit Seal   1800

A slumber did my spirit seal;
    I had no human fears:
She seemed a thing that could not feel
    The touch of earthly years.

No motion has she now, no force;   5
    She neither hears nor sees;
Rolled round in earth's diurnal° course,   *daily*
    With rocks, and stones, and trees.

WILLIAM WORDSWORTH   (1770–1850)

She Dwelt among the Untrodden Ways   1800

She dwelt among the untrodden ways
    Beside the springs of Dove.°   *river in England*
A Maid whom there were none to praise
    And very few to love;

A violet by a mossy stone   5
    Half hidden from the eye!
—Fair as a star, when only one
    Is shining in the sky.

She lived unknown, and few could know
    When Lucy ceased to be;   10
But she is in her grave, and, oh,
    The difference to me!

WILLIAM WORDSWORTH   (1770–1850)

The Solitary Reaper   1807

Behold her, single in the field,
    Yon solitary Highland lass!
Reaping and singing by herself;

Stop here, or gently pass!
Alone she cuts and binds the grain,   5
And sings a melancholy strain;
O listen! for the Vale profound
Is overflowing with the sound.

No Nightingale did ever chant
    More welcome notes to weary bands   10
Of travelers in some shady haunt,
    Among Arabian sands:
A voice so thrilling ne'er was heard
In spring-time from the Cuckoo-bird,
Breaking the silence of the seas   15
Among the farthest Hebrides.°   *distant northern islands*

Will no one tell me what she sings?—
    Perhaps the plaintive numbers° flow   *mournful verses*
For old, unhappy, far-off things,
    And battles long ago: 20
Or is it some more humble lay,°   *song*
Familiar matter of to-day?
Some natural sorrow, loss, or pain,
That has been, and may be again?

Whate'er the theme, the Maiden sang   25
    As if her song could have no ending;
I saw her singing at her work,
    And o'er the sickle bending;—
I listened, motionless and still;
And, as I mounted up the hill,   30
The music in my heart I bore,
Long after it was heard no more.

SIR THOMAS WYATT   (1503–1542)

They Flee from Me   1557

They flee from me, that sometime did me seek,
With naked foot stalking in my chamber.
I have seen them, gentle, tame, and meek,
That now are wild, and do not remember
That sometime they put themselves in danger   5
To take bread at my hand; and now they range,
Busily seeking with a continual change.

Thanked be Fortune it hath been otherwise,
Twenty times better; but once in special,
In thin array, after a pleasant guise,°   *in a pleasing way*   10
When her loose gown from her shoulders did fall,
And she me caught in her arms long and small,°   *slender*
And therewith all sweetly did me kiss
And softly said, "Dear heart, how like you this?"

It was no dream, I lay broad waking.   15
But all is turned, thorough° my gentleness,   *through*
Into a strange fashion of forsaking;
And I have leave to go, of her goodness,
And she also to use newfangleness.°   *try something new*
But since that I so kindely° am served,   *according to her nature*   20
I fain° would know what she hath deserved.   *gladly*

MITSUYE YAMADA   (born 1923)

A Bedtime Story   1976

Once upon a time,
an old Japanese legend
goes as told
by Papa,
an old woman traveled through   5
many small villages
seeking refuge
for the night.
Each door opened
a sliver   10
in answer to her knock
then closed.
Unable to walk
any further
she wearily climbed a hill   15
found a clearing
and there lay down to rest
a few moments to catch
her breath.

The village town below   20
lay asleep except
for a few starlike lights.
Suddenly the clouds opened
and a full moon came into view
over the town.   25

The old woman sat up
turned toward
the village town
and in supplication
called out   30
Thank you people
of the village,
If it had not been for your
kindness
in refusing me a bed   35

for the night
these humble eyes would never
have seen this
memorable sight.

Papa paused, I waited.   40
In the comfort of our
hilltop home in Seattle
overlooking the valley,
I shouted
"That's the *end?*"   45

MITSUYE YAMADA   (born 1923)

Marriage Was a Foreign Country   1976

I come to be here
because
they say I must
follow my husband

so I come.   5

My grandmother cried:
you are not cripple
why
to America?

When we land the boat full   10
of new brides
lean over railing
with wrinkled glossy pictures
they hold inside hand
like this   15
so excited
down there a dock full of men
they do same thing
hold pictures
look up and down   20
like this
they find faces to
match pictures.

Your father I see him on the dock
he come to Japan to marry   25
and leave me
I was not a picture bride
I only was afraid.

WILLIAM BUTLER YEATS   (1865–1939)
Crazy Jane Talks with the Bishop   1932

I met the Bishop on the road
And much said he and I.
"Those breasts are flat and fallen now,
Those veins must soon be dry;
Live in a heavenly mansion,   5
Not in some foul sty."

"Fair and foul are near of kin,
And fair needs foul," I cried.
"My friends are gone, but that's a truth
Nor grave nor bed denied,   10
Learned in bodily lowliness
And in the heart's pride.

"A woman can be proud and stiff
When on love intent;
But Love has pitched his mansion in   15
The place of excrement;
For nothing can be sole or whole
That has not been rent."

WILLIAM BUTLER YEATS   (1865–1939)
The Second Coming   1921

Turning and turning in the widening gyre°   *spiral*
The falcon cannot hear the falconer;
Things fall apart; the center cannot hold;
Mere anarchy is loosed upon the world,
The blood-dimmed tide is loosed, and everywhere   5
The ceremony of innocence is drowned;
The best lack all conviction, while the worst
Are full of passionate intensity.

Surely some revelation is at hand;
Surely the Second Coming is at hand;   10
The Second Coming! Hardly are those words out
When a vast image out of *Spiritus Mundi*°   *Spirit of the World*
Troubles my sight: somewhere in sands of the desert
A shape with lion body and the head of a man,°   *sphinx*
A gaze blank and pitiless as the sun,   15
Is moving its slow thighs, while all about it
Reel shadows of the indignant desert birds.
The darkness drops again; but now I know
That twenty centuries of stony sleep
Were vexed to nightmare by a rocking cradle,   20
And what rough beast, its hour come round at last,
Slouches towards Bethlehem to be born?

WILLIAM BUTLER YEATS   (1865–1939)
To a Child Dancing in the Wind   1933

Dance there upon the shore;
What need have you to care
For wind or water's roar?
And tumble out your hair
That the salt drops have wet;   5
Being young you have not known
The fool's triumph, nor yet
Love lost as soon as won,
Nor the best laborer dead
And all the sheaves to bind.   10
What need have you to dread
The monstrous crying of the wind?

YEVGENY YEVTUSHENKO   (born 1933)
Humor   1965
TRANSLATED BY GEORGE REAVEY

Tsars,
    Kings,
        Emperors,
sovereigns of all the earth,
have commanded many a parade,   *deformed slave who authored* Aesop's Fables   5
but they could not command
        humor.
When Aesop, the tramp,° came visiting   *deformed slave who authored* Aesop's Fables
the palaces of eminent personages
ensconced in sleek comfort all day,   10
they struck him as paupers.
In houses,
    where hypocrites have
left the smear of their puny feet,
there Hodja-Nasr-ed-Din,°   *19th-century Persian king*   15
      with his jests,
swept clean
   all meanness
      like a board of chessmen!
They tried   20
   to commission
      humor—
but humor is not to be bought!
They tried
   to murder   25
    humor,

but humor
      thumbed
           his nose at them!
It's hard   30
    to fight humor.
They executed him time and again.
His hacked-off head
was stuck on the point of a pike.
But as soon as the mummers' pipes   35
began their quipping tale,
humor defiantly cried:
         "I'm back, I'm here!",
and started to foot a dance.
In an overcoat, shabby and short,   40
with eyes cast down
       and a mask of repentance,
he,
  a political criminal,
now under arrest,   45
      walked to his execution.
He appeared to submit in every way,
accepting the life-beyond,
but of a sudden
     he wriggled out   50
        of his coat,
and, waving his hand,
      did a bolt.
Humor
    was shoved   55
      into cells,
but much good that did.
Humor went straight through
prison bars and walls of stone.
Coughing from the lungs   60
like any man in the ranks,
he marched
     singing a popular ditty,
rifle in hand upon the Winter Palace.
He's accustomed to frowning looks,   65
but they do him no harm;
and humor at times
     with humor
glances at himself.
He's everpresent.   70
     Nimble and quick,
he'll slip through anything,
       through everyone.
So—
  glory be to humor.   75
He—
  is a valiant man.

BIOGRAPHIES OF POETS

MATTHEW ARNOLD (1822–1888)—English critic, educator, and poet—graduated from Oxford and became inspector of the British schools for most of his life. As a poet, Arnold was inspired by Greek tragedies, Keats, and Wordsworth. In 1857 he began to teach poetry at Oxford and to publish numerous books on literary criticism. In much of his writing, Arnold took the position of the agnostic unable to accept traditional faith, wishing to replace doctrines that had become doubtful with great literature as a source of inspiration and moral guidance. His prose writings helped define the nineteenth-century ideal of high culture, which he saw as a synthesis of Judeo-Christian ethics and the classical dedication to reason and form.

MARGARET ATWOOD (born 1939) has said, "My life really has been writing since the age of sixteen; all other decisions I made were determined by that fact." Born in Ottawa, Canada, Atwood resides in Toronto but has lived all over Canada as well as in the United States and England. She studied at the University of Toronto and Harvard, and has taught and lectured widely. In addition to two collections of short stories and seven volumes of poetry, Atwood has published six novels, including *The Edible Woman, Cat's Eye,* and a chilling portrayal of a nightmarish dystopian future, *The Handmaid's Tale,* which won a *Los Angeles Times* award for best fiction and was made into a movie.

W. H. AUDEN (1907–1973) knew science, history, politics, philosophy, psychology, art, music, and literature. As a result, his poetry "is full of knowledge and wisdom and ideas" (Kenneth Koch). Auden believed that "living is always thinking." Born in the ancient city of York, Wystan Hugh graduated from Oxford University and became an important voice for the radical criticism of established society by the Marxist left. After serving on the Loyalist side in the Spanish Civil War, he emigrated to America in 1939 and became a U.S. citizen. His first collection of poetry, *Poems,* appeared in 1930. In 1948 he won the Pulitzer Prize for his collection *The Age of Anxiety,* an expression he coined to describe the 1930s. Auden saw poetry "as a game of knowledge, a bringing to consciousness, by naming them, of emotions and their hidden relationships."

BASHO (1644–1694) was a famous Japanese writer of haiku in the seventeenth century. His simple, descriptive poems evoke emotions.

WENDELL BERRY (born 1934) is a poet, novelist, and essayist who was educated at the University of Kentucky, where he also has taught for many years. Although Berry deals primarily with Kentucky and its people, "one would be hard pressed to dismiss him as a mere regionalist. . . . his work is rooted in the land and in the values of an older America" (Jonathan Yardly). Among his many titles are *The Broken Ground* (1964), *Findings* (1969), *To What Listens* (1975), and *Clearing* (1977).

ELIZABETH BISHOP (1911–1979), who said, "There's nothing more embarrassing than being a poet," was born in Massachusetts. Only four years old when her father died, she was taken to live with her grandmother after her mother suffered a mental breakdown. After graduating from Vassar, Bishop planned to enter Cornell Medical School, but poet Marianne Moore persuaded her to become a writer. She served as a poetry consultant to the Library of Congress (1949–1950) and taught poetry writing at Harvard. She received numerous awards, including a Pulitzer Prize (1956). Bishop's poetry has been called "both precise and suggestive . . . fantastic yet fanciful" (Louis Untermeyer).

WILLIAM BLAKE (1757–1827), a forerunner of the English Romantic movement, "could transmit his basic consciousness and communicate it to somebody else after he was dead—in other words, build a time machine," said poet Allen Ginsberg. Born in London, Blake was apprenticed at the age of fourteen to an engraver; his engravings illustrated many popular books of his day as well as his own poems. He began to write his richly symbolic, mystical poetry in his youth, and with the financial assistance of his friends published his first collection of poems, *Poetical Sketches,* in 1783. However, efforts to find a publisher for his second manuscript, *Songs of Innocence,* were unsuccessful. The last twenty-five years of his life were marked by extreme poverty; it remained for later audiences to appreciate the complex symbolism of his mystical, enigmatic poetry.

LOUISE BOGAN (1897–1970), born in Livermore Falls, Maine, was educated at Boston University. She served as consultant in poetry to the Library of Congress, taught at a number of universities in the United States and Austria, and served over twenty years as a poetry critic for the *New Yorker*. Her books of poetry include *Body of This Death, Dark Summer, The Blue Estuaries,* and *Collected Poems, 1923–1953,* which won the Bollingen Prize in poetry.

ARNA BONTEMPS (1902–1973)—American poet, novelist, editor, and biographer—was born in Alexandria, Louisiana and raised in California. A 1923 graduate of Pacific Union College, Bontemps first published his poetry in *Crisis* magazine in 1924. He turned to the novel, publishing *God Sends Sunday* in 1931, *Black Thunder* in 1936, and *Drums at Dusk* in 1939. His *Story of the Negro* received the Jane Adams Children's Book Award in 1956. In *Any-*

place but Here he gathered brief biographies of outstanding black Americans. He published a much-read biography of Frederick Douglass in 1959 and an anthology of poetry written by African Americans in 1963.

KAY BOYLE (born 1903), a native of St. Paul, Minnesota, lived much of her life in France, Austria, Germany, and England. Being in Europe at the beginning of World War II led her to write three books that described the unfolding war: *Primer for Combat, Avalanche,* and *1939.* Her novel *Generation without Farewell* deals with conditions in postwar Germany. Prior to the war, Boyle published a collection of short stories in 1929 and a novel the following year. She became an English professor at San Francisco State University in 1963.

ANNE BRADSTREET (about 1612–1672) wrote the first volume of original poetry published in the British colonies of North America. She had sailed for America from her native England after marrying at the age of 16. Her father, Thomas Dudley, became a governor of the Massachusetts Bay Colony. The mother of eight children, Bradstreet wrote an autobiography entitled *Religious Experiences.*

BERTOLT BRECHT (1898–1956), a German communist poet and playwright, has enjoyed a tremendous international vogue since his death. One of his German editors has said of him that "in poetry and drama he wrote the history of our land since 1918." As a young man in a country embittered by its defeat in World War I, Brecht joined the radical left in its criticism of exploitation and imperialistic wars. When Hitler's anticommunist crusade drove him into exile, he wrote grimly prophetic poetic commentaries on his countrymen's march into catastrophe. For a time he joined other refugees from Hitler's Germany in the United States, returning to East Berlin after World War II to serve the East German communist regime as head of the famed Berliner Ensemble. Plays like *The Caucasian Chalk Circle, Galileo,* and *Mother Courage* have become classics of the modern theater.

GWENDOLYN BROOKS (born 1917) was the first African American woman to achieve widespread critical acclaim as a poet. Brooks began writing poetry as a child in Chicago and had her first poem published at age ten in a children's magazine. In high school, she saw several of her poems published in *Defender,* a Chicago newspaper. In the early 1940s she won prizes for her poetry and published her first poetry collection in 1945. The first African American woman to be so honored, Brooks won a Pulitzer Prize for poetry in 1950 for her second collection, *Annie Allen.* Other works include *The Bean Eaters* (1960), *In the Mecca* (1968), and *To Disembark* (1981). Brooks became a major force in the movement to define black identity and to foster black pride.

ELIZABETH BARRETT BROWNING (1806–1861), who wrote "grief may be joy misunderstood," had a difficult young life. Born into a well-to-do family in Durham, England, as the oldest of eleven children, Barrett Browning was reading Greek at the age of eight and writing poems that imitated her favorite authors. At fifteen she suffered a spinal injury when she fell from a pony and was a partial invalid when she met the poet Robert Browning in 1845. The two fell in love immediately, but she had to elope to escape from her obsessively jealous father. Because of her health, the couple went to live in Italy. Her most famous collection, *Sonnets from the Portuguese,* love poems written to her husband, was published in 1850.

ROBERT BROWNING (1812–1889) was born in Camberwall, England. He decided to become a poet at seventeen and after setbacks became one of the best-known and most influential poet-sages of Victorian England. He was still receiving financial support from his family when in 1845 he met and fell in love with Elizabeth Barrett, one of the leading poets of the day. *The Ring and the Book,* a series of dramatic monologues based on a seventeenth-century murder, appeared in 1869 and finally brought him popular acclaim. His metrically rough and intellectually challenging poetry secured him a following of dedicated admirers, with Browning Societies surviving to this day.

ROBERT BURNS (1759–1796)—born in a small cottage in Alloway, Scotland, to a family of poor tenant farmers—knew poverty and exploitation at first hand. He was steeped in the traditional ballads and songs of his country, and he became for the Romantic poets the type of untutored, spontaneous, original genius throwing off artificial conventions. After years of trying unsuccessfully to earn a living as a farmer, he was offered a job as an overseer in Jamaica. To pay for his passage, he published in 1786 a collection of poems and songs entitled *Poems Chiefly in the Scottish Dialect.* Because of its tremendous success, he was able to give up his Jamaica project. Like the Romantic poets after him, he was fired with generous enthusiasm for the aims of the French Revolution, envisioning a world in which the aristocracy would be swept away and brotherhood and human dignity would prevail.

ROSEMARY CATACALOS (born 1944) is a bilingual Hispanic poet whose work has been reprinted in recent anthologies stressing multicultural themes. She was born in St. Petersburg, Florida, and grew up and attended a two-year college in San Antonio, Texas. She has conducted poetry workshops in schools throughout Texas and has published more than thirty chapbooks, or pamphlets, of students' work. Her collection *Again for the First Time* received the Texas Institute of Letters Poetry Award in 1985.

LORNA DEE CERVANTES (born 1954) discovered the world of books in the homes that her mother cleaned. "We were so poor . . . We were brilliant at wishing," she wrote in her poem "To My Brother." Born in San Francisco of Mexican descent, Cervantes published her first poetry collection, *Emplumada,* in 1981. Educated at San Jose State University, she is the founder of Mango Publications, a small press that publishes books and a literary magazine.

KAWAI CHIGETSU-NI (1632–1736) was a Japanese woman writer of the seventeenth century.

LUCILLE CLIFTON (born 1936) has said, "I am a Black woman poet, and I sound like one." Born in Depew, New York, and educated at Howard University, Clifton taught at several colleges, worked as a claims clerk in the New York State Division of Employment, and was a literature assistant in the Office of Education in Washington, D.C. Her first collection of poetry, *Good Times*, was selected as one of the ten best books of 1969 by the *New York Times*. Among her awards are the University of Massachusetts Press' Juniper Prize for Poetry, an Emmy Award, and creative writing fellowships from the National Endowment for the Arts. In 1979 she was named Maryland's poet laureate.

WILLIAM COWPER (1731–1800) was bullied as a child in school. As an adult, Cowper suffered from fits of depression aggravated by his obsession with the doctrine of eternal damnation. He found comfort for a time in his association with evangelical Christians (he coauthored the *Olney Hymns* still familiar to Methodists) but struggled with mental illness to the end of his life.

STEPHEN CRANE (1871–1900), admired for his harsh realism in the tradition of American naturalism, is best known for his imaginative reenacting of the traumas of the Civil War experience in his novel *The Red Badge of Courage*. Crane was born in Newark, New Jersey, and spent most of his youth in upstate New York. After attending college for two years, he moved to New York City to become a free-lance journalist. His fame as a writer grew in the same year with the publication of *The Black Riders*, a collection of free verse. "The Open Boat," one of his two most famous short stories, appeared in 1897. The other, "The Blue Hotel," was published the year before his death of a tubercular infection at the age of twenty-nine.

COUNTEE CULLEN (1903–1946) was a moving force in the Harlem Renaissance of the 1920s and 1930s, which made the work of poets like Claude McKay, Langston Hughes, and Helene Johnson known to a large public. Cullen's poetry, traditional in form, deals memorably with the joys and sorrows of African Americans. Born and raised in New York City, Cullen graduated from New York University in 1925 and received a master's degree from Harvard the following year. His first three collections of poetry—*Color, Copper Sun*, and *The Ballad of a Brown Girl*—were published in the mid-1920s. His only novel, *One Way to Heaven*, a description of life in Harlem, appeared in 1932. A selection of his own favorite poems, *On These I Stand*, appeared a year after his death.

E. E. CUMMINGS (1894–1962) believed that "poetry is being, not doing." One of the most provocative and unconventional of modern poets, cummings was born in Cambridge, Massachusetts, and educated at Harvard. During World War I, cummings served as a volunteer ambulance driver and was held briefly as a prisoner of war. After the war he spent several years in Paris studying art. A talented painter, he often exhibited his artwork. His first volume of poetry, *Tulips and Chimneys* (1923), was both criticized and praised for its unusual use of language and punctuation, which is reflected in the un-

orthodox use of lowercase letters in his name. "The effect of this experimenta-
tion is not to take the meaning away but to add or emphasize a certain kind of
meaning. His way of writing seems to call attention to the sense of each word,
so that each word counts and is important in the poem" (Kenneth Koch).

ANN DARR (born 1920) has said, "If I could write the way I want to
my writing would be a cross between that of Woody Allen and Pablo Neruda.
I want the poems to be honest and alive, as immediate as I can make them."
In addition to writing poetry, Darr has worked as a radio writer and actress for
NBC and ABC in New York and as poet-in-residence at several universities.
During World War II, she served as an air force pilot. "My dominant
metaphor has been flight in all of its meanings," she said.

NORA DAUENHAUER (born 1927) is a linguist and author of instruc-
tional materials in her native language, Tlingit. A native Alaskan, Dauenhauer
comes from a family of noted carvers and beadwork artists.

REUEL DENNEY (born 1913) has said, "When I learned to write, I
chalked criticisms of the household on the tile entry of the house. For example, slogans taken from fairy tales such as the Little Tailor's lampoon against
the castle holding him prison: 'Too much potatoes and not enuff meat.' Instead of being told that some children somewhere in the world didn't even
have potatoes . . . I was praised for my literacy. This was the start of my
writing, although I was not published until later, at sixteen or so." Born in
New York, Denney was educated at Dartmouth. He lives in Honolulu,
Hawaii, where he writes "for three to fifteen hours a week."

COUNTESS OF DIA (born about 1140) was one of the women troubadours of the Provençal courts in southern France, who provided counterpoint
to the usually male-oriented tradition of courtly love.

WILLIAM DICKEY (born 1928) "is a national treasure" says critic
Brown Miller, adding that "Dickey writes a rare and enviable sort of poem,
truly humorous and truly serious at once." Educated at Harvard and Oxford
universities, Dickey has taught at Cornell, San Francisco State, and the University of Hawaii. His award-winning work has appeared widely in periodicals such as the *New Yorker, Harper's,* and the *Atlantic.* He lives in San
Francisco.

EMILY DICKINSON (1830–1886) is now considered one of the greatest American poets, but only a few of her poems were published—and those in
edited and conventionalized versions—in her lifetime. After attending Amherst
Academy and a year in a seminary, she spent her life and died in the same
house in Amherst, Massachusetts, where she was born. In 1862, she wrote to
Thomas Wentworth Higginson, editor of the *Atlantic* magazine, enclosing
some poems and asking his opinion. Unable to deal with her strange, provocative poetry, he encouraged her to make her poetry more "regular." After her
death, 1,775 poems were discovered in a dresser drawer in her bedroom. "She
did in her poetry what she could never have done out loud," writes Louise

Bernikow. "She found a voice both original and strange in which to speak with the kind of honesty that exists in no other poet of her time."

JOHN DONNE (1572–1631), English poet, preacher, and religious prose writer, was born in London. He enrolled in Oxford; after converting from Roman Catholicism to the Anglican church, he was ordained into its priesthood in 1614. In 1621 he became dean of St. Paul's Cathedral in London, a position he held as an influential and compelling preacher until his death. When he was very ill in 1623, he wrote a series of essays called *Meditations*. His early love poems were probably written before 1614; his later religious poems were published in *Poems* in 1633. In recent decades, Donne's poetry and that of other metaphysical poets of the seventeenth century have been the object of much critical discussion. His poems appeal strongly to modern readers who prefer the challenging to the conventional, the complex to the superficial, the ironic to the sentimental.

H. D. (1886–1961), pseudonym of Hilda Doolittle, took on the "prophet's mantel in poetry, anticipating the spirit of the current feminist movement by a good half century" (Tom Clark). Born in Bethlehem, Pennsylvania, H. D. attended Bryn Mawr. In 1911 she went to Europe, where she lived most of her life. She began publishing when in 1913 Ezra Pound sent some of her poems to Harriet Monroe of *Poetry* magazine. H. D. soon became known as one of the leaders of the Imagist poets. She published six poetry collections, wrote several novels, and translated Greek literature.

RICHARD EBERHART (born 1904), critically acclaimed American poet, was educated at Cambridge and worked as a tutor to the son of the king of Siam, and as a businessman, a naval officer, a cultural adviser, and a professor. His books of poetry include *Selected Poems, 1930–1965* and *Gifts of Being* (1968).

T. S. ELIOT (1888–1965) was a chief architect of modern poetic theory and one of his century's most influential poets. Born in St. Louis, Missouri, he studied at Harvard, then settled in London in 1915, becoming a British citizen thirteen years later. His poetry departed dramatically from familiar conventions and techniques, notably in "The Love Song of J. Alfred Prufrock" and the epochal *The Waste Land*, which he dedicated to Ezra Pound. Eliot's later works include *Four Quartets* (1943), his plays *Murder in the Cathedral* (1935) and *The Family Reunion* (1939), and poems for cat lovers, which inspired a triumphantly successful musical. He won the Nobel Prize for literature in 1948.

LOUISE ERDRICH (born 1954) writes about American Indian traditions in her novels *Beet Queen* and *Love Medicine,* as well as in her shorter works. Part Chippewa Indian, Erdrich is intensely involved in native American land claims and other issues concerning native Americans. Born in Little Falls, Minnesota, she spent much of her youth on the North Dakota reservation where her father taught school. She was educated at Dartmouth and Johns Hopkins. She has collaborated with her husband, Michael Dorris, on a nonfiction book, *Broken Chord,* about fetal alcohol syndrome among American Indians.

MARTIN ESPADA (born 1958) was raised in a Brooklyn housing project and became an attorney and a poet, using the "power of the word to fight against what I consider to be wrong." He won the 1991 Peterson Poetry Prize for *Rebellion Is the Circle of a Lover's Hands.*

NELLE FERTIG (born 1919) is included in current collections of work by women poets.

DONALD FINKEL (born 1929) "is one of the few Americans," says Peter Meinke, "trying to extend poetry past the internal into the external world." Much of Finkel's work has been praised by the critics for its startling images and "comic extravagance." A New York native, Finkel has taught at the University of Iowa, Washington University, and Princeton. His numerous awards include the National Book Award for his 1979 poetry collection *The Garbage Wars.* Joseph Bennet wrote in the *New York Times Book Review* that Finkel is "so gifted he does not need subjects for his poems. . . . He has, above all, the gift of wonderment."

ROBERT FROST (1874–1963), born in San Francisco, moved to New England at age ten upon his father's death, and his poetry is closely linked with rural Vermont and New Hampshire. After briefly attending Dartmouth and Harvard, Frost worked as a shoemaker, schoolteacher, editor, and farmer. Unable to make a living, he took his family to England, where his first poetry collection, *A Boy's Will,* appeared in 1913. By 1914 his reputation had become firmly established through the publication of *North of Boston,* a collection containing what were to become some of his most popular poems, including "Mending Wall" and "The Death of the Hired Man." Frost won Pulitzer Prizes for poetry in 1924, 1931, 1937, and 1943. He developed a legendary reputation as America's best-known poet; he read "The Gift Outright" at John F. Kennedy's inauguration in 1960.

FEDERICO GARCÍA LORCA (1898–1936) was killed by the Fascists during the Spanish Civil War. Born in Andalusia, in southern Spain, Lorca spent some time in New York and Cuba in his early thirties. He is best known for his play *Blood Wedding,* which was first performed in Madrid in 1933. His early poems have been compared to "strange folk or fairy tales," and his New York poems have been described as "rougher and freer and less songlike." Kenneth Koch notes that "Lorca's poetry is always wild and strange in one way or another." Lorca believed his dreamlike images reached the complex truth that direct language does not reach.

DANA GIOIA (born 1950), whose surname is pronounced *"Joy*-a," was born in Los Angeles to a cabdriver and a telephone operator. Educated at Stanford and Harvard universities, Gioia has said, "Though most of my poems use rhyme or meter, they rarely follow 'traditional' patterns. I love traditional forms, but I find them slightly dangerous. Their music can become so seductive that one loses touch with contemporary speech, which is, to my judgment, the basis for all genuine poetry."

NIKKI GIOVANNI (born 1943) believes that "a poem is a way of capturing a moment. . . . A poem's got to be a single stroke, and I make it the best I can because it's going to live." Born Yolande Cornelia Giovanni in Knoxville, Tennessee, Giovanni was the daughter of a probation officer and a social worker. In 1967, she graduated from Fisk University in Nashville and later did graduate work at both the University of Pennsylvania and Columbia University. *Black Feeling, Black Talk,* her first volume of poetry, appeared in 1968, and in 1970 she established her own publishing firm. A prolific writer, Giovanni believes that "poetry is the most mistaught subject in any school because we teach poetry by form and not by content."

JUDY GRAHN (born 1940), born in Chicago, graduated from San Francisco State University. She has published eight books of poetry, including *The Work of a Common Woman* and *The Queen of Swords,* which was performed in San Francisco. She has also published books about poetry and language, as well as a novel, *Mundane's World.* The winner of several grants and awards, Grahn founded the Women's Press Collective in 1970 and has taught writing and mythology.

ANNE HALLEY (born 1928)—the daughter of a German mother and a Jewish father, both physicians—came to America in 1938 from Germany as a refugee from Nazism. Educated at Wellesley and the University of Minnesota, Halley studied with Mary Curran and Robert Penn Warren and was influenced in her early years by the English metaphysical poets. She lives in Massachusetts, where she has taught at several colleges and edited the *Massachusetts Review* out of the University of Massachusetts. Her work centers on women's concerns, the legacies of a German-Jewish past, social issues, and problems of language.

THOMAS HARDY (1840–1928)—a major British novelist *(Tess of the D'Urbervilles, The Mayor of Casterbridge)*—produced eleven novels and three collections of stories before he finally abandoned prose for his first love, poetry, in his sixtieth year. He produced delicately bittersweet poems until he was almost ninety. Critics, thinking his power had waned, did not take his poetry seriously until he published his epic, *The Dynasts* (1904), which established his reputation as a poet. The young poet Siegfried Sassoon wrote that Hardy recorded life with "microscopic exactitude . . . and a subtle ironic sense" of the tragic in human existence: "But his despair is mitigated by tenderness and pity for his fellows. With a wistful understanding he surveys the human scene." As an octogenarian, Hardy published *Late Lyrics and Earlier* (1922); his posthumous *Winter Words in Various Moods and Metres* was arranged by him before his death. Louis Untermeyer observed that, although his syntax was often clumsy, his poetry is "as disciplined as it is original."

JEFFREY HARRISON (born 1957) believes that "poetry is the lens through which the soul looks at the world, thereby keeping the soul alive." Harrison, an Ohio native who lives in Cincinnati, is author of the poetry collection *The Singing Underneath* and a contributor to many magazines. Educated at Columbia University and the University of Iowa, Harrison has taught English in Japan and has worked as a researcher in Washington, D.C.

ROBERT HASS (born 1941) was born and raised in San Francisco and studied at St. Mary's College in Oakland and Stanford University. He has taught at the State University of New York at Buffalo, St. Mary's College, and Berkeley. His first book, *Field Guide,* won the 1973 Yale Series of Younger Poets Award; he received a MacArthur Foundation award in 1985. "Hass believes that poetry is what defines the self, and it is his ability to describe that process that is the heart" of the pleasure his work gives his readers (Anthony Libby).

ROBERT HAYDEN (1913–1980), born in Detroit, Michigan, graduated from Wayne State University in Detroit and did graduate work at the University of Michigan. He later joined the faculty of Fisk University. *Heartshape in the Dust,* his first poetry collection, appeared in 1940. His 1963 collection *A Ballad of Remembrance* received the grand prize at the World Festival of Negro Arts. Hayden called his work "a form of prayer—a prayer of illumination, perfection."

SEAMUS HEANEY (born 1939) was born to a rural Catholic family in Northern Ireland, received a B.A. from Queen's University in Belfast in 1961, and taught in secondary schools and universities. His first published book, *Death of a Naturalist,* set his reputation of being a powerful "rural poet," a label he addresses in these lines: "Between my fingers and my thumb / The squat pen rests. / I'll dig with it." Heaney's poetry is steeped in Irish lore and history and noted for its "inventive language and sharp, immediate physical imagery." More than simply portraying the Irish countryside and folklore, however, Heaney is concerned with the poet's political role, seeing poets as "both helpless witnesses and accomplices in the fratricidal battles" of Ireland.

JOHN HEAVISIDE published his poem in the *Olivetree Review,* a publication devoted to student work and published at Hunter College of the City University of New York.

GEORGE HERBERT (1593–1633), a younger son of a wealthy aristocratic English family, began writing religious verse while an undergraduate at Cambridge University. Until the death of King James in 1625, Herbert enjoyed royal favor and participated in the life of the court. Undecided for a time between the uncertain promise of a career in public office and a career as a churchman, he eventually became an Anglican priest. His collected poems were published after his death in a volume entitled *The Temple.* Like other metaphysical poets of his time, Herbert introduced into religious poetry complex imagery and intense personal emotion.

ROBERT HERRICK (1591–1674) addressed lightweight conventional poems about love to imaginary Corinnas and Julias while leading a quiet life as a country priest. Born in London, Herrick was apprenticed as a young man to his uncle, a wealthy goldsmith. Later Herrick entered Cambridge, and at some point before 1627 he was ordained an Anglican priest. Two years later the king appointed him to a rural parish in a location he hated at first but grew to love. His *Hesperion,* published in 1648, contains 1,200 poems.

A. D. HOPE (born 1907), a native of Australia, attended Sydney and Oxford universities. A teacher and lecturer as well as a poet, Alec Derwent Hope has been called "one of the two or three best poets writing in English." Hope himself has said that "poetry is principally concerned to 'express' its subject and in doing so to create an emotion which is the feeling of the poem and not the feeling of the poet." Hope is interested in philosophy, biology, and history and claims he has "no very fixed convictions on anything." His most recent collection is *Selected Poems* (1986).

GERARD MANLEY HOPKINS (1844–1889) saw none of his poems published during his lifetime. Born in London, this English poet earned a degree from Oxford in 1867, one year after he had converted to Roman Catholicism. He then entered the Society of Jesus and was ordained a Jesuit priest. Troubled by what he saw as a conflict between his life as a priest and as a poet, he had burned all his poems when he entered the Jesuit order but began to write poetry again in 1875. His complete poetic works were published nineteen years after Hopkins' death by his friend, the poet Robert Bridges. Modern poets and critics soon provided a receptive audience for its complex diction, startling imagery, and intense religious emotion. His poems defied convention and are marked by what one of his editors called "a kind of creative violence."

LADY HORIKAWA (twelfth century) was a woman poet living in Japan in the 1100s.

A. E. HOUSMAN (1859–1936), born in Worcestershire, England, failed his final examinations at Oxford in 1881. Sometime during the previous four years he had changed from lively and outgoing to strictly reserved and melancholy, a change that culminated in this bitter disappointment. Working as a clerk in the Patent Office, he pursued studies on his own and contributed numerous articles to classical journals. Eventually he was named professor of Latin at Cambridge and published *A Shropshire Lad,* his major collection of poems, in 1896.

LANGSTON HUGHES (1902–1967) was a central figure of the Harlem Renaissance of the 1920s, a movement that examined and celebrated American black life and its African heritage. Hughes focused on what it was like to be black in America, a thread that runs through his work as poet, editor, and biographer. Born in Joplin, Missouri, Hughes attended high school in Cleveland, and his first published poems appeared in the school's literary magazine. He attended New York's Columbia University for a year and graduated from Lincoln University in Pennsylvania. His first poetry collection, *The Weary Blues,* appeared in 1926. In addition to numerous collections of poetry, Hughes wrote novels, short stories, plays, radio and motion picture scripts, and nonfiction. In his frequent lecture appearances at black colleges throughout the South, Hughes encouraged others to write. He also translated into English the poetry of black writers from other parts of the world. His own poetry has been translated into many other languages.

BEN JONSON (1572–1637), called by one critic "the most scholarly of all Elizabethan playwrights," worked for a time at bricklaying, his stepfather's trade. Jonson's real love, however, was the theater, and after military service he became attached to a company of actors as player and playwright. His *Every Man in His Humour* was performed in 1598, with Shakespeare in the cast. Jonson also wrote love lyrics and songs for his many plays and masques.

MARIE LUISE KASCHNITZ (1902–1974), like many German artists and writers, was censored and driven into exile by Hitler. Born in Karlsruhe, she was honored with some of the most prestigious German literary prizes after the war. In addition to writing short stories, essays, and poetry, Kaschnitz produced several radio plays. Her reflections of an aging woman in *Tage, Tage, Jahre (Days, Days, Years)* "define the high point of her literary achievement" (Marilyn Sibley Fries).

JOHN KEATS (1795–1821) died at age twenty-six from tuberculosis and became for later generations a symbol of the sensitive artist destroyed by a harsh world. Born in London, Keats gave up studying medicine for writing when thirty-three of his poems were published. He produced some of his finest poetry in 1818 and 1819, including "La Belle Dame sans Merci" and "Ode on a Grecian Urn." Admired for the rich sensuous imagery of his poetry, Keats was passionately concerned with the relationship between emotion and knowledge, between beauty and truth. He expressed a conviction shared by many Romantic writers when he wrote, "I am certain of the heart's affections and the truth of imagination—What the imagination seizes as beauty must be truth."

MAXINE KUMIN (born 1925) was born in Philadelphia, Pennsylvania. She earned her B.A. and M.A. degrees from Radcliffe and lives on a farm in New Hampshire. She published her first collection of poetry in 1961 and won the Pulitzer Prize in 1973 for her collection of poems entitled *Up Country*. She has written a number of novels and numerous successful children's books, several in collaboration with her friend, poet Anne Sexton. She has lectured at the University of Massachusetts, Columbia, Brandeis, and Princeton. May Swenson has called Kumin's work "large-hearted, articulate, and acute."

MELVIN WALKER LA FOLLETTE (born 1930) "believes in the sensuous body of the world," wrote Richard Eberhart, adding, "He finds his feelings of the greatest richness of life in three areas . . . youth, the love of small animals," and "the devotion to the idea of saints and sainthood." La Follette was born in Evansville, Indiana. He received his B.A. in creative writing at the University of Washington. He taught for many years at colleges in California, Canada, and Oregon. He also spent time in forestry work in various parts of the Pacific Northwest.

PHILIP LARKIN (1922–1985), a native of Coventry, England, was considered by some critics to be the finest English poet of his generation. Larkin began his studies at Oxford in 1940. After graduating, he became a librarian at the University of Leicester. In 1946 he published his first poetry collection, *The North Ship*, but it wasn't until 1960, with the publication of *The Less Deceived*, that he gained critical recognition. In addition to publishing many poetry collections, he served as editor of the *Oxford Book of Twentieth Century Verse* and was a recognized expert on jazz. Larkin once said, "Form holds little interest for me. Content is everything."

JAMES LAUGHLIN (born 1914) has made the writing of love poems and light verse his principal avocation. He is also well known as publisher of New Directions Books. Laughlin was friends with William Carlos Williams and e. e. cummings, and the influence of both poets is clear in his work. City Lights Books published Laughlin's *Selected Poems, 1935–1985*.

LI-YOUNG LEE (born 1957) has said, "I believe the King James Bible to contain some of the greatest poetry in the world and I hope to own some of its glory and mystery in my own writing one day." Lee was born in Jakarta, Indonesia, to Chinese parents "who were classically educated and in the habit of reciting literally hundreds of ancient Chinese poems." His father, jailed by then-dictator Sukarno in a leper colony, escaped, and the family fled to the United States. They settled in Pennsylvania, where his father became a Presbyterian minister. His volume of poems, *Rose*, appeared in 1986.

URSULA K. LE GUIN (born 1929), the daughter of an anthropologist and a folklorist, has been called "the best living writer of fantasy and science fiction." Her novels include *The Left Hand of Darkness*, *The Dispossessed*, and *Always Coming Home*. In addition to adult fiction, she has published poetry, children's books, and essays about her travels and her political commitments as a strong feminist, environmentalist, and champion of the dispossessed.

DENISE LEVERTOV (born 1923) has said she grew up in "a house full of books and everyone in the family engaged in some literary activity." The family's vast library and the diverse visitors to the house—"Jewish booksellers, German theologians, Russian priests from Paris, and Viennese opera singers"—were her education. Her father, a biblical scholar and Anglican priest, harbored the lifelong hope of the unification of Judaism and Christianity. Born in Essex, England, Levertov was a civilian nurse in London during World War II, then settled in New York in 1948 with her American husband. The influence of the American poet William Carlos Williams helped her to develop "from a British Romantic with almost Victorian background to an American poet of . . . vitality."

AUDRE LORDE (born 1934) describes herself as a "black lesbian feminist warrior poet." Born in New York City of West Indian parents, Lorde attended Hunter College and Columbia. She worked as a librarian and then taught at several colleges before becoming a professor of English at Hunter College in New York City. She lives on Staten Island with her companion and her two children. Her first poetry collection, *The First Cities* (1968), chronicles the effects of racism on African Americans. A more recent work, *Zami: A New Spelling of My Name,* Lorde calls her "biomytho-graphy." In what Claudia Tate calls "stunning figurative language," Lorde "outlines the progress of her unyielding struggle for the human rights of all people."

RICHARD LOVELACE (1618–1658) was born in Kent and studied at Oxford. An ardent supporter of Charles I, he was held in London as a prisoner during the civil war between the monarchists and the Puritan rebels. When the king was executed, Lovelace lost everything; he spent the remainder of his life in poverty. Most of his poetry was not published in his lifetime, but today he is one of the best remembered of the Cavalier (royalist) poets.

EDWARD LUCIE-SMITH (born 1933) was born in Kingston, Jamaica, and educated at Oxford. He went to live in London, working as a free-lance writer, an art critic, an anthologist, and a translator.

HUGH MACDIARMID (1892–1978) "effected, almost single-handed, a literary revolution," wrote David Daiches. "He . . . destroyed one Scottish tradition and founded another." In order to identify himself with the Scots' heritage, MacDiarmid changed his name from Christopher Grieve, his English name. Setting himself the task of reviving the great Scottish poetic tradition, he wrote the much-admired lyric poetic sequence *A Drunk Man Looks at the Thistle* in 1926.

CLAUDE MCKAY (1890–1948), who wrote militant poetry attacking the racism he encountered as a black immigrant to the United States, surprised some readers by converting to Roman Catholicism in the 1940s. "To have a religion," he wrote, "is very much like falling in love with a woman. You love her for her beauty, which cannot be defined." Born in Jamaica, McKay was a published poet before coming to the United States at age twenty-three. His 1919 poem "If We Must Die" helped inaugurate the 1920s Harlem Renaissance. His writings include an autobiography entitled *A Long Way from Home,* published in 1927.

ROD MCKUEN (born 1933) built a business empire consisting of four record labels, three book publishers, two music-publishing companies, a mail-order venture, and a clothing company named "Rod McKuen Casuals." A resident of Los Angeles, he has published many collections of poetry, composed musical scores, and written more than a thousand songs.

ARCHIBALD MACLEISH (1892–1982) was for a time a leading advocate of the role of poetry in contemporary society. Born in Glencoe, Illinois, he served in World War I in 1917–1918. He graduated from Yale in 1915 and received a law degree from Harvard Law School in 1919. He grew tired of law practice and turned to study literature, reading the works of the great early moderns, T. S. Eliot and Ezra Pound. President Franklin Roosevelt appointed MacLeish librarian of Congress in 1939, and he served as assistant secretary of state during the final two years of World War II. In 1953, his *Collected Poems*

1917–1952 won him his second Pulitzer. MacLeish taught at Harvard and at Amherst College.

ANDREW MARVELL (1621–1678) was known in his day for satirical commentary on political events; his poetry was not published until after his death. Today his "To His Coy Mistress" is one of the best-known poems in the English language. Twentieth-century critics rediscovered Marvell and other metaphysical poets (John Donne, George Herbert), championing their love of irony and paradox and their blend of intellectual vigor and passionate intensity. Born in Yorkshire, Marvell entered Oxford at the age of twelve. When the civil war broke out, he was appointed assistant to John Milton in the Cromwell government. After the monarchy was restored, he served in Parliament until his death.

JOHN MASEFIELD (1878–1967), a native of Herefordshire, England, was a young boy when his father, a lawyer, died. At fourteen Masefield was indentured to a merchant ship and became a wanderer for several years. Staying for a time in New York, he took odd jobs before returning to England at nineteen. After Masefield read Chaucer, he was determined to become a poet. Not until the 1911 publication of *The Everlasting Mercy* did he become famous. In addition to his poetry, he wrote more than a dozen plays, a book on Shakespeare, twelve volumes of essays, books for youths, and adventure novels.

PETER MEINKE (born 1932) was born in Brooklyn, New York. He served in the U.S. Army and received a B.A. from Hamilton College, an M.A. from the University of Michigan, and a Ph.D. from the University of Minnesota. Meinke's reviews, poems, and stories have appeared in periodicals such as the *Atlantic,* the *New Yorker,* and the *New Republic.* His collection of short stories, *The Piano Tuner,* won the 1986 Flannery O'Connor Award.

WILLIAM MEREDITH (born 1919), a native of New York City, graduated from Princeton in 1940 and served as a naval aviator during World War II. His award-winning poetry has been published in several collections, including *Ships and Other Figures, The Open Sea,* and *Earth Walk: New & Selected Poems.* He taught at Princeton and Carnegie-Mellon, and has been with Connecticut College since 1955.

EVE MERRIAM (born 1916) grew up in a suburb of Philadelphia. A 1937 graduate of the University of Pennsylvania, Merriam continued her studies at Columbia and the University of Wisconsin. In 1946 she published her first poetry collection, *Family Circle,* which received the Yale Younger Poets Prize. She wanted to share her lifelong love of words with children, so she began writing poetry designed for young people. The first of these collections appeared in 1962 under the title *There Is No Rhyme for Silver.* Other titles followed: *It Doesn't Always Have to Rhyme, Catch a Little Rhyme,* and *Independent Voices.*

W. S. MERWIN (born 1927), one of the most prolific poets and translators of his generation, was born the son of a Presbyterian minister in New York

City. Educated at Princeton, Merwin was influenced by poet Robert Graves, whose son he tutored in Majorca, Spain. Merwin has translated widely from Spanish, Portuguese, Latin, French, and Russian in both conventional forms and free verse. He has received numerous fellowships and awards, including a Pulitzer Prize in 1971 for his collection *A Carrier of Ladders*. He went to live in Hawaii in 1968.

EDNA ST. VINCENT MILLAY (1892–1950) began writing poetry as a child in Camden, Maine, encouraged by her mother, who had left her father when Millay was eight years old. While a rebellious student at Vassar, Millay dared the president to expel her, and he explained that he didn't want a "banished Shelley on my doorstep." She supposedly replied, "On those terms, I think I can continue to live in this hellhole." She graduated in 1917, the same year her first book of poems was published. In 1923 she won a Pulitzer Prize for her poetry collection, *The Harp-Weaver*. In addition to over twenty volumes of verse, she published three verse plays, wrote a libretto for an opera, and translated Baudelaire. Neglected for a time by critics who thought her poetry too traditional in form and too frankly emotional, she has recently been rediscovered by feminist critics as an early champion of feminist themes.

VASSAR MILLER (born 1924) calls poetry "an act of love." Born in Houston, Miller was educated at the University of Houston. She has published several poetry collections, including *Wage War on Silence*. Afflicted with cerebral palsy from birth, Miller has dedicated herself to poetry "and has demonstrated . . . that craftsmanship, religious fervor, and personal joy and agony can produce major poetry" (Chad Walsh).

CZESLAW MILOSZ (born 1911) "deals in his poetry with the central issues of our time: the impact of history upon moral being, the search for ways to survive spiritual ruin in a ruined world" (Terrence Des Pres). Milosz, a native of Lithuania, published his first book of poetry at age twenty-one. When Poland was invaded by Germany and Soviet Russia in 1939, Milosz worked with the underground Resistance in Warsaw, writing and editing several books published secretly. After the war, Milosz became a member of the new communist government's diplomatic service but left this post in 1951 and defected to the West. He joined the faculty at the University of California at Berkeley in 1960 and won the Nobel Prize for literature in 1980.

JOHN MILTON (1608–1674) was poet deeply involved in the political and religious turmoil of his time. Born in Cheapside, London he was steeped in classical literature and wrote some of his early poems in Latin and in Italian. After graduating from Cambridge, Milton traveled the continent, returning to England shortly before the civil war. Milton was an ardent supporter of the Puritan cause. He joined in the vigorous polemics of the time and published aggressive prose tracts on subjects including censorship. After the overthrow of King Charles I, Milton became Latin secretary in charge of diplomatic correspondence under the dictator Cromwell. He escaped death as a traitor to the crown after the restoration of the monarchy, publishing his monumental religious epic *Paradise Lost* in 1667. By this time he was completely blind and living in poverty. "Lycidas," the best known of his shorter poems, appeared in 1637.

GABRIELA MISTRAL (1889–1956) adopted her pen name from the names of two poets she admired, Gabriele D'Annunzio and Frédéric Mistral. Born in Chile, Mistral wrote about her concerns for children, the social condition of Chilean workers, and the social emancipation of women. Some of her books include *Sonetos de la Muerte* (1914), *Desolación* (1922), and *Ernura and Tala* (1923). In 1945 she was awarded the Nobel Prize for literature.

N. SCOTT MOMADAY (born 1934) is a Kiowa whose writing explores the history and culture of his people. Momaday was born in Lawton, Oklahoma. He graduated from the University of New Mexico in 1958 and received master's and doctoral degrees from Stanford. He began his academic career teaching English at the University of California, Santa Barbara, in 1973. He told the story of his rediscovery of his heritage in *The Journey of Tai-me* (1968)—republished with illustrations by his father Al Momaday under the title *The Way to Rainy Mountain*. His novel *The House Made of Dawn* won a Pulitzer Prize in 1969.

OGDEN NASH (1902–1971) gave pleasure to untold readers with a steady stream of irreverent light verse. Born in Rye, New York, Nash attended Harvard and worked as a teacher, a bond salesperson, and an editor for Doubleday Publishers in New York City. Later he joined the editorial staff of the *New Yorker*. His collected poems, *I Wouldn't Have Missed It,* appeared in 1975.

THOMAS NASHE (1567–1601), the son of a minister, was born in Lowestoft, England. After graduating from Cambridge, Nashe toured France and Italy and by 1588 was a professional writer living in London. Nashe wrote pamphlets to defend the Anglican church against attacks by the Puritans. He also wrote several plays and in 1594 published an adventure novel, *The Unfortunate Traveler*.

HOWARD NEMEROV (born 1920), American poet and literary critic, was born and raised in New York City. He graduated from Harvard and served in World War II with a fighter squadron in the British Royal Air Force. He has taught at Bennington College in Vermont and George Washington University in St. Louis. Known for its clarity and simplicity, much of his poetry sings the praises of nature and the simple life.

PABLO NERUDA (1904–1973) said, "I like the lives of people who are restless and unsatisfied, whether they are artists or criminals." Neruda himself lived a restless, adventure-filled life. Born "Neftali Beltran" in a small frontier town in southern Chile, Neruda took his pseudonym at a young age out of admiration for a nineteenth century Czech writer. When Neruda was still a boy, his father, a railroad worker, was killed in a fall from a train. At nineteen, Neruda published a book called *Twenty Poems of Love and One Ode of Despera-*

tion, which is still loved in South America. During that period, he said, "Love poems were sprouting out all over my body." In later years much of his poetry became political. He served as consulate in the Far East and Mexico and traveled widely. He became a member of the Chilean Senate, fleeing from dictatorship for a time. During his years of exile, Neruda wrote *Canto General,* which his translator, Robert Bly, called "the greatest long poem written on the American continent since *Leaves of Grass.*"

NILA NORTHSUN (born 1951) was born in Schurz, Nevada, of Shoshoni-Chippewa heritage. She coauthored *After the Drying Up of the Water* and *Diet Pepsi and Nacho Cheese.* She has written about the ironies of exchanging reservation life for city life.

SHARON OLDS (born 1942) has said, "One of the hardest tasks as a poet is to believe in oneself—or to act as if we do!" A self-described "late bloomer," Olds says she was thirty before she found her voice, her ability "to embody on the page thinking about an actual self." Born in San Francisco, Olds earned a B.A. from Stanford and a Ph.D. from Columbia. A winner of many awards, she has taught and given numerous readings at colleges and universities. Her poetry books are *Satan Says* (1980), *The Dead and the Living* (1982), *The Gold Cell* (1987), and *The Father* (1992). She writes with astonishing frankness and authentic emotion about being a child, a woman, and a mother.

MARY OLIVER (born 1935), was born in Cleveland, Ohio, and attended both Ohio State and Vassar. She worked as a secretary to the sister of poet Edna St. Vincent Millay. Her first collection of poetry, *No Voyage, and Other Poems,* appeared in 1963, then again in 1965 with nineteen additional poems. Her second collection, *The River Styx, Ohio, and Other Poems,* appeared in 1972.

WILFRED OWEN (1893–1918) wrote powerful antiwar poems during World War I—poems that are a lasting memorial and tribute to a generation destroyed in the trenches of Flanders and northern France. Owen was killed in action one week before the armistice, at age twenty-five. Born in Shropshire, England, into a devout, relatively poor family, Owen was educated at London University and enlisted in military service when England entered the war. In late 1917 he was wounded and sent to a military hospital. There he met the poet Siegfried Sassoon, who edited and published Owen's poems after Owen's death.

DOROTHY PARKER (1893–1967) has been called "the quintessential New York wit, known as much for what she said as for what she wrote." Parker often wrote bitter satire and showed empathy toward suffering. "The humorist has never been happy, anyhow," she once said. "Today he's whistling past worse graveyards to worse tunes." In addition to writing for the *New Yorker* and *Vanity Fair,* Parker wrote screenplays for Hollywood.

LINDA PASTAN (born 1932) was born in New York City and studied at Brandeis and Radcliffe. Her first poetry collection, *A Perfect Circle of Sun,* appeared in 1971. Other collections include *Five Stages of Grief* (1978), *AM/PM*

(1982), *Imperfect Paradise* (1988), and *Heroes in Disguise* (1991). Poet laureate of the State of Maryland, she has been honored with fellowships from the National Endowment for the Arts. The *Washington Post* noted that Pastan "writes with a music of her own—reinforced by overtones of Yeats and Frost."

OCTAVIO PAZ (born 1914), Mexican poet and critic, won the Nobel Prize for literature in 1991. He has lectured to large audiences in the United States and served as Mexico's ambassador to India, a post from which he resigned in 1968 in protest over the bloody repression of student demonstrators before the Olympic Games in Mexico City. He has written much about the dialogue between the North American and Latin American cultures. Published collections of his poetry include *Savage Moon* (1933), *Sun Stone* (1957), and *Selected Poems* (1960).

FRANCESCO PETRARCA (1304–1374) was a humanist of the early Italian Renaissance, participating in the rediscovery of the learning and literature of classical antiquity. His *Canzoniere,* a collection of songs *(canzoni)* and sonnets, started the vogues of Petrarchan love poetry that dominated lyric poetry in Europe for centuries.

MARGE PIERCY (born 1936) was born in poverty in Detroit during the depression. She was the first in her family to go to college and "took five years to recover." She has published eight novels, including *Woman on the Edge of Time,* a science fiction work in which she experiments with a "woman's language." She has also written a play, essays, and nine volumes of poetry. Recent works include a 1988 volume of poems entitled *Available Light.* When she is not giving readings and conducting workshops throughout the country, she writes in her Cape Cod home.

CHRISTINE DE PISAN (about 1364–1430), called "France's first woman of letters" by biographer Charity Cannon Willard, lived and wrote at the end of the Middle Ages. Born in Venice, Italy, she moved to Paris, France, at age four. There her family became part of the royal court, for her father, a scientist, was employed by King Charles V. At age fifteen she married but was widowed after ten years. Her first poetry collection, published by 1402, marked the beginning of a long literary career, during which de Pisan wrote lyrical and allegorical poetry, biographies of important political figures (including Charles V), textbooks, and books about women and government. She is also known for her role in a debate over contemporary negative attitudes toward women and for her championing of women's rights.

SYLVIA PLATH (1932–1963) was born in Boston of an Austrian-born father who was an instructor at Boston University and an expert on bees. She began writing early and sold several stories and poems to *Seventeen* magazine. A 1955 summa cum laude graduate in English from Smith, Plath earned an M.A. at Cambridge as a Fulbright scholar. In 1956 she married English poet Ted Hughes. *The Colossus,* published in 1960, was her only poetry collection to appear before she committed suicide. *The Bell Jar,* a quasi-autobiographical novel, chronicles the struggles of a brilliant young woman with radical alienation from her environment and her bouts with suicidal depression. Critic David Young says Plath "lived on a knife-edge, in the presence of a tremendous attraction to death and nothingness," Since her death, her powerful and disturbing poetry has been widely discussed and anthologized.

ALEXANDER POPE (1668–1744) became an arbiter of literary taste in the age of reason. Born into the family of a prosperous London merchant, Pope's formal education was largely confined to his own home. Excluded from universities discriminating against Catholics, Pope quickly demonstrated his ability to overcome obstacles and adverse criticism. His *Essay on Criticism* (1711), a discussion in poetic form of literary taste and style, established its author's reputation. He undertook monumental translations of Homer's *Iliad* and *Odyssey* by public subscription and became financially independent in the process. *An Essay on Man,* a versified compendium of the fashionable optimistic philosophy of his age, appeared in 1733.

EZRA POUND (1885–1972) was one of the great innovators and nonconformists of early modern poetry. He championed or inspired writers like Marianne Moore, T. S. Eliot, Robert Frost, William Carlos Williams, Ernest Hemingway, and James Joyce. Pound was born in Idaho and educated at Hamilton College and the University of Pennsylvania. Associated with the imagist poets, Pound translated Chinese, Latin, Japanese, German, French, Italian, Greek, Anglo-Saxon, and Provençal (thirteenth-century French) poetry. In 1945 he was arrested for treason because of radio broadcasts in Fascist Italy during World War II. Found unfit for trial by reason of insanity, he was committed to St. Elizabeth's Hospital in Washington, D.C., where he spent over ten years. His most ambitious and complex work is *The Cantos,* a vast, richly allusive collection of poems he worked on while in a prisoner of war camp near Pisa, Italy.

LEROY V. QUINTANA (born 1944) has said, "In many ways, I'm still basically a small-town New Mexico boy carrying on the oral tradition." Born in Albuquerque, Quintana was raised by his grandparents, who told him *cuentos*—traditional Mexican folktales—and stories of life in the Old West. "I seem to be tied to a sense of the past," he said. "My work reflects the 'sense of place' evoked by New Mexico. I hope I am worthy of portraying the land and its people well." Quintana, a graduate of the University of New Mexico, won the American Book Award for poetry in 1982 for *Sangre*. His other titles include *Hijo del Pueblo: New Mexico Poems* (1976) and *The Reason People Don't Like Mexicans* (1984).

JOHN CROWE RANSOM (1888–1974), both as a poet and a critic, shared in the redirection of modern literary taste associated with the rediscovery of the metaphysical poets of the seventeenth century. Born in Pulaski, Tennessee, Ransom was educated at Vanderbilt University and Oxford, where he was a Rhodes scholar. Ransom made a name for himself as both poet and critic in the 1920s and 1930s. He taught at Vanderbilt and then at Kenyon

College, where he was a faculty member for almost forty years. At Kenyon he founded and edited the *Kenyon Review*. He became a leader in what was then called the New Criticism, publishing *The World's Body* in 1938 and *The New Criticism* in 1941.

HENRY REED (born 1914), poet and playwright, was born in Birmingham, England. After earning a B.A. from the University of Birmingham in 1937, he worked as a teacher and free-lance writer. He served a stint in the British army and wrote poetry about his experience in cadet training, as well as about political events of the time. His only collection of poetry, *A Map of Verona*, appeared in 1946. Soon thereafter, he began writing radio plays, including the popular BBC "Hilda Tablet" series, a parody of British society in the 1930s.

KENNETH REXROTH (born 1905) has been a painter, essayist, radio and television performer, editor, and journalist as well as a poet. Born in Indiana, Rexroth was mostly self-educated. A guru of the Beat Generation, for many years he lived in San Francisco and has written extensively about California's High Sierra Mountains. "Some of his mountain poems are the best nature writing we have" (Hayden Carruth). Rexroth has translated from six languages and has written three volumes of critical essays.

ADRIENNE RICH (born 1929) was educated by her parents in their Baltimore, Maryland, home until fourth grade, when she entered public school. A 1951 Phi Beta Kappa graduate of Radcliffe, Rich won the Yale Younger Poets competition that same year for her collection *A Change of World*. Since then she has been awarded the prestigious Bollingen Prize and in 1974 was a cowinner with Allen Ginsberg of the National Book Award for poetry. She has published more than half a dozen books of poetry, including *Diving into the Wreck* (1973) and *The Dream of a Common Language: Poems 1974–1977*. An inspiration to feminist poets and critics, Rich collected some of her incisive, thought-provoking prose in *On Lies, Secrets, and Silence*.

RAINER MARIA RILKE (1875–1926), perhaps the most widely admired and translated of the twentieth-century German poets, was born in Prague to German-speaking parents. In 1898 he went to Russia, where he met Leo Tolstoy, author of *War and Peace*. In 1905 in France, Rilke served as secretary for the famous French sculptor Rodin, and the influence of this experience can be seen in his collection *New Poems*. When World War I broke out, Rilke moved to Switzerland, where he wrote *Sonnets to Orpheus* and the *Duino Elegies*. Critic Kenneth Koch has said of Rilke's power as a poet: "When Rilke writes about a subject, it is as if nothing were known about it, as if he started from the very beginning in order to understand deeply, for himself, the power or purpose or beauty of it."

THEODORE ROETHKE (1908–1963), grew up in Saginaw, Michigan, where his father and uncle owned a greenhouse; greenhouses would serve as prominent images in his poetry. He studied at the University of Michigan and Harvard, and he taught and coached tennis at a number of colleges. He sold his first poems for a dollar, but shortly thereafter his poetry appeared in several widely read magazines. He won a Pulitzer Prize in 1954 for *The Waking: Poems 1933–1953,* which was followed by the Bollingen Prize in 1959 for *Words for the Wind* and two National Book Awards. Abrasive in his criticism of contemporary culture and fellow poets, Roethke looked into the world of nature for sources of spiritual renewal.

CHRISTINA ROSSETTI (1830–1894), whose father had come to England as a political refugee from his native Italy, was born in London in a poor neighborhood. Rossetti had no formal education but was taught to read by her mother. From her earliest days she loved to write, and her grandfather had a number of her poems privately printed when she was twelve. Her first collection of poetry, *Goblin Market and Other Poems,* appeared in 1862.

LAURA ST. MARTIN (born 1957) has been anthologized in recent collections of contemporary American poets.

SAPPHO (about 620–550 B.C.), called "the tenth Muse" by Plato, lived on the Greek island of Lesbos, where she wrote passionate love poems addressed to younger women she may have taught. She was an aristocrat involved in controversial political activities which led to her being exiled twice. She married a rich merchant and bore a daughter. In 1073 A.D., a large collection of her verse was publicly burned by church dignitaries of Rome and Constantinople. However, some of her writing—as well as her legendary reputation—has remained intact.

ANNE SEXTON (1928–1974) encouraged writers to "put your ear close down to your soul and listen hard." Born in Newton, Massachusetts, she studied at Boston University and Brandeis. At twenty-eight, a suburban housewife, she suffered a nervous breakdown. Her therapist encouraged her to write, and she soon became a successful poet. She claimed that when she began to write she was reborn, for "suicide is the opposite of the poem." She wrote eight books of poetry; her *Live or Die* won the 1967 Pulitzer Prize. Sexton lived a troubled life, punctuated by suicide attempts and hospitalizations, until she finally took her life in 1974, mourned by fellow poets who thought of her as one of the great poetic talents of our time. "When I'm writing, I know I'm doing the thing I was born to do," she said. "I guess I listen for my melody. When it comes, I just turn . . . like a little dancer." A 1991 biography of Anne Sexton made the *New York Times* bestseller list.

WILLIAM SHAKESPEARE (1564–1616) is the foremost English dramatist of the reigns of Queen Elizabeth and King James I. Shakespeare was actor, playwright, and shareholder in a theatrical company at a time when the English stage enjoyed both royal patronage and popular support. He wrote some thirty-five plays for an audience that liked spectacle and was used to keen competition among theatrical companies and to rapid changes in dramatic fashions. A vast literature of comment, analysis, background information, and textual study has grown up around his works. His great tragedies—*Romeo and*

Juliet, Hamlet, Othello, King Lear, Macbeth—probe the paradoxes of our human nature and destiny. Little is known about his life: He was born in the small town of Stratford-on-Avon, and his formal studies ended with grammar school. At eighteen he married Anne Hathaway. He retired to his hometown at the end of his career.

PERCY BYSSHE SHELLEY (1792–1822), most iconoclastic of the younger Romantic poets, was born in Sussex, England, as the eldest son of a conservative country squire. He went to Oxford but was expelled for publishing a pamphlet that advocated atheism. This was but the first of many rebellions against convention and established institutions that marked his brief life. Shelley spent most of his adult life in Italy; many of his shorter and more famous lyric poems, such as "To a Skylark" and "Ode to the West Wind," he wrote in Pisa in 1819. One of his last poems is the elegy written to mourn the death of his close friend John Keats. Shelley himself, who had written "How wonderful is Death, / Death and his brother Sleep," died in a boating accident at age thirty.

CHARLES SIMIC (born 1938) came to the United States at age eleven from his native Yugoslavia. The son of an engineer and a dress designer, Simic has published twelve poetry collections. Robert Shaw of the *New Republic* said that Simic's poems are "at once weighty and evasive, and describing them is about as easy as picking up blobs of mercury with mittens on." Many critics have commented on the enigmatic quality of Simic's poetry: "I have not yet decided," writes Diane Wakoski in *Poetry,* "whether Charles Simic is America's greatest living surrealist poet, a children's writer, a religious writer, or simple-minded. . . . his poetry is cryptic and fascinating."

GARY SOTO (born 1952), award-winning Mexican American poet, believes that "writing makes the ordinary stand out, thus enabling us to build in some kind of metaphorical meaning." Much of Soto's writing includes the ordinary events of his childhood in Fresno, California. In addition to the prose memoir *Living up the Street,* Soto has published five books of poetry, including *Home Course in Religion* (1991). An alumnus of Fresno State and the University of California, Irvine, he joined the faculty at Berkeley. Soto says that literature "reshapes experience—both real and invented—to help us see ourselves—our foibles, failures, potential, beauty, pettiness. In short, literature helps define the world for us."

WOLE SOYINKA (born 1934) is associated worldwide with the struggle for justice and freedom in Africa. Born in Nigeria of Yoruban parents, this Nobel laureate writes plays, poems, and novels. He has worked as a teacher and served as secretary general of the Union of African Writers. His plays were first performed in England while he was a student at the University of Leeds. His poetry collection titles include *Idanre and Other Poems* and *A Shuttle in the Crypt,* which contains poems written while he was imprisoned during the Nigerian civil war.

WILLIAM STAFFORD (born 1914) grew up in small towns of central Kansas, hunting, camping, and fishing in the countryside. He earned a doctorate in English from Iowa State. A member of the United Brethren, Stafford became a conscientious objector during World War II. He worked in labor camps, an experience recorded in a prose memoir, *Down in My Heart.* In 1947 his first collection of poems appeared, and the next year he joined the faculty at Lewis and Clark College in Oregon. His third poetry collection, *Traveling through the Dark,* received the National Book Award in 1963. His poems often explore commonplace events; critics note, however, that on closer examination, Stafford proves to be "a very elusive poet with a distinctive private vision that slips through our grasp when we try to identify, summarize, or paraphrase it" (David Young).

WALLACE STEVENS (1879–1955), who commanded a large loyal following among readers dedicated to the cause of poetry, believed "the poem refreshes the world." Born in Reading, Pennsylvania, Stevens attended Harvard University and New York Law School. He began practicing law in 1904 and then joined the legal department of a Connecticut insurance company, retiring as vice president of the firm. His challenging, complex poetry appeared in journals as early as 1914; his first collection, *Harmonium,* appeared in 1923. His second collection, *Ideas of Order,* appeared thirteen years later.

SIR JOHN SUCKLING (1609–1642), who has been called "the most skeptical and libertine of the Cavaliers," was born the son of the secretary of state to King James I. Suckling studied at Cambridge and then traveled throughout Europe. A courtier with a reputation of brilliant wit, Suckling wrote four plays and a number of lyric poems. He became embroiled in political intrigue; he committed suicide in 1642.

JON SWAN contributed poems to the *New Yorker* in the 1950s and 1960s. He published *Journey and Return: Poems 1960* in the Poets of Today series.

MAY SWENSON (born 1919), a child of immigrant Swedish parents, was born in Logan, Utah. After graduating from Utah State University, she came to New York City and worked as an editor. She has received many awards for her poetry, which is noted for its freshness of perspective and experimental form. Some of her poetry collection titles are *Another Animal* (1954), *Iconographs* (1970), and *Poems to Solve* (1966), a volume for children.

JONATHAN SWIFT (1667–1745), a towering figure in eighteenth-century English literature, was born in Dublin, Ireland, of English parents. His father died shortly before he was born, and his mother gave him over to the care of a nurse. He was a rebellious and angry youth who barely graduated from Trinity College in Dublin. Swift was ordained a priest of the Anglican church, although he was more interested in politics than in the church. He wrote political tracts for the Whig party and later for the Tories, becoming editor of the

Tory newspaper. He castigated England's unfair treatment of Ireland and became a hero to the Irish. In 1726 he published *Gulliver's Travels*, a satirical masterpiece in an age of satire.

ALFRED, LORD TENNYSON (1809–1892), poet laureate of Victorian England, gave voice to characteristic assumptions and aspirations of his contemporaries. Born the son of a clergyman, Tennyson was educated at Cambridge. His first published poems appeared in 1830; in 1842 he published two volumes that included "Morte d'Arthur" and "Ulysses." His *In Memoriam* (1850), written after the death of a close friend, mirrored the religious doubts and earnestness of his time. His *Idylls of the King* (1859) became required reading for generations of high school students.

DYLAN THOMAS (1914–1953) called his poetry a record of his "struggle from darkness toward some measure of light." Born in Wales, Thomas had his only formal education in grammar school. When his first poetry collection appeared in 1932, he was hailed as a leading modern poet. His radio work in England and his numerous poetry readings at American college campuses made him a popular figure on both sides of the Atlantic. His passionate, visionary tone and wild flights of the imagination appealed to readers starved for mysticism and emotion. Alcoholism and lung ailments precipitated in his early death. Thomas once said that his poems, "with all their crudities, doubts, and confusions, are written for the love of man and in Praise of God, and I'd be a damn fool if they weren't."

UKIHASHI (seventeenth century) was a Japanese woman poet of the 1600s. Her work has been translated from the Japanese by Kenneth Rexroth and Ikuko Atsumi.

DAVID WAGONER (born 1926), "a master technician" (Daniel Halpern), was born in Ohio and educated at Penn State and Indiana University. An award-winning poet and novelist, Wagoner taught English at several colleges and made his home in Seattle. He has been praised for his witty and deep perceptions, as well as his "skillful manipulation of language" (Halpern).

ALICE WALKER (born 1944) has said, "All of my poems . . . are written when I have successfully pulled myself out of a completely numbing despair, and stand again in the sunlight." Born in the small town of Eatonsville, Georgia, Walker received her bachelor's degree in 1965 from Sarah Lawrence College. After graduating, she taught at several universities and worked for voter registration and welfare rights. Her novel *The Color Purple* (1982) made her the best-known black writer of her generation. In 1983, she published the essay collection *In Search of Our Mothers' Gardens*. Using language as catharsis and potential for growth is essential to Walker, who said, "No person is your friend (or kin) who demands your silence, or denies your right to grow and be perceived as fully blossomed as you were intended. Or who belittles in any fashion the gifts you labor so to bring into the world."

WALT WHITMAN (1819–1892), a giant of American and world literature, successfully created a public persona as the poet of democracy and the voice of an expansive vision of America. Son of a carpenter and farmer, he spent much of his life as a journalist in Brooklyn, Manhattan, and Long Island. In 1855, he published the first edition of *Leaves of Grass,* a milestone of nineteenth-century American literature. He celebrated the varied scene of contemporary America: the steamers and railroads and ferries, the carpenters and pilots and farmers, the cities and plains and mountains. He once said, "the United States themselves are essentially the greatest poem."

C. K. WILLIAMS (born 1936) was born in Newark, New Jersey, and was educated at Bucknell and the University of Pennsylvania. He established a program of poetry-therapy for emotionally disturbed patients at the Institute of the Pennsylvania Hospital in Philadelphia, where he also served as a group therapist in the treatment of disturbed adolescents. He has taught at Boston University, Columbia, and George Mason. He was awarded a Guggenheim Fellowship in 1974.

WILLIAM CARLOS WILLIAMS (1883–1963), writer of fiction, essays, and poetry, also had a full-time career as a physician. Born in Rutherford, New Jersey, Williams attended preparatory schools in New York and Switzerland and studied medicine at the University of Pennsylvania, where he met Ezra Pound. With Pound's encouragement, Williams began publishing poetry. Winner of many prestigious awards, including a National Book Award and a Pulitzer Prize, Williams worked in New Jersey as both a poet and a doctor until his death.

WILLIAM WORDSWORTH (1770–1850), in collaboration with his friend Samuel Taylor Coleridge, published the collection *Lyrical Ballads* in 1798. The poems in this volume and its programmatic preface broke with the poetic conventions of the eighteenth century and signaled the beginning of the English Romantic movement. Wordsworth, born in Westmoreland, was educated at Cambridge. He for a time was caught up in the revolutionary fervor of the French Revolution but became a voice of conservatism in his later years. He is best remembered for his poems that turn to the healing influence of nature as the antidote to the ills of city civilization.

SIR THOMAS WYATT (1503–1541) was the first to introduce into England Petrarch's sonnets of frustrated love, which started the sonnet vogue of the Elizabethan Age. Born in Kent, England, Wyatt was educated at Cambridge. His father was a joint constable with the father of Anne Boleyn, who was to become the second wife of Henry VIII and the mother of Elizabeth, the future queen. Wyatt was assigned his first diplomatic mission by Henry VIII in 1525 and led a busy life as a courtier and diplomat.

WILLIAM BUTLER YEATS (1865–1939) became known for poems drawing on the heritage of Irish myth and legend and developed a rich symbolic language in his later poetry. Yeats, who won the Nobel Prize for literature in 1923, is widely recognized as one of the most outstanding poets of the English-speaking world. An Irish dramatist and poet, he was born in Dublin. In the 1890s he became involved in the developing revolution against British rule in Ireland. Cofounder of the Irish Literary Theater, he wrote plays for its stage. From 1922—the year of the Proclamation of the Irish Free State—until 1928 he was a member of the Irish Senate. Poet Seamus Heaney says that "a Yeats poem gives the feeling of being empowered and thrilled."

AL YOUNG (born 1939) has said, "long before the printed word and stuffy ideas about literature turned up in my life, and certainly long before I became the willing ward of schoolteachers, I was sleeping with words." His love for language began in his childhood home in Ocean Springs, Mississippi, where "talk was musical. Clusters of people were forever talking with one another, telling stories, sharing experiences, observations, jokes, riddles, conundrums, and swapping lies." Young believes in the Kenyan proverb, "Talking with one another is loving one another." Because of his background, he "never outgrew the need for magic or the curative powers of language." Educated at the University of Michigan, Berkeley, and Stanford—where he was a Wallace E. Stegner Creative Writing Fellow—Young has worked as a free-lance musician and disc jockey, and has taught at Berkeley, Stanford, and the University of Washington. In 1982 he was named Distinguished Andrew Mellon Professor of Humanities at Rice University in Houston. In 1972 began editing with Ishmael Reed the *Yardbird Reader* and *Quilt Magazine*. Young has published four novels and two plays, in addition to four collections of poetry. Commenting on the power of poetry, Young said, "Word by word, line by line, season upon season, poetry keeps teaching me that the only time there is is now."

GLOSSARY OF
LITERARY TERMS

Abstraction   A generic, broad label that describes a large category—such as happiness, freedom, or honor. See *concrete*.

Alexandrine   A twelve-syllable line made up of six iambic feet (iambic hexameter). Edmund Spenser used the alexandrine in his Spenserian stanza, which is composed of eight pentameter lines followed by an alexandrine.

Allegory   A symbolic work in which characters, events, or settings represent moral qualities. The characters of an allegory are often *abstractions* personified. The meaning existing below the surface in an allegorical work may be religiously, morally, politically, or personally significant. Spenser's *The Faerie Queene* is an example of an allegory.

Alliteration   The repetition of the same sound at the beginning of words, as in "He clasps the crag with crooked hands."

Allusion   A reference in a poem to a historical or literary character, event, idea, or place outside the work. Allusion serves to tap indirectly into an association already existing in the reader's mind. Greek mythology has been a major source of allusion over the ages, and Biblical allusions also are frequent in English literature.

Ambiguity   A quality of certain words and phrases whereby the meaning is left unclear. Poets often use ambiguity deliberately to create multiple layers of meaning.

Anapest   Two unaccented syllables followed by an accented one, as in New ROCHELLE. The following lines from Percy Bysshe Shelley's "The Cloud" are anapestic: "Like a CHILD from the WOMB, like a GHOST from the TOMB,/ I aRISE and unBUILD it aGAIN."

Antithesis   A playing off of opposites or a balancing of one term against another, as in the point/counterpoint statement, "Man proposes, God disposes." "Thesis" and "antithesis" in the original Greek mean "statement" and "counterstatement."

Antonym   A word with the opposite or nearly the opposite meaning of another word. See *synonym*.

512

Apostrophe A dignified invocation to someone or something not present, often to a personified abstraction, like Liberty or Justice. Emily Dickinson employs apostrophe in her address to God: "Papa Above! / Regard a Mouse."

Archaic language Language that is no longer in common use. Unlike *obsolete language,* archaic words and phrases have survived but have an old-fashioned flavor. Used intentionally, archaisms can be useful in recreating a past style.

Archetype An image, character, or event recurrent in the literature and life of diverse cultures, suggestive of universal patterns of experience. According to psychologist Carl Jung, archetypes link common human experiences. Jung held that within the human race exists a "collective unconsious" formed by the repeated experience of our ancestors. The collective unconscious is expressed in myths, religion, dreams, fantasies, and literature.

Assonance Repetition of similar internal vowel sounds of final syllables, as in *break/fade, mice/light, told/woe.* See *consonance* and *half-rhymes.*

Author biography criticism See *criticism.*

Autobiographical "I" The personal voice through which poets share their personal experiences and feelings. Confessional poets use the autobiographical "I" to make public their private, often painful, experiences and observations. Use of first person point of view in poetry is not always the autobiographical "I," particularly when the "I" is more a *persona* speaking, rather than the poet personally. See *confessional poetry, point of view,* and *speaker.*

Ballad A songlike, narrative poem traditionally characterized by a recurring refrain and four-line stanzas rhyming *abcb.* Anonymous folk ballads were originally sung as the record of a notable exploit or calamity. From *balar,* "to dance," ballads are created both by individual composers and through communal activity. See *literary ballad.*

Blank verse Unrhymed iambic pentameter. Commonly used for long poems, blank verse has been employed by many poets over the ages from Marlowe to Wordsworth to Frost. Shakespeare used blank verse in most of his serious plays.

Caesura A pause or a break within a line of verse. From the Latin for "a cutting off," a caesura can occur at almost any point in the line, as the first four lines of Andrew Marvell's "To His Coy Mistress" demonstrate:

> Had we but world enough, ‖ and time
> This coyness, lady, ‖ were no crime.
> We would sit down, ‖ and think which way
> To walk, ‖ and pass our long love's day.

Carpe diem Latin for "seize the day," a poetic convention urging us to make use of the passing day, to live for the moment. This theme was common in sixteenth- and seventeenth-century love lyrics, as in Robert Herrick's lines, "Gather ye rosebuds while ye may / Old Time is still a-flying; / And this same flower that smiles today, / Tomorrow will be dying."

Circumlocution Indirect, roundabout phrasing, such as calling a "home" a "primary residence." A *euphemism* can be a form of circumlocution.

Cliché A term that has lost its freshness due to overuse, such as "strong as an ox," "tip of the iceberg," and "American as apple pie."

Closure A satisfying conclusion or sense of completion at the end of a poem.

Conceit An extended, elaborate and often farfetched analogy. Love poems of earlier centuries often featured conceits, comparing the subject of the poem extensively and elaborately to some object, such as a rose, a garden, or a ship.

Concrete Vivid, graphic images that appeal strongly to the senses, as opposed to generalized *abstractions*.

Concrete poetry Poems that use the physical arrangement of words on a page to mirror meaning (for example, a poem about a bell that is bell-shaped). Concrete poetry takes advantage of the visible shapes of letters and words to create a picture.

Confessional poetry Poetry that employs the *autobiographical "I"* as the poem's speaker for an often painful, public display of personal, private matters. Confessional poets such as Anne Sexton, John Berryman, and Sylvia Plath came into the forefront during the 1960s and 1970s. Although confessional poetry is most often associated with contemporary poets, poets over the ages, such as the ancient Greek poet Sappho, for instance, have employed confessional techniques.

Connotation The associations and attitudes called up by a word, as opposed to its *denotation* or straight, literal definition. For instance, the words "aroma" and "odor" both denote a "scent," but each word has a different connotation: "aroma" connotes a rich, pleasing scent, whereas "odor" suggests something pungent and foul-smelling.

Consonance Repetition of similar sounds in the final consonants of words, as in *torn/burn, add/read, heaven/given*. See *assonance* and *half-rhymes*.

Context The information surrounding a particular word or expression that often determines its meaning.

Conventional symbol A symbol with familiar, agreed-upon uses. For example, a rose conventionally symbolizes love.

Counterpoint A contrasting but parallel element or statement. See *antithesis*.

Couplet Two rhymed lines of verse. If set aside or self-contained, the two rhymed lines are called a *closed couplet*.

Criticism The study, analysis, and evaluation of works of art. Traditionally, literary critics employed **author biography criticism**, looking for the meaning of the work by examining the writer's background and historical milieu. The **New Critics** of the 1940s and 1950s moved away from this stress on context. Instead, they paid close attention to the intrinsic features of a work (such as imagery, symbolism, and point of view) and to how these contribute to meaning. Any such critical position focusing on the form and technique of a work is termed **formalist criticism**. In recent decades, many critics have once again widened their scope to consider the historical, personal, or sociological context of literary works.

Contemporary critics vary greatly in their approaches to literature. **Feminist criticism** examines representations of the feminine in all literature and often focuses on works written by women. **Marxist criticism** examines the political content of a work; it often examines how works either depict or contribute to the power struggle between the classes. **Language-centered criticism** looks closely at the characteristic or changing patterns of language in a work. **Reader response criticism** focuses on how the reader contributes to the meaning of a text. **Psychoanalytic criticism** traces in literary works the typical patterns of human development and consciousness first theorized by psychoanalysts such as Freud and Jung. **Myth criticism** examines the archetypal echoes and recurrent mythical allusions or themes in literary works.

Cumulative repetition   See *repetition.*

Dactyl   One stressed syllable followed by two unstressed syllables, as in BALti-more.

Dark humor   A paradoxical humor that often uses irony to find a comic angle on catastrophe, illness, and other events that usually defeat people.

Denotation   The literal definition of a word; its stripped-down meaning devoid of *connotation.*

Dialects   The regional variations of a common language that are still mutually intelligible, although some actually border on becoming separate languages.

Dialectic   The playing off of opposing forces or points of view.

Diction   The writer's choice and use of words.

Didacticism   In a poem, the presentation of ideas intended to instruct or improve the reader.

Elegy   A poem of mourning and lamentation. Elegies are most often sustained, formal poems with a meditative, solemn mood. Notable examples include John Milton's "Lycidas," Walt Whitman's "When Lilacs Last in the Dooryard Bloom'd," and John Berryman's "Formal Elegy."

Elizabethan Age   The English literary period named after Queen Elizabeth and lasting from 1558 until 1642, the year of the closing of the theaters. This "golden age" saw such literary figures as Shakespeare develop the beginnings of modern drama and an outburst of lyric poetry. Other notable names of the period include Sidney, Spenser, Jonson, and Donne.

Empathy   Identifying deeply with the experience, situation, feelings, or motives of another.

End rhyme   A rhyme in which the last words of two or more lines of poetry rhyme with one another. See *internal rhyme.*

End-stopped line   A line of poetry that ends with a period, colon, or semicolon. See *enjambment.*

Enjambment   The continuation of a sentence in a poem so that it spills over from one line to the next. See *end-stopped line.*

Epic poem   A long narrative poem that speaks to the listener in an elevated style and embodies the central values of a civilization. The traditional epic recorded the adventures of a hero and focused on a high point in history.

Some important epics are Homer's *Iliad* and *Odyssey,* the Old English *Beowulf,* the Spanish *El Cid,* and Virgil's *Aeneid.* See *lyric poem.*

Epigram   A concise, cleverly worded remark making a pointed, witty statement. From the Greek for "inscription," an epigram often contains an antithesis, as in "Man proposes, God disposes."

Euphemism   From the Greek for "good saying," the substitution of an indirect statement for a direct statement, often with the intention of sounding less offensive or more refined. Examples of euphemisms are calling a "janitor" a "sanitation engineer" or calling "death" "passing away."

Explication   The line-by-line explanation of a poem. Explication differs from interpretation in that it usually refers to a literal, step-by-step scrutiny of the language of a work, as opposed to a broader, more subjective look at its overall significance.

Extended (or sustained) metaphor   A metaphor traced throughout a work.

External evidence   Evidence outside a poem itself, examined in an attempt to understand a work's meaning. Characteristic themes in the author's other works or information found in the author's letters or interviews are common forms of external evidence.

Feminine (or double) rhyme   Two-syllable rhyme, with the first syllable stressed and the second unstressed, as in *ocean/motion, started/parted.* See *masculine rhyme.*

Feminist criticism   See *criticism.*

Figurative language   Language in which the poet means something more than what is literally stated. See *allegory, hyperbole, metaphor,* and *simile.*

Foot   A segment of verse composed of stressed and unstressed syllables. For different types of metric feet, see *anapest, dactyl, iamb, spondee,* and *trochee.*

Formalist criticism   See *criticism.*

Free verse   Poetry with no strong, regular pattern of meter or rhyme.

Ghazal   A traditional Persian (Iranian) poetry form made up of sequences of five to fifteen related couplets.

Grotesque   A poem characterized by bizarre, fantastic, or ominous characters or events.

Haiku   A traditional Japanese poetry form of three lines of five, seven, and five syllables each. Although haiku appears starkly simplistic, it offers serious, profound insight into a captured moment in time, often drawing on associations from nature's seasons, elements, and animals. Henry David Thoreau, Ezra Pound, Robert Bly, and Gary Snyder are a few of the western writers who have written short pieces aimed at capturing the spirit of haiku. See *tanka.*

Half-rhymes   Words that do not rhyme but distantly sound alike.

Hyperbole   A figure of speech using extreme exaggeration. From the Greek for "excess," hyperbole is often expressed as a simile, as in "he's as strong as an ox."

Iamb   A two-syllable foot with the stress on the last syllable, as in DeTROIT. Over the centuries, iambic meter with four or five beats to the line (iambic tetrameter and iambic pentameter) has become the most common meter in English-language poetry.

Idiom   The characteristic language style of a person or group of people. From the Greek for "peculiarity," idiom can refer to a regional speech or dialect or to the specialized vocabulary or jargon of a group such as doctors, lawyers, or scientists.

Image   A literal or concrete detail that speaks to the physical senses of sight, hearing, smell, taste, or touch. See *concrete*.

Incongruity   The quality of being composed of inconsistent, discordant parts. The *metaphysical poets* focused on incongruity in their works. See *irony, paradox,* and *polarity.*

Internal rhyme   A rhyme within a line of poetry. See *end rhyme.*

Interpretation   Moving beyond line-by-line *explication* of a poem and examining its major themes in order to see its larger human significance.

Inversion   The reversal of normal word order in a sentence or the reversal of the rhythmic stress in a poem.

Irony   An effect produced when there is a discrepancy between two levels of meaning. **Irony of situation** refers to a contrast between what we expect to happen and what really happens. **Verbal irony** refers to a deliberate contrast between what is said and what is meant. See *paradox,* and *hyperbole.*

Language-centered criticism   See *criticism.*

Literary ballad   A conscious imitation of a traditional ballad.

Lyric poem   A brief, compressed poem. See *epic.*

Marxist criticism   See *criticism.*

Masculine (or single) rhyme   A rhyme in which the final syllables of two or more words are accented and rhyme, such as *high/sky, leave/grieve, renown/gown*. See *feminine rhyme.*

Metaphor   A comparison between two essentially unlike things. With metaphor, the speaker treats one thing as if it were another, without the use of "like" or "as," as in these Emily Dickinson lines: "Hope is the thing with feathers / That perches in the soul." See *extended metaphor, organizing metaphor,* and *simile.*

Metaphysical poets   Poets of the seventeenth century whose work is noted for its complex imagery, demanding form, and abundant use of *incongruity, paradox* and *irony.* Famous metaphysical poets include John Donne, Andrew Marvell, and George Herbert.

Meter   An underlying regular beat in a poem. **Trimeter** is meter with three stressed syllables to the line, **tetrameter** has four stressed syllables, **pentameter** has five, and **hexameter** has six.

Metonymy   A figure of speech in which a term closely related to something serves as its substitute. For instance, the word "sword" means "military career" in the line "He abandoned the sword." See *synechdoche.*

Minimalism   A contemporary style of writing that tries to eliminate all rhetoric and emotion or at least to reduce these elements to bare essentials.

Modernism   A movement of the early twentieth century against the conventions of Romantic literary representation. In their search for new modes of expression, the modernists rejected the flowery and artificial language of Victorian poetry and began using concrete imagery and *free verse.* Famous modernists include Ezra Pound, T. S. Eliot, and Archibald MacLeish.

Mood   The emotional or psychological cast of a poem, generally produced by literary devices such as *tone* and *imagery.*

Myth criticism   See *criticism.*

Neoclassicism   The eighteenth-century revival of interest in classical Greek and Roman works. Neoclassical writers believed that sound judgment should guide and restrain the poetic imagination. They prized order, concentration, economy, logic, restrained emotion, correctness, and decorum. Notable writers of this period include Milton, Pope, and Johnson.

New critics   See *criticism.*

Obsolete language   Words and phrases that are no longer in use. See *archaic language.*

Octave   An eight-line stanza.

Ode   An elaborately crafted, stately poem fit for solemn subjects.

Onomatopoeia   The use of a word that sounds like its meaning, such as *pop, hiss,* or *buzz.*

Open form   A poetic form characterized by a lack of regular rhyme, meter, line length, or stanza form.

Organizing (or controlling) metaphor   A single extended metaphor that gives shape to a poem as a whole.

Ottava rima   From the Italian for "eighth rhyme," a finely crafted stanza consisting of eight iambic pentameter lines with the rhyme pattern *abababcc.*

Paradox   An apparent contradiction that, on second thought, illuminates a truth. See *incongruity, irony,* and *polarity.*

Parallelism   The repetition of similar or identical structures within phrases or sentences.

Paraphrase   Stating someone else's ideas in your own words.

Para-rhyme   See *slant rhyme.*

Parody   A humorous, mocking imitation of a serious piece.

Pastoral   A poetic tradition offering harried city dwellers a nostalgic vision of the idealized simplicity and leisure of country life. Pastorals were first written by the Greeks and continue to be written today. Traditional pastorals use courtly language to refer to the shepherds and the countryside. In modern terms, pastoral often means any poem about rural people and rural settings.

Persona   See *speaker.*

Personification   Figurative language that endows something nonhuman with human qualities, as in "the trees whispered in the wind."

Petrarchan sonnet   See *sonnet.*

Poetic diction   Language more elevated and refined than ordinary speech.

Polarity   The play of two opposites on a spectrum. See *incongruity, irony,* and *paradox.*

Prose poem   A poem written with the margins justified like prose.

Psychoanalytic criticism   See *criticism.*

Pun   A type of *word play,* sometimes on the similar sense or sound of two words and sometimes on different meanings of the same word.

Quatrain   A four-line poetic stanza.

Reader response criticism   See *criticism.*

Recurrence   The reappearance of themes or key elements that serves to echo issues and concerns introduced earlier.

Refrain   The same line (or group of lines) repeated at intervals in a poem.

Reiteration   Purposeful, insistent repetition in poetry or prose that reinforces a basic point.

Repetition   Recurrence of the same word or phrase used to highlight or emphasize something in a poem. Poets often use purposeful cumulative repetition for a rhythmic, building effect.

Rhetoric   The study of the content, structure, and style of literature, with particular attention paid to the effective or persuasive use of language.

Rhyme   Echo effect produced when a writer repeats the same sounds at the ends of words. See *end rhyme, feminine rhyme, half-rhyme, internal rhyme, masculine rhyme, sight rhyme, slant rhyme,* and *triple rhyme.*

Romanticism   An artistic revolt of the late eighteenth and early nineteenth centuries against the traditional, formal, and orderly *Neoclassicism.* Whereas Neoclassicism stressed the "order in beauty," Romanticism stresses the "strangeness in beauty" (Walter Pater). The writers of this time dropped conventional poetic diction and forms in favor of freer forms and bolder language, and explored nature, "organic unity," mysticism, the grotesque, and emotional psychology in their art. Some famous poets of this period include Blake, Keats, and Shelley.

Sarcasm   A bitter or cutting remark that moves beyond verbal irony.

Scansion   A system for charting the underlying beat, or meter, of a literary work.

Sentimentality   An oversimplified, emotional quality of a literary work.

Sestet   A six-line poetic stanza.

Shakespearean sonnet   See *sonnet.*

Sight rhyme   Words that coincide in spelling but not in sound, like *come* and *home.*

Simile   A comparison between two essentially unlike things, using "as" or "like" or "as if": "My love is like a red, red rose." Unlike the implied comparison of a *metaphor,* a simile says outright that something is like something else.

Slang   Colloquial, informal language not acceptable for highly formal usage.

Slant (or para-) rhyme   The near rhyming of words that distantly sound alike. See *assonance* and *consonance.*

Sonnet   An elaborately crafted fourteen-line poem in iambic pentameter. The

Petrarchan sonnet contains an eight-line stanza, or octave, with an *ab-baabba* rhyme scheme, followed by a sestet (six-line stanza) of *cdcdee* or *cdecde*. The octave often raises a question or states a predicament or proposition that is answered in the sestet. The **Shakespearean sonnet** generally is arranged as three quatrains (four-line stanzas) and a couplet (two lines), with the typical rhyme scheme of *abab/cdcd/efef/gg*. The **Spenserian sonnet** uses three quatrains and a couplet like the Shakespearean sonnet but employs a linking rhyme scheme more similar to the Petrarchan sonnet: *abab/bcbc/cdcd/ee*. Among the famous sonneteers in England and America have been Sidney, Wordsworth, Auden, Longfellow, e. e. cummings, and John Berryman. See *sonnet sequence*.

Sonnet sequence   A group of sonnets thematically connected. One of the most famous sonnet sequences (or "cycles") is Elizabeth Barrett Browning's *Sonnets from the Portuguese*, which explores her love for Robert Browning.

Speaker   The voice speaking in a poem, as distinct from the author as a person. Also called "persona."

Spenserian sonnet   See *sonnet*.

Spenserian stanza   A nine-line stanza used by Edmund Spenser. It follows the rhyming pattern *ababbcbcc;* the first eight lines are pentameter and the last is an *alexandrine* (iambic with six stresses).

Spondee   A metrical foot of two stressed syllables, as in HEARTBREAK or HONG KONG.

Sprung rhythm   An irregular rhythmic pattern developed by Gerard Manley Hopkins in which stressed syllables are followed by a varying number of unstressed syllables.

Stanza   A grouping of lines that traditionally marks the completion of a metrical pattern within a poem. *Couplets, tercets, quatrains, sestets,* and *octaves* are all types of stanzas. In *free verse* or *open form* poetry, stanza breaks mark shifts in meaning or theme.

Stress   An accent that makes one syllable stand out from the others in a word or phrase.

Style   An author's unmistakable personal choice of words, sentence construction, diction, imagery, tone, and ideas.

Symbol   An object or action that has acquired a meaning beyond itself. Symbols are often used to articulate the themes of a poem. See *conventional symbol*.

Synechdoche   A figure of speech that uses the part to stand for the whole, or the whole to stand for the part: "wheels" to mean "car" and "hired hands" to mean "hired people." See *metonymy*.

Synonym   A word that has the same or nearly the same meaning as another word. See *antonym*.

Tanka   A Japanese poetic form that, like *haiku,* fixes a moment in time, but is five lines long: three lines of five, seven, and five syllables each and two lines of seven syllables.

Tercet   A three-line stanza.

Theme   A recurring, unifying subject, idea, or motif; the primary idea being explored or general statement being made by a poem.

Thesis statement   A concise, memorable statement of what a written work is attempting to prove. The thesis statement often appears toward the beginning of the work but can also appear at the end. A thesis statement can be explicit, meaning it is stated outright, or implicit, meaning the work's theme is implied.

Tone   The implied attitude of a writer toward the subject, material, and reader.

Transition   A link that smoothly moves the reader from one stanza, paragraph, or idea to the next.

Triple rhyme   Rhyme in which the rhyming stressed syllable is followed by two unstressed syllables, as in *moralities/realities* or *meticulous/ridiculous*.

Trochee   A metrical rhythm with the stress on the first syllable, as in this example from Coleridge: "TROchee|TRIPS from|LONG to|SHORT."

Understatement   Lack of emphasis on the undercurrents or implications of what is being talked about. See *tone*.

Villanelle   A nineteen-line poetic form employing only two rhymes and repeating two lines at various intervals. Line 1 is repeated at lines 6, 12, and 18; line 3 at lines 9, 15, and 19. The first and third lines return as a rhymed couplet at the end. These intermeshing rhymes link five tercets rhymed *aba*. The poem ends with a quatrain rhymed *abaa*.

Word play   Witty or clever use of words. See *pun*.

ACKNOWLEDGMENTS

Margaret Atwood. "Dreams of the Animals" from *Procedures for Underground* by Margaret Atwood, © Oxford University Press Canada 1970. Reprinted by permission of Oxford University Press Canada. "You fit into me." From *Power Politics* (The House of Anasi Press, 1971). Copyright © 1971 by Margaret Atwood. Reprinted by permission of Stoddart Publishing Co. Limited, Don Mills, Ont.

W. H. Auden. "Musée des Beaux Arts" and "The Unknown Citizen." From *W. H. Auden: Collected Poems* by W. H. Auden, ed. by Edward Mendelson. Copyright 1940 and renewed 1968 by W. H. Auden. Lines from "Happy the hare at morning." From *The English Auden: Poems, Essays, and Dramatic Writings 1927–1939,* ed. by Edward Mendelson. Copyright © 1977 by Edward Mendelson, William Meredith and Monroe K. Spears, Executors of the Estate of W. H. Auden. Reprinted by permission of Random House, Inc. and Faber and Faber Ltd.

Amiri Baraka. "The Turncoat" from *Preface to a Twenty Volume Suicide Note.* Reprinted by permission of Sterling Lord Literistic, Inc. Copyright © 1961 by Amiri Baraka.

Bruce Bennett. "Leader." Copyright © 1984 by Bruce Bennett. Reprinted by permission of the author.

Wendell Berry. "The Peace of Wild Things" from *Openings,* copyright © 1968 by Wendell Berry, reprinted by permission of Harcourt Brace Jovanovich, Inc.

John Berryman. "Dream Song #14" from *The Dream Songs* by John Berryman. Copyright © 1959, 1962, 1963, 1964, 1965, 1966, 1967, 1968, 1969 by John Berryman. The Ball Poem" from *Collected Poems, 1937–1971* by John Berryman. Copyright © 1989 by Kate Donahue Berryman. Reprinted by permission of Farrar, Straus & Giroux, Inc.

Elizabeth Bishop. "The Fish" and "One Art" from *The Complete Poems, 1927–1979* by Elizabeth Bishop. Copyright © 1979, 1983 by Alice Helen Methfessel. Reprinted by permission of Farrar, Straus & Giroux, Inc.

Robert Bly. "Snowfield in the Afternoon." From *Silence in the Snowy Fields,* copyright © 1962 by Robert Bly. Reprinted by permission of the author.

Louise Bogan. "The Dream," "Women," and "Cassandra" from *The Blue Estuaries* by Louise Bogan. Copyright © 1967, 1968 by Louise Bogan. Reprinted by permission of Farrar, Straus & Giroux, Inc.

Arna Bontemps. "A Black Man Talks of Reaping." Reprinted by permission of Harold Ober Associates Incorporated. Copyright © 1963 by Arna Bontemps.

Kay Boyle. "October 1954" from *Collected Poems of Kay Boyle.* Copyrighted © 1991 by Kay Boyle. Used by permission of Copper Canyon Press, P.O. Box 271, Port Townsend, WA 98368.

Anne Bradstreet. "The Vanity of All Worldly Things" reprinted by permission of the publisher from *The Works of Anne Bradstreet,* edited by Janine Hansley, Forward by Adrienne Rich, Cambridge, Massachusetts: Harvard University Press. Copyright © 1967 by the President and Fellows of Harvard College. All rights reserved.

Gwendolyn Brooks. "The Bean Eaters," "The *Chicago Defender* Sends a Man to Little Rock," "We Real Cool," "A Song in the Front Yard," "Hunchback Girl: She Thinks of Heaven," "Piano after War," "Old Mary," "Truth," "The Preacher Ruminates behind the Sermon," "The Ballad of the Light-Eyed Little Girl," "When You Have Forgotten," and "The Chicago Picasso." From *Blacks* by Gwendolyn Brooks. Copyright 1945, 1949, 1953, © 1960, 1963, 1969, 1970, 1971, 1975, 1981, 1987 by Gwendolyn Brooks Blakely. "The Boy Died in my Alley" from *Beckonings* by Gwendolyn Brooks. Copyright © 1975 by Gwendolyn Brooks Blakely. Reprinted by

H. D. (Hilda Doolittle),"Helen" and lines from "The Mysteries Remain." From H.D.: *Collected Poems 1912–1944.* Copyright © 1982 by the Estate of Hilda Doolittle. Reprinted by permission of New Directions Publishing Corporation.

Rita Dove. "Daystar." Reprinted from Rita Dove: *Thomas and Beulah* by permission of Carnegie Mellon University Press, © 1986 by Rita Dove.

Bob Dylan. Lines from "It's Alright Ma." Copyright © 1985 by Warner Bros. Inc. Reprinted by permission.

Richard Eberhart. "The Fury of Arial Bombardment." From *Collected Poems 1930–1976* by Richard Eberhart. Copyright © 1960, 1976 by Richard Eberhart. Reprinted by permission of Oxford University Press, Inc.

T. S. Eliot. "The Love Song of J. Alfred Prufrock" and "Preludes." Published in *Prufrock and Other Observations* (1917). Reprinted from *Collected Poems 1909–1962* by T. S. Eliot by permission of the publishers, Faber and Faber Ltd.

Louise Erdrich. "Indian Boarding School: The Runaways." From *Jacklight* by Louise Erdrich. Copyright © 1984 by Louise Erdrich. Reprinted by permission of Henry Holt and Company, Inc.

Martin Espada. "Latin Night at the Pawnshop" from *Rebellion Is the Circle of a Lover's Hands.* Copyright © 1990. Reprinted by permission of Curbstone Press.

Lawrence Ferlinghetti. "Constantly Risking Absurdity." From Lawrence Ferlinghetti: *A Coney Island of the Mind.* Copyright © 1958 by Lawrence Ferlinghetti. Reprinted by permission of New Directions Publishing Corporation.

Donald Finkel. "The Sirens" from *The Clothing's New Emperor* by Donald Finkel (Scribner's, 1959) and "They" from *A Mote in Heaven's Eye* by Donald Finkel (Atheneum, 1975). Copyright © 1959 and 1975 by Donald Finkel. Reprinted by permission of the author.

Adelaide Foppa. Lines from "Words." From Alicia Partnoy, ed., *You Can't Drown the Fire: Latin American Women Writing in Exile,* © 1988. Reprinted by permission of Cleis Press.

Carolyn Forché. "Selective Service" from *The Country Between Us* by Carolyn Forché. Copyright © 1982 by Carolyn Forché. Reprinted by permission of HarperCollins Publishers.

Robert Frost. "After Apple Picking," "Mending Wall," "The Road Not Taken," "The Oven Bird," "Tuft of Flowers," "Acquainted with the Night," "Design," "Fire and Ice," "Neither Out Far Nor in Deep," "Nothing Gold Can Stay," "On Being Idolized," "Once By the Pacific," "One Step Backward Taken," "Stopping by Woods on a Snowy Evening," "The Night Light," "The Silken Tent," and lines from "Pertinax." From *The Poetry of Robert Frost* edited by Edward Connery Lathem. Copyright 1916, 1923, 1928, 1930, 1939, 1947, © 1964, 1969 by Holt, Rinehart and Winston. Copyright 1936, 1942, 1944, 1951, © 1956, 1958, 1962, by Robert Frost. Copyright © 1964, 1967, 1970, 1975 by Lesley Frost Ballantine. Reprinted by permission of Henry Holt and Company, Inc.

Tess Gallagher. "The Hug" copyright 1987 by Tess Gallagher. Reprinted from *Amplitude* with the permission of Graywolf Press, Saint Paul, Minnesota.

Federico García Lorca. "Half Moon." From Federico García Lorca: *Selected Poems of Federica García Lorca.* Copyright 1955 by New Directions Publishing Corporation. Reprinted by permission of the publisher.

Allen Ginsberg. "A Supermarket in California" from *Collected Poems 1947–1980 of Allen Ginsberg.* Copyright © 1955, 1980 by Allen Ginsberg. Reprinted by permission of HarperCollins Publishers Inc.

Dana Gioia. "California Hills in August." Reprinted by permission; © 1982 Dana Gioia. Originally in *The New Yorker.*

Daniela Gioseffi. Lines from "Some Slippery Afternoon" copyright © 1979 by Daniela Gioseffi. Reprinted from *Eggs in the Lake* by Daniela Gioseffi with the permission of BOA Editions, Ltd., 92 Park Avenue, Brockport, NY 14420.

Nikki Giovanni. Text excerpt of "Legacies" from *My House* by Nikki Giovanni. Copyright © 1972 by Nikki Giovanni. Text of "Nikki-Rosa" from *Black Feeling, Black Thought, Black Judgment* by Nikki Giovanni. Copyright © 1968, 1970 by Nikki Giovanni. Text of "The Drum" from *Those Who Ride the Night Winds* by Nikki Giovanni. Copyright © 1983 by Nikki Giovanni. All by permission of William Morrow & Company, Inc.

Louise Glück. "The School Children" © 1971, 1972, 1973, 1974, 1975 by Louise Glück. From *The House on Marshland* by Louise Glück, first published by The Ecco Press in 1975. Reprinted by permission.

Paul Goodman. "Haiku." From *Collected Poems* by Paul Goodman. Copyright © 1973 by the Estate of Paul Goodman. Reprinted by permission of Sally Goodman.

Judy Grahn. "They Say She Is Veiled" and "Helen in Hollywood" from *The Queen of*

Wands. Copyright © 1982 by Judy Grahn, published by The Crossing Press, Freedom, CA. Reprinted by permission.

Robert Graves. "The Frog and the Golden Ball." From *Collected Poems 1975* by Robert Graves. Copyright © 1975 by Robert Graves. Reprinted by permission of Oxford University Press, Inc. and A. P. Watt on behalf of the Trustees of the Robert Graves Copyright Trust.

Donald Hall. "My Son, My Executioner" from *Old and New Poems* by Donald Hall. Copyright © 1990 by Donald Hall. Reprinted by permission of Ticknor & Fields, a Houghton Mifflin Company imprint. All rights reserved.

Anne Halley. "Dear God, The Day Is Gray." Reprinted by permission from *The Massachusetts Review,* © 1960 The Massachusetts Review, Inc.

Daniel Halpern. "How to Eat Alone," from *Seasonal Rites* by Daniel Halpern. Copyright © 1979, 1980, 1981, 1982 by Daniel Halpern. Used by permission of Viking Penguin, a division of Penguin Books USA Inc.

Robert Hass. "Song." From *Field Guide* by Robert Hass. Copyright © 1973 by Robert Hass. Reprinted by permission of the publisher, Yale University Press.

Robert Hayden. "Frederick Douglass" and "Those Winter Sundays." Reprinted from *Angle of Ascent, New and Selected Poems* by Robert Hayden, by permission of Liveright Publishing Corporation. Copyright © 1975, 1972, 1970, 1966 by Robert Hayden.

Seamus Heaney. "Valediction" and "The Forge" from *Poems, 1965–75* by Seamus Heaney. Copyright © 1972, 1975, 1980 by Seamus Heaney. Lines from "The Republic of Conscience" from *The Haw Lantern.* Copyright © 1987 by Seamus Heaney. Reprinted by permission of Farrar, Straus & Giroux, Inc. and Faber and Faber Ltd.

John Heaviside. "A Gathering of Deafs" from *Olivetree Review 8* (Fall 1989). Reprinted by permission of the author.

Calvin Hernton. Lines from "The Distant Drum." From *The Medicine Man: Collected Poems* (Reed, Cannon & Johnson, 1976). Reprinted by permission of the author.

Robert Hershon. Lines from "How to Walk in a Crowd." From *Grocery Lists,* published by The Crossing Press, copyright 1972 by Robert Hershon. Reprinted by permission of the author.

A. D. Hope. "Coup de Grâce" from *Collected Poems 1930–1970.* © A. D. Hope 1966, 1969, 1972. Reprinted by permission of Collins/Angus & Robertson Publishers (Australia).

Lady Horikawa. "How long will it last?" translated by Kenneth Rexroth and Ikuko Atsumi. From Kenneth Rexroth: *Women Poets of Japan.* Copyright © 1977 by Kenneth Rexroth and Ikuko Atsumi. Reprinted by permission of New Directions Publishing Corporation.

Langston Hughes. "Dream Deferred" from *The Panther and the Lash* by Langston Hughes. Copyright © 1951 by Langston Hughes. "End" from *Selected Poems* by Langston Hughes. Copyright 1947 by Langston Hughes. Reprinted by permission of Alfred A. Knopf, Inc.

Ted Hughes. "Hawk Roosting." From *Lupercal* by Ted Hughes. Copyright © 1959 by Ted Hughes. Reprinted by permission of Faber & Faber Ltd.

Vincente Huidobro. "Ars Poetica." From Vincente Huidobro: *The Selected Poetry of Vincente Huidobro.* Copyright © 1981 by Vincinte Huidobro and David M. Guss. Reprinted by permission of New Directions Publishing Corporation.

Elizabeth Jennings. Lines from "Answers" and lines from "Song for a Birth or a Death" from *Collected Poems* by Elizabeth Jennings (Carcanet Press). Copyright © Elizabeth Jennings 1979, 1985. Reprinted by permission of David Higham Associates.

June Jordan. "Lullaby" from *Things That I Do in the Dark,* copyright © 1977 by June Jordan. Reprinted by permission of the author.

Donald Justice. "Time and the Weather" from Donald Justice, Revised Edition *Night Light,* copyright 1981 by Donald Justice, Wesleyan University Press by permission of University Press of New England.

Marie Kaschnitz. "Women's Program," translated by Lisel Muller, from *Selected Later Poems of Marie Kaschnitz.* Copyright © 1980 by Princeton University Press. Reprinted by permission of Princeton University Press.

Kawai Chigetsu-Ni. "Grasshoppers" translated by Kenneth Rexroth and Ikuko Atsumi. From Kenneth Rexroth: *Women Poets of Japan.* Copyright © 1977 by Kenneth Rexroth and Ikuko Atsumi. Reprinted by permission of New Directions Publishing Corporation.

Galway Kinnell. "Blackberry Eating" from *Mortal Acts, Mortal Words* by Galway Kinnell. Copyright © 1980 by Galway Kinnell. "For William Carlos Williams" from *What a Kingdom It Was* by Galway Kinnell. Copyright © 1960 by Galway Kinnell. Copyright © renewed 1988 by Galway Kinnell. Reprinted by permission of Houghton Mifflin Company. All rights reserved.

Ethridge Knight. "He Sees Through Stone." From *Poems from Prison* by Ethridge Knight, © 1966. Reprinted by permission of Broadside Press.

Maxine Kumin. "Nurture," copyright © 1987 Maxine Kumin, from *Nurture* by Maxine Kumin. "The Retrieval System," copyright © 1976 by Maxine Kumin, and lines from "Address to the Angels," copyright © 1978 by Maxine Kumin, from *The Retrieval System* by Maxine Kumin. Used by permission of Viking Penguin, a division of Penguin Books USA Inc.

M. W. La Follette. "The Ballad of Red Fox" from *The Clever Body* (San Francisco: Spenserian Press). Copyright © 1959 by M. W. La Follette.

Philip Larkin. "Born Yesterday," "Poetry of Departures," and lines from "Next, Please" are reprinted from *The Less Deceived* by Philip Larkin by permission of The Marvell Press, England. © the Estate of Philip Larkin, 1988.

D. H. Lawrence. "Snake," from *The Complete Poems of D. H. Lawrence* by D. H. Lawrence. Copyright © 1964, 1971 by Angelo Ravagli and C. M. Weekley, Executors of the Estate of Frieda Lawrence Ravagli. Used by permission of Viking Penguin, a division of Penguin Books USA Inc.

James Laughlin. "Junk Mail" from *Selected Poems, 1935–1985* by James Laughlin. Copyright 1945, © 1978, 1985, 1986 by James Laughlin. Reprinted by permission of City Lights Books.

Li-Young Lee. "Persimmons" copyright © 1986 by Li-Young Lee. Reprinted from *Rose* by Li-Young Lee with the permission of BOA Editions Ltd., 92 Park Avenue, Brockport, NY 14420.

Ursula K. Le Guin. "The Old Falling Down." Copyright © 1987 by Ursula K. Le Guin; first appeared in *Io;* reprinted by permission of the author and the author's agent, Virginia Kidd.

John Lennon and Paul McCartney. Lines from "Lucy in the Sky with Diamonds" by John Lennon and Paul McCartney. Copyright © by Northern Songs Ltd. All rights for the U.S., Canada, and Mexico Controlled and Administered by SBK BLACKWOOD MUSIC INC. Under License from ATV MUSIC (MACLEN). All Rights Reserved. International Copyright Secured. Used by permission.

Denise Levertov. "O Taste and See," "In Mind," "The Mutes," and "The Ache of Marriage." From *Denise Levertov: Poems 1960–1967.* Copyright © 1964 by Denise Levertov Goodman. "What Were They Like?" From *Denise Levertov: Poems 1968–1972.* Copyright © 1968 by Denise Levertov Goodman. "To One Steeped in Bitterness." From *Denise Levertov: Breathing the Water.* Copyright © 1987 by Denise Levertov. Reprinted by permission of New Directions Publishing Corporation.

Audre Lorde. "Now that I Am Forever with Child" and "Coal." Reprinted from *Chosen Poems, Old and New,* by Audre Lorde, by permission of W. W. Norton & Company, Inc. Copyright © 1982, 1976, 1974, 1973, 1970, 1968 by Audre Lorde. "Coping" and "Sister Outsider." Reprinted from *The Black Unicorn, Poems by Audre Lorde* by permission of W. W. Norton & Company, Inc. Copyright © 1978 by Audre Lorde. "Poems Are Not Luxuries." Copyright © 1982 by Audre Lorde. Reprinted by permission of the author.

Robert Lowell. "Skunk Hour" from *Life Studies* by Robert Lowell. Copyright © 1956, 1959 by Robert Lowell. Reprinted by permission Farrar, Straus & Giroux, Inc. Lines from "For the Union Dead." From *For the Union Dead* by Robert Lowell. Copyright © 1962 by Robert Lowell. Reprinted by permission of Farrar, Straus & Giroux, Inc.

Edward Lucie-Smith. "Afterwards" from *Confessions and Histories* by Edward Lucie-Smith (Oxford University Press, © 1964). Reprinted by permission of Rogers, Coleridge & White Ltd.

Hugh MacDairmid. "Weep and Wail No More." From *The Complete Poems of Hugh Mac-Dairmid,* edited by Michael Grieve and W. R. Aitken. Copyright © Christopher Murray Grieve 1979; © Valda Grieve 1985. Reprinted by permission of the author's estate.

Mary Mackey. "When I Was a Child I Played with the Boys." From *Split Ends,* © by Mary Mackey, 1974. Reprinted by permission of the author.

Archibald MacLeish. "Ars Poetica." From *Collected Poems 1917–1982* by Archibald MacLeish. Copyright © 1985 by The Estate of Archibald MacLeish. Reprinted by permission of Houghton Mifflin Company. All rights reserved. "The Genius" from *Songs for Eve* by Archibald MacLeish. Copyright 1954 by Archibald MacLeish, © renewed 1982 by Mrs. Ada MacLeish. Reprinted by permission of Houghton Mifflin Company.

John Masefield. "Cargoes." Copyright 1912 by The Macmillan Company, renewed 1940 by John Masefield. Reprinted by permission of The Society of Authors as the literary representative of the Estate of John Masefield.

Claude McKay. "If We Must Die." From *Selected Poems of Claude McKay.* Copyright © 1981 by the Estate of Claude McKay. Reprinted by permission.

Rod McKuen. "Thoughts on Capital Punishment." From *Stanyan Street and Other Sorrows* by Rod McKuen. Copyright 1954, © 1960, 1961, 1962, 1963, 1964, 1965, 1966 by Rod McKuen. Reprinted by permission of Random House, Inc.

Peter Meinke. "Advice to My Son." Copyright © 1965 by The Antioch Review, Inc. First appeared in the *Antioch Review,* Vol. 25, No. 3 (Fall 1965). Reprinted by permission of the Editors. Lines from "When I with You." Reprinted from *The Night Train and the Golden Bird,* by Peter Meinke, by permission of the University of Pittsburgh Press. © 1977 by Peter Meinke. "Sunday at the Apple Market" from *Inlet* (Virginia Wesleyan College). Reprinted by permission.

William Meredith. "A Major Work." From *Partial Accounts: New and Selected Poems* by William Meredith. Copyright © 1987 by William Meredith. Reprinted by permission of Alfred A. Knopf, Inc.

Eve Merriam. "Robin Hood" from *The Nixon Poems.* Copyright © 1970 by Eve Merriam. Reprinted by permission.

Thomas Merton. Lines from "Ariadne." From Thomas Merton: *Collected Poems of Thomas Merton.* Copyright 1948 by New Directions Publishing Corporation. Reprinted by permission of the author.

W. S. Merwin. "For the Anniversary of My Death" from *The Lice* —© 1963, 1964, 1965, 1966, 1967 by W. S. Merwin. "Separation" from *The Moving Target* —© 1960, 1961, 1962, 1963 by W. S. Merwin. Reprinted by permission of Georges Borchardt, Inc.

Edna St. Vincent Millay. "An Ancient Gesture," "Childhood Is the Kingdom Where Nobody Dies," "Pity Me Not," "I, Being Born a Woman and Distressed," and the sestet from "Oh, Oh You Will Be Sorry for That Word." From *Collected Poems* by Edna St. Vincent Millay, Harper & Row. Copyright 1923, 1934, 1951, 1954, © 1962, 1982 by Edna St. Vincent Millay and Norma Millay Ellis. Reprinted by permission of Elizabeth Barnett, literary executor.

Vassar Miller. "The New Icarus" from *Wage War on Silence,* copyright 1960 by Vassar Miller, Wesleyan University Press by permission of University Press of New England.

Czeslaw Milosz. "Incantation" © 1984 by Czeslaw Milosz. From *The Separate Notebooks* by Czeslaw Milosz, first published by The Ecco Press in 1984. Reprinted by permission.

Gabriela Mistral. "To Drink," translated by Gunda Kaiser. From *La Poesia Hispanoamericana desde el Modernismo.* Copyright © 1968 by the Meredith Corporation. Reprinted by permission of Gunda S. Kaiser, Alma, MI.

N. Scott Momaday. "Earth and I Gave You Turquoise" and "New World" from *The Gourd Dancer* by N. Scott Momaday. Copyright © 1975 by N. Scott Momaday. Reprinted by permission of the author.

Marianne Moore. "The Mind Is an Enchanting Thing." Reprinted with permission of Macmillan Publishing Company from *Collected Poems of Marianne Moore.* Copyright 1944, and renewed 1972 by Marianne Moore.

Ogden Nash. "Celery" and "The Hunter." From *Verses from 1929 On* by Ogden Nash. Copyright 1930, 1941, 1949 by Ogden Nash. "Celery" first appeared in the *Saturday Evening Post.* By permission of Little, Brown and Company.

Howard Nemerov. "The Great Gull" (Part II of "The Salt Garden") and "Lobsters," © 1967 by Howard Nemerov, from *The Collected Poems of Howard Nemerov.* Reprinted by permission of Margaret Nemerov.

Pablo Neruda. "The Fickle One" translated by Donald D. Walsh. From Pablo Neruda: *The Captain's Verses.* Copyright © 1972 by Pablo Neruda and Donald D. Walsh. Reprinted by permission of New Directions Publishing Corporation. "Childhood and Poetry." From *Neruda and Vallejo: Selected Poems,* edited by Robert Bly (Beacon Press). Copyright © 1971 by Robert Bly. Copyright © 1962, 1967 by the Sixties Press. Reprinted by permission of Robert Bly.

nila northSun. "Moving Camp Too Far" from *Diet Pepsi and Nacho Cheese* by nila north Sun, © 1977, Duck Down Press, Fallon, Nevada. Reprinted by permission.

Sharon Olds. "I Go Back to May 1937." From *The Gold Cell* by Sharon Olds. Copyright © 1987 by Sharon Olds. Reprinted by permission of Alfred A. Knopf, Inc. "The Death of Marilyn Monroe." From *The Dead and the Living* by Sharon Olds. Copyright © 1983 by Sharon Olds. Reprinted by permission of Alfred A. Knopf, Inc. "Quake Theory" and "The Possessive." Reprinted from *Satan Says,* by Sharon Olds, by permission of the University of Pittsburgh Press. © 1980 by Sharon Olds.

Mary Oliver. "The Black Snake." From *Twelve Moons* by Mary Oliver. Copyright © 1978 by Mary Oliver. By permission of Little, Brown and Company.

Gregory Orr. Lines from "Like Any Man", copyright 1988 by Gregory Orr, from Gregory Orr, *New and Selected Poems,* Wesleyan University Press by permission of University Press of New England.

Ovid. Excerpt from *The Art of Love,* translated by Rolfe Humphries. Copyright © 1957, Indiana University Press. Reprinted by permission of the publisher.

Wilfred Owen. "Dulce et Decorum Est," "The Parable of the Old Men and the Young," and "Anthem for Doomed Youth." From Wilfred Owen: *The Collected Poems of Wilfred Owen.* Copyright © 1963 by Chatto and Windus, Ltd. Reprinted by permission of New Directions Publishing Corporation.

Dorothy Parker. "Solace," copyright 1931, renewed © 1959 by Dorothy Parker, from *The Portable Dorothy Parker* by Dorothy Parker, Introduction by Brendan Gill. Used by permission of Viking Penguin, a division of Penguin Books USA Inc.

Linda Pastan. "1932–," "Posterity," "Sometimes in Winter." Reprinted from *Heroes in Disguise*, Poems by Linda Pastan, by permission of W. W. Norton & Company, Inc. Copyright © 1991 by Linda Pastan. "Anger" from *The Seven Deadly Sins* is reprinted from *A Fraction of Darkness*, Poems by Linda Pastan, by permission of W. W. Norton & Company, Inc. Copyright © 1985 by Linda Pastan. Lines from "After and Absence" are reprinted from *The Imperfect Paradise*, Poems by Linda Pastan, by permission of W. W. Norton & Company, Inc. Copyright © 1988 by Linda Pastan. Lines from "Emily Dickinson" are reprinted from *The Five Stages of Grief*, Poems by Linda Pastan, by permission of W. W. Norton & Company, Inc. Copyright © 1978 by Linda Pastan.

Octavio Paz. "Wind and Water and Stone," translated by Mark Strand. From Octavio Paz: *A Draft of Shadows*. Copyright © 1975 by *The New Yorker* Magazine. Reprinted by permission of New Directions Publishing Corporation.

Nils Peterson. Lines from "Bedtime." From *Writing the Natural Way* by Gabriele Rico (Tarcher, 1983). By permission of Nils Peterson.

Robert Phillips. "Running on Empty." Copyright 1984, Robert Phillips. Reprinted from *Personal Accounts: New and Selected Poems, 1966–1986* by Robert Phillips (Princeton: Ontario Review Press, 1986) by permission of the author.

Marge Piercy. "Simple Song." From *Circles on the Water* by Marge Piercy. Copyright © 1982 by Marge Piercy. Reprinted by permission of Alfred A. Knopf, Inc.

Sylvia Plath. "Daddy." Copyright © 1963 by Ted Hughes. "Metaphors" by Sylvia Plath. Copyright © 1960 by Ted Hughes. "Mirror" by Sylvia Plath. Copyright © 1963 by Ted Hughes. From *The Collected Poems of Sylvia Plath*, edited by Ted Hughes. Reprinted by permission of HarperCollins Publishers and Faber and Faber Ltd. "Frog Autumn," copyright © 1959 by Sylvia Plath. Lines from "Watercolor of Grantchester Meadows," copyright © 1960 by Sylvia Plath; originally appeared in *The New Yorker*. From *The Colossus and Other Poems* by Sylvia Plath. Reprinted by permission of Alfred A. Knopf, Inc. and Faber and Faber Ltd.

Ezra Pound. "The River-Merchant's Wife," "Alba," "In a Station of the Metro," "A Pact," and lines from "And Thus in Nineveh." From Ezra Pound: *Personae*. Copyright © 1926 by Ezra Pound. Reprinted by permission of New Directions Publishing Company.

Dudley Randall. "Ballad of Birmingham." From *Poem Counterpoem* by Margaret Danner and Dudley Randall, copyright © 1966 by Dudley Randall. Lines from "A Different Image." From *Cities Burning*, copyright © 1968 by Dudley Randall. Reprinted by permission of Broadside Press.

John Crowe Ransom. "Bells for John Whiteside's Daughter" and "Janet Waking." From *Selected Poems* by John Crowe Ransom. Copyright © 1924 by Alfred A. Knopf, Inc. and renewed 1952 by John Crowe Ransom. Reprinted by permission of Alfred A. Knopf, Inc.

Ishmael Reed. ".05." From *Chattanooga* by Ishmael Reed. Copyright © 1973 by Ishmael Reed. Reprinted by permission of Random House, Inc.

Henry Reed. "Naming of Parts." © The Executor of Henry Reed's Estate 1946, 1947, 1970, and 1991. Reprinted from Henry Reed's *Collected Poems* edited by Jon Stallworthy (1991) by permission of Oxford University Press.

Kenneth Rexroth. "Trout." From Kenneth Rexroth: *Natural Numbers*. Copyright © 1963 by Kenneth Rexroth. Reprinted by permission of New Directions Publishing Corporation.

Adrienne Rich. "Aunt Jennifer's Tigers," "Diving into the Wreck," "Novella," "Bears," and lines from "Planetarium." Reprinted from *The Fact of a Doorframe, Poems Selected and New, 1954–1984* by Adrienne Rich, by permission of W. W. Norton & Company, Inc. Copyright © 1984 by Adrienne Rich. Copyright © 1978, 1975 by W. W. Norton & Company, Inc. Copyright © 1981 by Adrienne Rich.

Rainer Maria Rilke. "The Panther" from *Selected Poems of Rainer Maria Rilke* edited and translated by Robert Bly. Copyright © 1981 by Robert Bly. Reprinted by permission of Harper-Collins Publishers.

Theodore Roethke. "My Papa's Waltz", copyright 1942 by Hearst Magazines, Inc. "The Waking", copyright 1953 by Theodore Roethke. "Root Cellar", copyright 1943 by Modern Poetry Association, Inc. "I Knew a Woman", copyright 1954 by Theodore Roethke. "The Meadow Mouse", copyright © 1963 by Beatrice Roethke, Administratrix of the Estate of Theodore Roethke, from *The Collected Poems of Theodore Roethke* by Theodore Roethke. Used by permission of Doubleday, a division of Bantam Doubleday Dell Publishing Group, Inc.

Carl Sandburg. "Grass" from *Cornhuskers* by Carl Sandburg, copyright 1918 by Holt, Rinehart and Winston, Inc. and renewed 1946 by Carl Sandburg, reprinted by permission of Harcourt Brace Jovanovich, Inc.

Sappho. "Letter to Anaktoria." Excerpted from "Invocation to Aphrodite" in *Greek Lyrics,* 2nd ed., translated by Richmond Lattimore. Copyright 1949, 1955, and 1960 by Richmond Lattimore. Reprinted by permission of The University of Chicago Press.

Anne Sexton. "Her Kind" and "Ringing the Bells" from *To Bedlam and Part Way Back* by Anne Sexton. Copyright © 1960 by Anne Sexton. "The Truth the Dead Know" and "To a Friend Whose Work Has Come to Triumph" from *All My Pretty Ones* by Anne Sexton. Copyright © 1962 by Anne Sexton. "Two Hands" from *The Awful Rowing Toward God* by Anne Sexton. Copyright © 1975 by Lorint Conant, Jr., Executor of the Estate of Anne Sexton. All reprinted by permission of Houghton Mifflin Company. All rights reserved.

Charles Simic. "Poem." From *Charon's Cosmology* by Charles Simic. Copyright © 1977 by Charles Simic. Reprinted by permission of George Braziller, Inc.

Louis Simpson. "American Poetry" from *At the End of the Open Road,* copyright 1963 by Louis Simpson, Wesleyan University Press by permission of University Press of New England.

Gary Snyder. "After Work." From *Gary Snyder: The Back Country.* Copyright © 1959 by Gary Snyder. Reprinted by permission of New Directions Publishing Corporation. "Old Woman Nature" from *Axe Handles* copyright © 1983 by Gary Snyder. Published by North Point Press and reprinted by permission of Farrar, Straus & Giroux, Inc. "Hay for the Horses" from *Riprap and Cold Mountain Poems,* copyright © 1958, 1959, 1965 by permission of Farrar, Straus & Giroux.

Cathy Song. "Lost Sister" from *The Picture Bride,* copyright © 1983. Reprinted by permission of Yale University Press.

Gary Soto. "Oranges." Reprinted from *Black Hair* by Gary Soto, by permission of the University of Pittsburgh Press. © 1985 by Gary Soto.

Wole Soyinka. "Lost Tribe." From *Mandela's Earth and Other Poems* by Wole Soyinka. Copyright © 1988 by Wole Soyinka. Reprinted by permission of Random House, Inc.

William Stafford. "At the Bomb Testing Site" and "Traveling Through the Dark" (copyright © 1960 by William Stafford), "Freedom" and "One Home" (copyright © 1969 by William Stafford) from *Stories That Could Be True.* Reprinted by permission of the author.

Wallace Stevens. "Anecdote of the Jar," "Disillusionment of Ten O'Clock," "Thirteen Ways of Looking at a Blackbird," "The Emperor of Ice Cream," and "Domination in Black." From *Collected Poems* by Wallace Stevens. Copyright 1923 and renewed 1951 by Wallace Stevens. Reprinted by permission of Alfred A. Knopf, Inc.

Mark Strand. "Eating Poetry." From *Selected Poems* by Mark Strand. Copyright © 1979, 1980 by Mark Strand. Reprinted by permission of Alfred A. Knopf, Inc.

Jon Swan. "The Opening," *The New Yorker,* April 2, 1960. Reprinted by permission of the author.

May Swenson. "Living Tenderly" and "Question" from *New and Selected Things Taking Place.* "Living Tenderly" by May Swenson, © 1963 and renewed 1991. "Question" by May Swenson, © 1954 and renewed 1982. Both used with permission of the Literary Estate of May Swenson.

Dylan Thomas. "Do not go gentle into that good night," "Fern Hill," "In My Craft and Sullen Art," "The Force that through the green fuse drives the flower." From *Dylan Thomas: Poems of Dylan Thomas.* Copyright 1939, 1946 by New Directions Publishing Corporation, 1945 by The Trustees for the copyrights of Dylan Thomas, 1952 by Dylan Thomas. Reprinted by permission of New Directions Publishing Corporation and David Higam Associates, Ltd. Excerpts from "Notes on the Art of Poetry." In *Texas Quarterly,* Winter 1961. Reprinted by permission of Harold Ober Associates Incorporated. Copyright 1961 by the University of Texas. Copyright renewed 1989 by Stuart Thomas and Wynford Vaughan Thomas.

Ukihashi. "Whether I sit or lie" translated by Kenneth Rexroth and Ikuko Atsumi. From *Kenneth Rexroth: Women Poets of Japan.* Copyright © 1977 by Kenneth Rexroth and Ikuko Atsumi. Reprinted by permission of New Directions Publishing Corporation.

David Wagoner. "Breath Test" and "The Other House." From *First Light* by David Wagoner. Copyright © 1983 by David Wagoner. By permission of Little, Brown and Company. "The Return of Icarus" and "Old Words" from *Collected Poems 1956–1976* by David Wagoner. Copyright © 1976 by Indiana University Press. Reprinted by permission of the author.

John Wain. Lines from "Apology for Understatement" from *Weep Before God.* Reprinted by permission of Curtis Brown Group Ltd.

Diane Wakoski. "On Experience and Imagination." "Introduction" from *Trilogy* by Diane Wakoski. Copyright © 1962, 1966, 1967, 1974 by Diane Wakoski. Used by permission of Doubleday, a division of Bantam Doubleday Dell Publishing Group, Inc.

Alice Walker. "New Face" (copyright © 1973 by Alice Walker) and "Women" (copyright ©

1970 by Alice Walker) from *Revolutionary Petunias and Other Poems*, reprinted by permission of Harcourt Brace Jovanovich, Inc.

J. R. Watson. "'God's Grandeur'" from *The Poetry of Gerard Manley Hopkins*, published in 1978 by Penguin Books, Ltd.

Richard Wilbur. "The Writer" from *The Mind Reader*, copyright © 1971 by Richard Wilbur, and "The Boy at the Window" from *Things of This World*, copyright 1952 and renewed 1980 by Richard Wilbur, reprinted by permission of Harcourt Brace Jovanovich, Inc.

C. K. Williams. "Hood" from *Poems 1963–1983* by C. K. Williams. Copyright © 1969, 1988 by C. K. Williams. Reprinted by permission of Farrar, Straus & Giroux.

William Carlos Williams. "Between Walls," "The Red Wheelbarrow," "Spring and All," and "This Is Just to Say." From William Carlos Williams: *The Collected Poems of William Carlos Williams, 1909–1939, vol. I*. Copyright 1938 by New Directions Publishing Corporation. "Landscape with the Fall of Icarus" and "The Dance." From William Carlos Williams: *The Collected Poems of William Carlos Williams, 1939–1962, vol. II*. Copyright 1944, 1948, © 1960, 1962 by William Carlos Williams. Reprinted by permission of New Directions Publishing Corporation.

Mitsuye Yamada. "A Bedtime Story," "Marriage Was a Foreign Country," and lines from "Masks of Women." From *Camp Notes and Other Poems* by Mitsuye Yamada, copyright © 1976, 1980, 1986 by Mitsuye Yamada. Reprinted by permission of the author.

William Butler Yeats. "Leda and the Swan" and "Sailing to Byzantium" (copyright 1928 by Macmillan Publishing Company, renewed 1956 by Bertha Georgie Yeats), "The Second Coming" and lines from "Easter 1916" (copyright 1924 by Macmillan Publishing Company, renewed 1952 by Bertha Georgie Yeats), and "Crazy Jane Talks with the Bishop" (copyright 1933 by Macmillan Publishing Company, renewed 1961 by Bertha Georgie Yeats). Reprinted with permission of Macmillan Publishing Company from *The Poems of W. B. Yeats: A New Edition*, edited by Richard J. Finneran.

Yevgeny Yevtushenko. "Humor" and lines beginning "Tsars, Kings, Emperors . . . " from *The Poetry of Yevgeny Yevtushenko*, translated by George Reavey. Translation copyright © 1965, 1967 by George Reavey. Reprinted by permission of Marion Boyars Publishers Limited.

Al Young. "Chemistry" from *The Blues Don't Change* by Al Young. Copyright © 1965, 1966, 1967, 1968, 1969, 1970, 1971, 1972, 1973, 1974, 1975, 1976, 1977, 1978, 1979, 1980, 1981, and 1982 by Al Young. Reprinted by permission of Louisiana State University Press. "For Poets" from *The Song Turning Back into Itself* by Al Young. Copyright © 1965, 1966, 1967, 1968, 1970, 1971 by Al Young. Reprinted by permission of Henry Holt and Company, Inc.

INDEX OF AUTHORS, TITLES, AND FIRST LINES

INDEX OF LITERARY
AND RHETORICAL TERMS